COLONIZATION

A STUDY OF THE FOUNDING
OF NEW SOCIETIES

BY

ALBERT GALLOWAY KELLER, Ph.D.

PROFESSOR OF THE SCIENCE OF SOCIETY IN YALE UNIVERSITY

GINN & COMPANY
BOSTON · NEW YORK · CHICAGO · LONDON

The Athenæum Press
GINN & COMPANY · PRO-
PRIETORS · BOSTON · U.S.A.

TO
WILLIAM GRAHAM SUMNER

χείρεσσι στιβαρῇσι πύλας νόου αἰὲν ὀΐγνυς·
ψεύδεα δ᾽ ἐχθαίρειν καὶ νηλέϊ θυμῷ ἐφορμᾶν
ὁπλότεροι πρὸς σοῦ ἐδάημεν· σοὶ χάρις ἔστω.

CONTENTS

INTRODUCTION

The main motive in writing this volume has been to provide a text-book for the study of colonization. It does not take one who essays to teach the subject long to see the futility of dilating upon this or that aspect of colonization when his students are not yet in possession of an adequate historical background; but this they seldom have. Their historical studies have generally been circumscribed, and envisaged from different standpoints; while colonization, if approached by the comparative method, must call for a wealth of historical allusion, widespread both as to place and time. In the absence of text-books, at least in English, of any adequate character, the instructor in colonization is therefore confronted by an ever-present dilemma: the assignment of widely scattered and disconnected collateral readings, or the devotion of a large part of his lectures to historical detail. The former alternative is, for practical reasons, next to impossible for classes of any size; and it is rendered in a higher degree impracticable, so far as comprehensiveness goes, by reason of the linguistic training which it must involve. In the field of colonial history, translations, especially from the less well-known foreign languages, are but few; and it is only by the rarest exception that even a German or French treatise can be utilized; for the undergraduate who ventures upon the actual use of even those languages upon which he has spent a good deal of time is commonly a prey to faint-heartedness and sore misgiving. Thus, at best, assigned readings must be of narrow scope. And as for the other alternative, in so far as he is obliged to introduce into lectures that from which a text-book ought to secure freedom, the instructor is compelled to exclude what he regards as more worth while and to sacrifice the continuity and logic of his exposition.

To meet such a need, felt personally, the following sketches of colonial history have been written. They have been condensed so far as their purpose seemed to allow, and include very little that appeared at the time of writing reasonably easy of access to serious students. Thus the whole of British and French colonization has been passed over, although there existed here an added deterrent in the intolerable lengthening of a task somewhat outside of the author's field, if such a pair of topics were to be included. It seemed likewise that the author would be able to add little to what is accessible to any one concerning the colonial activities of the Russians, Belgians, Americans, and Japanese. Consequently, of the moderns, only the Germans and the Italians are treated, and they in something of the appendix style; for until they are taken up the continuity of the narrative need show no essential breaks. An attempt has been made to treat the several colonizing states in slightly differing ways, while adhering, in the main, to one general plan; indeed, such shifting of emphasis has been almost unconscious in view of the fact that accessible material tended to show strength now in one direction and again in another. The treatment is not designed to be encyclopædic. Nor, finally, is any consistent endeavor made to bring everything up to date; for the present-day political, fiscal, and other details, publications on the order of the Statesman's Year-Book, with its references, can easily be consulted. What have seemed to the author from his point of approach to be the signal and salient facts and relations in the colonial history of the ancient, mediæval, and modern peoples have been set forth, with some pedagogic devices of partial repetition and the like, to meet the needs of the college student as these have been brought home by the experience of several years. The hope is not renounced, however, that this book may be useful to others than college students. The American collegian is, after all, simply a member of society *in posse* who is being put through a course of learning designed to fit him to become one *in esse*. In general, the kind of book upon any particular subject that may meet his needs ought to meet those of one who, in later life, it may be, is directing his own education along the same line. It is hoped that the information here assembled, and its arrangement, may prove of some utility to any one interested in colonization.

Naturally, however, any such fact-assembling must be referred to some set of guiding elective and systematizing principles; and these, in the present case, are such as appeal to the student of human societies. The study is one of that societal movement which commonly results in the formation of new societies in new environments, and so seems to the writer — though the question of nomenclature is naturally a matter of indifference — to be ranged rather under the social sciences than under history in any moderate and reasonable understanding of the term. There has been no attempt to get at new historical data, but rather to assemble what is known and arrange it under somewhat different categories, with an eye to any important relationships, newly or long recognized, that may emerge.[1] Hence the sub-title of this book.

And it may be worth while, perhaps, to go a little farther and indicate the place in a series of studies of man and human society which colonization as here treated is designed to occupy. It presupposes some such study as geography in its broader sense, including physical geography, the geography of man (anthropogeography), and the geography of trade; or, put more generally, since man is the center of interest, a study of environmental influences on man and human groups, and of the various topics of general anthropology. A geography of trade or of man comes inevitably to touch upon the trading settlement, which is in turn the commonest forerunner of the colony; and the science of society then reaches out to these frontier societies as in many respects peculiarly significant. The subject of colonization opens out, therefore, as a sort of special topic of the science of society (sociology), following, in so far as the exigencies of a curriculum will allow, upon the more general study of man and human groups. It is possible that the concreteness of these statements may serve to define the scope and method of attack of the present volume, as the more general considerations which precede may not.

Finally, although some attempt has been made to define a colony, there has been no systematic effort put forth to exclude from treatment everything that does not square with that definition, loose though it may be; this book deals with colonies and colonial empires in the common acceptance of these terms.

In the preparation of the following essays I have received aid from many colleagues and friends; the faithfulness of their wounds accounts for a large part of any value which these labors may have. The influence of Professor Sumner is ever present with his former disciples wherever their subsequent interests may lie; and I am conscious in particular that my first interest in colonies as frontier societies was awakened by his illuminating suggestions.

[1] See the Bibliographical Note, p. 599.

It is but fair, though I esteem it a great privilege, to dedicate this volume — and I wish it were a more mature and worthier offering — to him. Among younger men I hasten to mention Professor Edward G. Bourne,[1] to whose stimulating criticism and helpfulness and never-failing kindness I wish here to bear witness. I have also been privileged to profit by the advice and criticism of several other colleagues in the matter of details which fell within their fields ; such assistance I have derived from Professors Gregory, Emery, Day, Schevill, and many others. Formal acknowledgments are due to my colleagues on the editorial board of the *Yale Review*, and to the editors of the *Annals* of the American Academy of Political and Social Science, for permission to use material originally published in those journals.

A. G. K.

New Haven, Connecticut

[1] Now that this gifted and intrepid spirit is gone from among us, it is perhaps of interest, as bearing upon his many side-activities, to record the fact that all of the following chapters except X–XII and the first part of XIII were read in manuscript and criticised by him — Chapters II–IX during the early weeks of his last illness.

COLONIZATION

CHAPTER I

DEFINITION AND CLASSIFICATION

The word "colony" is like all other current terms of language in that it covers, as Whitney puts it, "not a point, but a territory." For the purpose of this book it will be necessary to make the term more precise; there seems to be no urgent need for restricting it artificially to cover a point, but it must be defined with reasonable sharpness within a portion of the field to which it has come to be applied.

EMIGRATION AND CONQUEST

The fundamental ideas of colonization are a movement of population and an extension of political power; because it is allied to them both, colonization is therefore to be distinguished on the one hand from migration, and on the other from conquest in the broad sense. The former distinction is not so difficult, for it is generally admitted that one area and society cannot rightly be called a colony of another when the sum of mutual relations does not include political dependence of the former upon the latter. No one thinks of regarding the Vandal groups in Africa as having been colonies; and if the Italian settlements in Argentina are so denominated, it is usually with the added qualification, "natural" (colonies), or the like. The other distinction is more troublesome; yet it may be said that in common understanding of the terms a dependency is scarcely a colony until it contains actual emigrants from the colonizing state; or, at least, until it looks to such settlement, or counts upon potential emigration. As long as the activity of the colonizing state is purely governmental, — as long as the immigrants are simply officials, — there is a province, perhaps, but no colony. However, by adding either of these fundamentals, emigration and conquest, to the other, the essence of colony is brought out. A group of emigrants in a foreign land may become a colony by the extension of political control over them, their possessions, and interests, on the part of the state of which they are citizens; and, on the other hand, a state-acquired domain or mere sphere of influence may become a colony through settlement by non-official members of the state's population. Both individual and governmental initiative and subsequent support are needful in the creation of a colony.

Formulating a working definition upon these terms, a colony is here understood to be a political dependency, settled or prospectively to be settled, to some degree, by the citizens of its dominant state. This, it will be noted, is a definition of a *type*: the following treatment may exhibit variations about the type, but to it return will constantly be made, in the belief that it represents a popular and at the same time sufficiently precise conception.[1] Cases where either of the two prime conditions is represented rudimentarily will be treated simply for the light which such immature, simplified, or abnormal forms may cast upon the typical or normal ones. More specifically, the definition would exclude as a whole from direct treatment such dependencies as the Roman provinces, the Arabian conquests in Africa, the Turkish vilayets, and the Chinese republican communities in the Malay Archipelago, although any and all of them might be drawn upon for side-lights and *in loco experimenti*, while it would include the territories of the United States, Russian possessions in Asia, and the like. The so-called "interior colonization" of the Germans would naturally be a misnomer on the basis of the definition suggested.

The portion of the "territory" connoted by colony and colonization being thus roughly defined, its limits can be sharpened in some degree by proceeding to a classification of colonies; for although this classification, being one of societies, might apply to groups which do not form colonies, yet, as a cross-classification, it should not be without its value in filling out the conception of the term "colony" itself.

[1] The etymological demonstrations in which some writers on colonies deal are of little or no value in framing a working definition. They are rather of historic interest. The etymology of *colonia* is of great value in forming a conception of the character of the Roman colonies; but the modern term "colony" conveys a dissimilar and modern conception, suited to the modern world and its organization.

Basis of Classification

It is a common conviction among students of the less complex forms of human society that the character of the latter is ultimately, if not immediately, determined by the conditions of natural environment.[1] For these conditions at once evoke the local form of the struggle for existence, that is, the industrial organization; and upon the latter rests a series of secondary social forms, such as systems of property-holding, marriage, and government. And it is further believed by those who hold this view that the influences of natural environment enter far deeper into the life of even the more evolved societies than is generally recognized. If now such a standpoint were taken, and natural environment were conceded, if only for the sake of argument, to be a sort of elemental determinant in the destiny of societies in general, it would be so *a fortiori* in respect to such special and peculiar forms of societies as colonies. For colonial societies are, by their wide diffusion over the earth, exposed to a great variety of environmental influences, under conditions where these can be the more freely gauged and estimated, owing to the essential constancy of other factors (e.g. race-character of the colonizers) whose diversity commonly obscures every such valuation. Here should be a chance for a striking refutation or vindication of more general views.

But it is not necessary for the present purpose to embark upon any such troubled waters in attempting to demonstrate wide generalities. Naturally, as has been hinted, the relationship between a society and its environment comes out most clearly in the case of the simpler human groups which are, as we say, "nearer to Nature"; but colonies are, at least in their beginnings, societies of relative simplicity, as yet unendowed with that accumulation of relationships, institutions, and so on, through which older human groups appear to have rendered themselves, to some extent, independent of natural conditions. If this is admitted, either through conviction or as a working hypothesis, then it should be possible to construct a useful classification of

---

[1] The views set forth in this classification represent a sort of composite impression derived from the reading of some years in anthropology, sociology, and colonial history. Hence it is impracticable, if not impossible, to fix the exact provenance of derived ideas. That which is owed to Darwin, Huxley, Spencer, Sumner, and other stock authorities will be easily recognized.

colonial societies upon the broader variations of the natural conditions to which they are or have been exposed.

Of these conditions climate is, in the present case at least, the vital and determining one. It is usually so, carrying with it, as it does, so many other factors whose variations are correlated with its own; for instance, flora and fauna, including among the latter the microscopic fauna of disease. Climate, though itself varying in accordance with several factors, and though it evades classification except by type, may still, for the purpose in hand, be broadly divided into *tropical* and *temperate*. But this distinction would be of no utility in classifying colonies, because too general, if these distinct types of climate did not condition the human struggle for existence in a manner so vital as to determine two distinct types of industrial organization, upon which in turn, as what follows is designed to show, there would regularly be developed two distinctly variant types of human society. Thus the classification based upon climate and attendant influences may be shifted over into a classification based upon the type of the industrial organization. Anticipating what is to follow, we should then distinguish the tropical and the temperate colony upon the ground of their common and basic occupation, agriculture, and might name them respectively the *plantation colony* and the *farm colony*.[1]

VITAL CONDITIONS

But there are not a few considerations and reflections of a more concrete nature that underlie the assertions ventured in the last paragraph; we turn now to what must be a rather rapid survey of the same. The new environmental influences felt by colonists most obviously condition the struggle for existence, perhaps, through their direct action upon the struggling individual or group; they create new vital conditions, conformity to which means life, health, fecundity, working power of body and mind, while inability to conform entails an absence of these same advantages. The issue is one which popular parlance rightly denominates one of acclimatization. The question of acclimatization is simplified in the colonial field because the important colonizing nations of the

[1] As this classification is based in large part upon data to be found in the succeeding chapters, it is suggested to the teacher that the first chapter might profitably be re-read by the student after completing the book.

world have been without exception nations of the temperate zone and mainly Europeans; hence the racial element is all but eliminated, and the colonists may be conceived as moving either into regions of a temperate climate similar to their own at home, or into the tropics. Climate transitional between these two types, and polar climates,[1] must be understood to exist, but need not confuse or add to the main and clearly marked types.

Let us first consider the vital conditions of the European colonist in another part of the temperate zone. From such a change he is likely to experience physical profit rather than detriment. What variations he encounters in physical conditions are seldom so great as to call for vital modifications in his constitution or mode of living, while on the other hand there exist the positive advantages of a life free from the crowding and over-competition of his fellows.[2] Conflicts with the native races have been, in the temperate colonies, short, though sharp, and the outcome never seriously in doubt; indeed, the aborigines have been but sparsely represented in temperate regions at all open to colonization.[3] The momentum of the inter-racial struggle and the elation of relatively easy and sweeping victories have often lent to the colonists a vigor that lasted on. That such change of environment is generally beneficial is indicated by the more rapid growth of population in the new country as compared with that at home, despite the ruder conditions met. It is also likely that the physical and mental quality of the population is bettered, partly no doubt because of the more unrestricted activity of natural, and perhaps of sexual, selection as compared with their impeded action under the régime of a higher development of the arts. There are fewer of those agencies, such as surgery, medicine, humanitarian institutions, and the like, by which man seeks to lessen the mortality of the less fit, and the selection of mates must rest more largely upon

[1] The really polar possessions of the Danes, Russians, Americans, and British have never assumed the real forms of self-supporting colonies. They are temporary camps of hunters, traders, miners, or missionaries, and if they deserve the name of colony at all, they represent aberrant and extreme forms.

[2] The many analogies between man's occupation of a new habitat and what is well known to naturalists concerning the migrations and struggles of plants and animals scarcely need to be pointed out.

[3] In Australia and America, for example. Such a country as China is taken to be not open to colonization. For the effects of contact upon the native stocks, see p. 269 below.

physical adequacy. Again, although nature yields a liberal return to sturdy effort, no bounty is offered regardless of industry and foresight. The temperate colony is one which invigorates the constitution of the immigrant race and at the same time coerces it into an incessant and wholesome activity in meeting and coping with difficult but not insuperable obstacles.

In a tropical country, on the other hand, there occurs a violent change in the life of the emigrant from temperate regions. The man animal is out of his habitat. A few years of unvaried tropical heat undermine the most vigorous constitutions, and acclimatization in the case of individuals is practically impossible. Even when the vicissitudes of the climate, including its diseases, are minimized by an artificial mode of life or by other means,[1] profound changes in the physical organism still appear. Of these the most important from a sociological standpoint is the general disturbance of the reproductive system, both in the direction of morbid stimulus and of decreased vitality. In the case of animals this perturbation, in consequence of what is often a very slight change of habitat, is fully recognized; it was used by Darwin as one of his causes for otherwise unexplained variation. This disturbance is often fatal to mother and child, owing to the decrease in vitality of both; pregnancy and parturition constitute a grave danger to European women, and, as is natural, the infant death-rate is high where the more stable constitutions of adults are wont to disintegrate. Population suffers quantitatively owing to the above causes, and to their deterrent action on immigration, especially of females; it also tends almost inevitably to take on a temporary and changing character as accession after accession dies off or is forced to withdraw. The quality of population also tends to retrograde, for lethargy replaces energy where life is both easy and hopeless; and before such a small and enfeebled society there stands always the menace of a numerical preponderance of native population incapable of being restrained by the unaided force of the immigrant merchants or planters. The conditions of the tropical colony are thus extremely unfavorable to both individual and society.

---

[1] I.e. by not living as the natives do.

POPULATION

A comparison of colonial population in one and the other type of colony, as determined by the vital conditions thus briefly indicated, reveals the following results. Emigration to the plantation colony is slight, and natural increase thereafter is inconsiderable. The colonists are few in number, do not contemplate an extended stay, and are represented preponderatingly by males; the racial unit is thus the individual, not the family.[1] The population is rendered by the climate and attendant influences unfit for strenuous labor, and is practically excluded from the direct working of the soil. Excesses are not infrequent, and the attempt to stimulate a languid physical organization by the use of alcohol is common and disastrous; incredible deeds of criminality that must have their origin in an unsettled nervous system are from time to time reported to an offended world. Relations, often irregular, with native women, especially on the part of the Latin nations, have produced a multitude of half-breeds, whose general character is but rarely an improvement upon that of either of the uniting races; for its objectionable qualities are likely to increase proportionately to the degree of contrast exhibited by the uniting hereditary elements. In general, the colonial population exhibits the characteristic symptoms of a group of animals transported into a habitat to whose strange conditions it is unable to adapt itself within a reasonable time; but because these animals are *homines sapientes*, they are enabled to adopt rational methods which limit the immediate and fatal action of natural selection.

The state of affairs in a temperate colony presents a marked contrast in almost all these particulars. Immigration is relatively strong at the outset; later, in consequence of the accelerated rate of natural increase the accession of periodic relays of population from without is not a matter of vital importance. The colonists are numerous and intend to stay; and since they include a considerable number of females, the unit is the family[1] rather than the individual. The climate invigorates the population, which is energetic, self-reliant, early of marriage, and fecund, and displays these qualities in its vigorous and healthy activity. The native

[1] The Portuguese in India, Dutch in Java, etc., compared with the English in North America.

population of the temperate regions is unable long to withstand the new and generally ruthless competitor. Mongrel races are.extremely rare, for the settlers marry within their own ranks, either before or after migration, and are not led by strange and unnatural conditions of life to associate irregularly with the natives. Hence the whole stock of the society is homogeneous and of high physical and racial quality.

INDUSTRIAL ORGANIZATION

The total diversity of vital conditions here indicated is also sufficient to effect the wide divergence between the temperate and tropical forms of the organization of industry to which allusion has been made. Here, however, dealing as we are in types, some narrowing of the field is possible. On looking over the colonies of the world, it becomes perfectly clear that of the industrial opera- tions which secure their existence, agriculture stands foremost. Only when the environment approaches the desert type does agriculture yield to cattle-raising; and since the savannas or steppes suited to the latter occupation are practically all of a temperate or sub-tropical climate,[1] agriculture is the only important primary form of the industrial organization common to colonies of all latitudes and altitudes, and so the only criterion of classification of adequate generality, not to mention importance. It is also the ultimate form to which any preliminary occupations may lead. Practically all colonies have their origin in trade, as Roscher[2] says; but exchange of life-supporting *products* is the form toward which it tends. There must be that wherewith to trade, and, if the colony is to be economically self-sufficient, there must exist first and foremost that wherewith to support life. Mining may last on for a long period, but it is not a basis upon which a normal society may continue to rest. The only self-sufficient vocation of man is that of working the earth and utilizing its primary or derived nutritious products. It is a significant fact that, as time goes on, all colonies where the soil will permit are forced into agriculture on their own account. Classifying by the forms of agriculture characteristic respectively of the temperate and of the tropical climate, therefore, one discriminates upon a character that is not

[1] Those nearest the tropics are, for example, the savannas of the Sudan, the Ilanos of South America, the interior semi-deserts of Australia, etc.   [2] Page 16.

transitory but ultimate. Hunting, fishing, and mining last but for a time; even cattle-raising tends relatively to decline as unoccupied or arid land is redeemed; whether the masters of the colony labor, or steal the results of others' labor, the occupation which assures combined societal existence, either directly or through exchange, is the vital one.

This fact has been recognized by the two most eminent writers on colonies, Roscher and Leroy-Beaulieu.[1] The former's classification (A, conquest colonies; B, trading colonies; C, agricultural colonies; D, plantation colonies) is faulty from the simultaneous employment of several criteria of discrimination: for example, in A the criterion is mode of acquisition or administration; in B, motive of settlement or acquisition. But C and D, to which in his discussion Roscher assigns a special importance, correspond to the distinctions contended for in this essay. Leroy-Beaulieu distinguishes colonies of (1) exploitation or plantation, (2) settlement or agriculture, and (3) mixed colonies. The first two categories correspond with Roscher's C and D above, and are in reality tropical and temperate agricultural colonies, although the alternative terms suggest also the predatory or sedentary tendencies of the population. No subordination of these alternative terms one to the other is indicated. The term "mixed colonies" represents an unnecessary effort to cover inevitable transitional forms, and does not aid in a classification which seeks well-marked types for purposes of exposition and clarification of thought.

Both authors, then, recognize the two types of colony mentioned above, — the tropical agricultural and the temperate agricultural; for this is what the terms "plantation colony" and "agricultural colony" really mean. These forms of colony might be denominated, to avoid confusion, *plantation colony* (tropical) and *farm colony* (temperate).

Agricultural Economy

It requires something more than the assertion, however, to prove that these two forms are marked enough to constitute the basis of a classification; that is, that they really possess a sort of generic value. Besides their direct action on man, as sketched

[1] Roscher, chap. i; Leroy-Beaulieu, II, part ii, book ii, chap. i. For a minute and involved classification, see Schäffle's, in Reinsch, pp. 19–20.

above, the natural conditions which center about climate exert other strong though less direct influences. First of all, they profoundly affect the medium upon which man works. For example, the tropical soil, flora, fauna, etc., are of types entirely distinct from those of temperate regions. This fact may be brought out clearly enough by proceeding at once to a general comparison of the industrial organization of tropical and temperate colonies, which will incidentally explain the coördinate terms "farm colony" and "plantation colony" already employed.

Owing to the diversity of natural conditions in the two regions, the tropical lands are fitted to produce with ease certain goods which either cannot be produced at all, or not without great difficulty and cost, in the temperate regions. To the northerners who were reaching out beyond the confines of their native habitat for the fuller satisfaction of their wants these tropical products (spices, sugar, coffee, etc.) were purely luxuries, but of a desirability measured by history-making efforts to attain them. Even now they remain largely luxuries, though their extended use has made them seem indispensable; they are not really so in the sense that life would be for many people impossible without them; they are not like wheat or corn. Another cardinal fact respecting tropical products is that those which pay are relatively few in number. Of a consequence, production is specialized, and, as a rule, must be carried out on the larger scale, extensively and with a strong labor force. Thus the characteristic tropical "plant" has been the *plantation* rather than the *farm*.

But this very form, of necessity taken by tropical production, implies a number of definite results which in turn enter as conditioning factors of production. First of all there arises the troubled question of tropical labor; tropical colonies are the home of the "native question." Vital conditions do not permit of the accomplishment of plantation labors at the hands of an unacclimatized race. But the disposition of the inhabitant of tropical regions is not industrious, and he has never been induced to alter his ways by the application of economic stimuli. However, the logic of what was conceived to be necessity would not be denied. The formula ran: The tropics must be developed; the native of the tropics is the only available agency for such development; therefore, whatever his will in the matter, he must work. The earliest form of compulsion was slavery of the local native; then, in certain regions where this native remained intractable, slavery of an imported native. / Plantation colonies have regularly been the seats of wholesale enslavement,/ and planters have championed such theory as was needful to support what was to them an indispensable actuality. But those who did not feel the necessity of the system were able to coerce those who did. The abolition of slavery then led to the development, where the former system did not persist, of various substitutes and subterfuges: contract-labor, debt-slavery, "compulsory labor," and the like,[1] all in greater or less degree disguised forms of coercion. Such compulsory production, however, under whatever form, was bound to suffer from the stock weaknesses of slave-labor,—lack of energy, purpose, and initiative. Thus tropical production has never lived up to such possibilities as it might have realized with an adequate labor supply.

But it has not been the native situation alone which has crippled the industrial organization of the hot countries. The Europeans had a well-founded distaste and fear, rather than love, of the new environment; and their presence in it has been prevailingly motived by a desire for wealth speedily gained.[2] They have exhibited, as a rule, no real interest in the region of their temporary sojourn. Taking into account the tendency of mankind to strike into courses offering least resistance, it is not surprising to find the system of plantation-culture to have been a ruthless and wasteful one, not only of soil but of men. It is what the Germans graphically denominate *Raubbau*. Agriculture presents the extensive rather than the intensive form, with all which that implies of non-restoration of soil, even non-rotation of crops, etc. Frequent and protracted absenteeism of sick or indifferent owners — who are often, indeed, mere shareholders in a company — has played its part in mismanagement and waste. A widespread indifference or cynicism respecting the fate of the human working-animal has prevailed; he has been regarded in general as an insentient factor in the accumulation of wealth. There has been but little concern for the future well-being of the land or people; the unexpressed, if not openly avowed, sentiment has been, "After us, the deluge!" This attitude is so characteristic of the plantation colony as to have led Leroy-Beaulieu and others to employ the alternative title of "colony of exploitation." It was natural enough for European

[1] Cf. pp. 580 ff., below. [2] Cf. pp. 258 ff., below.

peoples who invaded the tropics in quest of what they did not have at home to seize by any methods the spices, or the ivory, and depart.[1] They were not figuring on the long run, but the short; this is the main reason why they pursued their characteristic methods in the tropics alone, — there was comparatively nothing in the other type of environment to allure them. It took a different theory of life to render the cooler regions attractive.

The tendency in the tropics toward the specialized production of a few staples, and those usually incapable of being transformed into a local food-supply, has had, finally, for one of its results, a thorough-going economic dependence upon the dominant state, the importance of which in a political direction will presently be seen. This dependence is most clearly shown by the distress attendant upon either failure of the staple crop or interruption of communication with the mother-country or outside world. A lack of self-sufficiency is further shown in the failure of the population to provide for its own immediate and simple needs along the line of manufacture or small jobbing; or, in general, to develop any natural resources beyond those few that are immediately and highly profitable.[2] This species of economic dependence is of course quite different from that of a frontier society in the temperate zone which specializes in a certain kind of production, — for example, in that of corn, — to the temporary exclusion of such products of the mechanic arts as can be easily obtained by exchange with more settled sections.

A parenthetic word may here be introduced relative to the other extractive industry, mining. This is generally pure exploitation, at least for a time, wherever practiced; but it yet differs in form as between the regions where natives are numerous and where they are few.[3] Precious stones and metals were costly luxuries which attracted the adventurous exploiter, and in the tropical regions called for native labor and made for economic dependence. But this industry, because in itself it implies no definite and protracted settlement, is here passed over in favor of the more basic occupation.

Carrying out, now, the comparison with the farm colony, it is found, first of all, that the products of the new country do not materially differ from those of the home-land. Because they

---

[1] Cf. pp. 91 ff., below.   [2] Cf. pp. 221 ff., below.
[3] For instance, compare Peru and Australia.

represent more fully the extractive industries, the colonies with their raw products may be able so to supplement the mother-country as to encourage a progressive mutual diversification of industry on a grand scale; but the colonial society, under normal conditions, produces a variety of products, most of which are necessities of life designed for local consumption. Because these products do not afford immense profits by reason of their absence or rarity in the older lands, — because there is no great diversity of the conjuncture, — specialization and exploitation on the grand scale are seldom seen. The characteristic "plant" is the *farm* rather than the *plantation*.

Contrasts between the labor-situation and other important phases of the industrial organization may be signalized in a few words. The colonists themselves furnish labor of a high order, for they are healthy and sturdy, and efficient as few natives can be. Wholesale slavery, therefore, has been found unprofitable in temperate colonies, and has yielded, even though tried in a number of cases, as in New England, to a more effective system impossible in the torrid regions. The native-labor question does not exist; even in the mines the bulk of labor falls upon the immigrant race. Nor does the custom of improvident exploitation develop with any such generality as in the tropics; except in the short-lived fur-trade and in mining, motives of a different stamp[1] — economic, political, and religious — have led to establishments of a permanent nature. Foresight and economy in the use of natural advantages result, and agriculture is intensive rather than extensive. Absenteeism is almost unknown; the owners cannot afford to be absent if they would. The future well-being of the land is to the interest of all, especially as parents expect their descendants to succeed them, perhaps for centuries, in the enjoyment of their possessions.

And economic independence and self-sufficiency are, with few exceptions, marked. There is no great staple crop, relatively useless as a food-supply, upon the hazard of whose success or failure well-being or misery wait. Industry is diversified; the people are resourceful and inventive, practice simple manufactures as the forerunners of greater yet to come, and develop natural resources of all kinds that may make for their own success in the struggle for existence and comfort.

[1] As bearing upon the character of these immigrants, the relative loftiness of their motives should receive attention.

Types of Society

The colonial societies and social life built upon these contrasting forms of the industrial organization could not but reflect in the superstructure the lines of the foundation. The system of property-holding in land characteristic of the temperate colony is the small, inherited freehold; at first, the farm or clearing. This system, being the one upon which forms familiar to us all are built, needs little characterization beyond that afforded by its contrast with the system as developed in the tropics. The latter started with a larger unit and developed the estate-form and the domain of the chartered company. The tropical plantation was an undertaking beyond the power of the individual, and ownership thus became shareholding rather than individual possession or active partnership. The immediate concern of the owners was thus replaced by a remoter interest through functionaries of various kinds, absenteeism was thus encouraged, and such undertakings have taken on a marked speculative character. Brief reflection will show that these diverse forms were not the product of traditional legal prepossessions, except as these fell in with the demands of the new environment. Peoples as prejudiced against monopolies as were the Dutch promptly developed chartered companies; and the failure of the proprietary system in the English colonies is notorious.

Comparison is likewise challenged in respect of marriage and the family. The fundamental factors which rendered the conditions in the tropical colonies so different from those, say, of the New England settlements, were the great preponderance of males, and the feeble economic efficiency of such females as were present. The former factor led to formal celibacy, intermixture of races, and aberrations all but unknown in societies of the other type, — all this amounting to a negation of matrimony in the sense characteristic of the temperate colony. The other factor, economic inefficiency, minimized the importance of woman's status; the materfamilias had no such independent and influential position in the tropics as in the cooler regions. And where woman was absent or of little significance, there could be little of the family life and solidarity characteristic of many settlement colonies. Thus, as has been said, the individual was in one case the unit of population, in the other the family.

It is probably impossible to show any consistent contrasts between the religious ideas of one region and the other; but in the matter of missionary activities a distinction follows partly from the conditions already described.[1] In the temperate regions the native people were decimated or driven back in a fierce race-conflict, inconsiderate of their material or spiritual interests, almost before there had been time to institute propaganda; but in the tropical countries a distinct proselytizing type of religion has often appeared, stimulated as it was by the abundant and persistent native population. The necessity of adaptation to the needs and understanding of the latter has often induced, likewise, a modification of the alien toward the native type of religion. Actual or pretended solicitude regarding the spiritual weal of the native has disguised the selfish and economic motive rather more in the warmer zones than elsewhere. And, in general, in the tropics, the invading religion of the higher race has usurped and discharged, for good or ill, an important economic and political function but rarely approached in the colony of settlement.

Political dissimilarities between the plantation and the farm colony afford, perhaps, the most striking and evident basis of differentiation; and with these differences is closely identified the political destiny of the societies in question. For these reasons not a few classifications have been based upon such criteria of distinction; the latter are deducible, however, from the more fundamental basis here adopted. The economic dependence of the plantation colony has been explained already; its very life lies in exchange with the cooler regions — exchange not only of products but of men; and it is not infrequently dependent regularly or for varying periods upon the bounty of the mother-country. In the presence of a native population which far outnumbers its own, the colony is likewise dependent upon the support of the sponsor state; and its very riches under the typical policy of exclusion tempt foreign aggression. The colonizing power is often forced to take upon its shoulders enterprises which have proved too arduous not only for the individual but for large corporate bodies with practically unlimited power. These conditions promote constant outside interference and molestation, and keep the colony and its doings from

[1] Compare the missions in Spanish America and Central Africa with those in French and British North America.

lapsing into that happy state of obscurity where it may direct its own destiny. The peoples of such colonies gain no experience in managing their own affairs, and, if left to themselves, possess no body of norms or local precedents by which to gain an orientation. If they have become, by some contingency, nominally independent, their ensuing political form has been unstable and they have offered a standing temptation to aggression on the part of stronger nations.[1] This instability both before and after independence is the more marked if the presence of a mongrel population has already provided the unfortunate element of what might be called biological instability and incongruity. No tropical colony has ever yet proved itself capable of living up to a régime of representative institutions (self-government) or of independence, apart from the sponsorship of some state of the temperate regions. The terms "protectorate," "crown colony,"[2] etc., expressing a distinctly subordinate relation, are all but peculiar to the tropical lands.

The contrast with the other type of colony is pointed. The latter is economically independent; it is able early in its career to settle its own disputes with its native neighbors; it is not unwilling at times to challenge an older society to the arbitrament of the sword. But because it presents few immediate rewards to the conqueror, it generally escapes the latter struggle. It is not rich enough to evoke, and suffer under, so rigid a policy of exclusion and monopoly as has been so regularly applied to tropical colonies. In short, it can live its own life, without much aid, even though it demands help as of right when its advantage seems to lie in so doing. At other times outside interference is bitterly resented. The society not infrequently lives under a beneficial régime of neglect and even

---

[1] E.g. the Spanish American republics.

[2] As an example of a popular classification, which is practical, but of administrative rather than of scientific value, the following, based upon the degree of extension of control of the mother-country, may be cited: (1) colony proper, which may have representative or semi-representative institutions, or nothing of the kind (crown colony); (2) protectorate; (3) sphere of influence. Classifications of this kind simply darken counsel in the popular mind, for they envisage the colony from the administrative standpoint of the home government, and afford to the expert alone a clue as to the real nature of country and people. It depends largely upon the identity of the colonizing power, and to a certain degree upon chance, whether the form of administration is, within a reasonable period, adapted to the vital peculiarities of the dependency in question; i.e. whether this form is an index of the character of the colony or not.

contempt on the part of the native country, and is thus able to work out its own salvation. Not being hermetically sealed from the world, it learns from others, friends or rivals. The experience and suggestions thus gained are invaluable, and create a sense of self-sufficiency and power which in the course of time asserts itself in the forcible or peaceable acquisition of virtual or real independence. And since the population is homogeneous and politically experienced, the resulting state is fitted to take its place alongside the older states as a stable and safe government, not essentially different from its elders except in the qualities of vigor, however crude these may be, and possibilities of growth characteristic of a healthy society in a roomy and wholesome environment.

This political comparison is not complete unless supplemented by an alignment of the divergent social structures which grow out of the other conditions, mainly economic, already described. It has been suggested that the population of the tropical colony, taken as a whole, is unhomogeneous. The presence of native and mongrel races, the latter usually of all degrees of mixture, causes the population to cleave along various lines so as to create castes or classes of a marked order. This is the kind of growth upon which a rigid aristocracy is wont to develop. The large-scale production and system of *latifundia*, or extended estates, implying as they do an original aristocracy of wealth, contribute to the speedy appearance of social strata; and the system of slavery on the large scale causes the lines of cleavage of the society to widen into unmistakable chasms between "higher" and "lower." The adventurer class often finds its level in a sort of retainer relation; priests and missionaries form at times a sort of sacerdotal caste. And the scattering of population-groups in what might well be termed manors — a phenomenon due again mainly to the mode of production and the relations with subject races — lends still another characteristic feature of the aristocratic régime.

These conditions are all but reversed in the farm colony. The population is homogeneous from the outset, for the mediocre gains of the farm colony attract neither the very wealthy nor the helpless pauper; while for the former a large aggregation of capital will not pay, the man who has no capital and feeble instincts of industry has few prospects before him. Hence the original immigration is largely from the middle class, or what is likely soon to attain that station (e.g. indented servants), and a certain feeling of equality exists at the outset.[1] This is speedily augmented by the action of the characteristic economic conditions. Abundance of available land and the prevalence of the small holding render men independent of birth, landlord, and employer. Rents are low and wages must be high enough to tempt the laborer to remain in a position where he is not his own master. Efforts to transplant the retainer relation from the older lands have resulted in utter and ridiculous failure. Evasion was too easy, and livelihood, in consequence of individual effort, too well assured. Thus no social cleavage of moment occurred among the immigrants themselves, and in the absence of slavery or miscegenation on the large scale, an incalculably strong factor working against a democratic régime was excluded. The adventurer class clung to the outposts of civilization and actually discharged a service to the society comparable to that of the sappers and miners to an army. And, finally, the population was not indefinitely scattered, owing to a large-scale division of the land, but congregated in groups of farms, or towns.

This is a ground on which ideas of equality and democracy throve, as the wheat and maize throve in the soil; and to carry out the comparison in this detail, it was a ground as little fitted for aristocracy as was the soil for sugar, coffee, and spices. Such a society was enabled to receive elements of the most diverse and often objectionable kinds, and transform them to its type. And its

---

[1] It has not seemed necessary to go into a number of subsidiary points bearing upon this classification, — for instance, into the motives for emigration. Strictly speaking, there is no real emigration to most plantation colonies. It may be noted, however, that the very motives that lead to real emigration reveal in those who found the farm colony a very different temper from that displayed by those who go to the tropics. The latter are generally mere sojourners; they go out for wealth and wish no break with the metropolis, guaranteed as they are by its support. Genuine emigration, on the other hand, is motived by discontent with the old environment, — and such a sentiment must be strong to overcome the human tendency toward inertia or love of accustomed environment (home). Roscher (32 ff.) and Leroy-Beaulieu (II, 471 ff.) catalogue these motives. Taken in broad lines, the discontent with the old may be directed toward the economic conditions prevalent (over-population, and its attendant ills) or toward the political and social (dominance of a hostile political or religious faction, etc.). In any case there is a disposition to break with the old, ignoring the bonds once recognized. Home is not alone a certain congenial fraction of the physical environment; it is not alone a matter of latitude and longitude. Congeniality must extend to that which is less tangible, in group-life. Hence if the conditions of the colony are, or are made, different and more acceptable, the home feeling grows and the former sentiments of attachment and loyalty are displaced. This is another aspect of the " independence " of the settlers in the farm colony.

local and detached governments were able, even though with throes, to coalesce into a centralized and powerful state. The only strong and stable European offshoot societies are located in temperate regions and are developed farm colonies.

And these were evolved into their stable form, without as yet important exception, beneath the British flag : Canada, the United States of America, South Africa, Australia, New Zealand. This consideration would seem to cross a classification based upon environment by introducing the element of race-character, and perhaps national policy. These factors have been reflected upon, and, while their importance has been realized, they have been regarded as, in the large, distinctly ancillary to the criteria of classification adopted. Where have even the British developed a stable state in the tropical regions ? And have not the Germans and Italians in Argentina, or the Spanish-Americans in Mexico, made notable progress — even if aided somewhat in indirect ways by British and Americans — toward evolving (but only in a temperate region) a promising state ? It is no place here to argue upon the reasons why nearly all the eminent young states of the modern world have developed out of British colonies : opportunity seized, the capability of learning from the experience even of others, adaptability, indifference, — these and other less general elements have contributed to the astonishing results chronicled in British colonial history. The British, because of their race-character, conformed themselves and their methods more aptly to the conditions amidst which their colonial destiny launched them than did other colonizing peoples. But they performed no miracles in the setting aside of elemental forces of nature.

CONCLUSION

Returning from this digression, the discussion of classification, which has been developed chiefly with the purpose of getting the essentials of a colony before the mind, may be concluded in a word. The sharp and vital contrasts in primary and secondary societal forms, which have here been detailed, seem to afford a sufficient ground for assigning to the two types of colony distinguished by climate a separate and, as it were, varietal value. As colonies, or better, perhaps, as frontier societies, the plantation and the farm colony possess many characteristics in common. So closely allied varieties possess specific characters in common, although they may be, as varieties, sharply differentiated in a number of respects one from another. But the characters here selected have, to all appearance, such a determinative influence upon the characters by which colonies are more obviously or superficially distinguished, as to deserve precedence, from the genetic point of view, over the latter. From the practical standpoint, also, it could not be a misfortune to a statesman of a colonizing state to get clearly before his mind the essential diversity, in constitution and destiny, of colonies exposed to such diverse types of natural environment.

CHAPTER II

COLONIZATION OF A SIMPLER TYPE

The colonies and colonization of the ancients have this value for the social scientist, — they exhibit in their simpler form the groundwork of the complex structures and processes of a later day. In the social sciences, owing to the impossibility or impracticability of experimentation, such less complex instances, fairly representing an isolation of one or more factors, attain a special importance. The same might be said with perhaps even greater pertinence of the colonial operations of races widely alien to our own.

The chief writers on colonies have been criticised for not including in their treatises the colonial activities of primitive peoples, and the critic cites a brief list of facts calculated to illustrate these activities among certain African, Malay, and other tribes.[1] They are good enough so far as they go. The reader of ethnography often meets with cases of emigration and settlement consequent to pressure of population in certain tribal areas, or to the stimuli of economic gain; and occasionally observes an instance of what might well be called colonization, in a sense approaching that of our definition. The new society is not infrequently a strict reproduction of the old, and is sometimes temporarily united to the latter by a loose sort of political cohesion; or, as in the case of the ancient Peruvians, a deliberate governmental colonization may be observed. But all these instances tell us scarcely more than that men of lower races flee from an actual or impending catastrophe in the struggle for existence; or that they seek to raise their standard of living by temporary or permanent change of environment; or that they find the artificial shifting of population an effective means for consolidating the power of the state or community. Men of higher races, however, do all these things, and leave completer and more definite records of their activities. So

---

[1] Ratzel, Politische Geographie, pp. 143–145; cf. Wilken, p. 63; Van der Aa, "Koloniale Politiek" (*De Gids*, 1860); Letourneau, La Guerre, pp. 184 ff.; G. C. Lewis, pp. 96 ff.

that while no evidence germane to the subject — especially if it is calculated to simplify it — should be neglected, it is scarcely possible to make practical use of the scattered, fragmentary, and often largely inferential ethnographical data which are as yet available.

THE COLONIES OF THE CHINESE

These considerations, however, do not apply so well to the case of the Chinese. With them we are already within the field of history. Their activities, while they stand in no genetic connection with the evolution of what are called the modern or occidental systems of colonization, merit, from their very isolation and exceptionality, a brief mention.

That which would, in strictness, remove the case of the Chinese from our field is that, where popular initiative has been most strikingly exhibited, there extension of governmental control has been least; and conversely, where the authority of the government has been extended, there the whole movement has resembled the mere widening of political boundaries rather than colonization in any strict understanding of the term. The former of these alternatives is what has led Ratzel[1] to remark that " Chinese colonization is an exclusively economic and ethnographic affair. Nothing is more manifest than the incapacity of the Chinese to effect a military conquest and then to rule." This refers mainly to the extension of political control over districts already economically and ethnographically Chinese. The other alternative — boundary extension — is represented by the cases where conquest of territories adjoining the empire was followed by the attempt to further an economic and ethnographic assimilation.

The latter alternative may be considered first. Precaution in self-defense early prompted China to secure her boundaries by extending political control over neighbors who threatened them, — chiefly the unruly and restless nomad tribes of the northern and western steppes. At the outset the half-unconscious policy was one of conquest through civilization rather than by force of arms, a movement due less to pressure of population on land, and more to the desire for political influence in the steppe region. But although settlers and merchants came thus to form nuclei of culture in wilder lands, the necessity of more compelling agencies

[1] Chin. Ausw., p. 252.

soon became manifest; "in the steppes, in view of the peculiar character of their inhabitants, one must follow the rule : nothing or everything." Districts occupied in consequence of such necessity were secured by the founding of military colonies and by governmental measures such as the wholesale transfer of population between unruly districts and loyal sections of the empire. These colonies were generally prosperous and soon became agricultural or industrial in type; but of voluntary emigration there was little.[1] Individual enterprise played but a small part in operations of this nature.

Manchuria, Mongolia, Tibet, and Tonkin represent governmental activity of the order described. The policy followed was to assure the nomads or other natives of a semblance of freedom, which stood to them for its reality. Their leaders were sometimes placed in a position corresponding to that of Chinese mandarins; they not infrequently received their lands back in fief, tribute being exacted where practicable. The Chinese settlers promptly intermarried with the natives and gradually acquired possession of the best lands. They were favored in important ways by the government, which sought likewise to attract to permanent settlement both such laborers as had emigrated across the boundaries in search of employment, and criminals, chiefly political, who had been banished from the older society.[2]

In sharp contrast with the favoring policy of the government as here exhibited stand the restrictions imposed upon Chinese emigration which took its origin in individual initiative. To envisage these private motives it is necessary to realize, first of all, that the Chinese have been too firmly rooted in ancestral soil, and too little actuated by ideal considerations, to emigrate for any reasons short of the most obvious and vital, i.e. material ones. One of these was the discomfort and danger arising from the pressure of population on land, already alluded to;[3] and it must be realized, in order to gain a conception of the pressure, that what we call prudential checks to the growth of numbers have played but a vanishing rôle among a people the whole weight of whose superstition

---

[1] Ratzel, Chin. Ausw., pp. 56–59; Von Brandt, pp. 126–127, 137, 140 ff., 151 ff., 161 ff., 191–192. The Chinese influence advanced as far west as the Caspian (p. 138).

[2] Ratzel, Chin. Ausw., pp. 75–81 ; Von Brandt, pp. 136–139, 190–191, 521.

[3] It must be admitted, however, that emigration did not, as a rule, take place from the most thickly settled districts; contiguity to the territory to be settled played a considerable part in those days.

and tradition is thrown against celibacy and the restriction of off-spring.[1] Coöperating with this motive to emigration, and often directly derivable from it, were others arising from political discontent or friction;[2] but only when the latter reflected economic dissatisfaction did they rise into the importance of true motive forces. Religious motives were practically non-existent. For the consideration which, above all others, impelled the Celestial to pass the boundaries of his country was commercial gain. No governmental aid was here needed; such emigration pursued its course not only without state aid but despite state opposition. The Chinese government decreed from time to time against the departure of its subjects at the promptings of individual enterprise. It could not, however, prevent the gradual growth of a shipping-trade[3] for which environing geographical and other conditions provided so irresistible an incentive, nor that of a land-trade which was tempted ever farther by opening vistas of commercial profit. In spite of all restrictions the Chinese early made their way by sea not only to Japan and the Philippines, but throughout the Malay Archipelago and far into the Indian Ocean; and by land they penetrated at such a remote period and in such great numbers into the southern peninsulas that Siam and Cambodia are half-Sinicized, and India came to exhibit a strong ethnological and cultural strain of the same character.[4]

Something of the importance of the Chinese element in the colonies of modern nations will be seen in later chapters. Their movement to the adjacent islands and countries has been almost irresistible. Adherents of the Ming dynasty, settling in Formosa in the latter half of the seventeenth century (A.D.), led a colonial movement which practically conquered the rather strong Malay population of that island. In the Philippines and in Java the Chinese element has for centuries been of an importance quite disproportionate to its size; heavy taxation and extreme cruelty at the hands of Spaniards and Dutch were inadequate to secure relief from its hated though indispensable presence. In general the Chinese have functioned as itinerant frontier-traders, plantation

[1] Schallmayer (pp. 193 ff.) works these conditions with a somewhat precarious argument for "the biological value of Chinese civilization."

[2] Chiefly in the case of Formosa and the frontier provinces of Korea.

[3] Cf. Lindsay, I, 128 ff. This was after the conquest of southern China (220 B.C.).

[4] Cf. Von Brandt, pp. 544–545, 569 ff., 592 ff.; Ratzel, Hist., III, 171; Chin. Ausw., pp. 121 ff.

and mine workers and directors; not infrequently as large merchants and money-lenders; and as a successful, frugal, and clannish group[1] they have been, as a rule, cordially hated both by natives and by later European conquerors. Nevertheless, when reasonably and intelligently dealt with, they have proved to be industrious, law-abiding, and valued subjects. The Chinese immigrants were mostly males (except to some extent in Formosa, which by reason of the exception more nearly resembled a colony in the stricter sense of the term), and commonly consorted with native women, producing mongrel races which are, at least in the Philippines, of a relatively high quality. Native wives and their children were generally deserted when the adventurer had accumulated enough property to return to China and live at ease; yet from time to time the Chinese chose to remain permanently in foreign parts, and even constituted settlements modeled after the local political form of the fatherland.[2]

It is plain that the Chinese have displayed in vigorous form certain activities characteristic of so-called colonizing peoples; that they have formed what might be termed a potential colonial empire. Had the capacities and disposition of the home government admitted of an extension of control analogous to that exercised by much weaker European nations over more ephemeral European settlements in lands far less accessible, we might here be studying the Chinese settlements as full-fledged Chinese colonies. However, governmental activity of this kind is an evolved product, and China had not developed it.

One consideration connected with this potential colonial empire is of curious interest. Owing to the apparent power of the Chinese to live, labor, and procreate in any climate,[3] the so-called plantation colony in a hypothetical Chinese colonial empire would lose many of its distinctive features, as sketched in Chapter I. And it will be seen, at the close of this chapter, that the Chinese settlements fall in with those of the ancients in illustrating the effect upon the nature and results of colonization produced by the elimination of several factors often assumed to be of great moment in the modern and irresolvable product.

[1] The Chinaman does not easily assimilate to the environing type. He adapts himself with little difficulty to all climates, but retains his peculiar characteristics — language, customs, industry, commercial ability — under all governments and in all natural environments with only general modification.   [3] Cf. Bordier, Col., p. 59.

[2] De Groot, Het Kongsiwezen, etc.; cf. Knoop, "Krijgsgeschiedenis" (*De Gids*, 1860).

THE COLONIES OF THE PHŒNICIANS

The forms of migration and colonization thus far considered are not genetically connected with colonial systems familiar to us at the present day. They have been cited because they throw a side-light upon the latter, through their exhibition of the similarities and diversities of human motives and actions as displayed in similar social movements under widely diverging conditions. Attention now turns to the colonizing peoples whose activities lay in the Occident, and whose influence, consciously or unconsciously, has extended down to the present day and its modern systems.

Conditions of the Development of Trade

Of these peoples the first to found what may be called a colonial system were the Semites of the eastern shores of the Mediterranean, the Phœnicians.[1] If now we seek for the causes of that movement of trade, and finally of population, to which the Phœnician colonies owed their being, we find them rooted in conditions of actual or relative discomfort in the home-land. Phœnicia, with a coast-line of about two hundred miles (far shorter than that of Portugal), a maximum extension from the coast-line of some thirty odd miles, and with considerable unproductive soil, was not well fitted to support a growing population. And, in addition to this, there existed constant pressure from the directions of the neighboring empires, and not a few incursions; Phœnicia was not infrequently the unfortunate witness of Egypto-Assyrian collisions on her own ground. This meant not alone pressure of population but also political discontent; and all these factors contributed to render the native environment unsatisfactory and to motive an ever-augmenting attention to the lands which lay in sight across the sea. The Phœnicians became the first people of the West who were able freely to sunder their relations with the native soil and to

[1] Much of the following is condensed or adapted from the first chapter of the author's Homeric Society, and rests largely upon the authorities there used. Reference is also made to the Homeric Society as a study of one of the undeveloped societies of the Phœnician period, envisaged in good part from the standpoint of its relations with the Phœnicians. On Phœnician trade, Speck's Handelsgeschichte has been the general source and check. Busolt (I, 263 ff.) gives some attention to the Phœnicians in their influence upon Greek history. Professor Seymour's authoritative handbook of Homeric antiquities has appeared during the progress of the present volume through the press.

adapt themselves readily to the varying conditions of the outside
world, without at once losing their national individuality. To these
motives for emigration was added the positive incentive of commercial gain. Overland trade between the two great empires of
the time had long been in progress, and had been, at least in part,
in the hands of the Phœnicians. But when once the latter had
overcome the initial difficulties of the sea-route to Egypt, they
were increasingly disposed to sacrifice the land-traffic to the even
greater profits of a maritime frontier-trade. It is to be noted here
that Phœnicia was favored for the development of commerce
above either of the empires, both in geographical position and in
the possession of materials (cedar, etc.) for the construction of
ships. Moreover, in the very dawn of their history the Phœnicians appear already to be characterized by that restless energy,
persistence, audacity in enterprise, acuteness of intellect, commercial genius, adaptability, and general unscrupulousness which were
their distinguishing qualities in later time. Hence, with the inevitable advance of civilization toward the west, their country became the staple and they the middlemen and carriers for the whole
occidental world; and they were thus enabled to seize at the
outset and to maintain for ages the predominant position in a
rapidly extending frontier-trade.[1] The lucrativeness of such a
trade is proverbial. It matters not that they were adapters rather
than inventors; they reaped for centuries enormous gains from a
double exchange of commodities between markets of widely diverse conjunctures,[2] and speedily advanced their sphere of operations to include the limits of the then-known world. But a widely
developed trade implies trading-posts, and successful trading-
stations have ever formed favorable ground for the erection of
colonies.[3] This latter result was the more likely to take place, if,
as was not uncommon in the case of the Phœnicians, delays in
procuring a return-cargo led to temporary settlement, including

---

[1] Rawlinson, pp. 1 ff., 50 ff., 89, 129; Duncker, II, 70; Movers, II, part ii, 6 ff.;
part iii, 127 ff.; Pietschmann, pp. 7 ff., 252 ff.

[2] Cf. Lindsay, I, 22–23; Pietschmann, p. 291; Movers, II, part iii, 87 ff.

[3] Winckler does not believe that there was much emigration from Phœnicia
proper; he thinks that the settlers, in North Africa for instance, were peoples
racially related to the Phœnicians, who came to be thought Phœnicians because of
their connections with Tyre. The trading-colony, or fondaco (cf. p. 64, below), was
the typical form of Phœnician colony. See pp. 341 and 349–357 of Winckler's first
article.

tillage and the like. Starting out in search of the *murex*, from which the popular purple dye of the time was expressed, they were led by this motive, and in quest of metallic treasure, step by step across an island-dotted sea, until, with the lengthening of such easy stages, their nautical art and their confidence had grown able to cope with the more formidable distances and exigencies that lay beyond. In one's astonishment at the extent and daring of Phœnician enterprise he must not lose sight of the fact that these mariners were "children of destiny," and, even though apt scholars, were taught by Nature in one of her exceptional moods of suggestiveness, sequence, and complacency. These progressively established trading-stations, extending from the eastern to the western end of the Mediterranean, and beyond, were subjected, in the course of time, to a sort of unconscious selection whereby the most favorably located and circumstanced became actual settlements and colonies. Located on the coasts, at the mouths of rivers and in other eligible spots, these colonies became centers for the dissemination of culture in all its existing forms.

Characteristics of Phœnician Commerce

But no sufficient conception can be gained either of the colonies themselves, or of their influence upon the West and upon civilization, without at least a sketch of that stream of trade to which they owed their origin and of which they marked the successive courses and branchings. This commerce found its strongest incentive and richest rewards in the exchange of the characteristic commodities, crude and elaborated respectively, of West and East. It cannot be said that the eastern-bound traffic compared in any degree with the western-bound in the momentousness of its effects upon contemporary culture and subsequent history; but it was the desire for the raw materials of the West which constituted the predominant motive for the early extension of Phœnician trade. These unelaborated products were, in large part, metals or ores, and later, wool and grains. Copper was gotten from Cyprus in early times, and tin, — of such importance in a "bronze age," — from Spain, and, through direct or intermediary trade, from the Scilly Islands and southern Britain. Silver was derived largely from the fabulously wealthy deposits of Spain; and gold, lead, and iron, from points near and remote. Mining was a colonial occupation of the highest importance, and many of the settlements were as truly mining colonies as were those of the Spanish in America. Rare and curious products, such as ivory, amber, precious stones, feathers, and even apes and peacocks, made their way to Tyre and Sidon from such remote points as the Senegal and Gambia regions. The impression created in the East by this influx of commodities is vividly expressed in the Book of Ezekiel (chap. xxvii).

It is, however, to the stream of commodities which flowed from, rather than toward, the centers of civilization that the attention of the student of colonization is directed. The latter stream served to provide an already refined civilization with additional necessities and luxuries, but the former carried civilization where before it was not, and in its train came those results of commercial and colonial activity which have contributed so effectively to make the later world what it is. The western-bound [1] traffic consisted roughly of products of the arts, and, of these, manufactures formed the chief component: the various creations of metal work, textiles, wines, oils and ointments, spices, perfumes, dyes, drugs, and the like, — in brief, those products of the high civilization of the East which would progressively appeal to the evolving taste of the western peoples, starting with trinkets and baubles and leading up to the most refined of artistic creations. And to these products of the mechanic arts are to be added others of scarcely less significance, — those of domestication and breeding, i.e. plants and animals within whose organisms there had been accumulated, by the selective activity of man, elements of refinement and superiority. That the Phœnicians were the main agents in the spread of the noble grains, vines, and trees, and of some, at least, of the most useful domestic animals, admits of little doubt.[2] In the course of time the processes also of the arts of agriculture, domestication, manufacture, etc., followed in the wake of the products, if, indeed, they did not often come with them. And there can be no question but that the slave-trade and indiscriminate kidnapping practiced by the Phœnicians considerably aided in the latter result.[3] For one

[1] Phœnician traffic with the farther East does not concern the present argument, as it affected only indirectly the origin and life of the colonies.

[2] Lippert, I, 584 ff.; Rawlinson, pp. 38 ff., 243 ff.; Duncker, II, 287-300; Movers, I, 524-525; II, part i, 250; part iii, 83 ff., 316 ff.; Maspero, pp. 234 ff.; McCurdy, I, § 66; Pietschmann, pp. 245 ff., 287 ff.; Meyer, I, 226.

[3] Movers, II, part iii, 71 ff.; Maspero, pp. 248 ff.; Pietschmann, pp. 28 ff.; cf. Odyssey, xiv, 200 ff.

must realize that the slaves of this time, and indeed of all antiquity, were not necessarily racial, cultural, or social inferiors. Quite the reverse would be true if Egyptians, Hebrews, or Assyrians, kidnapped in the East, were sold in the West. Western masters learned much from such slaves; and if a westerner happened to undergo the same ordeal of loss of liberty in an eastern land, it would occasionally be possible, no doubt, for him to escape with a wealth of ideas and accomplishments acquired in his enforced contact with a higher culture. And thus, to some degree, would the dissemination of civilization be attained.

Nature and Extent of the " Empire "

This survey of the main lines of Phœnician commercial activity is sufficient to demonstrate the general groundwork out of which grew their colonial system, if it should be dignified by such a name. It cannot, in justice, be maintained that the Phœnician settlements and dependencies fully satisfy our definition of colony. Emigration, especially during the periods of Assyrian and Persian aggression in Phœnicia, was strong enough seriously to undermine the prosperity of the colonizing cities; but the extension of governmental control over the colonies was of a sort which would to-day be deemed shadowy, to say the least. One must reflect, however, that such extension of state control as that upon which as a criterion we form our judgments, is rendered possible only by the advance in power over nature, and especially by the development of speedy means of communication. By ship, Carthage was in early times as far from Tyre as is Australia from England, and Cyprus itself was at an equally great distance as far as administrative control through direct communication is concerned. Assuming, however, the sufficiency of means of communication in the setting of the age, there remains the significant and vital fact that Phœnicia was not a unified state with a central government. There was not so much as a capital. Authors tell us of the " hegemony " of Sidon, and then of Tyre;[1] and this word, as in later Greek times, precisely expresses the degree of governmental centralization to which

---

[1] Meyer, art. " Phœnicia," says that it cannot be shown that any other Phœnician towns, except Tyre, founded colonies. Cf. McCurdy, I, §§ 42–44; Movers, II, part i, 318 ff. The hegemony of Tyre covered the period of great Phœnician prosperity (ninth and eighth centuries B.C.). Winckler, I, 344 ff., 357; II, 439 ff.

the Phœnicians, and later the Greeks, attained. Not even inside
the single cities, which formed the largest political and colonizing
units, was centralization secured. This absence of national or even
local coherence and coöperation, and of centralized direction, is
heavy with fate for the "colonial empire" when there are enemies
in the field; but it does not necessarily prevent the growth of
such an empire under favorable conditions. In the early days of a
Phœnician settlement there existed a distinct relation of dependence — even unwilling and coerced dependence — of the new
settlement upon the mother-city; and there even arose a certain
recognizable solidarity between the complex of colonies and metropolises, worthy of the name of empire. This preliminary statement
of the reasons for employing "colony" and "colonization" in reference to the Phœnicians should receive justification in the more
specific account which follows.

"In the tenth century B.C. the navigation and trade of the
Phœnicians extended from the coasts of the Arabian Sea, from the
Somali coast, and perhaps from the mouths of the Indus as far as
the coast of Britain." [1] This extension of activity, immense, even
though it be cautiously discounted, implies a long past of commercial enterprise and attendant colonization. It is therefore with
less astonishment that we are able to accept the truth of the statement that Phœnician colonial activity began, with the settlement of
parts of Cyprus, as early as the thirteenth or fourteenth century B.C.
The movement was continued along lines of least resistance to the
then navigation (island-chains, etc.) toward the north-west, and the
islands of the Ægean and the coasts of Greece (Thrace, Eubœa,
Cythera) were visited and partially settled within a relatively brief
period. The Black and Adriatic seas, offering as they did comparatively unfavorable opportunities for lucrative commerce, were, for
the most part, neglected. However, by the time they had advanced
to the Adriatic the Phœnicians were able to leap the barriers of a

---

[1] Duncker, II, 302; cf. McCurdy, I, App. 3. It is of course impossible to assign
dates except with vague approximation. The chronology of the ancients was, as was
inevitable at their stage of civilization, legendary, conventional, and uncritical. See
Pietschmann, p. 287, note. The tendency of the older writers on ancient history
was undoubtedly toward the assignment of a too high antiquity, especially as regards
the activity of the Phœnicians. Movers (II, part ii, *passim;* part iii, 21 ff.), Duncker
(II, 54 ff.), Rawlinson (pp. 96 ff.), have been corrected by Pietschmann (pp. 27,
240 ff.), Meyer (I, 230 ff.), Maspero (pp. 244–246), and other authorities of a later
date. From the standpoint of the present volume the precise dating of these early
colonial movements, even if possible, is not a matter of essential moment.

narrow sea and to pass on to Sicily, Sardinia, the Balearic Islands, and Spain. They likewise visited the northern coast of Africa, opposite Sicily, and founded colonies, one of the earliest of which was Ityke, the later Utica. From these stations they pushed on through the Straits of Gibraltar and founded Gades (Cadiz), the extreme of their colonies (*ca.* 1000 B.C.); for, although they advanced beyond the straits both northward and southward, and even westward, there is no reliable record of further settlement in these outlying parts. The Mediterranean thus became a Phœnician sea, fringed with Phœnician settlements, and crossed by a network of Phœnician trade-routes.[1] Although our information concerning the actual life in these settlements and colonies is very defective, there can be little doubt that they were typical trading and some-times mining colonies, and came in the course of time to engage in agriculture for the support of life. Population was shifting during the "factory" period, and it was only during later and more settled times that Phœnician wives and families emigrated, and then in no considerable numbers. Free miscegenation with the natives must have been the rule, as will appear later. The local governmental form was probably that which regularly obtains in a group of merchants far from home, — an oligarchy of the older and more experienced. These general inferences are supported by the better-known case of Carthage, later to be cited.

Relations of the Colony and Metropolis

It is fitting now to examine the relations subsisting between the colony and its metropolis. The bearing of the means of communication upon this matter has already been noted, but definiteness may be given to that factor by a word upon Phœnician navigation. In the early periods the ships were very small and slow, and their effectiveness as vehicles of communication was halved by the impossibility of night-sailing. But this was soon remedied, and the Phœnicians also learned to sail into the wind, — a feat regarded as no less than marvelous in those days, — to steer by the north (or Phœnician) star, and to venture over untried seas. As early as the Homeric times Phœnician ships had taken on a magical

---

[1] On the tradition of the circumnavigation of Africa by Phœnician sailors dispatched by King Necho of Egypt, see Herodotus, IV, 42. Saco (App. I, 362 ff.) collects the opinions of scholars upon the reliability of this account.

character because of their relatively high speed and extensive voyages. Their advance in nautical technique was, relatively to that of their contemporaries, very great, but it did not suffice to draw the bonds of empire close, even in the latter days.[1] Thus it is clear that the very apparatus for the extension of metropolitan control, had this existed in the spirit of the age,[2] was yet inadequate. On the whole, however, the political bond seems not to have been much in evidence or attention; the ties between colonies and parent-cities were rather commercial and religious than political. "Most of the colonies of importance were held under a very mild form of the general system of vassalage. The tribute expected was light, and ships and sailors were more in demand than money for the fulfillment of the obligations to the mother-state."[3] Any relations in which Phœnicians figured are better understood if the fact be kept before the mind that the desire for actual, material gain overweighed, in the Phœnician temperament, all other considerations, especially those of large and unsubstantial ideals of "empire" and the like. When the sometimes sorely oppressed metropolis was dependent upon one of its colonies for contributions or trade in raw materials and foods, any defection would naturally be resisted with energy. Thus Utica was forced to resume payment of tribute, and the policy of monopoly and exclusion of alien rivals led to the employment of mercenaries in considerable numbers. In general the government of the metropolis was not so much averse to the exercise of coercion, as incapable of enforcing it.

If, however, the purely political bonds were thus weak, there certainly existed other ties of a rather intimate variety; quarrels between colonies, for example, were referred to the authorities of the metropolis for settlement. And if the purely political bonds were weak, it must be realized that the religious bonds of the period were of a far more vital and material character than those of modern times. The colonies made yearly presents, which were a

---

[1] Herodotus (IV, 86) reckons 700 stadia for a day-voyage and 600 for a night-voyage, aggregating 1300 stadia, or 150 miles, for twenty-four hours. Cf. Lindsay, I, 3 ff. The voyage from the Syrian coast to Gades occupied eighty days, even in Greek times. Pietschmann, p. 307; cf. Maspero, pp. 246 ff.; Rawlinson, pp. 57, 411–412, 467; Movers, II, part iii, 157 ff.; Pietschmann, pp. 27 ff., 283.

[2] Cf. p. 43, below.

[3] McCurdy, I, § 42; Meltzer, I, 144; Meyer, art. "Phœnicia"; Movers, II, part ii, 34 ff.; Lewis, pp. 108–109; Speck, III, part i, 173 ff. (on Carthaginian relations to Tyre).

sort of tribute to the state, to the temples of the metropolis ; even Carthage thus supported the worship of Melkarth in Tyre.[1] And the commercial bonds were at first the more closely drawn, inasmuch as the ways of trade converged in the parent-cities and commerce thereby attained its exclusive and monopolistic stamp. The solidarity engendered by all these alliances, when practically all merchants were natives of one small country, took the place, to some extent, of the political union now deemed, in the wide and cosmopolitan extension of trade, to be the *sine qua non* of colonial empire.

This semi-coherence tended to pass away with time, but was confirmed for a considerable period during the rise of the early competitors for that alluring traffic which had once been all but exclusively Phœnician. If the mother-country could have preserved and extended its independence and effected some adequate unification, and if the colonists had safeguarded the integrity of their blood, this clannish feeling of a monopolistic nation might have continued. That friendly feelings toward the country of origin were preserved for long periods is indicated by the continued migrations to the colonies, and by the welcome there extended to Phœnician fugitives during the encroachments upon Phœnicia of Sargon, Sennacherib, Nebuchadnezzar, Alexander, and others. But it was evident from the disposition and ideals of the Phœnicians that the formation of a colonial empire, in the modern sense, was outside of their purposes and endeavors. Temporary union for self-defense, to say nothing of the formation of any political aggregation, had to be forced upon them — as is evidenced by the case of the Carthaginian empire — by the exigencies of the struggle for existence. All the Phœnicians cared for was commercial gain : if in force, they had always pillaged, robbed, and practiced piracy ; if inferior in strength, they fell back upon pilfering, cheating, and kidnapping. They were known even to Homer as rogues and deceivers,[2] but were endured throughout antiquity for the sake of that which they brought within the reach of active and progressive, if rude, races.

One of the cardinal points of Phœnician policy was the preservation of their monopoly through the exclusion of rivals ; to this end they were ready to expose themselves to serious loss and danger.

[1] Meltzer, II, 149, 151 ; cf. Winckler, I, 342 ff.
[2] Cf. the *punica fides* of the Carthaginians, of which the Romans liked to tell. Speck, III, part i, 63.

This attitude came out more clearly when their monopoly, in its origin almost a natural one, began to suffer from the encroachment of much-tempted competitors. When at last the sources of their material prosperity were threatened they were eager to resist. However, in the palmy days of greater security they were willing to sacrifice all to economic profit; language, religion, customs, even integrity of blood — all the characteristics which distinguish a race or a people — were readily renounced for the gratification of an all-pervading passion for the accumulation of material wealth. It could not be otherwise but that the Phœnician colonies should thus lose their national character. And more : even the racial character of the settlements gradually merged with its environment, so that while the Hebrews, who pursued a policy almost diametrically opposed to the easy adaptability of the Phœnicians, have maintained their racial stamp into modern times, the Phœnicians as a people have long ceased to exist.[1] If, then, the specialized commercial spirit has been able to effect a result of this generality, it is no wonder that the inceptive or potential colonial empire disintegrated and melted away. But it was not left entirely to these broadly acting forces of nature to begin and conclude the process of decay. As in most such cases, the fatal sweep of the storm did not occur without an antecedent brewing, nor apart from ominous indications in previous periods. Even during the Sidonian hegemony (roughly estimated as extending to about the tenth century B.C.), the period of early expansion, the people first to profit by and imitate the activities of the Phœnicians had already replaced their masters in the eastern regions of the Mediterranean. By the thirteenth century the Greeks had driven the Phœnicians from the Ægean Sea. And during the glory-period of Tyrian supremacy which succeeded that of Sidon, the end was already foreshadowed. With a vigor to which they could offer but insufficient resistance, the Phœnicians were forced from the hitherto undisputed advantages of their position, and were encroached upon until

---

[1] Cf. Gumplowicz, Rassenkampf, pp. 332–333; McCurdy, I, §§ 39, 683; Duncker, II, 263; Rawlinson, p. 28; Maspero, pp. 214 ff.; Movers, I, 61; II, part i, 559–561. The Phœnicians did not resist the payment of tribute, provided there was a net commercial gain. "The Tyrians, like the other Phœnicians, were at all times ready to pay tribute to the Great King, whether he was Assyrian, Babylonian, or Persian. But in the present case [that of Sennacherib] it was not a question of allegiance, but of the abdication of maritime supremacy, and such preëminence Tyre was as little willing to forego as was afterwards her greatest colony, Carthage." McCurdy, II, 283–284.

there existed in the Mediterranean Sea another colonial empire
conterminous with their own.

To the activities of these new colonizers the account will presently
come; it is enough here to say that they overcame and forced back
the Phœnicians through the same methods of aggression practiced
by the latter throughout their history. But when the Phœnicians
had retired to a point where further withdrawal meant a complete
surrender of their share in the world-trade, they began to evince a
characteristically tardy willingness to unite and to fight for commercial existence. And, since the decline of the Phœnician cities
left the headship of this enforced confederation to the greatest
colony of the west, — Carthage, — the center of historical interest
moves, naturally enough, to that city and its destiny. Here, in the
strict sense of the word, leave is taken of Phœnician colonization.
But since the subsequent history of the quondam colonies is well
fitted to bring out several important considerations respecting
Phœnician capabilities and colonial policy, a sketch of this history
as it centered about the figure of Carthage is yet in place.[1]

Carthage as a Phœnician Colony

Carthage, the "new city," founded about 800 B.C., was already
beyond the early stages of a trading-colony — was, indeed, a large
and powerful city — before the Greeks thought of moving westward.
During the three centuries of upheaval and general insecurity which
followed the second elevation of the Assyrian kingdom in the first
half of the ninth century B.C., many a noble family and its retainers
and many a prominent business firm was transferred from Tyre,
the mother-city, to Carthage. The position of affluence and independence thus attained was increased by the results of Greek
aggression in the eastern Mediterranean, which interposed a foreign
and hostile element between the metropolis and its colony. And
so, because of its prosperity and power, Carthage came to usurp
the position of a common metropolis, as it were, for the colonies of
the west.[2] With the tardy recognition on the part of these colonies
of the true significance of the advance of the Greeks, at first under-
estimated, Carthage was led to assume a theoretical, if not actual,

[1] See especially Meltzer, I, 144 ff. Speck (III, part i) gives a very valuable general
account of Carthage and its dependencies.

[2] As Winckler (II, 449) puts it, Carthage gathered together "Phœniciandom" as
Tyre had done before.

protectorate over Phœnician interests; to direct united efforts where the spur of necessity had clearly demonstrated the need of concerted action, and to enforce coöperation on the part of recalcitrants. A quasi-imperial station was thus, as it were, forced upon her. She aided other colonies in their wars with native peoples, and in return possessed herself of part of their lands; she was even led to a certain amount of true colonization on her own account.[1] But it was as a willingly or unwillingly acknowledged head of a defensive coalition that she, like Athens in the Delian League, administered her empire.[2] The progressive advance of the Greeks to the shores of Sicily seems not to have aroused the Phœnician colonies to a sense of danger, but their abrupt appearance in the western end of the Mediterranean, and even in the Gades-region, awakened the Semites to the fact that their last and most treasured possessions were threatened; and before the Greeks could advance across Sicily, a line of defense had already been formed, facing the south and east, by cities under the protection of Carthage, and by allied native peoples. The Greeks were at first repulsed, and in succeeding times were held back from political advance both in the islands and on the coasts. To this end a system of alliances with Etruscans, Romans, and others was skillfully employed. Treaties went even to the modern extent of delimitation of spheres of influence, for instance in the relations of the Carthaginians with Massilia. The Carthaginian hegemony took on a more and more imperial aspect, and the administration a progressively centralized form.[3] From this time on the colonial quality of the settlements

---

[1] The Carthaginians had much difficulty with the nomad peoples of Africa, over whom they were unable to extend an unquestioned supremacy. They had, indeed, bought or rented their own ground from the natives and paid them an annual stipend up to the middle of the fifth century. They attempted to enlist native races in their armies from time to time, but above all tried to keep on good terms with them. Meltzer, II, 74 ff., 93, 104; Speck, III, part i, 37–50, 407; cf. Smith, pp. 13–21, 43 ff.; Lewis, pp. 110–112; Ratzel, III, 183–184. On the Phœnicians and Carthaginians in Spain, cf. Colmeiro, I, 29–43. On the rather close mutual relations of Tyre and Carthage, see Meltzer, II, 149–152.

[2] On the Carthaginian league or empire, see Speck, III, part i, 25–28, 33–36, 50 ff., 144 ff.

[3] Cf. Ihne, II, 5 ff. This author naturally envisages Carthage from the standpoint of its relations and conflict with Rome, summing up the comparison as follows (II, 461): "The main cause of the superiority of Rome over Carthage we have found in the firm geographical and ethnographical unity of the Roman state as compared with the chequered career of the nationalities ruled over by Carthage, and in the disjointed configuration of its territory, scattered over long lines of coast islands." This contrast serves to bring out from a somewhat different angle of vision several considerations upon which the present treatment lays stress. Cf. Speck, III, part i, 63 ff.

drops away, and states are pitted against states. The rise of
Carthage demonstrates, however, that there was in the trading-
settlements of the Phœnicians the possibility of the construction
of a closely knit colonial empire. The elements lacking to this
end, and cited above, are easily recognizable as functions of the
Phœnician character and of the contemporary stage of civilization.[1]

Temper and Influence of the Phœnicians

But, before leaving the Phœnicians and their activities, recognition must be accorded to the services rendered by them to civilization. Working from the sole standpoint of self-interest, they
neither harbored humanitarian and missionary aims nor felt the
necessity of utilizing them as cloaks to conceal their real motives.
Hence any " culture-mission " performed by them was discharged
with indifference, if not unconsciously. If their influence upon
later times was a powerful one, it represents the effectiveness of
the virtually isolated factor of trade, — a factor which, in later
times, it has been all but impossible convincingly to isolate. It
must be realized that the Phœnicians had largely to do with active,
receptive races, and no doubt effected changes in their culture with
the minimum of resistance. But it is likewise true that they had
no notions of what " ought to be," but contented themselves with
a tactful display of temptations to the acquisition of a higher
material civilization, this being a commercial activity which brings
its own rewards. It would be hard to do justice to the unconscious
culture-dissemination of the Phœnician settlements and colonies.
Most authorities would doubtless agree upon the general statement
that but for the Phœnicians Europe, and so the farther West, could
scarcely have become what they now are. From the trade-routes
of this people, both to the north and to the south, there radiated a
glow of enlightenment and civilization; and in their wake came
worthy successors in the task of race-education, whose arts and

---

[1] Speck (III, part i, 147), envisaging terms in a sense somewhat different from
that here employed, can write : " Kein anderer Staat der alten Welt hat das Kolonial-
system in solchem Umfange geübt wie Karthago, und für keinen zweiten sind die
Kolonien andauernd von gleicher Bedeutung geblieben. Der Staat bestand beinahe
nur aus Kolonien, war in solchem Masse auf sie begründet, das seine Existenz davon
abhing." This author calls attention to the wide extent of Carthaginian trade (III,
part i, 182 ff.), asserting (p. 182) : " Kein anderes Volk brachte gleichzeitig so
zahlreiche und mannigfaltige Waren in den Handelsverkehr wie die Karthager."

methods were based upon those of the path-breakers themselves.[1]
The same trade-routes continued to mark the widening highroads
of culture until the way was prepared for the great civilizing
agencies which proceeded westward with the extension of the
Christian religion. Owing to physiographical and ethnological conditions, this progress of culture turned to the north rather than to
the south. Possibly some indirect influences penetrated in the latter
direction; in any case it is certain that the African coast would
have exerted less attraction upon the later Moslem conquerors had
it not been brought within the civilized world, and made worth the
effort of conquest, by the initial activity of the Phœnicians.[2]

" Not only were the Phœnicians the originators of a worldwide
trade and of a farsighted commercial policy unrivalled in ancient
times, but their maritime supremacy has been the most enduring
known to men. Even that of Britain has not yet lasted one-fourth
as long." [3]

THE COLONIES OF THE GREEKS

After the Phœnicians, the next people to found colonial societies
on a large scale were the Greeks.[4] Their activities have been
touched upon in so far as was necessary to the preceding argument,
and may be reviewed the more rapidly for the reason that they
were so largely inspired by and patterned after those of the Phœnicians. The genesis of Greek maritime enterprise can be made out
in the Homeric poems, which, in addition, cast considerable light
upon early relations between Greeks and Phœnicians. The Homeric
Greeks are about as proficient on the sea as the earlier Phœnician

[1] Winckler (I, 340; II, 450) lays particular stress upon the fact that the Phœnicians were only intermediaries; he says that they had no more of independent
culture than does a harbor-town in comparison with the interior district to which it
affords an outlet. He likewise insists that the Phœnicians have been given too
much credit, because everything that came to the less-cultured nations from the East,
i.e. through trade, was referred by the recipients, who knew of no other, to a Phœnician source. Cf. Keller, Hom. Soc., pp. 10, 24, 89–90. The Phœnicians thus came
to be trade personified.

[2] Meltzer, I, 63 ff.; Pietschmann, p. 285; Duncker, II, 287 ff.; Movers, II, part ii,
4 ff.; part iii, 2 ff.; Meyer, art. " Phœnicia." " Wherever the Phœnicians had been,
the grandeur and audacity of their enterprises had left ineffaceable traces in the
imagination of the people." Maspero, p. 234.

[3] McCurdy, I, § 66.

[4] The greater part of what follows on the Greek colonies has been taken from
Beloch (Vol. I), Busolt (Vol. I), and Speck (Vol. II); where there is substantial
agreement between these authorities specific references to them are omitted.

mariners; they are just learning from the latter, who display the products and processes of culture to their eager eyes, and pour wild and competition-discouraging "commercial myths"[1] into their astonished ears. The Greeks venture on the sea, it is true, but their voyages are short and slow, and but rarely for trading-purposes; they are still the sought and not the seekers. From the Homeric narrative we are therefore able to apprehend the point of view of the lower and rising race in its contact with a superior civilization. This picture is but the reverse of the process as it has been viewed from the Phœnician side; the early colonial activities of the Greeks are the more readily understandable if the scope and nature of Phœnician commercial enterprise be kept in mind.[2]

MOTIVES OF EMIGRATION

At the outset, however, it would appear that the main motive for Greek emigration to and settlement in adjacent islands was less a desire for commercial gain than an impulse to escape the evils attendant upon pressure of population on land. Emigration because of political discontent played but a small rôle in these early ages, and trade-interests of an aggressive sort did not exist in the absence of industries sufficient to provide products for exportation. It was under such a system of folk-movements that the neighboring Ægean and other islands and the western coast of Asia Minor were settled, in the latter half of the second millennium B.C. The native peoples were absorbed or reduced to a subject class, and the various cities united their interests in a sort of religious league with its center at Mykale. By the eighth century, therefore, when the stream of emigration began to flow with stronger sweep over greater distances, the Greek race already occupied an area far larger than Greece itself, and some of the earliest settlements of the Ægean were ready to send out colonies in competition with those of the parent-land.[3]

[1] It seems probable that the tales of strange and vaguely localized tribes and monsters in the Odyssey may be in large part referred to the only mariners of the time well known to the peoples of Greece. These tales were certainly calculated to discourage travel upon the sea. It will be seen in later chapters of this book that other peoples who have held valued monopolies have utilized such means to hold off encroachment.

[2] Cf. Keller, Hom. Soc., chap. i, et passim; Letourneau, Commerce, pp. 426 ff.

[3] Hertzberg, pp. 3 ff. Speck (II, 166) says that "the external history of the Greek people consists essentially in an unbroken transmarine migration."

Meanwhile the simple motive for emigration in the sense of folk-movement had been superseded by a complex of incentives, of which the desire to escape the direct ills of over-population was but one. Commercial interests had sprung up with the advance in culture gained by contact with the East. These took form, first of all, in piracy, wherein the Greeks speedily came to surpass their old masters, the Phœnicians. Thucydides [1] notes that the older Greek settlements were established inland rather than directly upon the shores, in order to expose them less to piratical raids ; and even in his own time this historian had not seen the suppression of the freebooters. Another motive was the adventurous and wandering spirit which characterized the Greeks in their newly gained power of sailing the sea, and which, indeed, promoted settlement less in a direct way than indirectly through piracy. Motives of conquest were also involved in the complex of Greek incentives. And, finally, the development of factions in the home-cities had led, through consequent political dissatisfaction, to the voluntary or coerced withdrawal of considerable bodies of citizens.[2] But the primary motives remained rooted in the conditions of pressure of numbers and in the opening prospects of commercial gain through imitation of Phœnicians and their methods. It has been stated by some that the typical colony was of the agricultural type; and it is no doubt true that Greece was, by its physiographical nature, a land sure to suffer from limitations of agricultural and pasture areas. These limitations were felt the more because of the strength of the growth of population. There were many purely agricultural colonies and not a few fishing-stations, but a survey of the facts leaves no room for doubt that a large number of the inceptive undertakings were essentially commercial in nature and represented an effort to win a share in the lucrative operations hitherto monopolized by the Phœnicians. In the course of time the trading-stations acquired adjacent areas and took on a distinctly agricultural type, for the Greeks exhibited a tendency thus to identify themselves with land, which was almost as marked as the indifference of the Phœnicians to all else than exchange. The progress of the Greek colonies was

[1] I, 7 ; cf. 8.

[2] Speck, pp. 180–182. A writer on the term ἀποικία in Pauly-Wissowa distinguishes a third period of emigration and colonization, subsequent to the year 580 B.C. and lasting till the time of Alexander, where the predominant motive for movement lay in the stresses and calamities of war. This period, however, falls rather outside the scope of this discussion.

from trade to agriculture and cattle-raising rather than the reverse; and this, their ultimate form, in accordance with general principles explained above, rendered them of a type less dependent and ephemeral than that of the Phœnician colonies, and so differentiated them from the latter in an important respect.[1]

Relation of the ἀποικία to its Metropolis

In fact, the ἀποικία is not infrequently used as a type of the so-called "natural colony,"[2] — an emigrant group connected with the country of origin by no more definite bonds than those of a common nationality and culture. If this were strictly true, the ἀποικία could have small place in our present discussion. In their early history, however, and sometimes in their subsequent periods, the Greek colonies seem to have recognized bonds of a much closer character. In founding the colony, the activity of the metropolis was generally the determining factor. For, in addition to service in forwarding the emigrants to their destination, the parent-city appointed a director (οἰκιστής) for the colony, who supervised the settlement and established institutions for the settlers modeled directly upon those of the metropolis.[3] This bound the colony to the mother-community by ties of an intimate nature; and to these were added those of a common dialect, religion, body of customs, etc. Even the rivers, mountains, and other natural features of the new habitat were named after those of the home-land.[4] War of a colony upon its metropolis was regarded as a crime analogous to an assault of a son upon a father,[5] and the metropolis was, on its part, supposed to aid the colony in time of danger. Corinth, for example, afforded aid to the adult Syracuse through four centuries. The colony was represented at festivals in the mother-city by solemn embassies, and common intellectual interests — in poetry, art, and ideas in general — added to the more material solidarity.

The political dependence characteristic of trading-stations, with their sparse population and dangerous environment, gave the

---

[1] Speck, II, 180 ff.; cf. Ihne, II, 4–5.   [2] Roscher, pp. 44 ff.; Ireland, p. 3; etc.

[3] For the details of colony-founding, see Caillemer; Speck, II, 167 ff. The colonists generally emigrated willingly, but sometimes under constraint. Surveys implying the definition of titles to land were undertaken.

[4] The ἀποικία was really a "home away from home."

[5] Cf. Raoul-Rochette, I, 33–34, 44–45

metropolis an especial influence in the earliest times. Not infrequently the colonies paid tribute in return for protection, and were forced to submit to a certain amount of coercion, especially in times of danger. But with the divergence of interests the power of the metropolis declined, and became rather a respected and honored general influence upon trade and politics than a real rule. The mother-city sometimes rebelled against this consummation, and, in the case of Corinth, resisted it and formed what might be called a true, if miniature, colonial empire; but the non-centralization at home, and the inadequacy of means of transportation and communication, rendered an extensive empire almost as impossible for the Greeks as it had been for the Phœnicians.[1]

The loose relationship between metropolis and colony — so striking to one who has in mind the extent of metropolitan pretensions at the present day — was largely a function of the comparatively diminutive scale of areas and activities of the ancient times. Both Greek and Phœnician colonies were settlements of cities, "not of nations, not of kingdoms, nor of commonwealths on the scale of kingdoms." The emigrants were citizens isolated from their spheres of civic activity, not subjects who owed loyalty to a sovereign man or government in all places and at all times; the latter is an idea which demanded the mediæval environment to call it into being. The metropolis continued to lead its life as before; the colony began one of its own. Claims of actual dominance on the part of the older society did not enter into the category of possibilities harbored by the minds of the time. There was no need of a declaration of independence, still less of the severance of an irritating relation in wrath and by the sword; the falling-out of Corcyra and Corinth, by its very exceptionality and the popular feelings it engendered, contributes to the strengthening of the general case.[2] There was no necessary economic, political, or financial dependency, such as characterizes, as has been seen, the distant or tropical colony. No allegiance was implied; hence no constraint was felt in the acknowledgment of what would seem in a later age to indicate dependence, — of such names, bonds, and the like, as are not infrequently suppressed, ignored, or chafed

---

[1] In collateral confirmation of this principle it may be noted that the centralized monarchies of some of the colonies were able to hold in subjection their own sub-colonies if the latter were not too remote.

[2] Busolt, I, 305–307; Raoul-Rochette, I, 33, 48.

under in modern times.[1] The lasting tie between colony and metropolis, and the one which constantly recalled community of nationality and interests, was that of trade. And here we have the familiar relation of the supplementary markets of communities producing respectively elaborated and raw products. It is scarcely necessary to rehearse the details of Mediterranean trade, which have been indicated already in treating of the Phœnicians; for the Greeks virtually imitated the Phœnicians, then expelled them and took their places, at least in the eastern sections of the Mediterranean.[2]

Extent of Greek Colonization

The spread of Greek colonization might roughly be indicated by saying that it was practically conterminous with that of the Phœnicians, but also included certain districts to which the latter, with their exclusively commercial interests, gave less attention. From the eastern end of the Mediterranean to Sicily the Phœnician colonies were largely suppressed and replaced; beyond that point, toward the west, the settlements of both nations existed, occasionally in close proximity. The first Greek colonies, the results of irregular movements of population, had been located in Crete, the Ægean Islands, and on the coasts of Asia Minor; they were composed largely of emigrants from Attica, Bœotia, and other agricultural centers. But with the lengthening of distances and the development of shipping, the centers of dispersion had changed to such maritime districts as Chalkis and Eretria; and later to Megara, Corinth, Rhodes, Lesbos, and the Ionian coast-cities, among which Miletos was the most eminent. Owing to the resistance met with toward the south and east, the course of emigration had been directed predominantly toward the west, where its energetic currents rapidly drove before them the almost non-resisting Phœnicians. In this western movement the first great stage was Sicily, a fertile island, rich in hides, wool, salt, clay, asphalt, valuable stones, and other desirable products. Roughly

[1] Freeman, pp. 6–46 passim.

[2] Speck, II, 187–190. "Den Kern einer Kolonie bildete eine Schar von Auswanderern, die eine neue Heimat suchte und eine neue Polis begründete, welche zwar in einem Pietätsverhältnisse zur Mutterstadt blieb, sich jedoch als selbständiges Staatswesen entwickelte." Busolt, I, 281; cf. Raoul-Rochette, I, 36–42, 56–58; Lewis, pp. 107–108.

speaking, the Greek voyages to the west began with the eighth century, and by 700 B.C. Naxos and Syracuse had been founded. Corinth was especially prominent in these early western enterprises. The emigration to Sicily was large, and the early colonies were soon able to send out sub-colonies. New settlements were made in what was later known as Magna Græcia, the most important of them being Cumæ, Sybaris, Croton, Tarentum, and Neapolis.[1] By the middle of the seventh century the growth, prosperity, and aggressiveness of the Greek colonies, particularly of Syracuse, aroused the Phœnicians to their peril, and the struggle between the rivals began. However, the Greeks were not deterred by opposition from passing beyond the chief scene of conflict and founding settlements in the farther West. The most important of these was Phocæan Massilia (about 600 B.C.), which, with the aid of the metropolis, proceeded to surround itself with a series of daughter-settlements located especially on the south-eastern coast of Spain.[2] The Greeks thus secured the trade of the Gulf of Lyons and of the Spanish eastern coast, and even opened up routes for the overland transportation of Gallic and British products. Upon the southern shore of the Mediterranean they likewise established themselves in Cyrenaica and Barca, between the Egyptians and the Carthaginians.

It has been shown how the Carthaginians, called to assume the headship of a defensive Phœnician league, succeeded in blocking the hitherto irresistible advance of the Greeks. The details of this action need scarcely be given, for neither Carthage on the one hand, nor Syracuse on the other, after this time deserve the name of colony. No doubt the indefatigable activity of Dionysios I, had it met with success, would have opened up a broad field for further Hellenic expansion. And it is not without its significance that under pressure both Phœnicians and Greeks could coöperate among themselves for a common end; Dionysios received aid from even the old Greek metropolis in his struggles, which shows that the original bonds had not yet dropped away.[3] Nevertheless, interest in the western colonies as colonies can hardly be extended farther.

---

[1] Cf. Ihne, I, 376 ff.; Pauly-Wissowa, sub ἀποικία; Hertzberg, pp. 20–80; Speck, II, 168 ff.; Lindsay, II, 68 ff.

[2] For the commercial importance of Marseilles, see Pigeonneau, I, 18; Speck, III, part i, 55 ff.   [3] On the career of Dionysios, see especially Beloch, II, 155 ff.

Toward the south and east the Greeks found insuperable obstacles to settlement in the presence of the older empires and their influence. Even Cyprus was never fully cleared of Phœnicians. Before Egypt the Greeks first appeared as pirates, later as mercenaries; and in subsequent times they had factories, with rights of corporations, at the mouths of the Nile. This acquaintance with Africa probably suggested the settlement of Cyrenaica, but has little importance for our subject. Toward the north-east, likewise, attention was directed. Greek cities, especially Miletos, early conceived an interest in the Black and Marmora seas; of the former they made, with their many trading-settlements, an "hospitable sea."[1] There was, however, but little colonization in this region. The configuration of the coast enforced settlement in localities unprotected by nature from the inroads of barbarian tribes; and the Greeks, besides, never cared to dwell permanently outside of their native vine-and-olive type of physical environment. The Black Sea stations were not populous, and, for the most part, discharged the function of supply depots for grain, salt fish, and other raw products in demand at home. Somewhat the same may be said of the colonies in the northern Ægean.

If, now, the data of Greek expansion be summed up, "In a period of two centuries (*circa* 800–600 B.C.) the Greeks turned the Ionian Sea, the Propontis, and the Pontus into Greek seas, and founded settlements in the lands of the Scythians, Thracians, Italians, Kelts, Iberians, Libyans, and Egyptians. Greek merchants visited the courts of inland kings as far as the great mountain chains of Central Asia, in the Libyan oases of Egypt, the Po region, and that of Tartessus[2] on the Atlantic Ocean. The nation outgrew former narrow boundaries; Greek influence made itself effective in the whole Mediterranean region; the Hellenes took their share in the evolution of the world's history."[3] The process by which the Greeks spread civilization has already been indicated in speaking of the Phœnicians and their methods; but some differences in results may be seen by noting several characteristic features in the growth and life of the colonies.

---

[1] Πόντος Εὔξεινος. It was once called ἄξενος because of the rude tribes which surrounded it; Εὔξεινος may be a euphemism (Liddell & Scott, *sub* εὔξενος).

[2] The Phœnician Tarshish, the region about Gades.

[3] Speck, II, 73–74; cf. Busolt, I, 293; Beloch, I, 198. A full list of Greek ἀποικίαι is given under ἀποικία in Pauly-Wissowa. See for exhaustive details Raoul-Rochette.

CHARACTER OF THE COLONIES

When Cicero speaks of the Greek colonies forming a "border" about the seas,[1] his expression is descriptive rather than metaphorical; for the inland penetration of the colonies was very slight. This was natural enough in the trading-colonies, for commerce, as well as fishing and mining, affords gains to a limited number only; but even the agricultural colonies, or those which later took on the agricultural type, although they received a large immigration, remained essentially coast-settlements. The Greeks never cared to leave the sea and found an inland empire; perhaps their greatest inland expansion, if it may be so called, before the time of Alexander, occurred in Magna Græcia, across the peninsula of Italy. The colonial areas varied from four to twenty-four square miles; in North Africa they got no farther than eleven or twelve miles from the sea. It may be judged, therefore, that Greek influence proceeded but little farther through direct contact than Phœnician. And in the Greeks' relations to natives, since they had no "colonial system," variation was the rule — variation according to the strength and needs of the colonists and the state of settlement, on the one side, and in view of the military strength and disposition of the natives on the other. Friction was generally avoided, and simple relations of trade maintained; if, however, the colony received numerous accessions, it made itself mistress, through force or treachery, of the native peoples.[2] These were destroyed only in desperate cases; the Greeks preferred to keep them as slaves, or subjects without rights. Thus the significant influence of the Greeks upon later civilization was not exercised through conquest, political or religious, but primarily through the adaptable instrumentality of exchange. Thus far the cases of Greek and Phœnician are parallel.

It is noteworthy, however, that the Greeks maintained their national identity more successfully than did the Phœnicians, and that they impressed the type of specifically Hellenic civilization where the Phœnicians spread a less specialized form. This result is referable partially to the Greek character and partially to the condition under which colonization took place. For while the Greeks lusted for gain quite as much as did the Phœnicians, they

[1] De Republica, II, chap. iv.
[2] Speck, II, 185–186; Busolt, I, 271–272.

substituted in place of Phœnician adaptability a positive element of aggressiveness in the retention of their national characteristics. With all its city-economy,[1] Greece was more of a nation than was Phœnicia. There was a general loyalty to the Delphic god, who, it should be noted, relying as he did upon rather full information,[2] actively furthered and directed colonization; and the national games long formed a tie of an intimate nature. The distinction between Greek and barbarian was too strongly felt to admit of systematic neglect, for example, in miscegenation. The barbarians became Greek less through contact with Greek settlements than through the dissemination of the Greek tongue and culture — they became Greek by adoption, not by the infusion of Greek blood.[3] And the spirit of Greek institutions and customs was not allowed to lapse. It has been shown how a colony was modeled throughout upon its metropolis, and this went so far as to render an οἰκιστής from the original city all but indispensable in the founding of even a colony's colony. Strong instances of attachment between a colony and its metropolis are not infrequent; according to Plato, the two should form one entity, alike in language and laws.[4] This extended community of interests and life was broken in upon by no such catastrophes as separated the Phœnician cities from their colonies; in fact, constant and copious emigration to the colonies was a distinctively Greek characteristic. And since these colonies were real colonies of settlement, the general principles given above[5] apply to them, and show, on general lines, why they grew to states, while maintaining their individuality and leaving its strong impress upon the world.

Action and reaction are interwoven; for the economic and other effects of the opening of extended markets and the spread of nationality could not but affect strongly the land of origin.[6] Greece was better fitted for manufacture, mining, and trade than for agriculture; and her technical inferiority to the East gradually

---

[1] How all-absorbing in group-relations the conception of the πόλις was, can best be judged by one who has searched the Greek language for a term corresponding to "society" or "nation." It is only in the absence of an adequate Greek term that a linguistic hybrid such as "sociology" has become current. But "political" is a heritage which is retained, although with etymological inconsistency.

[2] Caillemer.

[3] Freeman (p. 11) draws a contrast with America, where the population of the United States has become European not by adoption but through a process of replacement.   [4] γένος ὁμόφωνον καὶ ὁμόνομον. Νόμοι, IV, 708.   [5] Pp. 17 ff.

[6] Beloch, I, 198 ff.

disappeared as this broad division of labor between metropolis and colony rendered possible an ever-sharpening specialization. She was enabled progressively to shift the center of gravity of her industrial organization away from the production of a food-supply and of raw materials of the arts. And the development of crowded centers of population, and of complex relations between men, forced changes of great moment in customs, laws, and government. Not only that, — which is a matter of Greek culture-history, — but the important colonial interests formed a new basis for Hellenic strifes, catastrophes, and combinations, and so of larger, if not more stable, political units.

The history of the colonies, so far as it is known, shows them prosperous. They were sufficiently adaptable to change unessential elements in their own constitutions, and not infrequently surpassed the home-land in the wealth and variety of their products, material and intellectual. Their original social forms, modeled upon those of the parent-cities, and consequently aristocratic in general nature, were not infrequently altered in the direction of adaptation to a rougher environment. Thus, especially in Sicily, and under pressure of hostile neighbors, a well-developed monarchy was established and long maintained. The more intimate details of colonial life are not well made out; this life was undoubtedly a rougher type of that exhibited by the metropolis, but identical with the latter in essential details. The great influence of material wealth should be especially noted; the colonies were often " timocratic."[1] The trading or agricultural colony, by whomsoever founded, represents a fairly consistent type.

It is because there existed between the colonies and metropolises a complex of ties vital enough to be transformed, in case of need, into actual bonds of political dependency, that the Greek settlements, like the Phœnician, give the impression of a colonial empire. But it appears that the characteristic factional spirit of the Greeks followed them directly into the newer settlements; and this internal dissension, even though suspended on occasion, was a quality fatal to the construction of a real empire.[2] The

[1] Caillemer; cf. Busolt, I, 271 ff.

[2] It would be unjust to pass over the two Greek "empires" that deserve the name, — the Athenian and the Macedonian. During their period of predominance the Athenians developed a form of offshoot society, the κληρουχία, very similar to the Roman colonia, presently to be mentioned in more detail as being a better represented type. This was an imperial dependency created for imperial ends,

rising Roman power reduced the several Greek states and colonies, as it were, one by one; and the arduousness and cost of this reduction did not approach those incurred in conquering the enforced but persistent and desperate league of Semites, which constituted the last hope of the Phœnicians in the West. So far as these cases *in extremis* go, they indicate less capacity in the Greek than in the Semite for the unification and extension of political power.[1]

THE ROMAN *COLONIAE*

In treating of the Phœnician and Greek colonies it has been possible practically to eliminate the element of metropolitan control over the new societies, for it existed only at the outset, by exception, or in vague and shadowy form. Nice discrimination might with some reason refuse to recognize in these peoples' enterprises a genuine colonial activity; and the same might be asserted with even greater reason regarding those of the Romans. The latter afford us, however, another experiment in the elimination of factors, and that in a sense converse with respect to the one just cited; for with the Romans emigration and trade were negligible and metropolitan control was a universal principle.[2]

whose settlers expropriated the natives of its regions, or functioned as a garrison among disaffected allies, while retaining most of the rights and duties of Athenian citizenship. The cleruchies were located chiefly in Eubœa, the Cyclades, the islands off the southern coast of Thrace, and the Chersonese; the number of families located in cleruchies just before the Peloponnesian War is estimated at 15,000. Hertzberg, p. 80; Caillemer; Beloch, I, 493 ff.; II, 274 ff., 279, 304; Lewis, p. 104.

The Macedonian settlements in the East were mostly garrisons, whose members generally intermarried or consorted with the natives. They can scarcely be denominated colonies in our sense, although their constituents of population, their later industrial and commercial activity, and finally their widely extending Hellenizing function give them a kind of colonial stamp. Perhaps they were as much colonies for a time as the Roman *coloniae*; their general type departs in only unimportant respects from that of the latter, as described below. But their ephemeral character makes them of less value to the study of colonization than their more developed aftertypes. See Hertzberg, pp. 81 ff.; Beloch, III, part i, 10 ff., 261 ff.

[1] Cf. Ihne, I, 377–378; Hertzberg, pp. 11–16.

[2] The bulk of the data here given on the colonies is derived from Brodrick, Ihne, Lewis, De Coulanges, Arnold, and the article "Coloniae" in the Pauly-Wissowa Encyclopädie. Cf. also Humbert, in Daremberg et Saglio, *sub* "Colonia." These encyclopædia articles furnish details and necessary references; the present treatment takes up the *colonia* mainly as a variant form. For a brief general treatment, see Brunialti, pp. 19 ff.

Motives for Founding the *Coloniae*

The stock motives for colonization were with the Romans relatively non-existent. Italy was never to such a degree over-populated during the Roman predominance that the rational utilization of the existing arts would not have afforded almost immediate relief. The commercial spirit entered but feebly into the situation, for mercantile activity scarcely existed in earlier times, and then and later, as is natural in a military state, was held in more or less of disesteem.[1] There were no religious or political reasons to impel emigration. The incentives, in short, which have most generally led men to a change of environment were but a vanishing quantity. All other motives were merged in the political and imperial one of group-aggrandizement, — the extension and confirmation of the authority of the Roman rule ; " the history of Roman colonization is the history of the Roman state.[2] Roman colonization was thus one of many governmental expedients in the struggle for empire ; the colonies were part of the machinery of conquest and subjugation. They did not precede the state and impel its extension to cover already existing national interests, but followed it, and, as outposts, secured its successive advances. Thus they formed, from one aspect, part of the machinery of provincial administration ; they were, in short, a series of garrisons, and in both the earlier and later periods were intended to be " non oppida Italiae, sed propugnacula imperii." [3] They " marked the growth of Roman dominion as the rings mark the annual growth of a tree." [4]

[1] " Despising commercial pursuits, they [the Romans] looked to Greece and other nations to regulate their over-sea trade and to supply their wants; and when their fleets obtained the dominion of the sea, their object was less to protect their rapidly extending maritime commerce than to consolidate and preserve their power and dominion upon the land. . . . As far as can now be ascertained, the supply of corn for the capital formed the chief and for ages almost the only article of commerce worthy of senatorial notice, as any scarcity in the supply of that necessary article invariably produced tumults among the people." Lindsay, I, 163, 170 ; cf. also pp. 109, 157, 177–179, 187–188. It was mainly the efforts of other peoples that made Rome a commercial center. One is inclined sometimes to suspect that the body of Roman commercial law subsequently developed was aimed in its application mainly at non-Roman merchants, etc. Cf. Speck, III, part i, 427 ff., 493, etc. ; Lindsay, I, 162 ff.

[2] Pauly-Wissowa, *sub* " Coloniae."

[3] Cicero, De leg. agr., II, 27, § 73. The colonists regularly went out " sub vexillo." Practically all the colonies founded under the Empire were strictly military. Brodrick, pp. 53, 54, 56.

[4] Ihne, I, 413.

Conformably with this their object, the colonies owed their origin not to individual initiative, but to deliberate official action; the right of creating colonies lay successively with the kings, the official representatives of the people, and the emperors. Even emigration to already formed colonies was excluded from the sphere of individual initiative. It is also to be noted that the colonies were not established in unsettled districts, but were generally located in the heart of towns, in newly conquered regions, where their presence provided a constant suggestion and example of subordination, as well as an intimate and uninterrupted exhibition of the advantages of Roman rule and civilization. Thus they were far from representing the tentative efforts of a growing people to expand into new habitats, or to "tap" a virgin region of trade; they were the guardians, and at times the buffers, of the empire, the last links between Rome and her dependencies, the objects of gradual incorporation. It is clear that we have here a form of colonization exhibiting a thorough-going contrast with those of the other Mediterranean nations hitherto considered. The principle of the Roman colony has been compared with that followed by the French in Algeria and the British in India.[1]

NATURE OF THE *COLONIA*

If the *coloniae* had been merely garrisons, they would have entered as little into the range of our subject as do the *provinciae*. Etymologically the word *colonia* designates an important, if secondary, character of the Roman offshoot societies; they were groups of cultivators.[2] When, during the earlier Italian conquests, the citizens of a town were dispossessed in favor of a Roman garrison, a part of their lands (often one-third) was given over to the farmer-soldiers as a sort of substitute for other remuneration. The *coloniae* likewise came to discharge the political and social

[1] Algeria: Lewis, p. 117. India: Brodrick, p. 64; De Saussure, pp. 268–269. Lewis, in the same place, says that the Greek colonies were somewhat similar to the English colonies in America, especially after the latter's independence.

[2] It is clear, of course, that the connection of this term with our own "colony" is etymological merely; it explains little or nothing in the modern term. See note, p. 2. For the previous history of the term, see Pauly-Wissowa, *sub* "Colonatus," "Coloniae"; cf. Lewis, p. 115, note 2. On the *provinciae*, see Arnold; Lewis, pp. 117 ff. The provinces form a very suggestive side-study for one interested in the general question of colonization. As for the *coloniae*, they were, in strictness, only special parts of their *provinciae*.

function, subordinate up to the time of the Gracchi, of providing for poorer citizens from whose presence the state desired relief; this function was strongly emphasized by the younger Gracchus, who wished to reëstablish an independent, land-owning peasantry.[1] It is clear that such colonization rested upon the family as its unit, especially as preference is regularly given to prospective emigrants with families.[2] After the Civil Wars the *coloniae* were further employed to afford a place of retirement, together with a sort of pension in land, for the veterans. Not infrequently, in later times particularly, the distinction between *colonia* and, for example, *municipium*, became legal or fictitious merely, implying no vital differences of any kind.[3] Thus the term changed during the life of the Republic and Empire, with the extension of security of rule in the wake of conquest. But the essential of *colonia* for the present purpose is the conception of a garrison-society maintaining itself by industry, and to a certain extent producing its kind, on the borders of the empire, and exercising a moral restraint rather than an actual coercion upon the surrounding population. Of the colonial types hitherto cited it resembles most closely the Greek cleruchy.[4]

The foregoing considerations form the justification of the statement that "the area embraced by Roman colonization was coextensive with the whole Empire." The first local conquests did not need colonies to secure them, but a large number were formed in more distant parts of Italy. A strong indisposition to extend the system outside of the peninsula was made manifest at the time of Caius Gracchus; indeed, the senate was committed to many steps in the direction of world-dominion before it was well aware of the fact. But this reluctance was made short work of by the emperors, who regularly followed up their conquests with the

---

[1] Ihne, IV, 455; V, 394.

[2] Brunialti, p. 26, note. Livy gives the numbers sent to several colonies as 300, 1500, 3000, and even 6000 (IV, 47; VIII, 21; X, 1; XXXVII, 57; XL, 26, 34). The assignments of land ranged from 2 jugera (a superficial measure equivalent to about one acre and one-quarter) to 140 a head (Id., IV, 47; VIII, 21; XL, 26, 34; Brunialti, p. 27).

[3] Such were all post-Hadrian colonies, "purely fictitious." Pauly-Wissowa, "Coloniae"; Lewis, p. 115.

[4] "The *Coloniae* were settlements of Roman citizens in Italy, who occupied a conquered town, divided the whole or a large part of the lands belonging to its citizens among themselves, and became the *coloni*, or cultivators of the lands thus appropriated." Lewis, p. 114. This definition covers mainly the earlier *coloniae*.

founding of colonies.[1] The latter varied in number with the turbulence of the locality, were sometimes very prosperous, as in Africa, and at other times short-lived and unsuccessful, as in Spain.[2] In the latter country troops had to be assigned for garrison-duty year by year.[3] All these colonies, with the provinces they guarded, were bound closely to Rome both by their interests and by the presence of relatively complete means of communication.[4] For Rome instinctively created for herself those bonds of empire for which the less imperial genius of Phœnicia and Greece had not clearly conceived the necessity; by her roads Rome held to herself not only her provinces but her colonies.[5]

Under this ever-present domination of the capital, however, the *coloniae* remained as they had begun, comparatively devoid of individual enterprise, initiative, and character. They had no life of their own, never conspired against Rome nor asserted independence. They clung to Rome with a "sort of passive, mechanical cohesion," [6] even after the imperial government had become weak and old; from having been self-governing above other sections of the empire, they suffered their privileges to lapse in the general gravitation of power into the hands of a single despot.

But little is known of the internal life of these garrison-colonies, and that may be summed up by saying that they constituted small replicas of Rome. Agriculture was practically the only industry. Miscegenation with natives doubtless occurred, but did not eliminate the need of fresh relays of emigrants to keep up the population. Theoretically these emigrants did not lose their Roman civic rights, but in practice such rights, culminating in the franchise, lay dormant. It is certain that as a whole the colonies possessed no capacities for self-transformation or development into

[1] Brodrick, p. 52; Arnold, pp. 2–3, 9. For the number of colonies founded at various periods and by different rulers, see Pauly-Wissowa, *sub* "Coloniae"; Brodrick, p. 50; Ihne, I, 455, 473, 543, etc.

[2] Cf. Martins, Civ. Iber., pp. 14 ff.; Colmeiro, I, 57 ff.

[3] Ihne, III, 373–374.

[4] The care taken by the Romans to afford material benefits to their colonies is evidenced, among other things, by ruins of aqueducts, cisterns, etc., in such dry regions as North Africa. See Brunialti, p. 31, note; p. 32, note. The careful enumerations and surveys which formed a part of the founding of the *colonia* defined the holdings of land and titles to it in a most satisfactory manner. It would be hard to discover another such matured and scientific system until the nineteenth century.

[5] Cf. Arnold, pp. 7, 14 ff.; Lewis, p. 127; Brunialti, p. 31.

[6] Brodrick, p. 77.

new states;[1] nor were they able, in the final time of trial, to aid themselves or Rome in any considerable degree. They were connected with Rome alone, and in a quasi-parasitic relation; they existed for her and fell with her; among themselves they had no common interests and no fellowship except in their common destruction at the hands of the invading races.[2] Hence Roman colonization represents no such grandiose and startling movement of population and no such generation of new societies as do the antecedent activities of the Phœnicians and Greeks.

ROMANIZATION: CASE OF GAUL

In their influence, however, upon the world-to-come the Roman colonies were far from insignificant. This their effect upon subsequent history was exercised by them rather as expedients in imperial administration than as colonies pure and simple; nevertheless it seems desirable briefly to consider this influence, even though it leads to a certain amount of digression from the subject in hand. In much later days colonial administration is occasionally hard to distinguish from imperial administration; but a suggestion of the system of which the *coloniae* formed part cannot fail to cast light upon their origin and their destiny as instruments in the spread of culture. It is in order, then, to show the methods of the Romans in dealing with and modifying subject peoples; and for this purpose it has seemed best to single out a particular people, the Gauls.[3] For while the activity of the Romans in Gaul may not be absolutely typical of them in the capacity now under consideration, it is sufficiently so for the present purpose; and it is the more in point because of its pervasive and enduring influence upon the disposition and tendencies of several peoples with whom any complete study of colonization must deal. Like the

[1] The *coloniae* conserved the form into which they were originally molded; they preserved what was distinctively Roman when Rome itself was "Roman" no longer. Pauly-Wissowa, *sub* "Coloniae." By way of comparison with the relations of Greek colonies to the metropolis, Brodrick's remark (p. 68) is apt: "The despotic character of the relation between father and son, as defined by the Roman jurisprudence, was amply realized in that between Rome and her colonies." Cf. Ihne, I, 413–414; Lewis, pp. 116–117. [2] Brodrick, pp. 77–82.

[3] Most of what follows on Gaul is derived from Fustel de Coulanges. The attitude of this author is pro-Roman, but his conclusions as here cited seem amply supported over a wide range of scholarship. His views find a rather more popular presentation in De Saussure's chapter on Roman Gaul. Cf. Brodrick, pp. 51–52.

Phœnician and the Greek, the Roman left his stamp unmistakable upon the rising races of his time; but it was impressed through agencies widely diverging from those of his predecessors.

It was a primary and vital condition of the Gallic conquest and subsequent history that the Gauls did not conceive the Romans to be enemies of their race. The sentiment of race-diversity was vague in those days, and what little there was in evidence was not accentuated and perpetuated by any marked external distinctions, such as were familiar in the ages succeeding the discovery of new worlds and races. Nor did the Gauls regard the Romans as ene-mies of their country, in the modern sense. There was no Gallic state, no national feeling; all was turmoil and encroachment of neighbor on neighbor, to say nothing of threatened irruption from the north. Hence the dominion of those who could guarantee security and peace, as it became better known, was accepted rather than repelled; subjugated on one side, the Gauls were freed on the other. The conquest, so far as fighting went, occupied but a few years, and did not degenerate into the petty but endless guerrilla warfare to which an irreconcilable people takes recourse. There were therefore no vital difficulties in the way of extension of Roman rule. Not only this, but, because they wished simply to govern, the Romans systematically escaped the consequences of an interfering and meddlesome policy.[1] "Assimilation" of the conquered district to the metropolitan model was an idea foreign to the ancients. Hence Gaul was not crushed by the conquest and its sequel, nor were the Gauls reduced to servitude; they retained, with few exceptions, their civil liberty, internal organ-ization, traditions, and habitudes. Most men of narrow horizon perceived no great change in their existence as a consequence of the conquest. If the Gauls had to pay taxes and furnish soldiers, that was nothing new to them; and discharging these obligations to the Romans, they were sure of the return they desired, — security

[1] The actuality of rule was preferred to its name, and consequent ostentation. Bordier (p. 165) quotes the Roman maxim in reference to colonies, "Non tam regendae sunt quam colendae"; adding, "Ce ne sont pas les lois qu'il nous faut, disent les colonies, ce sont les bras!" It must be understood, however, that the Roman citizens were those who profited most largely in a material way from the development of Gaul, receiving almost all the concessions, commercial privileges, etc. The great and rapid development of the country proves conclusively that the activity of the latter, even though often oppressive, was, conjoined with the advan-tages of Roman rule, a favorable factor. Pigeonneau, I, 22 ff., 29 ff.

and peace. The "Pax Romana" was something for which the provinces could afford to pay dearly, as is proved by their prosperity, even under the exactions of Roman rule in the hands of certain unscrupulous functionaries.

The Roman system of dealing with subject races was one of non-disturbance; such changes only were made in local forms as were necessary to complete subordination.[1] Even the exercise of sovereignty was mild, and it impinged upon the common people through old and familiar channels. In the case of Gaul, the country was, if not subjected, certainly administered and developed through the Gauls, somewhat as India has been through the Hindus; for with few exceptions the Gauls were left to themselves, and it is an evidence of their satisfaction with their destiny that they did not care to be free. Indeed, the "assimilation" policy originated in the subject people itself, starting with the richest and noblest families and working on through the population. The people passed with no great difficulties or throes from the state of subjection to that of citizenship. They became attached to Rome as to a native land; and their union with her was broken not by themselves but by another race. If Gaul was transformed from her former state, it was the will of the Gauls rather than of the Romans that this came to pass. Here again, then, as in the cases of the Phœnician and Greek colonization, we are drawn to note the absence of any preconceived ideal or "mission"; differing from their predecessors in many and characteristic respects, the Romans were one with them in the practicality of the ends which they set before themselves. The results were of far-reaching and wholesome effect in the one case as in the other.[2] For, as a matter of fact, as members of the Empire the Gauls renounced in favor of Roman characters most of

[1] Lewis, p. 119. Judæa, says this author (p. 120), presents a "lively image of the continuance of the peculiar laws and religious usages of a Roman dependency outside of Italy."

[2] Language and religion were respected, but the needs of trade, etc., brought about a use of Latin even among the higher classes of Carthage, however much the lower classes clung to their gods and native tongue. Rome did not try to modify everything by a sweeping *tabula rasa*, but altered the present and prepared for the future. Brunialti, p. 31, note, quoting from J. Toutain, Le città romane della Tunisia (French), Paris, 1896. Pliny (Hist. Nat., III, v) says of Rome: " . . . terra omnium terrarum alumna eadem et parens numine deum electa quae caelum ipsum clarius faceret, sparsa congregaret inperia, ritusque molliret, et tot populorum discordes ferasque linguas, sermonis commercio contraheret, colloquia et humanitatem homini daret, breviterque, una cunctorum gentium in toto orbe patria fieret." Cf. De Saussure, pp. 268–269; Van der Aa, *De Gids*, 1860, I, 833–834.

those national characteristics which race-educators have desired to remove or change; religion, language, law, customs, even names, were remodeled after or directly replaced by the Roman forms. The popular religion was not essentially different from that of Rome; Gaul not only adopted Roman gods, rituals, etc., but, following Rome's example, those of other Mediterranean nations as well. Druidism was, indeed, uprooted and proscribed, but it was hardly a genuine Gallic form. As for the Gallic language, it scarcely appears after the first century A.D. Rome never fought the Gallic tongue; in fact, the change in language was less a consequence of conquest than of an altered social status. The Gauls took up Latin " because they found interest, profit, and pleasure in its adoption." For their new and advanced status of culture Gallic was insufficient; it lacked terms corresponding to the things and ideas of a changed order. Latin was from the first, of course, the official tongue, and as the Gauls gradually entered into the empire as an integral and patriotic constituency, they naturally adopted the traditional speech of the Roman citizen. There is here afforded a case of the prevalence of that language which suits the situation over one which is spoken by the majority of the group.

In the matter of law the same gradual but sweeping change took place. After the conquest the Gauls retained their own law; the Romans, through the suppression of the Druids, simply replaced a sacerdotal with a lay justice, and a rigid and unmodifiable system, rooted in religion and ancestral custom, with one capable of consistent adaptation in the interests of the community. The Gauls were quick to perceive the advantages of security of individual property, freedom of contract, and, above all, of the impartial protection of all classes, which, under the Roman law, succeeded their own system of clientage, debt-slavery, etc. The capricious Druid justice was gone, and in its place was the responsible, reasonable, and accessible system of Rome, with its unheard-of right of appeal to governor, senate, and emperor. And when, by a natural process, the Gauls had entered the ranks of the Roman citizens, their own legal forms were already things of the past. But it should be noted that for two centuries and a half no constraint was laid upon them to become citizens; here again they were the seekers and not the sought. And the like is true when we consider the alterations which took place in the more general customs and habitudes of the subject people. They speedily renounced their hitherto proverbial warlike habits and disposition, and adopted the usages, mode of existence, and even the tastes of the Romans. They imitated them in such important activities as road construction, and freely built schools where Latin and Greek should be taught. The whole political education of the land was derived from Roman sources : a national political and religious unity was formed, and a compact and centralized government became traditional. This centralization was not attained, however, at the expense of local freedom ; for the cities administered themselves, and their councils were even able to exert a certain controlling influence over the proconsuls and governors.

The function of the colonies in the dissemination of Roman ideas and customs has already been noticed ; they were responsible in no slight degree for the transformations just described.[1] But these transformations, it should be clearly apprehended, were not a matter of racial mixture. From Gaul, for example, there was practically no emigration, permanent or temporary, to Italy, and but few Italians were introduced into this country through the colonies. If these intermarried, the Roman strain and traditions, passed on thus family-wise, could not have left much trace upon the population. The colonists, here, as elsewhere, were often of races other than the Roman ; and the functionaries did not care to establish themselves away from Rome, the great center of interests and careers. It was, therefore, neither the blood of the Romans nor their will and policy which produced the far-reaching changes whose result was the impressing on the western world, through the elevation of the backward peoples, of a sort of homogeneous stamp. It was the attraction of superiorities in the practical ordering of individual and communal life, — superiorities that were not heralded to others nor forced upon their attention, but which were self-evident. And here reflection returns to that vital condition of Roman influence upon subject peoples, — the absence of wide racial diversity in these ancient times. The superiorities of Roman ideas and systems were self-evident because the grades of civilization were not so distant one from another as to prevent easy passage from the lower to the higher. This was particularly noteworthy in respect to Gaul, but not untrue in the case of other

[1] " All that was valuable in the Roman Empire, transmitted through the colonies whole and entire, has long since been incorporated into the social life of modern Europe." Brodrick, p. 85 ; cf. Arnold, pp. 21, 45 ff.

lands. It is said that Rome succeeded better with races inferior in civilization to herself than with her equals or superiors.[1] What she would have done with a complex of races such as are represented within the British Empire we cannot know; her experiences in Africa held no great promise. But the essential factor in her influence on the world, as in that of the Phœnicians and Greeks, was the relatively high quality and remarkable potentiality of the civilizations with which she came into effective contact. And into this momentous work the *coloniae* entered as examples and nuclei of Roman civilization among ruder peoples; their importance is correspondingly great in the history of the contact of races through colonization.

MEDIÆVAL ITALIAN COLONIES

The troubled course of events which preceded and accompanied the dissolution of the Roman Empire was such as to preclude both state-directed colonization and that which takes its origin in individual initiative. Imperial colonization had, of course, reached its end together with the expansive power of the Empire, and could not reappear. The next series of social phenomena to which the name colonization may apply was almost purely commercial, and was connected in no slight degree with the great reactionary movement from west to east represented, among other results, by the Crusades.[2] Hitherto the general rule had been that the East should seek the West, resorting thither as the carrier of its own civilization; but when, in consequence of the great changes of the early Middle Ages, the East retired into itself and ceased to manifest the active initiative of former times, the hitherto relatively passive West began to reach out on its own account for that of which it now felt the lack.[3] Naturally enough this effort was directed at first along commercial lines; from the tenth century on through the Discoveries period the attention of the West was regularly and continuously directed toward the East, and finally toward that vicarious and, as it were, accidentally substituted East represented by America.

[1] Arnold, Introduction.

[2] The following is written mainly from Cibrario, Heyd, Prutz, Pigeonneau, and Sumner. Brunialti covers the period in an interesting chapter based largely upon Heyd.

[3] For the articles of mediæval commerce, see, besides Heyd, Pigeonneau, I, chap. iv; Cibrario, III, chap. ix.

The Mediterranean was, naturally enough, the theater of action for many decades ; and in view of Italy's central and commanding position, it is not surprising to find the eastern movement most strikingly developed in that country. The desire for the characteristic products of the East, stimulated under the Empire, manifested itself anew with the relative emergence of the West from a period of turmoil and confusion ; but the agency through which these products were transported, changed. During the early Middle Ages the trade-routes toward the East remained practically the same as those in use under the Empire ; but it suited the policy and pride of Byzantium to renounce the intermediary function and to force the westerners to acknowledge her commercial predominance by personal suit for the commercial favors which they desired.[1] This policy, like that later developed at Lisbon, was well calculated to raise up strong rivals, and amounted in the end to an abdication of the leading position which it was desired to hold. Of the diminutive city-republics which at this time flourished in Italy, Amalfi was the first to bridge over a gap thus widening between West and East ; the trade of the Amalfitans with the Levant began in the tenth century, or earlier ; and they were followed by the Venetians, and somewhat later by the Genoese, Pisans, and others. The activities of these four cities in the Levant were practically identical, but the historical importance of the Venetian and Genoese factories and colonies so far outweighs that of the Amalfitan and Pisan settlements that the latter may be excluded from more than casual mention, as may also, for the same reason, those of the Florentines, Sienese, Provençals, and Spanish.[2]

Settlement in the Levant : Motives and Extent

It has been suggested that the activities of the westerners were motived almost wholly by the prospect of commercial gain. The Italian settlements were at the outset trading-posts or factories of an almost pure type. In those days of undeveloped means of communication it was necessary for a merchant to go in person to the scene of his operations, and generally to remain there for a protracted period. Although protected by treaties with native

---

[1] Heyd, I, 64–65.

[2] Details in Heyd, I, 105 ff. *et passim* ; Lindsay, I, 232 ff., 473 ff., 522 ff. ; Wappäus, I, 118 ff. ; on the mercantile activities of the mediæval Jews, see Heyd, I, pp. 139 ff. For the French merchants of the Middle Ages, see Pigeonneau, I, chap. iv.

rulers, considerations of safety led such traders to cleave together; they even went so far as to have a military organization and defensive structures in those city-quarters in which their commercial purposes favored settlement. Under these circumstances the trading-colony was not infrequently tempted to a display of force in conquest. These two motives, the predominant one of trade and the derived one of conquest, lay at the bottom of Italian colonization in the Levant; other stock motives play but a small part in its inception and history.

The internal development of the Italian city-states brought it about that Venice should earliest attain a degree of political coherence which justified and rendered possible the turning of attention without. This advantage in time was augmented by the favorable geographical and topographical conditions which early assured her of safety from aggression and of a picked population of desirable refugees, together with the further advantage of relative nearness to the East. Some time before the Crusades the Venetians had already attained many grants in reward of aid lent to the Emperor of the East against the Saracens; their settlements came early to be regarded by him as those of allies rather than subjects. One of the earliest of these was in Byzantium, but from this central point they were scattered throughout the country, forming the outlines of a real "maritime empire."[1] Their influence was so strong that the emperor excluded from his domains any nation with which they were at war, thus considerably hampering the early operations of the Genoese and Pisans.

The latter competitors were later in the field, for they attained the requisite internal unity and organization only shortly before the Crusades. But such was the energy of the Genoese that they were not far behind their older rivals in sharing the gains of this great movement of peoples.[2] It was only with the Crusades, indeed, that the opportunity came to them both to found the characteristic Italian colony in the Levant; their timely and indispensable, if not disinterested,[3] services during the early Crusades enabled them

---

[1] Heyd, I, 120 ff.; Brunialti, p. 41; Cibrario, III, 275; Wappäus, I, 118 ff.; Sumner, Lectures.

[2] Cibrario, III, 278 ff.; Prutz, p. 377.

[3] The Crusaders and their trappings were the Italians' "back-freight." Sumner; cf. Heyd, I, 145 ff. "Pardessus observes that in reading the history of the period of the Crusades, any one would suppose that these expeditions were made merely to promote and extend their [the Italians'] commerce." Lindsay, I, 473.

to acquire wide and practically sovereign areas and rights in the most important trading-centers of the land of commercial, as well as of other, promise. To Venice, for instance, was granted as much as a third of such important cities as Tyre (capitulated 1124) and Sidon, to say nothing of extensive rights in Jerusalem, where, in consequence of many pilgrimages, business was very profitable. Even greater concessions were gained by the Venetians after the capture of Constantinople (1204), undertaken largely at their own instance as creditors for transportation services, and at which they assisted; the removal of the Doge to this station as a center of empire was at one time considered. Their ambition extended to the exploitation of the Ægean Islands and, in 1395, even to the seizure of Athens and Thessalonica; and their trading-settlements were gradually extended along the shores of the Black Sea.[1] They were well received in Egypt, Tunis, and Tripoli, and established regular lines of navigation to these coasts; through the Barbary settlements they were enabled also to share to some extent in the commerce of interior Africa. The Genoese and Pisans were at first mere novices, where the Venetians were masters; but the Genoese were not contented to follow afar off, and, after acquiring a commercial colony in Constantinople (1155), had speedily risen to be deadly and dangerous rivals for the monopoly hitherto enjoyed by their predecessors. For the strains of this great conflict the forces of the Amalfitans and Pisans were insufficient.

CHARACTER OF THE *FONDACHI*

Such was the general field covered by the Italian factories. Had they remained factories merely, they could have but little importance for the subject in hand; and they might have retained a more rudimentary form had it not been for the Crusades. The results of these quasi-migrations which concern this immediate contention were the presence of a large, if unstable, European population in the East, and, especially in the Holy Land, the substitution of political, legal, and other conditions modeled upon familiar European patterns for the more unfamiliar and difficult

[1] Canestrini, Il Mar Nero, etc., covers mainly the local Genoese colonies, — their government and legislation, products and commercial policy, decadence and fall. Cf. Wappäus, I, 183 ff.

Mohammedan systems. The East was no longer a foreign country; it was a complex of European nationalities, and a favorable ground for the development of security-loving trade.[1] Hence the Italian factories, through the presence of a considerable population, including whole families, became real Italian settlements; and the persistence of close, strong, and partisan relations between the several Venetian, Genoese, and other settlements and their respective cities of origin, formed the ties which bound together two real, even though diminutive, colonial empires.

In accordance with the terms of their treaties with eastern rulers, and grants from them, the citizens of the several Italian republics were assigned to different quarters in the cities of the Levant. Here was erected a warehouse, or *fondaco*,[2] which, in the smaller settlements, was likewise the courthouse, dwelling-house, and inn. The quarters were sometimes much more extensive, including a whole street or several streets, with official and private buildings, warehouses and salesrooms, churches, mills, slaughter-houses, baths, etc.[3] Venice is said at one time to have had fondachi in all the cities of importance in the Eastern Empire. But the life of the colonies was not always strictly confined to the cities; when they received, for instance from the Crusaders, a concession of one-third of a city, they likewise acquired claims on one-third of the surrounding land for a mile out. The larger of these domains were under the charge of overseers; in Syria the peasants did most of the cultivating, on shares, where their remuneration appears to have been a generous one (two-thirds to three-quarters of the product).[4]

The relation of the Italian *communes*, as they were called, to the dominant power of the region in which they were established, was an extremely independent one. They were states within states; were regularly exempt from the payment of full taxes, and often made no contribution whatsoever. Indeed, it was not uncommonly the case that they received a considerable share in the revenue of their cities, so that in the event of the local preponderance of one Italian city, another might be paying tribute to it. In the Holy

---

[1] Heyd, I, 180.

[2] From the Arabic *funduk* = Greek πανδοκεῖον (or πάνδοκος). See especially Simonsfeld, II, 3 ff.

[3] See Heyd, I, 167 ff., 445 ff.; II, 430 ff. A community of such relative magnitude was called a *ruga* or *vicus*.

[4] Heyd, I, 170 ff.; Prutz, pp. 377 ff.

Land during the domination of the Crusaders [1] the communes owed no feudal obligations and existed as equal and generally self-sufficient powers. During the period of their prosperity the colonies were relatively uncontrolled by the local governments, a fact which will emerge the more clearly from a consideration of their internal administration and relations to their cities of origin.

RELATION OF COLONY AND METROPOLIS

The influence of the metropolis was from the first supreme. The original grants and privileges were obtained by the mother-city, often as the rewards of considerable military and naval activity and expense; the buildings were erected at public and not private cost; the trade of the colonies was manipulated for the advantage of the metropolis. The colonies were treated as a piece of external domain; it was only at first that they elected their own head-men; as the factory grew into a colony, the magistrates were regularly appointed by the home-authorities. These officials were called at first *vice-comites*, later *consoli* (Genoese and Pisans) and *baili* (Venetians). In earlier times each colony had its supervisor; later a consul, or *bailo*, residing in the chief center of trade, was appointed for an entire region or country. After the capture of Constantinople, in which the Venetians afforded the Crusaders indispensable aid, the chief Venetian official of the region became the *podestà*, with the rank of despot or prince, and with a very high power delegated in the name and commission of the Doge. These vicegerents were chosen for a specified time and given complete instructions, the central power to which they were responsible, in the case of the Venetians, being the three *consoli*

[1] De Lanessan (p. 13) says that the Crusades were nothing but tentatives at the colonization of Syria, rendered unfruitful by climate, difficulties of communication, etc. Prutz (pp. 1–5) compares them with the operations of Alexander the Great. The religious and mystic elements which surround these enterprises should not blind us to their essentially worldly and economic character; nor is the comparison of the Crusader-states and the Italian communes without great value for the understanding of the latter. Nevertheless, there appears to be good reason for regarding these adventures as constituting a case of conquest rather than colonization; the relation of the Syrian governments to any possible metropolis or metropolitan complex (i.e. Christian Europe) is too vague to justify the use of the term "colony," even in a loose sense. Certain phenomena aptly bearing on the effects of a changed environment and the contact of races tempt one to include these curious settlements and governments; but for the same reason one might well include migration or conquest in general. See, for details, Prutz, especially pp. 1–32, 89–181, 314–354, 396–415.

dei mercanti, by whose general supervision a marked unity of policy was effected. This body was a sort of prototype of later Boards of Trade.[1] The post of consul, or *bailo*, was one of great honor and responsibility; in the lists of the *baili* of Syria occur many famous Venetian names.[2]

A large part of the official responsibility granted to local directors was due to the impossibility of receiving instructions from the metropolis at all times. To somewhat neutralize the personal power which attended such independence of function the governors were provided with counselors or councils without whose knowledge they should not act. Thus the superior officers, whatever their title, remained at least nominally subordinated to and controlled by the metropolitan government. The laws of the metropolis were, in addition, carried over with little alteration to the colonies. The communes administered their own justice, and their exterritoriality sometimes went so far as practically to disallow the authority of the former ruler of the district. Appeal could be made from an inferior officer to the *bailo*, and through him to the highest authorities at home. They were able to lay taxes, e.g. on industries, and sometimes, as has been mentioned, enjoyed large revenues from their share in public income. Because of this, and the fact that they were enabled to raise most of their own food, they were much less dependent upon European importation than, for instance, the Crusader-states.

MONOPOLY POLICY AND TRADE WARS

The temper of the communes was in consequence extremely free and independent respecting local control; they even insisted upon having their own clergy, from their own cities of origin. Their sense of nationality was very pronounced, not to say assertive; they stubbornly and successfully resisted the attempts of the

---

[1] *Casa da India, Casa de Contratacion*, etc. Cf. p. 228, below. As this volume does not pretend to follow the derivation of institutions, it is possible on occasion simply to hint at or suggest accepted or probable prototypes or aftertypes.

[2] Heyd, pp. 176 ff., 282 ff., 317 ff.; Brunialti, pp. 44, 59 ff.; Prutz, pp. 384 ff. The *Officium Gazariae* discharged the regulating function from Genoa to her colonies. Cibrario, pp. 292 ff. Many of the governmental measures regarding trade, such as the detailed directions given to ship captains (the keeping of the fleets together, etc.), foreshadow the policy of the later commercial and colonial powers. Cf. Brown, pp. 277–278; note, p. 71, below.

Crusader-rulers to lay hands upon the administration of justice, or, indeed, to direct the least important parts of their lives. They formed an element totally incongruous amidst the feudal régime of the knights and orders. They were in, but not of, the Crusades; after the acquisition of their privileges they took little part in succeeding wars against the Mohammedans. They exhibited no religious enthusiasm and but little of the intolerance and narrowness of the Crusaders; for their commercial motive was their strength. They were prudent and farsighted in trade, zealous for the interest of their several states, steadfast for their rights, and moderate in their living, — all of which made life in the East easier for them, as compared, for instance, with the ill-living Crusaders. They utilized their exceptional advantages to the utmost and profited accordingly. The exclusively commercial preoccupation was likewise, however, their weakness. Their policy was one of closed monopoly and "secret commerce"; all commercial operations were veiled in the deepest mystery, and the exposure of trade-secrets was severely punished.[1] Their trade-envy and insatiable greed led to recurrent, if not constant, and always savage, feuds with the Crusaders and with each other, by which the enemies of Christendom profited. The victories of these enemies caused a shifting of the trading-centers toward the end of the thirteenth century from Syria to Cyprus and Lesser Armenia.[2]

One great object and ideal, above all, lay before the Venetians and Genoese, — that of trade-monopoly, implying the ruthless exclusion or destruction of all competition. The pursuit of this policy naturally brought the Italians into conflict with the authorities in the Levant and with each other; the history of the colonies in Constantinople and elsewhere, to the very end of their existence, is one of intrigues, expulsions or massacres, and restorations, to say nothing of mutual friction and bloody wars. In the desperate struggles for the creation and maintenance of monopoly, Amalfitan hopes were early crushed, and the rôle of Pisa was cut short. The details of the fierce colonial wars of Genoa and Venice do not especially concern us; on the whole, Venice seems to have emerged with a residuum of advantage over her great rival, but not with

---

[1] Cf. Hunter, I, 218, 220; Sumner, Lectures.

[2] Heyd, I, 216 ff.; II, 3. For the relations with the Crusader-states, see especially Prutz, pp. 377 ff. An interesting account of "Christian and Infidel in the Holy Land" is given by Munro.

the power to crush her. But the essential bearing of this condition of affairs lies in its fatal effect upon the colonies themselves; for not only were they crippled and sometimes prostrated during the periods when conditions promised rich rewards to commercial activity, but they could in the end offer no unified resistance to the advancing Turks. Behind the trade-hostility there lay also a political hostility of city against city in Italy itself. Here again, as amongst the Phœnicians and Greeks, we have a city-economy, — a too small and restricted metropolitan unit. Political control was indeed extended over the persons and interests of subjects in foreign parts, such as neither Phœnician nor Greek had been able to encompass, but upon a scale insufficient for the erection of any considerable empire. The parent society, taken as a city-republic, was too small, and the complex of city-republics was so unhomogeneous as to refuse to cohere even in the face of destruction. The Venetians and Genoese allied themselves even with Spaniard and Ottoman [1] in order to prevail one over the other. When, now, the Turks took Constantinople (1453), and began to extend their conquests toward Egypt, the several Italian colonies were unable to make an effective resistance. Payment of tribute was their only safety; all their old preferential treatment was reversed in favor of taxation to the limit of endurance. Certain ostensibly favorable agreements were drawn up, but the rude and brutal invaders paid but little heed to them; the usual contempt of a warlike people for an industrial and commercial one was exhibited in an extreme form. The duties of consul became difficult and even dangerous; the Italians fervently wished the Greeks back in power.

DECLINE BEFORE THE TURKS

The gradual extension of Turkish conquests brought on actual war with Venice, which led (1479) to considerable losses of territory on the part of the latter. Individual traders suffered severely; many Venetians had been seized and imprisoned and much property arbitrarily confiscated. The Constantinople colony dwindled under such adverse circumstances and presently disappeared in consequence of another war. By 1500 but few of the eastern possessions

---

[1] Brunialti, p. 46.

of Venice and Genoa remained; the Black Sea colonies also disappeared under incursions of the Tatars and in consequence of the fall of Constantinople. The last great blow in the East was the Turkish conquest of Egypt (1517), followed by the disappearance of the fondachi and colonies in that country, upon which the last hope depended. Cyprus held out till 1570, and then it, too, was swept under by the wave of barbarism. In none of these cases were the Italian cities or colonies of material aid one to another.[1]

The colonies were gone, but not even *in extremis* was the trade-monopoly given up or modified. The Venetians struggled tenaciously for many decades against the inevitable. But by their very policy and its accentuation they had invited rivals into the field; the artificially elevated prices, in Europe, of the products of the East stimulated the western nations to repeated attacks upon the monopoly system. As long as the Mediterranean remained the center of activities, such efforts were of little avail against the preponderant maritime power of the Venetians.[2] But the center of trade was moving inevitably westward, and deserting a "thalassic" for an "oceanic" field. When, therefore, at the end of the fifteenth century both Portuguese and Spaniards broke through the cordon of restrictions by their discovery of independent and uncontrollable routes to new regions of supply, the supremacy of the Venetians was already obsolescent and doomed. In spite of the utmost efforts of the Venetians to demonstrate to the Turks the advantage and necessity of reasonably low transit dues and taxes, the latter, taking counsel of greed and ignorant lack of foresight, refused to be persuaded. The situation from the commercial standpoint became desperate, and in 1504 the Italians contemplated even the project of piercing the Isthmus of Suez, an undertaking beyond the possibilities of the age. The attempt to utilize more tortuous land-and-river routes to the Indies also proved

---

[1] Details in Heyd, I, 383 ff., 445 ff.; II, 158 ff., 257 ff., 313 ff., 381 ff., 427 ff., 505 ff. This book is by far the best authority for the period it covers; especial attention is here drawn to Anhänge I and II of Vol. II, which deal with the various products derived from the East, and their destinations.

[2] For some data on the maritime power of Venice, see Cibrario, III, 277 ff. He quotes (p. 277) Marin Sanuto, who assigns to Venice in the fifteenth century 36,000 sailors, 16,000 workers in the arsenals, and 3300 ships in commission (*giro*). For the commercial wealth of Venice, see Lindsay's figures (I, 480–481). Brown (p. 278) quotes an estimate of the annual revenue of Venice in 1500 as amounting to 1,145,580 ducats. Cf. Wappäus, I, 240, 262 ff., 317 ff.

impracticable,[1] and it was only through the inertia of custom and habit that a temporary respite from the inevitable was rendered possible. By a timely realization of changed conditions and by submission to them, Venice might have long retained a secondary importance in the commerce of the new period; but the old spirit of haughtiness and selfishness had persisted, and brought on the end the more speedily.

ITALIAN INFLUENCES UPON LATER AGES

The significance of the Italians and their colonies during the Middle Ages was in many respects analogous to that of the Phœnicians and Greeks in ancient times. They transported the products and ideas of civilization from East to West, and thereby unconsciously educated the westerners to a civilization which they could have evolved independently only through the lapse of ages. They likewise engaged to no small extent in the slave-trade, an activity whose results for the spread of civilization have already been pointed out in the case of the Phœnicians. Their function was not so vital as that of their early predecessors, for the seed had been long sown, and in addition the crusading movements had effected a certain contact of West with East;[2] but they nevertheless bridged over the chasm between the Occident and the Levant long before the Crusades, and they maintained such connection when protracted estrangement was threatened, and when degeneration might easily have taken place. But when the Italians' activity was waning, the West was ready to take its fate in its own hands, since it had acquired confidence in the effectiveness of its own initiative. It is not necessary to rehearse the details of this educative process, for they were analogous to those of preceding ages; but a word may be given to the commercial example of the Italians, so faithfully copied and maintained by the nations of the West.[3]

[1] The final struggles of the Venetians are treated briefly in Brunialti, capo iv, pp. 84 ff. The Venetians had an idea that the Cape-route trade would not last; that the Sultan would be obliged to lower duties and then their old trade would return. Sumner, Lectures.

[2] This contact was not exclusively beneficial, of course. Among other eastern products the plague is thought by some to have been transferred directly through the agency of the Crusades. Bordier, Géographie médicale, p. 256.

[3] The best presentation of this phase of the subject known to the author is that formerly given by Professor Sumner in unpublished lectures on "The Industrial Revolution of the Renaissance Period."

During and after the Crusades, in operations which demanded the movement of much capital, the Italians were led to the invention or practical application of many new and economical commercial devices, among them the bill of exchange, letter of credit, and other banking and credit devices.[1] Money, interest, speculation, and like topics occupied much of their attention, and practical applications along these lines did a good deal to break down bigoted mediæval notions derived from the intuitions and deductions of ecclesiastical visionaries. But the characteristically shortsighted ideas and practices connected with the maintenance of monopoly constituted, to its misfortune, a large part of the heritage from these talented peoples to the modern world. Many of the dogmas and doctrines later known under the collective name of the Mercantile System were original, as far as effective application goes, with Venice and Genoa. Because of admiration and emulation of Italian successes, these were eagerly adopted, and have persisted in force or as survivals down to the present day. It has already been mentioned that the colony was utilized strictly for the benefit of the metropolis, and to provide her not only with regions of active demand and supply, but with a profitable carrying and transfer trade. This trade was regulated in the most minute and arbitrary fashion;[2] for Venice insisted upon retaining for herself the so-called " active " as distinguished from " passive " commerce. The regulations, for example, to which traders of other nations living in Venice were obliged to conform, were no less than tyrannical as viewed from the standpoint of the present day.[3] In short, an unremitting and tireless effort was put forth to limit the movements of commerce and to confine the action of the great forces of exchange within local and selected channels.

One of the commercial expedients of the period under examination deserves special notice as the forerunner of many a grandiose enterprise of later times, — the joint-stock company with rights of sovereignty, that is, the prototype of the later chartered companies.[4] Amidst the strife of parties in Genoa, in the middle

[1] See Pigeonneau, I, 253 ff, 278 ff; Cibrario, III, 306 ff; Prutz, pp. 362 ff.
[2] Officers were required to take oath to obey instructions. Their routes were minutely prescribed, size of anchors and quality of rope scrutinized, etc. The ships were to stick together, refit at prescribed ports, etc. These vessels were, of course, convertible into men-of-war. Brown, pp. 277–278. [3] See Simonsfeld, *passim*.
[4] Hopf, in Ersch und Gruber's Encyclopädie, Part LXVIII, 308 ff., *sub* " Giustiniani"; see also Heyd, I, 509, 542 ff.

of the fourteenth century, it became necessary for the city to depend for its defense upon the efforts and capital of private persons. The latter were then allowed to farm certain revenues and to make any conquests they pleased until fully indemnified. The body of citizens who stopped the breach for the city were called *Mahonenses*, and the body into which they organized themselves *Mahona*, or *Maona*. The fleet raised by the Mahonenses sailed off to the east to protect the Genoese colonies in 1346, and in pursuance of their purposes of self-indemnification seized Chios from the Greeks and Phocæa from the Turks. Complaints to the Genoese government were met by a disclaimer of responsibility. And yet Genoa was to have complete jurisdiction over these acquisitions; though the profits were to go to the 29 Mahonenses for 20 years, the city could obtain full sovereignty by completing the indemnification within that period. By a treaty of 1363 with John Palæologus the Greek claims to Chios were renounced in return for tribute. The Maona was a real joint-stock company, and the shares were salable; by 1358 Chios belonged to eight men, only one of whom had been a member of the first company. When in 1510 the republic proposed to pay off its indebtedness, the company protested, and was finally for a consideration left in possession. They retained the island of Chios (chiefly valuable for its mastic) until, falling into arrears in their tribute, they lost it to the Turks; in 1588 the republic disclaimed to the Sultan all responsibility for the Maona. Claims for compensation were lodged against Genoa by the representatives of the Maona as late as 1805.

This instance is noteworthy in that it exhibits with especial clearness the function of the chartered company as a substitute for or a concealing medium of state action. It thus offers an anticipation of a phase of the chartered company most clearly exhibited in the resurrected type of recent decades, — a prototype in a sufficiently elaborated state to challenge comparison and suggest principles.

Whatever may be said of the influence of the Italians on the later world, it should be noted yet again that it was exercised without direct policy or intent. Although nominally participators in a great religious movement, the Italian cities had but one real motive for their activities, — that is, material self-interest.[1] In pursuance

[1] It should be pointed out that what was likely to have vitally differentiated the activity of the Venetians and Genoese from that of their predecessors was the fact

of this worldly end they effected significant political and social changes which followed upon the economic ones to which allusion has already been made. Their influence was far more lasting in the diffusion of culture than was that of the Crusades, however important the latter may have been; for when, with the loss of their cause in the ruin of their Syrian empire, the Crusader-states disappeared, the Italian colonies stayed on, resolutely holding together their mother-cities and their trading-areas, and thus preventing the deadly hatred incident to a religious war from "effecting a cessation of the most important culture-relations."[1] In Europe this commerce and its consequences helped to disintegrate the manor-economy by widening the horizon of individuals and of societies; it likewise aided in the shattering of the whole feudal system. The Italian monopoly unwittingly and unwillingly forced potential but diffident rivals into an activity which resulted in the ensuing great discoveries with their far-reaching effects upon subsequent history.[2] Italian activity, in short, ushers in what are known as modern times; and this momentous function was furthered not a little by the possibility of prolonged sojourn in eastern countries, with a consequent better knowledge of eastern civilization; that is, by the existence of the colonies whose origin and course has now been traced.

The Italians in the Discoveries Period

Nor must it be thought that, with the decline of the Italian supremacy, the influence of Italy upon the world's history abruptly ceases. This is not in the order of nature. Experience such as the

that they and their Saracen clients in trade professed two separate and irreconcilable religions. Former conditions about the Mediterranean of essential religious similarity and consequent tolerance had suffered a metamorphosis since the spread of Christianity and Islam. But because the Italians were led frankly to recognize the preponderant importance of trade over creed, whatever the danger to their souls of such a complaisant or mercenary attitude, they so subordinated the newly introduced element of hostility as practically to pursue their projects with the tolerance of Phœnicians and Greeks. Hence the essential similarity, as respects methods and results, of their activity and that of their pagan prototypes.

[1] Prutz, p. 393. For a comparison of the civilization of the Saracens and Crusaders, cf. Munro, Christian and Infidel in the Holy Land.

[2] If the Syrian tolls raised prices, including the large margin of profit, from one ducat in Calicut to from 60 to 100 in Venice, then, taking the average as 80, the Portuguese could get a market for whatever they could import at a profit just short of equal to that of the Venetians plus the tolls, say 79. This was a powerful incentive. Sumner, Lectures.

Italians possessed was not built up in a day; and under the mediæval system of mystery and secrecy respecting trade but little of
it had been transmitted. Of a consequence we find that Italy, as
represented by individuals, in a sense directed the progress of the
Discoveries. The detailed demonstration of this statement would
make a long story; but a few of the best-known cases, several of
which will appear in later chapters, may be cited by way of illustration. Prince Henry of Portugal is supposed to have derived,
through his brother, considerable information from Italian sources;
and, farther back, a Genoese, Pezagno, became admiral of Portugal.
The brothers Vivaldi discovered the Azores and Madeiras; Cadamosto operated under Prince Henry; the thirteenth-century journeys of the Poli took them to China. Two of the greatest discoverers
were a Genoese and a Venetian, — Columbus and John Cabot.
Men of lesser fame were Verrazano, Sebastian Cabot, Amerigo
Vespucci, Pigafetta, Toscanelli; not to mention many others, pilots,
map-makers, travelers, and the like.[1] If, now, some such list be
compared with one made up from names of any other single nationality, however actively the latter may have been engaged in the
operations of the early period, it will not suffer in comparison.
This is perfectly natural, and in the order of events; for human
progress depends always upon the accumulation of knowledge,
experiences, and dexterities. The Italians knew, and the westerners were ignorant; the latter had to secure their footing under
the guidance of the former before they were able to work out their
destiny upon the different lines determined by newly invaded areas
and newly experienced conditions of nature.

Summary of the Conditions of Colonization preceding the Discoveries

Before proceeding to the colonization of the modern times, it
seems useful to survey some general aspects of the subject as they
emerge from the study of the foregoing simpler cases, — cases in
whose evaluation, moreover, since sentiment cannot enter as in

---

[1] A brief chapter on the Italians during the Discovery period is given by
Brunialti (capo iv, 68 ff.), who quotes the old formula *Sic vos, non vobis* to charac-
terize their activities in the service of others. See also Major, p. 309; Bourne,
Spain in America, pp. 1 ff.; Roscher, Sp. Col. Sys., pp. 1 ff.; and any work on the
Discoveries period (e.g. Peschel, Ruge, Fiske), *passim*; cf. Cheyney, pp. 41 ff.

more modern phases, any other consideration than that of historical impartiality can scarcely find place. It has been possible here to study the course of colonization in the absence of several factors which have attained considerable importance in later times, and to which great significance has been uncritically assigned. In a whole series of phenomena it has been found that strict control on the part of the metropolis was unessential for the economic and other development of offshoot societies; indeed, so far as the converse case of the Roman *coloniae* goes, rigorous governmental supervision has tended to undermine the independent life and development of the new community. It has been seen, however, that the weakness of control, practically unavoidable under the conditions of the times, — in the absence of swift communication, in the relative feebleness of political units, etc., — has precluded, the case of Rome excepted, the existence of a real and persisting empire. In most of the cases considered, centralization of authority in a more than local metropolis has been consistently absent. Relations of colonies to parent-cities have been those of material interest rather than of political integration, and of a common civilization rather than of actual dependency. The argument of Freeman, above cited,[1] is susceptible of an application wider than that given by the author, whose specific comparison is that of Greece and Britain.

The motives for colonization reviewed have been preponderantly commercial, and as a consequence the colonies have regularly originated in trading-stations; important exceptions must naturally be made of the state-initiated enterprises of the Chinese and the Romans. Incidentally it should be noted that trade has not "followed the flag" to any convincing degree,[2] although military operations have at times removed obstacles against which a healthy trade has employed its own expedients in vain. Economic and political discomfort, as an incentive to emigration, has played a relatively unimportant rôle; it was rather to gain more abundantly than to avoid loss and misery that change of station has taken place. Among the stock motives the absence of religious discontent is noteworthy: there were no irreconcilable religious (or, indeed, political) dogmas in those days.[3]

[1] P. 43.

[2] That "trade and the flag" were not inseparable ideas to these non-conquering commercial experts lends color to the contention that their close association has something of affinity with the imperial disposition that does not care openly to proclaim its purposes.   [3] Cf. Keller, Hom. Soc., p. 17.

For similar reasons the "native policy" of ancient times was constructed to subserve the purposes of exchange, or was directed simply toward the maintenance of such subordination and order as a wider administrative experience had proved to be socially beneficial, if not indispensable. There was no idea of "culture-mission" or the like, and consequently no dogma, rooting in national egotism, of "assimilation." No moral or religious crusades were carried on through the colonies; diversity of customs and morals was regarded as natural and a matter of course, — though both customs and religions were nationally less differentiated than they have come to be in the eyes of later ages. The predominant commercial motive, and the imperial policy as well, counseled respect for the social forms of an alien people; hence the influence of the higher civilization upon the lower proceeded through example and suggestion rather than coercion. Participation in exchange between the complementary trade-areas of East and West was indeed enforced, as was the maintenance of peace and order (e.g. by Rome); but these were benefits, self-evident or speedily demonstrated, thus needing but little insistence. In short, influence was brought to bear primarily upon the economic life and industrial organization of backward peoples, while their secondary and derived social forms (marriage-system, property-tenure, etc.) were for the most part let alone. This is the secret of much of the success in the spread of civilization which has been noticed;[1] but such influence was, of course, of almost totally unconscious application. It was effective, because, falling in with the order of nature and evolution, it moved along lines of least resistance.

One makes haste to add that if the elder colonizing peoples appear to have attacked the question of elevating the less advanced races with better effect than have their successors, it is largely owing to the fact that the problem was presented to them in a form more easily soluble; for between the races that were brought into contact, especially around the border of the Mediterranean, there existed few contrasts of any significance. The like was true in the case of the Chinese and their ethnic environment. There were no obvious ethnological differences such as distinguish one race sharply from another, and the various stages of culture were separated by no impassable or discouraging chasms. If the eastern races had lifted themselves to a higher plane of material

[1] Cf. Keller, Soc. View, etc.

civilization, they yet retained in their religious forms and in their body of customs and *mores* an essential likeness to those of racially allied peoples. Even slavery was an institution totally different from that with which later ages have made us familiar : there was no "color-line" ; the system was one of "domestic slavery" in the main ; and the passage from freedom to servitude was easy, often turning purely upon chance. Hence that eternally vexatious and unsolved question of the treatment of a "lower race" was but faintly represented ; except in mining, we hear little of the labor supply or "native-labor question." If other than economic stimuli had to be applied, it was not the colonizing state that had to apply them, for the forces of trade impinging upon local controllers of labor were sufficient.

Another point well worthy of notice, and which really lies beneath the one just mentioned, as Chapter I is designed to suggest, is that the colonists before the Portuguese but rarely settled outside of their native climatic zone.[1] The Semites and Aryans colonized the shores of their own Mediterranean ; and as for the Chinese, no climate appears to affect them adversely to any great degree. Hence there have been brought into the discussion thus far none of the physical and social disturbances incident to a sudden and violent change in vital conditions. In other words, any of the colonies hitherto mentioned might have developed into what has been called the farm colony. One of the consequences of this condition has been already mentioned, — the absence of a "lower" race, or, as it might be stated from another point of view, the absence of the need itself for an acclimatized labor force. It is not surprising, therefore, if the foregoing types of colonies fall in rather strikingly with the temperate or farm colony in the matter of life, social forms, etc. ; but they differ from it markedly in one respect : instead of native wars and annihilation, an auspicious large-scale miscegenation, mainly of closely allied races, took place, this being due to the several facts that the seats of the colonies, conformably with their commercial purpose, were but rarely in relatively unoccupied country ; that the colonists were regularly too weak to indulge in extended conquests ; and that no such barriers to intermarriage existed as appeared in later times, when racial distinctions were more marked. Under these

[1] Hertzberg (pp. 86 ff.) develops this aspect of the Greek colonization to some extent.

conditions a greater modicum of success in the spread of a fructi-
fying civilization is the less to be wondered at. It was the Discoveries which, by opening up new parts of the world where
Europeans were subjected to new and strange conditions, immensely complicated the matter of colonization. In so far as these
conditions were new and strange, they drew in their wake new
necessities of adaptation; but it is hoped that the rehearsal of the
foregoing simpler phases of a now complicated and tortured social
movement cannot be without its utility for the better understanding of the modern forms, and the factors which condition them.

CHAPTER III

THE PORTUGUESE IN THE EAST

It has been shown how the monopolistic policy of the Italians was calculated to raise up rivals whose energy and eagerness would vary directly with the rigor with which monopoly was maintained; for it is when monopoly is at its climax of efficiency and tyranny that it offers the richest rewards to him who shall evade or break it. The strength and prestige of Venetian maritime power was great enough, indeed, to deter all rivals from the serious attempt to dispute Venetian monopoly within the Mediterranean,[1] but the extraordinary prizes of this monopoly were sufficiently alluring to other nations to overcome the inertia of things, and to motive those efforts along untried ways which were destined to set upon commerce an oceanic and cosmopolitan stamp, where before it had been mediterranean and relatively local. The successors of the Venetians would come into no less a heritage than the intermediary function between the two complementary trade-areas of East and West, — India and Europe, — a function which had been historically the making of the wealthiest and most powerful commercial nations. The incentive was sufficient to force a display of activity along indirect and unpromising lines, when the old direction of least resistance had been, to all intents and purposes, blocked.

In preceding pages it has been noted that merchants of countries west of the Italian peninsula had been drawn into commercial activity during the period of the Crusades and later, and that the inhabitants of western Europe in general had during this period experienced considerable enlightenment as to the nature of the Orient and its commerce. Some of these peoples, like the Germans, long received their dole of luxuries through the hands of the Venetians; others, Provençals and Iberians, made a more

[1] One might query why the Venetians did not fight the Portuguese for the possession of the ocean-route. But it must be realized that they were led by the inertia of things to cling to the old and familiar ways, especially since the new were so formidable and were for many decades of so little promise.

79

or less vigorous attempt to supply themselves at the source.[1] But it was the historical destiny of the Iberians to break the Italian monopoly and to found its aftertype on a grander scale.

Conditioning Factors of Iberian Colonization

The two streams of colonial enterprise which thus arose in Portugal and Spain can hardly be treated in isolation one from the other. They flow in parallel channels, and recurrent reference from one to the other is inevitable; and when one looks to their historical antecedents, he finds a number of determining and conditioning elements common to both. These may be briefly indicated before embarking upon an account of more detailed and local matters.

The status of the Peninsular peoples toward the end of the fifteenth century was in large part the outcome of centuries of war, on native soil, with an alien race; of conflicts culminating in 1492 with the reduction of Granada. These wars had effected a racial and national cohesion exceptional in its time, and visibly represented by the strengthening of monarchy,[2] and, later, by the formation of larger political units. They had likewise engendered a military spirit attended by the usual qualities of endurance, courage, skill in the use of arms, love of an irregular and venturesome life, and, too often, contempt for the arts of peace. And because these racial struggles were likewise religious wars, there had grown upon the people an ideal of religious solidarity which had within it the germs of intolerance and fanaticism. The spirit of conquest was commingled with that of crusade; the Iberian soldiers went out to win the temporal empire for the sovereign and the spiritual dominance for the faith. It is probable that the exaltation of mind under which they strove lent them a motive force with which their opponents found it difficult to reckon, and which the historian cannot well measure or define.[3]

In addition to these elements of strength, Spain and Portugal possessed undoubted economic vigor at the outset of their colonial

---

[1] Wappäus, I, 191–210, 277–309.

[2] " The Hanseatic confederacy, powerful as it might be, was but a confederacy; and Venice, however magnificent, was but a city. The really modern states of Western Europe had the germs of quite another force and power within them." Major, pp. 308. [3] Martins, Civ. Iber., p. 205 *et passim*; Major, p. 300.

careers. The Peninsula as a whole had benefited by the intelligent industrial example and legislation of its Moorish conquerors; for the latter, despite their military prowess and successes, were endowed with the habits and sentiments characteristic of an industrial society. The Moors, for example, were experts in the manipulation of arid soils, and were the repositories of both agricultural and other sciences during the Dark Ages. Under the protection of their Semitic brethren, likewise, the Jews for long years advantaged the economic life of the Peninsula by developing their characteristic financial functions. And even after the fall of Granada, the Moriscos, or conquered Moors, continued to confer benefits upon the Peninsula by their presence and activities. The very fact that they attained, under hard conditions, an industrial prosperity which in later times drew upon them the envy and greed of the Christians, witnesses to their economic efficiency.[1] Moreover, apart from the Moors, the Peninsula had by 1500 developed industries already of long standing, and of vitality rugged enough to have weathered the fantastic regulation of the Middle Ages.[2] A high quality of wool was produced in relatively enormous quantities; the olive was a prolific source of national wealth; silk was a prime asset of the Peninsula, and the manufacture of silken and woolen fabrics formed before 1500 a point of distinct industrial superiority. In short, the industrial population of the period formed a middle class capable of developing into a lasting resource and stay of any government. And to these several advantages was added a prosperous maritime commercial element susceptible of a high development under reasonably favoring conditions. When a series of momentous possibilities along many lines of activity was about to be opened by Da Gama and Columbus, the Peninsular nations were ready to play a considerable part in their realization. No European peoples were more closely unified and nationalized, and few save the Venetians and Genoese economically stronger.[3]

Although now the calamities and decline of Spain and Portugal cannot be treated conjointly, still, at the risk of anticipation, a few

[1] Colmeiro, I, 159–198; Lea, Moriscos, pp. 5 ff.

[2] Colmeiro, I, 233 ff.; cf. 349 ff.

[3] This is not believed by Leroy-Beaulieu (I, 3), who thinks that "no people were less fitted to colonize than the Spaniards." But he adds the limiting clause, "à juger les choses de notre point de vue actuel." The reader will be furnished in later pages with information and considerations upon which to base a judgment as to this contention.

general considerations growing out of the projection of the above factors upon the life of the sixteenth century may be noted. Both of the Iberian states were enticed or forced into efforts disproportionate to their population and economic strength, this being due in large part to royal and clerical incitement, to the inebriating and demoralizing effects following upon the Discoveries, and to miscellaneous unhappy combinations of circumstances of a less general nature. The destructive forces were at work before the sixteenth century began, but displayed themselves in aggravated and menacing form only toward its close. Then both states suffered from the incapacity and maladministration of kings who were always short of funds; from decline in quantity and quality of population and of industry, — in short, from the effects of the diversion of national life into uncharted ways. Under the influence of racial and religious hatred, and economic greed and envy, both nations drove from them economic assets of a high order: the Jews, expelled from Spain and Portugal in 1492 and 1496 respectively, and the Moriscos, banished in cruel fashion in 1609.[1] Both nations came to support a large parasitic element in the population in the persons of the clergy, and of the vagrants and mendicants attracted by a profuse and indiscriminate charity for which the Church stood as champion. The encouragement of such classes amounted to contraselection in the evolution of the national type, and aided the government in blocking industrial development. Idleness, venality, cheap ostentation, and superstition infected rulers and ruled.[2]

Each state collapsed in its own special way from the lofty position to which its earlier energy had elevated it; and that this decadence was decisive and irrevocable finds evidence in the subsequent history of the Peninsular peoples and their colonial empires.

[1] Martins, Os Filhos, etc., chap. vii; Hist. de Port., II, 13 ff.; Civ. Iber., pp. 266–271; Colmeiro, I, 250 ff.; cf. pp. 335 ff.; Varnhagen, I, 87–88. Upon the Moriscos, Lea is the special authority. The story of the oppression and expulsion of these valuable people and of the Jews cannot be gone into in this place, but will be found in all needed detail in Lea's Moriscos, especially chaps. i, iv, vi, vii, viii, x, and xi; and in his Inquisition, especially I, chap. ii, 84 ff.; II, 315 ff., 485 ff.; III, 1 ff. It will be noted that almost the chief activity of the Inquisition was the harassing of Jews and Moriscos. Even if the number of actual autos-da-fé was less than was once supposed, not running into the tens of thousands (cf. Inquisition, III, 551 ff.), yet the other penalties of torture, imprisonment, confiscation, etc., constantly overhung the predestined victims, rendering life and property insecure and so crippling all economic activity. In fact, "practically acquittal amounted to a sentence of not proven" (Inquisition, III, 107).

[2] Martins, Hist. de Port., II, 32, 113–116, 192–193; Civ. Iber., pp. 271–273, 283–286.

The general impression of the Portuguese and Spanish activities under consideration is that of an excessive and feverish energy, a prodigal over-expenditure of vitality, followed by an equally accentuated reaction and exhaustion. As one follows more specially the course of Spanish and Portuguese colonial enterprise, these general considerations are found to underlie not a few of the sets of conditions encountered.

PORTUGAL'S PREPARATION FOR COLONIZATION

If in the period immediately preceding the Discoveries the Peninsula as a whole had been gathering its forces, the same was true of its constituent political units, — Spain and Portugal. Each of these nations exhibited, moreover, the action of local forces making for internal coherence and the storage of energy.

Portugal had won its independence, after a series of wars, toward the end of the fourteenth century,[1] and had developed a centralized government of some strength Conflicts with an alien race had accentuated racial and religious homogeneity, and the genius of the King Affonso Henriques (1143–1183) was enabled politically to consolidate a land and people neither geographically nor ethnologically distinct from their neighbors. At the end of the fourteenth century, according to Stephens, Portugal formed a political and social entity more conscious of nationality than almost any other people of Europe.[2] This unity of purpose, conformably with the laws of state-development, proceeded to display itself outside the boundaries of the state, and at first along lines already familiar. Expeditions were led against the Moors of North Africa, and the idea of external dominion was, in true crusading fashion, commingled with the desire to extend the outposts of Christendom. The strength of the rising state was augmented also by the skillful use of foreign relations. A striking illustration of the essential analogy between the Crusades and the Moorish wars of the Peninsula lay in the fact that Portuguese kings were able to divert large bodies of itinerant Crusaders to their own local purposes. Even

[1] The battle of Aljubarrota, 1385, practically ended the aggression of Castile. Martins, Hist. de Port., I, 15, 158 ff.

[2] Stephens, p. 100; Hunter, I, 57 ff.; Martins, Hist. de Port., I, 67 ff "The grand movement, popular in its essence, of the fourteenth century, invigorated the nation and prepared it for the great period of daring navigation and grand discoveries." Corvo, I, 6.

the Pope declared that crusading in the Peninsula was as meritorious as in the Holy Land.[1] Of still greater and more lasting import were the relations between Portugal and England. Himself the founder of the house of Aviz and the consolidator of the realm, John I, by his union with Philippa of Lancaster[2] (1387), laid the foundation of an international relationship and sympathy which have often redounded to the advantage of the less powerful nation. Already in 1385 English archers had rendered material assistance in the attainment of Portuguese independence; and after the recognition of John as king (1411) and the completion of the era of consolidation, the cementation of this alliance through the more palpable and enduring bonds of trade went on with few interruptions.

The position of Portugal was scarcely favorable, under the conditions of the age, for the development of trade and shipping. Cut off from the Mediterranean, the scene of action of the time, the Portuguese felt the influence of the trade-movements already described only after the Italians had extended their voyages to Flanders and the North; and even then the Italian exclusion-policy allowed them but small share in the new operations. Portuguese sea-battles of the twelfth century showed courage rather than skill; it was not until the early fourteenth century that a real beginning of maritime activity was made.[3] From this time on the Portuguese, together with the Spanish, became more alive to the economic advantages enjoyed by the Italians in the trade with the East and with North Africa. On the part of both nations there emerged more and more plainly the tendency to outgrow the status of the passive recipient and to enter upon the lucrative function of the distributor. King Diniz (1279–1325) of Portugal, in addition to his unremitting efforts to repair the damage of the Moorish wars, through the development of economic resources, managed to check the overgrown power of the Church, and thus to lay the foundation of a strong and undisputed monarchy.[4] He also attracted Genoese shipbuilders to Portugal and employed an Italian as admiral of his fleets, thus making the first definite advance toward

---

[1] Stephens, pp. 48, 52–53, 61, 72; Martins, Hist. de Port., I, 84, 181.

[2] Daughter of John of Gaunt and granddaughter of Edward III. Hunter, I, 58 ff.; Martins, Hist. de Port., II, 130–131.

[3] Wappäus, I, 209–210; but cf. Martins, Hist. de Port., I, 26.

[4] The strife between the kings and the clergy was practically ended by 1360. Lavisse et Rambaud, III, 478–481; IV, 872–874; Martins, Hist. de Port., I, 118; II, 11, note. The popular title of Diniz was *Lavrador*.

maritime power; and in succeeding reigns, notably that of Ferdinand IV (1367–1383), numerous privileges and exemptions were granted to shipbuilders and sailors. This attention to sea-borne commerce went even to the extent of founding a marine insurance society. Merchants of all lands were attracted to Lisbon under this fostering policy, and John I, on attaining power, found the ground prepared for a solid advance in commercial development. This opportunity was not suffered to slip away.[1]

That the subsequent generations of astonishing activity on the part of Portugal, and her final degeneration as well, were the work of no single man, or group of men, the preceding argument is designed to indicate. It is in all ways probable, however, that the very strength of the monarchy as it existed in Portugal was at the bottom of a premature or exaggerated display of enterprise and aggression.[2] Fitted to play a part proportionate to her resources, Portugal was constantly forced into situations with which she was normally unfit to cope. And yet her royal directors were far from being unpopular; the sound or senseless ideals at which they aimed in their early contact with Africa and the East appealed to the spirit, or at least encountered no resistance on the part of their subjects; it was weakness of the flesh rather than unwillingness of the spirit that caused a falling-short.

HENRY THE NAVIGATOR

In some such way as this the spirit of the Discoveries period was epitomized in an influential member of the ruling house. This was Dom Henriques, son of John the Great and his English queen, a character more familiarly known in history as Henry the Navigator, — a prince who was enabled in an exceptional degree to direct the fortunes not only of his own country, but of the civilized world, with his own hand.[3] Raised in an environment of religious militancy,

[1] Wappäus, I, 351–364; Schäfer, I, 112 ff.; Danvers, I, 16 ff.; Hunter, I, 16–18. Major (p. 46) thinks that the expulsion of the Moors from the Peninsula, entailing as it did a dearth of objects of Oriental luxury to which the westerners had become used, " was one of the great stimulants to the search for a passage to India by the sea." He adds: " In this expulsion the Portuguese took the lead, and were consequently the first to feel the effect of the incentive." Cf. Martins, Hist. de Port., I, 165. [2] Cf. Hunter, I, 89 ff.

[3] The best accounts of Prince Henry's life and work will be cited below. Briefer estimates are Stephens, Story of Portugal, pp. 141 ff.; Bourne, Essays, etc., pp. 173–189; Zimmermann, I, 4–10. Martins (Hist. de Port., I, 166 ff., 183 ff.) gives Henry rather the character of a ruthless enthusiast.

its spirit was his, and his earliest independent efforts were spent in the endeavor to gather such information concerning the Moors of North Africa as would enable him the more crushingly to defeat them and to reduce the power of Islam. The salvation of souls was an object very near to his heart in his character of mediæval knight and crusader; his earliest ships were fitted out to injure the enemies of Christendom rather than to advance the worldly interests of Portugal or the king. Yet Henry was more than mediæval and unworldly; he was a man of scientific curiosity and of practical astuteness. He was versed in the geographical and other lore of his time and imbued with respect for that reasoning which proceeds from fact to theory, and which has become the special heritage of modern science. His knowledge, as a child of a new age, was the fruit of an accumulation of what had gone before; [1] like Columbus, he represented one of the results of the invention of printing. He was able to apprehend the import for the general advancement of culture of the extension of the geographical horizon and of nautical education, attained through the development of shipping. He saw at least some of the results to be expected from the establishment of easier and cheaper communication with the East.[2] He was aware of the seemingly secure but really precarious tenure of Venetian monopoly, and coveted for Portugal not only the souls but also the lucrative trade of the easterners.[3] He may not have seen that the discovery of a direct route to the Indies would "turn the flank of Islam," but he was convinced that it would neutralize the excessive advantages held by Italian cities, and, above all, by Venice. He stood, as it were, the inspired and clarified exposition of the time's awakening spirit,[4] and was for this reason enabled to wield the influence he did. As commander of the wealthy Order of Christ he controlled ample funds for his purposes, and, renouncing all else in the pursuit of his life-idea, retired to the rocky promontory of Sagres, there to pass his days.[5]

[1] The Arabs were "the most important helpers and informants of Prince Henry." Beazley, in Azurara, II, xlv; cf. pp. xliii ff.

[2] Wappäus, p. 145; Beazley, in Azurara, II, lvi ff., cxvii ff.; Major, pp. 47 ff.; Ruge, pp. 81 ff.; Martins, Os Filhos, etc., chap. iv; Hist. de Port., I, 167 ff.

[3] There also existed at this time a legend derived from the classics concerning certain Gold and Silver Islands in the Far East. The Portuguese later made several ineffectual attempts to find them. Ruge, pp. 207 ff.

[4] Cf. Leroy-Beaulieu, I, 41–42; Cheyney, pp. 43 ff., 76.

[5] That he took up his abode in Sagres in 1419 is doubtful, but he certainly remained there most of his life after 1437. Beazley, in Azurara, II, viii, xii; Martins,

In spite of considerable opposition accompanying and following his many reverses, he did not fail, such was his consistency of purpose and great force of character, throughout his life to inspire his followers with a spirit similar to his own. There is, in his case, more reason than usual for asserting the effect upon history of the work of a single man.

His activities came to be directed almost wholly to the attempt to circumnavigate Africa, — a feat reputed to have been accomplished in the remote past.[1] To this end he not only gathered about him the leading scientists of his time, but also secured the services of daring sea-captains and sailors.[2] In their wretched, insufficient sailing craft these mariners made their way, little by little, down the coast of Africa, were long daunted before the terrors of Cape Bojador, but finally doubled it (1434) and passed on toward the south. The long trend to the eastward represented by the Gulf of Guinea no doubt raised false hopes; it took until 1471, eleven years after Henry's death, to cross the equator. Yet he lived to see some of the wealth of Africa, if not of India, return to Portugal, and to experience, though it probably affected him but slightly, the sudden veering of a public opinion hitherto adverse to him (about 1442). The Madeira Islands had been occupied (after 1418), and endowed with the beginnings of their future resources; to these the Cape Verde Islands were added (1446) and the Azores (1449).[3] Slaves had been introduced (1441) into the great estates of the south of Portugal where the labor supply was depleted; this set free large numbers of men for the royal policy of adventure, but the cruelties attending the seizures had already embittered the natives of the African coast.[4] Whatever its immediate effects for

Os Filhos, etc., chap. iii. What he did was, in one of its most important aspects, to found a "school of sea-training." Cheyney, p. 76. These expeditions, owing to lack of private capital and enterprise, could not have been sent out without drawing upon some such funds as a prince might be able to control. Cf. Van der Chys, p. 117, note.

[1] See p. 32, note. Payne (Age of Disc., p. 12) doubts this, regarding Henry as little more than a crusader. But cf. Beazley, in Azurara, II, v.

[2] Seamen of Italy, Germany, and the Netherlands entered Henry's service in relatively considerable numbers. Major, pp. 308–309.

[3] It is scarcely necessary to take up in detail the history of these island groups. Being unoccupied, they were divided in feudal fashion into captaincies, and gradually settled by Portuguese, as a vacant portion of Portugal might have been settled. They soon became portions of Portugal and were administratively so considered. See Martins, O Brazil, etc., pp. 3 ff., 194; Corvo, I, 43 ff.; Saco, pp. 20 ff.

[4] Hunter, I, 61 ff.; Beazley, in Azurara, II, cix; Bourne, Essays, etc., pp. 173–189; Payne, Age of Disc., pp. 13 ff.

good or ill, the life of this determined and undaunted prince had seen a grand undertaking so far upon its way that non-cessation of effort was assured. Without his activities " the results of the great forty years (1480–1520) of Diaz, Columbus, Da Gama, and Magellan must have been long, might have been indefinitely, postponed." [1]

After the death of Henry the voyages to the south continued, with few interruptions, to extend their range, until the Cape was doubled by Diaz (1486), and until finally Da Gama swung clear around the southern tip of the continent and made his way to India (1497–1498). The details of these voyages are important to our purpose simply as they display from the outset the daring and reckless spirit of the Portuguese of the time. Shipping had been much improved in the hard school, and was now better adapted to the ocean and the exigencies of oceanic commerce. The sea had lost its imaginary terrors; navigation under strange skies had been learned. In short, a beginning had been made in the creation of a vehicle to meet the needs of a world-wide commerce.[2] The timely impulse of the single farsighted man had probably hurried on the evolution of the period at a greatly accelerated pace. When it was removed, exploration was indeed largely suspended for about twenty years; but it needed only a resumption of royal encouragement to stimulate it to the accomplishment of its ultimate object.[3]

It is noteworthy as illustrating the knowledge and purposes of the Portuguese that in 1487 two envoys were dispatched to pursue the overland route to India, and to search for the mysterious Christian potentate, Prester John. The latter, it was hoped, would prove an efficient ally against the Moors. It fell to one of these envoys, Covilhão, not only to reach India and to become the " theoretical discoverer " [4] of the Cape route — he sent back assurances

---

[1] Beazley, in Azurara, II, vii. Yet such was the slowness of progress in these early years that the forty-two years from 1418 to 1460 had added only 18 degrees of latitude to verified geography. Hunter, I, 69; cf. Roscher, p. 258, and note.

[2] Henry really founded, with the funds of his Order, the first real commercial and discovery company of modern times. Bourne, Essays, etc., pp. 173–179.

[3] The details of the voyages under Prince Henry's direction are to be found in Azurara, Discovery and Conquest of Guinea. In the second volume of this publication is included an excellent introductory essay by C. R. Beazley, who gives some space to the voyages subsequent to Henry's death, in completion of his work (pp. xxviii ff.). See also Major, pp. 317 ff.; Martins, Os Filhos, etc., chap. ix; Lavisse et Rambaud, IV, 800 ff.; Heyd, II, 506 ff.

[4] Hunter, I, 78–79; Whiteway, p. 16; Major, pp. 339–340; Martins, Hist. de Port., pp. 163 ff. For a résumé of the legends, etc., about ester John, see Ruge,

to Portugal that ships would of a certainty attain the termination of the continent, and he directed them to Sofala — but to discover Prester John in the king of Abyssinia, and to be retained by him under kindly restraint for the rest of his life.

Effects of the Discovery of the Cape Route

With the discovery of the Cape route, Portugal takes her place as the successor of Venice in the empire of commerce;[1] for, despite the efforts of the latter, her monopoly was already doomed when the ships of Da Gama had once anchored at Calicut. The center of the world's commercial activity again shifted toward the west, and its medium became the ocean which connects, not adjacent areas, but all lands of the earth. Local trade, with its relatively restricted interests, was a thing of the past, for in the distance lay the world-market and its limitless possibilities for the meeting of all nations and peoples.[2] The policy of Portugal, however, contemplated no such cosmopolitan aims. It has been shown how the ancient nations strove to maintain, through any and all means, the monopoly of trade, each for itself; and how the Italians invented expedients and fought for their realization, in the effort to exclude rivals. As was inevitable, the policy was adhered to by the new mistress of the seas. Prince Henry had no sooner realized the likelihood of success in his prime endeavor than he secured, from the only arbiter of the time, a clear title to all lands to be discovered from Cape Bojador "ad Indos." The Pope "represented after the fashion of that age what we now call the concert of Europe"; he exercised an authority which was "regarded as essential to the peace of Christendom," for Papal arbitration was the only course short of war. Even recalcitrant nations like England, under aggressive sovereigns like the Tudors, hesitated openly to assail a "settlement which had become part of the public law of Europe."[3] Hence India became Portuguese by fiat, and the

---

pp. 37 ff. Payne (Age of Disc., p. 11) says Henry hoped to unite forces with Prester John through the "Western Nile," — a geographic illusion, — and so turn the flank of Islam. [1] See p. 69, above.

[2] "Of all the changes which mark the transition from ancient and mediæval to modern history, none is so profound as that which has regrouped human life about the Atlantic as a new and grander central sea." Bourne, Sp. in Amer., p. 3.

[3] Hunter, I, 83, 84, 85. Under the conditions of the time, then, the Portuguese had a right to call intruders upon their dominions "pirates" (πειραταί), i.e. those who make (wrongful) tempts. Hunter, I, 86, note; Leroy-Beaulieu, I, 43-44.

Portuguese habitually spoke of it as theirs, despite their scanty occupation.

It is necessary here to anticipate slightly. When, in consequence of the discoveries of Columbus, Spain entered the lists with Portugal, it became imperative for the Holy See to construct some working agreement between these, its favorite children. This arrangement worked out eventually into the Treaty of Tordesillas (1494), whereby the non-European world was divided along a meridian 100, later 370, leagues west and south of any one of the islands known as the Azores or the Cape Verde Islands.[1] The Portuguese were excluded from areas west of this line, the Spanish from those east. In conformity with the spirit of the time, as will be seen, this to us stupendous presumption was regarded as a matter of course, and as indisputable. Its bearing upon the subject directly in hand is this : it justified the destruction of interlopers, and enlisted the superstitious and religious tendencies of the time in the maintenance of commercial and colonial monopoly. Its incompleteness may be passed over for the present ; the Portuguese had the East as a sphere of activity, the Spanish the West. It was time enough to consider and discover where the East and West must meet, when that question became a practical issue.[2]

Conditions in India

The marvelous good fortune of the Portuguese — for thus one must denominate the happy outcome in their colonial history of many an unplanned or ill-planned venture — attended them from their arrival on the scene of action. They landed propitiously both as to place and time. Calicut was part of a narrow strip of shore

[1] See especially Bourne, Essays, etc., pp. 193–217; Sp. in Amer., pp. 29–32, 71–73; Hunter, I, 83 ff.

[2] " Neither in the Papal Bulls nor in the Treaty of Tordesillas was there any specific reference to an extension of the Line around the globe or to a division of the world. The arrangement seems to have contemplated a free field for the exploration and conquest of the unknown parts of the world, to the eastward for Portugal and to the westward for Spain. If they should cross each other's tracks, priority of discovery would determine the ownership.

" The suggestion of the extension of the line around the globe and of the idea that Spain was entitled to what might be within the hemisphere set off by the Demarcation Line and its extension to the antipodes does not appear until the time of Magellan, and it is then that we first meet the notion that the Pope had divided the world between Spain and Portugal like an orange." Bourne, Hist. Introd., pp. 24–25; cf. Payne, Age of Disc., p. 23.

belonging to petty rajahs of whom its ruler, the Zamorin, was a sort of chief. Too feeble to offer a serious resistance, and with an eye to an increase of revenue, the kinglets welcomed foreign merchants; and having long been accustomed to differences of faith, they conceded freedom of religious belief and practice. And at the time of the Portuguese arrival united resistance was further weakened because of the encroachments of Mohammedan invaders upon the Hindu overlordship of the interior. The Mogul Empire was not yet firm; petty states were isolated and the Portuguese could deal with them with a free hand, and one by one. And the people, though in important respects more highly civilized than the Portuguese, were not only insufficiently advanced in the arts and almost unprovided with the modern weapons of war, but also exhibited in their military system certain customs of a chivalrous nature, e.g. antecedent declaration of hostile intent, of which the Portuguese were able to make consistent and unscrupulous use. These considerations, while in no way detracting from the courage of the Portuguese adventurers, rendered their task an easier one than had at first appeared.[1]

The mood in which the Europeans approached the East is well exemplified in the character of the first great leader, Vasco da Gama. A man of great energy and indomitable firmness, incorruptible in dealing justice, and of strong religious purpose, he added to his inflexibility a harsh manner and a cruel, violent, and revengeful character.[2] He dealt out justice untempered with mercy, and was utterly lacking in tolerance, and even in a formal and diplomatic courtesy. The striking success of his summary methods scarcely atoned for the friction and ill-feeling which they engendered. In conformity with the purpose of his voyage, however, Da Gama's immediate duty was the collection of such a cargo of spices as would verify the high expectations of his royal patron in Lisbon. Trade agreements were therefore made with the rulers of Calicut and Cochin; an attempt was made to fix prices once for all; and in the face of Arabic misrepresentation, and in spite of high-handed and hot-headed conduct on the part of the Portuguese,

---

[1] Whiteway, pp. 27–28; Lindsay, I, 152.

[2] ". . . so liegen auch bei Vasco da Gama als die treibenden Kräfte: ritterlicher Waffenruhm und die Verbreitung des heiligen Glaubens offen vor Augen; denn vielen, und darunter den Edleren, erschienen die indischen Kämpfe als heilige Kriege, als Kreuzzüge gegen den Erbfeind des Christenthums." Ruge, p. 190. The spirit of exploration had succeeded and absorbed that of the Crusades. Hunter, I, 58.

the ships were well loaded with pepper, cinnamon, and other local products. In exchange for his spices the Zamorin wished chiefly gold, silver, coral, and scarlet. In accordance with instructions, Da Gama likewise visited Cannanore and established a factory at Cochin, making arrangements for its protection during his absence, and for the purchase and storage of goods destined for the lading of the yearly fleets which it was planned to send. By reason of ignorance of local conditions and a tendency easily to take offense with a people whom he despised without in any degree striving to understand them, Da Gama managed also, at the end of his brief sojourn, to leave the Zamorin of Calicut his bitter enemy.[1] Beyond imposing the natives with brute force, his activity had been sterile of real results. The breach which he had made with the Zamorin was widened by the blundering incapacity of his successor, Cabral.[2]

Conditions of Navigation

Some more definite information concerning the nature of ships and navigation at the date in question will help to form a conception of both the advantages and the difficulties of the discoverers and their successors. Since the time of Prince Henry considerable advance had been made in the size and power of the vessels and in the outfit of the navigator. The fleet of Da Gama consisted of a flagship of 120 tons and about 80 feet long, two other vessels of 100 and 50 tons respectively, and smaller craft with munitions. The flagship had a very high bow and stern and possessed great floating power and strength, but was nautically deficient; it carried twenty guns.[3] The combined crews of the vessels came to about 150 men. Cadamosto says the Portuguese caravels of his time[4] were the best sailing ships afloat; there had certainly been much improvement since Prince Henry's early life, but when we read of

[1] The exclusion of Da Gama from the Indian enterprises from 1502 to 1524 is thought by some to have been a consequence of his rude and exasperating methods. Ruge, p. 188; cf. Whiteway, pp. 77–81; Martins, Hist. de Port., I, 212 ff.; Lindsay, II, 41 ff.; Danvers, I, 85 ff.; Hunter, I, 109.

[2] Whiteway, pp. 88 ff. It is noteworthy that Cabral sailed for India not as a discoverer and adventurer but as an ambassador, fitted to appear in state. Martins, Hist. de Port., I, 223.

[3] For further details of construction, see Danvers, I, 43–44. Here also (pp. 33 ff.) and in Azurara (*passim*; and Beazley's Introduction to II, viii ff.) are to be found the details of the voyages down the west coast of Africa, including the noteworthy one of Diaz. See also Martins, Hist. de Port., I, 209–210, and especially Lindsay, I, 547 ff.; II, 1 ff.   [4] He was in the service of Henry after 1455 and died in 1480.

"lateen sails on long poles suspended from the masthead," we are led to realize the essential backwardness of the arts of construction, and the corresponding hardihood of the navigators. Yet these constituted the new "ocean-going" type of vessel and were undoubtedly a great improvement on the galleys that went before.

The navigation of the time was also much advanced; this is proved partly by the fact that sailors dared to let land out of their sight. After the equator was crossed, also, it had been necessary considerably to modify the means of determining directions and bearings. The rude astrolabe had been improved and the constellations of a new hemisphere learned. Nevertheless, in the time of Da Gama and his successors navigation was a haphazard affair. To take an observation with an approach to accuracy it was necessary to land; this was done repeatedly by Da Gama on his first voyage. The compass was known, but its use was checked by the superstition of the sailors.[1] Without satisfactory charts and pilots dangers abounded, and although the efforts of Prince Henry had exorcised most of the ridiculous superstitions of preceding centuries, yet in their frequent calamities, due to storms and unseaworthy craft, the sailors, as Albuquerque remarked, "always had the pumps in their hands and the Virgin Mary in their mouths."[2] Voyages were lengthened out into years. Da Gama, it is true, covered the distance from Lisbon to Calicut between July 8, 1497, and May 20, 1498; but it took one unfortunate captain considerably more than two years, and several trials, to make the return-voyage.[3] And if the perils of the sea and of indifferent quality of ships and seamanship were overcome, there still remained the danger of encountering one's fellow-men. Every strange vessel was a possible enemy, and even friends, in the panic of ignorance and inexperience, could not be relied upon. On the Indian coast, ships blown into a wrong port became lawful prize; and during the wars succeeding the Portuguese entrance into the eastern seas, a rank growth of piracy was fostered.[4] The conditions of navigation, of which such instances as the above are typical, must be constantly kept in mind in order to form a just estimate of the Portuguese exploits and failures in the East.

[1] Hunter, I, 71; Major, pp. 58, 59.

[2] Whiteway, p. 46, note; a short description of the voyage to India is found in Martins, Hist. de Port., I, 306 ff.

[3] Beazley, in Azurara, II, cxi–cxii, cxliv; Whiteway, pp. 45 ff.; Lindsay, I, 547 ff.

[4] Whiteway, pp. 44–45, 47, 175–176; Martins, Hist. de Port., I, 282–283.

The Monopoly and its Defense

If the risks were great, the rewards could scarcely be regarded as disproportionate. The freight of Da Gama's ships covered the expenses of his voyage sixty times over.[1] Of Cabral's fleet only five vessels out of thirteen returned laden, but the cargo more than repaid the cost of the whole fleet. The elation and excitement in Lisbon may be imagined, for these were the first rich rewards of monopoly. At this time the Portuguese merchant-in-chief, that is, the king, assumed with Papal sanction the resonant title of Lord of the Navigation, Conquest, and Commerce of Ethiopia, Arabia, Persia, and India.[2] The very exuberance of self-confidence indicated by this rather premature assumption witnesses to the exceptional and exalted frame of mind in which the foremost people to grasp opportunities unparalleled in history approached their destiny.

It was the voyage of Da Gama, then, which brought to its definite fruition the work of Prince Henry. The first striking evidence of its importance was the readjustment of the markets and routes of the eastern products, which followed upon the safe return of this expedition.[3] The Venetians came after a time to perceive

[1] To get these spices was, says Ruge (p. 203), "das äusserste und letzte Ziel der portugiesischen Handelspolitik." For some discussion of the prices of pepper, etc., at this time, see Danvers, I, 64; Ruge, pp. 127–128, 201–203; and especially the tables of D'Avenel, *passim*. Cf. note 3 below.

Those who would gain a conception of the difficulty of attaining anything approaching exactitude of valuations in past centuries should read the opening chapters of D'Avenel, and consider the herculean toil evidenced in his treatise. In the present book no attempt could be made to secure such exactitude, and wherever prices are quoted or money-values transferred into modern terms, it must be understood that only rough approximations are presented.

[2] Hunter, I, 104. King Manuel displayed great ostentation in his embassy to the Pope, announcing the tidings; he attempted in some degree to assume the leadership of Europe, especially as against the Turks. Martins, Hist. de Port., II, 6 ff.

[3] The statement has been made that, in consequence of Da Gama's return, spice-prices experienced a sudden drop of 50 per cent or more. Cf. Adams, p. 289. If this statement is made to apply directly or by implication to more than local and exceptional conditions, it does not represent what one is led to expect from the first infringement of a monopoly-price. The Portuguese were actuated as little by philanthropic intent as had been the Venetians before them, and could hardly have bidden under the latter to any extent greater than was necessary in order to attract their customers away. Cf. note 2, p. 73 above. Some local flurries of a speculative nature might have been experienced, but, taxed as they were in transit, it is incredible that the Italians could have supported even for a few years such losses as the halving of prices would have brought upon them. The detailed tables of prices of eastern

that their worst apprehensions had been realized, that both their
center and their routes of distribution had been superseded; and
they made some approaches to the king of Portugal with a view
to saving at least a share of their disappearing commercial advantage. But it was not in the spirit of an age imbued with the
Italian theories to refrain from utilizing the immediate advantages
of the commercial upper-hand; coöperation was impossible, and
the struggle, now rendered practically hopeless for the Venetians,[1]
pursued its course. The scene of the conflict was transferred,
however, to regions nearer the sources of supply, and the opposition of the Venetians was felt, not directly, but indirectly in the
person of the Arabs and later of the Turks. The trade-routes
toward the west, mainly in the hands of the former, started from
Malacca and, diverging from its complementary port, Calicut,
passed into the Red Sea and Persian Gulf. At the entrance of
the former lay Aden, whence routes finally emerged into the Mediterranean, by way of the Nile or Suez, over Cairo and Alexandria;
it was by way of Aden also that the supplies of goods and the
ship-loads of pilgrims destined for Mecca and other Moslem centers
were carried. The corresponding port on the Persian Gulf route
was Ormuz, an island-city; from this point the trade-way passed
through Mesopotamia, then westward (via caravan) through Syria
to Beirut. Through these channels the Venetians obtained the bulk
of their Oriental products. More immediately, however, the Red
Sea traffic served the purposes and revenues of the Mameluke
Sultan of Egypt; and the latter speedily became aware of the
presence of the Portuguese in India through the complaints of
the Venetians, and, more effectively, through a decline in his own

products given by D'Avenel in Vol. IV (especially pp. 576–577) indicate a more
normal sequence of events, as do the figures of Thorold Rogers (III, 518–543; IV,
656–660). According to the latter authority, spices were cheapest in England, in the
period under discussion, from 1471 to 1490, while their highest quotations are for
1521–1540. The significant fact here is that the latter period follows closely upon
the date (1517) of the conquest of Egypt by the Ottomans, an event which, as has
been seen, practically put an end to Venetian competition. Cf. also Rogers, IV,
chap. xxiii; Heyd, II, 525–526, 531–532. D'Avenel's figures show no startling
changes in price-levels toward the end of the fifteenth century. In view of these considerations it seems to the present writer that the rather dramatic statement alluded
to at the beginning of this note does not fairly represent those general market-
conditions with which we are here concerned.

[1] In 1521 the Court of Lisbon refused an offer of the Republic of Venice to buy
up all the spices yearly brought to Portugal, over and above what Portugal itself
required. Hunter, I, 187. See p. 69 above.

revenues. To these causes of irritation was added the even more disquieting fact that the victorious activities of the Christians in the West were now to be transferred to a new and promising field. The Sultan accordingly threatened the Pope (Julius II) with war in the Mediterranean and the East, and with the destruction of the Holy Sepulcher, in case the activities of the Portuguese were not suspended. King Manuel was able to defy the Sultan through the Pope; and, in view of the concourse of enemies in the Mediterranean, the Sultan determined to crush the Portuguese in India, where they could count on no allies. The Portuguese learned in 1505 of these plans and of the formation of a considerable fleet designed to approach India the next year.[1]

THE "CRUSADE IN THE EAST": ALMEIDA

Although Vasco da Gama and the several captains who, up to this period, had succeeded him, had operated in behalf of the king, — for, from Prince Henry down, these enterprises had taken their direct origin in the royal initiative,[2] — they had worked almost wholly for commercial ends. Adventure was eagerly sought, but the idea of conquest and subjugation had not as yet appeared in any definite form. When Arab ships had been seized and plundered, religious hatred had been sated by a gruesome mal-treatment of the men, women, and children taken with the vessels; this activity might be called "religious piracy," were such a term self-explanatory. But when the Portuguese interests in India came to be threatened by the infidel, there appeared in the East, as there had appeared in the West years before, a centralization and unification of political and, through it, of religious strength and control. It is more than a picturesque fact that the first viceroy of India should have been a man who had won a high reputation with the Spaniards before Granada. To the Iberians a Moor was a Moor, and the best man to oppose the Moors of the East was one who had distinguished himself in conflict with those of the West. This man was Francisco d'Almeida, who was hurried

[1] Ruge, pp. 145–147. Hunter remarks that this conflict was "the third and last act in the long conflict between mediæval Christendom and Islam" (I, 115); King Manuel "knew that he had turned the flank of Islam, and that he had the sympathy of Catholic Europe in this final and greatest of the Crusades" (I, 116).

[2] Stephens (p. 176) says that nearly all the great Portuguese heroes of the period were of the noble classes.

off to India in March, 1505, to oppose the Sultan's movement; it is significant of the nature of this expedition that it drew support from Genoese, Florentine, and German merchants, but met only hostility from Venetian sources.[1] Almeida was fitted out with what was at that time a powerful force; there were over twenty ships and about 1500 soldiers pledged to a service of at least three years. Other squadrons followed, for national enthusiasm was aroused. After some inconsiderable reverses he managed to gain a complete naval victory at Diu (February, 1509); in this battle he commanded a fleet of twenty-three ships and 1600 soldiers. The Egyptian ships were attacked systematically, and sunk one after the other; the native auxiliaries and the city were spared, for the viceroy could not risk the hostility of the local potentate, and held, besides, to a general policy of friendly relations with the natives.

The impending danger which had called into activity the patriotic and religious zeal of the Portuguese was thus, at least temporarily, repelled. But the popular sentiment in Portugal was not satisfied with this; it demanded a general crusade against the Mohammedans in the East wherever and whenever encountered. It was not content with Almeida's idea of concentrating a power on the sea which would hold the most valuable parts of the Indian coast tributary to the Portuguese trade and government; it found its ideal, rather, in the offensive operations of Affonso d'Albuquerque, with which Almeida had no sympathy. Its goal was conquest and the propagation of the faith. Thus it may be said that the Sultan's attack precipitated in India a consolidation of Portuguese power similar to that effected nearer home in wars with the European and North African Moslems. Of this state of popular energy and aggression the radical Albuquerque expressed the spirit; so that with his accession to the governorship the hitherto uncertain policy of the Portuguese turned squarely toward conquest. At this parting of the ways it is useful to compare the variant policies of these two exceptional men, the first viceroy and his successor.[2] Almeida had started out with a threefold task: to secure a base for permanent occupation in East Africa; to effect the coercion of the Malabar ports and the construction of factories; and to break the Moslem

[1] Ruge, p. 147.
[2] Martins, Hist. de Port., I, 236 ff., 241–245, 269–270; Hunter, I, 118 ff., 135 ff.; Danvers, I, xxviii–xxx, 261 ff.; Whiteway, p. 16.

sea-power. By the construction of a fort at Quiloa and by the reduction of Mombasa his first purpose was realized; by the destruction of the Zamorin's fleet and that of the Arabs, not only were the Malabar ports rendered available to the Portuguese, but the influence of the latter was extended as far as Ceylon;[1] and as a consequence of the engagement at Diu the Indian Ocean was made for a hundred years a Portuguese sea. It is little wonder, therefore, that Almeida favored a sea-policy and opposed the foundation of garrisons, except at dominant points; for to his mind they simply depleted his power. He wished also to confine his operations to India alone, in order not to divide his forces; he believed it would be impossible for Portugal, with its small population, effectively to maintain a colonial empire under Portuguese administration. In this view, as will be seen, he was largely justified by the final outcome.

ALBUQUERQUE

Albuquerque's programme, on the other hand, representing the more alluring idea of empire and of a general campaign against the infidel, appealed to the king with a peculiar force; for it fell in with the spirit of an age of grandiose movements in both the temporal and spiritual fields. Albuquerque believed that the whole Moslem world was united against him; neither he nor the king realized the presence of a conflict between the Ottoman and Mameluke Sultans. He felt, therefore, that command of the sea was not enough to assure the Portuguese of the upper-hand; that a land empire alone could afford a sufficient base of operations during the ups and downs of a life-and-death struggle, especially in the case of a metropolis so distant as was Portugal at this stage of undeveloped communications. For this reason he wished to convert every captured district into a permanent possession; and, disbelieving in the utility of alliances with local sovereigns, he invariably planned to coerce conquered princes into acknowledging Portugal as a suzerain power. He aimed at the command of all the trade between East and West; but he intended to found such dominance entirely upon physical force, exercised directly and solely by the Portuguese. This demanded a cordon of fortresses

---

[1] Ceylon was visited in 1505 and conquered in 1515. Von Brandt, p. 511. A good general account of the penetration of the eastern seas by Europeans is given by this author.

and naval stations at strategical points, and also factories and colonies to meet the demands of an enormous development of exchange and to repair the wastage of life entailed by this general policy.[1] Almeida could not be accused of tenderness toward the Moslems; but the projects of Albuquerque looking to their discomfiture were no less than vast, not to say visionary. The old crusading spirit, as so often in Spanish and Portuguese colonization, was highly developed in both men. Albuquerque, for example, planned and actually attempted a reckless expedition for the purpose of seizing Mohammed's bones, to hold as ransom for the Holy Sepulcher, or to burn in public; and even contemplated with the utmost seriousness the diversion of the Nile into the Red Sea for the purpose of ruining Egypt. His actual activities in India were grouped about three main purposes: to intercept Moslem trade at its base in the upper Nile region and the Persian Gulf; to destroy Moslem trade on the Malabar coast by concentrating the commerce of that region in Portuguese ports; and to seize the fountain-heads of the spice-trade by taking Malacca. The Portuguese were intent upon diverting to themselves the profits in the spice-trade enjoyed by Mohammedans and Italians; that in the attainment of this end the unbelievers would suffer was an added incentive. In Albuquerque's mind these objectives went hand in hand with empire; "he supplied no new aim, he merely pointed out a new method of attaining an old object." [2]

Differing thus in his views from Almeida, Albuquerque got the ear of the king and was sent out in 1508 to succeed the viceroy; his title, however, was merely *governador*. He died late in the year 1515. Within the few years of his command, however, is to be reckoned the real glory-period of Portuguese dominance in India.[3] For this reason, and because during these years there emerged many a portent of the dull decades to come, it is fitting to dwell here somewhat at length upon details and chronicles of events.

[1] Hunter, I, 119 ff.; Danvers, I, xxviii ff.; Whiteway, pp. 169 ff.; the annals of Portuguese India are full, for example, of the costly sieges resulting from this policy.

[2] Hunter, I, 100 ff., 125–126; Whiteway, p. 16 (quotation); Martins, Hist. de Port., I, 251, 264. Leroy-Beaulieu (I, 46–47) regards Almeida's policy as the more sound; he cites the costs, enmities, jealousies, etc., of the conquest policy, and quotes a contemporary, Sir Thomas Roe (early seventeenth century), upon the disadvantages of the Portuguese policy as laid down by Albuquerque. Cf. also Martins, Hist. de Port., I, 298–299.

[3] An excellent brief article, "De Portugeezen in den Maleischen Archipel," is found in Encycl. Ned. Ind.

Albuquerque's Administration

The threefold purpose alluded to formed the basis of Albuquerque's action. He commenced operations with an attack on Calicut; but the ill-success of this and other early ventures led him to pause before Goa until he had restored the discipline and morale of his forces. The soldiers were drilled, and laxness in all branches of administration was corrected with characteristic decision and energy. Many enemies were thus made, but it was only during Albuquerque's last years that they succeeded in thwarting his designs. The disciplined forces were now turned against Goa, the headquarters of a league whose object was to eject the Portuguese from India, and prospectively a good base of operation for the Turks; it fell in November, 1510.[1] This result, as Albuquerque had foreseen, greatly enhanced the prestige of the Portuguese, not only in the East, where the native princes hastened to declare their allegiance, but in Europe as well. According to Albuquerque, the taking of Goa kept India in repose; the city became his capital and that of his successors. Its capture represented to the Portuguese the success of the endeavor to control the Malabar coast. But such local and defensive operations were but the beginning of Albuquerque's projects; it remained to lay hands upon the sources themselves of the Oriental trade. There had been a factor in Malacca, the great entrepôt of the Far East, since 1508, and the importance of this focus of trade-routes, rendered by geographical and meteorological conditions the terminal of converging sea-roads, was a cardinal belief in Albuquerque's mind. In 1511, as soon as his hands were free on the Malabar coast, he led an expedition which took Malacca, thereafter destined to remain in Portuguese possession for about a hundred years.

These operations at a distance were doubtless more important for Albuquerque's general plans, effecting as they did a stoppage of Mohammedan trade at the source, but it was an ideal dear to his crusading spirit to attack the infidel at his very doors. These were, so far as commerce was concerned, Ormuz and Aden.[2] His designs on Ormuz were revealed even before he became governor. Indeed, it had become increasingly apparent, since the arrival of the Portuguese, that the real and sole menace to their commercial supremacy came directly from the north. The native rulers were

---

[1] Martins, Hist. de Port., I, 260–262; Whiteway, p. 137.   [2] See p. 95, above.

regularly incited to opposition by Egyptian agents, and the king repeatedly urged an expedition to the Red Sea.[1] In 1515 the governor was successful in extending a sort of protectorate over Ormuz and its environs; a move which effectively closed the Persian Gulf to the Mohammedans. An attack on Aden, the key to the Red Sea route, failed after great expenditure of resources and lives, but the trade in these waters was greatly crippled by the possession of Goa and the other Indian ports, and by the constant activities of the Portuguese in the Indian Ocean. The Mohammedan ships were forced to sail around Ceylon and were often hunted out in waters even so remote. Thus the purpose of intercepting Mohammedan trade *en route* was largely realized; and the insecurity caused by the successes and restless energy of Albuquerque was an even more deadly blow. Ottoman resources were drained and Ottoman forces divided; this proved the saving of Europe itself.[2]

All these successes, crowded into the space of a few years, raised the renown of Portugal and of the governor to an extraordinary degree. At the end of Albuquerque's life Portugal was the undisputed mistress of the East, while in India peace was universal from Ormuz to Ceylon. The interior of the land " he left so quiet and well-ordered that there was never a nation left so completely conquered and subdued by force of arms as this was." [3]   Trade was not endangered by robbery; east of Cape Comorin the kings were at peace and friendly with Portugal, and even Malacca enjoyed repose. The kings of Siam, Java, and even China were glad to make peace with the redoubtable conqueror.[4] All these results were the outcome of a strong man's guidance; the Portuguese were as brave both before and after, but they never again swept all before them. A review of Albuquerque's personality and internal administration throws much light, partly by contrast, upon a century of Portuguese dominance.

ALBUQUERQUE'S PERSONALITY

He was a man of great sagacity and decision of character, as fearless elsewhere as he was in battle; his policy was therefore an intelligent, independent, and consistent one.[5] He was deeply

---

[1] Ruge, p. 177; on the " Rumes," cf. Payne, Age of Disc., pp. 27 ff.
[2] Hunter, I, 132.
[3] Danvers, I, 330.   [4] Id., I, 330–331.   [5] Whiteway, pp. 131, 169–171.

religious, strictly loyal, and incorruptible; and so, while he dealt hardly and to our eyes mercilessly with the enemies of the faith, he upheld against constant and treacherous opposition standards of rectitude in the colonial service. He had a talent for the business of administration; he labored incessantly himself, and required no less of his subordinates. And yet he was not so immersed in detail that he could not view his own activities in perspective, and look forward to and plan for a period of peace as the end and outcome of war. He was fortunately so far removed from Lisbon that his actions were not subject to control, even if he had wished it. The fact of it was that he resisted and resented interference, even from the king,[1] and it was owing to the high opinion of the latter that he had his own way so largely, to Portugal's profit, for the term of his command.

Turning to some of Albuquerque's measures, we find his character reflected not only in their excellences but also in their defects. He would not tolerate inefficiency or slothfulness in his subordinates; he constantly appealed to Portugal for a better quality of functionaries. He exclaimed in exasperation that the latter were so poorly trained that they were "not fit to purchase two-penny-worth of bread in the bazaar. A clerk trained in the counting-house of Bartholomew, the Florentine, would be more useful than all the factors the king has in India."[2] Disinterested himself, he pursued with vigor the detection and punishment of dishonest officials; he wished the temptation to unrighteousness to be removed by the extension of the term of offices from three to eight years. He himself, in spite of unexampled opportunities for amassing wealth, left scarcely any property behind.[3] All presents that came into his hands passed on to those of the king or queen. He had a way of summarily disposing, during his morning peregrinations, of many complaints and petitions; the parties were thus satisfied, and processes spared, which, in the ordinary channels, would have been indefinitely spun out and correspondingly involved and costly. He was interested, above all, in the development of

---

[1] He once retorted to the king, to whom he practically refused obedience from time to time, "But do not require of me every year an account of what I am doing, as if I were a tax-gatherer." Danvers, I, 263.

[2] Whiteway, p. 174; cf. Martins, Hist. de Port., I, 298.

[3] He made his will, and in leaving his last wishes to his successor his old humor flashed out: "I beg he will not put up my goods to auction: I do not wish my ragged old breeches to be seen." Whiteway, p. 166; cf. p. 174.

trade and the attendant advance in the well-being of the people. He even checked, so far as possible, the indiscriminate persecution of the Moslems, and granted passes to Arab ships for trade other than that in spices.[1]

It was, however, in his relations to the native population that his peculiar powers found their most striking expression. His personality was of the compelling sort which inspires the Oriental with awe and which he will follow blindly. The very heat of Albuquerque's temper and the swiftness with which action followed on impulse captivated the imagination of the Easterners, and the governor's herculean toil and notable successes were calculated to impress sturdier spirits than theirs. But Albuquerque was more : through quick perception or long experience he understood the workings of the native mind, and aroused their respectful admiration by repeatedly overreaching them in their own methods of intrigue and wile.[2] Albuquerque's insight into local conditions was generally unerring ; for example, he realized that in Malacca the Portuguese had replaced a foreign (Mohammedan) intruder, who was hated cordially, and so he exerted himself to appear, in contrast to his predecessors, friendly to the native dynasties.[3] And he was, though stern, approachable and just to a degree remarkable in his day ; his word was scrupulously kept, and a promised punishment or reward seldom failed to be meted out. If he himself oppressed, he did not allow the liberty to his subordinates ; his clear-headed judgment was not warped by fear or favor. His pithy and proverbial speeches circulated among all classes. An atmosphere of superstitious awe enveloped his striking figure ; and after his death the natives made pilgrimages and left offerings at his tomb to secure his aid against the oppression and injustice of his successors.[4]

[1] Whiteway, pp. 160, 162.

[2] According to Whiteway (pp. 24–25), these methods, successful only in a master's hands, reacted banefully upon the Portuguese. Among the moral causes of Portuguese decline, he says, " one of the most potent was the adaptation of the Oriental methods of diplomacy which placed Eastern and Western on the same plane, and in an intrigue the Eastern won." Another cause was " ingrained suspicion and distrust of each other," referable possibly to the same methods.

[3] Ruge, pp. 171–172.

[4] Whiteway, pp. 166–169; Hunter, I, 140. The Hindus still have fetiches which they call " Affonso de Albuquerques." Martins, Hist. de Port., I, 267.

Albuquerque's Policy

The policy of Albuquerque toward the natives is said to have been modeled upon that of Alexander the Great; his furious attacks in war and his deft treatment of the Orientals certainly bore likeness to those of the Macedonian.[1] It was his policy, after inflicting a thorough-going and unquestioned defeat, to bind the subject people to him through even-handed justice and even affection; and he never let slip the opportunity to impress the susceptible Oriental mind by pomp and ostentation. He left the administration of conquered countries to the natives, but kept the military and the revenues in his own hands. The general arrangements with princes were that the Portuguese should be allowed to erect fortresses, that merchandise should enter no Indian port save Goa, and that the natives should not receive Turks into their kingdoms; but inasmuch as the objects of the Portuguese were at first largely commercial, the tribute-system was not an exaggerated one.[2] The colonial, as distinguished from the purely commercial and political policy of Albuquerque deserves a word; as has been stated, he proposed to draw the men for the armies and navies, which would be rendered necessary by his policy as distinguished from that of Almeida, from colonies in India. He could not hope for any considerable emigration of women from Portugal; he therefore fostered unions between the Portuguese and the native women. This policy had been foreshadowed by Da Gama, and was one of the expedients of Alexander the Great. It is to be noted that the Portuguese were, in the home-country, accustomed to mixed unions and their offspring, and consequently there was little or no prejudice to overcome. "In every Portuguese settlement the married men rapidly became a caste to themselves with special privileges; all petty offices were reserved for them, and in Goa all the lands belonging to the King — a very large part of the area — were divided among them."[3] Albuquerque also encouraged the married men to engage in industrial pursuits. It is perhaps an anticipation to say that this policy was totally unsuccessful; as will be seen, the mongrel type thus formed tended to revert, in the absence of regular infusion of the blood of one of its constituent

[1] Danvers, I, 328 ff.
[2] Danvers, I, 255. For models of these treaties, see Hunter, I, 142 ff.
[3] Whiteway, p. 177; cf. p. 17; Danvers, I, 217.

elements, to the type of the country of its origin, and thus was unable to hold its own with sturdier races. Comparison is here challenged with the results which appeared in Brazil. These " colonies," in any case, amounted to little or nothing; they were a curse rather than a blessing.[1] In three places only did the Portuguese hold cities that had been transferred under treaty or as a result of conquest; these were Diu, Bassein with Salsette, and Goa, all upon small islands. Here only were the Portuguese masters; the consequence was that European settlers were relatively numerous and that these cities lost their native hue. Elsewhere the Portuguese came to dominate only so far from their forts, or the coast, as their guns would carry. Moreover, in spite of their familiarity with a relatively warm climate, and their proverbial temperance, the Portuguese succumbed in large numbers to the climate of India. Their dense ignorance of the laws of health, and the demoralization of their customs, effectually blocked all possible efforts toward neutralizing the changed environmental conditions.[2]

The relatively extended term of Albuquerque gave to Portuguese policy a fixity from which there was in form little subsequent deviation; but it will be seen that the same policy, in the hands of inferior men, took on a different aspect and led to disastrous results. The fact is that Albuquerque's policy was himself. He was an imperator, with the virtues and faults characteristic of the practically unlimited despot. His system was satisfactory, therefore, in his hands only; when his powerful grasp was relaxed, a thousand growing disorders, hitherto held at bay, began to compass the disintegration of the structure. These influences embittered Albuquerque's last days. After years of effort his enemies, often the victims of his inexorable insistence upon purity in the service, gained the ear of the king and effected his supersession. Officials whom he had cashiered were sent back in positions of power; one of his enemies was named as his successor.[3] " In bad repute with men," he exclaimed, " because of the King, and in bad repute with

---

[1] Martins, Hist. de Port., I, 260–262; Hunter, I, 162; Whiteway, pp. 24–25, 176–178; cf. p. 164, below. Leroy-Beaulieu (I, 42) says : " Ce ne furent pas de véritables colonies dans le sens étroit du mot, c'est-à-dire des établissements territoriaux destinés à être peuplés par les habitants de la métropole, ce fut une chaîne de comptoirs et de points de ravitaillement, défendus par des fortresses, qui constitua les célèbres possessions portugaises."

[2] Ruge, p. 199; Brunialti, p. 105; Whiteway, pp. 24–25; Lavisse et Rambaud, IV, 897.   [3] Danvers, I, 326 ff.

the King because of the men, it were well that I were gone." He had lived a life of toil and self-denial, had never been viceroy, was superseded as governor, yet he lifted up his hands to heaven, "giving many thanks to our Lord."[1] His was the old crusading spirit, the deep loyalty and ardent piety which lent strength to the Iberians to accomplish unheard-of deeds and die gladly for the King and the Faith. But in Albuquerque we have plainly an exceptional man, to whom the ordinary limitations of humanity do not apply. This was realized after his death. Too late King Manuel reversed the order for his retirement; regrets for the old warrior (he died at the age of 63) replaced the scanty recognition accorded him in life. For his capture of Malacca he had not received even verbal acknowledgment; but when he was dead, the superstitious awe of the natives invaded the thankless minds of the Portuguese. It was provided in his will that his body should be taken home to Portugal; but the Portuguese kings believed that India would be safe for Portugal only while his bones rested there, and it took a fulmination of the Pope to secure the carrying-out of his wishes (1566).[2]

Extent of the Empire

It is not in the plan of this treatise to pursue in detail the exploits or failures of Albuquerque's successors. In Albuquerque is found the climax of Portuguese power and glory in the East,[3] and already in his lifetime decline had set in, never to be seriously interrupted.

The centers of Portuguese influence in the East have been indicated in what has gone before. No additions of moment were made to the empire after the death of Albuquerque. As may have been gathered, the East African possessions received comparatively little attention from him; of these something will be said further on. An unsuccessful expedition or raid was occasionally directed toward the Red Sea coast or that of the northern Arabian Sea. The final capture and defense of Diu, in 1537 and 1538, by Nuno da Cunha deserves rank among the best exploits of the

---

[1] His words were: "Mal com os homens por amor d'elrey, mal com elrey por amor dos homens, bom é acabar." Martins, Hist. de Port., I, 266; Hunter, I, 128.

[2] On the life and activities of Albuquerque, see his Commentaries; also Hunter, Whiteway, Danvers, *passim*. References are given in these books to primary sources.

[3] "À cette date de 1515, la situation de Portugal est merveilleuse. Le petit royaume est devenu le premier des États maritimes." Lavisse et Rambaud, IV, 891.

Portuguese. Strong aid was lent to Diu by the Turks; the Portuguese recruits were a poor lot, yet the spirit and vigor of the commander roused them to truly heroic activity. As usual the sight of the Crescent spurred dormant energies to a sort of irresistible frenzy.[1] But the bulk of attention at this time was turned toward the farther East. Ceylon was approached in Almeida's time and was later brought into a subject relation. The Coromandel Coast, the region of Calcutta, and certain portions of Burma were visited in a desultory manner. In Albuquerque's time relations were joined with some of the rulers of Farther India and China. After taking Malacca, Albuquerque sent an expedition to explore the Moluccas (1511); factors were located in the islands and in 1564 Portuguese suzerainty was acknowledged.[2] Borneo was visited in 1530, and various expeditions penetrated to this and that island of the Archipelago, to New Guinea, and even farther. Toward the north-east they visited the Philippines, and in 1540 the first Portuguese came to Japan. In none of these cases were colonies founded, and there were few permanent factories. However, by 1571 the "empire," extending as it did from Africa to China, was thought to be too great for control from a single center. King Sebastian constructed three separate governments: that of India, including all territory from Cape Guardafui to Ceylon; that of Monomotapa, extending from Cape Corrientes to Cape Guardafui; and that of Malacca, covering the claims between Pegu and China. The head-official of the India department kept the title of viceroy; the others were called governors.[3] In 1580, by the accession of Philip II to the Portuguese throne, the whole Portuguese East came under Spanish influence and remained so for sixty years.

THE ARMY AND NAVY

The military operations of the Portuguese, especially during the first years of the sixteenth century, seem to our eyes remarkable; their forces were always small, but their achievements appear to have been accomplished with an almost ridiculous ease, and in a spirit of light-hearted confidence and daring. The losses of the

[1] Ruge, pp. 193 ff. Martins (Hist. de Port., II, 276 ff.) describes the wretched material upon which this commander had to rely.

[2] On the more detailed history of the Moluccas, see Argensola, *passim*.

[3] Danvers, II, 1 ff.; for a list of the viceroys and governors, see Martins, Hist. de Port., I, 291.

Portuguese were often of the most trivial nature, while their opponents suffered crushing defeats or annihilation.[1] This was so for almost a century, despite the growing demoralization of army and administration. The element of good fortune constantly favored the invaders, and came to be reckoned upon as a matter of course. Opportune arrivals of unexpected reënforcements, timely ravages of disease among the enemy, — such occurrences are the order of the day. Not a little of the success of the early periods is referable to that mood of confidence, rooted in the conviction of divine approval and strengthened by good luck, which attended what was in reality a crusade. The truly heroic deeds thus inspired brighten the annals of conquest. However, one must not be led by the prolixity of Portuguese descriptions to infer that even the majority of the engagements with the natives consisted of operations on the grand scale; many of them were merely " magnified street brawls." [2] Nor must too much importance be lent to the originally enormous advantage of the possession of cannon and fire-arms. The ordnance and matchlocks were more effective at first through the noise of their explosions than through the force or accuracy of their fire; indeed, they were often more dangerous to the marksman than to the target.[3] The Portuguese were, however, greatly superior in armor; the risk of the panoplied knight was suffocation rather than wounds. It must be realized also that their opponents were seldom well organized. The success of the Portuguese rested rather upon their past : the discipline and experience of the European wars, the endurance and fearlessness derived from facing new and strange vicissitudes, the conviction of superiority and of divine approval, — these are the qualities that enabled them to win with such apparent ease.[4] Indeed, much more peril lay in the voyage to India than in the fighting which came after; on the average, it is said, not 60 per cent of the men who left Portugal for India reached their destination : of Da Gama's 170 men only 55 survived to return to Portugal.[5]

During the century the Portuguese held an irregular coast-line of 15,000 miles; but this was solely through their navy. That

[1] See, for instance, Danvers, I, 480–481, 534–535, 565, 566, 567, 568, 571.

[2] Whiteway, p. 35; Hunter, I, 93–96.

[3] A shot fired point-blank by the Portuguese at the hull of an Egyptian ship in 1508 cleared the fighting top of its defenders. Whiteway, p. 39; cf. pp. 37 ff.

[4] See Danvers, I, 377 ff., 384, 473, 531, 545, 555.

[5] See Whiteway, pp. 47, 82.

invisible agent was always able to concentrate, strike, and disappear; it was assured of an unquestioned prestige, under local conditions, whatever became of the army.[1] And its successes against unmatched opponents lent it a world-wide and utterly disproportionate distinction. In spite of isolated exploits of great brilliancy, however, both arms of the service speedily declined in the sixteenth century. At the end of the reign of Manuel, "The Fortunate," decadence was already manifest throughout the Portuguese dominions.[2] Albuquerque is found to complain bitterly of the equipments and the men forwarded to him from Lisbon. The former were flimsy, and often old and patched; the latter were insufficient in number and of contemptible quality.[3] The miscegenation furthered by Albuquerque gradually lowered even this low quality; and the native auxiliaries, although they never came up to expectation, were often preferred to the Portuguese. After a time discipline was relaxed, and when the meager pay of officers and men ran behind and stopped, the army became a military mob, which sold its equipments and those of the military posts, and gambled away the proceeds. The old faith in the saints degenerated into vague and superstitious hopes of supernatural aid; the spirit of the earlier years was gone, and with it former good fortune. The amount of genuine bad luck met by the Portuguese early in the seventeenth century is almost as striking as was their good luck at the outset. The navy also suffered, although its decline was not so immediately self-evident. The vessels for the India defense and trade became ever more unwieldy, in the attempt to make them more imposing, and for decades their reputation rested upon nothing but the inflated prestige just alluded to.[4]

[1] Hunter, I, 134, 166 ff. To such relatively small advances as the Portuguese made in nautical matters the dictum of Foreman (pp. 12–13) can yet be applied, when he says that it is the modern scientific discoveries that have enlarged governmental areas and made larger ones as compact as the older and smaller ones.   [2] Corvo, I, 7.

[3] Danvers, I, 305–306. Albuquerque had more faith in his common sailors than in his officers; he called them "my cavaliers," and preferred to meet a crisis depending on them alone. Danvers, I, 275.

[4] On the original fear of the carracks, see Roscher, p. 256. The ships finally became floating castles that could not stand the India voyage. The *Madre de Deos* had seven stories, was 165 feet long and 47 feet beam. Hunter, I, 165; cf. pp. 160 ff.; Martins, Hist. de Port., I, 309, 316. The authors remark upon the progressively increasing casualties from shipwreck, capture by enemies, etc. Martins (O Brazil, etc., pp. 35–36) contrasts the extended period 1497–1612 with the critical years 1585–1597, and finds that the percentages of vessels lost in the India service by wreck or fire in the two periods were 8.4 per cent and 33.4 per cent; those of ships captured by the enemy

MONOPOLY POLICY AND DEMORALIZATION

All this witnesses for a demoralization of administration, center-ing, in last resort, in Lisbon, and in the king. This administration, if it should be so denominated, had in view but two points of policy : to secure the commerce of the East, and to render it as productive as possible. These really reduced to one and the same thing. It has been shown how the initiative in the discovery of the Cape route had been taken by royalty, and how the succeeding com-mercial operations had been prosecuted on the count of the king ; it was not in the spirit of the time, nor in the stage of material advancement of the people, that such a movement should rise from a popular origin. Hence the policy which directed it is primarily royal, and national only in the sense that royal direction was popu-larly accepted. The royal policy, in conformity with current com-mercial ideas, was monopolistic, in this showing its relationship with that of the republics of the Middle Ages. The system of " secret commerce " was continued, being remodeled, however, upon the new doctrine of exclusive right based on priority of discovery and confirmed by the highest tribunal of the age.[1]

Although the exploitation of this monopoly belonged to the king, the effects of his enterprises could not but be national. When, therefore, Da Gama returned from the East, laden with spoils, the effect upon all Portugal was galvanic. A limitless field for "conquest, commerce, and conversion" was opened, and by contrast the ordinary interests of the people seemed flat and unprofitable. The spirit of adventure, the impulse to gamble with unheard-of chances, combined with distaste for the common vocations of life and a certain ardor for the saving of souls, laid hold upon a people as averse to industry as they were predisposed to the life of hazard. Every one hastened to get a share in the exploitation of

---

0.5 per cent and 3 per cent. These vessels were of from 500 to 600 tons, carried crews of 120 and troops to the number of 250, and cost on the average about $20,000. Such losses must be referred largely to the general demoralization of the service. See also Hunter, I, 171.

[1] Hunter, I, 218–221 ; cf. Varnhagen, I, 36, 79, 86. Pilots, seamen, and chart-makers were long subjected to jealous scrutiny, restrictions, prohibitions, etc. ; and the stock " commercial myths " were retailed.

About 1534 one Botelho embarked from Diu, with a few men, in a bark $16\frac{1}{2}$ feet long, 9 feet broad, and $4\frac{1}{2}$ feet deep, and, without seamen or pilot, managed to reach Lisbon. The bark was immediately burned, that the possibility of performing the voyage in so small a vessel might not be discovered. Danvers, I, 409.

the East.[1] It is characteristic of the age, however, that the chroniclers give but little attention to trade and its development. Such
subjects, they felt, little befitted a "grave history"; and so accidental notices form the bulk of evidence along these lines. But it
is clear that the first operations in the East were immensely profitable. Characteristically these enterprises included a large element
of piracy, or, according to the ideas of the time, spoliation of the
infidel. There was, besides, the long-distance traffic, between
markets of widely diverse conjunctures, and likewise the port-to-
port trade in the East, in opium chiefly, and other local articles.
Tributes and ransoms were added components of income.[2] The
net annual revenue of the king from India in early days, despite
the peculation to which it was almost from the outset exposed,
is reckoned at about $750,000; it is said that the king's profit
should have been $2,100,000 per annum.[3] It was impossible, in
the face of such temptations, to anticipate or eradicate the most
wholesale corruption. The king was merchant-in-chief, because,
among a people to whom corporate enterprise was scarcely known,
he alone could control sufficient capital for the purpose in hand;
but his subjects were not slow to improve a subsidiary capacity.
The Portuguese monarchs were willing to admit their subjects into
the eastern trade; but only with the permission of the government, and into certain restricted branches.[4] The trade resolved

[1] Schäfer, III, 330 ff. Martins (Hist. de Port., I, 222) says, characteristically,
"All Portugal embarked for India in Cabral's squadron."

[2] "A pirataria e o saque foram os dois fundamentos do dominio portuguez, cujo
nervo eram os canhões, cuja alma era a Pimenta." Martins, Hist. de Port., I, 233.

[3] Hunter, I, 174–175. For some of the rich "hauls" of the Portuguese, see
Hunter, I, 170 ff.; Whiteway, pp. 143–144; Danvers, passim; Martins, Hist. de Port.,
I, 271 ff. Corvo (I, 9–10) calculates that at the end of the sixteenth century the
taxes and the monopolies of the Portuguese dominions rendered between three and
four million dollars, in modern money, and that the chief expenses amounted to 60 per
cent of this sum.

[4] Hunter, I, 104 ff., 175–176; Leroy-Beaulieu, I, 47–48. The great royal monopoly
was the pepper trade. "It was so jealously guarded that no authority in India could
enter into any agreement or make any peace that affected it. It was the cause of
most of the coast wars, for the Muhamedans strove by every means to load cargoes
of pepper for the Red Sea, and there can be no doubt but that not many years after
the time of Albuquerque all the Portuguese, from the Governor downwards, traded
illicitly in pepper. The prices paid by the King were those fixed when his ships first
visited the coast, before competition had raised them; naturally the King got the
worst stuff in the market; some sent home . . . was so bad that 33 years later it still
lay in the Lisbon warehouses." Whiteway, p. 171; Martins, Hist. de Port., II, 20.
On the conditions of cultivation of pepper, etc., see Wallace, chap. xix; on the other
desirable products of the East, Cheyney, pp. 11 ff.

itself then into a royal monopoly operated through hundreds of subordinates not susceptible of any adequate control from the far-distant metropolis. The mood of these officials, who were poorly paid in anticipation of their own activities in accumulation, soon became one of unscrupulous greed; and the vital conditions of life in the tropics further accentuated this attitude. All other motives merged in the dominant one of the speedy amassing of wealth; and corruption in all branches of the public service followed. Every one hastened to procure, through slander, bribery, flattery, and general parasitism, some post in the service whence he could derive gifts, extorted moneys, or other riches.[1]

Naturally enough the king lost heavily through this disposition on the part of his agents. The latter were at first allowed to load some small amounts of merchandise in the cabins, or to get a low percentage on the cargo; but this speedily became a competing private trade on a large scale, and the king's interests, especially in the distant Indian ports, were regularly sacrificed. As early as 1513 service on the royal ships was shunned, and private traders coerced native rajahs to sell to them, leaving the king to purchase at higher prices; private cargoes were disposed of before the king's goods had their turn.[2] The king struggled against these tendencies in vain. As early as 1524 the aged Vasco da Gama was again sent out to India, and for the few remaining weeks of his life quelled abuses with characteristic sternness.[3] A few officers, like Da Gama's son, Estevão, completed their terms with their means depleted; but the abuses suffered merely a temporary check. The old spirit was gone: it was no longer the desire of the soldier to shed his blood for King and Faith, but all sorts of rascality were excused on the ground of insufficiency of pay. The wages of the soldier were indeed ridiculously small. It was tacitly admitted that any one in India could add to his stipend by avocations of some sort; and in time the higher officials, representing the government and king, began to pay off officers or appease relatives or cast-off mistresses by the reversion of an office or the "gift of a

---

[1] Martins, Hist. de Port., I, 245–246, 304 ff.; Hunter, I, 175 ff.; Lavisse et Rambaud, IV, 898. The Portuguese government, despite the great sources of income that lay before it, was never properly solvent. Whiteway, pp. 175–176.

[2] In 1530 the Bengal voyage from Malabar yielded the captain £2450 and the king £78. Hunter, I, 177. Cf. Martins, Hist. de Port., I, 287.

[3] Danvers, I, 368–374.

voyage." [1] By such means the Indian administration, both in
Lisbon and in Goa, was thoroughly demoralized; in 1552 the civic
authorities of the latter capital appealed to the king, asserting that
" In India there is no justice, either in your viceroy, or in those
who are to mete it out. . . . There is no Moor who will trust
a Portuguese." [2]

DEMORALIZATION IN THE METROPOLIS

It is evident that such depravity of customs in that portion of
the nation's life which had to do with the colonies must have been
correlative with momentous changes in the metropolis itself. Allusion has been made to the decline of the ancient and solid character of the people before the prospect of sudden wealth. The
result was a general movement to the capital, which soon increased
in quantity and declined in quality of population; a movement
which early depleted the supply of labor in agriculture, and largely
increased the idle and dependent classes.[3] To meet the shortage
of labor, especially in the south of Portugal, natives of Africa were
introduced under a system of slavery, with the result that, through
race-mixture and otherwise, a heavy blow was struck at the homogeneity and quality of population in general.[4] The growth of
estates dispossessed the lesser nobility and gentry and caused them
the more surely to drift into the crowded centers, which, at that
stage of the arts, were the hotbeds of disease as well as vice. To
partially remedy this state of things the government came to use
India as a refuge for depraved and destitute clients; for one and
all tried to force themselves into a share of the royal monopoly by
besieging the doors of the influential. Young women were shipped

[1] According to Falcão, in 1612 the China and Japan voyage was worth $125,000;
that to Goa by Mozambique, $30,000; to the Moluccas, $35,000. Whiteway, pp. 74–
75. According to the same authority, at the same date the pay of the captain at
Sofala for three years was $4250, and the profits $285,000. The salary was a
matter of the utmost indifference, and not infrequently decreased. In 1550 the captain
at Ormuz received $3000 a year and $1580 as the salary of his guard; in 1612 the
captain's pay had sunk to $2000 a year, that of his guards had risen to $2700, and he
was allowed $4300 to recompense 40 hangers-on who were supported out of public
funds. Whiteway, p. 72.   [2] Hunter, I, 185.

[3] Stephens (p. 182) says that Lisbon trebled its population in 80 years, in spite of
unsanitary conditions and continuous pestilences. Martins, Hist. de Port., I, 175–176;
Hunter, I, 181 ff.

[4] Corvo (I, 13) gives the annual importation of slaves into Lisbon, from about
1535 on, as 10,000; into Portugal, in 1573, as 40,000.

off to India with dowries of office for those who would marry them; the multiplication of the forms of government employment was carried to a ridiculous extent, but the rapidity of their creation could not keep pace with the increase of applicants.[1] For all this, the wealth of the Indies poured into Portugal in prodigal abundance;[2] visible prosperity increased. Lisbon became the entrepôt of the western world. Yet at the same time the national wealth, which was neither pepper nor pearls nor gold, was well on in its decline. Prices of necessities rose very high; population fell off; famine and disease wrought periodic havoc. The régime of luxury sapped the vigor of the upper classes, and the lot of the sturdy peasant farmer became, with the growth of estates operated by slave-labor, ever more intolerable.[3] "All were, or aspired to be, *fidalgos*; they had themselves attended in the streets by a multitude of servants, although they often had nothing for the latter to eat."[4] The lower classes lived upon the higher in a subject relation, and the higher upon the royal favor; Portugal as a whole became dependent upon the India trade, and the development of natural resources fell away. It is clearly to be seen that if the accidental source of wealth should be removed, but little would remain to fall back upon. Nor ought the India trade itself to be regarded as a fountain of riches commensurate with its quondam reputation. The possibility of unreasonably high profits dazzled the judgment, for the policy of the time and of the frontier-trade was directed toward the realization of large gains upon small quantities of merchandise, rather than of moderate profits upon large quantities. For this reason the continuity and multiplicity of exchanges were sacrificed in favor of a disjointed movement from extreme to extreme; from the feverish activity at the arrival of the India fleet to the dullness and torpor of a sluggish interim. And the very object of the military equipment of the individual trading-vessels and of their joint movement increasingly failed of realization; for the concentration of the year's booty in a single fleet was a temptation hardly to be long resisted by enemies. By this preference for magnitude in commercial operations all possibility of the development of a steady and normal

---

[1] Hunter, I, 185; Martins, Hist. de Port., II, 27, 30, 165.

[2] Profits on wares sent from the East must have been enormous to bear all the costs of passage and transshipments. See Whiteway, pp. 7–8. For a list of the imports, see Martins, Hist. de Port., II, 23–24.

[3] Lavisse et Rambaud, IV, 900; Martins, Hist. de. Port., II, 19, 25–26, 73, 110–112; Lindsay, II, 44.   [4] Corvo, I, 13.

commerce, resting upon the humdrum business of the small dealer, was destroyed.[1] The function of the humbler occupations had been long regarded as sordid, and fit only for the Jews; and, at the very outset of their colonial career, the Portuguese had rid themselves of this element of their population. The royal interests and those of the Faith had decreed the expulsion of the people renowned in Europe for intelligence and commercial probity, in whose hands rested the whole machinery of commerce.[2] The Portuguese were thus unable to profit by the large opportunities placed in their path, except through a rude and awkward manipulation not differing in essence from that displayed by semi-civilized peoples.

CORRUPT ADMINISTRATION IN INDIA

In most respects the Portuguese policy of commerce and colonization is a mere replica of the Spanish, presently to be described in greater fullness; indeed, after the accession of Philip II to the throne of Portugal the two systems actually merge for many critical years. The motive forces which explain both cases have been indicated, in general lines, above.[3] Both nations tended inevitably in the direction taken, for private initiative scarcely existed, and when they had become habituated to their system, it was too late to change. In 1580, in consequence of pressure by the Dutch, succeeding the union with Spain, the royal monopoly was sold to the *Companhia Portugueza das Indias Orientaes*; but the success of this corporation and its successor a century later (1697: *Companhia do Commercio da India*) was wrecked against the opposition of spoils-seeking officials.[4] The environment was thoroughly unfavorable for the development of trade along evolved and modern lines; the abnormal gains of individuals brought only loss to the nation, which, as in the case of Spain, shouldered, or rather sank beneath, the taxation necessary to keep upon their feet a power and monopoly from which it derived no benefits. The material sent to India became progressively poorer in quality. The crown had realized at the outset that it must delegate an almost uncontrolled power to its representative in the East. This arrangement was

[1] Leroy-Beaulieu, I, 47–48; Whiteway, p. 18; Lavisse et Rambaud, IV, 899–900.
[2] See especially Schäfer, III, 13 ff.; p. 188, below.
[3] Pp. 80 ff.
[4] Hunter, I, 181–182; Danvers, II, 79–80.

very advantageous in the case of the few disinterested and incorruptible viceroys and governors, although, as has been seen, there developed a tendency to suspect such a man even as Albuquerque. It has been remarked how systematically the best officials in India were treated with ingratitude; the officers in question assert the fact and the chroniclers corroborate it. The reason lies, in good part, in conditions already reviewed: many regulations and decrees originating in the capital arrived belated because of the distance, or were ill-advised owing to ignorance of local conditions in India.[1] If the viceroy suspended or put off the execution of these orders, it was felt to be a contravention of royal power, an evidence of an unmanageable spirit aiming at independence; if an incorruptible ruler, like Albuquerque, cashiered disobedient nobles who had come to India simply to get rich with all speed, he created against himself at Lisbon an opposition unscrupulous of means in securing his downfall. Hence it was the energetic and faithful official who was most likely to be inconsiderately superseded, insulted, or even thrown into chains.[2] Already in Albuquerque's time the policy of shortening the tenure of offices in order to curb their incumbents was begun; and, often for good reasons, the attitude of the crown became increasingly one of suspicion. The natural tendency of European activity in the tropics is toward the speedy and improvident use of opportunity for exploitation; and to this tendency the policy of short appointments and low salaries lent a spur, if not a sort of justification. By 1518 governors had gotten into the habit of taking men out with them to fill all the more important posts; and there was established a sort of baleful rotation in office wherein each appointee tried to sweep the ground clear during his incumbency. It went so far that at times the new viceroys seem to have adopted a deliberate policy of discrediting and insulting the officers whom they succeeded. Hence the slanders, peculations, and general corruption already referred to. Naturally enough, any attempts to control the viceroy from Lisbon, or through a resident countercheck (intendant), simply rendered the administration cumbrous and immobile. Captains became merchants and shunned war; honor was travestied; they were even allowed, in the chronic

---

[1] For a conspectus of the laws, customs, revenues, number of parishes, etc., in India in 1584, see Menezes's "tractate." Here also (p. 139) is mentioned the *regidencia*, to whose Spanish aftertype attention will presently be called. Cf. p. 307, below.   [2] Ruge, p. 198; Danvers, I, 458.

insolvency of the Indian government, to repay themselves irregularly, and by acts of piracy which constantly neutralized efforts for peace. This went on until 1614, when the king ceased to struggle against the trend of the times ; he "suspended all royal grants and ordered the Viceroy to put up for sale by public auction all commands of fortresses, all other offices, and all voyages, and give them — on a vacancy occurring — to the highest bidder." This document "stands as one of the most remarkable state confessions of utter demoralization on record." [1] "D. João de Castro was the last man with any pretentions to superiority who held office in the early days of Portuguese connection with India, and the names of his successors for many generations, some indolent, some corrupt, some both, and all superstitious, are but the mile-stones that mark the progress along the dismal path of degeneration." [2]

SOCIAL CONDITIONS IN INDIA

The Indian government could do little, under the circumstances, for the welfare of the land. Harbor-works, lighthouses, charts, and other necessities and conveniences of commerce were neglected ; in later times the Portuguese actually depended upon the English and Dutch for their knowledge of channels and shoals. The very government was a sort of organized robbery ; and its example was not lost on the population.[3] The latter rapidly became Orientalized and worthless. Life in Goa, which was the type toward which existence in Portuguese India ultimately tended, was marked from early times by luxury, profligacy, and sloth. This luxury was the outcome of the enormous wealth of " Golden Goa " (*Goa Dourado*).[4] All the work was done by slaves ; the pursuit of a trade disgraced a man, and domestic labors ruined a woman's social status. The

[1] Whiteway, pp. 74–75. But it was in the spirit of the time and is actually defended by Montesquieu, Esprit des lois. Cf. Bourne, Sp. in Amer., p. 238. Menezes (p. 165) gives the net income from the estate of India (1584) as about $775,000.

[2] Whiteway, pp. 324–325; Martins, Hist. de Port., II, 275 ff., 293. De Castro was viceroy from 1545 to 1548. His views upon the conditions of his times are given in a letter to the king quoted by Martins (Hist. de Port., I, 294). This author contrasts him with Albuquerque and Almeida : " The government of India created three great men : Castro, who might be called a saint ; Albuquerque, whom the name of hero better befits ; Almeida, who is a wise administrator, an intelligent factor." Id., I, 236.

[3] Whiteway, pp. 42–43; Danvers, I, xxviii ff.

[4] According to a Portuguese proverb, the man who had seen Goa had as good as seen Lisbon : " Quem vio Goa excusa de vêr Lisboa." Hunter, I, 155.

only respectable livelihoods then were the Church, the army, government employ, or buccaneering. Gambling in all its forms provided recreation for idle minds and bodies; the *zenana*-system invaded the home, and domestic relations were corrupted. Vanity led to gorgeous display of eccentric apparel on the part of strutting idlers. In later times Portuguese women, hopelessly in debt, begged in the streets from gilded palanquins. This life in Goa was a magnificent type of the life of other Portuguese settlements. On account of scarcity of men in Portugal, outlaws were banished to India, and residence in the colonies provided the punishment for thieves and prostitutes. The newly arrived Portuguese soldiers, even of the better class, were not paid, were the sport of the older inhabitants, and either starved, begged, hired out as cutthroats, or deserted to native states and changed their religion.[1] It was this class of Europeans from which the natives of the East gained their early impression of western civilization, religion, and morals.

This "last crusade against Islam" was scarcely living up to its early renown. Turning more specifically to the religious activity of the Portuguese, the state of the case is not bettered. When Cabral sailed for India in 1500 he was liberally supplied with ecclesiastics to hold up his hands in the conversion of the benighted. The attitude of these evangelists may be stated in the words of Barros, the official historian: "The Moors and Gentiles are outside the law of Jesus Christ, which is the true law that every one has to keep under pain of damnation to eternal fire. If then the soul be so condemned, what right has the body to the privileges of our laws? . . . It is true they are reasoning beings, and might if they lived be converted to the true faith, but inasmuch as they have not shown any desire as yet to accept this, we Christians have no duties towards them."[2] Moreover, the Pope was empowered to turn over to the faithful all the material goods of the unbelievers, a doctrine whose practical application was not suffered to lapse. With a "repulsive mixture of unctuousness and rapacity" the religious orders set on foot an exploitation that could compare with the government's best efforts.[3] To the effects upon the natives we shall presently come; the religious organization was,

[1] Hunter, I, 155–158; II, 157 ff.; Whiteway, pp. 72–73, 261, 335; Martins, Hist. de Port., I, 273–274.

[2] Hunter, I, 106; Whiteway, p. 21 (quoted).

[3] Whiteway, p. 60.

besides, a great drain on the resources of the India government. The zeal of the friars found its outlet in building cloisters and then in filling them. The cost to the state of the purely religious establishments in Portuguese India was, about 1550, $35,000; by 1612 it had risen to $130,000 in the same limited area, other semi-religious establishments costing over $30,000 in addition. Religious property in land had extended widely; some attempt was made to check this development in 1635. The power of the clergy became little by little a menace to the state; the Jesuits retained armed bands in defiance of the government, intrigued constantly, and even with the Dutch and Moors. Such activities led to their expulsion from the Portuguese dominions, by Pombal, in 1759.[1]

RELATIONS WITH THE NATIVES

In considering the relations of the Portuguese to the native peoples, the three salient objects of the Portuguese should be recalled: these were "conquest, commerce, and conversion." The formula might well read "commercial conquest," for the trade-motive was really dominant. But in those days it was thought that a preliminary intimidation formed a good overture to successful exchange; consequently the Portuguese aimed at a régime of terrorism, and this was seconded by intrigue of questionable nature. Rival dynastic claimants were taken up and thrown over according to expediency; even Albuquerque employed the assassin to effect his ends. Conviction of the rectitude of the mission often excused the means. After intimidation or the attainment of political ascendency the Portuguese regularly extorted tributes, commercial exemptions, and privileges, and a correspondingly unfavorable treatment of rivals. They did not — in fact, could not — effect any religious changes. They pursued the rule of expediency, imposing, to use a modern expression, "what the traffic would bear." Above all, they worked out their monopoly of the spice-trade, first by securing a "most favored" position, and later, as their power waxed, by ruthless prohibitions, impositions, and exclusions. In more distant parts they descended periodically in force to collect tribute in spices, or as individual and favored merchants they frequented the native markets and fairs. As has been seen, they

[1] Danvers, II, 247, 253; Whiteway, p. 65; cf. index, sub "Botelho, Simão"; cf. pp. 154 ff., below.

seized all the entrepôts.[1] They lived, in short, in a commercially parasitic relation upon the native industrial organization, and as they were able to extend their power, they drained it of its vitality and bloom. It should be understood, for a clear comprehension of the Portuguese native policy, that the invaders, intolerant and ignorant, never understood or tried to understand either the superior or the primitive native life. Ignorance of the native languages persisted to a late period, and offenses against native customs, prejudices, and superstitions were the order of the time.[2] The Amboinese, once friends, were alienated by an attempted assault on the wife of a prominent native. They had adopted Christianity and begun to intermarry with the Portuguese, but after this time Ternate and Amboina were the sources of recurring calamities and expense.[3] The natives of the East hold much to ceremonial, religious and other, and were constantly shocked and insulted by the rude invaders. They suffered atrocious cruelties, even under the better officials; Almeida blew prisoners from his guns, "saluting the town with their fragments"; mutilations of men, women, and children were practiced in cold blood. Garcia de Noronha blinded fifteen relatives of the king of Ormuz by passing a red-hot bowl close to their eyes.[4]

In the course of time the relations of the Portuguese with native peoples resolved themselves into a series of unprovoked aggressions, attended by speedy retaliation.[5] Native allies conceived a deep contempt for the cruel, bigoted, and mercenary Europeans, and, as the Portuguese power waned, they fell away or went over to the Dutch and English. It was only the fleet, and rare good fortune, combined with lack of organization and inability to prosecute a siege, on the part of their enemies, that saved the Portuguese from destruction at the hands of the King of Atjeh, and other native rulers, during the sixteenth century.[6]

[1] They were peremptory with the most uncivilized peoples (e.g. of the Laccadives), where more powerful rajahs were treated with politic consideration. Hunter, I, 149. For their experiences in Atjeh, see Veth, Atchin, pp. 60 ff.

[2] Martins, Hist. de Port., I, 215; see especially (p. 294) the letter to the king of J. de Castro (viceroy, 1545–1548); Whiteway, pp. 29–31.

[3] Danvers, I, 537–538, 550; Argensola, passim.

[4] Hunter, I, 139 ff.; Whiteway, p. 165. The accounts teem with worse instances.

[5] Danvers, II, 92–98.

[6] Ataïde (1568–1571) suppressed a dangerous coalition with a skill and firmness worthy of the earlier time. Lavisse et Rambaud, IV, 893; Zimmermann, I, 68 ff.; cf. Danvers, I, 480–481, 534–535.

ACTIVITIES OF THE CHURCH

To the other agencies that constantly provoked the natives was added the activity of the Church. It should be realized that an exaggeration of severity was natural in the Portuguese in India, owing to their ingrained hatred and fear of the arch-enemy of Christianity, Mohammedanism; Islam was already in the East, and its superior hold upon native peoples was coming to be realized. Hence the Portuguese proceeded in the East with a severity unknown in Brazil. To this element there was likewise added an ecclesiastical cupidity, stimulated by possibilities of material gain that did not exist in America. The clergy understood the natives as little as the laymen, and fulminated against everything that bore a heathen, and especially a real or supposedly Mohammedan tinge. After the time of Manuel, fanaticism became more unbridled; in 1540, under orders of the king, all the Hindu temples in the island of Goa were destroyed, and the ecclesiastics hastened to seize the confiscated lands. In 1560 Goa was made an archbishopric, and the first inquisitors were dispatched to harry the resident Jewish refugees from Portugal.[1] The recommendations of the first provincial council of Goa, in 1567, adopted by the state, at the command of the Church, for the conversion of Mohammedans and Hindus, give some idea of the aggression of the Church upon the native organization. No Christian could have infidel servants in his house, or employ infidel doctors or barbers; neither Hindus nor Mohammedans could have any public worship, all their priests were banished, and even the twice-born Hindu was forbidden to wear the sacred cord of his caste; the Hindus were obliged to attend church in squads of fifty, on alternate Sundays, to hear long sermons on the benefits of the Christian religion. The viceroys were instructed to favor converts in all ways, temporal as well as spiritual; inheritance was made to follow the kinship of faith rather than that of blood; the native Christian could demand all the privileges of the Portuguese citizen; female converts could claim heritages as if they had been males. Political power was taken, as far as possible, from the unconverted, and justice was practically denied to non-Christians. "Those who were not Christians must wear a distinctive dress, and must not ride on a horse or in a palanquin or carry an umbrella in Goa or

[1] Lavisse et Rambaud, IV, 899; Corvo, I, 8.

its suburbs." As a result of these and other senseless regulations, based upon clerical influence, Goa and the surrounding islands were, as early as 1561, practically depopulated of natives.[1] By 1729 native commerce was ruined, owing to the horror which local merchants, especially Moors, had of another clerical institution, the Inquisition; for the latter had been utilized freely for secular, not to mention private, ends, under guise of effecting religious purity and homogeneity. Its abolishment in India, in 1814, came too late to atone for or neutralize its evil consequences.[2]

Of course the corruption of the clergy and of the original disinterestedness of faith occurred, for the most part, in the centers of Portuguese power. Much unselfish effort was put forth in the outlying parts by men of the Xavier stamp. The Portuguese undoubtedly spread Christianity abroad in the East Indies, both among the Buddhists and the common heathen; and their converts, when in rare cases they were treated decently, were the firmest prop of their domination.[3] Xavier, indeed, during his activity in the East at the end of the sixteenth century, boldly assailed the India administration and exposed its corruption. Considerable missionary activity was put forth in China, and many brave lives sacrificed in Japan and in the Archipelago. But what the Portuguese gained by courage and devotion in war and in the missions, they lost by avarice and attendant shortsightedness of policy, and through the scandal which the unbridled passions of a low class of representatives brought upon the nation as a whole.[4] The resident Portuguese, for there were some, offer a typical case of race-degeneration.[5] Illicit relations with native women were common; Albuquerque had a son by a negress. There was never any considerable immigration of European women, and consequently no family life of a normal type. Jorge Cabral (1549) was the first governor who had his wife with him in Goa.[6] Miscegenation had been a policy since Prince Henry's time, both in Portugal and the dependencies, and had shown only evil results in both cases; these consequences were naturally accentuated in the tropical environment.

---

[1] Whiteway, pp. 65–67.

[2] Danvers, I, xl, xli. Autos-da-fé were practiced with ostentation and cold cruelty. Since Jews did not exist in sufficient numbers, the institution was speedily turned against native victims, especially Mohammedans. Corvo, I, 86.

[3] Van der Aa, *De Gids*, 1860, I, pp. 853–854; Danvers, II, 130 ff.

[4] See Ruge, pp. 213 ff.   [5] Tylor, Anthropology, p. 19.   [6] Whiteway, p. 321.

INFRINGEMENT AND COLLAPSE OF THE MONOPOLY

It is clear that by the opening of the seventeenth century the Indian Empire had been long ready to disintegrate under the impact of a sufficient shock. By this time, as will later appear, the nations of central Europe had come to perceive the true state of the Portuguese power. After 1600, therefore, they appear with progressive frequency in the East and deal ever more deadly blows to the waning power of the Portuguese.

Portugal's first competitor in the East had been the sister Iberian nation, Spain. It will be recalled how a preliminary division of the field was made through the offices of the Pope, in the treaty of Tordesillas.[1] This settlement appeared to be satisfactory until, in 1521, the voyage of Magellan led the Spaniards to the Moluccas, and until it became evident that part of South America fell within the Portuguese sphere. The Spice Islands being the ultimate objective of both nations, it became expedient to determine the full perimeter of the great circle of which the famous Demarcation Line formed half. For this purpose a learned council was summoned at Badajoz and spent a long time in futile wrangles over a problem whose settlement was beyond the scientific powers of the age.[2] The Portuguese introduced a further element of discord by their attempt so to manipulate the meridians as to include both Brazil and the Moluccas within their hemisphere. It is questionable what outcome would have been reached had not Charles V converted the uncertain Spanish claims into hard cash by selling them to the Portuguese for 350,000 golden ducats (about $850,000).[3] However, in these centuries peace between mother-countries did not preclude constant strife in the colonies, and the Spanish and Portuguese alternately expelled each other, concluded agreements, and bandied prohibitions throughout the sixteenth century.[4] Even the union of Spain and Portugal in 1580 did not put a stop to petty warfare.[5] The effects of this union with Spain can be better appreciated after a review of the

---

[1] P. 90, above.

[2] Bourne, Sp. in Amer., pp. 130–131; cf. note 2, p. 99, above.

[3] Convention of Zaragoza. Hunter, I, 189; for details of the history of the Moluccas, cf. Argensola.   [4] See Danvers, I, 388, 458, 463 ff.

[5] For the conditions leading to the accession of Philip II, see Martins, Hist. de Port., II, chaps. iii, iv (a presentation rather picturesque than accurate); Stephens, pp. 243 ff.; Hume, Spain, especially pp. 171 ff., 250 ff.

Spanish colonial system; but it may be said here that it exposed Portugal, for sixty years, to the results of all the follies and enmities of Philip II and his successors, without affording any compensating advantages. Philip II promised to keep the Portuguese intact in their nationality and policy, but by the nature of the case this was impossible. Because of this union the aggression of Portugal's competitors was considerably hastened; for the Dutch, English, and French were thus given a pretext, if not a reason, for the general development of hostilities in the East and in Brazil. Nevertheless it would be wrong to charge to the union of the crowns anything more than an acceleration of an already advanced decline.[1] For when the Portuguese had laid hand upon the trade of the East, they set about what turned out to be a deliberate education of potential competitors. First of all they stimulated the imagination and cupidity of the Dutch and English by the secrecy and ostentation of their trade. They depended upon the bugbears of papal disfavor, an impregnable navy, and a deliberate exaggeration of the terrors of the deep to hold competition at a distance, so far as the India voyage was concerned. They early prohibited the sale of charts to foreigners, and the service of Portuguese seamen in foreign navies.[2] In order to distract attention from the possibility of approaching the East, the coastwise traffic was renounced; complacent in seeing the ships of all nations flocking to the harbor of Lisbon rather than seeking the East, and besieging the Casa da India,[3] the Portuguese disdained the function of distribution and constituted Lisbon harbor as a terminal. Thus both the Dutch and the English not only conceived most highly colored, though vague, views as to the profits of the India trade, but were actually forced to develop a coastwise shipping, which was the best of training-schools for the development of sea-power. The weaknesses of the Portuguese were learned, and isolated adventurers even dared to infringe their monopoly. Experience taught the truth about the commercial myths regarding the dangers of navigation, and with the Protestant movement the papal authority became non-existent. War with Spain at the end of the sixteenth century discovered the inferiority of the then combined Iberian

[1] Danvers, I, xl ff.; II, 39 ff.; cf. Leroy-Beaulieu, I, 49–50. Martins (O Brazil, etc., p. 35) says: "One can affirm that India would have been lost even if the Philips had not reigned in Spain; just as one can affirm that Brazil has been preserved *despite* the rule of the Braganças in Portugal."

[2] See p. 67, above.   [3] See note, p. 228, below.

navies; then the English and Dutch, debarred access to the Lisbon market, went to the East to trade for themselves. And "the course of trade was the more easily diverted as there was no skeleton of custom formed out of existing trade-routes to retard the decay of Portugal."[1] The fate of the Venetians had overtaken their conquerors; monopoly had again raised up an agency for its own destruction.

The losses of the Portuguese in the East in consequence of the penetration of competitors into those regions will be treated from the standpoint of the dispossessors. The empire needed but a touch to make it fall; the incompetence, treachery, and corruption displayed in these latter days eclipse the isolated acts of heroism. Illicit traffic with the enemy was common; the revenues of the government were minimized through smuggling and misappropriation. The restoration, in 1640, did not materially change the situation, for the harm had been done long before, and decline went on without interruption.[2] Muscat was lost in 1650; Colombo in 1656; Cochin and Cannanore before 1663; Bombay was ceded to the English in 1661.[3] The Dutch gradually expelled the Portuguese from the Malay Archipelago, until at last they held (and still hold) only part of Timor. The Portuguese have retained from its cession in 1556 up to the present the inferior port of Macao in China: it enjoyed a passing importance before the cessation of the coolie-trade.[4]

In 1670 the Portuguese met for the first time the invading forces of the Mahrattas, before whom the Mogul Empire had crumbled; and between 1737 and 1740 they lost nearly all of their northern provinces. Commerce was practically swept from the sea by Arab pirates and by the rival Europeans.[5] The Napoleonic era, whatever may have been the grandiose Indian projects of the Emperor, brought nothing but misfortune. From 1844 on,

[1] Whiteway, p. 18; cf. Danvers, II, 65 ff., 105 ff.; Leroy-Beaulieu, I, 48; Hunter, I, 221 ff. Martins (Hist. de Port., I, 303) says that, despite the signs of decomposition, the apogee of commercial empire came at the end of the sixteenth century.

[2] Danvers, II, 172–173, 222 ff., 237 ff.

[3] The concessions and privileges acquired by the English are deplored by Martins (Hist. de Port., II, 138 ff.); cf. Hunter, I, 191 ff.; II, 190 ff.

[4] Corvo (IV, 131 ff.) discusses the history and final abolition of contract-emigration over Macao; his attitude is one of great hostility to the system — in fact, as Minister of the Marine, he was himself responsible for the decree of abolition. He says that this move was not prejudicial to the prosperity of the station (p. 167).

[5] Danvers, II, 367, 373–374, 402, 413.

Portuguese India has consisted only of Goa and the dependencies of Daman and Diu. Goa was largely in ruins in 1780, and it was only in the middle of the nineteenth century that any real effort was made to better the conditions of these remnants of the empire. Such improvements have been executed mostly through British enterprise; they consist of roads, a railroad to British Indian centers, steamship service, telegraphs, etc.[1] It is difficult to see any future for the few Portuguese possessions in Asia.

PORTUGUESE AFRICA

The fate of Portuguese Africa has been reserved, in the interest of clearness, for a place by itself. The African stations were at the outset simply halting-places upon the opening, and finally opened, India way. The early explorers of the west coast brought back some native products, and a number of slaves; but with the attainment of the ultimate object these lesser enterprises passed into abeyance. The African stations took a position distinctly ancillary to the Asiatic; an occasional expedition in search of rumored gold mines, and a number of brushes with the Kaffirs and other natives, saved their history from being entirely tame. With these halting-places must also be reckoned some of the oceanic islands, such as St. Helena and Tristan da Cunha, and naturally the contiguous coast islands, such as S. Thomé, Principé, Fernando Po, and Annobom. Most of these posts, calculated as they were to meet the needs of navigators who hugged the coast, became anachronisms under a more developed system. They were, besides, situated among peoples too barbarous to become large buyers and sellers, and in districts which were insufficiently fertile to overcome the aversion of the Portuguese to agricultural labors; they were consequently but feebly occupied, were sometimes used as penal colonies, and were easily seized by enemies.[2] In 1520 the

[1] Danvers, II, 442 ff., 475 ff.; Martins, Civ. Iber., 305 ff. For the decline of Portugal itself during the Napoleonic period, see Martins, Hist. de Port., II, 250; for the conditions of an earlier period (1706–1750), see Branco, pp. 33 ff., 45 ff., 109 ff.; for a sketch of Portuguese colonial administration, etc., in the nineteenth century, see Danvers, I, xliv ff.; Zimmermann, I, 216 ff. The most exhaustive handbook on the Portuguese colonies is that of Corvo, of which Vol. I, after a brief introduction, treats of the Cape Verde Islands, S. Thomé and Principé, and Angola; Vol. II, of Moçambique; Vol. III, of African civilization; and Vol. IV, of the Asiatic colonies. A late treatise, modeled upon the German Kolonial-Handbuch, is that of Vasconcellos.

[2] Leroy-Beaulieu, I, 42; Johnston, pp. 28 ff.; Martins, O Brazil, etc., pp. 271 ff., 283 ff. The latter author says (Civ. Iber., p. 263) that within twenty-five years after

Portuguese held Quiloa, Zanzibar, Mombasa, Sofala, Mozambique, and other ports of call; but by 1698 the Arabs had retaken every stronghold north of the last-named factory, while the Dutch had occupied the Cape, and other nations had encroached on the west coast. The development of the slave-trade was what kept the settlements alive for many generations; in particular, their proximity to Brazil afforded especial advantages in a traffic which even compensated in some measure for the loss of the India commerce.[1] Guinea and the Congo and Angola districts were in early days the chief theaters of the trade, which reached its apogee in the seventeenth and eighteenth centuries. From the middle to the end of the eighteenth century, from Benguela and Loanda alone, 642,000 slaves were exported; in 1770 the revenue from the Angola export was $150,000. From 1817 to 1819 it was $177,000, while other income scarcely reached $25,000.[2] Interest in these human products brought about a general neglect or decline of the African possessions as respects agricultural and other development; exploited almost solely in the interests of the slave-trade, they lapsed into insignificance when it was crushed.[3] A certain evasion was practiced by shifting the trade to Mozambique, but it was allowed no respite by its active enemies, and in 1810 and 1869 the Portuguese finally and with reluctance abolished respectively the trade and the institution.[4] As time goes on and civilization advances in these parts of Africa, illegal evasions are being more and more restricted.[5]

ANGOLA

Angola constitutes, according to Johnston, "certainly the most successful of the Portuguese attempts at the colonization of Africa."[6] The Portuguese are inclined to esteem it above the rest of their possessions; this, however, witnesses rather to the

the discovery of India the Portuguese could no longer hold their African stations against the foreigner.　　　[1] See p. 145, below.　　　[2] Corvo, I, 15–16.

[3] Leroy-Beaulieu, I, 50–51; Corvo, I, 150. Yet Martins (O Brazil, etc., p. 191) and Corvo (I, 24 ff.) seem inclined to minimize this effect. For the prostration of S. Thomé and Principé, see Corvo, I, 100, 105, 111–113, 121–124, 135–136.

[4] Corvo, II, 344–345. Yet "before 1849 the port of Mossamedes was nothing more than a factory for the embarcation of negroes for Brazil, America, and Cuba." Id., I, 288.

[5] But compare the recent disclosures of Nevinson, who has observed in Angola conditions that recall the worst features of evasion.

[6] Johnston, p. 44; cf. Martins, O Brazil, etc., pp. 98–99, 192, 224 ff. The latter author is clear upon the possibilities of free negro labor. Id., pp. 219–221.

unenviable status of the latter than to the exaltation of the former. For decades the country was passed over in favor of India; it was not until 1575 that its conquest began, chiefly under Paulo Diaz, and its reduction, even in semblance, took a century. In fact, Angola is still merely a "land of war and trade"; of settlement, there has been practically none.[1] From the early years of the seventeenth century the Portuguese attempted, through the establishment of fairs and markets, to call some trade into being; a species of fetichistic Christianity resulted in still earlier times from the activities of questionable missionaries. Even these enterprises were rendered well-nigh impossible of accomplishment by the excessive mortality of the Portuguese and by the general corruption of the service. Although São Paulo de Loanda was founded in 1574, it took a long time to master the country down to Benguela, and until 1840 to reach the present limits.[2] Emigrants will not go to Angola, even from the Cape Verdes; the convicts exiled thither in earlier times proved a doubtful benefit; both men and capital for economic development are lacking.[3] All the "significant works of civilization" have been conspicuous by their absence; "there did not exist in Angola, until 1877, any organization in the service of the public works"; not a road was projected between 1862 and 1877. The country had been torpid after its "long past of indolence and ignorance." [4] A great deal of this misfortune is referable to the existence and cessation of the slave-trade; for during its existence it smothered all other enterprise, and with its cessation little of importance was left. Because of the trade, Portuguese Africa suffered the incursions of the Dutch and the hostility of the British, and laid up for itself a heritage of rancor on the part of the abused and demoralized negro population.[5] However, in later times the country had been favored by the execution of public works, chiefly roads, of a very necessary character. Portuguese writers differ in their estimate of the colony's possibilities, but they are unanimous in their condemnation of the governmental policy and its supineness.[6]

[1] Corvo, I, 192 ff.

[2] On the mortality of the African climate and the attempts to minimize it, see Martins, O Brazil, etc., pp. 248 ff.; Corvo, I, 140. A somewhat favorable view is presented in a letter to Martins by a Portuguese colonist in Quelimane. Id., p. 235, note.   [3] Corvo, I, 47.   [4] Id., pp. 214, 227, 236.

[5] See p. 147, below; Corvo, I, 150, 200, 287–288, 290.

[6] Corvo, I, 230, 268. Corvo sees a "brilliant future" for Angola (I, 153). Martins regards Portuguese Africa, as a whole, as unprofitable, and, for the Portuguese,

MOZAMBIQUE

As for Mozambique, its history has been even less edifying. " The savage state which three centuries of our rule, more or less direct, did not avail to transform ; the lack of activity and of energy in the labor of the natives ; their unruly tendency toward war and violence ; the lack of European or even Asiatic colonization ; the disastrous influence of the Mohammedan Arabs who for many centuries have weighed East Africa down ; the lack of capital and of commercial activity ; the fatal consequences of the horrible and sterilizing slave-trade ; the errors and vices of the administration ; the lack of facilities of transport for merchandise ; the monopolies and exclusions which have embarrassed foreign transactions, industrial activity, and competition, — all these, in fine, have contributed to the lack of development of and profit by the powerful resources, the immense material riches, of Mozambique." [1] The white population is a vanishing quantity and enterprise almost non-existent. Mozambique appeared of some account in Portuguese eyes only when the journeys of Livingstone in the middle of the nineteenth century had directed British attention to that region. The Portuguese then made some costly attempts to unite their east and west coast possessions ; but the advance of the British could not be withstood. The Portuguese gained a slight advantage from the biased decision of Marshal MacMahon, who awarded them the whole of Delagoa Bay (1875), and from the construction of the railroad to the Transvaal. But their attitude is one of complaint rather than action in the face of British pressure. Little of the Mozambique trade is in Portuguese hands ; even the Portuguese chartered companies in East Africa have been capitalized by the English and French ; Mozambique has yielded a deficit regularly from 1508 to our own time. Exchange is hampered in all of Portuguese Africa by the imposition of unreasonable customs dues.[2]

One especial attempt by the Portuguese government to aid settlement in East Africa deserves mention. This was the effort to introduce, in the so-called *prasos da coroa*, a sort of proprietary

hopeless. The British might be able to make something of it. O Brazil, etc., pp. 197 ff., 212–213, 215, 222–223. Ribeiro, in a work upon The Portuguese Colonies, their Present and Future, presents a much more optimistic outlook. Reported in the U. S. Consular Reports, No. 1996, July 6, 1904.

[1] Corvo, II, 355 ; cf. pp. 263, 278, *et passim.*
[2] Johnston, pp. 45 ff. ; Martins, O Brazil, etc., p. 97.

system not unlike that of the early *doações* in Brazil.[1] Fertile crown land, chiefly on the banks of the Zambesi, was given for three lives to women who were descendants of European Portuguese parents, and who must marry European Portuguese husbands. The *prasos* were limited in extent to three square leagues, and males were excluded in the succession But the project came to naught, owing to labor difficulties, the invasion of the slave-trade, and other practical difficulties ; new concessions were prohibited in 1838, and the institution was abolished in 1854. It is severely condemned by Corvo and others ;[2] of course it was well-nigh impracticable in tropical Mozambique. However, it was resurrected in 1890 under a more strict regulation, and is said to have attained a limited success.[3]

Portuguese Influences in Africa

It can hardly be contended that the Portuguese have consciously exerted any influence for Africa's weal ; but they have unintentionally conferred some notable benefits by their additions to the articles of local food-supply and comfort. Fruits like the orange, lemon, and grape ; sugar-cane, maize, manioc, tobacco, and like plants, at least in superior varieties, were introduced ; likewise some animals, in particular, swine.[4] The fact is that the conditions obtaining in India were present here too on a smaller scale ; for, as Corvo says, " The early Portuguese did no more than substitute themselves for the Moors . . . in the parts that they occupied on the coast ; and their influence extended to the interior very slightly, unless, indeed, through some ephemeral alliances of no value whatever, or through missionaries, or without any practical or lasting results. The true conquest is still to be made." [5]

[1] See pp. 133 ff., below.

[2] Corvo, II, 119–121, 243.

[3] Zimmermann, I, 192–193.

[4] On Portuguese Africa, see, besides Corvo, Johnston, pp. 28 ff. ; Keltie, pp. 32 ff., 136 ff., 401 ff. Some successful attempts at improvement in Abyssinia are said to be referable to the period of strong Portuguese influence in the sixteenth and seventeenth centuries. Ratzel, Hist. of Mankind, III, 226.

[5] Corvo, II, 125–126. This volume is dated 1884. The quotation may be found in Keltie, p. 57. For the luxury and corruption of an earlier period of decline, during the seventeenth century, see Corvo, II, 67.

CHAPTER IV

THE PORTUGUESE IN BRAZIL

The exploits of the Portuguese in India, because of their connection with the "golden East," and their semi-religious character, have drawn the attention of the world, not only in earlier centuries but in a later age as well. The imagination of their contemporaries was captivated by phenomenal successes in the realization of aims that existed or came to exist in the minds of all. The Portuguese had, to all appearance, successfully consummated the connection long striven for between the trade-areas of East and West, and were in consequence the envied holders of exclusive commercial advantages. That the worth of this monopoly was consistently overestimated, simply added to the power and reputation of its possessors. And, in subsequent time, the romantic tale of Portuguese achievements, bereft by distance of any unpleasant or sordid aspects, had exercised a peculiar fascination upon recounters and their audiences. The "wealth of Ormus and of Ind" is familiar to those whose interests lie far from markets and colonies. And yet, when the tale of the exploits in India is done, we have the really enduring contributions of the Portuguese to the history of colonization still to consider.

Vasco da Gama, relying upon the accumulations of nautical experience made by the captains who had preceded him, and profiting by his own special knowledge, provided Cabral, who commanded the next Indian fleet, with sailing directions which, to catch the south-east trades, carried him far toward the west.[1] In the pursuance of this course, or in fortuitous deviation from it, Cabral made the coast of South America. He thus discovered (April, 1501) what proved to be the New World, on the count of Portugal, some nine years after the voyage of Columbus; and the occurrence was thought important enough to warrant the return of one ship to

[1] Varnhagen, I, 17 ff.; cf. Rio-Branco, p. 105; Martins, Hist. de Port., I, 217–218; Payne, Age of Disc., p. 35. For a brief description of the voyage of Yañez Pinzon, see Bourne, Sp. in Amer., pp. 69–70; reference to the third voyage of Columbus, id., p. 47.

convey the news to Portugal. Cabral was unable, of course, to estimate the magnitude of the new acquisition. He conceived it to be
another of the Antilles Islands, and named it *Ilha da Vera Cruz*.
This was subsequently modified to *Terra da Santa Cruz*, and finally
changed, upon the discovery of a dyewood similar to the valued
brazil-wood of the East, to *Brazil*.[1]

EARLY CONDITIONS OF THE CAPTAINCIES

The only appeal which Brazil could make to Portugal was on the
score of profits from the forests, and even of these but little is heard.
It is characteristic of the age and its aims that the Portuguese
repeatedly tried to get around or through Brazil toward the west,
and thus it was presently (1501) discovered that the supposed island
was part of a very large land-mass. For many years, however,
Brazilian harbors were little better than substitutes, along a more
satisfactory route, for the declining African stations. Preoccupation with the riches of India anticipated any vital interest in a rough
and virgin land. The government sent out colonists, but at first
rather with a view toward its own relief than toward Brazil's betterment, for the exiles were mostly convicts and women of ill repute.
Little more was done during the first decades of the sixteenth century than to establish small settlements or factories on the best
harbors. According to Varnhagen, the earliest real colony was at
São Vicente, near São Paulo. But it was already the intention of
the government that the fleet which should hold and defend the
Brazilian coast should be supported out of local resources. The
money which Portugal could spare for such objects had been swept
into the current that set toward India.[2]

However, as time went on, the original nuclei of population
received additions from the voluntary immigration of a much
better quality of colonists. These were represented in large part
by Jews, who had fled from Portugal to escape the Inquisition,
and who proposed to make their homes in Brazil.[3] This growth

---

[1] It is perhaps significant of the relative predominance in Portuguese minds of the
commercial over the religious aspects of their new possession that in this christening
the "gainful wood" (*lenho lucrativo*) thus supplanted the "sacred wood." Varnhagen,
I, 24; cf. pp. 17–24; Watson, I, 91 ; Zimmermann, I, 117–118.

[2] Varnhagen, I, 18–20, 30, 43, 53 ; Stephens, pp. 220 ff., 347.

[3] Zimmermann, I, 119. Leroy-Beaulieu (I, 51–52) assigns great importance to this
element in the population. Stephens (pp. 227 ff.) says that Brazilian colonization was
essentially popular, not royally or otherwise artificially initiated.

of population and the increasing interest of the French in South America gradually attracted the attention of the Portuguese to their lightly esteemed dependency. The necessities of development and defense were met, in the absence or impossibility of a display of individual initiative, by the adoption (1532) of a semi-feudal system of proprietary grants or fiefs. The proprietors (*donatarios*) were lords who should defend the country and settle it on their own counts, thus releasing government resources for the India enterprises. In pursuance of this expedient the whole dependency, back theoretically to the Demarcation meridian, was divided by lines running parallel to the equator into fifteen sections, forming twelve hereditary captaincies of from 600 to 12,000 square leagues in area.[1] These were distributed to favored persons, and so differed in size with the favor shown. The powers of the donatarios were, roughly speaking, somewhat more than vice-regal. The home government exercised over them a sort of protectorate with limited control, in return for the payment of a few taxes and the right of instatement at every change of possession; the donatario could issue land-grants, found cities, name officials and judges, and exercise other similar powers. The colonists were assured only of protection of property, freedom of trade with the Indians, and non-extradition on account of former crimes. Catholics of all nations were allowed to settle, but non-Portuguese were discouraged from trade by various restrictions.[2]

The history of the captaincies is for the most part a dull chronicle of life on a small scale. Few of them actually prospered. The donatarios were eager, of course, to get people to come with capital and take up land; but their efforts met, on the whole, with little success. The scattered and backward native population[3] offered but few inducements to traders. No one believed that Brazil had any value. Two ships a year conveyed from Portugal the aforesaid men and women of questionable character,[4] and

[1] A map of these *doações* or *capitanias* is given in Varnhagen, I, opp. p. 88; a list with dates, in Martins, O Brazil, etc., p. 10.

[2] The details of the system are to be found in Varnhagen, I, 60–63, 72 ff.; Watson, pp. 155 ff.; Zimmermann, I, 119 ff. The idea was earlier utilized in the Azores and Madeira Islands (Martins, O Brazil, etc., pp. 3 ff.), and later, in the form of the *prasos da coroa*, in Mozambique (Corvo, II, 119–121, 243).

[3] See Martins, O Brazil, etc., pp. 133 ff.

[4] Of these the donatario of Pernambuco wrote to the king (1546): "These people are worse than the plague; therefore I beg you, for God's sake, to spare me this poison in the future." Quoted in Zimmermann, I, 124.

brought back wood, parrots, and other curious products. The scanty European population, exhibiting scarcely any of those qualities of energy and self-sufficiency which we have come to associate with the term " settler," took to the ways of the natives in its attempt to conform to an environment which it could not control; native products were raised, and native arts and crafts were imitated. Fusion of races began early, and several varieties of half-breed came soon to be distinguished. On the part of the government no effort was directed toward exploration. The interior was unvisited and unknown; the whole colony was systematically neglected. Portuguese indifference under the proprietary system " recognized the independence of Brazil before colonizing it." [1]

A great deal of this adversity was directly chargeable to the régime of the donatarios, and when, toward the middle of the sixteenth century, Brazil had come to be regarded as of some importance to Portugal, the fact was immediately recognized. The original division has been made on too sweeping a scale and with little or no discrimination; the grants were too large, and no reservation of land for future assignment had been made. The massing of smaller holdings about the ports would have concentrated population and encouraged industry, whereas the system adopted had effected the exact reverse. The donatarios, also, had been given too much authority. It was impossible for the supreme power from across the Atlantic to control the virtually separate governments of the captaincies. The lives and property of the colonists were at the mercy of the several lords, and the many complaints made to the king witness for the fact that some, at least, of the captains did not fail to take advantage of the situation. Even where they were honest, the donatarios were generally pitiful failures. Those in northern Brazil had almost all come to grief by 1550, and misunderstandings with the natives and miniature wars of all kinds constituted the order, or rather disorder, of the day. In view of all this the king was led in 1549 to revoke the powers of the captains while leaving

---

[1] Varnhagen, I, 74; cf. pp. 98, 170–172. Velasco (p. 566) reports the following of Brazil in 1574: "Christians in this land live in a space of 350 leagues close to the coast, and they do not settle in the back-country because the Indians do not allow it, and at the same time because they wish to be near the sea for purposes of trade." In all the captaincies " they have sixteen Portuguese towns, in which there are 2340 inhabitants."

them their grants, and to appoint over them a governor-general, who should regulate abuses and correct and unify ill-considered and divergent policies. The seat of government was fixed at Bahia.[1]

This move led, of course, to the break-up of the captaincies, although the latter would inevitably have passed away with the growth of population. The system was, like that of the chartered company, simply a governmental makeshift. The donatarios displayed the semblance of administration and defense until the state had satisfied itself that it was worth while to take over the burden. This persuasion was reached when the India dream had begun to betray its illusive nature, and when Brazil had commenced to attract the attention of European rivals.[2] "Little by little the kings of Portugal recovered all these fiefs through inheritance, purchase, or otherwise. The last captaincies still existing under feudal régime were bought back by the crown in the eighteenth century in the time of D. José I and Pombal.[3]

The fundamental charge against the captaincy-system was, of course, its artificiality, or, to put it another way, its contravention of natural development. The provinces were crudely ruled off on the map with little or no regard to natural conditions. The stream of emigration was split up into a number of currents, each setting under direction toward the locations in each captaincy upon which, for sufficient or insufficient reason, the donatarios had pitched. Consequently, as Martins says, settlement started in several distinct centers of "social ossification," and the colony tended to subdivide itself into a number of disconnected areas.[4] Thus a variety of small centers of feeble development, and therefore exposed to many special exigencies, took the place of several strong and populous nuclei in localities naturally selected as favorable to man and his activities. Again, the attempt to impose an aristocratic system upon a virgin country was sure to encounter the fate reserved for such attempts, under similar circumstances, throughout the history of colonization. The efforts of noble Portuguese houses to transplant their less promising offshoots beyond the

[1] Varnhagen, I, 69–71, 192, 200; Watson, I, 155–158; Zimmermann, I, 125 ff.

[2] Cf. Martins, Hist. de Port., I, 52.

[3] Rio-Branco, pp. 110 ff.; Watson, II, 239; cf. Martins, O Brazil, etc., p. 13. For a list of the early governors of Brazil, see Martins, O Brazil, etc., p. 25, note.

[4] O Brazil, etc., pp. 126, 127; cf. p. 12. This tendency was later accentuated in consequence of the "adventurous hunt for Indians and mines."

seas in the natural course of events came to naught.[1] The establishment of the capital at Bahia was a further exhibition of the
same artificial methods ; although cartographically central among
the scattered nuclei already mentioned, Bahia was the focus neither
of economic development nor of population. It took a time of
stress, forcibly calling attention to the superiority in these respects
of the southern provinces, to secure the removal of the capital to
Rio de Janeiro.[2] One must, however, realize that at the outset
the southern provinces were regarded as relatively unimportant,
since they contributed none of those tropical products which alone
appealed to the Portuguese. The flow of population to these regions
was slight and almost unnoticed before the gold discoveries.

The man chosen to be the first governor-general was D.
Thomé de Souza, and the selection was apparently a happy one.
He attended to the much-neglected interests of the crown, reduced the excessive power of the donatarios, and established
better relations with the Indians. He also saw the value of the
"new Christians" (*novaes christiãos*) and tried to protect them.
Without using his position to justify undue interference, and leaving locally established government, where it was stable, alone, he
yet punished prevalent acts of atrocity with great severity and
labored always to curb the mutual hostility and to effect the consolidation of the almost independent captaincies.[3] His administration is looked upon as one of the landmarks in Brazil's early history.
Under his successors, although they were in general men of an
inferior stamp, population increased and the state of the colony
became more satisfactory. This was more particularly the case
during the governorship of Mem de Sá (1558–1570).[4]

INDUSTRY AND TRADE

At the very outset of their acquaintance with Brazil, as has
been said, the Portuguese, judging that country and India according to the same criteria, regarded it as of comparatively slight
value. Of the one local product which appealed to them with any
force, relatively but small and variable quantities could be gotten
at the coast. For the native population of Brazil were and remained practically insensible to economic stimuli, presenting in

---

[1] See Martins, O Brazil, etc., p. 12.   [2] See p. 160, below.
[3] Stephens, pp. 225 ff.   [4] Or *Men* de Sá, as Varnhagen insists (I, 233)

this a complete contrast to the Eastern peoples to whom the Portuguese were used. In the East, European demand impinged upon the native rulers, and these took measures to secure an increasing output ; but in South America, as the Portuguese knew it, there was no native organization to receive and transmit pressure. A certain amount of settlement and of production under European management was thus in Brazil an almost necessary condition for the development of trade. It has been seen that the earliest settlers were largely convicts and fugitive Jews ; the latter, with characteristic resource and industry, speedily introduced the cultivation of the plant which furnished in time the staple of Brazil, — the sugar-cane. Sugar-production once started in a favoring environment, plantations developed rapidly and yielded good profits. Each plantation demanded a rather numerous European personnel,[1] and since the Portuguese government, in its low appraisal of Brazil, spared it a good part of that petty regulation which discourages individual initiative, a number of desirable emigrants were gradually attracted across the seas. Because Brazil had shown no promise of wealth in gold and silver, it had for a time been on the verge of official abandonment. It was the " wholesome neglect " which fell to its share that saved it in some degree, especially during its early years, from the system of ruthless exploitation under which tropical dependencies have so often languished.[2]

In spite of the fact that the Portuguese frequented this tropical climate with some impunity, it soon became clear that they were incapable of doing justice to the sugar-industry without aid. They were not numerous enough, many were physically unable to put forth the effort required, and almost all were by character unfitted. They began early to have recourse to native labor, and experienced little difficulty in coercing the rude and mutually hostile Indian groups to their will. The Portuguese have always taken readily to

[1] Watson, II, 120.

[2] " A policy of rational freedom exempted agriculture, industry, and commerce from vexatious restrictions, opening the colony to foreigners upon the payment of light differential duties. The imposts were moderate, the monopolized articles few, and the movement of individuals from one captaincy to another, or from any one of them to foreign parts, was free. Such was the first constitution of Portuguese America. . . . " Martins, O Brazil, etc., pp. 10–11. In fact, after 1640 and the loss of the Oriental empire it was seen to be useless to prohibit the cultivation of spices, etc., in America. Id., p. 67. It was much later (eighteenth century) that limitation of Brazilian production in the interest of Portugal took place. Zimmermann, I, 172 ; Stephens, pp. 227 ff.

the slavery system, and here it was in many ways indispensable to the preservation of economic life.. But it was not put into operation unopposed; if in their material preoccupations the Portuguese as a whole had ceased to think much about the extension of the faith, there was among them a class of professional zealots who claimed to think about nothing else, — the Jesuits. This powerful order set itself strongly against Indian slavery, for it contemplated the organization of the untouched savages, their segregation from demoralizing association with Europeans, and their conversion *en masse*. The incompatibility between the economic needs of the planters and the religious aims of the Jesuits manifested itself in the early days of the Portuguese settlement, and the story of the collision of the two conflicting interests forms a good part of the history of the colony.

The country was, then, primarily an agricultural one, and sugar and woods long formed its major exports. About 1580 São Salvador had 57 sugar-works, exporting annually 2400 hogsheads; Pernambuco had 50. In addition to sugar, many products for a prevailingly local use were raised. The orange, lemon, and palm trees grew well, likewise the cocoa and tea plants; there were also some valuable Indian foods like manioc. Cattle and horses, imported from the Cape Verdes, throve and multiplied. Aside, therefore, from a single main staple, Brazil grew many other products valuable for the maintenance of life. All through the sixteenth and seventeenth centuries the colony proceeded toward a more settled and extensive agricultural economy, and although only an occasional portion of its immense periphery was settled, the stations were of a common type. The colony became constantly more valuable to Portugal; for one thing, the mother-country enjoyed its exclusive trade. Toward the end of the sixteenth century about forty-five ships came to Brazil annually for sugar and brazil-wood, and Portugal likewise monopolized the coasting trade.[1] When the decadence of India had now become apparent, it was realized that Brazil was the most valuable national possession, and it went steadily on in its development, despite checks presently to be mentioned, until its trade with Portugal equaled that of Portugal with all the countries of Europe.[2]

---

[1] Watson, pp. 251–252; cf. Martins, O Brazil, etc., p. 67.

[2] Varnhagen, I, 303; Leroy-Beaulieu, I, 53. In 1688, "the fleet which sailed from Bahia was the largest which ever left that port, and yet it did not contain tonnage

In spite of the value of Brazilian sugar, however, the Portuguese trade policy was, at least in comparison with the Spanish, liberal. Non-Portuguese were early handicapped by certain disabilities, but these were not prohibitive, as is proved by the constant increase of foreigners and their factories from the sixteenth century on. Commerce was subjected to the system of regular "caravans," but this was rendered but slightly oppressive because of the number of ships allowed and the number of stations visited.[1] Here again the treatment accorded to Brazil was markedly distinct from the measures that hampered the India trade. In fact, the Brazilians embarked so eagerly in commerce that the civil and judicial officers and even the clergy showed great readiness to become involved in speculation.[2] The settlers, too, had something to say about the system. In 1649 when a privileged company was founded, commanding a large number of armed ships and a regiment of infantry and artillery, the merchants of Rio and Bahia were able by their representations to secure needed reform, and finally the suppression of the organization (1720).[3]

What has been said is perhaps enough to establish the fact that for two hundred years Brazil's development followed the line of agricultural production and exchange. It is not surprising, therefore, to find the writers on Brazil adopting a sort of self-congratulatory vein as they remark upon the lateness of the discovery of the country's mineral wealth. For, as they say, Brazil's very poverty and its consequent neglect gave it the opportunity for an unhurried, natural development as a transplanted portion of the Portuguese nation, and as a result they adduce the conservation in Brazil of the Portuguese language, the Catholic religion, and many another national character which causes the powerful western state, now that India is gone, to reflect glory upon its diminutive metropolis, and to lend it economic and other support.[4] This is an *a posteriori* judgment with the usual excellences of its kind ; the Portuguese of the sixteenth and seventeenth centuries felt nothing

sufficient for the produce. . . ." A further indication of commercial advance lay in the betterment of the currency (1694). Watson, II, 109.

[1] These were six in number, — Lisbon, Oporto, Rio de Janeiro, Paraíba, Olinda, São Salvador. Pombal replaced the caravans with privileged companies. Leroy-Beaulieu, I, 53.   [2] Watson, II, 116–117.

[3] Rio-Branco, p. 135 ; Varnhagen, II, 37 ff.

[4] Leroy-Beaulieu (I, 52) says : "Portuguese colonization in America, at least during the first two centuries, differs much from Spanish colonization and approaches rather the English system." A brief series of comparisons follow.

but chagrin at their commonplace colony, when they compared it with the golden soil of Peru. There were from the outset certain rumors of mineral wealth, and convictions that "the ground of Brazil and of Peru were the same," but for generations no verification appeared.[1] The discoveries for which the pioneers longed and toiled were delayed until the eighteenth century.

The history of the colony, from the time of Mem de Sá (about 1570) until the period just mentioned, shows little worth remark upon the purely administrative side. The doings of many decades are really massed about two great and protracted struggles, — that between the planters and the Jesuits in regard to the labor supply, and that of the Portuguese colonists as a whole with the aggression of foreign nations, chiefly France and Holland.[2] That the former and internal contest was subject to periodic truces, during which erstwhile enemies worked shoulder to shoulder in a common cause, goes almost without saying, if one recalls the traditional qualities of the Portuguese when forced to the defensive.

SOCIAL CONDITIONS

Of the quality of the European population in Brazil something has already been said. Taking into account the fact that Brazil was at the outset practically a penal colony, it is not difficult to understand why the ecclesiastics soon found themselves obliged to raise a voice against the depravity of religion and morals. There was no honor in the public business, but in its stead a "cynical egoism." Justice, good faith, and confidence had fled the land; robberies and assassinations were everyday affairs. The average of crime was for some time higher than in Portugal itself.[3] This state of things was peculiarly characteristic of the time of the captaincies. But there were other influences at work to modify the character of the population, and one was the change of natural environment. The climate of tropical Brazil proved hurtful to many Europeans, and

---

[1] "There existed a conviction that the 'ground of Brazil and that of Peru were the same.' . . . But it did not please God to ordain that this should be confirmed before Brazil was more secure. The expeditions which were undertaken did not come to anything. And it is lucky that they did not, for the discovery of mines in the interior when there were still so few people on the coast, would have left the latter district deserted, and the French would have perchance seized upon it." Varnhagen, I, 214; cf. Leroy-Beaulieu, I, 54–55. [2] Watson, II, 112.

[3] Watson, I, 122, 253; Varnhagen, I, 203–204, especially pp. 185–189.

new diseases or new forms of old ones constantly appeared. Of the children born not one in three lived until the Portuguese mothers had learned to adopt native methods of care-taking.[1] If, in spite of these facts, it is said that "in no instance have Europeans suffered so little by transplantation from their own country into one of very different climate as did the Portuguese in Brazil,"[2] the implication is that other Europeans suffered excessively rather than that the Portuguese escaped well-nigh scathless.

Out of this tropical climate and other physical influences arose also the plantation-system of agriculture, to which some allusion has been made, and its general adoption and prosperity had pro-duced a singular modification of customs on the part of what had been at one time a fairly laborious and economical element of the population. "In the more flourishing settlements . . . nothing could exceed the luxury of the female costume, the wives of the planters being attired in silks and satins covered with the richest embroidery, with pearls, rubies and emeralds. . . . The ladies of Bahia were so indolent of habit that on going abroad they had to lean on their pages lest they should fall. Even the men — if men they might be called — were unable to descend the declivity on which Bahia stands, and were carried down on a contrivance called a serpentine, that is to say, a hammock suspended from a pole, a slave attending meanwhile with a parasol."[3] About 1560 gaming had to be prohibited under severe penalties, for it had become a prevalent vice of an idle people.[4] The officials gambled with the opportunities of the colony itself in no less consistent a manner, and the governors, appointed generally upon a three-year term as in India, enriched themselves by every means. The underpaid functionaries were almost compelled by their exigencies to be dishonest. Even the priests, except the Jesuits, were chiefly engaged in securing gain.[5] The population was vain of material successes, but raw and uncultured, and it was still very small toward the end of the seventeenth century. The number of Portuguese who held this vast area subject should not be over-estimated. Until mining led them inland they held small coast stations only ; spaces equal in size to an average European kingdom are still uninhabited. During the seventeenth century the numbers were " so scanty that it seems strange that the Portuguese could have at the same time contended

---

[1] Southey, I, 345. [2] Watson, I, 252–253. [3] Id., II, 121.
[4] Varnhagen, I, 252. [5] Southey, I, 345; Watson, II, 114–115.

successfully with a foreign invader and with hostile tribes in the interior." [1] In 1585 the settlements had a population of about 57,000, of whom 25,000 were whites in scattered groups, 18,500 civilized Indians, and 14,000 African slaves,[2] and the next century saw relatively slight increase.

RELATIONS WITH THE NATIVES: THE LABOR QUESTION

The whole system was based upon the domination and exploitation of the reduced country and people. For reasons assigned, the vital condition of economic existence was a cheap labor supply, and the natives were early enslaved. Against this outcome the Indians struggled with all the desperation of the American savage, preferring death and race-extermination to a servile station and labor. By the influence of the Jesuits their case was repeatedly brought before the king and state, and from early times orders of various kinds looking to their freedom were emitted from Lisbon. Without a strong local agency for their enforcement these would have been of no avail, and as it was they were again and again rendered null and void by the necessities and self-will of the colonists. The natural conditions demanded native slavery, and it took all the force of the most powerful of religious and political brotherhoods to stem the tide.[3] The planters grew to hate the Jesuits as the authors of their misfortunes, and did not fail to assert that the fathers profited largely by their discomfiture. Yet it is to be noted that the Jesuits were not opposing slavery as an institution, but the specific enslavement of the Indians, of heathen whom they wished to gather into the fold while they were still uncontaminated by contact with the lambs already technically in, but not as yet wholly above suspicion.

Whatever the theories, the facts speak for themselves. The colonists at first repaid themselves for their labors in reducing the country by drawing upon the physical forces of the conquered.[4] But as the plantation grew, these products of "just wars" were not numerous enough, and periodic slave-raids comparable to the better-known *razzias* of Africa were the regular thing; these were

---

[1] Watson, II, 119; cf. p. 112.

[2] Rio-Branco, p. 116.

[3] Watson, I, 161–163; Varnhagen, I, 257 ff. A good general sketch of the Indian situation and the conflict of planters and Jesuits is given by Zimmermann, I, 128 ff.

[4] Martins, O Brazil, etc., p. 50.

attended by an enormous waste of life under cruel treatment and exposure. As slaves the Indians were not able to perform the hard labor imposed upon them and to which they were totally unused, and they died away as a race beneath it. At first the colonists were allowed to enslave at will; later King Sebastian issued a clerically inspired regulation (1570) declaring all Indians free "excepting such as should be taken in war made by command of the king or governor, or such as were aggressive cannibals." In still later times many similar decrees were published, but these were almost invariably made to suit every individual occasion.[1] As in the Spanish Indian legislation, the intent was of the best, but the force of natural conditions in the distant colony completely negatived its realization. Even the so-called free Indians, who had voluntarily submitted to the Portuguese, were forced to leave their families destitute of support, while they raised and prepared tobacco on the plantations.[2] The aggressions of the Europeans rendered the efforts of the Jesuits in collecting the coast-natives into villages, there to civilize them under a paternal direction, a constant disappointment. Continued raids and fomentation of inter-tribal strife brought it about that by the end of the sixteenth century both missionaries and slave-raiders had to penetrate much farther into the interior in quest of converts and captives.[3] This was particularly marked in the district of São Paulo; in this relatively temperate climate the inhabitants (Paulistas) exhibited a superior energy and persistence in the enslavement and extermination of the natives. Attacked by the exasperated savages, they retaliated in a seven years' war (1592–1599), in which about three hundred villages were destroyed and thousands of Indians slain or enslaved. Man-hunts of this nature then became periodic, and the Paulistas gained a disgraceful reputation for their exploits in a bad business. The bewildered natives, a prey to epidemics of disease strange to them,[4] with everything going against them, became panic-stricken and intractable, choosing death in preference to the hazards of the strange and

[1] Watson, II, 82–83, 85, 115–116; Varnhagen, I, 173 ff.; Zimmermann, I, 128 ff.

[2] Watson, II, 84.

[3] Watson, I, 258. Varnhagen (I, 174–178) regards the early enslavement as a civilizing process, and asserts that the tales of cruelty represented exceptional cases, many of which were punished; the effects of a mistaken humanitarianism, sustained by the Jesuits, were deleterious.

[4] Peschel (Races of Man, p. 151) quotes from travelers, who assert that the Portuguese "deposited the clothes of scarlet-fever or small-pox patients on the hunting-grounds of the natives, in order to spread the pestilence among them."

repulsive fate forced upon them.[1] The Jesuits, seeing the futility of their strenuous and for the most part disinterested efforts for the natives, were gradually driven to the conviction that it was impossible to proceed with the conversion and civilization of the latter so long as the civil authorities should have any power over them. During the seventeenth century, under the leadership of the single-minded and energetic Vieyra, their efforts to secure the sole authority over the Indians were unremitting. They gradually gained extensive control; large sections of the aboriginal population were delivered entirely to them, and they enforced their authority with characteristic fearlessness.[2]

The jealousy of the settlers now passed the bounds of repression. They were so given over to the slave-system that they could no longer provide for themselves. A biological differentiation of function, as it were, had left them, like Darwin's slave-making ants, in a sort of parasitic relation to a subject race. " Men of noble lineage could not bring their children to the city because they had no slaves to row their canoes." On account of the activity of the Jesuits many planters " had no one to fetch them wood or water, and were perishing for want of slaves to cultivate their lands." Respect for law, heretofore manifested at least in form, broke down, threats of separation from Portugal were uttered, and a general tumult of hostility to the Jesuits broke out. The mob dragged the fathers from their cells, forced a resignation of control over the Indians in favor of the civil authorities, and undertook the speedy deportation of the whole order. A skillful governor, Segueira, managed to uphold authority without an appeal to force (1662), but the planters did not forget their day of triumph, and the Jesuits never again dared so imperiously to assert their dominance in the colony's affairs.[3] Thus their struggles against the enslavement of natives on the plantations were of little ultimate avail, and the outcome of their subsequent efforts to save their protégés from the mines was, as will presently appear, still more disastrous, at least to themselves.

The Indians constituted the labor force nearest at hand. Their conquest and capture afforded an employment which had been, and is said still to be, congenial to the Portuguese as a people.[4]

---

[1] Rio-Branco, pp. 127 ff.; cf. Martins, O Brazil, etc., pp. 25–26; Watson, II, 97–98, 115–116, 270.

[2] Watson, II, 85, 88–89; Leroy-Beaulieu, I, 52; Martins, O Brazil, etc., p. 30, note.

[3] Watson, II, 92–94.   [4] Watson, II, 81–82.

Their initial cost was, especially at the outset, negligible. Hence the prevalence of Indian slavery and the resistance to its abolition. However, from the earliest years of its occupation, Brazil had been the destination of an increasing number of African slaves, chiefly from the Guinea coast.[1] The various hindrances thrown by government and clergy in the way of the enslavement of the Indians caused the less tenacious or more law-abiding of the cultivators to have resource to the imported labor supply. And it was speedily recognized that the negro was far superior to the Indian for the purpose at hand. Indeed, it has been observed through history that the former race, both by physique, resistance to environment, and temperament, has been almost preordained to serve its more energetic fellows. But the great difficulty was that the planters could not afford the initial cost of the negroes, evident as was their superiority.[2] There was no opposition to negro slavery, *per se*, however, on the part of any one, and it steadily increased with the decline or liberation of the natives. By 1585 Pernambuco counted some 10,000 African slaves, Bahia 3000 to 4000. Elsewhere they were relatively few in number, for they found their greatest usefulness on the sugar-plantations. At one time in the seventeenth century the proportion of negroes to whites in Bahia was estimated at twenty to one, but this was by no means true of Brazil as a whole.[3] It need scarcely be said that this trade in human working-animals exhibited the stock features of heartlessness and incredible cruelty. The voyage from Guinea was relatively short, but its terrors were manifold. There are not lacking those who believe that the scourge of yellow fever was fixed upon Rio de Janeiro and other American ports by reason of the dumping of filth and diseased corpses from the slavers into the waters of the harbor and its environs. Once at work, however, the very value of the negroes insured them against such harshness of treatment as fell to the lot of the unadaptable and generally obdurate Indians, and with their increase there were added to the constituents of population several new varieties of mongrel, and a body of runaways or bush-negroes, who ranged the forests in a condition of dangerous tribal independence.[4]

[1] Varnhagen, I, 182.

[2] Watson, II, 111 ; Martins, O Brazil, etc., p. 52..   [3] Watson, II, 116–117, 121.

[4] Martins, O Brazil, etc., pp. 62–63. For the negro "republic" of Palmares, which attained its greatest vigor about the middle of the seventeenth century, see Watson, II, 110–111, 134 ; Martins, O Brazil, etc., pp. 64, 66.

Foreign Aggression

The internal struggle over the labor question was not allowed, in the course of events, to monopolize the attention of government and people. The more northern nations of Europe were gradually losing, as the sixteenth century wore on, both their respect for the papal awards to Spain and Portugal and their fear of the exaggerated naval power of these once irresistible states. Plucking up their courage, they began to infringe, first of all upon the Spanish and Portuguese possessions on the Atlantic. From the time of the discovery of Brazil the French had occasionally visited the region; indeed, it was their appearance in this quarter which incited in the Portuguese a realization of the possible value of their neglected acquisition in America. The first serious attempt of the French to establish themselves in what is now Brazil occurred in 1558, when an adventurer, Villegagnon, occupied an island in the bay of Rio de Janeiro. He was actively encouraged by Coligny, and was left unmolested by the Portuguese for four years. "Some ten thousand Huguenots were ready to emigrate with their arts had they been sure of meeting with toleration, but the governor's arbitrary proceedings ruined the project." By this time the court at Lisbon had been aroused by the Jesuit Nobrega to a realizing sense of the rivalry of the French, and after some hard fighting the latter were expelled from their position. Several subsequent attempts of the French in the same region were speedily thwarted; Rio was again taken by them in 1711, but was held for a brief period only. It was not until the latter half of the seventeenth century that they actually established themselves in Cayenne.[1]

If the French peril was a serious one, that which attended the appearance of the Dutch came near to being fatal. Up to the incorporation of Portugal by Spain (1580) the Portuguese and Dutch had been common enemies and combatants against the latter power, but with the accession of Philip II to the throne of Portugal, both this and other fortunate *rapprochements* were terminated. For sixty years Portugal was destined to share the odium of Spain and to receive blows delivered at her. Dutch

[1] Watson, I, 160–161; II, 106–108, 184; Varnhagen, I, 36 ff., 329 ff. A chapter on the Huguenots in Brazil is given in Parkman's France and England in North America, Part I ("Pioneers of France in the New World," chap. ii); cf. Payne, Age of Disc., pp. 49–50.

successes in the East had led to the formation of the West India Company (1621), one of whose main objects was the harassing and conquest of Brazil. The difference between the enterprises of the Dutch and the predatory expeditions of the French and English speedily became apparent to the Brazilians; they found, to their astonishment, that the Dutch intended to stay. This situation roused the national spirit in the contests with the Hollanders as it had not been stirred in the brushes with other Europeans.[1]

The history of the Dutch occupation of Recife (Pernambuco) and six provinces of Brazil might be more fitly taken up from the standpoint of the West India Company and its career.[2] The Portuguese steadily opposed the Dutch occupation, and, owing to the shortsighted and parsimonious policy of the company, with some success. The turning-point came in 1640 with the separation of Portugal from Spain and the accession of the house of Braganza, an event which detached Portugal from the destiny of Spain, and ranged her again among Spain's enemies, among the chief of whom were the Dutch. The altered situation was at once recognized in form, and a truce for ten years was arranged between the States-General and Portugal (1641). This, however, was illusory. A year was given for notifying the truce to the Dutch authorities in the Indies, and aid was afforded to Portugal against the common enemy; but the interval was employed in pushing forward the Dutch conquests in Brazil, and in seizing São Paulo de Loanda in Angola, the source of the entire supply of slaves for Brazil.[3] This, besides cutting off a lucrative trade, was a severe blow to the prosperity of the plantations; and after the recall of Count Nassau from Brazil the policy of the Dutch became less and less conciliatory, and the exasperation of the Portuguese more pronounced. In Maranhão, Bahia, and Pernambuco the people began to work for their own deliverance. The general revolution was headed by João Fernandes Vieira, a very wealthy planter, operating in the region of Pernambuco. It was not at first a universal movement, for many thought it hopeless and wished for peace at any price; but the impolitic procedures of the Dutch, who in their inability to reach the actual insurgents began to oppress the lukewarm who

[1] Martins, O Brazil, etc., pp. 39-40.   [2] Cf. pp. 413, 453, below.

[3] The pretext given for this action was disbelief in the permanent separation of Spain and Portugal. It must also be borne in mind that peace concluded between European nations never strictly applied, in these earlier periods, to their respective colonies.

had stayed at home, speedily rendered a neutral status untenable. The party of Vieira gathered momentum, and advanced from guerrilla warfare to battles and sieges. The West India Company provided insufficiently against the danger, and the outcome was not long delayed. The Dutch, hampered by the English war, were driven by 1654 to a surrender of all their holdings on the coast of Brazil, and further activity on the part of Holland was discouraged by the attitude of England and France. In 1661 negotiations were concluded whereby the Dutch renounced attempts on Brazil in return for certain considerations in money and trade and the restoration of their captured cannon.[1]

Thus ended the most serious danger to Portuguese dominance in Brazil. Under a more enlightened policy on the part of the Dutch the whole destiny of the country might have been altered. But an outcome of the kind described was quite characteristic of the West India Company. Of course the violence and disorder of the period were very unfavorable to the economic prosperity of Brazil; in partial compensation, however, certain distinct advantages emerged from the Dutch occupation. First of all, the Brazilians attained a sense of self-sufficiency and power and a consciousness of unity not experienced before. Like the Spanish-Americans of a later period, they had expelled a powerful invader practically unaided, for Portugal, though in sympathy with the insurgents, did not dare to offend her Dutch allies against Spain by openly lending aid. Thus the Brazilians felt, in a sense, that they had attained their political majority. Portugal realized the changing conditions, and in 1645 the colony was made a *principado* by the designation of the king's eldest son and presumptive heir as Prince of Brazil.[2] During this period of misfortune the Brazilians came also to realize the nature of the Inquisition[3] as a check upon the country's development, and were able better to secure commercial

[1] On the Dutch in Brazil, see Watson, II, pp. 1 ff.; Varnhagen, I, 335–404; Zimmermann, I, 138 ff.; Edmundson, in Eng. Hist. Rev., XI (1896), 231 ff.; XIV (1899), 676 ff.; XV (1900), 38 ff. [2] Varnhagen, I, 246; II, 2.

[3] The Holy Office, as has been intimated, never attained a firm footing in Brazil; but it interfered more or less regularly in affairs. Immediately preceding and during the union with Spain its influence waxed, and it assumed at times an independent judicial power. About 1702 a second period of vigor ensued, and between 1707 and 1711, 160 persons were seized and persecuted. The total number of colonists condemned by the Office acting in Lisbon was about 500. At times physicians, lawyers, and even ecclesiastics came under its displeasure. Autos-da-fé were relatively infrequent. Varnhagen, II, 179–183.

and other enterprises against the peril of confiscation of capital, ecclesiastical interference, and like impediments. A Brazil company, in imitation of the Dutch company, was created, against clerical opposition, and aided considerably in bringing the war to a successful end.[1] It should be said, too, that the Brazilians profited by the fact that the Dutch introduced, as it were, their country to Europe. The conquerors not only described Brazil, in the course of their commercial operations, to people to whom it had been but a name, but they also made Brazilian products, chiefly sugar and rum, familiar articles in European markets. Their charts and records of soundings remained in use up to a very recent time. It can hardly be said that the Dutch occupation exerted otherwise any considerable influence upon the future of the country. The Hollanders furnished an example of industry and extreme domestic cleanliness to a people who had a good deal to learn along these lines. They also benefited the country by their experience in the treatment of damp soils, in horticulture, in the construction of public works, and in other lines. But they had not time to develop any of these things to the full, nor did they intermarry to any great extent with the Portuguese, for difference of religion presented insuperable obstacles. They were in the country twenty-five years, but " when they departed they left little or no trace behind them either in religion, language or manners."[2] In fact, the departure of the Hollanders was signalized by a reaction toward Catholic fanaticism, and oppression of the Jews and Protestants.[3]

There was no ominous menace to Brazil from other enemies than the French and Dutch. During the Spanish predominance English fleets occasionally raided the coast, notably in 1582, 1586, and with most damage in 1594. Although considerable booty was secured, none of these attacks threatened the conquest of the country.[4]

The Gold and Diamond Discoveries

An attempt has been made thus far to clear up the perspective of Brazilian history previous to the eighteenth century; for with the end of the seventeenth the general trend of development in this colony takes a decided turn which provides a convenient break

[1] Watson, II, 71–72.
[2] Watson, II, 118. Life in the interior still remained distinctly primitive. Id., II, 266.   [3] Varnhagen, II, 42.   [4] Watson, II, 254–258.

in presentation and an apt point of departure for the ensuing narrative. Hitherto the colony had been almost wholly devoted to agriculture and the exchange of agricultural products;[1] but with the eighteenth century there is injected into its life the new element of the exploitation of the mines, destined here as elsewhere to set a characteristic stamp upon social development. But it is to be noted in the case of Brazil, as has been intimated already, that, unlike the majority of gold- and jewel-producing countries, it had already worked out two centuries of development along other and substantial lines before the rush of prospectors and the formation of mining communities could introduce disorder and a perversion of steadier and more normal development.

Hopes of a second Peru were early indulged, but the seventeenth century was well on to its end before any real promise was disclosed. A succession of arduous exploring expeditions culminated in 1693 with the exhibition of some promising specimens of gold,[2] and the consequent establishment of a smelting-house. The district toward which attention was turned was Minas Geraes, and, although the section was uninviting, it speedily became the Mecca of those who were impatient of laborious methods in the acquisition of wealth. The stampede for claims was so wild that special regulations had to be passed as early as 1702 limiting grants and defining tenure.[3] The plantation system was all but ruined; farms were deserted and ran to waste; negroes were transferred, by an excess of demand for their services, from the sugar-producing areas to the mines. The rise in the price of raw sugar disabled the refining industries, and the French and English in the West Indies, taking advantage of the situation, began to invade the European market hitherto supplied almost exclusively from Brazil. With the decline of the staple commodity, general trade suffered a great reverse.

[1] Martins, O Brazil, etc., pp. 15–16, summarizes the early development of Brazil as follows: "a) First material of colonization: convicts and Jews deported by the sovereign; escaped criminals; colonists assembled by the donatarios; in Brazil, enslaved Indians, and everywhere Guinea negroes, exported as instruments of labor. b) Species of colonial enterprise: agriculture, characterized almost exclusively by the culture of cane and the manufacture of sugar. c) Social constitution: feudal, by way of territorial grants, seigniories or captaincies; or by mercantile monopolies, as in Guinea; conjointly with the governors-general as representatives of the sovereign. Ecclesiastical organization; in imitation of the kingdom, in bishoprics and parishes. Free missions, chiefly of Jesuits." For the status of Brazil at the end of the seventeenth century, see Varnhagen, II, 92 ff., 136 ff.

[2] For the earlier efforts, see Martins, O Brazil, etc., p. 78, note.

[3] The regulations in force about 1710 are rehearsed in Varnhagen, II, 103 ff.

Some attempts were made to remedy this situation, but they were presently given up, for the Lisbon government was not hard to persuade that mining was more profitable than sugar-raising.[1] The old preoccupations which had once rendered Brazil inconsiderable to the Portuguese now exalted it to a position of superlative importance. With the development of the mines, then, it may be said that Brazil ceased for the time to be an agricultural colony. And the discovery in 1730 of the diamond fields, also in the Minas Geraes, carried the change considerably farther. Brazil fell back from its dignified status as a producing and developing region into the position of a California or a South Africa.

The results of heightened interest on the part of the home government began at once to make themselves visible. The crown demanded its fifths and marked out its allotments, and, as was inevitable under the conditions, it gradually enacted more and stricter regulations in its effort to control the illicit export of gold dust. All the gold was to pass through the royal smelting-house. Restrictions of the entrance of foreigners to Brazil were rendered more stringent than before, and even the Portuguese were required to exhibit passports. The ineffectiveness of the crown levies on the gold production led in time to the substitution of a poll-tax upon slaves; and yet, in spite of its strenuous efforts, the government was constantly defrauded. In the case of the diamonds, the system of the royal fifths was found impracticable from the first, and a capitation tax on slaves was early adopted. The diamonds were to be remitted in the royal ships only, one per cent on their value being charged as freight. It was necessary likewise to limit the output of diamonds, for within two years their price in Europe had declined seventy-five per cent.[2] The state undertook to reserve the diamond country and to limit the extraction, and the profits thus derived were very large. Between 1700 and 1820 Portugal consistently drew from the takings and taxes in gold mines and diamond fields a revenue upon which rivals looked with undisguised envy.[3] However, prosperity based upon such

[1] Watson, II, 171–174; Varnhagen, II, 174 ff.

[2] Leroy-Beaulieu (I, 55–56) defends upon economic grounds this limitation of output, at the same time stigmatizing the means adopted by the government. Cf. Watson, II, 171–172, 186–190, 244–245; Martins, O Brazil, etc., p. 80.

[3] Definite estimates of such income are, of course, impossible. Eschwege calculated the total product of the fifths as about $65,000,000. They are thought by others to have reached a minimum of $2,000,000 annually. See note appended to this chapter.

hazardous undertakings is apt to be illusory. It has been calculated by a competent authority that the value of the diamonds
extracted between 1740 and 1820 scarcely equaled the product of
eighteen months derived from the sugar- and coffee-plantations.[1]

The social effects of the discovery of the mines were naturally
very marked. The passion for gambling with large hazards induced
a general movement among the population towards the uncertain
and away from the secure and substantial. In a certain sense the
temper of the Portuguese in India was reproduced. That this
movement was not more disastrous than it was, is referable largely
to the tardiness of the discoveries, as occasion has already been
taken to show. Of course the mining districts themselves were
the centers of turbulence, irregularities, and disorder. In the arid
interior conditions of existence were very hazardous. Life in the
diamond fields was about synonymous with sojourn in a desert.
The necessaries of life rose to famine prices. Men were driven by
a shortage of food to cultivation or cattle-raising, occupations which
were often found to be more profitable than mining. However,
the great enticements of the golden harvest led to a considerable
settlement,[2] much of which was referable to the immigration of
the stubborn, independent, often half-Indian Paulistas. In 1776
Minas Geraes had a population of some 320,000.[3] The temper of
the miners was lawless from the outset, and they had to be quelled
again and again by governmental forces, as well as constantly spied
upon and restrained in the interest of the crown revenues. Insurrections against such restraints were put down only after prolonged
resistance, and by summary methods. Again, the large importation
of negroes into Minas Geraes rendered race-conflicts the order of
the day, and special effort had to be put forth to check the formation by escaped slaves of dangerous predatory bands. However,

[1] Eschwege, quoted in Leroy-Beaulieu, I, 55–56.

[2] " Brazil attracted, early in the eighteenth century, the entire Portuguese emigration. The rapidity with which this emigration developed was such that Dom João V
. . . promulgated a decree in 1720 in order ' to prohibit the yearly migration from this
country to the captaincies of Brazil of so many people . . . chiefly from the province
of Minho, which, from being the most populous, to-day finds itself in a state of not
having enough people to cultivate the soil, or to perform social services.' " Corvo,
I, 15.

[3] Watson, I, 269. Martins believes that the very names of the new mining settlements, which are mainly of local origin and seldom Portuguese, witness a progressive
nationalization or assimilation of the stream of immigration. O Brazil, etc., p. 85 and
note. He also thinks the frontier education was one that strengthened the love for
independence and at least indirectly contributed to the emancipation. Id., p. 79.

despite the perversion of law and order that resulted from the gold and diamond discoveries, the outcome of the movement toward the interior was a progressively increasing exploration of the country, its resources and waterways.[1]

THE EXPULSION OF THE JESUITS

One of the consequences of the gold discoveries was, naturally enough, the accentuation of differences regarding the treatment of the natives, for not only were slaves of all kinds in demand at the mines, where their position could scarcely be better than on the plantations, but the penetration of the interior and the rapid growth of European population worked toward the infringement of that isolation in which the Jesuits desired to keep their actual or prospective converts. The idea of the Jesuits, which perhaps appears more typically in the Paraguay missions,[2] was to keep the Indians under their own tutelage and in a life of repose under discipline. They divided the country systematically, and their *aldeias*, or industrial missions, rose at regular points over the whole. They labored excessively, building churches and establishing schools, learning native tongues and translating into them the prayers of the Church. Their system was mild and paternal; they neither corporally punished their charges nor would they sell or otherwise part with them. They did much to introduce civilization among the Indians, and, in order to make their work secure and to spare bad examples, they strove to keep the settlers at a distance.[3] In this they were aided by the laws of Pedro II (1667–1706), which forbade Portuguese to dwell in the missions. However, the Indians in Brazil, still subject to civil authority, never clung to the fathers as did the Guaranís of Paraguay; nor could the settlement of the whites be prevented, when strong enough motives for such establishment were once developed. But the activity of the Jesuits, hateful as it was to the planters, and the legislation secured in favor of the Indians, were not without their influence. For when the mines were opened the effect upon the condition of the natives was far less disastrous than would have been anticipated. This was partially due, of course, to the increased use of negro labor.[4] The

---

[1] Watson, II, 171; Martins, O Brazil, etc., pp. 19, 32–34, 80–81.
[2] Cf. pp. 287–294, below.   [3] Watson, II, 267.
[4] Id., pp. 170, 201–202; Varnhagen, II, 93 ff.

natives' sphere of rights had been extended, and with fewer qualifications as time went on. It is a curious coincidence that the
Indians were made unqualifiedly free before the law almost coincidently with the expulsion from Brazil of their old-time defenders,
the Jesuits (1758).[1]

It has been shown how the popular mind became inflamed
against the Jesuits in consequence of the determined efforts of the
latter to prevent the settlers from taking full advantage of what
seemed to them a naturally provided labor supply. It was practically impossible to persuade the planters that the Jesuits were disinterested antagonists. The conviction grew apace that the aldeias
were simply competing plantations, worked at a merely nominal
cost by converts adroitly turned into slaves. There was much
color to this persuasion, for the missions did not lag behind in
production. The planters felt that they were being overreached
even before the opening of the mines, and when, in consequence
of this latter event, they lost a large proportion of their workers,
and the price of negroes rose, their exasperation over the relatively
prosperous status of the Jesuit plantations steadily increased. The
Company had become "a true industrial association with which no
single capitalist could compete."[2] It had acquired or assumed a
degree of political power, in the attainment of its economic strength,
which galled the settlers, especially in the southern provinces
where population was more dense. The fathers were driven from
the south first of all, and then from the Bahia region. They were
not secure even in the extreme north.[3] It is probable, therefore,
that with the growth of population Brazil would alone have rid
herself of her incubus, but it was from the metropolis which had
fostered the Jesuits that final relief came.

King John V (1706–1750) had been the unresisting tool of the
Society,[4] but with the accession of José I (1750) the situation
changed. Carvalho, the Marquis of Pombal, became the dominant
figure of the new reign, and, in the estimation of some, the most
eminent statesman of his time.[5] Of his many projects, those which
touch vitally upon our subject were the freeing of the Indians in
Brazil and the universal and merciless pursuit of the Jesuit order.

[1] Martins, O Brazil, etc., p. 30, note; for a general account of the Indian legislation, etc., see Zimmerman, I, 136 ff.

[2] Varnhagen, I, 260; cf. pp. 257–261; Martins, Hist. de Port., II, 185; Rio-Branco,
p. 131.   [3] Martins, O Brazil, etc., pp. 70–73.

[4] Cf. Branco, Port. na Epocha de D. João V, passim.   [5] Watson, II, 232.

Pombal's object in freeing the Indians was that they should blend with the Portuguese population in Brazil; his hostility to the Jesuits resulted from his desire to strengthen the monarchy both in Lisbon and in the colonies.[1] In 1757 the temporal power of the mission was suppressed. The Indians were definitely freed in 1758, and the aldeias were transformed into villages under common law. Naturally the Society suffered much from this cancellation of its means of support, being reduced almost to penury. Lay directors were appointed to carry out the royal purpose of Christianizing and civilizing the Indians; needless to say, they neither possessed the preparation nor gained the successes of the Jesuits.[2] But there was more opportunity given for the amalgamation of races, and it was improved. "This is the true reason," says Varnhagen, "why the Indian type has disappeared almost absolutely from our provinces."[3] From this time on little is heard of the natives, for, as will be seen, the possibilities of African slave-labor began to engross the attention of those who had hitherto made requisition upon the Indians.

As for the Jesuits, the reasons for their expulsion from Portugal and the colonies go back to a series of wide-reaching activities of which the championing of the Indians was but one. "For two hundred years the Society had exercised unbounded influence over kings and courts. Its machinery for governing was so perfect, and its system was so subtle, that it began to appear to statesmen that unless this ambitious order were speedily and effectually opposed it must soon dominate Christendom. . . . The doctrines of Ignatius Loyola admitted of nothing short of an absolute obedience. . . . Kings were afraid to act without the approbation of an Order whose system of *espionage* was so complete as even to baffle secret confidential intercourse between sovereigns and statesmen. No one Catholic monarch felt himself strong enough single-handed to throw off the humiliating yoke."[4] Meanwhile the economic and political strength of the order waxed steadily; it had already, and

---

[1] Rio-Branco, p. 146; Martins, Hist. de Port., II, 204–205; cf. pp. 207–208; cf. also Branco, pp. 109 ff.

[2] Watson, II, 236–237; Martins, O Brazil, etc., pp. 72–73; Rio-Branco, pp. 148–149.   [3] Varnhagen, I, 205.

[4] Watson, II, 232. For an extremely eloquent arraignment of the Jesuits, see Martins, Civ. Iber., pp. 289–294; Hist. de Port., II, 85–100, 147 ff., and elsewhere in this author's works; somewhat the same judgment, with special reference to the Jesuits in the Philippines, is passed by Montero y Vidal (II, 141 ff.).

with considerable success, resisted the royal authority in India. A strong desire to free his country from this element led Pombal to seize the Jesuits in Portugal and ship them off to the Papal States (1759), and to decree their expulsion from Brazil together with the other colonies, an operation which was carried out in America with considerable gusto, and, it is said, with much brutality.[1] Their expulsion from France (1764) and Spain (1767) followed, — events which attest the widespread misgivings occasioned by their economical and political activities.

The ignominious exit of the Jesuits from Brazil must not divert attention from the great services performed by them before, having become conscious of the power of their well-knit organization, they yielded to the temptations of wealth and power. They performed herculean toil in their attempts to better the condition of the natives, and their preaching was not wholly in vain, even amidst the exigencies of frontier-life. By 1750 no hostile tribes remained on the banks of the Amazon throughout its entire course. Such as had not submitted to the missionaries had retired into the interior.[2] We may pause here to note that, partly because of the activities of the Jesuits, Brazil had suffered from none of the direful native wars common in the earlier stages of a colony's life. The teaching of the Jesuits and their paternal system may have unduly hampered the development of initiative on the part of their proselytes. Their methods may often have been questionable and their lives scandalous. It is significant, however, that the natives could with difficulty be induced to leave the missions and work for the settlers. The Jesuits were often, no doubt, especially in later decades, examples of apathy and inculcators of superstition, but "the conquest and colonization of Portuguese America in the sixteenth and seventeenth centuries is in large part their work. As missionaries, they succeeded in winning thousands of Indians for civilization, and the native race became, thanks to their devotion, a considerable factor in the formation of the Brazilian people." [3]

One of the outcomes of Jesuit opposition to Indian servitude was the growth of African slavery and the slave-trade. Despite the cost of the negro, the colonist was forced to use him, when the fathers had gained their day of success and had drawn the native

[1] Watson, II, 233–234, 237–238; Leroy-Beaulieu, I, 52–53; Martins, Hist. de Port., II, 147–148, 153, 182 ff.; Varnhagen, II, 194 ff.   [2] Watson, II, 158–159, 199–202.
[3] Rio-Branco, p. 149; cf. Watson, II, 114–115, 123; Varnhagen, I, 202, 243.

peoples into the missions under their paternal protection. But it was the edicts of Pombal, freeing the Indians and giving them actually or prospectively the same rights as the Portuguese, that lent to the negro slave-trade an impetus hitherto unknown.[1] " In the first years [1755 ff.] of the existence of the *Companhia do Grão-Pará* the import of slaves into Brazil amounted to 100,000 per annum; of these 22,000 to 43,000 had Rio as their destination. . . . From 1759 to 1803 the colonial registers give, as consigned from Angola to Brazil, 642,000 negroes. The income from the exportation of negroes is estimated at 160 contos [$160,000]. . . . From 1817 to 1819 the average shipment for Brazil was 22,000, and, despite the legal cessation of the traffic, as late as 1839 there still issued from Angola 35 cargoes of slaves."[2] These great numbers were demanded partially in consequence of a heavy death-rate on the passage and in the colony. To get 65,000 slaves to Brazil it was necessary to start with some 100,000, and of the 65,000 some 3000 to 5000 died in the first two months after arrival. The profits of the trade were of course high ; " the mine of negro labor was worth as much as or more than the New World mines of silver and gold." "The colony acquired decidedly and definitively the character common to all the [plantation] colonies of North America and the Antilles, — abandonment and extinction of the indigenous races, colonization by whites, and negro slave-labor."[3] The results for Brazil of the prohibition of the slave-trade and the activities of the British cruisers were similar to those experienced by those other American districts which were devoted to tropical agriculture. If the outcome was less disastrous, it was because part of Brazil was a true settlement colony, and because even the tropical portions had gotten a start early in the country's history.

[1] Varnhagen, I, 181–185; cf. Martins, O Brazil, etc., p. 30, note.

[2] M. de Sá, O Trabalho Rural Africano, quoted in Martins, O Brazil, etc., p. 56, note. The close natural connection between Brazil and the source from which it drew its indispensable labor supply, the West African stations, should receive especial attention. Cf. p. 127, above. When the Dutch occupied Brazil (see p. 147, above) they were led as a matter of course to acquire the slave-stations; after their departure the Portuguese again managed to secure these complementary districts. See Martins, O Brazil, etc., pp. vii, 37–38.

[3] Martins, O Brazil, etc., pp. 54, 58–59, 73, 75 ; Leroy-Beaulieu, I, 53.

Conditions Preceding Independence

The gradual exhaustion of the mines toward the end of the eighteenth century allowed the colony, though with some distress, to return to its former and interrupted course of material development. Abandonment of the famous, but now sterile, source of wealth was hard, and it took almost a quarter of a century to give it up. It is during this period of transformation that Brazil, by the fact of its separation from Portugal, passes from the field of our researches. However, before it ceased to be a colony, Brazil had already turned back toward the type of life in vogue before the gold discoveries. The province of Minas Geraes had been the first to suffer from the decline of the mines and the ensuing economic crisis. Early in the nineteenth century, while its inhabitants were vacillating between the mining of failing deposits and agriculture, many parts of the province were practically in ruins. Apathy and abandonment of all effort were all but universal.[1] In time, however, it was seen that cotton, coffee, tobacco, and other products of the soil promised a better and more solid yield than had the mines at their best. With this turn of the tide population began to grow with great rapidity again, and export and coast trade took on new life.[2] The opening up of the interior had followed the development of the mines and had not ceased with their virtual abandonment. King José I and Pombal had always had the interests of Brazil at heart, and the latter benevolent despot had formed in 1755 a commercial company for Maranhão and Pará which had aided much in the exploration and colonization of these regions.[3] Pombal likewise curbed the power of religious establishments other than those of the Jesuits, and rendered life in Brazil more endurable for the Jews.[4] By 1800 Brazil had a population of 3,200,000, half negro-slaves; in 1817–1818, 3,817,900, without counting children under ten years of age. Of these, about 1,000,-000 were whites, 260,000 civilized Indians, 526,000 mulattoes or free negroes, and 1,930,000 slaves. In 1800 Brazilian exports

---

[1] Martins, O Brazil, etc., pp. 86–89.

[2] Id., pp. 168–170.

[3] Watson, II, 238–239; Rio-Branco, p. 146.

[4] Watson, II, 242–243. Official corruption, was, however, rife. The desire to get rich quickly invaded the minds of the colonial appointees as it had in India. The population was still raw and illiterate. Zimmermann, I, 173 ff.

and imports amounted to over $11,000,000 and $10,000,000 respectively.[1]

The advance of the Portuguese toward the interior in consequence of the discovery of gold and diamonds revived the old contentions whose settlement was the object of the treaty of Tordesillas.[2] The Demarcation Line had been respected neither by the Portuguese in Brazil nor the Spanish in the East Indies. Spain had kept the Philippines and exacted an indemnity or purchase-price for the Moluccas. Admitting these facts as evidence of a western shift of the Pacific demarcation meridian, Portugal could claim a good part of Patagonia, Paraguay, and the Plata region. But by a treaty of 1750, a division which rested upon the principle of the maintenance of present holdings, boundaries essentially the same as those of to-day were established. Unrealizable pretensions based upon the famous papal bull were thus abandoned; the temper of 1493 had long passed. Portugal renounced any rights to the navigation of the Plata, and all trade between the two nations was forbidden.[3]

Factors Leading to Independence

In order now to understand the impelling forces of that movement which made of Brazil an independent state, it is necessary to recall the fact that a certain part of the country lay within a temperate region, and as a result of vital and other conditions was fitted to work out the line of development natural to such environment. This favored district was the south. From early times its population had been superior in quantity and quality to that of the tropical regions, and the fact that the mines lay within it lent it a still greater attractive power. "Mountains, rivers, mines, men, geography, and human choice coincided to give to the region of São Paulo-Minas the supremacy over all Portuguese America."[4] This district was at first neglected as especially unpromising according to the ideas of the time. It came, however, to a position of leadership in all Brazilian history: in the exploration of the interior,

---

[1] Rio-Branco, pp. 149–152; cf. Watson, II, 268; Martins, O Brazil, etc., pp. 68–69. An estimate quoted in Humboldt's Essai (II, 855) gives, for 1776, 1,900,000; and for 1798, 3,300,000 (800,000 whites, 1,000,000 Indians, and 1,500,000 negroes). The latter figures are said to be too low, and the Portuguese informant judges 4,000,000 to be nearer the truth. [2] P. 90, above. [3] Watson, II, 144, 218, 220; cf. p. 212.

[4] Martins, O Brazil, etc., p. 125; cf. Stephens, pp. 163 ff.

in Indian wars and slave raids, in mine discovery, in the beating off of attacks from without. The Paulistas were the most energetic, stubborn, and independent component of the population of the colony. As contrasted with the north, the progress of the south was less speedy but more solid; while in the north attention turned to an exotic culture dependent upon an imported labor supply, the south exhibited a system approaching that of "free colonization." The north still formed a Portuguese "plantation," while the south had acquired many of the rudiments of a developing nation. This supremacy was recognized by the transference of the capital in the middle of the eighteenth century from Bahia to Rio de Janeiro.[1]

The temper of this region was never tractable. It was quarrelsome rather, violent and revolutionary, particularly after the infusion of the miner element. When the eighteenth century was drawing to a close, the ground was already prepared for almost any degree of political assertion. The principles of the French Revolution and the example of the American united to render the Brazilians more uneasy; indeed, a revolution broke out in Minas Geraes in 1789, which witnessed in some degree to the receptivity of the Paulistas for the doctrines of the French philosophers. It was repressed with needless severity.[2] Now it was precisely during this disturbed period that the great European struggles impinged indirectly upon the local situation, and with a result unique in the history of colonization. For, in consequence of Napoleon's activities in the Peninsula, the crown of Portugal itself was forced to emigrate into its great transatlantic possession, thus completely perturbing the antecedent status of affairs. Socially, a veritable experiment in the admixture of oil and water ensued; the Portuguese "mandarinate" was brought into close proximity to the

---

[1] Martins, O Brazil, etc., pp. 31–32, 46–48, 75–77. "The Brazilian nation evolved in colonial fashion (*colonialmente*) in the north, but organically and spontaneously in the south. Semi-independent, the region of S. Paulo-Minas with the great bay of Rio-Janeiro, the national capital of a future empire, was working out in obscurity an organic structure; while the Brazil of officialdom, of brilliance and opulence, the Brazil of the viceroys and governors, was seated in the north, in Bahia and Pernambuco. That Brazil, however, was not geographically the center of the empire. Its climate seemed to condemn it to the eternal condition of a colony dependent upon an exotic culture and upon African slavery, or to the unhappy lot of a Jesuit Paraguay." Martins, O Brazil, etc., p. 76. For the general status of Brazil at the end of the eighteenth century, see Varnhagen, II, 236 ff.

[2] Martins, O Brazil, etc., pp. 101–104; Rio-Branco, p. 151; cf. Varnhagen, II, 269 ff.

Paulista type, rude and democratic. There was likewise an inversion, as it were, of political relationship between Portugal and Brazil, whereby the latter became the dominant state and the former the dependency.[1] Rio de Janeiro constituted, to all practical intents, the capital of the Portuguese empire. Results of great significance could not fail to follow upon this situation.

The royal family of the Braganzas arrived in Brazil early in 1808, thus realizing a transference of the court projected by John IV in the seventeenth century, by Da Cunha in 1736, and by Pombal in 1761. The country at once, and by the logic of the situation, became an independent empire. The king hastened to issue a series of decrees assuring to Brazil such industrial and other advantages as the metropolis had possessed : agriculture, manufacture, and commerce were put on their feet and encouraged, foreigners freely admitted, departments, courts, and councils established, roads built and exploration furthered, schools, libraries, and scientific projects supported. In 1815 Brazil was accorded the title of Realm. For seven years the country was administered directly by local officials under a local sovereign; this event was extremely opportune, for it had the merit of placing in evidence and politically sanctioning an inevitable and imminent change of Brazil's status.[2] It also had a more lasting effect in binding the various Brazilian provinces together, both politically and economically (through the construction of roads and other means of inter-communication), as the Spanish South American colonies, for example, were never united.[3] And when the king, against his will, was forced by the insistence of England to return to Lisbon, he left behind his oldest son, Dom Pedro, as regent of the realm.

For all the benefits of the royal sojourn, however, the Brazilians were glad to see it end. The European court was an exotic plant in the rude new country, and the ways of the aristocracy palled upon the hardy settlers of the Paulista type. There was nothing in common between the two. When now the Lisbon Cortes opposed the royal policy, voted the suppression of schools and higher courts, ordered the dissolution of the central government

---

[1] Martins, O Brazil, etc., p. 94 ; Leroy-Beaulieu, I, 56–57 ; Varnhagen, II, 297 ff. ; Zimmermann, I, 411.

[2] Martins, O Brazil, etc., p. 94. For the emigration of the Braganzas, see also pp. 90 ff. ; Rio-Branco, pp. 154–155; Watson, II, 263 ff.; Leroy-Beaulieu, I, 56–57 ; general sketch of the period in Zimmermann, I, 175 ff.   [3] Watson, II, 260, 270.

in Rio and the recall of Dom Pedro, and tried to break Brazilian unity by attaching each province separately to the metropolis, an almost universal movement in favor of Brazilian autonomy set in. Dom Pedro, in response to overtures on the part of the people of Rio and São-Paulo, declared (January, 1822) that he would remain in the country. The Portuguese troops who opposed the resolution were allowed to depart for Portugal, and the prince, after proclaiming the independence of Brazil (September 7, 1822), was acclaimed first perpetual protector, then constitutional emperor (October 12). It was impossible for the metropolis to resist this culmination, for it had " a smaller population and perhaps less wealth than its colony. It resigned itself cheerfully to an inevitable fact," [1] and Brazilian independence was recognized in 1825.[2]

Achievements of the Portuguese in Brazil

The achievements of the Portuguese in Brazil deserve a word of notice in perspective, and by way of comparison with those of other peoples operating under similar conditions. The case is well put by Leroy-Beaulieu : " The end of the eighteenth century and the beginning of the nineteenth brought to Brazil none of those calamities which broke over the English and Spanish possessions. Portugal followed in all the European conflicts the destiny of England, the mistress of the seas, from which it resulted that free circulation between the metropolis and the colonies was never interrupted : Brazil was in a position to gain rather than to lose during the maritime wars of the Europeans, for these smote the sugar islands of her rivals while leaving her intact. If the separation of Brazil and Portugal came to pass without violence and almost without shock, this must not be regarded as a fortuitous circumstance. It was not alone the diminutiveness and powerlessness of the metropolis which rendered the transition so easy ; the colony was ready for independence, and, when it had detached itself from its trunk like a ripe fruit, it did not cease to grow and prosper. The fact is that the Portuguese administration in Brazil, despite its errors and faults, . . . had not been very oppressive ; liberty had been the cradle of colonization. The abundance of

[1] Leroy-Beaulieu, I, 57 ; figures for the decline of Portugal's commerce in Martins, O Brazil, etc., p. 249.

[2] Rio-Branco, pp. 163–164; for the activities of José Bonifacio and the character of Dom Pedro, see Martins, O Brazil, etc., pp. 107, 111–116.

fertile lands, the absence of exaggerated regulation, the feebleness of the *main morte*, had allowed the colony, in spite of certain restrictions and monopolies, to reach conditions which were normal and appropriate to an adult age." [1] Brazil was likewise saved from the Inquisition, the Santo Officio, "from that *Status in Statu* whose dictation, superior to all law, diminished the majesty of the king, the power of the government, the justice of the courts, the ecclesiastical authority of the prelates, and the liberty of the people — liberty not only to discuss but even as it were to think. No special inquisition was ever created in Brazil." [2]

"The relations of Portugal with Brazil are, besides, much more familiar, more intimate, more frequent, than those of Spain with her former colonies in America. This has been seen by the number of Portuguese who [still] emigrate to Brazil. Several years ago the trade with Brazil represented about one-sixth of the export and one-seventeenth of the import movement of the total trade of Portugal. . . . In the Indies a jealous, narrow, and ambitious policy lost no time in ruining the edifice of Portuguese power; in Africa a disgraceful and degrading trade afforded Portugal a debasing wealth; in Brazil alone the Portuguese demonstrated themselves colonists. They managed to blend the spirit of adventure in a just degree with practical patience and laborious perseverance, and they thus succeeded in realizing one of the aims, if it is not the sole object, of colonization, the creation of a great state, rich, industrious, and free." [3]

These statements may serve to bring out the special achievements of the Portuguese in America as distinguished both from those of other nations in the New World and from those of the same nation in the Old. It is probable that Leroy-Beaulieu, in his partisanship for the Latin nations [4] and his solicitude for their future and the persistence of what is distinctive in their culture,

---

[1] Leroy-Beaulieu, I, 56. It should be realized that Brazil is about ninety times the size of Portugal. Cf. Watson, II, 113.

[2] Varnhagen, I, 88. [3] Leroy-Beaulieu, I, 58, 59.

[4] He also applauds the Germans and Scandinavians for their efforts in the colonial field, remarking (I, 186, note): "Il ne faut pas désirer la disparition des espèces ou des races, quand elles ont des qualités solides. Or, l'amoindrissement de son rang relatif dans le monde, l'abaissement indéfini du coefficient qu'il représente dans la population totale du globe, équivalent presque pour un peuple à sa disparition." He adds, more concretely (p. 187, note): "On a trop longtemps laissé le monde entier livré aux Anglo-Saxons, c'est une cause d'appauvrissement futur pour la civilisation humaine."

somewhat exaggerates the favorable case of Brazil. But it is clear enough, nevertheless, that, partly because the colony furnished a favorable environment, partly because it was let alone, partly because it was treated with less incompetence than ordinarily, partly for a number of lesser reasons, Brazil has become an independent nation whose kindly feeling for the metropolis, unbroken by bloody revolutionary struggles, is an international asset; for it adds much to the importance of an otherwise insignificant parent state. Continuous infusions of Portuguese blood, due to an immigration motived not by governmental but by popular initiative, have gradually overcome the native strain of what was a largely mongrel population, and a fortunate reversion toward the more developed ethnic component, with its happier adaptation to modern conditions, has ensued. The contrast with the outcome in the Portuguese East is sharp. In Brazil there has arisen a new and powerful sponsor for that in language, religion, customs, and literature which is Portuguese. To a certain degree a nation and its life have been transplanted, and a new society, inheriting its distinctive characters from an old, has come into a relative fullness of strength.

Conclusion of Portuguese Colonization

After all, however, there has been but a single and brief period during which Portugal was enabled to hold the center of the stage in the working-out of the world's history, and that was when she had succeeded in making the first direct contact between Europe and Asia, the West and the East. Fitted for some such desperate exploit, and through its achievement the objects of envy of the rest of the western world, the Portuguese could not maintain through cool and rational means what they had gained by dash and the impetus of enthusiasm. Even the Portuguese historians were wont perpetually to confuse personal heroism with political achievement.[1] Administration was beyond the intrepid pathbreakers, facing as they did a situation which called for the handling of problems new to men. It would have been hard in that age to have found any people in Europe which would have met the new situation untrammeled with the convictions, prejudices, and other intellectual handicaps to which Portugal largely owed her disasters.[2] Portugal was in truth the fine flower of the

[1] Hunter, I, 92; cf. Martins, O Brazil, etc., p. 95; Whiteway, pp. 24–25.
[2] Cf. Martins, Hist. de Port., I, 296; for a list of the causes of Portuguese decadence, see Corvo, IV, 88 ff.

age ; all wished to do as she was doing. There was not so much incongruity between the specifically Portuguese methods and the medium in which they were applied and failed, as between the general methods characteristic of an undeveloped age and the new environment suddenly thrown open — of world-wide commerce, distant empire, and the contact with alien races. The transition from that mediterranean or "thalassic" stage of commerce and colonization to the oceanic stage was sure to cause throes of misunderstanding, and failure in adjustment. Portugal was destined, for reasons stated, to be the first to plunge into a task far beyond her power of numbers or grade of discipline. Thus she did not reach the goal, but fell back, becoming as the years went on less and less able to dominate the situation, deriving a waning benefit from the relics of her old empire. She spent her strength before the race was really begun. In her decline she has been unable to attend properly to matters now regarded as fundamental in colonization : preparatory works of various kinds (roads, surveys, harborworks, etc.), hygienic measures, educative systems, and enterprises of all kinds. She has fallen into a more or less dependent relation with the nation which was able to seize the dominant place in the modern world-movements of trade and colonization, — the British.[1] Amidst these failures, however, Brazil stands forth as a success due to largely uncontrolled and natural development ; it is only the more visionary, or the practical in more visionary moods, who anticipate for it the menace of the Anglo-Saxon encroachment, or fear political interference on the part of the United States of America.[2]

NOTE ON BRAZILIAN REVENUE

For various reasons it is impossible to get any exact figures for the revenue derived from the gold mines of Brazil. Reckoning must start out, for the most part, from the amount of the government fifths as a basis. These are not always distinguishable from other items of revenue, and for other reasons are uncertain. No calculations such as those of Humboldt for Spanish America are available, and when the attempt is made to ascertain the total production of the mines, estimates enter for the most part into the region of rough guesswork. The amount to which the government was defrauded is indeterminable, although it is known to have been large. The case is much worse when the diamond revenue and production are considered ; here the system of taxation

[1] Corvo, I, 140; IV, 59–60, etc.; Leroy-Beaulieu, I, 59. Martins, citing statistics, speaks of the "denationalization" of Portuguese commerce with the colonies. O Brazil, etc., p. 197, note ; cf. Hist. de Port., I, 16.

[2] Cf. Leroy-Beaulieu, I, 58.

varied between two incommensurable bases, and evasion was still more difficult to detect.

The subjoined collection of estimates can give, therefore, no more than a
general idea of the situation; it is given for what it is worth. Watson[1] says
that the fifths of gold from Minas Geraes were assumed to amount to 100
arrobas (over 3200 pounds); in 1753 they reached a value of nearly $2,000,-
000. That year the fleet from Rio de Janeiro was believed to have brought
home gold, silver, and goods worth $15,000,000. The bullion and jewels sent
to Lisbon in 1754 were estimated at a million *moidores* ($6,500,000). On an
average of sixteen years the royal fifths exceeded 100 arrobas. Stephens[2]
gives the following: entire amount of gold extracted, $225,000,000; yearly
revenue to crown from fifths, $1,500,000. Martins[3] says that D. João V (1706–
1750) received about 130,000,000 *cruzados* (over $50,000,000) from the gold-
works, and, among other items, swelling this figure, 40,000,000 cruzados
($16,000,000) from diamonds. The same author[4] states that Eschwege cal-
culated the total product of the fifths at $64,800,000. They rendered about
$2,000,000 annually; some think double that sum. In 1809 Minas produced
for the fifth over 4800 pounds of gold; and in 1820 the total product of the
revenue was scarcely $240,000, the value of 440 kilograms.[5] Martins's cata-
logue of estimates, containing some rather inaccessible data, is translated in
full below. All these calculations should be taken *cum grano*; they should
be compared, by one who wishes a greater precision, with those of Humboldt
for Spanish America. It should also be realized that these sums appeared far
greater in the eighteenth century than they would at the present time. For
purposes of comparison the following facts may be appended: value of fine
gold per ounce at the present time, $20.67; gold production of the world: 1885,
$108,435,600; 1895, $198,763,600; 1900, $254,576,300; 1904, $347,000,000.
Whole stock of gold in the world, about $6,150,000,000.[6] A cursory review
of various national crop reports will show the superiority of agriculture and
other kinds of economy, once despised in comparison with the mining of precious
metals.

ESTIMATES OF THE YIELD OF GOLD AND DIAMONDS

(Translation from Martins, O Brazil, etc., p. 83, note.)

The insufficiency of the registers and the importance of contraband render
impossible the determination of the sum of production of the Brazilian mines.
We give, however, certain selections upon the topic.

Humboldt, in his Essay on New Spain,[7] calculates thus:

From 1699 to 1755 there came registered to Europe .	480,000,000 piasters
From 1756 to 1803 there came registered to Europe .	204,544,000 piasters
Not registered	171,000,000 piasters
Total	855,544,000 piasters
Gold in coin and the arts in Brazil	?
Production from 1803 to 1815, yearly (30,000 marcos) .	4,360,000 piasters

---

[1] II, 244.   [2] P. 348.   [3] Hist. de Port., II, 151.   [4] O Brazil, etc., p. 84, note.
[5] Other estimates are to be found in Branco, Port. na Epocha, etc., p. 99; Martins,
O Brazil, etc., p. 83, note.   [6] *Moody's Magazine*, December, 1905, p. 20.
[7] Essai, II, 643–644.

The mines of Goyaz apparently produced annually (middle of the eighteenth century) 150 arrobas of gold.

Ayres do Cazal says that the first fleet of Cuyabá looted by the Payaguas in Paraguay (1730) bore 22,000 libras of gold; and that in 1731 there went out from Matto-Grosso to S. Paulo 25,600 libras.

In 1773 the gold produced in Minas weighed 118 arrobas, and from 1773 to 1812 the total was 6895 arrobas, worth 85,000,000 cruzados.

From 1752 to 1773 the total registered production was 6400 to 8600 kilos per annum, and the contraband more than as much again.

Here are the figures of Chevalier:[1]

ANNUAL PRODUCTION OF AMERICA	BRAZIL	OTHER COUNTRIES
At the beginning of the century . .	kilos 3,700, fr. 12,744,000	kilos 10,418, fr. 35,885,000
Before the discovery of the California mines . .	kilos 2,500, fr. 8,611,000	kilos 12,715, fr. 43,796,000

The following are the tables of Baron von Eschwege in his *Pluto Braziliensis*:[2]

EXTRACTION OF GOLD

Minas Geraes	1700 to 1820	35,687 arrobas
Goyaz	1720 to 1730	9,212 arrobas
Matto-Grosso	1712 to 1820	3,107 arrobas
S. Paulo	1600 to 1820	4,650 arrobas

This excludes contraband, confiscation, etc. The total production of Brazil might have reached from 1600 to 1820, 63,417 arrobas of a value of 391,000 contos of reis.

In 1735, according to Constancio, the diamond mines produced a million and a half of cruzados annually. The district of Diamantina (Minas) yielded, in 1808, from 20,000 to 25,000 carats, and in 1809 the treasure of Rio allowed D. João VI to decree an annual sale in London of 20,000 carats to guarantee the debt-charges.

Up to 1794, according to the *Correio brazilienze*,[3] the total expense of the extraction had arisen to 6185 contos, the product being 48,547 oitavas [eighths of an ounce] of diamonds. The work was, as is known, a royal monopoly, and the diamonds went, on the count of the national finances, to Amsterdam to be cut and sold. From 1802 to 1819 they were adjudicated to the service of the loan raised in Amsterdam, and the firm of Hope was the consignee. During this period the house in question received 348,926 carats, liquidating 8,810,479 florins. This sum, however, does not represent the total production; there must be added the value of diamonds of greater size and price, preserved in the Treasury, and all those which circulated in the hands of individuals in the Reino-unido.

---

[1] Cours d'Économie Politique, III, 397, 401. Martins's figures are wrong. [2] P. 33.
[3] Nos. 79, 81, and 111. See a chart of A. Patricio de Anderlecht, in the *Padre Amaro*, London, 1821, t. IV, 343.

CHAPTER V

THE BEGINNINGS AND THE SETTING OF SPANISH COLONIZATION

In passing from the colonial enterprises of the Portuguese to those of the Spanish, strong contrasts due to racial differences in the two peoples are conspicuously absent; and the same may be said of those rooting in antecedent history. The common motive forces which led to the exploits of the two Iberian nations have been reviewed in a former passage.[1] It is necessary only to recall the religious unity and political coherence forced upon them by the western crusade against the Moslem invader; the enthusiasm, love of adventure, taste for gambling with large hazards, impatience with a humdrum existence, and the overpowering greed begotten of preceding generations of war and rapine; and finally the benefits derived from the presence and efforts of an alien industrious people, and the deep national disaster incurred or about to be incurred through its expulsion. These considerations being recalled, it is possible to turn without further preliminaries to the more special and local conditions of Spain in order to find what particular preparation lay behind her activities in the Discoveries period and later.

POLITICAL AND RELIGIOUS UNIFICATION

The case is not so simple as that of Portugal. Politically the provinces which were to become Spain had never been soundly welded together; their union was more accidental than natural or inevitable. The need of concert against the Moors appealed, with the gradual retirement of the latter, chiefly to the South. It was really the much opposed union of Ferdinand and Isabella (1469), rather than any inherent necessity, which represented the drawing together of the two leading kingdoms. Nevertheless this union powerfully furthered political concentration under a strong

[1] Pp. 80 ff., above.

monarchy.   Ferdinand, upon whom had been conferred the grand-mastership of the three military orders, Santiago, Alcántara, and Calatrava, came thus to be the "sole and only leader of the old chivalry of Spain, as of its modern military system." The two sovereigns, united in their purposes, grasped the situation and constantly built up their power by breaking that of the nobles and by resolutely repressing disorder; "the unity of the king and queen was so entire, and the personality of each so strong, that for purposes of external policy Castile and Aragon were already Spain." [1] The subsequent extension of the Spanish dominions but added to this power. "It placed them on a pedestal high above the strongest nobleman, or the wealthiest ecclesiastic; it gave distance and atmosphere to royalty. Yet this very extension would have been impossible or dangerous had not king and queen resolutely increased also the intension of their power." [2]

However unhomogeneous by nature the several districts of Spain may have been, there is no doubt that the Catholic Sovereigns soon attained a position from which they could dispose of the forces of Spain as of a nation politically unified. Indeed, the political unity seems as a practical factor to have surpassed the religious, in spite of the aftermath of passion following upon the Moorish wars; [3] for these sovereigns, perhaps not deliberately but in any case opportunely, played upon the religious interests common to all sections, interweaving with the success of their grand crusade against the Moorish kingdoms many a strand of political loyalty to themselves, and extending their rule through actual conquest.[4] In many ways the cementation of religious unity appears to have been merged into or even to have been secondary to the establishment and preservation of the monarchy; the Inquisition was later employed as an effective political agency, and in Spain, as in few other Catholic countries, the sovereign dominated the Church.[5] At the same time, as will be seen, the religious motive flowed in a powerful current through the minds of individuals, high and low, and through the life of the nation at large. Certainly at the end of Ferdinand and Isabella's reign an effective coherence

[1] Hume, pp. 1, 12–14.

[2] Id., pp. 11, 19–24, 29–30; Martins, Civ. Iber., pp. 179, 220; Haebler, Wirt. Bl., p. 7. The same process was carried forward by Charles V and Philip II. Haebler, Wirt. Bl., pp. 12–16.   [3] Cf. Colmeiro, I, 219.

[4] Navarre, for instance, was conquered in 1512.

[5] Hume, pp. 128–131; cf. Fabié, p. 41.

along all lines had been secured; "with a disciplined infantry, a guileful diplomacy, a powerful Church, Spain was fully equipped for the conquest of territory or the control of opinion."[1]

ECONOMIC STRENGTH

The question of the economic strength of Spain at the entrance of her world-career still remains. The opinion has been offered that both Spain and Portugal were led by enthusiasm for King and Church into enterprises which placed too severe a strain upon their material resources. This does not necessarily imply that Spain's economic development was relatively backward, for it is morally certain that there was no nation in Europe that could have coped with the new and dangerous situation with which Spain was presently to find herself confronted. To one who pauses in amazement over the absurd restrictions placed upon industry and trade by the casuistries of the mediæval system, the periodic and capricious alteration of the coinage and other ill-advised and unfair measures, it seems well-nigh impossible that any economic development whatever should have taken place;[2] but one must reflect that the prescriptions of the canons weighed upon all European nations except the most advanced and skillful of evaders, and really represented an honest though blundering attempt at the solution of the rising problems of society. Despite all these drawbacks, it would be difficult to show that Spain, upon the eve of the Discoveries, was not economically as well prepared for her opening career as were several other states of later times with which it has been the custom to compare Spain to her disadvantage.[3] The period of Spanish decline, once believed to have been in full swing before the sixteenth century, was yet to be ushered in; in fact the exigencies of the opening century were largely responsible for its coming.

Traces of industrial development in Castile and Aragon were slight up to the fourteenth century, when some protection was

[1] Hume, p. 30; cf. Leroy-Beaulieu, I, 3; Clarke, pp. 353–356; Cheyney, pp. 79 ff. For an eloquent but perhaps "impressionistic" account of the factors of royalty and the Church, see Martins, Civ. Iber., pp. 158 ff.

[2] Colmeiro, I, 405 ff.; chaps. xlv, xlvi, xlvii, l, etc.

[3] The Spanish and Portuguese were confronted with a series of problems for whose solution they were, as was the rest of the western world, by education unfitted. The Dutch and English, in a later time, profited by their errors. Martins, Civ. Iber., pp. 261–263.

extended to the arts and crafts. Unable to maintain the level of
Moorish agriculture, the Spaniards allowed aqueducts and other
irrigation devices to remain in the ruins to which war had reduced
them, and turned their attention more particularly to an occupation
which made fewer demands upon their warlike minds and unsettled
dispositions, — cattle-raising. It cannot be denied that the physical
character of the Peninsula favored sheep over grain; but the
extensions of privilege granted to the owners of flocks over the
cultivators of ground were plainly excessive, and they choked
whatever agricultural development was possible. Valencia supplied
but one-third of her own needs along this line, and Catalonia and
Aragon were almost wholly dependent upon importation from
Sicily, the Balearic Islands, and elsewhere. Castile, depending
upon her ill-treated Moriscos, managed even to export a little grain
up to the time when the latter were crushed and expelled. In the
fifteenth century the chief raw products of Spain were wool, wine,
and iron.[1] Industries were far from being self-sufficient, for almost
all industrial products were imported; the realization of the fact
that "wealth was being drawn from the country" to pay for them,
motived the efforts of Isabella to build up industries, although as
respects agriculture and cattle-raising no great departure from
traditional policy was attempted.[2]

Of all those occupations whose pursuit builds up national material
wealth, commerce was as little neglected as any. Spain had lain
in the path of trade for many centuries and could not but have
profited by her position. Cadiz (Gades) had been famous in Phœnician times; and the Italians of the Middle Ages had met a fierce
competition, especially in the African trade, from the merchant-
shipping of Barcelona. The parts of the Peninsula accessible from
the sea had been visited and enriched by the sojourn of Phœnician,
Greek, Carthaginian, Roman, and Arab. In the first half of the
fourteenth century regulations of Castilian commerce with England
and the Netherlands occur, and in 1348 the barbarous "strand-law"
was abolished.[3] Barcelona entered the field somewhat earlier, and
the inhabitants of other districts learned more of the sea with the
extension of their fisheries. The very need of imported food

[1] Colmeiro, I, 300 ff.; II, 112 ff.; Haebler, Wirt. Bl., pp. 8, 22–26, 32–35. On the
Consejo de la Mesta, see also Hume, p. 84; Clarke, p. 356.

[2] Haebler, pp. 8, 47; Hume, pp. 85–86.

[3] Wappäus, I, 348; Lindsay, I, 471, 548–549, 554 ff.

and other products forced the development of commerce, and Ferdinand and Isabella, as soon as their hands were freed from wars, are found to have directed close attention to the requirements of a sea-borne traffic.[1] Indeed, as has been seen, the very entrance into the heritage of the Moslems could not but open the eyes of the conquerors to its value. Whatever may have been the weakness of the Spaniard in the matter of industrial pursuits, he certainly experienced an economic awakening as well as a spiritual revival and an access of loyalty to a centralized power during the course of the decades which just preceded the capture of Granada.[2]

Comparison of the Spanish and Portuguese Discoveries

In judging of Spain's preparedness to meet her destiny, one finds himself laying more stress upon the religious and political, rather than upon the economic factors. Yet it is not the strength or weakness of any special factor, economic or other, upon which judgment must be rested, but rather the sum total of all the elements which combined to constitute national strength or weakness. Thus judging, Spain is found to have been strong for an inspired effort, but to have possessed scarcely enough stamina to react against a severe and enduring strain. It is plain, in any case, from what has been said, and from a closer study of Spain's economic conditions in the fifteenth century, that a display of individual initiative was as little to be expected in Spain as in Portugal. This fact, and the concentration and exaltation of the royal power, led naturally, in one case as in the other, to the lodgment of the new enterprises in the hands of the sovereigns. What we miss, however, in the case of Spain, is the presence, as in Portugal, of a directing mind, reaching out in a series of tentatives leading to an ultimate and at length consciously visualized aim; there was no Spanish Prince Henry. But the fact is that Henry the Navigator performed his service, not for Portugal alone, but for the whole of

---

[1] Colmeiro, I, 377 ff., 391 ff.; Haebler, Wirt. Bl., pp. 44–46.

[2] " The period during which Spanish territory was divided between the Christians and the Mohammedans appears, from the standpoint of social enlightenment, the most hopeful in the history of the Peninsula. The process of race affiliation and assimilation had begun, and, through the mingling of the elements present, there was forming a new nation, big with the prospects of great material achievements and of splendid cultivation. . . . Its resources for establishing a high grade of civilization appear to have exceeded those of any other Western nation at that time." Moses, p. 10.

Europe ; and that the final success of the Spaniards in the West represents one of the forms of a grand dual consummation of which Da Gama's exploit was the more immediately evident. For it is plainly stated by the son of the Genoese discoverer of America that the latter attained many of his ideas, and their final clarification, while in Portugal. Columbus married the daughter (and the pair lived with the widow) of one of Prince Henry's captains, and he came into a certain sea-dog heritage thereby.[1] As is well known, he tried his fortune first of all at the Portuguese court, and there attained a degree of success represented by a treacherous attempt at appropriation of his ideas. His grand projects were in so far not the dreams of a visionary, but an increment of constructive imagination, added to the persistent, steady, and dogged perseverance of the Portuguese-English prince, who avowedly built upon the accumulated experience and wisdom of the past. It is with a sense of satisfaction that one perceives the continuity of the efforts of these two men, and feels himself justified in discounting once again the asserted value of intuition and inspired speculation over commonplace toil in the world.[2] At the same time the attainment of Columbus cannot but convey an impression of the accidental and fortuitous which that of Vasco da Gama does not.

The cases of the two nations and their discoverers may be aligned for comparison and contrast by the consideration that, in Spain, Columbus was really the talented source of a novel enterprise, while Da Gama was simply an agent — one of many — in the elaboration of a settled policy.[3] For Spain Columbus furnished the ideas and put them into practice, receiving material aid only from

[1] Hunter, I, 76–77 ; Major, pp. 347–348 ; Beazley, in Azurara, II, xxxv.

[2] For the studiousness of Columbus, see Bourne, Sp. in Amer., p. 11. Haebler (Amerika, p. 335) says that the only part of the enterprise of Columbus which was peculiarly his own, was his decision to steer across a trackless, endless ocean, in the knowledge that weeks or months would pass before land would be seen. Columbus was thus the way-breaker from the "thalassic" to the "oceanic" stage of navigation. Cf. Foreman (p. 30), who credits the Portuguese with the exploits of Magellan and Elcano as well.

[3] " It is not difficult to understand why the king of Portugal should have hesitated to accept the proposition of Columbus. Nearly seventy years of continued effort on the part of the Portuguese to realise the great conception of Prince Henry afforded substantial proof of their conviction of the soundness of that conception. . . . That route, therefore, . . . was identical with their hopes in the future as well as their predilections in the past." Major, p. 354. It is equally clear that Columbus could hope for no interest on the part of Genoa and Venice, whose preoccupation lay in keeping the Oriental trade in its old channels. The discoverer turned naturally to the states bordering on the ocean. Payne, pp. 21–22.

the government; for Portugal, Da Gama simply carried out royal instructions. The prospects of realization lay for both in the support of royalty — the hopes of Columbus were centered on kings alone. Columbus carried in his own mind the religious obsession of the time and place, and through it appealed most strongly to Isabella;[1] his plans and pleas looked to the regaining of the Holy Sepulcher, to the extension of the Faith; and with the queen who sent him, material considerations seem to have played a relatively insignificant rôle. Prince Henry and his successors were crusaders, too, and fervent in the Faith; Albuquerque's designs on the bones of the Prophet haunted him; but an unmistakable strain of commercial sagacity existed in Henry and was impressed upon the policy he bequeathed to those who took up his work. For these and other reasons the Portuguese exploits not only give the impression of being consistent outgrowths of the national system, with more momentum at first than those of the Spanish, but they likewise appear to fall into a more logical sequence with the earlier movements of trade and of national expansion.

EFFECTS OF THE DISCOVERY OF AMERICA

America as an outlet for Spain's forces was thus opened by a foreigner, suddenly and without warning.[2] The results were probably more accentuated in Spain than in Portugal. For while to the bulk of the people in either country the Discoveries came, as it were, unawares, the directors of the Portuguese voyages had always had Africa, with its possibilities, before them, and, in the later decades of the fifteenth century, had been seeing more and more light toward the consummation of what became their highest and final purpose. Spain, on the other hand, with no series of experiments to rely upon, and no continent to skirt, was really dependent upon chance, or, as piety would have it, upon Divine Providence for her position in the new world-order that was being evolved. There was no chance to duplicate the performance of Da Gama, for the vice-gerent of God had assured to the Portuguese who were able and

---

[1] Bourne, Sp. in Amer., pp. 76, 79, 82, etc.

[2] The romantic story of Columbus has been told often and well; for this reason, and because our present studies center about collective rather than individual enterprise and activities, no rehearsal of the discoverer's life is attempted. See Bourne, Sp. in Amer., pp. 8–25, 47, and bibliography. On his rights and those of his early successors, see Fabié, pp. 13 ff., 27 ff., 86.

willing to defend it a monopoly of the fruits of Prince Henry's activities. The exaltation of mood that followed upon the supposed attainment of the East by Columbus can be the better apprehended for these considerations. In spite of all, Spain was not to be left out; she, too, was to have a chance to serve God and herself on the grand scale. The reception of Columbus by people and sovereign witnesses to this attitude. As Martins, somewhat extravagantly, puts it: "Men thought of the millions of souls to be won for God! Of the mountains of gold to bring home! Of the great battles, the vast kingdoms to conquer! They saw all the crosses, commanderies, riches, captaincies, and glory. This shower of fortunate possibilities fell upon a nation in the plenitude of life, in the meridian of force, and in the ardor of faith. All the future captains of the Indies were formed in that moment. Columbus revolutionized the anterior direction of the current of national genius, directing it to that world which he discovered." [1]

THE DEMARCATION

The first move of the Catholic Sovereigns was to assure their permanent possession of the "East" as it had been opened up to them despite the sanctioned monopoly of the Portuguese. Might not the new lands be claimed from them by the king of Portugal by virtue of the bull secured from a former Pope? [2] As has been previously narrated, they succeeded so far as to cause the issuance of a new bull by Alexander VI (May 4, 1493), which recognized in the new worlds a dual "sphere of influence" of the two favored Catholic nations. This outcome was not palatable to King John of Portugal, and he would have fought Spain if he had dared. The Portuguese did not wish to be restricted to the original 100 leagues west of the African islands, for this would have prevented them from taking advantage of the trade-winds to evade the calms of the African coast. Spain yielded to Portuguese representations, and the demarcation meridian was shifted 270 leagues farther west by an agreement of June 7, 1494. As will be understood, the instruments, charts, etc., of the time were inadequate for the measurement of longitude and so for the exact fixation of any such

---

[1] Martins, Civ. Iber., p. 238. It is interesting to note that the fortunes of Columbus at the Spanish court remained dubious until it was seen that Granada was about to fall. Then only the new crusade, substituted for the old, was in order. Cf. Haebler, Amerika, pp. 356, 357; Moses, p. 15.   [2] See p. 89, above; cf. Saco, pp. 52–53.

demarcation; of a consequence disputes were sure to arise. These appeared unmistakably after the voyage of Magellan (1521), when it became necessary to fix the other half of the great circle of which the Atlantic meridian was part. A council summoned at Badajoz in April, 1524, failed to settle the question. The Portuguese were really served by uncertainty, for if the line were measured from the eastern end of the Azores archipelago they would lose recently discovered Brazil; if from the western end, the Moluccas. Charles V finally sold his rights to the latter islands, so that the Portuguese actually gained both their objects, and the dispute fell into oblivion.[1]

The appeal of the two European nations which first systematically approached the newly discovered regions, to the great political and religious arbiter of Europe, the Pope, set in motion a train of consequences which may here be foreshadowed. The policy of exclusion, as has been seen, was not new; but the invocation, to secure such exclusion, of that which alone stood for international law, gave to the long-prevalent national policy a wider significance. A policy sanctioned by the head of Christendom, and consistently enforced by the states most prominently in the eye of the western world, was sure to be erected into a sort of universal and unquestioned dogma. The triumphal progress of this dogma through the succeeding centuries can be traced in the narrative which follows.

EARLY POLICY OF SPAIN

The words of Columbus and others make it clear that the original intentions of Spain with regard to America were approximately those of Portugal in the case of India;[2] she appears to have been more eager to gain native converts, but she was as keenly alive to the getting of spices and gold. However, after some years of disappointments, it was recognized that the *Nuevo Mundo* was not the East, and that cloves, cinnamon, and other Oriental spices were not to be found.[3] And it was not so very

---

[1] For an excellent brief treatment of the Demarcation, see Bourne, Essays in Crit., pp. 193–217; cf. also p. 159, above.

[2] Cf. Payne, p. 24. Instances will appear in what follows of the Spanish tendency to utilize Portuguese models. Indeed, it is often through the better-known Spanish types that one arrives at some conception of the Portuguese.

[3] Premiums offered by the government in 1529 for the collection of cloves, ginger, cinnamon, and other spices seem to indicate that hope was not yet extinct. Bourne, Sp. in Amer., p. 217; cf. Fabié, pp. 163–164.

long before it became evident that there was no easily accessible passage through the new land-mass to the much desired destination. There were few who cared to contemplate a voyage over the course of the redoubtable Magellan. Consequently Spain was unable, after all, to compete with Portugal for the heritage of Venice. It was early discovered, however, that gold was to be found in the New World, and that there existed people whose bodies could be utilized by a parasitic organization to acquire the gold, while their souls were being inducted into the true faith. The relation of Spain to America soon reduced itself to the simple old terms, Conquest and Conversion, herein recalling the Portuguese attitude toward India and Africa. Any extended parallelism between the operations of the two nations is not, however, to be made out, owing to a diversity of colonial environment, both physical and ethnic, and to differences of national strength. There was no spice-trade in America, the conquests were far more thorough-going, the subject peoples upon a much lower stage of culture; there was no competing religion of a high order as in the East, for a long time no European intruders, and never any such disastrous period of foreign administration as the year 1580 initiated for Portugal.

THE CONQUESTS

The interest of the Spaniards in agricultural development and in actual settlement was slight.[1] The plantation system came to some development in later times, when certain products had attained an unforeseen importance, but these articles were largely luxuries and of tropical origin.[2] The great temperate regions of North and South America were uninteresting and repellent; such lands, yielding neither gold nor tropical products, were denominated "worthless territories";[3] the discoveries of De Soto, Coronado, Cabeça de Vaca, Ponce de León, De Solis, and Cabot were not followed up;[4] it was those of Cortés, Pizarro, and their lesser aftertypes that received instantaneous recognition, for they opened alluring avenues for the unleashing of the spirit of adventure and

[1] See p. 207, below.

[2] See pp. 10 ff., above. The expedition to Florida was condemned by the objection, "For what purpose do we need such products as are identical with those of southern Europe?" Roscher, Sp. Col. Sys., p. 2.

[3] *Tierras de ningun provecho.* Peschel, Races of Man, p. 211.

[4] See Bourne, Sp. in Amer., chaps. v–xi; Watson, I, 91 ff.

the satisfaction of greed.[1] The conquests of the Spaniards deserve
to be termed magnificent; they are as wonderful as the exploits of
the Portuguese under the early viceroys. The martial spirit of the
Spaniards, as of the Portuguese, has been traced to their antecedent
training;[2] it was also derivable to no small degree from their
nature and natural conditions. "The Spaniards were admirable
military material. Sober and temperate, they were more easily
provisioned than any European troops except the Turks. . . .
Spanish troops . . . have always been celebrated for marching
powers. Peculiarly uneducated, they had remarkable natural intelligence in soldiery. . . . They distinguished themselves especially in
the attack and defence of fortresses, and in retreats."[3] The value
of these qualities, and of the superior resistance of a more southern people to the strains of a tropical climate, will appear in any
account of the American conquests. Such admirably adapted
soldiers of fortune, the Spaniards found in America an extended
and, on the whole, easy field for their purpose of exploitation.
From the original headquarters, Santo Domingo (Española), conquerors licensed by the kings reached out to Cuba (1511) and
Florida (1513); to the Isthmus (Balboa, 1513) and Venezuela (1527);
and, greatest of all, to Mexico (Cortés, 1519) and Peru (Pizarro
and Almagro, 1531). Later years saw the invasion of Lower
California (1534), the Plata regions (1534), and of Chile (1535).[4]
The Spanish power came actually to be felt from Florida and
Louisiana to Tierra del Fuego, excluding, of course, Portuguese
South America.[5]

In order to render more definite the motives and procedures of
the Spanish conquests, it may be useful to recall certain aspects
of those two great enterprises, accounts of which, from the hand
of Prescott, have made them household words. Each of these
expeditions represents an outcome of individual adventure, rather

[1] Haebler, Amerika, pp. 378 ff. "The importance of New Granada in the eyes of
the Spaniards lay in its being the source whence the best emeralds were procured."
Watson, II, 151.   [2] Pp. 80 ff., above.

[3] Hume, p. 29.

[4] Bourne, Sp. in Amer., pp. 159 ff.; Haebler, Amerika, pp. 378 ff.; Watson, *passim*.
On the significance of the term "Florida," see Bourne, Sp. in Amer., p. 175.

[5] "Under the pressure of the immense excitement which resulted from the discoveries of Columbus, the entire eastern coast of the American continent, from
Labrador in the north to *Terra del Fuego* in the south, was explored within about
thirty years from A.D. 1492." Watson, I, 105. For the great changes of the Discoveries
period, see Bourne, Sp. in Amer., pp. 190–191.

than a deliberate state-enterprise;[1] the luster of the unknown always attracted the Spanish commanders, for they could from the nature of the case conduct no definite program like that of Albuquerque. Cortés, it is true, made use of royal troops, but in reckless disregard of the commands of his superior, the governor of Cuba; it was, indeed, the victory of Cortés over the government's punitive expedition which gave him the strength to subdue the Aztec empire. Pizarro and Almagro were in effect merely the active members of a triple partnership, for which De Luque secured the financial support.[2] Both expeditions represented gambling with large hazards for the sake of golden prospects whose realization was relied upon to excuse irregularities; the case of Balboa shows what might have happened to the conquerors. That the brigandage of Pizarro should be invested with a religious character, begun as it was under the patronage of the Holy Trinity and the Virgin, and with the sacrament of communion, is in line with the spirit of the age.[3] The insignificant number of the followers of Cortés and Pizarro is again evidence of the essentially adventurous nature of their enterprises, as well as of the self-reliance and military daring of this nation of seasoned soldiers. Cortés had about 400 Europeans with him, and Pizarro 168.[4] Even though the Spaniards were superior in weapons and discipline, and were enabled besides to impose upon the superstitions of the natives with their horses, guns, and negro attendants, yet the odds were overwhelmingly against them.[5] In both cases these odds were reduced by acts of reckless boldness in the seizure of the persons of the semi-divine rulers, and by a policy of alliance with conflicting factions. Again, predominance once established, it became the object alike of Cortés and of Pizarro to secure by any

[1] "A fact of great importance in revealing the economic characteristics of Spanish rule in America was, that discoveries and settlements were usually made, not at the expense of the state, but with private funds. If at any time the crown made advances for the support of an expedition, it was regarded as a loan to be repaid out of the first proceeds of the undertaking; and assurance was given that the settlements should remain under Spanish authority." Moses, p. 262. Cf. the case of Pizarro, id., pp. 111–113.   [2] Haebler, Amerika, pp. 379 ff.   [3] Cf. Watson, I, 111, 116; Moses, p. 111.

[4] Cortés had also 200 Indians, 16 horses, and 14 cannon; Pizarro had no allies at all. Haebler, Amerika, pp. 370, 380; Watson, I, 124.

[5] The natives thought the horsemen were centaurs, and stood aghast to see the beast and man parts separate themselves. And, as is well known, they at first regarded the Spaniards as beings of a divine nature, come in accordance with an ancient promise of their god Quetzalcoatl. Haebler, Amerika, pp. 370–371; cf. p. 289. Cf. Bourne, Sp. in Amer., pp. 151–157; Zimmermann, I, 267 ff., 285 ff.

means the treasure which would enrich themselves and secure justification at court. In both instances, finally, the state asserted itself, sequestered the conquerors or their representatives, and entered into a wider activity in governmental exploitation.

These cases are but types of what the rest of the explorers hoped to do; that personal adventure and self-aggrandizement were the driving motives is rendered the more likely by the fact that, of all the explorers, few besides Cortés possessed a station, education, and other qualities which raised them above the type of the poor and ignorant soldier of fortune. Pizarro, Balboa, and others were plainly ruined men, grasping at straws to gain reinstatement. The prevalence and effectiveness of these motives is attested by the number and extent of the expeditions, and in turn cast light upon the material qualities and predisposition of the Spaniards as indicated above.

Conquest in the hope of exploitation may then be regarded as the primal activity of the Spaniards in the New World. For many years this exploitation had reference almost exclusively to mineral wealth; hence the relations of Spain to America, although they were begun in the hope of reaching the East and its spices, really stand apart from the series of national enterprises resulting in colonization, which, from the Phœnicians to the Portuguese and Dutch, were centered about the acquisition for Europe of the products of the Orient. If, however, the conquests had been effected in somewhat irregular ways, and through, as it were, unauthorized agents, it was not in the disposition of the Catholic Sovereigns that they should be thus administered. When Cortés had been recalled to a position of inactive elevation at court, and the pretensions of the Pizarro family had been finally disposed of, the monarchs laid a heavy hand upon their continental possessions in the New World, as they had upon the island-empire of Columbus. Henceforth direction in all particulars, whether effective or not, emanated from Spain, and no one subject was allowed to hold the center of the stage for any extended period.

In Spain the tidings of the discoveries and then of the conquests had been, naturally enough, productive of great popular excitement. Columbus had about as much difficulty in keeping down the number of his complement for the second voyage as he had in raising a scanty crew for the first.[1] The various motives that have been

---

[1] Haebler, Amerika, p. 360.

mentioned contributed to this result ; but that material considerations overweighed all others is made probable by the decline of
enthusiasm when the life of romantic adventure and quickly
acquired wealth failed immediately to materialize. After hopes
had been again raised in later years the hand of the state had
already descended in restriction of freedom of emigration.

The Early Strength of Spain

Before, now, the colonial policy of Spain is further considered,
it seems in place to isolate as far as we are able the colonial activities of Spain from her other activities. It is always a fascinating
problem to attempt to determine the effect upon a country and
people of a colonial career ; and it is the more so in the case of
Spain in view of the fact that her subsequent and tragic fate has
not infrequently been explained to be, at least in good part, the result of her New World conquests and of their attendant reactions
upon the mother-country, its organization and people. Unquestionably the over-sea enterprises carried in themselves, or in their
wake, many contributing causes to Spain's subsequent misfortune ;
but these cannot well be estimated unless they are disengaged so
far as possible from other and much more serious causes for such
an extraordinarily dire result.

Some discussion of the preparedness of Spain for her colonial
activities has already been set forth. In 1500 Spain was really
strong, not only in her religious and political unity and enthusiasm,
but also in her economic organization. This state of affairs suffered
little diminution during the early decades of the opening century.
The king, as real head of the State and Church, increased in power,
and was, in the time of Philip II, about as nearly unlimited in
action as the head of a relatively civilized state may ever be ; and
on the whole this was with the approval of the people. No Spanish
king was more popular than Philip II. That such a state of the
popular mind was induced by fetichistic adoration of what was
royal and ecclesiastical, rather than by any rational considerations,
but added to its fervor and contagion. Economically, too, Spain
continued strong for some decades, albeit partly, as before, upon
borrowed force. She profited, among other things, by a foreign
king whose whole education and experience inclined him to go
counter to the restrictive ideas of the more genuinely Spanish

sovereigns. However, before the time of Charles V,[1] Ferdinand and Isabella strongly favored industry, especially as it formed the basis of trade ; for example, they founded a consulate in 1494 in Burgos, the first of a series whose services to Spanish trade were signal. This attitude was maintained by Charles, within whose reign falls Spain's period of greatest commercial energy. The immigration of foreign artisans was encouraged by him and his predecessors, despite the opposition of the Cortes. " Manufactures, chiefly wool and silk, increased tenfold in the course of a century ; the great fairs drew buyers from foreign lands ; it seemed as though the inborn Spanish dislike of commerce and industry had been overcome " [2] These conditions lasted on into the time of Philip II ; it is difficult to determine the date at which decline may be said to have set in, but the situation was still hopeful in 1560. " Spain was at that time not only at the climax of power, but also at the summit of her prosperity, and she owed this far more to trade and industry than to the gold of Mexico and the silver of Potosí. The wool industry alone supported almost a third of the Spanish population, and in Castile itself it occupied the inhabitants almost exclusively." [3] With all this came the growth of the merchant marine and the navy — one and the same thing, for the most part, in those days ; Spain " in the time of the Catholic Kings possessed over a thousand merchant ships, and there was no nation whose maritime power equalled ours." [4] Wars were fought by Charles in defense of trade or for its extension, and his treaties with England witness his preoccupation with commerce.[5] And if the growth of a national literature is to be regarded as an outcome of the quickening of national life, the time of the three consecutive Philips calls for an antecedent period of economic and other power.[6] In what degree these phenomena were referable to entrance upon the colonial career itself will be clearer presently ; naturally enough, there was a baffling interplay of causes and results, actions and reactions.

SPANISH DECADENCE AND ITS CAUSES

It would be safe to say, however, that the forces which made for decadence had begun to turn the scale by the middle of the

[1] The Emperor Charles V was King Carlos I of Spain, but he is referred to in this book under the better-known title.

[2] Haebler, Wirt. Bl., pp. 10, 47, 49–50, 58–59.; Clarke, p. 357 ; Colmeiro, II, 185–188, 197 ff.   [3] Haebler, Wirt. Bl., pp. 66 ff. ; Colmeiro, II, 185.

[4] Colmeiro, II, 465.   [5] Haebler, Wirt. Bl., pp. 54–55.   [6] Cf. Hume, pp. 246–247.

sixteenth century. Colmeiro finds the first indication of the decline of manufacture in Valladolid in 1537, and offers evidence to show that within twenty years of that date Spain could no longer meet the domestic demand for textiles.[1] Whatever the date preferred for the first visible signs of decadence, all reliable accounts would agree that its progress was clearly manifest by the end of the century in question, that it was astonishingly rapid, and varied by remarkably few reactions toward the former, if fictitious, prosperity. Details of Spanish history do not appertain to our discussion; given a realization of the fatal sweep of Spanish destiny, it is desirable here only to rehearse the probable causes other than those which might be called specifically colonial. The authorities make little question but that the destructive agencies were in the main of a political nature; if the government had been a fortunate one, or even an indifferent one, such deep destruction would scarcely have been entailed.[2] In so far as the people stood behind the kings in their ill actions and policies, results were, of course, inevitably the outcome of race-character and education. That the Spanish were predisposed to a religious and political autocracy we have already seen. When, therefore, it is asserted that the causes of decadence were mainly political, the meaning is that they emerged in the form of unthwarted measures, decrees, etc., to which subsequent damage may be aptly and logically referred. There were, however, other misfortunes of a political nature which appear to have been as nearly fortuitous as such things may be; which would scarcely have existed but for the fact that certain men, and not others, were the Spanish kings. These should be cleared from the path first of all; plainly they are not referable to the colonial career.

"ACCIDENTAL" CAUSES

Spain suffered from the Hapsburgs because of their hereditary peculiarities and degeneracy; genius in Charles V speedily ran down into the gloomy and self-immolating conscientiousness of Philip II; and the grotesque defectiveness of the impotent, lolling-tongued, pin-hunting Charles II was but a question of time and inbreeding

[1] Colmeiro, II, 186–188; cf. p. 440.

[2] "Hätte die nationalökonomische Einsicht der Regierung und der Landesvertreter nur einigermassen Schritt gehalten mit dem grossartigen Aufschwunge des Unternehmungsgeistes im Volke, so wäre der Verfall Spaniens um Jahrhunderte verschoben, wenn nicht unmöglich gemacht worden." Haebler, Wirt. Bl., p. 35.

from the insane Juana, mother of the first Charles. The morbid mind of Philip II was at the bottom of many positive regulations of a harmful nature, and the progressive imbecility of his successors threw a baneful influence into the hands of unworthy panders and dependents. The fact, again, that Charles V became Roman Emperor, and that he and Philip II were drawn or tempted into foreign wars of a costly nature simply because they were the descendants of certain ancestors, was, in a certain sense, a matter of chance; but it was responsible in large measure for the economic downfall of Spain. Taxation for Peninsular and American projects could never otherwise have been so ruinously high; the loyalty to King and Church would not have been so extravagantly drawn upon. The disastrous wars in the Low Countries might have been avoided if Charles had not been a Hollander and Philip a monomaniac upon the subject of his divine mission.[1] The personal character of the latter, in particular, furnished a specific cause for governmental aberrations during a crucial period. Conscientious to a degree, he was slow, distrustful, secretive; modest and laborious, he was so conscious of divine inspiration as to become rigid and unadaptable in methods. Early and late he toiled at his desk; matters of the smallest importance were exhaustively discussed with uninspired spirits who could endure and thrive upon such a deadly routine. Men of parts and initiative were shut out from control of affairs, and all free play of intelligence and intuition was paralyzed. Questions of broad principle were excluded by a mass of sordid minutiæ. Delay was inevitable under such a system of grinding, dragging toil; ambassadors fretted and fumed and lost opportunities, for instructions were delayed, between the deliberations of Philip and the inadequacy of means of communication, for weeks and months. Jealous of his divine prerogatives, Philip hoped to make of a man like Farnese a mere machine; "cold half-confidence and semi-veiled distrust were given in grudging return for slavish obedience to the orders of an anchorite a thousand miles away." The Duke of Medina Sidonia protested his unfitness for the command of the great Armada, but Philip insisted; having in mind the very fact of the duke's incompetence and self-distrust, he "doubtless hoped to command the Armada from his cell in

---

[1] Hume, pp. vi–vii, 194–196, 299–302, 306–307, 317; for the strains incident upon Philip II's establishment of claims to the throne of Portugal, see id., pp. 171, 250–254, 279–285.

the Escorial."[1] For his own purposes likewise, Philip fomented jealousy and distrust among his secretaries. Yet "the nation gave him credit for all his laborious good intentions in its behalf, and loved him accordingly ; but it credited him with a wisdom he did not possess. No country in the world has ever been so completely ruined as Spain was by the avoidable faults and follies of its governors."[2]

Before leaving what might be termed the accidental causes of Spain's decline, mention should likewise be made of the pure bad luck which attended her upon her downward path, as it accompanied and dragged down Portugal in hers. Pestilence, floods, hurricanes, earthquakes, and other calamities well-nigh impossible to foresee swept the empire with all the thoroughness and diabolical timeliness of mischance when the tide of men's affairs is no longer at flood.[3]

POLITICAL CAUSES FOR DECLINE

Here are grave causes for a nation's decline ; but they are only a beginning. It will be recalled that the Spanish people had exalted the ever more centralized power of the king to the position of a fetich, and this is in itself a sufficient explanation of their non-resistance to many a wild and vicious decree. In the royal measures now to be recounted, the status of popular feeling must bear its share of responsibility, for those who in other countries and under other conditions might have restrained disastrous policies, in Spain lent them rather support. Ignorance and superstition led the people to refer the rolling up of their calamities rather to God than to themselves, and in truly primitive fashion to seek a reconciliation through propitiation rather than relief as the result of rational analysis and action logically based upon it.[4]

---

[1] Hume, pp. 189, 180.

[2] Hume, pp. 136–137 ; for the above general characterization of Philip, see pp. 119, 122, 134, 136 ff., 169–170, 180, 189–196; Haebler, Wirt. Bl., pp. 15–16; Blok, III, 449–450. For a striking characterization of Philip, see the play "El Haz de Leña," by Nuñez de Arce; the introduction in Schevill's edition is important.

[3] Hume, pp. 306–307.

[4] Haebler, Wirt. Bl., p. 17 ; Martins, Civ. Iber., p. 263. "It is the fatal delusion that liberty and national welfare depend solely upon good government, instead of good government depending upon united and coöperative individual exertion, that has brought the Spanish nation to its present state of deplorable impotence." Foreman, p. 219.

The most disastrous enterprises of the kings, taking origin in religious prepossessions, were the insistence upon a single faith at home and the attempt to enforce conformity abroad; the oppression and expulsion of the Jews, Moriscos, and foreigners from Spain; and the religious wars in other parts of Europe. The general causes leading to the banishment of the Moriscos have been dwelt upon before; here it is necessary only to recall the fact that beneath the religious hatred lay motives of a more material nature, — jealousy, covetousness, irritation at habits of industry and frugality; fear, fictitious or real, of political plots, — motives whose very character witnesses to the solid economic virtues and energy of the subject race. The case of the Jews was similar. The whole procedure reduced itself, industrially speaking, to skimming off the cream of the population; it was, indeed, even more serious than this. For the state was further relatively weakened by the strengthening of such national rivals as received these exiles with their specialized dexterities and handicrafts. The expulsion of Moriscos and Jews from Spain ranks with the persecution of the Huguenots in France as a grand, even if inevitable, political blunder. Together with this goes also the oppression of the Low Countries, and the consequent emigration, largely to England, of their skilled artisans.[1] And as for the religious wars in which Spain undertook to champion Catholicism, they form a whole section of European history and require no detailing. Those which bear most closely upon colonial affairs, and which were in many respects the most disastrous, were the attempted reduction of the Low Countries and the ambitious enterprises directed against England.[2] And to the count of disasters arising out of religious conflicts must be presently reckoned the reverses in America and elsewhere, referable in good part to the exasperation of Protestant nations at the arrogant pretensions of the Spaniards, and at their cruel bigotry, — a quality doubly happy in its results in that it served God by burning or dismembering alive His human enemies, while at the same time it destroyed for His adherents a brood of hateful competitors.

[1] Colmeiro, II, chap. lv; Haebler, Wirt. Bl., p. 164; Hume, pp. 16–18, 152–155, 210–213; Moses, p. 15; Clarke, pp. 359–360. See pp. 81–82, above.

[2] Hume, pp. 130–131, 184, 206–208, 218–219, 232–243, 267–268; cf. pp. 256, 370, below.

Treatment of Foreigners

Relations with foreign merchants were marked by less cruelty, but were scarcely more rational. Owing to the character of their past, the Spanish were as little fitted by training as by nature for the discharge of the more specialized economic functions. There was little or no native business talent, and the hidalgos, with their strong military and other biases, despised and hated it in others; for the treatment of the foreign merchants the sovereigns were assuredly not solely to blame. Ferdinand and Isabella encouraged the presence in Spain of German, French, and Italian colonies; to propositions of exclusion presented by the Cortes, Ferdinand averred that Spain could not do without the foreigners. For it was they who supplied the capital and the apparatus of production and exchange, and farmed the revenues; and they were the more indispensable after the expulsion of the Jews. Indeed, as time went on, they became the real support of the empire, and after the death of Philip II their activities were absolutely essential to the maintenance of the public credit.[1] But it is little surprising that the Spanish looked with increasing distrust and exasperation upon the rich monopolies enjoyed by the foreign capitalists, notably the German Fugger, and that repeated attempts were made to force them to surrender or to disgorge. These attempts met with little success in view of the royal necessities and policy, but they did drive the foreigners to an ever-increasing haste and unscrupulousness in the piling-up of profits. The whole situation made for the progressive decline of what economic strength Spain had, and the general attitude toward producers and exchangers made of the latter a group of rapacious and predatory aliens where they might have become active factors in a sturdy economic life. The fact that all this was inevitable in the setting of the time excludes the colonial career as a specific cause.

Treatment of Jews and Moriscos

Some writers have asserted the causal relation between the treatment of foreigners, and especially the expulsion of Jews and Moriscos, and the subsequent numerical decline in the Spanish

[1] Colmeiro, II, 208–212, 235–236, 258–259, 567–568; Haebler, Wirt. Bl., pp. 51, 165–171; Hume, p. 87. On the dependence of Spain upon foreigners for a labor force and for transport facilities, see Haebler, Wirt. Bl., pp. 81, 83–84; Hume, p. 285.

population. Emigration to the Indies has likewise been taken to explain this disaster. The inefficiency of the latter factor as a cause will be shown presently;[1] and as for the former, it should at least be set in a more precise relation to that which it is supposed to explain. The number of Moriscos expelled is variously estimated from 300,000 to 1,000,000; Lea, who has made the subject a matter of exhaustive research, decides that 500,000 is not far from the truth. The number of Jews expelled is reckoned as low as 200,000, but more generally at between 400,000 and 800,000.[2] This represents unquestionably a heavy quantitative loss in material strength, but it does not at all sufficiently explain the subsequent decline. Since Darwin's time, and before, there has been no doubt as to the possibility of the rapid increase of any species up to the limits assigned by its life conditions. Of a consequence it is to these latter that the careful observer is bound to look for an explanation of Spanish depopulation. History is full of cases where the ravages of wars, plagues, and other calamities have been succeeded by a national fecundity under freer conditions which speedily filled all gaps in the ranks. He would miss the full significance of the expulsion in question, however, who failed to note that men make, to a large degree, their own life conditions, and that it was precisely that part of the population which represented the most energetic and successful assault upon natural conditions which was driven from the scene. That is to say, while the quantitative injury to population consequent upon the expulsion was almost negligible, the qualitative injury was no less than ruinous.[3] And the same line of argument may apply with equal force to the withdrawal from the propagation of the race, through religious celibacy, through the ambition to be an hidalgo, or even through army service, of the most promising of the Spanish youth.[4] The quality

---

[1] P. 210, below.

[2] Colmeiro, II, 62; Hume, p. 213; Lea, Moriscos, pp. 359 ff.; Inquis., I, 84 ff., 131 ff., 142; III, 231 ff., 317 ff., 388 ff.; Haebler, Wirt. Bl., p. 153; Moses, p. 15.

[3] To gain a clearer conception of what the merely quantitative loss meant to Spain, her 500,000 exiles might represent to us a loss of 4,500,000 to 5,000,000 in a population of 80,000,000. But since the United States are so largely industrial, these figures would have to be considerably increased in order correctly to parallel the qualitative loss suffered by Spain. Add now the results of persecutions, insecurity of vocation and trade, etc., and the whole foots up to an appalling calamity. The practice of infanticide attained considerable development at this time.

[4] Schallmayer, pp. 111 ff., 223 ff.; Darwin, Desc. of Man, p. 144; Galton, pp. 356 ff. Still, sacerdotal celibacy was "more an ideal than a fact." Bourne, Sp. in Amer.,

of the population declined, its vigor was sapped, and the result could not fail presently to appear in a diminution of numbers. Under Philip III the number of marriages is said to have decreased almost one-half.[1] The degree of depopulation is a matter of dispute; Haebler gives the total population of the Peninsula in 1723 as 5,777,900, — about three million below the figures for 1594, and one million below those of 1541.[2]

LEGISLATION AND REGULATION

It has been stated that the woes of Spain were due prevailingly to bad government, supported or at least unchecked by public opinion. The expulsion of the Jews and Moriscos was merely the climax of a course of class-legislation, and the latter was by no means confined to the period in which class meant race. It is now in place, with no further specific reference to Jew and Morisco, to pass in review, as hastily as consideration for clearness will permit, the main types of legislation to which Spain's calamities were due. It is to be noted, first of all, that the government, partially in consequence of its sense of divine guidance and universal responsibility, was, through all the earlier colonial period, possessed of a very monomania for regulation; regulation not alone on the grand scale, but also upon one of pitiful and incredible pettiness, whose sordid and fatuous detail the specialist alone is called upon to follow. In general, however, regulatory measures touching the industrial organization turned upon theory derived from mediæval sources; or represented contradictory experiments in time of trouble, pursued with no adequate idea of economic laws; or took their origin in an ever more insatiable hunger for revenue. Out of her past Spain retained contempt for agriculture, industry, and trade, especially upon the small scale; while, therefore, such vital improvements as those of irrigation, communication, and transportation were neglected, the government spent its efforts in making detailed and rigid rules for the movement and sale of goods, with the result

p. 307. For a general treatment of the subject, see Lea, Sacerdotal Celibacy, especially chaps. xix, xxi, and pp. 392–393.

[1] For a discussion of depopulation in Spain, together with proposed remedies, see Colmeiro, II, chaps. lv, lvi, pp. 12 ff., 43 ff., 156 ff.; this author is corrected to some extent by Haebler, Wirt. Bl., pp. 146–157. See also Hume, pp. 212 ff., 297; Martins, Civ. Iber., pp. 261–262; Blok, III, 131 ff.

[2] Wirt. Bl., p. 158. For summaries of the causes of this decline, see id., pp. 153–154; Colmeiro, II, 15–17; Martins, Civ. Iber., p. 261.

of crushing free competition; for trade was thus subjected to a system of costly and harassing examination. In contrast with the modern system, the object was the protection of the consumer;[1] and it was pursued well-nigh as vigorously as the safeguarding of the producer has been in the United States. Preference was accorded to the gild system, under close scrutiny; frauds, actual and imaginary, were guarded against; prices were regulated, exportation prohibited. All this left no time to keep the currency sound, or even to suppress or buy off the pirates of the Mediterranean; and the immediate result, as far as the machinery of government was concerned, was an endlessly complicated bureaucracy.[2] The harassment of this detailed regulation, whose repetition witnesses to the resistance and evasion which it met, fell almost wholly upon the useful classes; it fostered rather than harmed the beggar and the priest.[3]

When, now, such ill-advised measures had produced a paralysis of economic life, the inexperienced government of an ignorant and passive people was driven to make changes whose appropriateness could be but a matter of chance.[4] All sorts of political nostrums in the hands of unpractical theorists or charlatans (*arbitristas*) were applied; unprincipled favorites swayed the royal mind. The accumulation of church-property went on apace; law-suits, to retain what little they had, ruined the poor, while sumptuary laws were ineffective in restraining extravagance. Policies were adopted and reversed with the utmost inconsequence.[5]

But it is when revenue considerations are added to our category that the worst economic conditions come to light. Multiform and exacting taxation, both at the boundaries and within, ground down the productive part of the community. Monopolies; alteration of the coinage; repudiation of debts, and other forms of governmental

---

[1] Owing, no doubt, to the preponderance of the upper middle class in the Cortes. See p. 195, below.

[2] Colmeiro, II, 167–178 (the *Mesta*), 180–183, 235, 237–239, 241, 244, 267–272, 296, 472–474, 487 ff., 498, 583, 585 ff. (*arbitristas*); Hume, pp. vi–vii, 85–86, 197–198, 244, 265; Clarke, pp. 356–357; Haebler, Wirt. Bl., pp. 62–63.   [3] See p. 82, above.

[4] " The afflictions of the Spanish monarchy went on increasing, toward the end of the sixteenth century, without the public men of the government being able to conjecture why, despite the treasures of the Indies, the realm was so poor. . . . Every one clamored for the remedy and no one came to the rescue with rational counsel." Colmeiro, II, 504.

[5] Colmeiro, II, 190, 197 ff., 252–253, 259–260; Haebler, Wirt. Bl., pp. 17–19, 35–36, 40–43; Hume, pp. 86–87, 197–198; Martins, Civ. Iber., pp. 261–263.

dishonesty ; forced loans ; confiscations at slight provocation ; the reduction of interest rates ; the indiscriminate farming of the revenues, inducing deep corruption, — these were some of the forms of the financial policy. Unpaid soldiers who plundered right and left, and an army and navy supplied with deteriorated and useless stores, were some of the visible signs of bankruptcy and corruption. For while the revenues were unreasonably large, that part of them which was left for the government, after they had passed through many unscrupulous hands, was rarely sufficient to meet immediate needs.[1]

Attempted Reform

Two centuries of this kind of thing were enough to have ruined a prosperity more firmly rooted than that of Spain. When, therefore, in the eighteenth century, under Philip V and especially under Charles III, sincere and intelligent efforts were made to reverse an inveterate policy and to neutralize its effects, it was already too late to mend. "The status of the monarchy at the beginning of the eighteenth century was such that one political writer compared Spain to a building which was afire in many parts at the same time, so that it was necessary to rush to the aid of them all."[2] Philip V (1700–1746) attacked with vigor most of the evils detailed above ; not always wisely, but with good intent. He owed much to his French ministers — indeed, Spain seems to have been not infrequently rescued from herself by the suspected foreigner. And even at this late day the nation rallied with unexpected patriotism and strength. Ferdinand VI (1746–1759) carried the reforms still farther ; and the ministries of Ensenada (1743–1754) and of Aranda (1766–1773), the latter under the enlightened Charles III, represented a greater return to prosperity than could reasonably have been expected. At this period came the expulsion of the Jesuits. But the death of Charles III (1788), "the only good, great and patriotic king that Providence had vouchsafed to Spain in modern times,"[3] allowed the scepter to fall once more into incompetent hands, directed by contemptible favorites. Then

[1] Haebler, Wirt. Bl., pp. 14, 135–138; Colmeiro, II, 26, 542; Hume, pp. 181 ff., 193–196, 208–210, 214–215, 226–227, 257 ff., 285.

[2] Colmeiro, II, 215; cf. Hume, p. 222.

[3] Hume, p. 411. Aranda was at first minister of Charles IV (1792), but was speedily removed.

comes the age of Napoleon, with all the misfortune it brought to Spain, to be followed by the general prostration of the nineteenth century, and the final disappearance of the " Empire " at its end.[1]

TAXATION

Inasmuch as the administrative evils detailed were grouped so consistently about over-taxation, and because the greed for revenue fell upon the colonies as upon victims devoted, it is fitting to enter somewhat more fully upon the system of taxation before taking up the more general economic and social factors of Spanish decline. One relation stands out in the raising of revenue : taxation varied directly, not with the development of the colonial empire, but with the extent and frequency of the foreign wars which resulted largely from the policies enumerated. Ferdinand and Isabella, although their intentions were of the best, found it necessary to resort to extraordinary taxation to carry through the conquest of Granada ; and their successors, plunged into ever greater expenditures of the same kind, were never able to carry out the last wish of Isabella with regard to the repeal of these taxes (*juros*). No successful attempt at reduction came under the Hapsburgs ; in contrast to the later impositions, those of the Catholic Sovereigns seem light and reasonable.[2] Charles V became more and more deeply entangled in foreign wars, and was obliged, against his will, to raise the means to prosecute them. And yet, in his time, owing to the threefold rise in prices, with a corresponding fall in the value of money, the tax-payer really contributed lesser values than at the opening of the century. Despite, however, the larger sums at his disposal, Charles was not infrequently unable to follow up an advantage, or even to pay his troops, and when he passed over the rule to Philip he transferred with it a considerable increase in the public debt. No doubt this was due in some considerable degree to the dishonesty of the collectors, who absorbed at times almost a half of the contributions.[3] But it was to Philip II and his successors that Spain owed the relentless draining of her resources before which her recuperative powers failed. Philip's extraordinary demands for the pursuit of the several phases of his divine mission

[1] Colmeiro, II, 87–109, 218–225; Hume, pp. 327–328, 351, 356, 381–382, 388–391, 399 ff.

[2] Colmeiro, II, 539–540, 565, 578–579; Haebler, Wirt. Bl., p. 108.

[3] Haebler, Wirt. Bl., pp. 64–65, 109, 117–118, 163; Colmeiro, II, 546 ff., 556, 558.

were combined with the most reckless system of collection — a constant farming out of future revenue at ruinous rates to foreign capitalists — and a feebleness of conscience strongly contrasting with its morbid strength as exhibited elsewhere in his life. Colossal sums were sunk in religious wars, to say nothing of uncounted ducats that were swept away by misfortunes frequently recurring and not to be forecasted. The king at one and the same time depended upon Genoese bankers, and frightened them into unscrupulousness and rapacity by arbitrary and oppressive measures. His finances grew steadily more hopeless, until, as a virtual pauper, — had he not been a king, — he left behind him a debt of a hundred million ducats.[1] And the favorites who ruled Spain under the later degenerate Hapsburgs pursued toward the same end of ruin, but sordidly and with rascality, the policy dictated to Philip by a certain morbid and ignorant, but high-minded, narrowness and bigotry.

The most obvious source of revenue was, naturally, the Cortes ; and the *servicio*, the subsidy demanded at each of its sessions, was paid with astonishing submission. At most the king had to listen first to a series of petitions and complaints. The servicio ran regularly, under Philip II, into millions of dollars.[2] Aside from this triennial tax however, the government leaned directly and constantly upon the people. The most hateful of the food-taxes was the *millones*, introduced in embryo by Philip II (1590) in consequence of the Armada disaster ; an excise which was increased and developed, and which for over two hundred years weighed (at length to the extent of one-eighth of the value) on wine, vinegar, meat, and oil, the principal food of the people. Debasement of the coinage also fell with severity upon the cost of living.[3] A further extravagant method of raising revenue was through the *juros* whose suppression Isabella had wished : "The Crown raised a loan, and assigned the product of certain estates or taxes in payment of interest, often at the rate of ten per cent." Naturally, the foreign capitalists were most likely to profit by this. And there were sold besides such favors as the legitimization of illegitimate children, titles, newly made positions in councils, and the like — anything that would add to income.[4]

[1] Haebler, Wirt. Bl., pp. 123–130, 131 ff., 134.

[2] Colmeiro, II, 541 ff., 583 ; Haebler, Wirt. Bl., p. 111 ; Hume, pp. 26–27.

[3] Colmeiro, II, 233, 542 ff. ; Haebler, Wirt. Bl., pp. 129–130 ; Hume, pp. 179, 201 ff., 271–272.

[4] Hume, p. 27 ; Colmeiro, II, 579–580 ; Haebler, Wirt. Bl., pp. 115–116.

One of the heaviest and most ill advised of the taxes was incident upon trade, and through it, of course, upon production : the *alcabala*, which became no less than a tax of ten per cent upon all exchanges of commodities, *ad valorem*, and usually farmed. Such a tax needs no comment.[1] In addition, agriculture was severely taxed because Philip thought it could bear it ; the farmer's very plow and hoe were not safe in his own hands.[2] The internal and external customs-dues rendered legitimate commercial profit extremely hazardous and smuggling very profitable ; applied to the Netherlands they infuriated a merchant-people and incited to war.[3] And by various moves, which threatened an indefinite postponement of payment or even a repudiation of the state's debts, the foreign merchants resident in Spain were rendered insecure, and so the more ready to impose upon an ignorant people. Even ecclesiastical taxation (*subsidio*) was not totally excluded.[4] Between the year of his accession and 1573 Philip had well-nigh doubled the state-income.[5]

It is plain that the country was being systematically and cynically bled of its resources of all varieties. This process explains a very large part of the decline of national vigor in the sixteenth and seventeenth centuries. The time of Philip III brought peace, and the age of the Bourbons real efforts toward reform, but the strain had been too prolonged and too pitiless ; resiliency was gone. "Finally," says Colmeiro, "the deplorable state of our treasury during the whole of the domination of the house of Austria, and its extraordinary obligations, owing to wars, in the eighteenth century . . . had accumulated deficit upon deficit until the Spanish nation was oppressed with the weight of a debt of 13,250,207,506 reals."[6] Expenditures constantly outran income, however unreasonably the latter might be increased. The extravagance of the palace under Charles II (1665–1700) and Philip V (1700–1746) formed a marked contrast to the parsimony of Philip II.[7]

[1] Haebler, Wirt. Bl., pp. 73 ff., 110–111, 118–122 ; Blok, III, 83 ff. ; Hume, pp. 135, 157–159, 198–200, 245–246. "Bread paid three times over, as corn, as meal, and as manufactured." Clarke, I, 356.

[2] Haebler, Wirt. Bl., pp. 37, 39–40 ; Blok, III, 132 ff.

[3] Hume, pp. 159–160 ; cf. pp. 155, 227–228, 271 ; Haebler, Wirt. Bl., pp. 54–55, 62–63, 77–81 ; Colmeiro, II, 261–262.   [4] Haebler, Wirt. Bl., pp. 70–72 ; Hume, p. 27.

[5] Haebler, Wirt. Bl., p. 122 ; Blok, III, 155 ff. ; for a general sketch of Philip's exploits in tax-laying, see Haebler, id., pp. 118 ff.

[6] Colmeiro, II, 584 ; cf. pp. 544–545, 565, 570, 575–576 ; Haebler, Wirt. Bl., pp. 87–88, 134–135, 138–143.   [7] Cf. Hume, pp. 286–287, 382.

Economic and Social Causes for Decline

In the rehearsal of what have been called in a broad sense the political factors leading to national impoverishment, a sufficiently threatening set of conditions has been disclosed. In order, however, to get the effects of Spain's colonial career into a proper perspective, it is necessary still to consider several important factors which might be called economic and social, and which represent popular persuasion and habits of thought and of action rather than a definite state-policy. The national economic character of the Spaniards was such as in any case to have rendered their supremacy but short-lived in an era characterized by the steady gain of the industrial and commercial type over the military.[1] The attitude of regarding the industrial organization as a contemptible appendage upon the social structure persisted during the centuries that succeeded the Discoveries period, and it placed industry and commerce at a disadvantage only partially portrayed in the actual statutes and their implications. Mediæval ideas, together with prejudices against the Moors, and the inevitable teachings of their own militarism conspired to create and nourish this disesteem of the gainful occupations (*oficios viles y baxos*). The Spaniards were not alone among the nations in this view, but being so largely hidalgos, or aspirants to that station, they naturally formed an extreme and unadaptable case. The law made the matter worse, because it reflected this attitude, and custom and precedent backed the law up strongly. The infamy of labor might even pass on to one's family, or carry with it exclusion from office. This political ignominy of toil is one of the reasons why the interests of industry and commerce were never adequately represented in the Cortes.[2] It also explains the tendency of the whole population toward display and luxury, for these were the badges, as the example of the upper classes proved, of a respectability unsullied by usefulness.[3] And the curse of vagabondage itself, though referable in part to love of adventure, was really the result of such contempt for and discouragement of industry. "The *caballero*, before whom peace closed the path of glory and fortune, enlisted in the crusading armies, or

---

[1] Cf. Martins, Civ. Iber., pp. 255–256.

[2] Colmeiro, II, 26–27; Haebler, Wirt. Bl., p. 61; Hume, p. 136.

[3] Colmeiro, II, 26; Leroy-Beaulieu, I, 37; for the sumptuary legislation and its causes, see Colmeiro, II, 524–537; Hume, p. 170.

placed himself in the service of a foreign prince at whose side he could go on in the profession of arms ; and the villein, accustomed to live and thrive on the spoils of the enemy, suffered the yoke of labor with impatience. Even though he had formed the resolution to stay at home and gain by his industry the support of his family, he was prevented by conditions : now by the lack of land from becoming a cultivator ; now by the gilds and their ordinances if he set out to make himself an artisan ; and again by the shortage of his capital if he wished to follow the example of the merchant. And, finally, the laws which left liberty and property all but unprotected, the exclusive and monopolistic privileges, the royalties and dues, the alterations of the coinage, the insecurity of the roads, the confusion of the taxes, and the whole medley of economic errors characteristic of that period, condemned him to enforced idleness." Thus mendicancy became worse and worse during the sixteenth, seventeenth, and eighteenth centuries.[1]

Even the attempts to favor the industrial vocations resulted in no progress ; for they started out from the mediæval prepossessions of a people that knew nothing of industrial progress and could not, economically speaking, think rationally. So that while other European nations, through the forced and recurring inconsistencies of their own practice, made heavy inroads into whatever obsolete theories they professed, — and were at last obliged to make the theories square with the objective facts, — Spain long clung to traditional doctrines with the virtuous consistency of inexperience.[2] Among the professions social selection favored types whose dominance in the world was already a thing of the past, and whose association could not form a national structure fit long to compete under the new conditions imposed upon the strife of nations. Spain "put her money on the wrong horse" when she favored over the merchant the soldier or priest. Naturally, as time went on and the young refused to disgrace themselves with toil, the

[1] Colmeiro, II, 21.

[2] Louis XIV said of Spain : "It is sufficient in Spain that an abuse be old-established for it to be scrupulously maintained without any care being taken to consider whether a thing which perhaps may have been good in the past is bad for the present." Hume, p. 320. In 1678 (treaty of Nimeguen), when Spain was utterly bankrupt and humiliated, "the overwhelming grandeur and wealth of its own monarch continued to be an article of national faith ; and his clemency in letting his enemies off so easily, a matter for admiring congratulation upon his magnanimity." Id., p. 294. See also Colmeiro, II, 243, 246–248 (gild system), 139 (system of inheritance, etc.).

proportion of political hangers-on and sycophants, of priests or commoner mendicants, increased. Corruption and the undermining of moral standards gained headway year by year. That the colonial enterprises were responsible for all this can therefore be denied; it would have been in all but degree the same, had America never been discovered.

Religious Causes for Decline

Submissiveness to the exactions of the kings has several times been noted as a Spanish trait; and the importance assigned to the minister of the faith by a loyal, ignorant, and superstitious people invited economic and social consequences of an extreme type. So many landholders had been led, especially in the frequent times of stress, epidemic, or of expectation of the end of the world, to insure themselves for the life to come, that by 1600 a large portion of the best land in Spain had come into the possession of the Church; and once there it became inalienable. The phenomena, then, of the *latifundia* were not long delayed in their appearance, for the dispossessed migrated to the towns and too often became sturdy ruffians therein. " Ecclesiastical amortization absorbed the larger and better part of the landed property, and against this rock all the forces of agriculture were shipwrecked. The clergy afforded liberal succor to the poor; but its blind and indiscreet charity often fomented sloth and its unproductive monopoly of the land rendered labor sterile." [1] Not only that: "in reality there were many who took the habit and entered religious institutions, fleeing from the labors and miseries of the world in order to enjoy the sweetness of idleness; and not because they were led to this life through devotion, penitence, or the love of a life of contemplation. These are the words of the Council of Castile in 1619." [2]

As time went on this double process of robbing industry of the best lands and the land of its complement of workers proceeded apace, being rather strengthened and justified than weakened by later developments: it was not until a much later time that Church and State were shorn to any considerable degree of their land-monopoly.[3] Again, careers for the ambitious seemed to become

[1] Colmeiro, II, 160; cf. pp. 28 ff., 131–133, 139, 146–148; Haebler, Wirt. Bl., p. 153. The ecclesiastical rights even struck at the royal power. Colmeiro, II, 157–158.

[2] Colmeiro, II, 151.

[3] Colmeiro, II, 159 (Philip IV); cf. pp. 131–133, 162–163; see the account of the report in 1618 of the Council of Castile, in Hume (pp. 221–222).

less and less attainable except through the Church. "In justice," says Colmeiro,[1] "we ought to condone the inclination of the Spaniard of the seventeenth and eighteenth centuries to take refuge in the religious establishments. Those professions which held out hopes of fortune were few. The toga and the uniform appealed very aptly to the vanity and presumption of the *caballeros* and *hidalgos*, while agriculture, the mechanic arts, and commerce were suitable only to an humble station, inasmuch as they were regarded as lowly occupations. The Church was a neutral field, where noble and plebeian mingled and became indistinguishable. All, ascetic as well as worldly, proud and modest, lazy and diligent, wise and ignorant, found in the Church a harbor of refuge from the storms of the age, without thereby renouncing, however, the opportunity of embarcation upon the high sea of the Court, and upon functions and offices of greater honor and authority, when occasion, acceptable or unavoidable, should have cast them into the tumult of affairs. Spanish history is full of cardinals who became ministers, of prelate-ambassadors, or bishop-presidents of Castile. It offers us the example even of a mere priest like Pedro de la Gasca, named pacificator and governor of Peru; and of certain good and simple ecclesiastics sent out to check the insolence of the captains, administer justice, and bring order and accord into various parts of the Indies."

The religious loyalty of the Spaniards, strong as it was, did not remain proof against the very evident evils of this exaltation of the power of the Church; in 1619 the Council of Castile proposed that licenses should be necessary for new religious foundations, and that a minimum age limit should be set for those entering the religious life.[2] But it was not until the eighteenth century that the great estates were broken up and sold under full property rights. And as for the numbers of the religious, an estimate of Dávila, reported by other authorities to be moderate, assigned to Spain (about 1623) 9000 convents and 100,000 persons of ecclesiastical status — 30,000 of the secular and 70,000 of the regular clergy. In 1768 the census showed 148,815 curates, monks, nuns, etc., and in 1787, although certain semi-connected persons were not counted, there still remained 138,761. In 1797 the number had decreased by 15,000.[3] To gain a correct impression of the

[1] II, 154–155; cf. Haebler, Wirt. Bl., p. 154. [2] Colmeiro, II, 150; Hume, p. 222.
[3] Colmeiro, II, 149; cf. II, 52. This author was not able to find the reported estimate of Dávila, and regards the above numbers as excessive. Upon scanning the

strain brought upon the nation by these establishments, it must be
realized not only that most of the members of the orders were
withdrawn from any profitable service to society, but that it was
really the pick of the population that was thus cut out from social
service, and in theory from the propagation of the race. They had
to be supported by an already over-burdened laboring-class, yet
they consistently interfered with and injured the useful occupations.
When the Inquisition was at its climax of power and ferocity, they
systematically forced from his place in the society any one who
possessed activity and independence of mind enough to fall into
religious or political heresy.[1]

Nor must the interruption or stoppage and the consequent
demoralization of labor, caused by the over-development of religious exercises, fail of mention; it is even to this day a distinct
hindrance to the growth of industry in Spain. Festivals and holidays in honor of this or that saint took up a large fraction of the
working days of the year; Campomanes counted ninety-three
fiestas in the year, and Colmeiro,[2] reckoning 8,000,000 laborers at
a minimum wage of two reals a day, foots up the annual loss at
1,488,000,000 reals. The almost 800,000,000 days' labor sacrificed per annum, with the resulting irregularity in habits, and the
acquired taste for amusement, are of course far more striking and
serious than any loss calculable in money. Again, the hours of
labor were always short, and tended to become shorter; in Aragon,
in 1640, the working hours were five per day, and what was done
was scanty, costly, and poor.[3]

It is indeed hard to see where the workers of this society were,
or to what economic support it owed the deferring of its decline.
For while the lower classes starved rather than work, the upper
had to be restrained from a senseless luxury by repeated sumptuary
laws. It is not surprising, under these conditions, that a great
burst of immorality in nobles, clergy, and common people followed

---

Teatro the present writer found no such specific estimate, but counted up about
2000 convents and 40,000 *religiosos* alone. Figures for the nunneries, hospitals, etc.,
were incomplete, but it is not difficult to believe that the estimate given in the text
needs comparatively little discount, especially when it is compared with Colmeiro's
figures for the eighteenth century. Dávila says (p. 308) that in all the parishes, convents, hospitals, etc., which he has named, no fewer than a million masses are said
each year. The tone and matter of the *Teatro* are certainly evidence of the strength
in numbers and in social importance of the clergy.

[1] Hume, p. 304; cf. Galton, pp. 357–359; see p. 188, above.
[2] II, 53–54.   [3] Colmeiro, II, 23.

upon economic decline : petty vanity, venality, all kinds of corruption, looseness of sexual relations, and other vices from which the nation had formerly been relatively free, invaded all walks of life.[1]

The Colonial Career as a Cause for Decline

No considerable part of the factors that made for decline, and which have now been recounted, can be charged to the colonial career. They lay in the constitution of the race, in the results of mediæval and later European systems and complications, theories, and institutions ; they were sufficient to have ruined Spain even though America had never been discovered. The effect upon them of the colonial enterprises was, at the most, contributary ; not creative, determinative, or even prominent. They were there already. What the colonial experiences did was to evoke, as a special case, a pronounced and striking exhibition of what had come to be the national way of doing things ; and if it stimulated fateful impulses and policies not elsewhere so active, it is in this sense only that it may be considered to have hastened an evil destiny. For example, the possession of the colonial empire drew Spain into hostilities whose cost had to be covered by an added increase of taxation ; but this was largely because the external possessions afforded Spain a stage in plain sight and directly in the path of her most enterprising rivals, upon which her hateful and obstructive policy could be displayed. Possibly the enlarged sphere of Philip II's accountability to God may have intensified his effort to live up to his destiny.   Such effects were, however, relatively insignificant ; and with reference to the taxation, to which the authorities refer so large a part of Spain's exhaustion, it will presently be seen that the metropolis was far from being required to expend money on America ; the New World was rather an abused source of income.

It is reasonable to believe that the effect of the Discoveries was to enhance the characteristic feeling for King and Church, bearing witness as they did to the world-power of both ; and both were no doubt stimulated to an extravagancy of self-confidence and presumption for the very reason that they saw themselves the holders of such universally envied advantages.[2] We of the present day can scarcely call before the imagination a semblance of the excitement

[1] Colmeiro, II, 524 ff. ; Hume, pp. 169–170, 221 ff.
[2] Cf. Roscher, Sp. Col. Sys., p. 42 ; Leroy-Beaulieu, I, 35–36.

and elation of the period under review;[1] comparison may be made perhaps with the emotions excited here and there by the gold discoveries in the Transvaal and Alaska, or, farther back, in California and Australia The pretentious titles assumed by the king of Portugal after the attainment of India[2] reflect an exalted frame of mind, and the pious ecstasies of an Azurara betray excitement before the prospect of extended religious dominion. Perhaps the additional prestige thus lent the Spanish rulers rendered them less assailable for criticism in their series of unfortunate measures. In fact, it was the very refusal of Spain to adapt herself to the conditions of a new destiny which made the colonial career so disastrous. She was not alone in mistaking her way in an uncharted course, but she occupied a bad and almost unique eminence in that she seemed to learn nothing by experience. Conditions were not studied with the idea of better coping with them. Other nations managed to dodge and shift ground and adapt, — profiting not infrequently by the mishaps undergone before their eyes by Spain, — but Spain pursued a course of rare and ruinous consistency.[3]

Taking up now the larger economic and social effects of the colonial career, which are here distinguished for the sake of clearness from the more purely political or administrative, the case becomes considerably less simple and evident. A larger share in Spanish decline seems referable to the relations with America ; and it is possible to appreciate the standpoint of those older Spanish observers of affairs who used to query whether the Indies had not been a curse, and not infrequently answered themselves in the affirmative.[4] For, first of all, the discoveries and conquests opened an illimitable range for the adventurous military and missionary spirit, thus promoting the diffusion over a wide and uncertain field of such forces as might have been rendered productive if closer confined. Beside the prospective treasures of the Indies, former wealth seemed of little account. The Spanish non-industrial type and ideal attained thus a new lease of life when the situation at home was already calling for their effacement. If the military and ecclesiastical professions in Spain were at the saturation-point

---

[1] Cf. Bourne, Sp. in Amer., pp. 190 ff.   [2] See p. 94, above.

[3] The unavailing efforts of the Netherlander Charles V to limit the application of mercantile doctrines are significant. Haebler, Wirt. Bl., pp. 11–14.

[4] Cf. Colmeiro, II, 421, 440–442 ; Haebler, Wirt. Bl., p. 30.

there was chance enough in the Indies; thus Cervantes and other contemporary writers represent the situation.[1] Of a consequence, as in the less-known case of Portugal,[2] the tendency to dependency and sycophancy was largely increased, and the steps of every man of importance were dogged by hangers-on hopeful of undeserved chances in life. The plain tendency toward corruption in public affairs was naturally increased; and the demoralization of the people under the régime of unreasonable luxury for some, incredible but unresisting poverty, devoid of all self-respect, for others, and indiscriminate charity for social parasites, was intensified. In short, the social shortcomings, natural or acquired, were enhanced all along the line by the entrance into Spanish life of the new factor of romance and hazard represented by the acquisition of America.[3]

THE MERCANTILE SYSTEM

Neglecting minor effects, which are either deducible from the rather extended treatment already accorded, or will appear in the ensuing narrative, there yet remains one prominent factor in Spain's decline to which, from Adam Smith down, a considerable degree of importance has been assigned, especially by economists. This is the effect of the mercantile system as adopted by Spain in her relations to her colonies. One of the stock illustrations of the fallacy of the seventeenth and eighteenth century views regarding the identity of money (coin) and wealth has been afforded by the fact that Spain, although the recipient of an uninterrupted golden stream from the New World, yet grew steadily poorer and more miserable, declined in population, and sunk from a position of preëminence to one of humiliation and degradation. It was partially to get this contention into a proper setting that the causes for the

---

[1] Roscher, Sp. Col. Sys., p. 3; Leroy-Beaulieu, I, 37. It is perhaps superfluous to point out, in this connection, the great importance for the study of colonial affairs of the impressions preserved in contemporary literature.

[2] See pp. 113 ff., above.

[3] Cf. Martins, Civ. Iber., pp. 255–256; Colmeiro, I, 253. "The highest ambition of the nation in its golden age was to be to Europe just what the nobility, the clergy and the army were to single nations. Consequently there was an enormous preponderance of personal service in the industrial organism, and much of this was purely for ostentation. Nowhere in the world were there so many nobles, so many officers, civil and military, so many lawyers and clerks, priests and monks, so many students and school-boys, with their servants. But as truly, nowhere in the world were there so many beggars and vagabonds." Roscher, Sp. Col. Sys., pp. 3–4.

decline of Spain have been so extensively recounted ; and now, admitting freely the disastrous nature of any such economic prepossession, the reader is in a position to draw his own conclusion as to its share in the whole process. Plainly, however harmful, it could have constituted only one factor among several scarcely less effective. Taking the matter up upon its own account, it is noteworthy, first of all, that Spain never developed the mercantile system *in extenso* ; never so far as did England, for example. She naturally followed her prototypes, the Italians and Portuguese, in their policies of monopoly and exclusion ; she regarded the colonies, in practice at least, as destined to subserve the necessities and desires of the metropolis. But the Spaniards were not enough of an industrial and merchant people to adopt unconsciously, or even as the result of rational reflection, any but the crudest and most obvious phases of the system.[1] The crudest dogma of the mercantilists was probably that which confounded the metallic species of wealth with the general term, and this view, largely because they had the bullion, and because they knew they were, on that account, envied and feared by the rest of Christendom, the Spaniards applied in an extreme.[2]

THE INFLOW OF BULLION

It has been shown how, in default of spices and like products, the whole attention of the Spaniards in the New World was turned predominantly, and at first almost exclusively, to the search for precious metals. Anticipating somewhat,[3] it is fair to say that between 1525 and 1825 a quantity of bullion was entered via Spain upon the markets of the world, which utterly dwarfed any former experience of the race. The contemporary and subsequent literature of Europe reflects the impression made upon the western world by this period, and in particular by its opening episodes. Inasmuch, now, as the circulation of commodities between Spain and

---

[1] Cf. Roscher, Sp. Col. Sys., p. 42 ; Leroy-Beaulieu, I, 26 ; Moses, pp. 300–301.

[2] See pp. 227 ff., below. " While heaven was exerting itself to rain gold and silver to slake the burning thirst of our forebears, the doctrine prevailed which regarded the precious metals as the sum of all the temporal riches of life, the blood of all peoples and nations, and the nerve of all the powers of the earth. The art of governing consisted in retaining the rivers of gold and silver which flowed from the Indies, and in hoarding up their abundance in Spain without spilling a drop for the benefit of foreigners." Colmeiro, II, 437–438. For a comparison of the " metal-policies " of Spain and England, see Moses, pp. 300–301.   [3] See pp. 208 ff., below.

the rest of the world was impeded, not only by the desire to hoard gold, but also by the advancing feebleness of Spain's industrial life, and by the artificial barriers placed in the path of trade, money tended to stagnate along the avenues of exchange. An immediate effect was an extraordinary rise of prices which outdid that of the first half of the sixteenth century. It must be understood that before the influx of gold prices had already gone up by reason of the industrial conditions of Spain; between 1519 and 1565 they rose on the average about 300 per cent. Double prices were complained of as early as 1528. But whereas money was by 1558 down to one-third of its earlier purchasing power, it declined between that date and 1632 to one-fifth.[1] Wheat rose from 110 to 952 maravedís, and the other grains kept the pace.[2] Naturally a considerable impulse was given to industry by this prevalence of high prices; but real wages soon experienced a decline. Meanwhile it cost so much to produce in Spain that foreigners could pay the heavy dues demanded of importers and yet undersell the Spanish producers.[3] Thus was the periodic flood of gold which accompanied the returning galleons drained away, and with the greater speed as Spain was forced the more consistently to rely upon foreign producers to supply her needs.[4] And so the Spanish coins came really to flood the world, being found in China and Japan, the East Indies, Persia, Constantinople, Cairo, and Barbary, — "destinations of the larger part of the silver of Spain, because scarcely any other coin was current among those remote tribes than pieces of eight (*reales*

[1] Haebler, Wirt. Bl., pp. 160 ff.; cf. p. 32; Colmeiro, II, 445, 451. By 1558 Philip II was acting upon the theory that coin had fallen 40 per cent in value. Colmeiro, II, 449. The general level of prices in Europe from 1200 to 1800 is treated by D'Avenel in his monumental work. He says (I, 15–16) that prices began to rise about 1500 and were speeded after 1525 through the incoming of American bullion. The value of money fell one-third between 1530 and 1560; then about one-half by 1600. The price of merchandise tripled in 70 years. The following table is taken from notes on pages 27 and 32 of Volume I.

PURCHASING POWER OF THE PRECIOUS METALS COMPARED WITH THEIR PRESENT (1890) VALUE TAKEN AS UNITY

1451–1500 6	1626–1650 . . . . 2.50
1501–1525 5	1651–1675 2
1526–1550 4	1676–1700 . . . . 2.33
1551–1575 3	1701–1725 . . . . 2.75
1576–1600 . . . . 2.50	1726–1750 3
1601–1625 3	1751–1775 . . . . 2.33
	1776–1790 2

[2] Colmeiro, II, 232.

[3] Haebler, Wirt. Bl., p. 15; cf. pp. 52–53; Leroy-Beaulieu, I, 38; Cunningham, pp. 518–520; Clarke, p. 357.　　　　[4] Colmeiro, II, 443–447.

de á ocho) and Castilian doubloons. It was for so short a time that we enjoyed the treasures of the fleets and galleons that they dampened our soil without watering it." [1]

The natural results of this constant inflation of the stock of bullion were economic instability, insecurity of trade, and a great amount of social misery; and when to such natural inflation, if it may be so called, were added periodic capricious alterations of the currency on the part of king and irresponsible favorites, the case was by so much the worse.[2] What the Spaniards, and indeed all the nations of the time who were not shaken in their dogmas by being forced constantly to test them in practice, failed to see is what one of their own writers of 1684 stated so clearly: "The most necessary metal," the anonymous one asserts, "the most noble, precious and sure which has ever existed or will exist, is the sweat of the brow; it ought to be designated the unique element in the conservation of realms. For where this metal shall be wanting, gold and silver cannot hold their place, since it is alone the sweat of the individual which constitutes the universal coin of the world." [3] Instead, however, of adopting rational means for delivering themselves from the results of price-inflation, recourse was had to acts of legislation aimed at the symptoms alone; and such price-regulation simply aggravated the economic ills.[4]

The cult of the metals was certainly pursued to the extreme; but the other dogmas of the mercantilists seem to have suffered

---

[1] Colmeiro, II, 439. " The permanent gain from the treasure went to the countries which could employ it as capital for industrial or agricultural development. This Spain could not do. Even in the Low Countries her system forced a migration of industry. Foreigners were forced to go into banking and their failure in this witnessed to the fact that the treasure was passing into foreign hands. Thus the prosperous element were the Dutch, who used this treasure of Spanish America as capital in commercial shipping and industry." Cunningham, p. 521 ; cf. Colmeiro, II, 440–442 ; Hume, p. 305. Realization of these conditions brought the doubt referred to (p. 201, ,above) as to the real value to Spain of the Indies. " En fin algunos llegaron á poner en duda si el descubrimiento y conquista de las Indias había sido, un bien ó un mal para España, puesto que al cabo si nosotros cogíamos las flores, los demás reinos y provincias de Europa se llevaban el fruto."

[2] " There is another powerful cause of dearth which has been passed over hitherto by the political writers, and which nevertheless played a very prominent part in the general rise of the prices of our goods and products, namely, the frequent alterations of the money. With their eyes upon the inflow of the riches of America, they do not note that the value of merchandise rose proportionately with the decline in weight and quality of our *escudos* and *reales*." Colmeiro, II, 452 ; cf. pp. 492–494.

[3] Colmeiro, II, 227–228. Other isolated pamphleteers urged the same views ; cf. pp. 226–227, 452.   [4] Haebler, Wirt. Bl., pp. 32, 35–36 ; Clarke, p. 357.

considerable attack and modification. Colmeiro[1] says that the rigor of the system was tempered as far as the theories regarding the precious metals would permit. Haebler, a more modern authority and of great weight, sees in the operation of mercantilism, especially as it demanded the exclusion of foreign merchants, a "strong factor" in Spanish decadence.[2] But touching this exclusion, the Spanish, as has been seen,[3] were never, even in their early history, fond of strangers; and it seems doubtful if an economic theory not reënforced by the uncommon intolerance, bigotry, and race-hatred of the Spanish could explain the rigor of the treatment accorded to aliens, from the Jews and Moriscos on. Again, the foreigners were never entirely excluded, and were even the objects of favorable discrimination in the time of Charles II (latter half of the seventeenth century).[4] The fact is, as Haebler says in another work,[5] that Spain was economically too weak to react against conditions: "If Spain had been an economically sound state, it would have been as little likely to collapse in consequence of the superfluity of gold and silver as in actuality England has been harmed by the treasures of India." "It is certain," says Colmeiro,[6] "that other industrial nations of Europe suffered from the same or similar errors; but they corrected themselves with greater timeliness, while we persevered for a long period in the policy which consummated our ruin."

[1] II, 226–227.
[2] Haebler, Wirt. Bl., p. 14.
[3] See pp. 187 ff., above.
[4] Haebler, Wirt. Bl., pp. 89–90.
[5] Amerika, p. 418.
[6] II, 452. "Bending every energy for years to stay the tide of change and progress, suppressing freedom of thought with relentless vigor, and quarantining herself and her dependencies against new ideas, conservatism grew to be her [Spain's] settled habit and the organs of government became ossified. Policies of commercial restriction which were justifiable or at least rationally explicable in the sixteenth century lasted on, proof against innovation or improvement, until the eighteenth century and later." Bourne, Hist. Introd., p. 48.

CHAPTER VI

SPANISH AMERICA: POPULATION, INDUSTRY, AND TRADE

In the conclusions to which the foregoing account of Spain and Spanish policy have led, we now possess a setting or perspective for the colonial career itself. For a nation like the Spaniards, it has been seen, the first and most engrossing interest in any new world must have lain in the large element of hazard and adventure which it offered. The expeditions and conquests were motived by the desire for wealth won speedily in the opening up of a mysteriously attractive Unknown. How far and with what sincerity the crusading spirit entered into the situation will appear a little later; but earlier experiences in the subjection of the Moors had certainly made the Spaniard aware of the great material advantages to be gained by reducing empires such as Montezuma and the Inca held. Enterprises reached out in all the directions indicated by rumor as the approaches to more developed and richer civilizations; and the booty thus gathered was so large as to afford a certain realization to the visions of Columbus. Naturally the state had always received a generous share of such takings,— a share which sometimes stood for propitiation on the part of insubordinate adventurers. Even at the outset the government as represented by Columbus had demanded gold in quantities which were beyond the power of the natives to furnish.[1] The yield to the king from Pizarro's enterprise reached, reckoned as a fifth, almost a million ducats; the Inca's ransom is estimated as having been the equivalent of $17,500,000, and out of this ransom Pizarro paid to every knight of his army 8000 pesos[2] and to every foot soldier half of that amount. These values are enhanced when it is realized that the precious metals at that time possessed purchasing power considerably above that of later periods.[3]

[1] See p. 262, below.

[2] Bourne (Hist. Introd., p. 50) renders the Spanish *peso* as *dollar*, adding: "The reader will bear in mind the varying purchasing power of the dollar. To arrive at an approximate equivalent, ten may be used as a multiplier for the sixteenth and early seventeenth centuries, and five for the middle of the eighteenth century." Humboldt (Essai, II, 648) gives the Inca's ransom as 3,838,058 piasters.

[3] Haebler, Amerika, p. 382; Watson, I, 130; Roscher, Sp. Col. Sys., p. 41.

MINE-PRODUCTION AND REVENUE

When, now, the acquisition of the gold came to turn upon extraction rather than upon looting, the state laid its hand with vigor upon an obvious source of revenue, and the regular fifths-system was put into operation. The mines proved almost from the first to be a source of incredible metallic wealth; after the conquest of Mexico the average annual output about doubled; and with the discovery of the quicksilver process, their productivity was greatly augmented. "The mine-owners promised to freight the ships of the New Spain fleet to the masts with silver if they could only get enough quicksilver"; the inevitable effect of this was the stimulation of the Almadén mines in Spain (held from 1563 to 1641 by the Fugger) and a considerable consequent increase in royal revenue.[1] Then came the discovery of the astonishing Potosí deposits (1546), and the takings in the precious metals soared to undreamed-of amounts. In the earlier and less productive period (1506) the annual importation of gold into Spain reached a value of some $1,200,000; this had risen by 1556 to 700,000 ducats for the crown alone.[2] The royal taxes from the Potosí deposits alone amounted, from 1556 to 1783, to over 3,000,000,000 reals, while from 1754 to 1791 there were coined in Lima over 3,000,000,000 reals, and from 1792 to 1813 over 2,200,000,000.[3] Estimates given by Watson[4] fix the annual import of Spain in American gold and silver at $20,000,000, while Peru yielded the crown some $5,000,000 annual revenue. In the latter half of the eighteenth century the fifth of the annual product of the mines was reckoned as $7,425,000, and the king's net revenue from America as $6,750,000.[5]

The estimates of Humboldt, taking into account his sagacity, wide experience in Europe and America, and general scientific reliability, probably form the best guesses at our disposal upon the matter in question. He estimated the annual yield of the mines of New Spain at $23,000,000;[6] the total yield from 1493 to 1803 at

---

[1] Haebler, Amerika, pp. 415–416; during the time of Ferdinand, however, the colonies had yielded only 50,000 to 70,000 ducats. Id., p. 114. On early mining concessions and their terms, see Fabié, pp. 49, 86, etc. On the mines in general, see Humboldt, Essai, II, book iv, chap. xi. An attempt to infringe upon the royal fifth was punishable by death. Watson, I, 121.

[2] Bourne, Sp. in Amer., p. 104; Haebler, Wirt. Bl., p. 114.

[3] Colmeiro, II, 429.   [4] II, 139, 145.   [5] Bourne, Sp. in Amer., p. 239.

[6] This estimate is the same as Bancroft's. Bourne, Sp. in Amer., p. 298, note.

5,706,700,000 pesos, and the total annual production at the beginning of the nineteenth century at 43,500,000 pesos, or about
ten times the known production of the rest of the world. The
average annual production, as calculated by the same authority, is
represented in the following table :[1]

1492–1500	250,000 pesos
1500–1545	3,000,000 "
1545–1600	11,000,000 "
1600–1700	16,000,000 "
1700–1750	22,500,000 "
1750–1803	35,300,000 "

To these figures Colmeiro[2] adds the following from the Spanish
minister of finance, Canga Argüelles :

Entered into the public treasury:

1808–1814	30,000,000 pesos
1814	5,439,275 "
1816	100,000 "
1818	2,472,627 "

It must be understood, as mentioned above, that in any estimates
of, or based upon, the royal fifths, a large element of error is represented by the constant evasion and peculations[3] which were invited
both by the richness of the field exploited, by the monopoly policy
of the government, and by the system itself of collection and supervision. Occasionally, on the other hand, even under Charles V,
the whole cargo of the bullion-fleets was confiscated to meet a
pressing emergency.[4] But, even if the total receipts in bullion of
king and private importers are discounted by a large percentage,
they must have represented a powerful and consistent attraction
away from the development of a settled industrial economy. It
was in the order of events that a non-industrial people should have
been so dazzled by these extraordinary yields of metallic treasure
as never to have seriously considered the immensely larger and
steadier profits to be gained through the more commonplace and
less picturesque vocations of agriculture and trade. The results of
such prepossessions upon Spain have been indicated ; and they
were, in many respects, duplicated in the colonies. But the latter

[1] Humboldt, Essai, II, chap. xi, 652. Quoted in Bourne, Sp. in Amer., p. 301 ; cf.
Cunningham, Econ. Change, p. 518.   [2] II, 435–436.

[3] Watson, II, 139; see also note appended to chap. iv, above. For thefts from
the mines, see Humboldt, Essai, II, 555.

[4] It was in 1535 that Charles first confiscated all the precious metals brought by
the fleet. Haebler, Wirt. Bl., p. 114 ; Hume, p. 89.

suffered also from the increasing demands for revenue of a government which could get less and less at home, and from the debasing
effect of the constant endeavor to evade or circumvent such
demands.[1] This last result will appear more clearly when the
general policy of monopoly and restriction is considered.[2] Nevertheless, "the Spanish colonies fulfilled their purpose down into
the eighteenth century. They provided the mother-country with the
financial resources of which it stood in unconditional need to maintain its position in the European concert, — and so abundantly that
the envy of all other countries was awakened and they were induced
not only to go into colonial enterprises on their own accounts, but
also to relieve the Spaniard of as many as they could of his
colonial prizes."[3]

Emigration to America

In view of the attitude of both state[4] and individuals toward the
New World, it is not difficult to understand why early emigration
was of so poor a quality. Indeed, it is doubtful if the word
"emigration" should be used either of the early movement of the
Spaniards to the New World, or of that of the Portuguese to
India. The motive of the incomer was, in both cases, to return,
as soon as return with a competence was possible; and the women
who accompanied the earlier voyagers were extremely few. The
description given by Columbus of the insurgents of 1498, even
though discounted considerably, is witness for the fact that emigration began most unpropitiously.[5] Leroy-Beaulieu[6] distinguishes
two classes which took part in the founding of the Spanish colonies :
adventurers recruited especially from the nobility and army, men
whom the end of the Moorish wars had left without employment
or resources ; and the clergy who were to convert the pagans.
Doubtless these were the main classes recognized ; it was the
intention of the Catholic Sovereigns " to give the posts and offices
to *caballeros*, *hidalgos* and *gente principal* and to distinguished and

---

[1] Cf. Watson, II, 139.   [2] See pp. 226 ff., below.   [3] Haebler, Amerika, p. 419.
[4] Haebler (Amerika, p. 368) opposes the old view that the whole state policy was
directed predominantly and continuously toward the acquisition of metallic wealth.
At first, naturally enough in the setting of its time, the government neglected everything else in favor of the advantages which it hoped to gain from the support of
Columbus's schemes. But metal exploitation was not "from the beginning and continuously the directing view-point of the Spanish colonial policy."
[5] Bourne, Sp. in Amer., pp. 49–50.   [6] I, 4.

prudent persons of good family," so that the "conquest and pacification of those lands and the colonization of the New World
might be entrusted to the flower of the nobility and virtue of
Castile." Nevertheless, Ferdinand found it necessary later, in
order to keep up a declining emigration, to commute sentences of
death or mutilation to perpetual or limited sojourn in the islands.
"There went, besides, the soldiers of fortune, men of valiant
spirit and of endurance, tested, some of them, in the campaigns in
Italy and Flanders, men of stout heart who fought with the hope
of enriching themselves with the spoils of war, and never admitted
that they were content with their lot, since, although they received
great favors, they held their services poorly paid. And when the
fervor of the discoveries and conquests was over, there began the
emigration of the plain and common folk, in part honorable and
laborious, in part stow-aways and license-evaders or vicious criminal adventurers." [1] In any case they came, not to labor, "but as
conquerors who take possession of the wealth and the persons of a
vanquished people and force the latter to labor for their profit. In
such a system it is understandable that if the conquest was rapid,
the settlement was slow." [2] Of the elements here mentioned the
clergy is reserved for a later treatment. But the results of having
the nobles, with their lofty contempt of labor, as constituents of
the early colonial bands appear even in the time of Columbus's
second voyage. When most of the laborers became disabled, in
consequence of the climate and of the hardships, the Italian admiral
adopted the un-Spanish recourse of ordering the gentlemen "to
take hold and work, under threat of severe penalty. To add the
degradation of labor with their hands to their suffering was too
much for the Spanish hidalgos, and Columbus never escaped from
the resentment engendered at this time." [3] The history of the
insurrections, factions, and acts of violence, and the tales of
deeds of lust, cruelty, and general scoundrelism certainly betray
the abundant presence in the society of degraded and degenerate
elements.

RESTRICTION OF EMIGRATION

During preparation for the second voyage of Columbus the
climax of national excitement over the Indies was evidenced, as
has been noted,[4] by the throngs which besieged the authorities for

---

[1] Colmeiro, II, 379–380; cf. Haebler, Wirt. Bl., pp. 29–30.
[2] Leroy-Beaulieu, I, 5.   [3] Bourne, Sp. in Amer., p. 40.   [4] P. 180, above.

permission to embark. At that time it was necessary to adopt certain restrictive regulations, and these, although the fever of popular interest never again approached so nearly to delirium, became the prototypes for a policy of restriction of emigration which was adhered to and extended during the whole period of colonial predominance and beyond.[1] From the time of Charles V, no Spaniard could go to the Indies without express permission from the crown, and then for only a stated time ; and " whoever sought permission had not merely to furnish a sufficient reason, but to present in addition satisfactory proofs regarding his morals and especially that neither he nor his ancestors for two generations had been punished by the Inquisition (law of 1518)."[2] This restriction-system was not palatable to Charles V, who granted numerous exceptions in favor of all the subjects of his kingdoms and lordships, and even admitted the Welser and Fugger families within the pale of the monopoly.[3] But under Philip the lines were more sharply drawn ; for example, the permission granted was usually limited to a certain province, and the journey had to be as nearly direct as possible. Emigrants had to reside in the locations and practice the vocations indicated in their licenses. Creoles educated in Europe required official permission to return ; shipmasters had to declare under oath that they had on board no unlicensed person.[4] The details of these restrictions occupy seventy-three laws in the code.

From what has been said of the disposition of the Spanish, and of the quality of the early emigration to the Indies, it is not difficult to derive the reasons for this legislation ; and although it represents over-detailed regulation, it was not entirely uncalled for. From this point of view the conscientiousness of the Spaniard stands in not unfavorable contrast with the indifference of the Briton.[5] However, it must be borne in mind that these motives were not all. There was a monopoly to be safeguarded and an empire to be held, and held in subjection ; and the secretiveness which developed many ages before in the dissimulation of profitable trade-advantages had descended unquestioned to the Spanish.

---

[1] Haebler, Amerika, p 360
[2] Leroy-Beaulieu, I, 6; Roscher, Sp. Col. Sys., pp. 17–18; Moses, p. 56. Restriction of movement within the Peninsula had been previously applied. Haebler, Wirt. Bl., p. 155.   [3] Bourne, Sp. in Amer., pp. 243, 245; cf. Colmeiro, II, 380.
[4] Roscher, Sp. Col. Sys., pp. 17–18; Moses, pp. 58–63.
[5] Cf. Bourne, Sp. in Amer., pp. 246–248; Haebler, Amerika, pp. 416–417.

It is of course unjustifiable to depend upon the prescriptions of Spanish law-codes in determining the conditions in the colonies; but despite probable suspensions and infractions of the regulations, and occasional panic flights from the relentless tax-gatherer,[1] it is probable that emigration to the colonies was, through all the period of Spanish dominance, very slight. The population of the home-country was neither numerous nor enterprising enough to break over the barriers. Annual emigration from Spain to the captaincy-general of Carácas was estimated as one hundred at most; during the sixteenth century the entire movement from Spain to America is thought not to have much exceeded a thousand or fifteen hundred. "About 1546 there were in Peru upwards of 6000 Spaniards; four years later there are said to have been in all the New World only 15,000."[2] In 1574 a competent official enumerates in the New World some two hundred Spanish cities and towns, containing, together with stock-farms and plantations, about 160,000 Spaniards. In the city of Mexico there were about 15,000 Spaniards of all vocations; in Vera Cruz, 200 Spanish families; in Yucatan, 300 householders; in South America, some 13,500 households; in Quito, 400 families; in Lima, 2000 families.[3] Although the error in these figures may be considerable, the fact is patent that emigration was slight; and it is to be feared, despite the efforts to rule out turbulent adventurers anxious only "to get rich quickly, and not content with food and clothing, which every moderately industrious man was assured of,"[4] that the type appealed to by the logic of the situation was generally a disappointment.

One other fact to which reference has been made[5] as a distinctive characteristic of the non-settlement colony is that the emigrants, such as they were, were almost wholly men. The objects of emigration — adventure, etc. — excluded nearly all women who were not objectionable; and these, as we have seen, the conscientious Spanish laws refused to foist upon the colonies. The privilege of going to the Indies was strictly withheld from all single women; and it was even difficult to return and get a wife who had been left behind. At the same time, married men were encouraged to

[1] Haebler, Wirt. Bl., p. 153.

[2] Roscher, Sp. Col. Sys., pp. 17–18; Bourne, Sp. in Amer., p. 250.

[3] Bourne, Sp. in Amer., pp. 196, 198–200 (from Velasco).

[4] Bourne, Sp. in Amer., p. 246.

[5] See p. 14, above.

take their wives.[1] The net result was, naturally, a prevailing absence of Spanish women, married or marriageable; and the inevitable results followed. And when, with the attainment of the temperate altitudes, real colonies of settlement could have been developed, this phase of the restrictive system, or a predisposition brought about by its earlier effectiveness, still prevailed to keep the unit of the society the individual, or the family based on a mixed union, rather than the family as known at home. The natural increase of the pure Spaniards in the New World was bound therefore to be negligible.

Despite this general policy, however, there were sporadic provisions for the encouragement of emigration which had actual settlement as its object. Columbus himself took over prospective settlers; and, in April, 1495, the sovereigns actually adopted a plan of voluntary assisted emigration to Española. Here, however, the rights of the admiral were infringed and the monopoly system prevailed: "It is melancholy to observe to what extremities Columbus was reduced to get colonists beyond those numbered on the royal pay-list." [2] Whether the sovereigns would have succeeded in attracting a satisfactory quantity and quality of settlers remains doubtful, for, although their terms were extremely liberal, the lot of the cultivator was not hard at this time in Spain. Naturally, however, a like liberal-mindedness regarding colonization was not to be expected of Philip and his successors. In 1518 most liberal offers were made in the hope of inducing workers to go to the New World and help take the pressure off the natives: free passage and living on shipboard; lands and live-stock on arrival; relief for twenty years from the alcabala and nearly all other taxes; premiums for production, etc. Again, in 1529, "a new plan was tried, — that of establishing feudal lordships.[3] If any one would take over to Española fifty married couples, twenty-five free whites and twenty-five negro slaves, build a church and fort and

[1] Moses, p. 59. "In striking contrast to the subsequent policy of Louis XIV in Canada and Louisiana and of the English generally, the emigration of single women to the colonies was not favored in the later legislation, and the king reserved to himself the power to grant the necessary license if exception was to be made. It was therefore inevitable that there should be an excess of white men in the colonies and that marriage with Indian women should be common. It was Humboldt's estimate in 1803 that not one-tenth of the European-born Spaniards in Mexico were women." Bourne, Sp. in Amer., pp. 265–266.

[2] Bourne, Sp. in Amer., pp. 45–46, 215–216.

[3] Cf. pp. 133 ff., above.

support the clergyman, pay the freight and supply provisions for the emigrants, build their houses, give each couple two cows, two bulls, fifty sheep, one mare, ten pigs, and six chickens, and make the settlement within a year, completing twenty-five stone houses within five years and fifty within ten — he was to receive an area of about sixty square miles, with its mines (subject to the king's royalty of one-fifth), its fisheries, one-fifth of the royal income from the territory, the right of patronage for the church, etc.; and finally his family should be raised to the nobility and granted a coat of arms."[1] But this proposition ran counter to the prevailing impulse of the time, namely, to steer straight for the mines; no toilsome industry could compete with the visions of a Potosí.[2]

CONSTITUENTS OF POPULATION

Of a consequence, colonial wealth and population early tended to concentrate upon the plateaus and in the high valleys of the Cordilleras. The life-conditions in lower altitudes had been found questionable by Columbus, even in the islands; and the Atlantic shores of both Americas were considerably worse. Neglecting the " worthless regions " which lay outside the tropics, the only healthful and at the same time wealth-producing areas were the interior altitudes; and it was only there, of all of Spanish America, that a numerous population was to be found.[3] That these conditions were persistent is proved by the figures given by Humboldt for the period of his visit (about 1800). There were then, for every hundred inhabitants, the following number of whites: in New Spain (excluding the so-called interior provinces), 16; in Peru, 12; in Jamaica, 10; in the city of Mexico, 51; and, for purposes of comparison, in the United States, 83.[4] It must not be understood, however, that the distribution of the Spanish immigrants was, in any sense, an even one. It was a town population above all else which they formed; and even the dwellers in rural districts tended to cohere into villages. This phenomenon is due to a number of causes, some of which will appear presently; Leroy-Beaulieu[5] sums them up as follows : " When, in a new country, one sees the population flowing wholly to the towns, he may be sure that local production is feeble, that the majority of the colonists are useless

[1] Bourne, Sp. in Amer., pp. 217, 249 (quoted from Saco, pp. 147–149).
[2] Cf. Roscher, Sp. Col. Sys., p. 41.
[3] Leroy-Beaulieu, I, 18.   [4] Roscher, Sp. Col. Sys., p. 18.   [5] I, 7.

persons, speculators or functionaries, not workers, and that there is beneath them a vanquished population exploited for the profit of the victorious class." In addition such agglomeration was a national trait of the Spanish and no doubt represented in part the result of having lived long amidst a hostile vanquished people; but it was very ill adapted, in any case, to the development of industry. Probably also the government had some interest in restraining whatever diffusive tendency the population exhibited.[1]

If, now, the early settlement by the Spaniards was so slight and was subject to but inconsiderable natural increase;[2] and if, owing to restrictions of emigration from Spain, which, it must be supposed, allowed of comparatively little evasion, the number of new recruits was never large; and if, finally, the pure Spaniards and the native-born Spaniards, or creoles, tended inaptly to gather in unnaturally large groups; then it is evident that the constant and determining constituent of the population, biologically speaking, must have been the native element. It was too large to be eradicated, except in isolated stations such as the islands; being acclimated, it was almost everywhere present; but, since it usually possessed less civilization and unity than the Europeans, it was prevailingly and hopelessly subject. Class-division between the two strata of population was therefore inevitable. Owing, however, to the exigencies of the type of settlement practiced by the Spaniards, —a form demanded, so far as the tropical areas were concerned, by the very nature of things,[3]— and to the fact that they had never acquired, or had lost as the result of experience, any aversion to race-mixture, the immediate result of their contact with the native Americans was a large-scale miscegenation. But the inevitable consequence of this was the addition of a third sub-division or class to the population. Nor was this all: the introduction of negro slaves resulted in the course of time in the creation of several other species of mongrel, each of which had a more or less clearly defined position in the society. Social distinctions between the Peninsular Spaniards and the creoles completed the class-stratification. The main constituents of the population, taken as ethnic and social types, were as follows; their several political abilities and disabilities will provide a topic for a later page.[4] The Spaniards who had arrived from Europe were called *chapetones* (or *gachupines*); and

---

[1] Leroy-Beaulieu, I, 6–7.

[2] For the influence of altered environmental conditions upon national increase, cf. Darwin, Orig. of Sp., II, 26.   [3] See pp. 4 ff., above.   [4] Pp. 312 ff., below.

next in order came the *criollos* (creoles) or the descendants of
Europeans (or even Africans) settled in America, a class which
early exhibited the degeneracy characteristic of a parasitic and
unacclimated stock. A third class was formed of mongrels of
Europeans with the aborigines or (later) with the negroes ; these
were called respectively *mestizos* and *mulatos*, and the former multiplied so rapidly as to constitute a very considerable portion of the
population of Spanish America. It may be said in passing that the
same phenomenon took place, but in a far less degree, in the Philippines.[1] Next in order were the *negros*, and finally the last and
lowest class, the *indios*, or natives. And, naturally, there came to
exist between these main components of population many transitional grades which approximated to one or the other class or constituted small anomalous groups.[2]

During the earlier periods the Indian element, so far as numbers
are concerned, was, of course, predominant. In 1576 a reasonably
reliable estimate gives for the New World the following figures :
Spaniards (and creoles), 160,000 ; Indians, about 5,000,000 ; negro
slaves, 40,000 ; and a " large number of mestizos and mulattoes."
In the city of Mexico the proportion of Spanish to Indians (1574)
was 15,000 against 150,000 ; in the province north of Mexico, 130
against 114,000, counting merely the tribute-payers ; in South
America, 13,500 "households" against 880,000 tributaries ; in
Lima, 2000 families against an Indian population of some 25,000.[3]
The estimate of Humboldt, over two hundred years later, gives
some idea of what the course of development had been. He reports
the proportion of whites to the whole population which is quoted
above,[4] and later the following figures.:[5]

	INDIANS	WHITES	NEGROES	MESTIZOS
In Mexico	3,700,000	1,230,000	. . .	1,860,000
In Guatemala	880,000	280,000	. . .	420,000
In Colombia	720,000	642,000	} 387,000	1,256,000
In Peru and Chile . . .	1,030,000	465,000	. . .	853,000
In Buenos Ayres . . ,. .	1,200,000	320,000	. . .	742,000
In Cuba and Puerto Rico .	. . . .	339,000	389,000	197,000
	7,530,000	3,276,000	776,000	5,328,000

[1] See p. 346, below.   [2] Watson, II, 132–135 ; Roscher, Sp. Col. Sys., p. 20 ;
Bourne, Sp. in Amer., pp. 266–267 ; Colmeiro, II, 391–392.

[3] Velasco, in Bourne, Sp. in Amer., pp. 196–200, 196–197 (quoted) ; cf. pp. 278–279.
[4] P. 215.

[5] In Roscher, Sp. Col. Sys., p. 18. There were scarcely any negroes in Mexico.
Humboldt, Essai, I, 130. For the proportion of the elements of population in the

For a later period (latter half of nineteenth century) Roscher assembles the following percentages : [1]

	Whites (%)	Indians (%)	Mixed (%)	Negroes (%)
Mexico	12.5	60.	27.5	(included in "mixed")
Central America .	5.0	56.	38.	1.
Panama	5.5	7.2	87.3 (mestizos, 74.6)	(included in "mixed")
Ecuador . . .	8.	50.		
Peru	14.	57.	29. (mestizos, 22.)	(included in "mixed")
Venezuela . . .	27.5	23.3	44.	5.2

Reflection upon the foregoing figures will show no very serious error in estimating the averages of the constituent elements of the mainland population as follows : Indians, not much less than 50 per cent; mestizos, about 33 per cent; whites (a shifting population), less than 20 per cent; negroes, not over 5 or 6 per cent. Though rough approximations, these percentages are close enough for the present purpose.

RACE-MIXTURE

In view of the fact that the pure Spaniards and negroes constituted such a small fraction of the population, it is plain that the prevailing ethnic mixture, the mestizo, was bound to revert toward the Indian component.[2] It had only caste considerations to preserve it from this fate; for it appears improbable, from the biological standpoint, that this newly formed cross should have so differed from other such mixtures as to have been able to preserve its new character by breeding strictly within itself. Despite a later more free influx of the European element, the reversion referred to seems to have taken place.[3] Whether the Spanish-American mixture, in its varying proportions, was a favorable one, is a difficult question. Anthropologists as a rule look with little favor upon a mixed race whose parent-components are widely diverse in their stages of evolution, however much they may enthuse over the results of a blend such as has occurred between European stocks in the United States. The present generally unstable status of the Spanish American "republics" is often popularly referred to the character

Antilles as against other parts of America, see id., p. 116. The proportion of men to women in New Spain is given (id., p. 138 ; cf. p. 140) as 100 to 95.   [1] Sp. Col. Sys., p. 18.
   [2] According to Humboldt (Essai, I, 135) seven-eighths of the "castas" were mestizos. Moses, pp. 196, 285; Ratzel, Hist. of Mankind, II, 27 ; Darwin, Variation, etc., II, 64 ff. But cf. Darwin, Descent, p. 196.   [3] Cf. the case in Brazil, p. 164, above.

of an unfortunate hybrid race.[1] Judgment as to the constitutional
quality of this population should be reserved, however, until the
conditions under which it lived and developed have been carefully
scrutinized. It is certainly important to try to appraise the Spanish-
American stock, for there has never existed in historic times any
other such experiment in the mixture of really alien races. The
natural lack of antipathy to such miscegenation exhibited by the
Iberians, combined with the natural and artificial conditions inherent in the physical and climatic environment and in the Spanish
system, all contributed to produce an *experimentum in extremis*.[2]
It may be asserted in a general way that the parts of the former
Spanish empire which rank to-day with the colonies of pure European race are, above all, the temperate Argentine region, and, in
addition, such other sections of South America as have become
the objectives of German, Italian, and other immigration. No
Spanish section proper, excepting Mexico, can lay claim to a population comparable in qualities and efficiency with that of the other
European colonies in temperate regions. Again, the population of
the really tropical colonies of the Spanish can scarcely bear comparison with that of India or Java, despite the evident misrule
long practiced in the latter. Any such comparison, however, is
very hazardous, for the multiplicity-of-causes error must be constantly guarded against. In its net results race-mixture plus other
factors seems scarcely to have produced a favorable human type
in Spanish America; taken at its very best it has not represented
a striking success. Even the French writers who advocate the
policy in their North African colonies are inclined to admit this.
The biological value of a cross is established to some degree
by its fecundity; and in this respect there is, if one accepts
the statement of Bernard Moses, a marked contrast between the
Spanish-American race and, for example, the crosses between the
closer related stocks of the United States. This student of Spanish
America asserts [3] that " at the end of any considerable period, the
increase in the English colony, even when allowance has been made

---

[1] Cf. Colmeiro, II, 391–392; Darwin, Orig. of Sp., II, 1 ff.; Bordier, Col., pp. 47–
54; Le Bon, pp. 52–56.

[2] The government favored miscegenation to encompass the fusion of the two
races, thus "avoiding the extinction of the natives which has taken place in the
countries occupied by the other nations of Europe." Fabié, p. 52.

[3] Pp. 309–310. Humboldt (Essai, I, 65) shows the slower growth of Mexican
population.

for different physical conditions, will be found to have far outrun the increase of the combined Spanish and native populations."

INTERRELATION OF CLASSES

A marked suspicion and antipathy characterized relations between the population-constituents named. This was largely due to the policy of Spain in fostering antagonism which existed in the nature of things. Naturally the Spanish officials held in contempt the creoles and especially the mestizos who formed the industrial element in the colonies; the mixed races felt superior to the native or negro stocks from which they had sprung;[1] the negroes, rejoicing in greater physical strength and in the favor of their masters, treated the Indians with insolence and scorn; while the latter, in their unenviable position, hated all their oppressors and insulters in varying degrees.[2] Plainly there was no hope of this caste-system developing anything approaching a homogeneity of population, especially under the policy of inculcation of antipathies practiced by the metropolis. The fact that marriage between the different degrees of color was considered a *mésalliance* naturally prevented any speedy obliteration of such class distinction.[3] Again, the local Spanish spirit of provincial pride and distinction had invaded the New World; "everywhere in Spanish America there existed the most violent antipathy between the inhabitants of the coast and those of the mountains, as, for example, Vera Cruz and Mexico; the former were accused of being frivolous, the latter of being slow. Few countries contain in themselves such numerous differences in climate and mode of living as the *tierra caliente* and *tierra fria* in Spanish America, the inhabitants of which despise each other heartily." The separate colonies too were all so different from one another as to have little natural sympathy.[4]

[1] "The aversion between mulattoes and negroes was as great as that between whites and negroes. The civil position of every class depended mainly and naturally upon the greater or less whiteness of their complexion. *Todo blanco es caballero*." Roscher, Sp. Col. Sys., p. 21.

"The different shades were classified with minute attention, not only by the force of custom but also by the law. When there was only a sixth of negro or Indian blood in the veins of a colonist, the law granted him the title of white: *que se tenga por blanco*. Each casta was full of envy for those above and of contempt for those below." Leroy-Beaulieu, I, 11; cf. Roscher, pp. 149–151. [2] Watson, II, 132–135.

[3] Roscher, Sp. Col. Sys., p. 20; Colmeiro, II, 291–292. "If the Spanish emigrant rose in fortune, he would marry into a wealthy creole family; if he fell, he would marry into one of the blends." Bourne, Sp. in Amer., p. 267.

[4] Roscher, Sp. Col. Sys., p. 21; cf. Leroy-Beaulieu, I, 11.

INDUSTRIAL ORGANIZATION

Having obtained some idea of the constituents of population, interest now centers upon the way in which the society thus formed pursued the struggle for existence. As for the Spaniards themselves, it has been shown how, at the outset, attempts to develop agriculture were rendered futile by the overpowering attraction of the life of adventure; and to this negative factor a second was added through the inability of the immigrants to withstand the climatic and other environmental changes to which they were subjected.[1] Plantation development in the hands of the whites alone was practically an impossibility; it could succeed only through the aid of better-adapted human organisms. Likewise the old disdain for manual labor persisted unbroken — fostered rather by the New World conditions. During a considerable period, therefore, the colonies remained dependent upon the metropolis for the very means of existence, this period coinciding with the impulse to Spanish industries alluded to above and bringing with its conclusion the decline of the same.[2]

Economic insufficiency, of an at least temporary nature, was an inevitable consequence of the natural conditions and of the temper of the invading group. For in the islands the stock conditions of the tropical colony prevailed, and in those areas where altitude corrected latitude, attention was turned for long decades almost exclusively to the mines.[3] In the mining-industry, as in most of their occupations in America, the Spaniards were owners, overseers, and directors, rather than performers, and the story of the mines, despite the humanity of the laws, is in good part the story of the oppression and decline of the native races.[4] In a general way the mines were opened and operated by private individuals or groups, on the condition of paying a fifth of the output to the crown. The methods were crude, particularly before the application of the quicksilver process, and wasteful of life; of the output something is said in another place.[5] Great fortunes were undoubtedly gained

---

[1] For the vicissitudes of the early period, see Bourne, Sp. in Amer., pp. 25–26, 34–37, 204–209, 217–218; Roscher, Sp. Col. Sys., p. 2.

[2] P. 182, above. Cf. Colmeiro, II, 255–256, 399–400; Clarke, p. 356; Haebler, Wirt. Bl., pp. 30–32, 34–35, 56–59; Amerika, pp. 367–368; Cunningham, pp. 518–519; Hume, pp. 83–85.   [3] Cf. p. 12, above.

[4] See pp. 265 ff., below; Bourne, Sp. in Amer., pp. 261–264.

[5] Pp. 208 ff., above. The quicksilver process was introduced into Mexico in 1566, and into Peru in 1574. Encycl. Brit. sub " Silver, Mexican process." For the introduction

by individuals, especially since the fifths were notoriously evaded. The whole atmosphere was that of the fortuitous or aleatory, hazard replacing rational calculation aimed at the development of solid economic resource; the whole body of the conquerors and their immediate successors, overwhelmingly attracted by the prospect, through a lucky discovery, of sudden wealth, paid but scant attention to the development of any form of tame industry. In fact, about the only agricultural resource of the Spanish island-colonies, before the wider extension of the empire, was the production of sugar, in which they depended almost entirely upon native labor. The later inclusion of areas where maize, maguey (agave), cacao, vanilla, cochineal, etc., could be produced, naturally rendered the settlements less dependent.[1] Moving thus from the islands and the coasts to the plateau-country, they encountered climatic, topographical, and other conditions remarkably like those of the homeland. So far as nature was concerned, there was no reason why a considerable development of agricultural economy should not have taken place. But the national character of the Spanish, and the restrictive policy extended over them, prevented this. Cortés alone among the conquerors seems not to have been utterly consumed by the desire for gold.[2] It is doubtful if the temperate-zone products would have been much developed in the absence of the native or mixed elements in the population; that agriculture was a distinctly secondary consideration in Spanish minds is proved by the fact that " the regions which were best adapted to agricultural colonies, as, for example, Carácas, Guiana, Buenos Ayres, were neglected by the Spaniards for centuries."[3] It was apparent to no one that the potato, — of which the first European discoverers were Pizarro and his band, and which was thus known to Europe only after 1526, — and the febrifuge quinine, introduced to Europe by the Jesuits, in 1639, were worth far more to the world than Potosí.[4] Whatever the purpose of the government,[5] the popular objective was not production but exploitation.

of the amalgamation process into the Potosí region, Humboldt (Essai, I, 624) gives the date 1571. [1] Haebler, Amerika, p. 399; Bourne, Sp. in Amer., pp. 298–299.

[2] Roscher, Sp. Col. Sys., p. 2, note 3.

[3] Roscher, Sp. Col. Sys., p. 2 ; see pp. 316 ff., below.

[4] Quinine, as then made, was worth in Europe in 1640 a hundred crowns ($125) a pound; during the colonial period it was practically the sole article of export of Quito. Watson, I, 113, 155.

[5] See p. 214, above; cf. Bourne, Sp. in Amer., pp. 216–219, 249–250; Watson, I, 136.

As a consequence it was not until recourse was had to a levy upon the vital forces of the conquered, that anything of significance was accomplished in the way of agricultural production. Then, despite the ruthless using up of these vital assets in the mines, the interior mainland, chiefly Mexico, began to exhibit signs of economic self-sufficiency and even of affluence.[1] But the cultivation of the ground never received in the early days any such impulse as it did in the tropical plantations of other nations ; the fleets carried away from New Spain and the islands certain amounts of natural products other than metals, but the development of such a mine of agricultural wealth as Cuba remained rudimentary until a fatal breach had been made into the restrictive system by which commerce had been tight-bound.[2] In fact, it can hardly be said that the Spaniards founded any plantation colonies with security in the sixteenth and seventeenth centuries. The superior attractiveness of Mexico and Peru early drained away the Spanish population of the islands, so that by 1574 the number of the Spanish in the city of Santo Domingo, for example, was only about 1000, and Havana harbored only 50. Santiago had fallen from 1000 to 30.[3] Colmeiro says,[4] having in mind chiefly tropical production, that the whole of Spanish America remained sterile in Spanish hands ; "in the middle of the eighteenth century Martinique and Barbados produced more for France and England than all the islands, provinces, kingdoms, and empires of America for the Spaniards." Allowing for a considerable degree of exaggeration, and realizing that this result was due to a number of contributing causes, it is inevitable that the observer should conclude that for three centuries the plantation-agriculture of Spanish America was a failure.

Besides agriculture there was one other productive vocation in the colonies, namely stock-raising. The climate and soil combined to favor this occupation, which was besides more congenial to the

---

[1] See pp. 303 ff., below; Bourne, Sp. in Amer., pp. 198–200, 298–300.

[2] Bourne, Sp. in Amer., p. 250 ; cf. p. 299. "The Spanish settlements, despite all efforts of the government to the contrary, had long remained little more than permanent trading-stations. In barter with the natives the settlers accumulated what objects of value they could, and, always with native aid, they dug and washed for precious metals. But no matter how often the government sent seeds and plants over the ocean, cultivation did not prosper; for the natives did not understand it, and the colonists on their part regarded such occupation as beneath them. And because, now, valuable products of the soil were present only in limited quantity, the barter-trade was soon exhausted." Haebler, Amerika, p. 399. The foregoing has especial reference to the islands.   [3] Bourne, Sp. in Amer., pp. 197–198.   [4] II, 421.

restless hidalgo.[1] Moreover, the cattle throve in the new environment, as superior animals naturalized into regions whose fauna offer
little competition are wont to thrive.[2] They lived in a half-wild
state ; the horses in particular soon showed a tendency to reversion
from domestication, the visible outcome of which was represented
by the droves of wild horses of the more northern plains. Nevertheless beef was cheap, and considerable exports of hides were
made long before the present stock-breeding areas of the Pampas
were opened.[3]

It does not appear that the small results attained by agriculture
and stock-raising are referable in any important degree to the
application directly to them of restrictive regulations, mercantile
or other. In fact, it was for the interest of Spain that the colonies
should produce sugar and other tropical products for her, and it
was only such important temperate-zone products as grapes and
olives which were looked upon with disfavor as duplicating those
of the Peninsula. Charles V and Philip II favored even the hide
and raw-wool industry of the New World.[4] Indirectly, however,
the restrictions on commerce impinged with force upon all forms
of production. And to these restrictions were added by the constitution of the Spanish system the unfavorable conditions represented
by the extension of ecclesiastical and private estates (*mayorazgos*),
and by the collection of tithes.[5]

The case is similar in respect to the manufacturing industries ;
no such direct restriction was intended as that of the English in
North America. Spain had few manufactures for which she sought
either a supply region of raw materials or a demand region for
finished products. Consequently she is found to have favored,
though to little purpose, the development in the colonies of the
mechanic arts, such as spinning and weaving, sugar-refining, and
the like.[6] Where restrictions were actually put in force and with

---

[1] Cf. p. 171, above.

[2] Darwin, Orig. of Sp., I, 100–101, 136 ff., 225; cf. Bourne, Sp. in Amer., pp. 218,
on the wild hogs in Española.   [3] Bourne, Sp. in Amer., pp. 200, 298–299.

[4] Roscher, Sp. Col. Sys., pp. 42–43; Moses, p. 284; Watson, II, 213. But the
colonies were mainly dependent for their subsistence. Watson, II, 153.

[5] See pp. 297 ff., below; Leroy-Beaulieu, I, 22; Watson, II, 131–132.

[6] Colmeiro, II, 395–396; cf. Roscher, Sp. Col. Sys., p. 42 ; Leroy-Beaulieu, I, 24,
26. The exportation of manufactures to the colonies was subject to absolute prohibition, "in order to start there at once manufactories for silk, cloth and leather-work
which might relieve the mother-country of care for the colonies." Haebler, Wirt. Bl.,
p. 62; Bourne, Sp. in Amer., p. 300.

widely deleterious results, it was for local reasons, and not infrequently with a view to the protection of the natives;[1] of the
mercantile system as applied to dependencies but few and vanishing traces occur. When the colonists complain of restrictions, it
is largely those of trade which they have in mind. Nevertheless,
as might be expected, the growth of manufactures was slower even
than that of the other vocations.[2]

In fact, the Spaniards in the New World were, for many decades,
either exploiting the mines or living in some other sort of unproductive parasitic relation upon the native population.[3] Aside from
the priests, who really pretended to return some equivalent to the
natives, and often did so, the Spaniards and creoles seem to have
been interested chiefly in squabbling for property, preferment,
offices, or titles,—in floating about on the surface of the economic
currents from which they derived, without return service, such
livelihood as they could. For instance, one traveler stated that
"the whole population of Spanish America was divided into two
classes: those who ruined themselves by law-suits and those who
enriched themselves by the same means." In a population of
31,000, Carácas had 600 judges, lawyers, and clerks. "There is
no one, white or almost white, who does not desire to be a lawyer,
priest or monk; those who are unable to give such scope to their
pretensions aim, at least, at being notaries, secretaries, clerks of
church-sacristans, or attachés of some religious community, such
as lay brothers, pupils, or foundlings. Thus the fields lie deserted and their fertility arraigns our inactivity. Cultivation of the
soil is despised. Every one wants to be a gentleman or to live in
idleness."[4] It was many years before cultivators, industrials, and
merchants gained numbers and a station in society such as secured
for them any consideration in comparison with the adventurers,
clergy, and officials.[5]

[1] Roscher, Sp. Col. Sys., p. 43; Leroy-Beaulieu, p. 24.

[2] "Until far into the second half of the sixteenth century no kind of industry
could gain a foothold in the colonies." Haebler, Wirt. Bl., p. 59.

[3] As early as 1508, the colonists, after petitioning the government for other favors
and exemptions from interference, request that the artisans be required to resist the
temptations to secure allotments of Indians, and desert their trades. Bourne, Sp. in
Amer., pp. 217–218. Thus the very logic of natural conditions may be seen to have
militated against industry.

[4] Depons (II, 63 ff.; and I, 186) in Roscher, pp. 156–157.

[5] Cf. Leroy-Beaulieu, I, 4–5.

TRADE-RESTRICTION

The markedly non-productive character of Spanish America, whatever its more general ethnic, economic, and social causes, was certainly accentuated by the cordon of restrictions imposed upon exchange, especially as between the mother-country and the colonies. In the latter areas there was at first little question of local exchange, insomuch as they were economically dependent upon Spain for supplies purchasable by the export of treasure and other articles destined to pass through but few hands. But with the growth of production, a merchant class, composed mostly of European Spaniards, slowly arose. It is difficult to discover the relative numbers of this class; in Vera Cruz (1574) there were 200 families of Spaniards, all merchants and shopkeepers;[1] but in the New World as a whole the merchants certainly formed but a small minority. They appear, however, not to have been heavily taxed or oppressed. The alcabala was introduced in 1558, but on the low basis of two per cent; and although this was later raised,[2] it seems never to have produced any special outcry. A subsequent consideration of the other taxes levied in America[3] will show that inter-colonial exchange was not singled out for unreasonable treatment; indeed it was, strictly speaking, too insignificant to draw attention except as it suffered indirectly through its connection with the general exchange between Spain and America.

To this topic we now turn; and it is here that we meet the extraordinary system of restriction which has riveted the attention of economists from Adam Smith down. In the earliest years Charles V is found to be, as usual, the exponent of a liberal policy: under Isabella only Castilians had been allowed to enjoy the fruits of the new Castilian discoveries; Ferdinand had extended such privileges of emigration and trade to Aragon; but Charles granted them to all his subjects without distinction of nationality (1526). In the first decades succeeding the discovery there appear to have existed the beginnings of a lively trade between Spain and the colonies; certainly the period of Spain's prosperity under Charles[4] is referable in no insignificant degree to the stimulus of having to provide and being allowed to provide the means of comfort and luxury for adventurers and colonists who had considerable wealth

---

[1] Bourne, Sp. in Amer., p. 199.
[2] Haebler, Wirt. Bl., pp. 118–119.
[3] Pp. 314 ff., below.
[4] See p. 182, above.

together with extravagant tastes, and who would not engage in productive industry. Large exports to America of wines, manufactures, and other characteristic products of the Peninsula were imperatively demanded. Restrictions were removed from agriculture and manufacture, and even beggars and vagabonds were impressed into the factories of Valladolid, Zamora, and Salamanca.[1] In 1518 fear of foreign competition had so far disappeared that the prohibition of the importation of silk-fabrics was removed. There was a considerable shifting of occupation toward industry and trade.[2] The result was a rather lively exchange between the mother-country and the colonies; for example, about 1550 Cadiz and Seville exported 140,000 centners of wine to America. The colonial demand exceeded Spain's power of supply, and the competition of foreigners was invited; Charles V admitted certain Germans, as has been seen, into the colonial trade.[3]

Monopoly Policy

But the course of things at home did not admit of a normal development from these beginnings.[4] "On the whole, it appears that the large colonial demands for food on the one hand, and the large supplies of foreign manufactures on the other, prevented a healthy reaction of commercial on agricultural and industrial development; Spain was left exhausted by the feverish activity which had been temporarily induced, and which passed away."[5] Even during the reign of Charles it was found necessary, in view of the European situation, to begin the process of restriction, a policy much more in harmony with Spanish prepossessions than that of freedom; and under Philip it was developed rapidly and with general approval. Neither Spaniards nor Portuguese had ever emerged from the spell of the monopoly system of the Middle Ages, typically represented by that of Venice. "The colonial system," says Colmeiro,[6] "was nothing else than the extension of the common code of Europe to the American dominion. The economic régime of the ancient world rested upon privilege and prohibition, and just as the provinces of a single kingdom were divided and separated by customs-houses, thus also the colonies

---

[1] Haebler, Wirt. Bl., pp. 57, 59; Bourne, Sp. in Amer., p. 287; Hume, pp. 83–85.
[2] Haebler, Wirt. Bl., p. 57; Colmeiro, II, 255–256.
[3] Pp. 187, 212, above. Cf. Haebler, Amerika, p. 367; Cunningham, p. 518.
[4] See pp. 204 ff., above.   [5] Cunningham, p. 520.   [6] II, 423.

lived apart from the mother-country, excepting for the bond of a reciprocal commerce." It should be noted, however, that the Spanish took as a model the Portuguese system rather than the more remote Venetian; they were expecting to meet with conditions similar to those encountered by the Portuguese in India: large cities and prosperous states admitting of an extended trade. Hence, among other things, the apparatus for the direction of trade and the preservation of monopoly, and especially the *Casa de Contratacion,* or House of Trade, modeled upon the Portuguese *Casa de Guiné,* the forerunner of the *Casa da India.*[1] To this and other devices for securing monopoly attention will presently be given; but the broad consideration to be borne in mind as the chief factor leading to restrictions of many kinds is the monopoly policy itself. This policy has appeared already in the history, commercial and colonial, of all the anterior peoples who in succession or as rivals controlled the exchange between the East and West, or, to express it in its final terms, between the complementary trade-areas of the tropics and cooler regions. Exclusion of others from such rich advantages was entirely natural, upon an undeveloped stage of economic and social progress; it represents, indeed, an ineradicable motive of self-seeking in the battle of life as waged by individuals and groups; in the minds of most, if not all nations its inferiority to a more generous and cosmopolitan policy still awaits practical demonstration. What is peculiar to the Spanish system and its prototypes is the crude, extreme, and baldly consistent exhibition of the exclusion-principle rather than that principle itself.

THE SEVILLE MONOPOLY

The expression of the exclusion-principle as respects foreign nations is reserved for a later page;[2] it is rather in its application as between sections of the Spanish dominions that it now engages our attention. The most obvious example of this is the reservation of the trade with the Indies, at first (until 1529) exclusively to Seville, and later to that city and Cadiz. Such a proceeding was

---

[1] Haebler, *Amerika,* p. 392; cf. p. 66, above. It is a disappointment to the author not to be able to furnish at least a brief account of the Portuguese *Casa*; but considerable effort expended in the search for materials has failed to yield, as yet, any results of importance. Inquiries made in the Peninsula by a colleague have been so fruitless as to suggest that the *Casa da India* is a matter of curious interest rather than of historical importance.   [2] Pp. 242 ff., below.

plainly after the Portuguese model, for the India trade of Portugal
had been centered at Lisbon. " This preference for Seville came
from the fact that it was the only large place in the kingdom of
Castile that could carry on ocean-commerce and at the same time
had a considerable river trade. Then, again, since the kingdom of
Castile alone had borne the expense and dangers of the discovery
of America, it wanted to have all the profit of it." [1] Further
reasons for the exceptional status of Seville, less plainly dictated
by a monopoly policy, are to be found. The establishment of the
Casa de Contratacion in 1503, for example, was the outward and
visible embodiment of a policy of strict supervision; and the need
for such control was found in the estimation and collection of
royal and royally assigned revenue. The discovered lands "were
regarded less as the territorial growth of Spain or Castile than as
an extension of the royal domain of the Castilian kings"; and the
income transferred by the sovereigns to the great admiral had to
be strictly accounted. It was the natural result, upon a stage
where the machinery of revenue-collection was yet crude, to persist in the mediæval idea of a "staple-port," and to force all
income-producing currents of trade through a "narrows" where
they could be estimated and levied upon. Again, in an age where
piracy was rife, and merchant-ships, sailing upon the ocean at their
own risk, could not yet be differentiated from war-craft, it was in
the nature of national insurance that inspection of vessels, crews,
and passengers should be rigidly enforced; and it was easier to
control all this, and later the religious character of emigrants,[2]
from a single office, more highly organized. The weight of motives
other than fiscal is witnessed by the fact that for some time the
trade to the Indies was not taxed.[3]

However, the monopoly idea is implicit in some degree in all
these considerations, as it had been in making Cadiz the staple of
the preceding Barbary trade. It was in the spirit of the place and
time. With all his liberal ideas, Charles V, who up to the end of
his reign meditated an assault upon the Seville monopoly,[4] was
yet obliged to decree, "on pain of death and confiscation, that
every Spaniard, embark where he would, must direct his journey
back from America only to Seville; and soon the journey out was

[1] Roscher, Sp. Col. Sys., pp. 32–33; Leroy-Beaulieu, I, 27.   [2] P. 212, above.
[3] Haebler, Amerika, p. 410; Wirt. Bl., pp. 50–51; Hume, p. 88.
[4] Haebler, Wirt. Bl., p. 53.

permissible only from Seville." The very fact that the starting-places were not at first designated, although the final return-destination was, and that " in particular all gold and silver, all pearls and precious stones could be brought only to Seville,"[1] betrays the early development of the monopoly idea as distinguished from that of benevolent supervision. Again, when, in 1529, Coruña, Bayona, Avilés, Laredo, Bilbao, San Sebastian, Cartagena, and Malaga received permission to send out vessels to America, the latter were obliged to return over Seville.[2]

The benefits conferred by this monopoly upon the favored city were all that could have been expected. In 1552 the import-restrictions were greatly reduced and Seville became the entrepôt of a stream of trade, artificial though it may have been, whose terminals were the countries of Europe on the one hand and America on the other; the merchants of Seville thus reaped a double gain, acting as they did as factors for foreigners who were excluded both in person and in proxy from the colonies. The more Spanish industry declined the more decidedly did the commercial operations at Seville take on the character and afford the easy gains of a transit-traffic, " so that Seville became the richest and most populous city of the monarchy as well as an inexhaustible treasure-house for the crown. . . . At a time when throughout Spain the decline of trade and industry gave cause for the most serious complaints, the merchant-population of Seville were erecting, in quick succession, truly monumental edifices."[3] Many a time a single returning fleet brought them back more than a thousand millions of maravedís, and "not a few of their daughters became the ancestresses of newly vivified noble families which in their traditions harked back to Pelayo."[4] But Cadiz began to put forth rival claims for the American trade as early as 1550, and after 1680 was plainly preferred by commerce. The sanding-up of the Guadalquivir, and the greater draught of vessels, which made it impossible for them to pass the bar of San Lucar, combined to render Seville obsolete. The official change was delayed only until 1717, and brought with it the end of this city's prosperity. The system of the staple was yet maintained for about fifty years.[5]

[1] Roscher, Sp. Col. Sys., p. 32.
[2] Colmeiro, II, 402; Haebler, Wirt. Bl., p. 54; Bourne, Sp. in Amer., p. 283.
[3] Haebler, Wirt. Bl., pp. 75–76; cf. Roscher, Sp. Col. Sys., p. 44; Clarke, p. 356.
[4] Haebler, Wirt. Bl., p. 69; Colmeiro, II, 401–402.
[5] Colmeiro, II, 402, 408; Haebler, Amerika, p. 425; Wirt. Bl., p. 76.

It is difficult to disengage the effects of one measure of restriction from the whole, but it may be said that the rest of Spain suffered from the excess of favor and opportunity vouchsafed to Seville; "naturally this transit-trade of Seville helped on the decline of Spanish industry by drawing from it, to the advantage of foreign countries, an important part of its commissions."[1] "The error lay in the persistence with which, after the great discoveries and conquests, . . . the commerce of the New World was still concentrated in Seville or Cadiz; in governing the much according to the rule of the little, and in converting an ephemeral ordinance into a perpetual privilege. Thus the Indies came to be the patrimony of a single city of the realm; and the interior provinces of Spain, and those which occupied the littoral of the Cantabrian or Mediterranean, could hardly enjoy the benefits of trade with America by reason of the re-imposition of tolls in transit, of the municipal duties and other taxes, and of the rise in charges for transportation,[2]— all of which made our manufactures dear and inclined the scales of competition in favor of those of the foreigners."[3]

THE CASA DE CONTRATACION

Reserving for a later page[4] the effects upon the colonies of the single-emporium policy, we now turn to the consideration of other manifestations of the all-regulating activity of the government. The general supervision of communications and trade will appear most plainly, perhaps, in an account of the agency designed to carry them out: the House or Board of Trade, the *Casa de Contratacion*. This organization was established at Seville in 1503, and at first appears to have been designed to look after the trade-interests of the crown, under the contracts with Columbus; later it extended a progressively augmenting control over the whole of the trade with the colonies, including all correspondence connected therewith.

---

[1] Haebler, Wirt. Bl., p. 76.   [2] *En razon de los portes y fletes.*

[3] Colmeiro, II, 408. "Of the manufactures exported to America, the greater part (it is said nineteen-twentieths) was made in England, Holland, France, etc., and the Spaniards themselves, apart from their own illicit trade, had only two kinds of profit from it. In the first place the national treasury secured the considerable customs which had to be paid in transit through Spain. Second, the merchants, ship-owners, etc., gained from the many charges which were added to the price of the goods and were paid again by the Americans. In order to avoid . . . the customs an immense partial smuggling was carried on at Cadiz." Roscher, Sp. Col. Sys., p. 44.

[4] Pp. 237 ff., below.

Increasing as it did in authority, it likewise took on judicial and administrative functions, acting as an adjunct to the Council of the Indies (*Consejo de Indias*), but in such manner that it disposed of all minor business independently. It was "at once a board of trade, a commercial court, and a clearing house for the American traffic"; [1] it "regulated the number of ships and the bulk and value of their freights, received and distributed the precious metals and the merchandise from the Indies," and kept itself informed regarding the extension and possibilities of trade. A certain amount even of instruction was associated with its other activities; especial attention was given to nautical subjects and the education of pilots.[2] An efficient agent of trade-supervision and extension was thereby created, and constituted, in the time of Charles V, an object of envy and emulation even to a Henry VIII. "No ship was permitted to sail from Spain to America, or land from there, until it had been inspected by the officers of the Casa and had received a license. Of everything a most careful register was kept." [3] "The historical significance of the organization known as the Casa de Contratacion lay in the fact that for a long time it held the key to the New World" and enabled the Spanish king to apply the extraordinarily rigid system of commercial restriction which has drawn invectives from economists of the succeeding centuries.[4]

THE FLEETS AND GALLEONS; THE FAIRS

But the Casa was only one agency, however important, in the general apparatus of regulation, here applied to trade; it constituted the sleepless eye of the Seville monopoly, and was later transferred with the latter to Cadiz. Regulation and cramping restriction did not, however, begin and end at the Peninsular terminal; it accompanied the vehicles of commerce to the colonies, determining schedules, routes, destinations, and manner of sailing to and fro, impressing its characteristic stamp upon markets, methods of exchange, and all the other factors and phenomena of trade. During

---

[1] Armstrong, II, 47; cf. Haebler, Amerika, pp. 391–395, 412; for its officers and personnel in general, see Bourne, Sp. in Amer., pp. 222–223; for early legislation concerning it, see Fabié, pp. 42–45, 71–73, 104 ff., etc. Moses (chap. iii) has made a rather exhaustive study of the Casa.

[2] Hume, p. 88; Bourne, Sp. in Amer., p. 222; Roscher, Sp. Col. Sys., p. 32.

[3] Roscher, Sp. Col. Sys., p. 32.

[4] Moses, p. 50. This author regards the system of restriction as the most rigid ever framed.

the earlier years this influence extended but little beyond the European terminal; under a proper license, a vessel might sail when she willed, and whither.   But with the increase in the number of pirates and their insistence and skill in following the scent of spoil, need was felt of the mutual protection of association during voyages.   Charles V decreed in 1526, and Philip II more urgently in 1561, that the ships should sail in company.   Thus were organized the famous *flotas* and *galeones*, companies of merchant vessels to which, in order to insure complete safety, there were assigned regular convoys of war-vessels.[1]   The establishment of the fleets, as of other factors in the restrictive system, seems to have been almost wholly in the interests of trade ; but this complex of paternal measures was sure to increase in rigidity and oppressiveness as the Spanish kings, in their increasing financial embarrassment, became alive to the fiscal possibilities of America.   The collection of dues was facilitated by the fleet system; wholesale confiscation, whether contemplated or not, was easier.   Moreover the control of emigration, and so the detection of prospective settlers of tainted faith, became more certain.

The definite legal establishment of the system was the work of Philip II; his ordinance of 1561 required the annual equipment, mainly in Seville and Cadiz, of two fleets and a naval escort for the Indies — one for New Spain and the other for Tierra Firme (northern coast region of South America).   The former started in April or May ; the latter in August or September, later in March. The sections parted at the island of Dominica, and made rendezvous for the return at Havana, putting in at the Azores to learn if the coast of Spain was free from pirates.   Six or more ships might procure a license for return without waiting for the rest.[2]   All the details of navigation were laboriously prescribed, and the destinations of the various vessels were scheduled; little or nothing was left to chance or to the free play of initiative in taking advantage of unforeseen opportunity.   One or more ships were detailed to the several islands and smaller mainland ports, but the great majority proceeded either to Vera Cruz or to Puerto Bello on the Isthmus. These ports became to the New World what Seville was to Spain,

---

[1] Colmeiro, II, 401–404 ; Haebler, Wirt. Bl., p. 54; Amerika, pp. 413–415. The flotas had Vera Cruz as their destination, the galeones went as far as Puerto Bello. Professor Bourne informs the author that he regards the distinction usually made between the flotas and galeones as an imaginary one.

[2] Bourne, Sp. in Amer., pp. 284–285, 288.

and with results the more deleterious, as discrimination was exercised over wider areas and more helpless victims.[1]

A natural issue of this primitive system of distribution was the fair at the terminals; under the conditions no regular market in the modern sense could exist. There was an annual fair at Vera Cruz, but the most pronounced type was that of Puerto Bello, by which practically all of South America was supplied. Here the products of the Peruvian fleet were exchanged, during forty days, for those brought by the galleons; the period was one of tremendous activity, of feverish effort to take advantage of a strictly limited contact with the outside world; bales of goods and billets of silver obstructed the streets. Great profits were made during the exchange of goods worth up to forty million pesos, but the period of the fair was bounded on both sides by a long "dead time" of commercial stagnation. The evils of the system were inevitably enhanced by the crowding of many people into notoriously unwholesome ports and by the untoward economic conditions incident to the whole situation.[2]

The fact that the fleet system had been employed by the Portuguese, and later appealed, at least in modified form, to the Dutch and English, seems to mark it as a device of some generality, and as probably finding its justification, therefore, in general rather than local conditions. This conclusion seems to be reasonable when the insufficiency of the ships for ocean-voyaging, the small nautical skill, the increasing prevalence of corsairs upon the southwestern coast of Europe, and, above all, the universal adherence to the monopoly principle, are recalled. Here, again, Spain exhibited a profound conservatism and maladaptability. "Staples, caravans, trading-companies, — these are arrangements which serve admirably only for the beginnings of trade and for the lower stages of civilization; but Spain tried to perpetuate them in her colonies. Indeed, where not only the state but the whole society rests upon mediæval principles — i.e. a caste-system, absence of a single nationality, great power of the church — there it is that the impossibility of much departure from these principles, even in trade, appears. Highly artificial governments, which are at the same time conscious of their own weakness, have from of old felt the need of

[1] Cf. p. 238, below.

[2] The mortality of Spaniards was high, and the atmosphere was one of merciless greed. Cf. Bourne, Sp. in Amer., pp. 291–293; Colmeiro, II, 403–404.

limiting trade, as far as possible, to a minimum; — trade which binds peoples together, and which might introduce, along with foreign wares, foreign ideas and influences as well." [1] In other words, the fleet-and-fair system was another of the anachronisms to which Spain, with characteristic consistency, clung; that it contravened a normal development is shown no less by constant attempts to evade its restrictions [2] than by the animation of economic relations which followed close upon its extinction.

FURTHER RESTRICTION : THE PRIVILEGED COMPANIES

But before passing judgment upon this phase of the general system of monopoly and regulation, it will clarify counsel to pursue Spanish trade restriction into a few of its remoter outreachings.   For example, the forwarding of goods beyond the Isthmus was subject to police-regulations even more hampering than those described. The whole trade with the Philippines was forced into one vessel per annum, and short periods of feverish activity lapsing out of and back into lassitude marked the commercial life of that colony ; the other details of regulation as disclosed in America applied, *mutatis mutandis*, in the Asiatic region.[3]   Again, there was absolutely no provision made for direct trade with Buenos Ayres or Chile ; their products and supplies must perforce go via Peru and its yearly fleet to Panama ; " if a settler on the bank of the Rio de la Plata wished some article of European production, for a long time the route by which it could reach him in the course of legitimate trade was from Seville to Porto Bello, across the Isthmus of Panama, from Panama to Lima, and from Lima across the continent to its destination." [4] " From 1535 to 1579 direct trade between Buenos' Ayres and Spain was prohibited. Thereafter the policy vacillated between absolute prohibition and the permission of a few vessels specially licensed." [5] In fact, police measures were applied generally to the communications between the several American provinces ; [6] this was doubtless due prevailingly to political considerations, but it impinged severely upon the development of trade and largely neutralized its beneficial influences.

---

[1] Roscher, p. 165.   [2] Bourne, Sp. in Amer., p. 286.   [3] See pp. 347 ff., below.
[4] Moses, pp. 285–286 ; cf. pp. 208–209 ; Watson, II, 208 ; Roscher, Sp. Col. Sys., p. 36 ; see p. 318, below.
[5] Bourne, Sp. in Amer., p. 290.   [6] Leroy-Beaulieu, I, 6, 18–19 ; see p. 245, below.

The monopoly principle worked out into still another form, deemed detrimental by the colonists and by students of the subject, namely, privileged companies. It did not take certain favored commercial houses long to attain practical control over the limited trading-system; "especially so when the merchants of Seville from the time of Charles V, and those of Mexico and Lima from the time of Philip II, became privileged corporations with an elected prior and consuls at their head. For example, the trade with the silver fleet was in the sole possession of eight or ten large Mexican houses." Naturally these organizations were interested, conformably with the policy of the day, in keeping the market understocked; their policy was "to raise prices to the point where reduction in the amount of sales would have caused them more of damage than the costliness of the merchandise would have returned in profit." And the interests of the several companies were effectively enough pooled to allow of no inconsistency of policy between them. The whole arrangement was not so different from that of the Dutch and English companies of the seventeenth century.[1] In spite of this fact, however, the régime of the privileged companies was less oppressive than that of the government; in 1728 the trade of Carácas was surrendered to a company organized at Guipúzcoa (*Compañía Guipuzcoana*) because the government was discouraged in its efforts to overcome smuggling. The very existence of this company depended upon its being able to stop the operations of foreign traders and to transfer to itself the exchange which they were carrying on; so it armed its ships and actually succeeded in considerably limiting the contraband traffic; it also promoted trade, for its restrictions, while rigid, were mild in comparison with what went before. Carácas, apart from the company, had connection with the Canary Islands by one registered ship, and enjoyed free trade with Vera Cruz; yet for the sixteen years before the founding of the company not a ship had sailed from Carácas for Spain, and in twenty years only five from Spain to Carácas. Under the more moderate restriction the cattle business trebled in a short time, the cocoa-trade doubled, and the price of cocoa in Spain fell fifty per cent.[2]

[1] Roscher, Sp. Col. Sys., p. 34; Leroy-Beaulieu, I, 28; cf. Colmeiro, II, 454 ff.; Watson, II, 142.
[2] Roscher, Sp. Col. Sys., pp. 37–38, and note; cf. Watson, II, 156; Moses, pp. 166–170. The *Compañía Guipuzcoana* retained its privileges until 1778.

But the companies were only relatively beneficial. Their history justifies the condemnation accorded them by modern economists. " They live upon monopoly, become weakened through extravagance and poor direction of business and perish oppressed by the weight of their debts, involving in their ruin many individuals and families. . . There is no doubt that Charles III followed the counsels of a wise and generous policy in dictating laws and regulations to secure free trade of the metropolis with its colonies ; and it was right here, and by that exercise of discretion, that he gave the *coup de grâce* to the companies existing in 1765, — a clear proof that their life is the death and their death the life of general trade." [1]

RESULTS OF RESTRICTION

If this can be said of the companies, it is of course doubly true of the still more evil system which they occasionally replaced. But the latter was so firmly established and so tenaciously and tyrannously maintained that it could scarcely disintegrate as a result of agitation and resistance within the empire; the power that broke it finally struck from without, and its interference was invited by the very height of pretension and presumption exhibited by the system. Nevertheless there was resistance within, even though it commonly took the form of connivance with foreign invasion. The colonies suffered progressively from restriction as they advanced in population and resources ; they were the victims of irrational exploitation and needed but slight contact with freer systems in order to realize it. " The clearest result of this organization of commerce was to diminish the supply of European goods in America without other compensation than the enormous profits made by a corporation of merchants." [2] While at the outset any system was good that provided safe supplies, even though they were very dear, for a small dependent population, as time went on the inadequacy of the means employed pressed home in ways both direct and indirect. The old-time tendency to prefer large profits upon a small movement of merchandise became more glaringly anachronistic as colonial production increased and diversified. The effect on colonies of such restriction has been shown up more spectacularly as a result of the sturdier resistance of the English colonies in the temperate zone against that policy which culminated

[1] Colmeiro, II, 462–463.   [2] Leroy-Beaulieu, I, 29 ; Bourne, Sp. in Amer., p. 294.

in the Navigation Acts. In Spanish America the fleet system and what went with it were all but prohibitive of any great development of colonial exportation; by them the life of the colonies as expressed in trade was restrained upon a stage from which the dominant people of the future were already emerging. The colonists petitioned in vain against the impregnable fortification of vested interests and the rooted governmental system of suspicious surveillance.[1]

But the realm was hermetically sealed that the victor might the more conveniently prey upon the victim; "the supplying of a great kingdom was carried on like the provisioning of a blockaded fortress."[2] Free competition being thus eliminated, and in the relative superfluity of gold and silver, prices in Spain were at first five times, and even, at the end of the sixteenth century, thrice those in the colonies. "Toward the end of the eighteenth century, Varinas tobacco cost, in Spain, four times, and in the rest of Europe seven times as much as in America."[3] The rising reservoir of American commodities was restrained by an ever-sufficient and rigid barrier from overflow upon the waiting markets of the world. Meanwhile the holders of the monopoly gained from 100 to 300, and in some cases 500 per cent from this frontier-trade and its artificial restriction.[4] Of course the means of communication, even with the metropolis, were entirely insignificant. It is not sufficient to explain the small exportation of the colonies, particularly in bulkier objects, by discanting upon freight-charges and by recalling the fact that ships were small and consequently must carry great value in small bulk ; prices were high enough in Spain to cover heavy costs, and numbers and frequency of vessels and voyages could and would have made up for size had the system approached that of freedom. But it was precisely number and frequency that engaged the invidious attention of the regulators. "When the trade of Seville was at the height of its prosperity, both fleets did not carry more than 27,500 tons, while, for example, in 1836 the little island of Mauritius [under a free system] sent 17,690 tons to England and received 18,576 tons from her.[5] The

---

[1] Cf. Bourne, Sp. in Amer., pp. 217–218.

[2] Humboldt, quoted in Roscher, Sp. Col. Sys., p. 34.

[3] Haebler, Amerika, pp. 412, 414–415; Bourne, Sp. in Amer., pp. 283–284; Roscher, Sp. Col. Sys., p. 34.   [4] Colmeiro, II, 404; Roscher, Sp. Col. Sys., p. 34.

[5] "Thus a little island lost in the Indian Ocean with a population of less than 150,000 had . . . a commercial movement much more considerable than that of the whole of Spanish America during the best times of the system of the galleons and the silver fleet." Leroy-Beaulieu, I, 29.

last silver fleet arrived in 1778 ; previously, the annual exportation from Vera Cruz reached, on an average, 617,000 piastres ; after 1787, 2,840,000 piastres annually. The total exports to and imports from Spanish America in 1778 amounted to 148,500,000 reals, carried by about 300 ships, and paying duties of 6,500,000 reals. Ten years later the trade-movement had risen to 1,104,500,-000 reals yielding 55,000,000 in duties." As occasion will appear later to show, a similar buoyancy under removal of pressure was exhibited by Cuba.[1]

The fleets were small and slow ; they were intended, as the term " silver fleet " indicates, to carry mainly one kind of product, that of exploitation. They did not follow out even the meager yearly schedule ; "during the latter part of the sixteenth century the regularity of the voyages of the fleets to New Spain was disturbed by the war with the Netherlands and England, so that only eleven fleets arrived at Vera Cruz in the last twenty years of the century." [2] The policy of Spain which led her into constant strife with other nations [3] thus impinged upon the bound and helpless colonies ; in fact, the fleet system, concentrating masses of treasure as it did, tempted aggressors to render its activity less regular and efficient. In the absence of competition this agency stamped the commercial development of the colonies with the character of discontinuity and artificiality. The words of Leroy-Beaulieu,[4] already quoted in connection with the Portuguese, aptly apply to the present case : " Une surexcitation extraordinaire quand un de ces vaisseaux arrivait, suivie de la plus grande torpeur dès que ce vaisseau était parti. La continuité des échanges, leur multiplicité, l'abondance des transactions plus que leur importance : voilà ce qui donne au commerce de l'essor, ce qui en entretient l'activité, ce qui le rend productif et progressif."

Even supposing the Spanish system to have been favorable to agriculture and manufacture in the abstract, or as local vocations, the narrow and selfish policy persisted in respecting exchange could not but have rendered such favors in effect illusory and even cynical. Interference was ever poised to pounce upon commerce which strayed from the paths whose treading meant wealth for the few. The provinces were all cut off from one another, for inter-colonial exchange had no picturesque side, but was simply low-lived

---

[1] Roscher, p. 166; cf. Bourne, Sp. in Amer., pp. 287–288; p. 330, below.
[2] Bourne, Sp. in Amer., p. 286.   [3] See p. 200, above, and pp. 242 ff., below.
[4] I, 48; see p. 114, above.

trade.[1] The special aggravation of the situation lay in "the fact that the mother-country, to which the colonies were chained in all economic matters, was, after the middle of the sixteenth century, really retrograding";[2] so that the life of the new societies was joined to the destiny of one already becoming decrepit to the degree above described.[3] It is comprehensible, then, why the colonies got along better, despite the absence of the fleets, in wartime, and why prosperity followed the throwing off of Spanish rule.[4] With more specific reference to Buenos Ayres, one writer declares: "The trade restrictions which were imposed upon the colonies, instead of permitting them to start with the advantages of the achievements of European civilization, in many cases drove them back to the barbarism of the aborigines, and doomed them to go over again the painful way up to civilization, which their ancestors had trod in Europe. To go from Spain to America, except to a few privileged places, was not merely to go into exile, but even to renounce civilization."[5]

DISINTEGRATION OF THE RESTRICTIVE SYSTEM

The pressure against the restrictive system as described, applied largely from without, but also consequent in part upon enlightenment within, began to take visible effect early in the eighteenth century. Ports were opened to merchants during wars, however speedily they were closed with the beginning of peace; the English were admitted to the Puerto Bello fair, with the result that smuggling speedily increased. "The galleons fell rather rapidly from 15,000 to 2,000 tons (about 1737). After 1740 permission was granted to fit out so-called register-ships in the intervals between fleet and fleet, especially to such parties as had a share in no fleet. About 1748 the galleons were entirely given up; now one could sail directly to Chile and Peru around Cape Horn, and Panama and Puerto Bello collapsed. But on the other side trade was still fettered to the monopoly of Cadiz and paid high royal licenses." In 1765 the West Indies were opened to all Spaniards and to a number of different ports under a duty of six per cent; this system was extended to Peru, Chile, Buenos Ayres, New Granada, and Guatemala

---

[1] Leroy-Beaulieu, I, 26; Roscher, Sp. Col. Sys., pp. 33–35; Bourne, Sp. in Amer., pp. 291–292; cf. pp. 195 ff., above, and 316 ff., below. [2] Roscher, Sp. Col. Sys., p. 35.

[3] Pp. 182 ff. Enlightened Spanish opinion protested against the system under discussion as destructive to Spain. Colmeiro, II, 410–411.

[4] Roscher, Sp. Col. Sys., pp. 31–32. [5] Moses, p. 286.

in 1778, and finally, a decade later, to New Spain. "The more important a colony was for the mother-land, the later was it resolved to open it to free trade. Furthermore, the duty on many classes of goods was lowered, and in 1774 the previously existing prohibition of internal trade between Peru, Guatemala, New Spain and New Granada was removed."[1] An experiment in opening all Spanish harbors to trade (1748) resulted in so many bankruptcies in the ranks of the pampered Cadiz houses that it had to be given up.[2] In 1778 the transatlantic commerce experienced a complete transformation: the fleet system was renounced finally and the Cadiz-Seville monopoly done away with. In place of the latter, nine of the most important ports of Spain were granted the right to send ships to the colonies, while across the ocean no less than twenty-two harbors were opened to direct commerce with the metropolis. And a reasonable system of taxation of trade was introduced.[3]

The end of the eighteenth and the first years of the nineteenth century saw, therefore, the initiation of a liberal policy. This was mainly the work of the one modern Spanish king, Charles III (1759–1788), and his ministers, Aranda and Gálvez. The measures carried through by his government resulted in a great expansion of trade which reacted powerfully upon agriculture and industry. Scientific expeditions, the most notable of which were those of Alexander von Humboldt and his companion Bonpland, were instituted at royal initiative. "Upon this field the Spanish colonial policy ranked among the enlightened."[4] But reform, however well-intentioned and extensive, could not measure up to the demands of a set of provinces so long repressed, and now at length alive to all the possibilities of freedom as taught them by other peoples; in a short time they were working out their own salvation, and in the injured and hostile state of mind engendered by separation in strife and bloodshed. Spain's later trade-relations with her former colonies have never been large; she has received little or no preferential treatment, contrasting unfavorably in this respect with Portugal in the latter's relations with Brazil.[5]

[1] Roscher, pp. 169–170; Watson, II, 143–144; Leroy-Beaulieu, I, 32–33.

[2] Roscher, Sp. Col. Sys., p. 39, note.

[3] Haebler, Amerika, pp. 425–426; Bourne, Sp. in Amer., p. 297; Watson, pp. 212–213.

[4] Haebler, Amerika, p. 427. But Spain still reserved many special privileges for herself; Watson, II, 212–213. For a list of the exports and imports at Vera Cruz for 1803, see Roscher, Sp. Col. Sys., p. 44, note.   [5] Cf. pp. 162–164, above.

CHAPTER VII

SPANISH AMERICA: RELATIONS WITH FOREIGNERS AND NATIVES

It is in the plan of this book to supplement the more general survey of the Spanish system as applied to the colonies with a rather more special account of the outlying parts of the empire. The history of these outer areas shows enough variation from that of New Spain and Tierra Firme needlessly to confuse a perspective of the colonial system, while it seems adapted, considered apart, to throw certain side-lights upon that which is more general. Hence our treatment of the restrictive system will proceed, with only casual reference to Buenos Ayres and Chile, Cuba and the Philippines, directly to the external influences leading to its collapse.

THE EXCLUSION POLICY

It has been explained how this system introduced limitations as respects places, means, and times; discriminations also against persons and groups within the empire have been involved in the monopoly idea. Conformably, however, with Spanish prepossessions, the most severe discrimination was bound to be that directed against foreigners, especially as these were heretics. Here, again, we find the Emperor Charles initiating the system in a cosmopolitan spirit that evoked Spanish displeasure; he improved upon the extension granted by Ferdinand, and, taking advantage of his imperial station, opened trade with the New World to all his many and varied subjects.[1] The emperor's theory was that the new lands, for other reasons as well as fiscal ones, needed forces for their development, and he could not fail, as a Netherlander, to see that these could not be furnished by non-industrial Spain. Hence he enlisted two of the strongest industrial factors of the day, the German families of the Fugger and Welser, in the opening-up of America, and was willing to admit rather generally those who were

---

[1] P. 212, above; Bourne, Sp. in Amer., p. 282.

not foreigners to him, however alien they were to Spain. This course was reversed as time went on and the participation of foreigners was viewed with increasing disfavor. Monopoly ideas were in the spirit of the time and not in Spanish minds alone: " Foreigners were excluded from trade with our colonies, as our men were from theirs, for in the whole world the policy of monopoly in favor of the mother-country was held to be a wise one." [1] After Charles the rigidity of the exclusion of aliens developed apace. By 1592 all unnaturalized foreigners were prohibited from going to the Indies, and this policy was adhered to until the downfall of Spain's rule on the mainland. With what success this was accomplished may be judged from the account of Humboldt (about 1800): in five years' travel he happened upon but one German resident; and he found the inhabitants of remoter provinces hardly able to conceive that there could be Europeans who did not speak Spanish.[2]

It should be realized that, in spite of the difficulties in the maintenance of pretensions to such monopoly, Spain was at the outset abundantly able to defend her title. She was regarded in the early sixteenth century as unquestionably the first land-power as well as the first sea-power in the world; and even the prowess of the individual Spaniard was greatly feared. Her only competitor was Portugal; and avoidance of collision with the latter was sought in the provisions of the treaty of Tordesillas.[3] This reputation was enjoyed for some time after it had ceased to be justified, and did not lose its menace until after the defeat of the Invincible Armada in 1588. Of a consequence the captains were few and daring who despised the early apparatus to secure exclusion possessed by the Spaniards. And to this material discouragement of invasion was added the powerful menace involved in the confirmation by the Pope of the Spanish, as of the Portuguese, monopoly. It took the Reformation to shatter this supernatural sanction, and it was a long time, despite the incitement of rich booty, before the passing of old attitudes and the fading of the survivals of former piety had removed all hesitation about invading the forbidden regions.

---

[1] Colmeiro, II, 397–398; Moses, pp. 162–164; Zimmermann, I, 329 ff.
[2] Cf. Bourne, Sp. in Amer., pp. 246–247.
[3] Roscher, Sp. Col. Sys., p. 29; cf. pp. 90 and 123, above.

The Safeguarding of the Monopoly

The Spaniards, then, "claimed to be the absolute lords of the traffic with the Indies and regarded all participation on the part of foreigners as a manifest usurpation."[1] The very envy which their American possessions provoked confirmed them in this attitude; consequently their disposition toward foreign interlopers was a compound of arrogance, self-righteous bigotry, and rage. It motived such proceedings against invading groups as the massacre in cold blood of the French in Florida (1564–1567),[2] and such cruel treatment of isolated foreigners as the Inquisition alone knew how to allot. "Until the middle of the seventeenth century the Spaniards treated the entry of any foreign ship into American waters as a crime. Shipmasters who were stranded on their shores were frequently executed or sent to the Mexican mines for life." And when, later, aliens were tolerated in America, their orthodoxy was subject to recurrent and exasperating scrutiny on the part of the Holy Office. " Later suspicion was aroused respecting the colonists themselves; the idea was to impede that introduction of foreign ideas which sometimes accompanies the merchandise from foreign ports. The laws were Draconian and the practices pitiless. Commerce with the foreigner, in the absence of express permission, was prohibited on pain of death and confiscation."[3]

In these and many other restrictions the spirit of the monopoly-holder is revealed; for they cannot be justified by benevolent intent, nor explained purely as the outcome of religious tenets or of economic theories, even if the mercantile system be included. With regard to the latter, Leroy-Beaulieu[4] says : " It is almost exclusively to that morbid and chronic state of distrust and suspicion that the exclusive and restrictive organization imposed by Spain upon the commerce of her colonies must be attributed; it is an error to see in all these restrictions an application of the mercantile system — for such a view rests upon a confusion of periods. It is perfectly possible that in the long run false economic theories had grafted themselves upon the political motives which had brought

---

[1] Colmeiro, II, 416–417.

[2] Bourne, Sp. in Amer., pp. 176–180, 189; Roscher, Sp. Col. Sys., p. 29; Leroy-Beaulieu, I, 23.

[3] Roscher, Sp. Col. Sys., pp. 28–29; Leroy-Beaulieu, I, 23; Moses, pp. 62–63.

[4] I, 24.

forth the commercial system of Spain, but it is inexact to assert
that this system found its first cause in the said economic theories.
It was with the purpose of excluding foreigners, not of favoring the
manufacturers of the metropolis, that Spain applied such strict
regulation to the relations of America with Europe." "A state
which conceals within itself numerous and important conflicting
elements, and can remain master of them only by means of a very
artificial governmental machinery, will always be inclined to restrict
as far as possible the intercourse of its own people with foreigners." [1]
To what extent such conditions prevailed in Spain and the colonies
it has been the aim of much of the foregoing to show.

The very constitution of physical nature in Spanish America
lent itself aptly to the enforcement of measures of exclusion such
as could never have been maintained so successfully, for example,
along the coast north of Florida. The experience of the Dutch
West India Company seems to bear this out.[2] Owing to the tropical
climate and its concomitants, especially yellow fever, the coasts
of New Spain and Tierra Firme were practically uninhabitable for
Europeans, or even Indians; and those of Peru and Chile were
largely desert for lack of rain. Of a consequence the population
was concentrated upon interior plateaus; and the highlands were
accessible, in the absence of rivers of any claim to navigability,
only by means of very steep and tiresome mountain roads. Moreover, there were but two passable harbors on the eastern coast of
New Spain: Vera Cruz and Campeche, both controlled strategic-
ally by Havana; and New Granada had scarcely any outlets on
the Gulf. The Isthmus, even after Magellan's passage, effectually
closed the whole Pacific coast, and its two harbors, Puerto Bello
and Panama, provided, with the few above-named, ideal points of
supervision for the whole stream of trade. Again, the very
approaches were difficult, for the prevailing winds of the Gulf
seriously impeded navigation upon its sixteenth- to eighteenth-
century stage, and the voyage down the west coast of South
America was long and tedious.[3] And, finally, the Spaniards held
all the island harbors, thus controlling way-stations as well as
terminals. Realizing the strength of its position, the government
made no effort to improve upon natural conditions; it accentuated

---

[1] Roscher, p. 158.   [2] Cf. pp. 413 ff., below.

[3] "Ulloa relates a popular anecdote of a ship-captain who married a wife in Payta,
but before he arrived in Callao had a son who was able to read; and the distance
covered amounted only to 140 leagues." Roscher, Sp. Col. Sys., p. 22, note.

them rather, and preserved them. No port was allowed within eighty-five leagues of the mouth of the Orinoco; the roads and harbors were purposely neglected. After the reign of Charles V a possible passage through the Isthmus was neither sought nor desired.[1] Internal communications were thwarted or actually prohibited. The provinces were in effect removed to the greatest distance possible both from each other and from Europe; and those which could not be so isolated (Carácas, Orinoco region, Buenos Ayres) became objects of the systematic neglect of the mother-country. It was felt that foreign influence called forth objectionable leanings toward independence; and, as a matter of fact, the movement for separation did begin in Carácas and Buenos Ayres.[2]

Despite all these elaborate devices for purging off the foreigner, the Spanish could not keep him out of America any more than they could do without him in Spain. In fact, a large percentage of the gains of Spanish merchants came from activities as middlemen between the productive nations of Europe and Spanish America; and even from commissions as agents of the foreign merchants.[3] Whatever mercantilists there were among the Spanish must have been shocked to find that Spain's commerce was "passive" with all the nations of the world and "active" with the Indies alone.[4] Attempts were made to shorten the rôle of the foreign producers, and in particular a decree was issued early in 1603 "which imposed an additional tax of 30 per cent upon the import and export of all wares whose owners were not in a position to demonstrate that neither the goods nor the vessels had had any connection with the Netherlands nor were destined for any such. This was all that was needed to bring the passive trade also of Spain to complete ruin, for even without this she possessed no longer any active trade. Even without the new tax-vexations every incoming or outgoing ship was subjected no less than seven times to visitation and control on the part of the most diverse authorities, and

[1] Charles V supported the wish of Cortés and Pizarro for the finding of a passage or the piercing of the Isthmus; even Philip II cherished similar ideas at first, but later forbade even the mention of such a canal. The Spanish Cortes ordered the cutting through of the Isthmus in 1814. Roscher, Sp. Col. Sys., p. 30, note 5.

[2] Roscher, Sp. Col. Sys., pp. 29-31; cf. p. 36. "We are told that ... the Spaniards, in order to impede the intercourse by land between the provinces, had left isolated Indian races on the intervening frontiers intentionally unconquered. ... " Id., p. 22.

[3] Colmeiro, II, 418-419.

[4] Roscher, Sp. Col. Sys., pp. 43-44; Colmeiro, II, 440.

was naturally compelled just so often to pay now larger, now smaller sums. . . . But Henry IV of France retorted to the Spanish measures by a general prohibition of trade with Spain. The natural result of this was that the tax-decree had at once to be suspended; and then one nation after another obtained exemption from the measure through new trade-agreements."[1]

THE INFRINGEMENT OF THE MONOPOLY

In the attempt to maintain exclusion in the colonies it speedily became evident that the Spanish were contending with two parties whose interests were one: the foreigners and the colonists. The exaggerated respect for the Spanish arms had decreased rapidly toward the end of the sixteenth century, when it was seen ever more clearly that Spanish pretensions were analogous to those of the Portuguese in respect of their emptiness; and the old reverence for and fear of the papal sanction was yielding before more rational thinking. But it was just about this time that the monopoly was enforced most strictly, and so, to all appearance, must be most rich and powerful. It is precisely when a monopoly bears this reputation that it is about to become the object of general assault and attempted infringement, for it promises the greatest premiums for its own breaking. The first open blow was struck at the monopoly system during the third war between Spain and France, just before the middle of the sixteenth century; thus France seems to have led the movement through her privateers. And she followed it up in a more covert way by secretly encouraging the corsairs whose presence off the southern and western coasts of the Peninsula had supplied one of the original motives for the fleet system.[2] But the defense of the Spaniards upon the European side of the Atlantic, though not always effective, was too good for her adversaries; so the pirates turned their attention to the source of wealth, the colonies, and thither they were followed by adventurers who were at first none the less pirates because they did not fly the black flag and did make some pretense at trade.[3] Foremost of these

[1] Haebler, Wirt. Bl., pp. 79–80.

[2] Of these *buccaneers* and *filibusters* Haebler says (Amerika, p. 424): "These homeless and lawless robber-bands were composed of subjects of all countries and rulers; Spaniards alone could find no place in their society. While they associated peacefully with other nations, they pursued everything Spanish with the most appalling hatred. Therefore the enemies of Spain often employed and in part protected them."

[3] Haebler, Amerika, pp. 419–420.

came the Dutch and English, the former fresh from the exposure
of the Portuguese pretensions and from the wars of independence
from Spain, with their legacy of contempt and hatred of the
oppressor; the latter long trained in the school of seamanship and
piracy that flourished with royal connivance under the name of the
Channel Rovers, and preyed with peculiar satisfaction upon the
property and subjects of the monarch most hated and feared, and
presently to be conquered. It is but natural that the mode of
approach to Spanish America should have exhibited in about equal
degree the components of open hostility and of evasion; the one
passed readily into the other according as the aggressors were
superior or inferior to the local Spanish defense. For example,
advantage was taken of the well-known demand in the Spanish
colonies for negro slaves [1] in order to introduce there, often with
the acquiescence of the Spanish authorities, cargoes of Africans
plundered from the Portuguese on the Guinea coast. During this
operation, however, the importers were keenly alive to any chance
for offering violence; and if it presented itself, they managed often
so to provoke the Spanish as to lend to their own aggression the
character of defense from unwarranted attack. In the sixties of
the century in question this kind of trade was entered into by numerous English ships; and Drake did not hesitate, under favorable
conditions, to make a real attack on Nombre de Dios and Panama
(1572).[2]

If we seek to distinguish evasion through contraband trade from
direct hostilities, we find, first of all, that certain outlying regions,
as, for instance, those of the Orinoco and La Plata, offered the
most promising objective points: "everywhere the finest opportunities to land, but nevertheless a thin population and neglect on
the part of the Spaniards. It was therefore in these places that
the Spanish revenue system received its most grievous wounds
from smuggling." [3] But the invasion speedily extended from the
outskirts toward the center, being favored by the colonists: "There
was joined to the necessary scarcity of goods the oppression of the
gild-ordinances which hindered the manufacture of fabrics, hats
and any other article of clothing destined for our American
dominions, in the variety suitable to the difference of climates,
while the foreigners succeeded in gratifying the taste and even the

---

[1] Cf. p. 280, below.   [2] Haebler, Amerika, pp. 420–421.
[3] Roscher, Sp. Col. Sys., pp. 36–37.

caprice of the consumers." [1] In other words, the foreigners catered
to local demand and profited largely, while the colonists got from
them alone what they wanted, both in quantity, quality, and time.
Of a consequence contraband trade became very popular, and presently the West Indian possessions of Holland, as well as those
of England and France, became smuggling-stations on a very
large scale. "Shortly before 1740 the English alone are said to
have had as much share in the Spanish colonial trade in ways
prohibited as the Spaniards themselves had in the authorized
ways." [2] Spanish political writers complained that the foreigners
were the ones who really benefited by the trade with America,
being free in their illicit traffic from the taxes which handicapped
the Spanish industries. [3] It need be added of the contraband trade
only that it increased and penetrated beyond the power of the
government to check it — a state of affairs self-confessed in the
founding of the *Compañía Guipuzcoana*. [4]

THE ASIENTOS: ILLICIT TRAFFIC

One of the methods by which the thin edge of the steel was
inserted between the armor-joints of the restrictive system was
the extortion of commercial privileges as the result of success in
war. Spain was pretty generally vulnerable because she was constantly at war or on the verge of it ; and quite often her antagonists
were the Netherlands and England, when she usually ended by
having to make concessions. Neither rival had any scruple about
driving the wedge home, but it was the English who secured the
lion's share of advantage. The Dutch effected entrance, through
the treaty of Münster (1648), into the ports of the Indies, East
and West, and other such considerable concessions were wrung by
force ; but the most spectacular and disastrous was that secured by
the English in the so-called *Asiento* of 1713 (Peace of Utrecht).
The Spaniards had never been able to supply their colonies with
a requisite labor force to take the place of the freed Indians ; [5] it
has been seen that foreign captains got almost their first insight
into American conditions by providing slaves to whom even the
authorities could not refuse entrance. During the personal union
with Portugal (1580–1640) slave-trading contracts were awarded to

---

[1] Colmeiro, II, 415–416.
[2] Roscher, Sp. Col. Sys., p. 37 ; Bourne, Sp. in Amer., p. 294 ; Moses, pp. 288–292,
cf. pp. 316 ff., below.   [3] Colmeiro, II, 415.   [4] Cf. p. 236, above.   [5] P. 282, below.

Portuguese, since the latter held the supply-areas on the African coast.[1] Such contracts for slave-importation were termed *asientos*, of which the most famous was the Asiento secured by the English. Reservation is made of its bearing upon the slave-system for a later treatment;[2] but its service in disintegrating the monopoly system, as applied especially to commerce, was certainly signal. For not only did the English secure the right of importing 4800 slaves per annum for thirty years, but, a still greater concession, they were for that time to be regarded and treated, in suspension of the laws excluding foreigners, "as if they were subjects of the crown of Spain"; the only restriction being "that there shall not reside in any one of the said ports of the Indies more than four or six Englishmen."[3] Moreover, England was to be allowed to send one registered ship of five hundred tons burden to Puerto Bello, a concession of which the factors of the English South Sea Company took advantage by covertly increasing this ship's capacity and by accompanying her with transports which kept out of sight by day and from which her cargo was rendered marvelously inexhaustible by night. By such means, by more direct smuggling, and by the competition of the *Compañía Guipuzcoana* and other like privileged organizations, the commerce of the fleets was sapped until all they had to carry was the king's royalty of one-fifth of the product of the silver mines.[4] In 1735 Philip V was shortsighted enough to forbid to the merchants of Mexico and Peru the making of remittances of funds to Spain in order that they might be sent merchandise in return; "and in reality the colonists did not send these by the fleets and galleons to Cadiz but, through the factors of the English Company, to London, employing deception in revenge for violence."[5]

In this and other ways the English obtained an exact knowledge of the tastes and needs of the colonists, and could extend their smuggling from Jamaica over an extraordinarily wide range. Spain suffered increasingly by comparison, in the eyes of the colonists, for she could not if she would supply their needs; so that presently Holland followed England, Curaçao began to compete with Jamaica,

[1] Bourne, Sp. in Amer., p. 273. Ships trading in slaves were exempt from examination or duty. Hume, p. 374.   [2] Pp. 280 ff., below.

[3] Bourne, Sp. in Amer., pp. 243 ff.; Moses, p. 275.

[4] Bourne, Sp. in Amer., pp. 274-275, 295-296; Colmeiro, II, 420-421; Leroy-Beaulieu, I, 30-31; Roscher, Sp. Col. Sys., p. 38; Watson, II, 143; Moses, pp. 273-283.

[5] Colmeiro, II, 420.

and in time every manufacturing nation of Europe, and even the
North American colonists, had part in the Spanish American trade.[1]
Even at the beginning of the eighteenth century "the contraband
for the Spanish colonies had risen to the dignity of an institution
and had attained a degree of regularity and of organization which
the world has not known either before or since."   And the result
for the colonies themselves was most happy.[2] For Spanish trade,
on the other hand, this meant ruin.   The Dutch gained control of
all the commerce of Carácas ; it will be recalled that from 1712 to
1728 only one vessel had left Carácas for Spain, and from 1708 to
1728 but five had sailed from Spain to Carácas.   While of all the
countries of the world Carácas produced the most cacao, and Spain
consumed the most, the Dutch had the trade entirely in hand.[3]
"The direct traffic of Spain in the New World had so diminished
that, in the eighteenth century, the number of ships which each
year left our ports in cargo for American ports did not reach
forty, while those of other nations passed the number of three
hundred."[4] It is plain that through the smuggling alone the integrity not only of the monopoly system, but even of the empire
was dangerously menaced.

TERRITORIAL AGGRESSIONS

For their illicit trade the English, Dutch, and French, not to
mention the buccaneers, needed headquarters and a base ; but
the attainment of such foot-holds implied territorial aggression ;
and this, since the occupation of such stations must ultimately be
an open one, meant overt hostilities.   The most natural locations
for the contraband stations were the islands ; and the occupation
of these, especially the smaller ones, was easier because Spain, pre-
occupied with the regions of treasure-promise, accorded them little
attention.   During the early part of the sixteenth century they had
been occasionally visited by Spanish hunters of Indian slaves, but
were later deserted and left uninhabited. As early as 1605 the
English took possession of Barbados, and in 1623 actually settled
in St. Kitts ; while during the years immediately following, the
English, Dutch, and French laid hand upon almost all the smaller
Antilles.   Even Denmark and, for a brief period, Sweden seized

---

[1] Roscher, Sp. Col. Sys., pp. 38–39 ; Moses, p. 283 ; Watson, II, 143.
[2] Leroy-Beaulieu, I, 30 ; Moses, pp. 169–170.
[3] Leroy-Beaulieu, I, 32.   [4] Colmeiro, II, 418.

and held diminutive islands. Up to 1670 Spain regarded all these enterprises as attacks upon her empire, and punished them, where opportunity offered, accordingly.[1] Protests were of no avail, for European governments could disavow; none of them could control its own pirates, or assumed to do so. And besides, to refer still again to an important consideration, a state of peace in Europe did not at all imply at this period an analogous condition in the colonies, then, in effect, far more remote than now.[2] So that, even during the periods when open wars were most carefully guarded against, predatory expeditions were a regular thing in American waters ; and when actual war broke out, these naturally increased very markedly. After 1585 scarcely a year passed when English fleets in greater or less numbers did not harry the coasts of Spain and of the colonies. And after the defeat of the Invincible Armada had caused the halo to fade from Spanish naval prestige, they began to compete for the actual control of the sea. " The expeditions of 1595, 1597 and 1616 against Guiana, conducted by Raleigh, were the first serious efforts of the foreigners in the South American continent not only to occupy the coast, but also to penetrate the interior." [3]

One of the constant temptations to which the nations who held these little empires in the Antilles were subjected was to try issue with the silver fleet; for, as in the case of the Portuguese sea-caravans, the concentration of treasure provoked an irresistible inclination to test the strength of its convoy. But this was redoubtable enough to resist anything weaker than a regular navy, the employment of which meant open war. Pirates and privateers hung about the treasure-ships and, despite reverses, managed to cut out an occasional prize to their great profit, but it was only in time of war that the fleet as a whole was actually attacked. However, there were sufficient wars to lend plentiful occasion for such a wholesale enterprise ; the Dutch in 1607 resisted the demand that a truce should be effective on both sea and land, for they were expecting to intercept the silver fleet off the Azores and were loath to give up the favorite device of fighting Spain with her own money.[4] In 1627 they actually took the fleet from New Spain, and besides this time secured large booty from it on many other occasions ; while England followed hard after with numerous

[1] Haebler, Amerika, pp. 423–424 ; cf. pp. 300, 340, below.
[2] Cf. p. 147, note 3, above.   [3] Haebler, Amerika, p. 421.   [4] Hume, p. 207.

and damaging lesser attacks. In 1671 Morgan and the buccaneers stole the accumulated hoard of silver at Puerto Bello. The fact that the fleet was often discontinued in time of war shows the extent of the depredations feared.[1] The periods of war likewise introduced the peoples of the outlying districts of the empire to foreign merchants, and with great profit and edification upon both sides. In 1702, for instance, during the War of the Spanish Succession, certain ships authorized by Louis XIV passed through the forbidden Straits of Magellan from St.-Malo to Lima; and since they found the country destitute of the European merchandise it required they were enabled to realize 800 per cent upon their cargoes.[2] Because contraband could not be restricted so closely during wars, the latter really brought prosperity to the colonies.[3]

The first point-blank attack upon the empire was that of Cromwell in 1655, directed at Santo Domingo (Española) and culminating with the permanent occupation of Jamaica; this was dictated largely by the personal prepossessions of the Protector,[4] and was not repeated in so direct a manner until the capture of Havana in 1762. But the extent of the British contraband trade which developed from privileges accorded under the Treaty of Utrecht galled the Spaniards so sorely that reprisals and mutual recriminations were the order of the day. Hostilities were openly initiated by the sack of Puerto Bello and other exploits of Vernon in 1739, and for once a vigorous reaction took place. Vernon was repelled from Cartagena, and Spanish corsairs took English merchantmen in a few months to the value of $1,170,000. All Englishmen were expelled from Spain and trade with them was strictly prohibited. The force of this resistance was due largely to the temporary predominance in Spain of wise administration under the statesman Patiño, who had imitated the policy of England and Holland.[5] But the former burden of misrule always rolled back with irresistible inertia, and in 1762, after carrying everything before them and capturing Grenada, St. Vincent, St. Lucia, and Tobago, the English took Havana and treasure to the value of $15,000,000, an enormous quantity of arms and stores, and twelve ships of war; in the same year Manila surrendered to an English fleet. The one instrument

[1] Colmeiro, II, 401; Hume, pp. 290–291.
[2] Colmeiro, II, 421; Bourne, Sp. in Amer., pp. 294–295.
[3] Leroy-Beaulieu, I, 31; cf. p. 251, above.
[4] Haebler, Amerika, p. 424; Hume, p. 277; cf. Woodward, pp. 129–130.
[5] Hume, pp. 374–380, 395; cf. p. 256, below.

possessed by the Spaniards which upheld their monopoly in earlier times, and after the divine dispensation securing it had lost its force, was their navy. It has been seen that through most of the sixteenth century Spain was the first naval power in existence; and the union with Portugal, her only serious rival, in 1580, considerably augmented the size of the fleets at her disposal. Besides policing the New World, she was able to muster 164 vessels, well equipped and manned, to fight the Turks at Lepanto (1571), and shortly thereafter 130 sail with 10,000 men on the occasion of fitting out the Invincible Armada. Again, — for the merchant-marine of those days was much more than a cipher in war-times, — she had, even under the Catholic Kings, over 1000 merchant-ships. The contrast, seventy years after the Armada, is sharp: "in 1656 the whole squadron of Spain was reduced to six galleys in poor repair, the miserable remnant of the sixty which some writers suppose her to have had in 1535."[1] And as for the merchant-vessels, they were mostly replaced by those of foreign nations.[2] This represents a disastrous decline, and an efficiency in the maintenance of former advantages diminished almost to nothing.

DECLINE OF THE SPANISH SEA-POWER

Throughout our preceding studies in the field of commerce and colonization, that metropolis seems to have held the center of the stage which possessed the most efficient, if not the largest, marine. Cases still to be cited demonstrate the same fact, that commercial and colonial empire go with the prevailing sea-power. It is sometimes difficult in a limited field to judge which one — the empire or the navy — was the factor that called forth the other as a result: whether, to put it in a more modern form, trade followed the flag, or the flag trade. However, there is no question, given a colonial empire founded, as most of them have been, upon trade and across the sea, that under conditions of competition a strong navy is all but indispensable for its preservation. It is no wonder, then, that Spain could not defend or hold her colonies, even though Spanish America was geographically isolated and approachable through a few points only.

---

[1] Colmeiro, II, 465–467; Haebler, Wirt. Bl., pp. 56–57, 81.

[2] Haebler, Wirt. Bl., p. 85; Colmeiro, II, 440, 471; Roscher, Sp. Col. Sys., pp. 43–44.

The decline of the much-needed navy is but another phase of the disastrous destiny which fell upon Spain in consequence of conditions and policies detailed above. The deterioration of the merchant-marine, and of the navy as well, scarcely needs explanation after the restrictive policy is fully apprehended : " in general the causes for the decadence of Spain in the seventeenth century also hold good for her retrogression in navigation, for without agriculture or flourishing manufactures no commerce is possible, and without commerce there is no merchant marine or navy." [1] " The lack of competition condemned this marine to immobility : it made no progress and was in the eighteenth century what it had been in the sixteenth." [2] These quotations give the core of the matter, but some attention may be called to a few selected details of unwise policy and stubborn conservatism. Naturally the régime of taxation and of minute and suspicious regulation smote the Spanish ship-builder and seaman as they did the rest of the useful members of society ; [3] but assuming all this, which was general and need not be repeated, it is to the special system of restriction represented by the fleets and galleons that attention is now directed. First of all, as respects the merchant-shipping, the size of the fleet was limited ; it needed not to be large, for there was not much product of Spanish industry to take, and foreign goods were, on principle, anathema ; again, the return cargo made demands that were no greater. But few ships were needed, and if there had not been some evasion of the system, still fewer would have been called for even by the trade of a hemisphere. Thirty for the year was a fair average ; and as almost all of the other trade possible for Spaniards was discouraged, it is no wonder that presently less than half of the ships in Spanish harbors were Spanish, and that there was scarcely any Spanish merchant-marine left outside of the fleets.[4]

Under the system quality was called for with about as little urgency as number. As all the ships had to go together, the pace was that of the slowest ; all were armed to a greater or less degree and lumbered heavily, like floating castles, upon their way. The naval escort of the fleets consisted normally of nine galleons and eight frigates, manned by 1500 persons, of whom 950 were marines ;[5]

---

[1] Colmeiro, II, 470 ; cf. pp. 468–469.
[2] Leroy-Beaulieu, I, 36.   [3] Cf. Colmeiro, II, 468, 470–471.
[4] Haebler, Wirt. Bl., p. 85. For a general treatment of the Spanish shipping, see Lindsay, I, 554–620.   [5] Bourne, Sp. in Amér., pp. 286–287.

and the average length of the voyage for the whole aggregation, from Spain to Mexico, was over ten weeks for the estimated 6500 miles.[1] The small demands of the system, and the early security of the monopoly, allowed the persistence of obsolescent models, both of merchant and war vessels. Great transformations had indeed taken place since Columbus set out with a flagship of at most 280 tons and two only partially decked tenders of certainly less than 150 and 100 tons; but the changes were more striking to the eye than profitable for the type. Like the Portuguese carracks, the galleons imposed at first by their very size and unwieldy bulk, and for decades there appeared to the backward and unpractical Spanish no need, present or prospective, of change. Even the arts of seamanship, at first so great a care to the Casa de Contratacion,[2] were suffered to become antiquated. The whole decline of the navy, which had been rapidly retrograding under cover of an inflated reputation, became evident with the destruction of the Invincible Armada; for here the question as to the best adapted type of vessel and of naval tactics was settled, for that stage of history, once and for all. It is not necessary to go into detail respecting the defeat of the Armada, for the story has been often and eloquently told, but it may be said, in a word, that the Spanish vessels were out-sailed, out-maneuvered, out-generaled; for one light blow received many severe ones, and were finally destroyed or forced into a long and disastrous homeward journey around Scotland. Much even of their ill-fortune harked back to the incompetence fostered by the system of the recluse who sent them.[3] By the time of the last Austrian king the sovereign had no ships to protect trade any more than his subjects had them to trade with; merchants lost courage and ceased to struggle, for their ships disappeared into the hands of foreigners and trade was destroyed almost as thoroughly as agriculture and industry had been.[4] In the eighteenth century some attempt was made to revive the merchant-marine by imitating the English Navigation Acts, but the whole situation was so bad as to admit of little alleviation.[5]

---

[1] Colmeiro, II, 470 ff.; Leroy-Beaulieu, I, 36. "The voyage from Panama to Lima [1500 miles] usually took two months, and it continued to Chile, two more. This was partly owing to head winds and adverse currents, for the return voyage could be accomplished in less than half the time." Bourne, Sp. in Amer., p. 288. On the crossing of the Pacific, see p. 348, below, and refs.

[2] Bourne, Sp. in Amer., pp. 222-223.　　[3] Cf. Woodward, pp. 29, 61; p. 184, above.
[4] Hume, pp. 271, 304-305.　　[5] Cf. Colmeiro, II, 471-472.

THE CONTACT OF RACES

When Roscher says[1] that the Spanish colonies were originally pure conquest-colonies, he has in mind, as his following treatment demonstrates, chiefly the phenomena of the contact of races. This is the topic which is now to engage our attention for a considerable space; for this contact of races called forth what are in many respects the most characteristic phases of the Spanish colonial system;[2] and its outcome, for better or worse, has determined the destiny, at least for centuries to come, of a large section of the human race.

When the Spanish arrived, even in their relatively insignificant numbers, in America, they started the first case in history of the permanent contact of two races widely separated in civilization, this contact taking place within the habitat of the lower race. The Mediterranean colonizers had never encountered this eventuality; and the Portuguese did not locate in India, Africa, or the Malay region in sufficient numbers to create the conditions of real race-contact. In India, indeed, they met a race in many ways their superior in civilization. But the Spaniards found an ethnic strain, whatever its origin, which was new to the civilized world; and they lived beside it, molded its life, and intermingled with it for many years and decades. To it they applied, instinctively or with conscientious consistency, a policy or lack of policy which was the outcome of their own separate Aryan, European, and local history. It may be said, in partial anticipation, that the case was analogous in the Philippines.[3] So that we have in the Spanish colonies, if we care so to view the situation, the first historical meeting, upon a scale that deserves the name, of two of the great varieties or sub-species of the genus Homo.

[1] P. 133.

[2] The most noteworthy brief account of the Indian policy of Spain is from the hand of the veteran authority, Henry C. Lea. It offers corroborative evidence for the argument of this chapter and opposes "the attempts at exculpation which have been fashionable of late years." The narrative is built about the biography of Las Casas, to whose testimony a just amount of weight is given. Dr. Lea begins and ends his article with practically the same statement: the Spanish relations with the Indians show the essential mildness and good will of the powers at Madrid, but they likewise form an example of "how the kindly intentions of governments, expressed in beneficent legislation, may be rendered nugatory when administration is intrusted to unworthy hands or when sufficient influence is brought to bear by those who profit from abuses."   [3] See pp. 347 ff., below.

The Conflict of the Economic Need and the Religious Motive

The Spaniards started out, naturally enough, with no conception of the real state of the case : they expected to encounter a numerous and highly cultured Oriental population, with whom they could trade advantageously, taking to themselves all the gains formerly reaped by the Arab, Turk, and Venetian middle-man; and likewise to find the old enemy, Islam, with which they were prepared to try issue. In other words, while conquest was in mind, it was not exactly the kind of subjugation later carried out; and if religious aims were cherished, they were directed upon the old lines of crusade rather than upon that of such conversion of primitive heathen as Prince Henry had projected for non-Mohammedan Africa. There was need, therefore, of a considerable readjustment of views and intents when the truth began to dawn upon the minds of sovereigns and people. The first natives encountered by Columbus, and exhibited through specimens in Spain, were a curiosity. Though called "Indios," they were regarded as outlying Oriental tribes, as the natives of islands off the coast of the Grand Khan; there were no especial designs upon them, but rather sympathy for them, and pity, and the pious desire to insure them the hopes of a Catholic heaven.[1] The designs were on the more remote and cultured states and their trade, and had no gold appeared in Española this attitude might have persisted longer. Certainly one of the most impolitic things Columbus ever did was to send these wards of the Church home as slaves.[2] The queen could not support this policy, modeled as it was upon that of the Portuguese; and even in her will, as if foreseeing what was to come, she recommended with especial earnestness the protection of the natives against the greed of their conquerors.[3] The key to the queen's attitude lay in her strong religious nature, wherein material advantages weighed but little when their attainment was conceived to be detrimental to the extension of the faith.[4] Had the discoverers encountered

---

[1] The following provision (1503) may serve as an example of paternalism: the governor was to order that the Indians "no se bañan con tanta frequencia como solían, porque los Reyes eran informados de que eso les hacía mucho daño." Fabié, p. 52.   [2] Bourne, Sp. in Amer., pp. 50–51; Zimmermann, I, 232, note.

[3] Haebler, Amerika, pp. 395–396.

[4] Cf. the instructions of Columbus, the very first of which read: " Que procure la conversion de los Indios á la fe." Fabié, p. 18; Zimmermann, I, 232; cf. Bourne, Sp. in Amer., p. 207.

Moslems in America, the religious and material motives would have been in accord, mutually reënforcing each other, as they did with the Portuguese in India; but as it was, these two great driving factors are found to have worked at cross purposes with the Spaniards, as they did with the Portuguese in Brazil, producing through many decades an inconsistency between legislation and execution, and a constant strife between the champions of conversion and those of production and trade.

Thus, with the disappointing encounter with a primitive race and with the scent of the precious metals to disconcert the situation, the unscrupulous discoverers threw off the mantle of religion, or rather adapted it to new purposes; these as yet good-natured islanders should be used in getting gold, for, after all, they were the conquered, and were likewise about to owe their salvation to their lords.[1] Apparently, to judge by the fate of the first colony Columbus left, this idea of superiority to such a strange and foolish race speedily worked out into appropriation of all they had, including their women.[2] Then came Columbus, preoccupied with the necessity of proving his discovery to be something, as values were then reckoned,[3] — if not spices, at least gold, — and the divergence between the "theoretic" policy of Isabella and the "practical" working-out of an economic and political problem was already begun. For many subsequent decades of the Spanish rule, the exploiters of the colonial resources were driven to employ the natives as their instruments, while the home-powers, with churchmen at their elbows, were laboring over the drawing-up of benevolent and humanitarian legislation whose underlying purpose was native well-being and conversion. As in Brazil, the clergy sought the scene of the combat, fought bravely for their charges against the inertia of an unfavorable economic conjuncture, gained some successes, especially by acquiescing in the substitution of another slave-labor supply — in short, held up on the ground the less materialistic policy with which the authorities were disposed to treat the natives at the start.

[1] Martins (Civ. Iber., p. 242) quotes from Lope de Vega :

No los lleva cristiandad
Sino el oro y la codicia.

[2] Bourne, Sp. in Amer., p. 42; Zimmermann, I, 235. In Peru there was, after the conquest, no protection whatever for the women of the country, from the Virgins of the Sun, down. Watson, I, 173.

[3] Bourne, Sp. in Amer., p. 44.

SUBJUGATION

The subjection of the islanders was but a slight matter; but when the emerging motives of adventure and the search for metallic booty had, as above described,[1] drawn the Spaniards to the mainland, the conquests, in the full sense of the word, began. Subjugation, so far as the natives were concerned, was carried through with remarkable ease, except in the case of the Araucanians of Chile; wherever else the Spaniards set seriously to work to reduce the tribes, success soon attended their arms. Without going into detail, it may be said that the American Indians had never advanced to the stage of strong and coherent state organization: "The Aztec power was a military despotism exercised by three confederated warlike tribes, who lived upon the plunder of their enemies and the tribute of their subjects. War for food and war for victims for their sacrifices was their chief occupation." Their subjects were ever ready to revolt; and before the enlightened and resourceful Cortés, their resistance speedily disintegrated.[2] Similarly in the only other region of high indigenous culture, Peru, no national opposition was met; the overthrow of the theocracy meant the demoralization of the state and the breaking-away of its dependencies. The same inability to prosecute a siege to the end, upon a primitive stage of military and other development, saved the Spanish in Cuzco, as it had the Portuguese over and over again in the East.[3] The Caribs (= cannibals) of Tierra Firme afforded considerable resistance to the Spaniards for a time, but later, like other tribes of the tropics, became the victims of slave-raids; nothing was made out of the natives of the north of Mexico, of Texas, Louisiana, and Florida,[4] except through missions, and the same may be said of those of the south temperate zone. Indeed, it was here that constant setbacks were experienced through the protracted Araucanian wars. For, beginning with the first expedition of Almagro, in 1535, the Araucanians, a peculiarly patriotic and invincible people, kept up, through intermittent wars, a successful resistance of encroachment upon their rights, until the treaty of 1780 secured them tranquillity for the rest of the colonial period.[5]

[1] Pp. 177 ff.　　　　　　　[2] Bourne, Sp. in Amer., pp. 154–155, 157, 354.
[3] Watson, I, 128 ff.　　　　[4] Cf. Bourne, Sp. in Amer., pp. 160–161.
[5] Watson, I, 97, 162 ff.; Moses, pp. 155–156; Zimmermann, I, 343 ff.

Conquest, then, of the native population may be said to have been confined to the islands and to Mexico and Peru. What contact occurred elsewhere, unless merely ephemeral, was almost wholly the work of the missions; and this, for the present, is left out of account. As spoils of their conquests, the Spaniards took possession of the private and corporate wealth of the conquered, and were soon led, in the absence of labor force, to levy also upon their vital powers, — that is, to introduce the system of slavery. It has been seen that this was first done in the islands, and in the desire to get gold; but it was the possession of the Mexican and Peruvian mines, as a result of the historic conquests, which first lent to the slave system a stimulus heretofore unknown. The metallic treasure must be gotten, but the Spaniards were too few and could not or would not work; hence the native, who did not want to work either, must. Although, then, the mines were not in a tropical region, the situation closely approached that which is characteristic of the tropics; there were plainly no results to be attained unless the natives were enslaved. Here is where the colonists' needs and the government's desires came into conflict, and, whatever the laws, there was no question as to what the practice would be.[1]

"The Indians were considered, during different periods of Spanish colonization, under three different aspects: at first as genuine slaves whose lot was uncontrollably in the hands of the Europeans; then as serfs attached to the soil and subjected to the corvée and to pecuniary and personal obligations; and in the end as freemen, not however possessing full civil rights, but remaining under the tutelage of their superiors, and incompetent to make a valid contract above a certain limit."[2]

ENSLAVEMENT

Under Ferdinand, and even in later times, it was lawful to enslave cannibal tribes, or those taken in armed resistance to cultivation and Christianity;[3] during the first turbulent years, then, when there was practically no control, and what little there was had fallen, at Isabella's death, into the hands of the lukewarm and more grasping Ferdinand, the ancient right of the victor was generally applied. This speedily degenerated into slave-hunting

[1] Cf. pp. 12 ff. and 142 ff., above. [2] Leroy-Beaulieu, I, 12.
[3] Haebler, Amerika, pp. 397–398; Fabié, p. 55.

pure and simple, for the oppression exercised in Española early reduced the working force of that island, and rendered a substitute necessary. Hence the terrible raids through the islands and, later, the general deportation of whole tribes to the mines.[1] "In the early times of the conquest the Indians were abandoned without defence to the rapacity of the Spanish adventurers."[2] The plainly exceptional Cortés managed to control conditions in Mexico to a considerable extent; but in Peru the same ruthlessness was the rule. "When Peru was divided amongst the conquerors, each of the latter was eager to obtain an instantaneous recompense for his services. Men accustomed to the carelessness of a military life had neither the industry to carry on any plan of regular cultivation nor patience to wait for its slow returns. Disdaining to profit by the certain results of agriculture in the fertile valleys, they selected for their habitations the mountainous regions, which abounded in the precious mines. In order to develop these, many hands were wanted; and the natives were accordingly driven in crowds to the mountains. The sudden transition from the sultry valleys to the penetrating air of the higher altitudes combined with inordinate labor and scanty nourishment to produce an unwonted despondency, under which they rapidly melted away."[3] And where slavery was not ostensibly in vogue, it was represented by an unreasonable tribute-system. Gold was demanded where gold was not, at least in sufficient quantities; a friendly *cacique* (chief) in Española "offered to put an enormous tract of land under cultivation for growing grain if the admiral would only not demand gold, but Columbus needed gold to demonstrate that the colony would be profitable"; even when he reduced the gold-tribute one-half, he was still demanding the impossible.[4]

The original idea was to handle the Indians as free subjects of the crown, and, aside from the tribute, to hold them to paid labor through their caciques, thus imposing the Spanish system upon the semi-feudal native one.[5] But there were several fundamental

[1] Haebler, Amerika, pp. 194, 389; cf. Bourne, Sp. in Amer., pp. 38, 43. How the Spaniards utilized the superstitions of the natives for their own ends is again illustrated by the reported fate of some Bahama islanders. They thought the white-faced, bearded Spaniards were messengers from the over-sea heaven of their ancestors, come to take them there. Upon the assurance of the Spaniards that this was true, they came into the vessels in crowds. But when they later found themselves in the gold-mines of Española they fled to the mountains or sea, or killed themselves. Zimmermann, I, 249.

[2] Leroy-Beaulieu, I, 12.   [3] Watson, II, 127; cf. Bourne, Sp. in Amer., p. 254.
[4] Bourne, Sp. in Amer., p. 44.   [5] Id., pp. 206, 353; Zimmermann, I, 246.

difficulties in this system, the chief of which were that the Indians did not wish to labor either as long or as hard as the impatient exploiters wished, nor at the occupations which the latter desired; and that, in the limitation and simplicity of their needs, they responded but feebly and irregularly to the economic stimulus of wages. And the Spaniards, for their part, were but little disposed to employ economic stimuli where others, far more effective, were suggested by the very logic of the situation; they did not intend to forego the high rewards of unquestioned power over a despised race for the sake of religious or metaphysical scruples which they did not share, held by unpractical people who could not coerce.[1]

But in order to get the native situation before one still more comprehensively, it is necessary to reflect not only upon the general character and disposition of the Spaniard and his government, but also upon the personality of the Indian and the temperament of his race. Even a cursory study of the native American reveals the fact that he has never been successfully enslaved. Slavery in the sense of any wholesale appropriation of the enemy's vital forces did not exist upon the continent prior to its discovery; the stages of the arts and the development of governmental organization would not admit of it. Torture of male prisoners was more likely than their preservation, even through adoption; a tribute-relation, as imposed by the Aztecs, was scarcely endured. The race had been schooled to submissiveness as little as to agricultural labors. Hence the ineffectiveness of the Indians under the wage-system and their irreconcilability to that of slavery; the latter appeared to them repulsive and unendurable, and to escape from it the Indians of Spanish, as of Portuguese America, did not balk at the extremest recourse, as their swift decline in numbers testifies. The newly-met scions of long-separated human groups were therefore in no position to fall easily into some mutually satisfactory relation; the ethnic strains were so estranged as to demand indefinite years of wrangling and oscillation before mere proximity could be transformed into anything approaching kindly feeling and unity of purpose. As has been seen, the problems set by the contact were solved, if at all, mainly by either miscegenation or the elimination of one of the warring components. What example and education did, we have yet to inquire.

[1] Cf. pp. 258 ff., above, and 277 ff., below; Keller, Sociol. View, etc.

THE REPARTIMIENTOS AND ENCOMIENDAS

The first modification of the rough-and-ready methods through rational control was represented by the attachment of the Indian to the soil, or his elevation to a sort of serfdom. Columbus had been obliged in 1497 to compound with certain insurgents on the basis of allotments to them of lands which carried with them the enforced labor of the Indians. This was a system rendered familiar in the Peninsula through the Moorish conquests, where it embodied the recognition of the rights of victors over the vanquished.[1] The earliest designation given to such an allotment was *repartimiento* or "distribution"; and the repartimiento was employed extensively, under royal order, by Ovando (1502–1509). He allotted to one Spaniard fifty, to another one hundred Indians under their chiefs; and still other such groups to cultivate lands for the king. These assignments were accompanied with a patent reading: "To you, so-and-so, are given in trust ("se . . . encomiendan") under chief so-and-so, fifty or one hundred Indians, with the chief, for you to make use of them in your farms and mines, and you are to teach them the things of our holy Catholic faith." It is plain that the eye of the Spaniard was upon the labor force at least as much as upon the land; and for generations, as it turned out, upon the possibility of enforcing labor rather than of effecting conversion.[2] The evils of this system, as applied to a refractory race, will presently appear; Isabella, with characteristic sincerity of purpose, was led to abolish the practice, "but after her death and about the year 1509 it was re-established under the dissembling title of *encomienda*."[3]

[1] Bourne, Sp. in Amer., p. 206; Colmeiro, II, 381; Moses, pp. 110–113. "The American conqueror with his encomienda of Indians differed little from the Andalusian or Valencian noble with his Moorish vassal peasantry." Bourne, id., p. 256.

[2] Bourne, Sp. in Amer., p. 210.

[3] Colmeiro, II, 383. *Repartir* is a plain colorless word meaning to divide or distribute; *encomendar* implies benevolent intent, i.e. to give in trust.

From the standpoint of the Spanish Americans the assurance to the Indians of the rights of free subjects could only mean the ruin of the colony. For the Europeans either could not labor (in the hotter regions) or would not where they could, since their whole philosophy of life militated against anything of the kind. Of a consequence, productivity in the colonies was unthinkable without native labor. "But the Indian was not to be moved, without a certain measure of compulsion, either to a degree of industry adequate to the needs of the colonies, or even to a lasting relation of friendliness to the colonists. But this was absolutely necessary if the civilization of the natives, and above all their conversion to Christianity, so strongly emphasized from the outset in the history of the discoveries, were to be successfully carried out. Therefore both lay and clerical authorities united in the declaration that the concession of

Decline of the Native Population

It is plain that the encomienda, neglecting for the present its religious and social aspects, really represented compulsory labor, perhaps in a somewhat milder form, under a more palatable name. The natives, whether or no, were to work the allotments of their lords or the king. But, in the relative unattractiveness of agriculture, this meant, especially under the earlier repartimientos, labor in the mines. At first the term of this service lasted six months, and later eight, involving, since the mines were generally from thirty to two hundred and fifty miles distant, separation of families and excessive burden on the wives.[1] The labor in the mines was difficult and the rations scanty ; great cruelties were unquestionably practiced ; and the effect upon the physique of the miners was very serious. The lot of subjected peoples whose enforced services have taken the form of working in mines has been, throughout history, an unhappy and baneful one; and here, where the masters were rude adventurers in the possession of resources out of which they were anxious to extract only the maximum of immediate profit, the chance of mitigation was slight. Las Casas no doubt exaggerates many of the ills of which he speaks ;[2] but we possess clear testimony as to the character of the early treatment of the Indians, before and for a time after the establishment of the allotment system, in the fact of their practical extinction in certain wide districts.

Depopulation proceeded most rapidly in the Antilles, as was natural. The islands were the first meeting-ground of the two races, and the islanders were less numerous in proportion to the invaders ; upon the continent, especially in Mexico, the efforts of Cortés and of the clergy were interposed to mitigate the violence of racial collision where the victor knew scarcely more pity for

---

unlimited freedom to the natives meant the ruin of the colonies, in ways both spiritual and economic. Out of the negotiations which took place in this way and that, over the subject, there emerged finally the system of repartimientos and encomiendas. Under this system the personal freedom of the natives was recognized, it is true, in principle. But in order to promote their education up to the European type of civilization and their conversion to the Christian doctrine, they were assigned (re-partir) to individual colonists, or put under their protection (encomendar)." Haebler, Amerika, p. 396.   [1] Bourne, Sp. in Amer., pp. 210–211 ; Watson, II, 135.

[2] Las Casas went to the Indies in 1502. He began preaching against Indian slavery in 1514, and published his book on the "destruction of the Indies" in 1552. For his work as it bore on the question of African slavery, see Saco, pp. 92 ff.

the unmatched victim than beast does for beast.[1] But in the Antilles the native race was almost annihilated. In the first three years of conquest the population of Española was supposed to have been reduced by at least two-thirds.[2] Peschel, an experienced ethnologist and a critical historian, after weighing all the evidence, places the population of Española in 1492 at less than 300,000 and at over 200,000. In 1508 the number of the natives was 60,000; in 1510, 46,000; in 1512, 20,000; and in 1514, 14,000. In 1548 it was doubtful if 500 natives of pure stock remained, and in 1570 only two villages of Indians were left. A similar fate befell all the islands.[3]

The fate of the natives upon the mainland was not so swift or so sweeping. The accepted impression has been that prompt decline took place there also; and this view seems to be correct. Colmeiro says,[4] with some exaggeration, doubtless, that "the population of the Indies diminished with such rapidity that America, in the course of two hundred years, seemed little more than a desert. Mexico and Peru . . . were, toward the middle of the eighteenth century, all but uncultivated and depopulated." That there was a great decline in the native population of the mining-regions or near them during the earlier years of occupation no one seems to deny. Velasco, whose report dates from 1574, says[5] that "in all the discovered districts the natives were at the outset much more numerous than since, for in many provinces where there used to be a great multitude of them, they have almost totally ceased to be." He goes on to enumerate the causes of this result, among which figure war, self-destruction, flight to the mountains followed by starvation, illnesses, and bad treatment. Labor, especially in the mines, was excessive, and was supplemented by toil in pearl-fishing, agriculture, and the erection of buildings. Humboldt says[6] that this was particularly the case in Peru, where evil conditions had persisted down to his own times; fatigue, shortage of food and of sleep, and strains upon the physique in consequence of sudden changes of temperature in moving from lower to higher

---

[1] In 1574 the upland Indians were increasing in number, while those of the plains were diminishing. Bourne, Sp. in Amer., p. 199.

[2] Bourne, Sp. in Amer., p. 44; according to Fabié (p. 58), the native population of Española was reduced much, but probably not to one-tenth of its former number, as Las Casas says.

[3] Velasco, p. 94; Bourne, Sp. in Amer., pp. 213–214; cf. Haebler, Amerika, p. 397

[4] II, 387. [5] P. 26. [6] Essai, I, 72.

altitudes had depopulated Peru to such a degree that its status in 1800 was considerably worse than that of Mexico. As for actual numbers, Humboldt, discarding early and extravagant estimates, accepts 600,000 for the native population of Peru in 1793 as against 1,500,000 in 1575.[1] This estimate is certainly a favorable one as compared with those of Velasco and the viceroys.[2] The viceroys Castel-Fuerte (1736) and Superunda (1756) remark on the decline of the natives, charge it to the work in the mines, and suggest remedies; the latter calls attention to the absolute dependence of the Spaniards upon the natives and mentions his misgivings as to latent conspiracy.[3] The conduct of the Spaniards from the outset seems to have been of the most savage and ruthless type, following few of the dictates of humanity or even economy. " The provident arrangements of the Incas in behalf of their subjects were suffered to fall into decay. The granaries were emptied; the flocks of llamas were wantonly slaughtered; whilst the lives of the Indians themselves were held so cheap that they were not only systematically worked beyond their strength until they died, but were even occasionally hunted by blood-hounds for the mere amusement of their conquerors." It is no wonder that they were always ready to rise against their oppressors.[4] In 1780, indeed, there

---

[1] Essai, I, 55.

[2] An examination of the reports of the viceroys and of Velasco's compendium has yielded the following figures for the Indian population in the viceroyalty of Peru:

1574	680,000 tributaries (Velasco, p. 400); of these
	190,000 tributaries in the audiencia of Quito (Velasco, p. 405)
1590 (circa)	311,257 tributaries (Relaciones, II, 333)
1761	143,363 tributaries (612,780 persons) (Memorias, IV, Appendix, p. 15)
1796	608,894 persons (Memorias, VI, Appendix, p. 9)

The viceroy who reports for 1796 accepts a general decline of 1,000,000 up to that date (Memorias, VI, 77), and adds that the number of mestizos is 244,436 (Memorias, VI, Appendix, p. 9). It will be noted that the alternative estimates for 1761 furnish a rough multiple (nearly 4½) by whose employment the " tributaries " can be converted into " persons."

As to the comparative reliability of these estimates a word might be said. Perhaps the accounts of the viceroys are the most reliable documents, as these officers in their reports to their successors had little reason for misrepresentation, conscious or unconscious. Humboldt was a model observer, a thoroughly trained scientist, and a man of the world of wide and varied experience; few authorities merit more confidence. It is possible that he was led to present the more favorable aspects of affairs, especially in view of his evident conviction that conditions were on the straight road to betterment. Velasco is very highly esteemed by Professor Bourne (cf. Sp. in Amer., pp. 196, 335) and seems to the author as reliable as an official recorder in that age could be expected to be.

[3] Memorias, III, 132; IV, 88–89, 94, 100.   [4] Watson, I, 173.

occurred an uprising under the Inca Tupac Amaru, who had long attempted in vain to alleviate the lot of his race; and the result was the annihilation of the whole Inca tribe (1783), a general campaign of extermination, numerous inhuman deeds of violence, and the unspeakable embitterment of the Indians in general.[1]

The case in Mexico was not so bad, for Mexico benefited, after the first shocks of the conquest, from the sagacious rule of Cortés; it was nearer to Spain, and so more easily controllable. Humboldt compares it, to its great advantage, with Peru, in respect of the treatment of the natives. He states, however, that the numbers in the region of the city of Mexico were, in his time, only a third of the old population, and that the condition of the Mexican cultivators in the sixteenth and seventeenth centuries was very pitiable. Better treatment and a consequent increase in population came only in the eighteenth century, and especially in its latter half under the administration of Charles III and Gálvez. Humboldt's optimistic opinions refer almost wholly to contemporary conditions; in 1793 the total population, he thinks, was fully 5,200,000, and in 1803, 5,800,000; and these numbers he regards as above those of the pre-Spanish period.[2] Endeavoring to get actual figures for native population, one finds that for 1570 Velasco[3] gives to New Spain (i.e. the archbishoprics of Mexico, Tlaxcala, Guaxaca, and Mechoacán) 691,000 Indian tributaries, or about 3,000,000 persons. Two hundred and twenty-three years later (1793) Humboldt[4] takes the Indian population to exceed 2,500,000, exclusive of half-breeds, remarking that it has increased considerably in fifty years.[5] What it was before the time of Charles III we are left to infer.

[1] Humboldt, Essai, I, 112–113; cf. Zimmermann, I, 371–372. The figures of the latter author, since, in the absence of references, they could not be checked, and since considerable carelessness or credulity appears in his work, have been, for the most part, neglected. Those given in the preceding reference, however, have been found, by chance, to be nearly correct in so far as they refer to the end of the eighteenth century. Hence the following data are added for what they may be worth. Zimmermann says (I, 370) that in 1573 there were 11,199 laborers for the Potosí mines, but that in 1673, although the same regulations were in force, there were only 1674; that encomiendas of 1000 grown men were reduced in a century to 100.

[2] Essai, I, 56, 57, 65, 73, 194; cf. Colmeiro, II, 387, note.

[3] Pp. 182, 187, 207, 227, 240.   [4] Essai, I, 76.

[5] Humboldt's estimates allow for errors of under-enumeration where Velasco's do not. If the Indians form, as Humboldt says (I, 76), two-fifths of the total population, and the uncorrected whole is 4,483,529 (I, 57), the number of Indians would be, uncorrected, less than 2,000,000. As for the concealment in returns, to cover which he adds one-sixth or one-seventh, he remarks (I, 58): "Dans le nouveau continent,

Conditions elsewhere on the mainland are more difficult to determine and are not of special importance.[1] It is clear enough from the above that depopulation took place with great rapidity preceding the thorough establishment of control, and especially in those regions (of plantations and mines) where a labor force was in imperative demand.

CAUSES OF DEPOPULATION

When, now, the attempt is made to determine, with some approximation, what part of so disastrous a result was due to the Spanish system, it is necessary first of all to clear the ground by recognizing and then excluding certain general factors, ethnological and other, and their probable consequences. The phenomenon of the decline of a native race in contact with one more highly civilized is not, as has been previously shown,[2] an exceptional occurrence during the last four centuries. It occurs, indeed, in spite of policies of a benevolent character which have actually been put into execution. Under such conditions, decline seems to be owing to nothing tangible and remediable, but to the inevitable workings of biologic and other laws the action of which is generally very obscure, but which is clearly set into operation by more or less evident or subtle changes in environmental conditions. The introduction of the micro-organisms of disease, for example, among peoples never rendered even slightly immune through the action of natural selection; the introduction of strong alcoholic drinks, or of drugs, among tribes whose intoxicants were weak in their alcoholic content or whose narcotics or stimulants were mild, — these are results of contact which have been responsible for much mortality and degradation among native peoples. And there is a further consequence of contact which is all the more determinative because it occurs unconsciously and as a necessary function of the diversity of the culture of the races thus brought together. The travelers report the natives, though not directly ill-treated, and even though favored, as dying of homesickness, or *nostalgia*, as it has been

comme dans l'ancien, le peuple considère tout dénombrement comme le présage sinistre d'une opération de finances." For birth-rates, etc., in Mexico, cf. I, 61 ff. ; for the easy conditions in the mines, II, book iv, chap. xi.

[1] Since Velasco (p. 2) assigns 1,500,000 Indian tributaries to all Spanish America, and 680,000 plus 691,000 to Peru and New Spain, there remain only some 130,000 for the other districts, of whom there were some 80,000 to 90,000 in Chile (p. 514; cf. p. 551).

[2] Pp. 5 ff., above.

called. What this means, however, is not that they have been removed from their habitat, but that gradually their environment has been so altered that they are no longer adapted to it, or feel at home in it: a hunting-tribe is surrounded by cattle-ranges or farms, for example, and subjected to the civilized institution of private property in land. Now it is a well-recognized biological fact that alteration of environment is likely to find one of its first visible effects in derangements of the reproductive system;[1] and whether or not this be true of man in the case of a change such as the one under consideration, there certainly is involved a thorough alteration of the conditions under which the struggle for existence is pursued, and this cannot fail ultimately, in event of the usual inability of the native to rise at once to a much more evolved stage of the arts, to have its effect upon numbers and strength of the population.

Considering these more general points, now, in their relation to the Spanish-American contact, it is possible to assign great mortality to the introduction of diseases, especially the eruptive diseases, the chief of which was small-pox. In 1518 the natives died from this disease "like sheep with the distemper"; it appeared in Mexico at the outset of the conquest and swept off in some provinces half the population, seeming to be particularly fatal to women. Again, the Indians always suffered severely from the inferior eruptive diseases such as measles, for they possessed no knowledge of the means of treatment, but usually employed the steam-bath and cold plunge for all illnesses indiscriminately. The same may be said of diseases of the respiratory system; other epidemics also, including finally yellow fever, resulted from the presence of the Europeans in the local environment. And the famines consequent to conquest, besides bringing their own special and perhaps unavoidable mortality, simply enforced the ravages of disease.[2] It is, however, perfectly evident that maladies could not have produced the extreme and continuous depopulation to which reference has been made; such quantitative injuries to population are speedily made up, if the life-conditions are otherwise favorable.[3] Diseases have occurred in colonies of other nations, and in the later history of the Spanish colonies, but without such extended

[1] Cf. Darwin, Descent, pp. 185 ff.

[2] Bourne, Sp. in Amer., pp. 212–213; Colmeiro, II, 387–388; Haebler, Amerika, p. 397; Watson, I, 219; II, 127.   [3] Cf. p. 188, above.

consequences. Nor could the innocent or willful introduction of alcoholic poison have played any considerable rôle in Spanish America; for the Spaniards were peculiarly temperate, even in the use of their own light wines, and could not have introduced in very considerable quantities the consuming " fire-water " which demoralized the more northern tribes. Again, the change of environment brought about unconsciously by the encroachment of the bearers of a new régime of civilization, by the steady transformation of the region into one of a higher industrial economy, could not have occurred, in any generality, the immigrants being what they were in numbers and character, in Spanish America. The causes of depopulation must have been more local and direct than those which have been cited.

In fact, the common explanations of this phenomenon are based upon such local considerations. The savagery of the conquests and raids; resulting famines; [1] heavy taxes; the greed for immediate gain which did not scruple at overloading the natives with hard and unaccustomed labor, and even impossible tasks, while stinting them regularly in their food; the imposition of similar labor in particular upon women and children; the separation of families; the transference of plain-dwellers to the mountains,[2] — these are causes not necessarily inherent in race-contact, but which easily explain a great mortality and race-decline. It is also clear that the effects of the actual wars of conquest and their train of woes may be eliminated from consideration as enduring factors of depopulation; their effects could not have been so persistent. What is left are the divers manifestations of selfish greed in the exploitation, particularly in plantation and mine (hence chiefly in the islands, in Mexico and Peru), of a practically defenseless subject race. Whatever the legislation, this was the fact.[3] The very actions of the natives reveal the state of the case: they fled to inaccessible places, and there died or dragged out a miserable existence; they renounced cultivation at the risk of starvation, if only they might

---

[1] Haebler, Amerika, p. 398; Bourne, Sp. in Amer., p. 211.

[2] Bourne, Sp. in Amer., pp. 212, 214; Haebler, Amerika, p. 367; Watson, II, 126–127, 131; cf. Letourneau, Commerce, p. 214.

[3] Colmeiro (II, 400) inveighs especially against the system of allotments of merchandise made by the officials for the Indian families. The latter were obliged to receive goods in quantities and at a high price, and, not being able to pay at once, they were drawn into an oppressive debt-relation which hampered all progress and filled the breasts of the natives with hatred "against the metropolis, and against the infamous alliance of commerce and justice."

injure the Spaniards; they destroyed themselves in numbers; in their misery and despondency they even reduced an already declining birth-rate by renunciation of procreation or by infanticide.[1] It does not seem just to charge these truly pitiable results, without qualification, to the monopoly-system;[2] had such destruction persisted through centuries and throughout the colonial world, such an explanation would have been rendered more apposite, for the monopoly-idea, as has been seen, was universally in evidence. But the haste in getting wealth, and especially metallic treasure, was more generally determinative of the character of the early race-contact than any defined system could be; and this it was which motived irrational oppression. No doubt the frame of mind which found institutional expression in the system was bound, given conditions of contact with a subject race, to pursue such an advantage in the competition of life with thorough and consistent unscrupulousness; but it is difficult to see any direct causal connection between the upholding of a monopoly in favor of Seville, or the fleets, or Vera Cruz, or Spain as a whole, and the wantonness of the destruction of the Indians at the hands of the rude adventurers who constituted the vanguard of the Spanish in America.

PROTECTIVE LEGISLATION

Indeed, as a system of any kind became more workable, the figures given indicate that the decline of the native population was retarded rather than accelerated; the instances of extreme depopulation were confined in the main to the opening, or least-controlled, periods in the history of the colonies.[3] Where there was intelligence

---

[1] Bourne, Sp. in Amer., pp. 43, 210–211; Haebler, Amerika, p. 397; Peschel, Races, p. 151; Watson, II, 126. They were quite willing to take their chances elsewhere than in heaven if, as they were informed, the Spaniards were to frequent the latter place.

[2] "The most probable cause of the diminution of the Indians is the oppression itself of the colonial system, which limited the progress of agriculture, hindered the establishment of factories and looms, rendered commerce sluggish, and, in fine, choked up all the springs of public wealth in order to perpetuate an absurd and ruinous monopoly. Without adequate means of subsistence, the population not only could not increase but could not maintain itself on the old level. The ill treatment of the Indians and the unseasonable wars with the barbarous tribes are simply concomitants of the main trend of events." Colmeiro, II, 388.

[3] The true sign of real and permanent increase in population, says Humboldt (Essai, I, 64; cf. p. 102; Velasco, p. 26), is the increase of means of subsistence. This was evidently taking place at the end of the eighteenth century. Preceding conditions can be inferred from the foregoing description of the industrial organization in Spanish America.

and a strong hand, such oppression of the natives was much less pronounced. In Mexico, for example, the desire of Cortés, which was that of the crown, was to avoid such wasting of the population as had taken place in the islands; the encomienda system was limited to four generations, after which the encomiendas would revert to the crown. The tribute demanded was not to be more than that which was supported under Aztec rule.[1] Not a few other regulations were carried into effect to the betterment of the natives' lot. But that the encomienda system, however modified by the many edicts incorporated in the *Recopilacion*,[2] effected anything approaching eradication of evils may be seriously doubted. The whole economic and social conjuncture was against control of the Indian question: the colonists needed a labor force in order to realize their purposes of exploitation, and it was unthinkable that men of their stamp should not utilize the one at hand, and the more ruthlessly as it was cheap and helpless. Under the facilities of communication of the day, especially as abridged for an enormous empire with a thin and scattered population by the Spanish system of isolation, there could be little respect for a distant, poorly informed,[3] and slowly operating control. Add the inefficiency and vacillation of the Spanish authorities, and the picture of incompetence to carry legislation into effect is nearly complete. Finally, the very representatives of metropolitan control, the governors and viceroys, were largely imbued or soon infected by the spirit of their subordinates and outdid them in their own line; or were weak and inefficient, and over-ridden or intimidated even when their intentions were good. The difficulties of even the able, determined, and conscientious representative of the crown will presently appear, as well as the benefits assured to the natives by his occasional interposition. The rapid succession of the viceroys and governors rendered the development of any consistent policy all but impossible.

In fact, it was, in good part, "the persons, not the laws, which nourished the propensity for war and conquest; so that whether a governor was clever and prudent or stupid and impetuous determined the good or ill treatment of the Indians. In the city of

---

[1] Bourne, Sp. in Amer., p. 256; Leroy-Beaulieu, I, 12; Zimmermann, I, 300 ff. Elsewhere the encomienda-tenure became in some cases even shorter.

[2] Recopilacion de Leyes de los Reinos de las Indias, a collection of legislation made in 1681. Colmeiro, II, 382–383.　　　　[3] Cf. p. 305, below.

Mexico, for example, several years after pacification and subjection to our rule, the greater part of the Indians had learned nearly all the vocations of Castile, and were accomplished silver-smiths, lapidaries, painters and intaglio-makers, knew how to read and write, wove textiles of silk and wool, made hats, and bettered the cultivation of the fields. Others enjoyed exorbitant privileges and scarcely recognized vassalage to the crown; but all lived at the mercy of the encomenderos who held them in the status of slaves, or of the alcaldes [1] who tyrannized over them, making them work for them and appropriating the fruits of their labors. In a word, inasmuch as the laws and royal decrees broke down with distance from the metropolis to the colonies, the condition of the Indians was bound to be, and was in reality, very precarious." [2]

This is the key to the whole matter of Indian administration. The native laws were exceptionally humane, among those of all history; alone among modern nations Spain "tried to put into practice in her relations with conquered peoples the precepts of humanity, justice, and religion." [3] But they could not be enforced with any regularity. "Whilst excellent laws and regulations for the well-being and proper treatment of the natives of America were constantly being enacted in Spain, we nowhere read of wholesome examples being made of the wrong-doers, who treated these laws as a dead letter. Even the laws and regulations, good and well-meant as they were, were not the result of the reaction of public opinion against the ill treatment of the Indians, but were brought about by a few humane ecclesiastics who had been helpless eye-witnesses of the atrocities." [4] The laws were often merely protests; their recurring injunctions are to be taken in general, especially in their repetition,[5] rather as registered criticisms of an anterior state of affairs than as really effective measures of future control which can be assumed to have been carried out. The "Protector of the Indians," even when he was a Las Casas, was almost power-less. "In practice the treatment of the Indians was by no means always in accord with the beneficent purpose of the laws." [6]

---

[1] Local judges with some executive powers; cf. German *Richter*.

[2] Colmeiro, II, 385–386; cf. Roscher, Sp. Col. Sys., p. 9; Moses, p. 96.

[3] Leroy-Beaulieu, I, 11.   [4] Watson, I, 70.

[5] "The laws upon this point [i.e. the duties of the encomendero] are explicit, but were the customs in conformity with the laws? . . . These laws are so often repeated, the same prescriptions return so frequently with so few years' interval, that one may well ask himself whether they were not perpetually violated. Great abuses must have taken place." Leroy-Beaulieu, I, 13.   [6] Roscher, Sp. Col. Sys., p. 9; cf. Watson, II, 135–136.

LAS CASAS: THE NEW LAWS

What has been said is perhaps enough to indicate that Spanish Indian legislation was scrupulous from the earliest time. Slavery was limited and finally abolished in 1530; the tributes were made more reasonable and protectors of the Indians appointed; the encomenderos were required to protect, educate, civilize, and convert their charges; and their conduct was carefully prescribed, even to the point of requiring their speedy marriage, restraining their presence in the Indian villages, prohibiting absenteeism, and so on.[1] Although regulation necessarily proceeded in a tentative way, striking at abuses as they cropped up, there was already, by the end of the first fifty years after the discovery, a considerable body of Indian laws.[2] It was at this time, however, that the famous attack of Las Casas[3] upon the native policy was delivered to Charles V. If one credited its utterances to the full, as they were credited at the time and for many decades after, there is nothing left to say except that the enforcement of benevolent legislation had been thus far totally impotent. It is impossible here to dwell upon the life and work of Las Casas, but it is perfectly evident to one who runs that his arraignment reveals the feverish and neurotic tone of the reformer possessed of a fixed idea; of the forerunner of calmer and more constructive men—one whose destiny seems to be to evoke popular enthusiasm or rage by which the latter may profit. Of a consequence his statements call for considerable correction for error.[4]

Nevertheless there is, in his work, enough concrete evidence that can scarcely be false, even though it is selected, to demonstrate that the laws had been of comparatively slight effect. And that the more elementary and fundamental of these statutes had been consistently set aside is made conspicuously evident by the resistance encountered in their enforcement when reëmbodied in the so-called "New Laws" of 1542. The emperor had allowed Las Casas, who had been sent out by Ximenes as early as 1516 as Protector of the Indians, an almost free hand; and the latter had incorporated and reaffirmed in his new code all the most stringent,

[1] Colmeiro, II, 382–383; Bourne, Sp. in Amer., pp. 259–260; Leroy-Beaulieu, I, 13.
[2] Fabié's Ensayo covers the legislation of this period.
[3] Brevissima Relacion de la Destruycion de las Indias; a "voluminous plea" prepared for presentation in 1540, and published in 1552. Cf. Bourne, Sp. in Amer., p. 257.
[4] Cf. Bourne, Sp. in Amer., p. 257, where the author denominates Las Casas the "Lloyd Garrison of Indian Rights"; Watson, I, 75.

because the most axiomatic, of the preceding legislation, garnished, of course, with certain favored measures of his own. The New Laws, for example, absolutely re-prohibited the enslavement of the Indians; all slaves whose masters could not prove a just title were to be liberated. They also attacked the semi-slavery of the encomiendas, for it was really from personal dissatisfaction with his own rôle as an encomendero that Las Casas set out. "Encomiendas belonging to officials, churchmen, and charitable institutions were to be given up; encomenderos who had abused their Indians were to forfeit their holdings; no new encomiendas were to be granted, and existing ones were to lapse on the death of the holder." [1] In short, the laws were aimed squarely against the exploitation of the man-resources of the New World. The details, given this attitude, were negligible; it was precisely upon this main contention that the issue between the legislator and the colonist was joined. The colonist was confronted by the dilemma of working himself, which he could not or would not do, or resisting the removal of the only means he had for realizing anything for his past enterprise, services, or toadyism. Even if the freed natives would work for wages, which, and with considerable reason, he doubted, yet he rebelled against paying for what had been done so much more simply by the old system. Consequently the New Laws were received with deep hostility by the colonists. In Mexico they were incapable of enforcement, especially as concerned the limitation of the encomiendas; "that the attempt . . . did not lead to bloodshed in a popular uprising in Mexico was in large measure due to the wise discretion of the viceroy, Mendoza," who deferred the execution of the laws. Attempts at enforcement, nine years later, encountered as undiminished opposition. Even the ecclesiastics were, with rare exception, "in favor of continuing the encomiendas, and opposed to the liberation of the Indians." [2] The laws were published in Mexico, March 24, 1544, and Charles V granted the desired revocation October 20, 1545.[3] Their application was delayed, especially in Peru; trouble was seen to be imminent in that newer and more turbulent province, and in 1542 it was resolved to appoint a viceroy and a royal audiencia, through whom the new legislation might be carried into effect. In spite of the

[1] Bourne, Sp. in Amer., p. 255; Moses, p. 101.   [2] Moses, pp. 101–104.

[3] Bourne, Sp. in Amer., p. 255. The crown had tried already (1523) to forbid the granting of repartimientos in Mexico, and to revoke those already granted, but the order had to be withdrawn. Moses, p. 95.

resistance, shortly before, to the attempts of Vaca de Castro to limit the repartimientos, it was probably not foreseen by the government that the projected laws struck at the very foundation of the colonial society. But "the Spanish settlers in Peru, with remarkable unanimity, felt that the enforcement of these laws would deprive them of whatever material advantages and prospects they possessed"; and they lent the more attention to the projects of Gonzalo Pizarro.[1] The task of crushing this incipient rebellion and of introducing the New Laws was intrusted to a tactless man, De Vela, whose attempt at execution of the latter speedily led to armed collision and his death. Pizarro thus gained control of the whole of Peru. This remarkable manner in which Pedro de la Gasca restored allegiance to the crown (1546–1548) does not pertain to the present subject, but it is sufficient to say that he disposed of Pizarro and gained a perfectly free hand. Yet even he did not see his way clear to the enforcement of the prohibition of personal service, for this measure, above all else, had been the cause of the rebellion. He was forced to compromise and managed to leave the condition of the Indians "on as good a footing as colonial exigencies might admit of." To a man of any perception, as soon as he had arrived on the scene, the impossibility of carrying out the Laws to the letter became immediately self-evident. The rougher type of the frontier would not endure the diminution of what they conceived to be meager payment for great and admittedly arduous services; "and more than one governor, in the effort to enforce respect for the laws touching the encomiendas, was thrust aside by his decivilized contemporaries."[2]

EFFECTIVENESS OF GOVERNMENTAL CONTROL

That the New Laws did not shatter the encomienda system, as was designed by Las Casas at least, is evidenced by the fact that in 1574, out of 160,000 Spaniards in the New World, 4000 were

[1] See p. 304, below.

[2] Watson, I, 172, 175, 206; Haebler, Amerika, p. 397; Moses, pp. 102, 122 ff. "The crown had . . . to adopt some other policy than uncompromising coercion, or run the risk of losing Peru completely." Moses, p. 126. Naturally enough, the pretext of humanitarianism and religion was employed in justifying the repartimientos. As it was "evident that the colonists could not support themselves without the services of the Indians, the ecclesiastics and the leaders of the expedition [Pizarro's] all agreed that a *repartimiento* of the natives would serve the cause of religion, and tend greatly to their spiritual welfare, since they would thus have the opportunity of being initiated in the true faith." Moses, p. 115.

reckoned to be encomenderos. The Indians were divided into 3700 repartimientos belonging to the king or private persons. In the bishopric of Tlaxcala there were 200 Indian villages containing 215,000 tributaries divided into 127 repartimientos. Of these, 61 belonged to the crown and 66 to private encomenderos. In Yucatan there were 300 householders, of whom 130 were encomenderos. In Lima, of 2000 Spanish families, 30 held encomiendas; the Indians of the district, 25,000 or 26,000 in number, were divided into 136 repartimientos, of which six were royal.[1] But while the argument thus far tends to demonstrate the ineffectiveness of the earlier laws, and while their repetition after the middle of the sixteenth century implies that enforcement still remained lax in many places and times, it is not meant to assert that they were of no avail. The Spanish government never gave up, nor did the clergy; and after the empire was brought into a more settled order, this persistence had its effects. What retarded the process was, on the one hand, the deleterious effect of the monopoly-apparatus, which set back the development of such ease and frequency of communication as would have enabled the metropolis to overcome, among other disadvantages, its remoteness from its scattered provinces; and on the other, the character and personnel of the local administration, to which attention will presently turn.[2]

The government did not cease to scrutinize and attempt to control the encomenderos. It was not in the character of Philip II, at least, to stay his hand in a matter of regulation which appealed to his conscience and to his European clerical advisers, simply because the individuals to be regulated objected almost as one man. So the attempted regulation of the encomiendas goes on through the decades; several typical examples may be given. "No encomendero could own a house in his village or stay there more than one night (law of 1609, 1618); not even his nearest relatives or his slaves could enter the encomienda (law of 1574, 1550, and often). He was forbidden to maintain any industrial establishment in the encomienda (law of 1621), or to take into his house any of the inhabitants (law of 1528)." Indians were on no account to be sold

---

[1] Bourne, Sp. in Amer., pp. 196–200. The figures are from Velasco. The terms *encomienda* and *repartimiento* were all but synonymous in the time of Las Casas. Id., p. 206, note 4.

[2] P. 310, below. "Under the conditions of communication . . . the actual practice of Mexico was determined rather by the wishes of the local authorities than by the will of the king of Spain." Moses, p. 96.

by the encomenderos. None of the officers of the government might participate in the system of enforced labor, even indirectly. The Indians were compelled to labor in mining, road-making, cattle-raising, maize-culture, and like production of necessities, but were exempt from plantation service where the vine, olive, and sugar-cane were cultivated, and from labor in factories and sugar-mills. In Peru not over one-seventh, in Mexico one twenty-fifth of the Indians could be summoned to general service; and for that of the mines (*mita*) only those within a radius of thirty miles. Natives were not to be transported from the plains to the elevated regions. The imposition of irregular personal services (carrying in a litter, for example) and of porterage in general was forbidden; it was not intended that the natives should continue to be beasts of burden. General injunctions are liberally interspersed to suggest the proper attitude of mind in all these matters.[1]

Unquestionably the conditions of the natives were bettered as the government gradually got the situation in hand; hence they were better off in Mexico than elsewhere. In some cases the mita was shown not to be excessive by the fact that the *mitayos* worked overtime to gain the high wages promised.[2] A competent author-ity states that "in the last years of the Spanish colonial rule there were in general scarcely any well-founded complaints about the situation of the Indians : a certain status of minority and depend-ence, where it existed, was due far more to the outcome of the natural situation and of generations of ancient usage, than to that of the perverted application of the laws."[3] Nevertheless the en-comienda system did not appeal, even in a mitigated form, to Gálvez and Charles III (1759–1788), and the king abolished it.[4]

It is much to be doubted whether the well-meaning Spanish legislation ever possessed an apparatus of local enforcement of a character thorough-going enough to insure the desired economic treatment of the Indian, except in certain restricted districts and where the pressure to secure mine-workers was not so urgent. Leroy-Beaulieu[5] ventures the opinion that "when once the Crown of Castile could by its laws curb the undisciplined bands of the

[1] Roscher, Sp. Col. Sys., pp. 4–6; Bourne, Sp. in Amer., pp. 260–261 ; Colmeiro, II, 382 ff.; Watson, II, 135.

[2] Haebler, Amerika, p. 399; Leroy-Beaulieu, I, 12 ; Roscher, Sp. Col. Sys., p. 6.

[3] Haebler, Amerika, p. 409.

[4] Cf. Humboldt, Essai, I, 102. Gálvez was *visitador-general* to America (1761–1774) and was appointed *Ministro Universal de Indias* in 1775.   [5] I, 12.

first invaders, the lot of the Indians was so far alleviated that one might ask himself if the conquest had not, at least for the Mexicans, bettered their destinies." But, as Leroy-Beaulieu at once adduces the suppression of human sacrifices, he is evidently reflecting upon Spanish successes in conferring positive and largely immaterial benefits rather than upon actual results attained in thwarting unscrupulous demands upon the life-forces of the natives. In 1803 Humboldt gained an impression of Indian life which is expressed by the words "une grande misère." [1] It is very difficult to see where the position of the Indian was economically better under the Spanish régime than it had been under native rule. What the Spanish laws did, where they did anything, was to soften the rigors of a slavery or semi-slavery that was formerly unknown and to render this service endurable instead of utterly destructive. The fortunes of the Indians took a sudden and great fall as the result of the discovery; they were restored in part by the benevolent laws, where enforced; but that they ever reached their status under the pre-Columbian conditions, who could maintain? Spain is to be praised for her efforts rather than censured for their only partial success. What colonizing people would cast the first stone? The passions unleashed in such a contact of races as that in Spanish America were inherent in the situation and in human nature; and since it was the first important case of its kind in human history, the task of control was the more difficult. But that to which the conquered owed their misfortunes was not disease, nor any other impersonal cause, but the avidity of the conquerors, leading to reckless exploitation of the conquered.

Negro Slavery

One of the indications, however, that the Spanish laws were, at least for a time, locally effective is afforded by the early introduction of a slave-labor supply from without; for if they had had a free hand with the Indians, it is probable that the Spanish would have been slower in taking up with the slavery of the negro, despite

[1] Essai Politique, I, 103: "Les Indiens mexicains, en les considérant en masse, présentent le tableau d'une grande misère." They are "in a state of extreme abasement" (p. 106; cf. pp. 59, 82, 108, etc.). To the present writer it seems clear, in view of Humboldt's many other expressions of pity, etc., respecting the Indians, that his remark (p. 100) should not be interpreted in the sense taken by Professor Bourne (Sp. in Amer., p. 263); in aligning the Indians' status with that of the lower classes in Europe, Humboldt purposes only a comparison of evils.

the latter's superiority for their purposes. Some such agency for effecting the development of natural resources was indispensable if the Spaniards were to profit by either the mines or the plantations. As early as 1510, when the severity of the labor in the mines began to tell on the Indians, a few negroes were introduced; they experienced a high death-rate, but were so much more efficient than the Indians that in 1511 measures were taken to encourage their direct shipment from Guinea. This trade naturally developed with the decline of the Indian tribes of the islands, and perhaps with success in protecting them by law; "in the whole export-trade which Spain maintained with her colonies there was still only one article which could measure up in importance with quicksilver, and that was the negro slave." The method of procuring negroes was by letting out a contract or asiento, the first of which appeared in 1517. During the union of Spain and Portugal (1580–1640) these asientos were granted largely to the Portuguese as the holders of the sources of supply;[1] and it was the Asiento of 1713, as will be recalled, which really opened Spanish America to the British.

What the Spanish government was trying to do was to satisfy at the same time "the demands of economic production and humane feeling"; and in this case it was "by sparing the Indian at the expense of the African" that the reconciliation was to be made. The agitation of Las Casas furthered this policy powerfully; for, like the agitators in Brazil, his opposition was not to slavery as slavery, but to the enslavement of the Indians.[2] However, negro-slavery never became widespread outside of the tropical regions, the Antilles, and the northern coast region of South America;[3] according to Humboldt not over a hundred negroes were imported annually into Mexico. Figures given above[4] indicate the negro-component of the population of various districts. In general it may be said that the demand for negroes varied according to the development of that prime tropical employment, sugar-production. "The

[1] Bourne, Sp. in Amer., pp. 270–273; Haebler, Amerika, pp. 416–418. Saco treats most fully the whole subject of slavery in America; for early conditions, cf. pp. 61 ff.; for the asientos, cf. pp. 110, 146, *et passim*.

[2] Bourne, Sp. in Amer., pp. 270–271; Colmeiro, II, 389; Haebler, Amerika, pp. 400, 417.

[3] Humboldt's figures for the total number in South America are 776,000. Bourne, Sp. in Amer., p. 275. Carácas took by far the larger portion of those who reached the mainland; there were, in 1822, 387,000 on the mainland, of whom Carácas possessed 218,400. Roscher, Sp. Col. Sys., p. 10.

[4] Pp. 215 ff.; cf. Bourne, Sp. in Amer., p. 278.

development of the sugar industry and the growth of slavery were dependent upon each other, especially after the mines in the Antilles gave out. Each trapiche, or sugar-mill, run by horses or mules, required thirty or forty negroes, and each water-mill eighty at the least. Had the commerce of the islands been reasonably free, plantation slavery on a large scale would have rapidly developed, and the history of Hayti and the English islands would have been anticipated a century by the Spaniards."[1] But despite the relief supposed to have been given to the Indians, the Spanish government did not favor the wholesale introduction of the negro; in earlier days a ratio of slaves to whites of over three to one was regarded as dangerous. The asiento-holders did not introduce much over 3000 slaves a year between 1550 and 1750. A sequel of insurrections, one finally culminating in the establishment of the negro-state of Haiti, testifies to the justification, though distant, of some of the misgivings. Naturally, however, the planters, bent on gain and caring little for larger policies, took precautions hardly, clamored for more slaves, and were willing to get them by any means that were effective. There resulted the contraband operations of the English and French corsairs to which allusion has been made.[2]

Because of their value, due partially to their rarity, but more to a race-temperament which is adapted to the slave-status, the negro received kindly treatment, and really ranked above the native in the scale of castes.[3] "The Spanish laws and the administration favored emancipation at every turn," with the result that there existed a "large number of free colored people everywhere in the Spanish colonies." If the Spanish system had not been so restrictive as to paralyze plantation-production the case would probably have been different. "In general the slaves were not overworked for the same reasons that kept their masters from overwork"; and in the dulling of interest in tropical production lay also the reasons for omission of all severe measures looking toward security from uprisings.[4]

---

[1] Bourne, Sp. in Amer., p. 272 ; cf. Roscher, Sp. Col. Sys., p. 10, note.

[2] Bourne, Sp. in Amer., pp. 275–276; cf. p. 207 ; Haebler, Amerika, pp. 399–400; p. 247, above.

[3] Cf. p. 217, above. The Spanish term *castas*, it must be understood, does not connote the rigidity and exclusiveness which are associated with the word when used in reference, for example, to India. The castas are rather the ethnological divisions of the population. Cf. Saco, pp. 225 ff.

[4] Bourne, Sp. in Amer., pp. 280–281 ; Roscher, Sp. Col. Sys., p. 10, note ; Leroy-Beaulieu, I, 17. Nevertheless the mortality of the negroes was high. Saco, p. 130.

CHAPTER VIII

SPANISH AMERICA: MISSIONS, CLERGY, GOVERNMENT

INDIAN VILLAGE LIFE

Returning now to the consideration of the Indians, the question of their labor as slaves or serfs yields place to the more general one of their treatment outside of their connection with the services of the encomienda, that is, in their villages or in the missions. Ovando, in 1503, had been instructed to establish the Indians in villages, assigning them lands which they could not alienate, appointing a protector, erecting school-houses, and the like. This was largely for the purpose of restraining them from their tendency to withdraw from any sort of relationship with the Spaniards;[1] later, this village system was more widely extended in regions as yet but sparsely occupied by the Europeans. Here the natives remained subject to their own caciques, whose tenure was hereditary and who in general had charge of such part of the administration as directly touched the natives, while the supervision of the whole lay in the hands of several local or native officials (*alcaldes* and *regidores*) who were annually elected by the residents. These offices were not purchasable as in the Spanish towns, and were filled, in Humboldt's time, by respectable and conscientious men. One of the duties of the protectors was the collection of the revenue; and they were especially to guard against oppression of the natives at the hands of their chiefs.

Thus, while the towns and their Indian inhabitants were subject to Spanish laws and magistrates, the inner life of the village went on along traditional lines; the society was regulated, however, especially as to its external relations, with considerable care. Like the Portuguese, the Spaniards looked with suspicion upon the kind of European who might through trade or otherwise come into contact with the Indians; police regulations restrained Spaniards, mestizos, negroes, and mulattoes from settlement in the villages;

[1] Bourne, Sp. in Amer., pp. 209–210. On the early Indian legislation, see Fabié, pp. 34–35, 79, 87 ff., etc.

and a law of 1600 forbade even merchants to sojourn therein over two nights. No Indian, again, might live outside his village, or change his dwelling-place without permission of the authorities, — regulations which were intended in part to restrain relapses into the barbarism of the hunter's life. The provision that Indians could not own weapons or ride on horseback probably rested upon similar considerations. No wine was to be sold in the villages, and the alcoholic content of the native *pulque* was not to be increased by adulteration. The attention to be paid to conversion dictated regulations as to the presence of churches and priests, the expenses of whose maintenance came from the encomendero, royal or other; schools also, for the teaching of Spanish, were directed to be opened. For all these benefits the Indians were supposed to pay little, being exempted entirely, for example, from the alcabala.[1] In short, the so-called "reduced"[2] or village Indians remained in a protected status. "On account of their ignorance, and weak minds," they were treated with indulgence, as perpetual minors; "as late as Humboldt's time the laws of Isabella and Charles V. were still in existence — laws which declared the Indians minors for life, so that, for example, they might not, on their own responsibility, contract debts of over five dollars. *No pueden tratar y contratar.* Neither their real estate nor their personal effects could be sold except in due legal form (law of 1571), and the law gave its consent then only when it found the trade advantageous to the Indian. On the other hand, guilt in a criminal case could be pronounced only on the agreeing testimony of six Indians because of their great and universally prevailing lack of truthfulness."[3] Here, again, we have a system which is a credit to the good intentions and honor of the Spanish government, and to which, in all likelihood, approximation was made in proportion as the Spanish jurisdiction was settled and fortified. But it is clear that the net result must have been the hindrance of the development of industry in America, and so must have been generally combated or evaded upon the ground.[4] Naturally, as the encomiendas reverted

[1] Leroy-Beaulieu, I, 14; Bourne, Sp. in Amer., pp. 258–259; Roscher, Sp. Col. Sys., pp. 6–7; Watson, II, 135–136.

[2] *Reducir* means "to convert to the Catholic faith." A *reduccion* (reduction) was "el pueblo de indios convertidos á la verdadera religion (neophytorum oppidum)."

[3] Roscher, Sp. Col. Sys., p. 7. The Indians were not expected to emerge from this minority. Leroy-Beaulieu, I, 13–14.

[4] Cf. Leroy-Beaulieu, p. 14; Bourne, Sp. in Amer., p. 263.

gradually to the king, the administration of the villages became more direct and so probably more strictly in accord with the legal enactments.

EXTENSION OF RELIGIOUS INFLUENCE

The provisions which have been but casually noted hitherto respecting the conversion and religious training of the Indians call for some special mention. It was, as has been seen, one of the chief preoccupations of Isabella, as revealed in the first of the directions given to Columbus, that the heathen should be converted; and she adds that Friar Buil and others shall accompany the discoverer to assist in good works.[1] To Ovando, again, the injunction was given that the Indians should not be disposed against Christianity.[2] In other words, the attitude of the Spanish in America was not to be the militant one characteristic of the collision of Christianity with Mohammedanism, as, for example, in the Portuguese East; it was to be paternal, inspired by pity called forth by ignorance of the faith, and adapted to a state of intellect scarcely able to comprehend the dogmas of the Church. For this reason, again, the religious policy of the Spanish does not preserve a direct sequence from the Crusades as did that of the Portuguese as represented typically by the activities of Albuquerque. Columbus expected something more nearly like the experiences of the Portuguese; he had no idea of coming upon a whole new and virgin field. But when the truth began, at least in part, to dawn upon the Spanish kings and church that here lay an almost limitless opportunity for the exercise of the positive function of religious construction practically *ab origine*, the accession of zeal in the conquest of souls set on foot a series of missionary enterprises hardly matched, of their kind, in history. " The work of conversion . . . followed upon the heels of conquest, indefatigable friars devoting every moment to preaching, baptizing and learning the native languages . . . Every town, Indian as well as Spanish, was by law required to have its church, hospital and school for teaching Indian

---

[1] " Que procure la conversion de los Indios á la fe: para ayuda de lo qual va Frai Buil con otros religiosos, quienes podran ayudarse de los indios que vinieron para lenguas. Para que los indios amen nuestra religión, se les trate mui bien y amorosamente, se les daran graciosamente algunas cosas de mercaderias de rescate nuestras: i el Almirante castigue mucho á quien les trate mal." Fabié, p. 16.

[2] Bourne, Sp. in Amer., p. 207.

children Spanish and the elements of religion." [1] Naturally the friars extended their ministrations first and most directly over the Indians of the towns and villages ; but the really independent portion of their activity had to do with those natives who had not been "reduced" to village life and placed under the systematic control of encomendero or government. The most striking enterprises of the priests were those *misiones* which preceded or lay without the extension of the power of the state. In wide regions relatively or totally unoccupied by Europeans, they alone represented the forces making for civilization and conversion ; thus they constituted, as Humboldt pointed out, a sort of intermediary status between the true colony and what might well be called, from the standpoint of civilization, the desert.[2]

They were thus part of the apparatus of conquest ; the forerunners too often, and quite against their will, of the soldier and the exploiting slave-raider, cultivator, or merchant. That the religious motive was utilized as a cloak for more material ones, during the conquest, has been already indicated ; the very attack upon the Inca was rendered ostensibly more justifiable by his expressed contempt for the Bible and for the bishop who sought, *stans pede in uno*, to explain to him the doctrine of the Trinity. Likewise the missions had to be repeatedly restrained from converting the Indians by force ; regulations to that effect were put forth, "and yet as a matter of fact it was quite customary for missionaries, whenever slaves (*poitos*) seemed necessary, at the head of their soldiers and converted Indians (*Indios reducidos*) to make inroads upon the territory of the heathen in order to seize young people there (*entrada, conquista de almas*)." [3] For all this, however, the methods of conversion were generally peaceable ; despite their own enthusiasm for the faith, the friars seem to have taken a sane view of their self-imposed task and its possibilities and impossibilities. They allowed the Indians the gratification of their simple vanity in their long hair, indulged them as no Spaniard would have been indulged respecting confession, penances, feast-days, hearing of masses, fasts, marriage within spiritual relationship (*parentela spiritualis*), and so on. Even the eating of human flesh was overlooked. The Indians were regarded as children and

---

[1] Bourne, Sp. in Amer., pp. 303, 304.
[2] Cf. Haebler, Amerika, p. 401 ; Leroy-Beaulieu, I, 15.
[3] Cf. pp. 142 ff., above; Watson, I, 127 ; Roscher, Sp. Col. Sys., p. 9 (quoted.)

so treated; theoretically at least the Inquisition never had to do with them.[1] There were never any real prosecutions for heresy, for who could treat the vagaries of a child as significant enough to bear that name? This policy has been called humane, and it was doubtless so; but it was either blundered into with rare fortune or deliberately adopted with extraordinary discernment. Mere conversion, that is, the acceptance of the newly introduced cult and its adaptation to local conditions, is not so very difficult for a native people not under the dominance of some more than primitive religion; it is when the customs and habitudes (*mores*)[2] sanctioned by the respective religions come up for adjustment that the real strains of contact appear.[3] It is here that an uncompromising rigidity on the part of the more developed system may result in the destruction of all possibility of modifying the less evolved, and it was just here that the Spanish clergy introduced their principle of indulgence and forbearance.

THE MISSIONS

If now the work among the wild Indians was successful, "they were gathered together in a village called a mission, where, under the increasing supervision of the friars, they were taught the elements of letters and trained to peaceful, industrious and religious lives. In fact, every mission was an industrial school, in which the simple arts were taught by the friars, themselves in origin plain Spanish peasants. The discipline of the mission was as minute as that of a school: the unmarried youth and maidens were locked in at night; the day's work began and ended with prayers and the catechism; each Indian, besides cultivating his own plot of land, worked two hours a day on the farm belonging to the village, the produce of which went to the support of the church. The mission was recruited by inducing the wild Indians to join it, and also by kidnapping them. Spanish America from California and Texas to Paraguay and Chile was fringed with such establishments, the outposts of civilization, where many thousands of Indians went through a schooling which ended only with their lives. In the process of time a mission was slowly transformed

[1] Roscher, Sp. Col. Sys., p. 7. Negro slaves were treated with similar clemency. Id., p. 10, note.   [2] Cf. Sumner, Folkways.

[3] E.g. the Spanish found the polygamy of the chiefs especially difficult to deal with. Bourne, Sp. in Amer., p. 304.

into a 'pueblo de Indios' . . . and the mission frontier was pushed out a little farther." Later the whites gradually established themselves among the Indians. "The missions become Spanish villages, and the natives lose even the remembrance of their natural idiom. Such is the progress of civilization from the coasts toward the interior — a slow progress shackled by the passions of man, but sure and uniform."[1] It was not until after the conquests were over (middle of the seventeenth century) that the missionary enterprises really began to discharge these important functions. But after that time, with their forts or *presidios*, guns and cavalry, they formed for the government, and with little cost to it, the best of outposts.[2] In their influence as nuclei of civilization they were remotely similar to the Roman *coloniae*.

The tact of the friars in not insisting upon instantaneous and absolute change of old habitudes has already been accorded some attention. But as explanatory of the really astonishing influence exerted by them upon their charges, decided emphasis must be laid upon the fact brought out in foregoing quotations, namely, that the basis of their whole system was industrial. It was their demonstration of success in the organization of industry which held their charges to them. The Indian, particularly of Mexico, was quite able to see the aptness of new agricultural methods and mechanic arts, and valued them and the greater ease of living consequent upon their exercise enough to be willing to accept all the religious paraphernalia and ceremony which, in this case, accompanied them. The missionaries preserved, first of all, the natural resources which had often previously been wasted : their strict regulation protected game and favored domestication and breeding. Then they got together from 200 Indians (in the inland missions) up to from 800 to 2000 (near the sea), and engaged them in a style of production clearly superior to that which they had been practicing, but yet easily maintainable under the priests' direction. "The finest mission of New California, San Gabriel Arcángel, still in 1834 numbered almost 3,000 Indians and possessed 105,000 head of horned cattle, 20,000 horses, and over 40,000 sheep ; they harvested annually 20,000 *fanegas* (20,000 to 40,000 bushels) of

---

[1] Bourne, Sp. in Amer., pp. 305–306 ; and Humboldt, quoted in id., p. 306. For a brief description of the mission, with references to more detailed accounts, see Roscher, Sp. Col. Sys., p. 12.

[2] Roscher, Sp. Col. Sys., pp. 12–13.

corn, 500 barrels of wine, and as much brandy." [1] " The foundation, the maintenance, and, up to a certain point, the prosperity of such establishments is one of the most notable facts of Spanish colonization.   These little societies were productive beyond the personal consumption of their members : they carried on a rather notable commerce in foodstuffs and in articles for exportation; they exchanged this surplus of production for ornaments for the church. They thus responded, although in a measure peculiarly limited, to the two mercantile desiderata of colonization : they furnished Europe with the raw products, and they drew upon Europe for manufactured articles : they constituted a region of demand and of supply." [2]   In other words, they attracted their charges, through the example of their own efforts and productions, and by means of this limited participation in the trade of the outside world, within the range of influences which profoundly modified the industrial basis of their social organization.   They assembled the natives into relatively large aggregations and then set before them a standard of economy somewhat higher than their own, but not so lofty that its benefits were not immediately self-evident.   In short, they began and continued their enterprise with the direct effort to modify the organization of industry, — to better organize the struggle for existence, — introducing changes in the matter of religion, marriage-system, etc., with tactful deliberation.[3]   This is one of the more general reasons for their success in dealing with a situation before which so many peoples have failed.

SECLUSION OF THE NATIVES

In fact, the *misioneros* seemed to feel that immediate and full contact with a higher civilization could do only harm to their charges.   Consequently the seclusion practiced in the villages found its extreme type in the mission ; and it was expressly stated that it was the enlightened people (*gente de razon*) with whom the natives were not to have intercourse.   The padres superintended the traveler during his sojourn and speeded him forward as soon as possible ; usually a single night's lodging was the extreme of tolerance.   Thus, too, was trade controlled : " the missionary, who did not himself disdain to trade, was to form the only connection

[1] Roscher, p. 143; cf. Leroy-Beaulieu, I, 15.
[2] Leroy-Beaulieu, I, 16; cf. Roscher, Sp. Col. Sys., p. 13.
[3] Cf. Keller, Sociol. View, etc.

between the mission and the outside world." [1] In view of the character of Spanish emigrants in the earlier periods such a strict policy of seclusion seems somewhat justified; on the other hand, the very presence of the Indians gave point to many of the conscientious government's restrictions of movement imposed upon the Spaniards.[2] But the policy led to frequent collisions with secular authorities, and, had production with a view to exportation reached any considerable development under the Spanish system, doubtless the same phenomena of conflict between clergy and settlers observed in Brazil would here have been repeated.

On the whole, and despite the fact that the clergy deteriorated somewhat in morals in the new environment, the control of the Indians seems to have been in good hands. Here again the omnipresent governmental regulations forbade the missionaries to accept any perquisites whatever beyond their small salaries; and, although such prohibitions were here eluded, as they were on other fields, still the picture of the priests is one, in general, of the endurance of " the greatest hardships with almost indescribable resignation "; of " silent and pious enthusiasm." [3] There was, in the Spanish dominions, scarcely any temptation to actual competition between the missions and the planters, and consequently the former did not exhibit the worldliness and lust for power characteristic of many of the aldeias of Brazil. Whatever the artificial seclusion, the geographical was too thorough-going to admit of much participation in the struggle for wealth, even though the missions had been climatically so situated as to have produced the tropical products upon which attention centered. By the time, too, that the mission had been included within the slowly expanding area of intercourse with the outside world, it was no longer a mission.

The services of the clergy in the education of the natives, aside from the important training given in industry, have been indirectly touched upon in the foregoing. Indeed, the mechanic arts were themselves taught in the city schools. Both the crown and the Church were solicitous for education in the colonies, not only for the Indians but for the rest of the population as well. To this we shall revert. But the instruction as given in the missions was

---

[1] Roscher, Sp. Col. Sys., pp. 13–14; Leroy-Beaulieu, I, 15–16.

[2] Bourne, Sp. in Amer., pp. 247–248.

[3] Pöppig in Bourne, Sp. in Amer., p. 14; for the immorality of the clergy, see p. 299, below, and p. 188, note 4, above.

necessarily slight, consisting of reading, writing, singing, and the like.[1] At the most it may have given an initial impetus to some individuals of more than ordinary powers, who might then take advantage of a higher instruction from which they were not debarred, but to which they were, rather, invited.

THE JESUIT REDUCTIONS IN PARAGUAY

Before closing the topic of the missions, it remains to sketch briefly the history of the most reputed of them all — the Jesuit Reductions in Paraguay. The Jesuits had been active in America from early times, but rather more in the Portuguese possessions than in those of the Spanish. In particular they had been endeavoring to rescue the Guaraní Indians from the persecution of the Portuguese slave-raiders and the colonists of Asuncion and Buenos Ayres. Finding that the commoner method of simply collecting the Indians about them in the wilderness really acted as a temptation to raiders, whom they could not resist without organization, and whom the state could not quell in that distant corner of the empire, they strove for a certain autonomy and grant of local power. They attained such an exceptional status in 1608, when Philip III assigned them a field in Paraguay, which was under no civil power, and where they might, exempt from colonial control, undertake the civilization and conversion of the Indians on the grand scale. Two friars arrived in 1610 and established the first reduction, called Loreto, upon the upper Paraná; the neighboring natives were invited to resort there to receive instruction and become members of the community. It is not surprising that they did so in numbers, for the contrast between the ways of the Jesuits and those of the European settlers and raiders was such as to attract confidence.[2] Once in control of their charges, the Jesuits speedily put into operation a most skillful adaptation of the communism natural to primitive tribes who have never yet attained to an agricultural economy. Their model might well have been in many respects the Inca state with its denial of private property and with its universal obligation to labor. And for this society they created a defensive force which gave it the character of an independent state and secured it against its enemies for many years.

[1] Bourne, Sp. in Amer., pp. 308–309.
[2] Haebler, Amerika, pp. 403–406; Watson, I, 266–267. For a fairly complete though rambling treatment of the Jesuits in Paraguay, see Zimmermann, I, 377 ff.

Roscher [1] provides the best brief sketch of the internal relations of the reduction: "In every mission the Indians chose their own *gobernador*, although, naturally, subject to the veto of the priest, to whom, likewise, all the punitory sentences of the *gobernador* had to be submitted for confirmation. These punishments had altogether the character of church penances. Usually the affairs of the mission were divided between two monks; the elder had the spiritual oversight, the younger the secular economic control. With great shrewdness the Indians were formed into a military organization and, allured by the splendor of uniforms, titles and the like, they came to constitute a well-constructed machine. All foreign necessities were paid for by the sale of Paraguay tea [*maté*] which the order managed 'because the Indians are too timid.' Then, too, the laborers and such people worked under the direction of the priest, and even the public slaughter-house was managed by him. Work on the *conuco* [i.e. on the common land] claimed two days of every week. The beginning and ending of a day's work were marked off by church ceremonies; likewise the hour and manner of meals, dress, and so on were arranged once for all by the mission. 'The missionaries,' says Duflot de Mofras, 'had solved the great problem of making work attractive. They had brought the Indians to the realization that, grouped about the mission, they were safer from the attacks of hostile tribes, and that they could maintain themselves more comfortably and plentifully from the light and varying work of the mission than from the insecure and dangerous spoil of the chase and of robbery.' In every mission there was a special house, called *beaterio*, where women of bad repute were kept under surveillance; here also resorted childless married women during the absence of their husbands. In similar cloistered seclusion young maidens (*monjas*) were reared up to marriageable age. The missionaries, too, had charge of the diversions, combining with them instruction in all kinds of vocal and instrumental music. One may see how ably the community of property which obtains among almost all quite rude peoples was here retained, and yet was freed from its natural defects by a remarkably appropriate organization of labor."

It should be noted that the Jesuits employed the same tactfulness exemplified by the missionaries above described, but in a degree exhibiting even more insight and discernment. The communal arrangements, the pomp of uniform and title, the ceremonies

---

[1] Pp. 145-146; cf. Haebler, Amerika, pp. 405-407.

dividing off the day, the seclusion of young women, the attention paid to diversion and play, — these and many other minor details could not have gone astray in their effect upon native predispositions. The compulsion to light labor was taken, again, as the basis operandi; "the monks followed the only intelligent course for missions among heathen — they realized that conversion has to begin with civilization."[1] Since the Jesuits had all the power, they were responsible for all the general results of their experiment. So far as the natives were concerned there seems to have been little question that they found it satisfactory; for they consistently followed the fathers and made every attempt to retain them when the state decreed their recall. The reductions grew in numbers and population, so that by the end of the seventeenth century there were forty large establishments, the greatest of which contained from 15,000 to 20,000 souls. At a very early period of their dominance the order controlled a military force of 7000. That the growth of these stations was so rapid during their first quarter-century was due in great part to the desire for protection against the furious Paulista raids of that period; and that this protection was found efficacious admits of no doubt.[2] What the Jesuits have been blamed for is that they made of their charges mere apes and parrots, incapable of progress and invention if left to themselves. The old accusations against communism, that it destroys emulation and individual initiative, were lodged against the reduction. Again, the protests were directed against the rigorous seclusion policy, for in this the Paraguay Jesuits rivaled all other missionaries because they had the power to do so. They admitted no European even within the bounds of their reductions, "and, having themselves no ties of kindred by marriage or otherwise with those around them, remained a distinct class apart. Their disciples were not even instructed in the Spanish or any other European tongue, save so much, perhaps, as was implied by their being taught to patter certain prayers by rote."[3] But this amounted, the critics of the Jesuits have regularly asserted, to the inducing of a mental and moral imbecility in a group held in virtual servitude for ulterior ends. One author[4] puts it thus: "One of the two following causes appears reasonable, — either the administration of the Jesuits was

---

[1] Haebler, Amerika, p. 406.
[2] Haebler, Amerika, p. 407; Watson, I, 269, 271, 276, 279; p. 144, above.
[3] Watson, I, 272; cf. pp. 271–277; p. 287, above.   [4] Watson, I, 278.

contrary to the civilization of the Indians, or they were such a people as were incapable of emerging from their primitive state of infancy."

To such comments the Jesuits bluntly replied " that the Indians could not have been developed out of the condition of perpetual childhood; that a larger measure of individual freedom would only have injured the individual and general weal." [1] It is probable that they were correct in principle; and it is likely also that the objections of the colonists were based upon something more solid than a theoretic dispute concerning the best way to exercise benevolent intent toward the savage. But the experiment was to produce no demonstrable result.

Expulsion of the Jesuits

The colonists had not welcomed the interference of the Jesuits with their own way of working out the Indian question, and as the reductions waxed in numbers and prosperity their discontent and jealousy, fostered doubtless by the sight of Jesuit ambition and independent policy, took on more ominous proportions. For here, as elsewhere, the inevitable success which attended the first intent, vigorous, and fearless onslaught of the strictly disciplined monks, was speedily metamorphosed into characteristic presumption and odious self-sufficiency. Without following out the details, it may be said that the settlers determined to possess their own Indians and to put an end to Jesuit pretensions to actual empire, and that out of the resulting situation, together with a boundary dispute with Portugal in Brazil, rose the War of the Seven Reductions (1753–1761). Certain Guaranís were obliged to remove from seven missions located in territory ceded to the Portuguese; they were insufficiently provided for, became wearied and exasperated, and finally resisted the treaty; and the other twenty-four reductions showed sympathy. The Jesuits then became the scape-goats, being held by the treaty-commissioners to persuade the Indians, and at the same time distrusted by the latter as the causes of all their troubles. War was declared untimely, and probably under local pressure, upon the Seven Reductions. The Jesuit Provincial then addressed to the authorities, in the name of the order, a general resignation of control of all the communities; but it was not

[1] Haebler, Amerika, p. 407.

accepted. The fathers were summoned by the government to deliver up the revolting reductions without resistance; they were the sole cause of the rebellion and would otherwise be guilty of high treason. And when, finally, Spain and Portugal had grown weary of the demarcation question, the priests were required to collect the scattered remnants of the natives and encourage them to repair their ruined towns and recultivate their devastated country.[1]

In 1767 came the expulsion of the Jesuits and the "last significant phase in the native-policy of Latin America."[2] After this time, in Paraguay as elsewhere, the lay authorities controlled the Indians together with the rest of the population. The impoverishment of the Paraguay communities under the shortsighted exploitation of the controllers, who "regarded the goods of these communities as a mine which they might not be allowed to work but a short time," bears witness again to the real virtues of the Jesuit rule. The Jesuits were more intelligent than their successors; they were skillful, moderate, and economical; "they looked upon the towns as their own work, and regarded them as their peculiar property and sought to improve them."[3]

Conclusion of the Spanish Native-Policy

Returning now to a final glance over the Spanish native-policy and its results, it is necessary to recall not only the economic, social, and religious aspects of the case, but also to retain within the perspective that prime phenomenon in the contact of races in Spanish America, miscegenation. Viewed in the large we have, then, first of all, the creation of what might rank as a mongrel race, the Spanish-American. Opinions are still too widely divergent regarding the suitability of this race to world-conditions to allow of the determination of a consensus. But that it constitutes a really important advance in the process of the modification of humanity toward the necessary type of the future, few would assert. If the evolutionary process consists, in the last analysis, in weeding out races which are less fit to compete in the larger struggles of a later age and of a world more fully occupied, then there seems here to have been called into being a new nondescript,

[1] Watson, II, 222–231; cf. I, 279.   [2] Haebler, Amerika, p. 409.
[3] Moses, p. 235; cf. Fabié, p. 22.

whose ultimate fate is not so clean-cut as that of either of its racial components. The Spaniards, unlike the more northern peoples, particularly those of English origin, have been willing to depart from the European standard and affiliate with a lower race; "in Spanish America, the Spaniards have mingled their blood with the blood of the natives, and have compromised with them in the formation of political and religious institutions. The English policy has tended to exterminate the barbarians; under Spanish dominion the Indians have, indeed, perished in great numbers, but those who have survived have entered to form a constituent part of the new nation." [1] Whether the Spanish policy, however well it compares in immediate effects with the uncompromising practice of the English and of the Americans of the United States, represents a process suited to world-conditions, is a question which must await a definitive answer in future generations.

When now the results of Spanish native-policy, aside from race-mixture, are made the subject of reflection, it is seen that there could be no such conflict of races as has so generally occurred in temperate regions. In the tropical areas of Spanish America, excepting the islands, the native element remained strong or the mixed race arose; there was naturally no formation of European communities to compete with and destroy the natives. In the limited areas of the islands the natives disappeared before temporary or shifting concentrations of greater numbers; there was here no conflict and competition of societies. On the Mexican and South American plateaus there were no factors in the environment which were prohibitive of the development of the farm colony. Communication with the outside world was difficult, but no more so than in many another colony of settlement. To be sure, the natives declined before the hardships of labor in the mines; but here again, for reasons of Spanish character and policy, real European societies were not founded. Hence there could not have been an advancing frontier of the English type, "with its clean sweep, its clash of elemental human forces"; with its results of a home established "for a more advanced civilization and a less variously mixed population, and its justification like that accorded perforce to the inexorable processes of nature." [2] The temperate plateaus of the New World make the impression, if the terms be allowed, of unsettled colonies of settlement.

[1] Moses, pp. 306–307.   [2] Bourne, Sp. in Amer., p. 306; Moses, p. 306.

Since, then, there was no real race-conflict resulting from the impact, in the struggle for existence, of rival societies, there was left a free field for the religious and benevolent operations of the exclusively male communities of the clergy; and there resulted that gradual and all but unconscious advance of frontiers which has been described.[1] The missionary had time to exert an unhurried influence before the settlers were upon his heels, introducing economic and social factors into the situation which would not have been consonant with his aims, or methods, or even presence. Consequently, even though the assertion be not accepted that "as the child physically and mentally passes rapidly through the earlier development of the race, so the natives of New Spain in a generation and a half were lifted through whole stages of human evolution,"[2] yet it is freely admitted that, as within limited districts much was done speedily, so over greater areas a good deal was accomplished, though in slower tempo. If such uplifting of a native race has not been matched on earth, if it is "one of the great achievements of human history,"[3] it must still be recognized that many of the uniquely favoring conditions were neither created by the Spanish nor consciously taken into account. What the Spanish system did was, negatively, to keep out those who might have competed with the natives, with results analogous to those commonly met with in settlement colonies, — and the object of this exclusion was dictated only partially by religious and benevolent purposes respecting the natives; and what it did positively was to intrust the latter to the clerical agents selected. The importance of the clergy and the tactfulness of their measures were certainly very great; clerical successes in America cause Roscher,[4] with other cases likewise in mind, to assert that "barbarous peoples who are unable to maintain their complete independence are most gently subjected by a strong Church."

CLERICAL ORGANIZATION

Although the most important part of the work of the Church in America has now been sketched, the method of presentation has

---

[1] Pp. 287 ff., above.

[2] Bourne, Sp. in Amer., p. 201. It is perhaps captious to point out that the strength of this comparison, granted that it is not calculated to carry an argumentative weight not sustainable by analogy, rests in a confusion of ontogenetic, phylogenetic, and societal evolution.   [3] Bourne, Sp. in Amer., pp. 195–196; cf. pp. 196–201, 303–304, 353–354.

[4] Sp. Col. Sys., p. 15.

not yet admitted of an account of the general clerical organization, apart from its purposes. The chief characteristic of the Church in Spanish America is, perhaps, its subjection to the crown. "Because no monarch of the world was esteemed so Catholic as the Spanish, so none had such a power over his country's church with the permission of the pope. . . . This influence was even much greater in America, a papal donation. No priest could go to America without the express permission of the king (law of 1522 and later). The ecclesiastical patronage of the whole of the Indies belonged exclusively to the crown; by it all bishops were nominated to the pope, and all canons to the prelates (law of 1508). Again, no papal bull could extend to America except by permission of the Council of the Indies. One of the most important prerogatives was the royal sale of indulgences; similarly the annates flowed not into the papal but into the royal treasury." Members of the religious orders went to America in most cases at the king's expense, and remained under his jurisdiction. "The long list of ordinances limiting the movements and general activity of the members of the religious orders indicates to what marvelous lengths and into what minute details Spain's restrictive system extended." [1]

As in Spain, the clergy was composed of the regulars, or members of orders, and of the seculars of all grades; the regulars held the large monasteries in the cities and were likewise distributed up and down the country in smaller groups, and their fields and those of the seculars were carefully delimited. Clerical labors consisted mainly of parish work in Spanish towns, teaching and parish work in Indian villages (doctrina), and the specific mission work. The different orders followed divers policies: the Dominicans employed fire and sword, purposely destroying many of the monuments of earlier culture, though they preserved others; the Franciscans attached little importance to science, but preached with fervent love; the Jesuits, admitted in 1664 to missionary work, pursued a more varied policy, and did much for geography, philology, and the like. [2] Despite the strict control of the king, who had triennial reports from his officers upon the number and activity of the monks, the extent and power of the church-establishments increased

[1] Roscher, Sp. Col. Sys., p. 11; Moses, pp. 61–62; Watson, II, 136–137; Bourne, Sp. in Amer., pp. 302–303. The annate was the first year's revenue of bishops or other ecclesiastics.

[2] Bourne, Sp. in Amer., pp. 304–305; Roscher, Sp. Col. Sys., p. 17; Watson, II, 137; Moses, pp. 61–62.

with great rapidity, especially in the second half of the sixteenth century. In 1600 there were in New Spain 400 convents of the several orders and 400 districts in charge of clergymen.[1] The economic burden entailed by the presence of the clergy was very oppressive, for "it enjoyed more extended tithes here than in other places and they were collected with greater precision. As early as the year 1501 the payment of the tithes had been ordered in all the colonies[2] and the method of collection regulated by law. All the products of agriculture were subjected to this tax; sugar, indigo, and cochineal as well as maize or wheat." Such a land-tax, in a new country, according to Leroy-Beaulieu, is "essentially prohibitive of cultivation." Again, the extension of the mortmain was a distinct obstacle to production; "in new countries where the lands have not enough value to be leased, the ill-cultivated possessions of the mainmorte constitute often vast expanses of poor pasture which arrest the agricultural development of the districts wherein they are located. The mainmorte was incredibly developed in Spanish America."[3] The Church "held about one half of all the property in the colonies, and was directed by men not always in the fullest sympathy with those interests on which the material prosperity of society depends. On the economic affairs of Spanish America, as on those of Spain, the church cast the blight of its dead hand." In 1576 Lima, for example, contained five monasteries and two convents, a convent for mestizo girls and a house of sisters of charity, and two large and rich hospitals, one for Spaniards and one for Indians; this for a population of some 2000 Spanish families and 26,000 Indians.[4] And as the power of the clergy increased, constant defrauding of the crown occurred; the Jesuits, by far the richest and most powerful order, were conspicuous for such practice until their expulsion in 1767.[5]

POLICY AND INFLUENCE OF THE CLERGY

But what the Jesuits usually were in their private life, many of the clergy certainly were not. Isabella's purging of the morals of the clergy was not sufficiently drastic to render them proof against the temptations of new conditions, and concubinage became a not

---

[1] Moses, p. 251; Zimmermann, I, 337.   [2] For that date, "all the colonies" means practically Española.   [3] Leroy-Beaulieu, I, 22.

[4] Moses, p. 311; Bourne, Sp. in Amer., p. 200; Zimmermann, I, 342.

[5] Zimmermann, I, 337, 366 ff.

uncommon thing, as practiced by regulars and seculars in the New World. Morals in general were much relaxed among a class of religious adventurers whose chances at home had been small. As late as the reign of Ferdinand VI (1746–1759) an edict was issued prohibiting regulars of any denomination from taking charge of parishes.[1] In reckoning up the services of the clergy in civilizing the Indians, some attention should be accorded to this aspect of their case, although such irregularities probably affected the outcome but little, one way or the other.

Except for the Indians, the Church displayed as little tolerance in America as in Spain. Reference has been made to the treatment of heretics when military operations or chance threw them into Spanish hands; and it has been shown with what care the genealogies of prospective emigrants were scrutinized in order to select only the spotless. It is probably a testimony to the early strictness of this examination that the introduction of the Inquisition into Spanish America was not authorized until 1569, and that its history there was relatively free from the grim spectacles often viewed in Spain. The Holy Office began promptly upon its arrival in 1574 "by pouncing on all of Hawkins's men who had been put ashore in 1568 that could be got hold of"; the first Mexican auto-da-fé was celebrated in that year. But in general it could find but small game amongst a population scarcely intellectual enough to doubt, and spent most of its efforts in harrying foreign heretics, Jews, witches, and bigamists. In an activity of 277 years the Inquisition put to death in Mexico forty-one unreconciled heretics; in Peru, within the same period, there were celebrated twenty-nine autos-da-fé, fifty-nine persons being burned at the stake. As for the Indians in their relation to the Inquisition, there was a law conferring upon them exemption from its searchings; for their misdemeanors were adjudged to be those of childish irresponsibles, and over them was held the threat of the rod rather than that of the more terrible apparatus of the Holy Office.[2]

The ecclesiastical censorship was wielded with vigor, the entire control of the press being given, with detailed prescriptions, into the hands of the Inquisition. Heavy fines and temporary banishment were the punishments of booksellers who could not produce a catalogue of prohibited books, or who sold one of them; travelers

[1] Bourne, Sp. in Amer., pp. 306–308; Watson, II, 137–138.

[2] Moses, pp. 310–311; Bourne, Sp. in Amer., pp. 243–244, 312–314; Zimmermann, I, 341–342.

crossing the frontier with such an article in concealment suffered a fine of 200 ducats. The agents of the Inquisition might enter private houses at any hour of day or night in the search for prohibited books or any similar articles. Thus the Inquisition came to exercise a repressive influence upon the growth of ideas and civilization comparable only with that of the state as directed against commerce and external communication. And when, in the eighteenth century, an intellectual awakening was actually threatened, the Office made haste to tighten the strait-jacket; the catalogues of prohibited or expurgated books grew to include the works of 5420 authors. On the lists occurred the names of the leading thinkers of the century.[1] Whatever the clergy may have done for the Indians, its influence could not have conduced, under such a system, to any great advancement for people of greater possibilities. The higher education which they professed to give was, for many generations, merely scholastic and theological. It was owing largely to the Jesuits that advance was made in the scientific study of the native languages, and in some other fields. The Inquisition had no special objection to the pious and orthodox study of geography, linguistics, ethnography, and history, and it was almost inevitable that a knowledge of these subjects should be forced upon the clergy, particularly the *misioneros*, in their work. In fact, it is hardly just to credit the clergy in general with scientific intent; their preservation of certain material, like their destruction of much more, was a casual and almost accidental consequence of their main preoccupation — the civilization and conversion of the Indians. It is lucky that certain information highly prized by a later age happened to be desirable for the realization of their then purposes. There was created, certainly, a considerable educational plant. In later times, doubtless, knowledge was pursued for its own sake, and it cannot be denied that notable authors occasionally appeared; but the whole educational system was vitiated by the persistence of mediæval prepossessions and was unfit to rear up a people to take its place in the modern world.[2]

Whatever the destiny of Spanish America, the Church has contributed largely to make it what it has been and will be; for the religious coherence of Spain and her colonies was much stronger than the political could be made, despite all the bonds forged by

---

[1] Roscher, Sp. Col. Sys., p. 31; Bourne, Sp. in Amer., p. 314.
[2] Cf. Bourne, Sp. in Amer., pp. 308–316; Haebler, Amerika, pp. 401–402.

the colonial policy. For "when the struggle for Spanish independence came, . . . the bond of ecclesiastical union and sympathy remained, always drawing a large part of several nations back to allegiance with Spain. . . . Even after the Spanish-Americans had achieved their political independence, they remained still•in a strong ecclesiastical alliance with the mother-country." [1]

COLONIAL ADMINISTRATION

Much has been said, from time to time, in the foregoing, concerning the policy and actions of the government. Some of its agencies, as these controlled the activities under discussion at the time, have been described. But, as in the case of the clergy, it has seemed best to reserve for this later place an account, in its main and general lines, of the machinery of government. And the attempt to gain a perspective of its development will carry us back once more to the time of the descóbridores and conquistadores. "During the process of exploration and settlement, authority in America rested in the hands of leaders of expeditions and colonies, who usually bore the title of *adelantado*," a title formerly applied to the commanders in the wars against the Moors, and whose use in the New World may stand for a certain transference of the crusading spirit to a new field.[2] Who the adelantados were, by what means and under what circumstances they attacked their enterprises, and with what successes, has already been indicated.[3] Gradually, however, the conquests reached their limits, and, first locally, then more generally, the passion for discovery, which had been fed by fancy and by hope of the acquisition of fabulous wealth through the opening of strange and unheard-of sources, found for the Spaniards no further promise of satisfaction. "In its place emerged the serious and difficult task of organizing the endless extent of territory of which they now possessed some knowledge, even though it was merely superficial. The epoch of the *conquista* had come to an end, and that of the *coloniaje*, the colonial economy, had begun." [4] Roughly speaking, the close of the period of conquest may be taken as 1550.[5]

[1] Moses, pp. 311–312.
[2] From *adelantar*, to further, or extend. Cf. Moses, pp. 68–69.
[3] Pp. 177 ff., above.   [4] Haebler, Amerika, p. 391.
[5] The expedition of Orellana (1541) was the last important example of the El Dorado enterprises. Ruge, p. 455. Of course the area of conquest extended more

THE CONQUISTADORES

When it came to organization, however, the immediate destiny of the colony depended largely upon the personality of the conqueror; Mexico and Peru may be taken, as the most valued conquests, to afford the most striking contrast. In Mexico the determining factor, despite greater nearness to the metropolis, was Cortés, for he combined the qualities of the superior organizer with those of the intrepid leader. In all his exigencies Cortés "revealed such inflexibility of resolution, never-failing presence of mind, unwavering self-control, such readiness to strike or to conciliate as best fitted the case, such consideration for his own men and for the conquered, such constructive statesmanship, such downright business ability, such scientific and practical interest in geographical exploration that he is easily the greatest of the conquistadores, if not the ablest man that Spain produced in that age." In consequence of his enlightened efforts the country began to possess an organized means of defense, the rebuilt city of Mexico came in a few years to have thousands of inhabitants, and a network of smaller European settlements spread over the whole country of Montezuma.[1] The shocks of conquest and the heavings to and fro, back to a state of relatively stable equilibrium, were thus minimized, and Mexico gave little cause for uneasiness and anxiety.

The case of Peru was very different. The first attempt to establish royal control ended in total failure; Peru came near to acquiring independence, an example which, according to Hume,[2] the other colonies would speedily have followed. Francisco Pizarro had been given in 1529 the practically absolute authority of captain-general, and permission had been accorded him and his associates to extend their conquests at their own expense. But Almagro's jealousy of what he regarded as undue preferential treatment of Pizarro, matched with the latter's envy of the former's successes in Chile, led to internal strife; and the quarrel was carried on by Almagro's son after Pizarro had inflicted a traitor's death upon the father. Upon such an unsettled society came now, in 1544,

slowly, and in the outlying regions or the mountains native tribes either retained their barbarous independence unbroken or regained it from time to time. Watson, II, 147.

[1] Bourne, Spain in America, p. 157 (quoted); Haebler, Amerika, pp. 375-376; Moses, p. 79.   [2] P. 91.

the viceroy De Vela, with commission to put the "New Laws" respecting Indian freedom and rights into execution. Resistance to these measures was rendered more bitter by reason of the abrupt and tactless proceedings of the viceroy; largely in consequence of such discontent the last of the Pizarros, Gonzalo, was forced into what was practically a rebellion, as its head. The viceroy was taken prisoner and Pizarro proclaimed governor and captain-general until the king's pleasure should be known. Pizarro could easily have made himself an independent sovereign at this time, for his authority was undisputed from Quito to Chile, while the mines of Potosí supplied a royal revenue. But, fortunately for the crown, he vacillated, hesitating to throw off his allegiance, until the plenipotentiary Gasca managed to work upon Spanish loyalty and won the empire back for the king.[1] And at length, after the final cessation of the civil wars (1555), the lawless society was brought into order by the vigor and severity of the viceroy Mendoza.[2]

Transfer of the Metropolitan System : the King

When, now, the control of the king began to replace the licensed conquests of the adelantados, the common phenomenon of the application of metropolitan political institutions to the colonial field at once appeared. "The whole drift of Spanish political life in the sixteenth century . . . was toward the strengthening of the power of the crown and the loss by the Cortes of its legislative function. . . . The government of Spanish America was pre-eminently monarchical." From what has been recounted concerning the power of the Spanish sovereigns it is not difficult to understand how " Spanish America did not belong to Spain, but was a part of the hereditary domains of the sovereigns of Castile as heirs of Queen Isabella, with which the cortes of Castile had little more to do than with the kingdom of Naples or the Netherlands." Hence it is more clearly to be seen that the king was little susceptible to control in the management of his own; that while " the laws of Castile were made by the king with the advice of his councils . . . the laws of Spanish America were made by the king through the Council of the Indies." A monopoly such as that of

---

[1] Moses, pp. 111–113; Haebler, Amerika, pp. 384 ff.; Watson, I, 117–119, 134–136, 140–141, 177–182, 187–188, 190–197, 203–204; Zimmermann, I, 319 ff.; see p. 277, above.

[2] Moses, pp. 134–137; Watson, II, 127–131.

Seville was his to give.[1] "The colonies of Spain, although the funds for their original settlement were largely private, were, like the Roman colonies, creations of the central political organization, and were upheld and controlled by a power outside of themselves." They were from the outset, at any rate, equipped with ample legal machinery, built upon the genuine Spanish pattern.[2]

One of the main characteristics of the colonial administration, perfectly in consonance with the policy of a Philip II, was its secrecy. No reports were published, and the inquisitorial powers of the Church were enlisted in the maintenance of mystery. Of course this is another outgrowth of the exclusion policy, especially as respects foreigners; Count Revillagigedo was seriously blamed for publishing statistics of Spanish American population, and thus informing rival nations of the small number of Spaniards in the colonies. Because of this absence of information the most mistaken opinions prevailed in Europe respecting the Spanish colonies; "while, in the sixteenth century, every one exaggerated their prosperity, their riches and population, in the eighteenth every one depreciated them beyond measure." In fact, the principle of secrecy, combined with the deliberate neglect of means of communication, referred to in another place, actually left the government itself poorly informed of affairs in the colonies; so that sometimes it became aware of important happenings only through the reports of foreigners.[3] The other determining characteristics of the administrative policy will appear in a review of the agencies employed, but it may be said preliminarily that, together with the Spanish institutions, came also the Spanish political habitudes of mind; besides secrecy there existed suspicion, the tendency toward minute regulation, and other characteristics of the metropolitan administration.

The Council of the Indies

Taking the king, now, to be the source of all legislation and government, the body nearest him was the *Consejo de Indias*, the Supreme Council of the Indies, founded by Ferdinand in 1511, and

[1] Bourne, Sp. in Amer., pp. 228, 221; Haebler, Amerika, p. 395; Moses, pp. 18–22, 298–299; cf. 295–296; Watson, II, 127, 131.   [2] Moses, pp. 298–299; Hume, p. 91.
[3] Leroy-Beaulieu, I, 21; cf. pp. 18, 23; Roscher, Sp. Col. Sys., p. 35; p. 245, above. This was not so bad in the earliest years, but later the development of means of relatively rapid communication was looked upon as a highly dangerous innovation. Moses, pp. 64–65; Roscher, Sp. Col. Sys., p. 22.

finally organized in 1542. "This board originally embodied all financial, police, military, ecclesiastical and commercial authority, and at the same time served as a high court of appeal in civil actions. . . . Endowed with the entire royal prerogative, it had, at all times, to remain in the neighborhood of the court. New laws could be passed only by a majority of at least two-thirds. For a century the Council of the Indies was universally and deservedly held in the greatest esteem. Its members were chosen preferably from those who had held high offices in America with distinction." [1] The Council was a most dignified body, therefore, and it performed its tasks in a worthy manner, collecting information, initiating schemes for improvement, nominating all officials, civil and ecclesiastical, and calling them to account, and otherwise controlling and supervising large policies and details. A worthy monument to its activities and intentions for two centuries is formed by the *Recopilacion de Leyes de los Reinos de las Indias*, a body of law evidently dictated by the broadest considerations of humanity. Its industry and the seriousness with which it took its functions are indicated by the fact that it was to meet five hours daily, except on church holidays; however numerous the latter, the Counselors certainly labored well and long as compared with a considerable part of the population.[2] But it must be recognized that the Council came to constitute the most stubborn conservator of the traditional policies whose effects have been passed in review; so that when, under the Bourbons, more liberal measures were adopted respecting America, it had to be suppressed. It was succeeded by a Ministry of the Indies, which in turn passed away under Charles IV, through the distribution of its functions among the five ministries of the state. The Council was at this time resuscitated in outward form, but its utility was gone.[3]

The Viceroy and Audiencia

This body, in its period of vigor, conferred all offices in America and held accountable every incumbent, from the loftiest down. The most important of all the officers was, naturally, the king's representative, the viceroy. This official possessed by delegation the entire royal authority, and his person was surrounded by retinue

---

[1] Roscher, Sp. Col. Sys., pp. 25–26; Bourne, Sp. in Amer., pp. 224–225; Saco, pp. 66 ff.   [2] Bourne, Sp. in Amer., pp. 225–226; Watson, II, 130.

[3] Leroy-Beaulieu, I, 20, 30; Roscher, Sp. Col. Sys., p. 26, note.

and ceremonial of a truly pompous character. Nevertheless he was hedged about with checks of many kinds, for the independence necessarily granted him because of the remoteness of the colonies from the mother-country made him a shining object for the perennial suspicion characteristic of the Spanish administration. To secure unity and sequence of policy the colonial affairs were directed first by Fonseca, then by the Council of the Indies, and the viceroy's duties were at length specified to such an extent that over seventy laws in the *Recopilacion* are devoted to him. Again, there was set over against him the *audiencia* or court of appeals, presently to receive notice, and the whole clerical organization. Even Columbus, with his extensive grants, never afterward duplicated, had been given full instructions, and the tendency to regulate gained strength with time.[1] One of the most obvious methods, practiced also by the Portuguese, of curtailing opportunity for the viceroy, was the limitation of his term, which was fixed at three, later at five, years, subject to royal extension. The first two viceroys reigned fifteen and fourteen years respectively; but from 1535 to 1821 sixty-two incumbents held the office, averaging a little over four and one-half years. Again, persons of very distinguished rank were seldom appointed. Numerous apparently petty restrictions hedged about the private life of the viceroy; inspectors were sometimes sent out; and, finally, the viceroy, upon his retirement from office, was subject to the *residencia*[2] or inquest into his conduct during his term. "The Council of the Indies appointed for this a particularly prominent jurist, who had to be ready for months to receive charges of every kind against the outgoing official. The justice of these charges was decided in Spain, and no viceroy or other officer could receive the slightest new appointment without first successfully meeting this test." Vaca de Castro was detained twelve years as state-prisoner, while his conduct was being laboriously analyzed, although in the end he was approved and granted due honors. "The wellnigh proverbial ingratitude of the Spanish court towards its great discoverers and conquerors is at bottom nothing more than the painful introduction of the later colonial policy of permitting no one to become

---

[1] Haebler, Amerika, pp. 393 ff.; Roscher, Sp. Col. Sys., pp. 23 ff.; Bourne, Sp. in Amer., pp. 229–230; Moses, p. 87; Watson, II, 128 ff.

[2] The Portuguese practiced the "regidencia" in India, but apparently upon inferior officers. Menezes, p. 139.

too powerful." [1] Comparison with the case of Albuquerque and others of the Portuguese viceroys and governors is here challenged. And what is said respecting the viceroy applies to the captain-general, who was simply the "king of a smaller kingdom." No efforts, however, to break the essential power of the viceroy really succeeded, limited though he may have been.[2]

The position of the conscientious viceroy was one of arduous labor and trying responsibility; he had, among other duties, to contribute toward the continuity of the colonial policy a general report embodying information and counsel for his successors.[3] Mendoza was granted in 1535 a salary of 6000 ducats, and 2000 for the expenses of his bodyguard. In the seventeenth century the viceroy of New Spain received 20,000 ducats, and of Peru, 30,000. In the middle of the eighteenth century the salary of the viceroy of Mexico was raised to 60,000 pesos, 12,000 of which he was expected to devote to his captain-general. The captain-general of Carácas held office on the average seven years and received 9000 pesos. Naturally perquisites might add considerably to these stipends. The viceroyalty of Peru appears from the above to have ranked as a higher dignity than that of New Spain; successful viceroys in the latter province were often promoted to Peru.[4]

The check which was set up as the most definite and tangible counterbalance to the viceroy who might be wielding, or suspected of planning to wield, too much power, was the *audiencia*. In Española a court independent of the governor was established (1510) to hear appeals from the decisions of the governor's justices; this is taken as the beginning of the audiencia, "a body which also became the mouth-piece of colonial needs by presenting memorials to the Council of the Indies." [5] On the mainland the adelantados were superseded by the audiencias, or balanced by them. In 1527 it was thought prudent to curtail the power of Cortés, and the conviction that no single minister would be able

---

[1] Roscher, Sp. Col. Sys., pp. 23–24; Bourne, Sp. in Amer., pp. 229–232; Watson, p. 183; Moses, pp. 86–87, 90–91, 144. The residencia was of varying efficiency. Bourne, Sp. in Amer., p. 232.

[2] Bourne, Sp. in Amer., p. 331; Moses, pp. 107–108.

[3] The Relaciones and Memorias cited in the bibliography of this book.

[4] Bourne, Sp. in Amer., pp. 229–231, 331; Roscher, Sp. Col. Sys., p. 41; Moses, pp. 86, 90.

[5] Bourne, Sp. in Amer., pp. 227–228. On the germ of the audiencia, legally considered, cf. Fabié, pp. 53 ff. This author (p. 24) regards the instruction given to Columbus as the prototype of all succeeding legislation.

to do this led to the selection of a collegiate body.[1] The audiencia in general was a sort of council of state, corresponding roughly to the Council of the Indies in Spain. It had great restraining power over the viceroy, for the Spanish government turned to it for information as to his conduct; "that in some respects the powers of the viceroy and the audiencia were co-ordinate may be seen in the fact that each without informing the other might correspond directly with the king." The audiencia acted in place of the governor in case of absences or vacancies, and its commands were regarded as if they emanated from the king himself. Persons who felt wronged by viceregal decisions could appeal to the audiencia; the fact that in important cases such appeal was carried to the Council of the Indies reveals the kinship of the two bodies. Again, the audiencia exercised a direct supervision over the economic, religious, and other conditions of its district, for one of its members was delegated every three years to make a thorough inspection, extending even to the testing of the purity of drugs in apothecary shops. The closest attention is said to have been given to the selection of proper men for the audiencia; because of their high rank and good salary they were more than ordinarily independent, and uncommon precaution was taken to detach them from social connections and business relations calculated to impair their impartiality.[2]

The political divisions of the empire, after the conquests were over, were based upon the viceroyalties and audiencias. "In the year 1574 the Spanish American world was officially described as consisting of two kingdoms: New Spain, comprising the main-land and islands north of the isthmus, and also that part of South America which is now Venezuela; and Peru, comprising the isthmus and all the territory from New Spain to Patagonia except Brazil." A third viceroyalty was added in 1718 at Bogotá, the capital of New Granada, the later Colombia, and a fourth in 1776 at Buenos Ayres. The other lesser divisions of the empire, most of them dating from the eighteenth century, were the captaincies-general: Guatemala (1527); Venezuela (1773); Cuba (1777); Chile (1778). The American audiencias were, in the seventeenth century, under Philip IV, eleven in number: Santo Domingo,

[1] Moses, pp. 69, 80.
[2] Roscher, Sp. Col. Sys., pp. 24–25; Bourne, Sp. in Amer., pp. 232–234; Moses, pp. 69–72.

Mexico, Panama, Lima, Guatemala, Guadalajara, Bogotá, La Plata, Quito, Chile, Buenos Ayres.[1]

CHARACTER AND RESULTS OF THE SYSTEM

It is not necessary for our purpose to pursue the colonial administration into its subdivisions — the " governments," the municipal councils (*cabildos*), officials, etc.[2] The characteristic of the whole system, both in the large and in its details, was perennial regulation from above, constant balancing and counterbalancing of power. The system was like a complicated machine calculated to make of each member of the government an obstacle to the action of the other members.[3] "This official system, with its good and bad features, had taken very early and deep root in Spain,"[4] and could not well escape transference to America. And, aside from this system, one most ill-adapted to a new country and a more undeveloped society, the colonial official personnel was very far from being a model one. The praiseworthy intent in respect to appointments, voiced in the precepts of many of the laws, did not materialize at all prevalently in practice. With such sovereigns as Spain had for many critical decades, men feeble and degenerate and swayed by unscrupulous favorites, it would have been little short of miraculous if the colonial appointments had been exemplary. Aside from their inapplicability under the economic and social conditions, the Spanish laws lacked, then, a medium of interpretation and enforcement in the personnel of the colonial functionaries. " It was impossible for the best governors to put into practice measures which were of the most incontestable utility to the public interest, while magistrates with small scruple had full facility in enriching themselves and their favorites." As to the captains-general, "their power soon became very limited and nothing at all remained to them but a grand ceremonial, an enormous patronage and the chance to enrich themselves in a thousand illegal ways."[5] Again, one of the regular sources of the royal revenue was the sale of offices as the latter increased in number with the expansion of the

---

[1] Bourne, Sp. in Amer., pp. 229, 232, 331; Watson, II, 128; Moses, p. 161.

[2] Cf. Bourne, Sp. in Amer., pp. 234–237.

[3] Merivale, in Leroy-Beaulieu, I, 19.

[4] Roscher, Sp. Col. Sys., p. 23.

[5] Leroy-Beaulieu, I, 19; Roscher, Sp. Col. Sys., p. 41; Moses, p. 96; cf. Bourne, Sp. in Amer., p. 242; Zimmermann, I, 340, 355–356.

king's domain (1557 on); whatever may be said in extenuation of this practice, it was certainly one the exercise of which was not destined to educate and equip a society or series of societies for the struggle of the sequent age. It is one thing to demonstrate a practice of this kind as natural in the setting of its time — so is cannibalism — and it is thus scientifically futile to pass moral judgments upon it; but it is equally profitless to seek to excuse or to have recourse to the *tu quoque* retort.[1] It is not that the Spanish system was morally bad; it is that it was hopelessly anachronistic and unsuitable; persisting in doleful consistency where the powers of the next age were adaptive, it virtually retrograded and became survivalistic.

For one thing, it taught the Spanish-American societies in no respect that self-reliance, visibly shown in the power of self-restraint and self-government, in the poise, which the nations that succeeded Spain as lords of affairs have in general so steadily exhibited. One author, who is inclined to minimize all the factors except education, puts the case as follows : " Under the rigid rule of the Council of the Indies and its subordinates, the great body of the people in the Spanish colonies learned only one lesson, and that was the necessity of obedience. The power of self-direction or self-control they had no opportunity to acquire. They only learned to follow; not because they saw any reason for going in one direction rather than in another, but because they were dominated by a superstition or habit favoring obedience, born of long subjection to absolute rule, and of inexperience in matters of public concern. The result of this was to make possible quiet and orderly conduct, as long as the power of the parent state remained unshaken; but it did not prepare the way for independent national action. When, therefore, the tie of allegiance to Spain was severed, the communities were like a ship without a rudder or ballast. There were no points of advantage that could be used to give them consistent movement in any direction. They were subject to the shifting currents of uninstructed prejudice. While the bulk of the people were willing to render obedience, they were without the means of determining to whom it should be rendered. They were perfect material for the demagogue, or the pliant tools of revolutionists. The Spanish-American attempts at self-government have, therefore, in most cases had a sorry outcome; not because

[1] Cf. Bourne, Sp. in Amer., pp. 237–239.

of any original incapacity in the stock, but because of the lamentable political education which the dependencies received during their three centuries of bondage to Spain."[1] The Spanish colonial government was the product of anterior and contemporary Spanish history, embodying the working-out in a new and ruder environment of the system evolved in an older and non-progressive land. It was only under the sought-for seclusion that it could stand; light and knowledge were inconsistent with its endurance.[2]

Class Discriminations

One of the interesting phases of this futureless system was the class division which it fostered; here again appears the policy of distrust, working out into the principle of *divide ut imperes*. The class distinctions were, as has been seen,[3] partially racial or social, and so inevitable; but there was no attempt made to amalgamate the unhomogeneous elements. Quite the opposite: the lines of cleavage were accentuated and demarked. " Mexico," says Humboldt,[4] "is the land of inequality." For example, the European Spaniard (chapeton or gachupin) was consistently favored over the American-born Spaniard (creole). " Legally the creole was on complete equality with the chapeton; but, as a matter of fact, until 1637 only twelve of the 369 bishops had been creoles, and until 1808 only one of fifty viceroys of New Spain had been a creole. Wappäus knew of only four creoles among 160 viceroys, and only fourteen among 602 captains-general or governors. To the excluded this must have been all the more irritating, since they had in their midst a numerous and brilliant nobility."[5] " It was in the *cabildos* (municipal councils) only of all the machinery of government that the Spanish creoles had a prominent or controlling share." The effects of such preferential treatment may be judged from the fact that the republicans of Buenos Ayres, upon lifting the standard of revolt, stated such exclusion to be one of the chief of their grievances.[6]

---

[1] Moses, pp. 302–303; cf. Bourne, Sp. in Amer., pp. 235, 263; Darwin, quoted in Roscher, Sp. Col. Sys., p. 46.

[2] See pp. 322 ff., below; cf. Leroy-Beaulieu, I, 5.

[3] Pp. 215 ff., above.   [4] Essai, I, 103.

[5] Roscher, Sp. Col. Sys., pp. 19–20. The single creole viceroy was Juan de Acuña, Marquis of Casa Fuerte (1722–1734). Humboldt, Essai, I, 203.

[6] Bourne, Sp. in Amer., pp. 236–237; Leroy-Beaulieu, I, 9.

The intention behind this policy was to keep the " old Spaniards," as the natives of Spain were called, so loaded with favors and honors as to secure in their envied status one of the surest guaranties of Spanish-American dependence. On the other hand the native-born were to be held as far as possible in a pliable status of simplicity and ignorance : " the viceroy, Gil de Lémcs, uttered to the colleges of Lima this characteristic language : ' Learn to read, to write and to say your prayers : this is all an American ought to know.' " [1] " The tremendous pride and stiff ceremonialism which characterize the Spaniards in Spain had developed here incomparably more, so that all cordiality was smothered beneath it, and, more than that, numberless family quarrels, denunciations, etc., resulted from it." [2] A special mark of favor granted to the chapeton was the feudal estate or fief, a grant taking origin from the time of the conquistadores, when it was assigned to the families of the latter or to court favorites. The fiefs were extensive and proved a great detriment to production, but, since the government held the more to such grants as the provinces were more distant, they seem to have been the visible expression of misgivings as to the growth of a very considerable agricultural and creole population. The political accentuation of class distinction led also to the inordinate love of titles and rank, especially among the creoles, and the consequent or correlative contempt for productive employments. But the dissemination of discord was effected within the lower social groups as well as the upper, and at the same time care was taken to deprive the former of their natural leaders. The implacable antipathy between Indians and negroes, for example, was made into political capital ; any general union to shake off the common yoke was rendered almost impossible.[3]

In short, as respects governmental treatment of class distinction, Spanish America represents a " classic ground for the so-called official aristocracy." [4] " By the establishment of a numerous nobility which sustained a rigid system of entails, by the constitution of a powerful clergy endowed with all the old temporal privileges in all their fulness, by the omnipotence of the royal

[1] Leroy-Beaulieu, I, 9, 10; Watson, II, 132 and ff.
[2] Roscher, Sp. Col. Sys., p. 22.
[3] Roscher, Sp. Col. Sys., pp. 19–21 ; Watson, II, 134.
[4] Roscher, Sp. Col. Sys., p. 23. This author regards the independent bureaucracy in Spain as a bulwark against arbitrary despotism, " and the class exclusiveness and arrogance of the numerous officials as a help to independence against temptation."

functionaries, by the restrictions of all sorts presented to the initiative of her subjects, Spain had wished to found *an old society in a new country* : in that phrase can be summed up the whole of Spanish colonization." [1]

COLONIAL REVENUE

Before following the later stages of Spanish policy in Spanish America to their final outcome in revolution, it is perhaps in place to introduce a few facts concerning the sources of revenue in the New World aside from the mining royalties. The importance of the latter, and the expedition shown by the state in laying hands upon them, have been discussed; it should be mentioned that, in Peru at least, the demand for a large revenue stood constantly in the way of establishing a good government. Whatever her humanitarian aims, Spain had to have the ducats, and "in her decline toward bankruptcy was practically insatiable." [2] But, with reference to the taxes apart from the fifths, they were much the same in kind as those in Spain: the alcabala; export and import duties (about 15 per cent); convoy-tax; receipts from the sale of offices and indulgences; monopolies of gunpowder, salt, tobacco, and quicksilver [3]; and a part of the church income. "In 1746 the total revenue of New Spain was estimated at 3,552,680 pesos. A little less than half a century later, in 1796, it had risen to $19,400,000, of which probably $3,500,000 represents the king's mining royalties, leaving about $16,000,000 from taxation from a population of five million." [4] This would not have been severe in the absence of the restriction which, as has been seen, checked the development of economic strength; and if it had borne equally upon the poor and the wealthy. Naturally the mining royalties received the most attention; and the other taxes, notably the alcabala, were not so severe as in Spain. But it is impossible to believe that any such complex of dues was not detrimental in the extreme to the development of the new societies.

What revenue the crown actually derived from America it is difficult to say; some estimates of the yield of the mines have

[1] Leroy-Beaulieu, I, 5.
[2] Moses, pp. 137–138.
[3] On the quicksilver royalty and its yield, cf. Roscher, Sp. Col. Sys., pp. 44–45.
[4] Bourne, Sp. in Amer., pp. 239–241; Watson, II, 145.

been given above. But the collection of statistics made by Roscher [1] from Humboldt and others certainly demonstrates a considerable hiatus between the gross and net revenue. Of course the king possessed the equivalent of income in the opportunity afforded him by the well-paid offices, loaded often with perquisites, which, in lieu of other gifts, he could bestow upon distinguished men or favorites.[2]

[1] "The actual surplus which, in Humboldt's time, flowed into the treasury at Madrid from the colonial administration was estimated at the following amounts: from New Spain, from 5,000,000 to 6,000,000 piastres annually; from Peru, 1,000,000 at the highest; from Buenos Ayres, from 600,000 to 700,000; and from New Granada, from 400,000 to 500,000. In the remaining provinces the expenditure was at least equal to the receipts; in fact, regular appropriations (*situados*) of probably 3,500,000 had to be sent annually to the Spanish West Indies, Florida, Louisiana, the Philippines, and Chile to help out their domestic administration. From Lima a contribution of 100,000 pesos went to Santiago and Concepcion every year, half in silver and half in supplies for the garrison there. Valdivia received annually 70,000 pesos likewise from Lima. The supplementary contribution for San Domingo is said to have amounted to 200,000 silver piastres annually, or from the beginning of the eighteenth century to 1784, inclusive, to about 17,000,000. Before the establishment of the Guipúzcoa company two-thirds of the expenditure of Carácas, Maracaibo, and Cumaná had to be supplied from Mexico. Taken all together the exports from Spanish America towards the end of the eighteenth century amounted to 9,800,000 piastres more than the imports. Whatever portion of this is not to be reckoned in the above-mentioned government surplus must have flowed into the hands of private individuals in Spain." Roscher, Sp. Col. Sys., p. 40; cf. Bourne, Sp. in Amer., p. 241; Leroy-Beaulieu, I, 36.

[2] Roscher, Sp. Col. Sys., p. 41; Hume, p. 396.

CHAPTER IX

SPANISH AMERICA: BUENOS AYRES, THE REVOLUTION, CUBA. THE PHILIPPINES. AFRICA

One section of the Spanish American empire still awaits disposition in the general scheme of Spanish theory and policy: the temperate regions of the south, Argentina, Paraguay, and Chile. These areas have been thus isolated, aside from certain inevitable references to them, because, by reason of their physiographical and other natural conditions, they clearly exemplify a special phase of Spanish colonial history and policy, and were thus marked out for a specifically different destiny.

EARLY CONDITIONS

The Plata was discovered by Magellan in 1519, but it was not until 1534 that any attempt at colonization of the region took place; Almagro made a campaign in Chile in 1535–1537, and Santiago was founded by Valdivia in 1541; Irala penetrated the Paraguay region (in search of treasure) in 1540. But any effective settlement in any of these districts was long delayed; in Buenos Ayres, for example, until 1562.[1] It will be recalled that the Spaniards took but slight interest in regions which furnished neither precious metals nor articles of production complementary to those of European origin. Apropos of voyages toward regions north of Florida, a member of the Council of the Indies remarked: "What need have we of these things which are common with all the peoples of Europe? To the South, to the South, for the riches of the Aequinoctiall they that seek riches must go, not unto the cold and frozen North."[2] Hence the development of what is now the United States of America was not seriously considered, and for many decades and generations the southern regions of South

---

[1] Haebler, Amerika, pp. 385–386, 414; Moses, pp. 147–148, 192; Watson, I, 98–103, 148–150; Bourne, Sp. in Amer., pp. 192–193; Zimmermann, I, 326–327.

[2] Quoted in Bourne, Sp. in Amer., page 142; cf. Haebler, Amerika, pp. 385–386, 402.

America were left to unaided and actually impeded settlers, and to the missions. In consequence of such neglect, the settlers of Buenos Ayres early undertook the management of their own affairs, electing as leader a notable man, Irala, who organized the colony and extended its borders (1537).[1] In Chile, Valdivia established a form of feudalism similar to that introduced in Mexico and Peru, and fought the first wars against the Araucanians.[2]

Emigration to Buenos Ayres and Paraguay was never large, and included few European women ; relations with the natives were cordial, and miscegenation was prevalent as it was in no other Spanish American district. Therefore the population always exhibited a predominance of the Indian stock, even though the number of those actually denominated mestizos was small, and, especially in Paraguay, " became characterized by Indian rather than by Spanish traits." [3] Otherwise the stock phenomena of the temperate colony are in evidence : the Indians were, between 1580 and 1740, gradually pushed back from the littoral, but with comparatively little violence ; then, from 1740 to 1881 they were warred upon by the now more numerous and powerful race. They could not become civilized, and miscegenation seems to have been their single, though partial, preservative.[4] In Chile, on the other hand, the temper of the natives admitted of no close affiliation ; their relatively advanced civilization declined before the depredations of the Spaniards and in consequence of prolonged wars. So that while the usual racial mixtures occurred in Chile, the white element exhibited a predominance scarcely duplicated in Spanish America.[5] Conditions of racial contact were in Chile more nearly analogous to those found elsewhere in temperate colonies than to those characteristic of any other part of the Spanish empire.

[1] This was done with the sanction of Charles V. Moses, pp. 192–193; Watson, I, 103–104; Zimmermann, I, 326 ff.

[2] Cf. p. 260, above ; Moses, pp. 147–148 ; Watson, I, 148–150.

[3] Moses, p. 196 ; Haebler, Amerika, pp. 387, 403 ; Watson, I, 104, 271–272. Velasco (p. 551) gives to the Plata region for 1574 only three Spanish settlements of about 400 inhabitants, almost all encomenderos, and more than 2000 mestizos. The census of the Buenos Ayres colony in 1776 gives the following elements of population (Daireaux, I, 45) :

	TOWN	COUNTRY
Spanish	15,719	9,732
Indians	544	1,542
Mestizos	674	} 1,020
Mulattoes	3,153	
Negroes	4,115	630

[4] Daireaux, I, 49 ff., 60 ff.   [5] Roscher, Sp. Col. Sys., p. 19; Watson, II, 165–166.

But the rapid growth of these regions was contravened not only by the general indisposition of the Spaniard for the humdrum existence of the farm colony, but also by Spanish policy itself. As has been seen, Argentina and Chile were regarded commercially and politically as mere appendages of Peru; they constituted the extreme frontier and were accessible only via the Isthmus and Lima.[1] This roundabout route of trade so enhanced prices at the destination that Argentine life of the early periods had to order itself in the most simple manner: "in contrast with the conditions of civilized life which the denser population of Peru made possible, the life of the sparse and slowly increasing population on the plains of Buenos Aires drifted toward a state of barbarism."[2] The value of the unlimited herds was little better than nil; "in the early years of the eighteenth century, even after the port of Buenos Aires had been opened to the extent of admitting two small vessels annually, an ox was worth one dollar, a sheep from three to four cents, and a mare ten cents. The prices had risen to this amount from a still lower point under the influence of the demand made by these vessels for hides, strengthened by the larger demand of the contraband trade of the English and Portuguese." But this manner of seclusion was not destined to endure; when Buenos Ayres became in time one of the chief terminals of contraband traffic, it did not fail speedily to realize the enormity of the system to which it had been subjected. "It was clear enough to the people of the Argentine that to them a closed port meant poverty, and a free port prosperity." Their opposition to the Spanish policy, and, in fact, to the Spanish rule, which appeared in the beginning of the nineteenth century, "was no sentimental opposition, but rested on the hard basis of economical considerations."[3]

The first real recognition of Buenos Ayres came in 1620, when it was declared a separate colony, though still subordinate to Peru, to comprise all the regions of the Plata below the confluence of the Paraguay and Paraná.[4] There was some wealth in the Argentine region, and it was gradually laying solid foundations for its future importance and prosperity. But the latter did not actually appear until, in 1776, Buenos Ayres was erected into a viceroyalty and

[1] Cf. p. 235, above; Moses, pp. 188–189.

[2] Moses, p. 207; cf. pp. 208–209, 268–270; Watson, II, 208; Bourne, Sp. in Amer., pp. 204, 290–291.

[3] Moses, p. 287; cf. Watson, II, 207.

[4] Watson, I, 204 ff., 265; Haebler, Amerika, p. 414.

delivered from some of the vexatious conditions of its former subordinate status.[1] It thus became a preferred port for trade with the southerly colonies, for vessels bound for Chile and Peru were now allowed to proceed by the Cape Horn route. Under these new laws, Buenos Ayres "speedily took an equal place, by reason of the wealth of its agricultural and pastoral economy, beside the richest colonial provinces of Spain." Freedom of trade stimulated all industry.[2] This economic movement gained such momentum that not only could restriction not be re-introduced, but the days of political submission to a distrusted rule were numbered.

Contrasts with the Northern Colonies

A point of clean-cut distinction between the Buenos Ayres region and those farther to the north appears in the treatment of the natives. The Spanish emigration to the former district, small as it was, was motived by intentions of settlement. Had it been unrestricted and included both sexes, the fate of the natives must have approached that observed elsewhere under conditions of contact in regions where the more civilized race can live and reproduce itself rapidly.[3] As it was, the native policy of the settlers was one of fellowship leading to miscegenation. Of the natives no very great labors were demanded, for there were no mines or tropical plantations, and the isolated community provided merely for its own simple needs; thus the Indians labored moderately as cultivators or herdsmen,[4] or, in remoter districts, came under Jesuit control in the reductions. Naturally the settlers resisted the interference of the latter, even though the natives were not in such a degree indispensable to them as to the miners and planters. But the motives for ruthless oppression and exploitation of the human working-animal were, owing to environmental conditions, conspicuous in their absence.

One of the results of the breaking of the policy of seclusion by the contraband trade, which, besides, affected the Indians through the wasteful War of the Seven Reductions, was the boundary dispute with the Portuguese in Brazil.[5] Early in the eighteenth century the governor of Buenos Ayres, being reprimanded by the viceroy of Peru for the negligence or connivance of his government with

---

[1] Watson, II, 216; Zimmermann, I, 374 ff. [2] Haebler, Amerika, p. 426.
[3] Cf. p. 5, above. [4] Watson, I, 266, 271–272; Haebler, Amerika, p. 403.
[5] Cf. pp. 159 and 294, above.

the smugglers, asserted that the contraband traffic could not be stopped; that either the markets must be thrown open to legitimate trade, or that the Portuguese must be expelled from Uruguay (Banda Oriental). After considerable strife the treaty of 1750 was adopted; it stipulated that Portugal should cede to Spain the whole eastern bank of the Plata, and in return should receive the seven missionary towns on the Uruguay. Hence the War of the Seven Reductions; later negotiations fixed the holdings, as has been seen, according to the principle of actual occupation.[1] These strifes had been largely fought out by the settlers themselves, and had inspired in them a certain degree of self-confidence and independence, in addition to that engendered by carrying on traffic with impunity in direct violation of Spain's restrictive commercial regulations, and by frequently electing their own officers.[2] Isolation and neglect were bringing forth their fruits of alienation and disaffection. But the years 1806 and 1807 saw further developments which strengthened the sentiment of self-sufficiency. The English, in the course of their struggle with Napoleon, saw fit in 1806 to make a descent upon Montevideo and Buenos Ayres, then colonies of a prospectively Bonapartist kingdom. No especial difficulty was experienced in reducing the towns. But, although almost totally unaided by the mother-country, the settlers and Indians, under the Frenchman Liniers, managed to expel a strong English force from Buenos Ayres and to negotiate the evacuation of Montevideo as well. The results were inevitable; a dominant power had been worsted, and without aid, and the natural conclusion was that the colony could take care of its own interests. Moreover, it was unwilling to give up the gain from freedom of trade with England, which it had enjoyed during the occupation. Yet no voice was raised at this time in favor of separation;[3] if there were such ideas, they were as yet inchoate. Buenos Ayres simply profited by her strength, and by the end of the colonial period had attracted immigration, and increased to such a degree that the population numbered about 800,000, of whom only about a half were Indians. Chile experienced a more commonplace and uneventful development, was more hampered, as being less isolated, by the activity of the government, — for instance in the policy of granting great entailed estates, — but afforded in general a smaller replica of the

[1] Watson, II, 209 ff.; Moses, pp. 213 ff.; cf. p. 159, above.
[2] Cf. Moses, p. 188.   [3] Watson, II, 272 ff.; Zimmermann, I, 437 ff.

conditions on the eastern coast. In 1787 Santiago contained over 40,000 inhabitants and the number was rapidly increasing.[1]

It is clear that the cases of the southern colonies, especially that of Buenos Ayres, constituted as distinct a divergency from those of the other Spanish colonies as did the history of the Portuguese São Paulo district from that of the rest of Brazil. The general explanation has been given in treating of the latter case, and in more general terms in our preliminary classification of colonies ; [2] it is largely a matter of physical, especially climatic environment. The situation is well set forth by Leroy-Beaulieu,[3] whose remarks are worth reproducing *in extenso*: " It is an observation of Humboldt that there is no country in the world where the social status is subject to such a degree to the influence of climate and of the disposition of the soil as it is in Spanish America. The examination of the physical constitution of the different provinces is, in fact, indispensable to the understanding of their economic organization. In the extreme northern and southern districts, in the interior provinces of Mexico, and in the Pampas of the Plata, immense plains, somewhat dry and of temperate climate, became the seat of a pastoral population. The domestic animals of Europe multiplied in astonishing fashion in these pasture-lands, and came to constitute the chief wealth of the colonists. The latter originated, for the most part, from the pure Spanish race. The Indians were few in number in these districts, and they manifested a warlike disposition which preserved them from subjection ; and on the other hand, the poverty of the colonists prevented the introduction of slavery. The creole in these regions obeyed the law which in our day governs colonists of European origin : he isolated himself from his companions in order to have a larger space and one sufficient for the pasturage of his immense herds. This is the way the shepherds of the Cape or of Australia are doing. A perpetual struggle against the Indians and a rude life of labors and watchings tempered with vigor these scions of the old Castilians. Towns . . . were rare and served only as refuges against Indian invasions. This pastoral civilization became eminently useful to Europe through the primary products, wools and hides, with which it supplied European manufactories.

[1] Moses, p. 148; Watson, II, 164–165; Roscher, Sp. Col. Sys., p. 19.
[2] Cf. pp. 14 ff., above.
[3] I, 16–17.

"The hot and fertile regions with easy access to the sea, like Guatemala and Venezuela, presented a quite different civilization : there the great wealth of the inhabitants consisted in the products of exportation characteristic of the tropical climates, — coffee, cotton, sugar, cacao. The status of society then approximated to that of the West Indies. The whites enriched themselves through the product of their plantations, which increased much in quantity and value during the eighteenth century. Manual labor was performed by the Indians in places where they were numerous, by the mixed races which were so common in certain provinces, and especially by the negroes." Here is a fundamental contrast in colonial life-conditions, and a further justification of the segregation of the real settlement colonies of the Spaniards from those depending upon the mines and the plantations — for the latter two may be treated as allied species of the exploitation colony. The economic, social, and political consequences of the contrast have been set forth in general terms in a preceding chapter;[1] and they are yet clearly in evidence in Spanish America as the first century after emancipation draws on to its close. The only relatively stable states of Spanish America at the present time are those whose life-conditions have allowed of free immigration and unimpeded propagation of European stocks ; and of these states, the most progressive, despite its past disadvantages of remoteness and other drawbacks, is Argentina.

But Argentine self-sufficiency and independence were a result of isolation as well as of climatic and allied conditions. This factor was of great importance; for whereas Mexico, a prevailingly temperate colony, lacking isolation, was less insistent upon independence, the neglected Carácas, a tropical colony, became one of the chief centers of revolt against Spain. But we move on to consider briefly the immediate antecedents of the revolutionary struggle, limiting attention still to those colonies which won independence in 1825, that is, to Spanish America in the narrower sense.

MOVEMENTS TOWARD INDEPENDENCE

It is clear that the Spanish system, as we have come to see it, was not calculated to harmonize with the spirit of a more modern age — that its great menace was enlightenment. But, however

[1] Pp. 7 ff., above.

strictly guarded against, enlightenment was bound to come; the penetration of the once almost absolute seclusion of the colonies through contraband trade, the asiento-agreements, and otherwise, soon afforded the Spanish Americans food for reflection and for a comparison of their own status with that of the rest of the colonial world. Indeed, it is not at all impossible that the liberal policy of Charles III, inspired by Aranda (1766 and following) and continued by Gálvez after 1775, contributed rather to the break-up of the empire than to its preservation; for it was too late to put new wine into old bottles. Moreover, the subsequent vacillation back to the old policy completely nullified preceding wisdom, so far as the retention of the colonial empire was concerned, and made of the liberal régime a simple incident in a consistently anachronistic policy.[1]

With the acquisition of knowledge of the outside world there early came to the Spanish-Americans the stirring story of the American Revolution and the foundation of a great republic based upon principles which their resentment of the Spanish policy led them to regard as the sum of truth and political desirability. Upon the heels of this movement, itself in great part a revolt against a political and economic "system," came the more feverish French Revolution, enacting into a universal dogma the rights of man, and constituting a violent and infectious reaction against the mediævalism inherent in royal rights, caste-systems, and other principles fixedly embodied in the Spanish system. The creoles and mestizos had long chafed against political discrimination and were quite ready to subscribe to any and all of the principles of the new political evangel. That Spain lent aid to the American revolt but stimulated this attitude. Tumults arose in Peru and Buenos Ayres immediately after the American Revolution, and anarchy reigned for months. Agitators arose in the chief cities, the foremost of them being General Miranda of Carácas, who approached England, France, and Russia in behalf of the colonies, and under whose leadership the *Gran Reunión Americana* was formed in London.[2]

[1] For the liberal reaction of the latter half of the eighteenth century, see Leroy-Beaulieu, I, 32–34; Bourne, Sp. in Amer., p. 316; Hume, p. 396; Zimmermann, I, 362 ff., 429 ff.

[2] Hume, p. 407; Watson, II, 272; Humboldt, Essai, I, 115; Leroy-Beaulieu, I, 10; Zimmermann, I, 436 ff. The basis of the treatment of this whole period is the work of Mitre as condensed by Pilling.

In the meantime Spain was in no condition to control the situation; during her constant wars " the colonies had been allowed to go on in their own way, Spanish governors and officials, clerical and lay, plundering right and left, with little or no thought of the benefit of the people over whom they ruled." In 1783 Aranda had plainly before him the prospects of the separation of the American colonies.[1] But it was again, as in the case of Portugal, the European wars which brought the situation to its climax. " The terrible shock given the mother-country by Napoleon was . . . the principal cause for the revolt of the colonies : the captivity of the old royal house, the elevation of the Bonapartist dynasty, the frightful war with France, and finally the rapid alternation of absolutist and constitutional rule through revolution in Spain herself. As a result the old carefully transmitted structure of colonial institutions, ideas, and policy was thrown completely out of joint. The keystone, as it were, was removed. This was the more markedly the case since many of the highest colonial officials exhibited a significant vacillation between the legitimate kings and the usurper. Because at the same time the mother-country was in such pressing need of the political help of the English, it was now impossible to repel their commercial invasions of the colonial markets. . . . In addition, after the restoration of general peace in Europe, the English both privately . . . and as a part of public policy . . . favored strongly the separation of the Spanish colonies from the mother-country." [2] It was believed that the colonies were anxious to throw off the yoke of Spain, and attention and aid were accorded to Miranda and others in the prosecution of their projects. Trafalgar (1805) had destroyed the navy, almost the last vestige of the apparatus of colonial control, and the end, whatever the attempts to avert it, could be only a matter of time.[3]

It does not lie within the province of this book to trace the history of the revolutionary struggle ; except for its general aspects, or as it throws light upon what has gone before, it scarcely forms a part of the subject of colonization. But it cannot be otherwise than enlightening to realize, among other things, that the strength of the revolutionary movement appeared (1810) in Argentina, its origin, however, having taken place in the Carácas region ; that the struggle displayed a marked ferocity of character and left

[1] Hume, p. 396 ; Zimmermann, I, 363, 429.
[2] Roscher, p. 176.   [3] Watson, II, 271–272 ; Zimmermann, I, 436.

behind it a legacy of lasting hostility; and that the revolutionists were effectually aided by foreigners, especially the English, and in a less degree by the emancipated Americans.[1]

GRIEVANCES OF THE COLONISTS: THE REVOLUTION

What the colonists fought for was the overthrow of the Spanish system of restriction. A manifesto issued in 1818 cites the main points of contention. It demanded the following: equality of rights with the inhabitants of the metropolis (this being the protest of the creoles against the discrimination they felt ever more strongly[2]); entire liberty of cultivation and of manufacture; liberty of importation and exportation as respects all the ports of Spain and of friendly countries; freedom of commerce between Spanish America and Asia; the same liberty with the Philippines;[3] the abolition of every governmental monopoly, an indemnification to be made through taxation; liberty to exploit the silver mines; reservation of half of the public functions for American Spaniards (this point being designed to fortify the one first cited); the establishment of a *junta* in every capital to see to it that this latter disposition should be always carried out. "Such were the just demands of the malcontents. And it was not alone the upper classes, it was the mass of the people itself which was penetrated by the necessity of these reforms."[4] What they wanted was liberty — freedom — as the repetition of the term indicates. The repeated discrimination against the native Spaniards and the mestizos in favor of the exploiting class, the European Spaniards, is what made the struggle so fierce and relentless.

Mitre, the first constitutional president of the Argentine Republic, gives the following synopsis of the Revolution.[5] "In the year 1809 the first tremors of the revolution began to be felt simultaneously in the two extremities and in the center of South America; the fact that its several forms were identical, their immediate purposes the same, and their aims analogous, reveals as of long standing an innate predisposition and an organic solidarity

---

[1] Roscher, Sp. Col. Sys., pp. 30–31; Leroy-Beaulieu, I, 10; Moses, p. 187; Zimmermann, I, 442 ff.

[2] For the resentment of the creoles, cf. Humboldt, Essai, I, 114–115.

[3] Cf. pp. 347–349, below.

[4] Leroy-Beaulieu, I, 34; cf. Roscher, Sp. Col. Sys., pp. 26, note; 46–47.

[5] Hist. de San Martín, I, 8–9.

of the living whole. In 1810, simultaneously, without a mutual understanding between the parties, and as if in obedience to an inborn impulse, all the Spanish American colonies rose in insurrection, proclaiming the principle of self-government, the germ of their independence and liberty. Six years later all the insurrections in South America had been smothered (1814–1816) and the United Provinces of the Rio de la Plata alone had kept their footing. The latter, after expelling from their soil all their former masters, declared their independence before the world, and, through making common cause with them, gave to the conquered colonies the signal for the great and last conflict. In 1817 the Argentine revolution, which had become an American movement, developed a plan of campaign, and a policy of emancipation that were to embrace the continent. The revolutionists took the offensive and wrought a change in the destiny of the struggle that had begun; they advanced across the Andes and freed Chile, and then, united with Chile, gained control of the Pacific, liberated Peru, and carried their delivering arms to the equator, thus assisting the Colombian revolution to its triumph. This vigorous forward movement made itself felt in the northern extremity of the southern continent, which, in its turn, conquered and expelled the champions of the metropolis, evolved through the same phases as the Argentine revolt, assumed the offensive, crossed the Andes, became generalized as an American movement, and converged toward the center — where the two forces of emancipation effected their union, as has been said. The strife remained confined to the highlands of Peru, the last refuge of the Spanish domination already wounded unto death in the battles of Chacabuco and Maipú, Carabobo and Boyacá. From this time on, Spanish American independence ceased to be a military and political problem and became simply a question of time and of persistent effort. The Spanish American colonies were free in fact and by right, through their own strength and without external aid; they fought alone in the face of the country's absolutist powers in alliance against them, and from the colonial chaos arose a new world in due order — a world crowned by a sky in which gleamed the polar and the equatorial stars. Few times has the earth presented a similar political genesis, few times an historical epic more heroic."

It should be noted that whenever the Spaniards effected any pacification, it had been attended by such cruelties and was followed promptly by such tactlessness of policy that the temper of the revolt was strengthened rather than impaired. Heavy forced loans, confiscations of patriots' property, and trials for high treason attended the restoration of Spanish authority. Yet it must be admitted that the situation was not much helped by the few exhibitions of a different spirit : what freedom was allowed, for instance to the press, was at once used in spreading separatist ideas. In general, however, the successes of the counter-revolution meant the reaffirmation of the essential features of the old system.

In Mexico, Iturbide won over the soldiers and had himself proclaimed in 1822 the Emperor Augustin I; this ill-advised move was, however, but the overture to the formation, in 1824, of the Republic of the United States of Mexico, with a constitution modeled upon that of its northern neighbor. In 1819 Florida had passed into the hands of the United States of America. By 1824 all the former colonies upon the mainland were lost to Spain. But the end might have been yet delayed had it not been for the active partisanship of England; she, and to a lesser degree by reason of feebler strength, the United States, had aided with men and credit upon many former occasions. Trade interests in the final and complete invasion of the old monopoly were combined with sentimental sympathy, and any number of formal governmental prohibitions on the ground of the friendship of England and Spain could not avail. President Monroe recognized Colombia as an independent state at the end of 1823, and England withstood a continental alliance whose purpose was to support Spain. The Monroe Doctrine was promulgated at about the same time ; and in 1824 English consuls were dispatched, first to Argentina, then to Mexico, Chile, and Colombia. Upon January 1, 1825, the independence of the republics was recognized by England and so stood as a *fait accompli*.[1]

Thus was the hampering monopoly system finally broken, and largely through the agency of the rising commercial and colonial world-power, Great Britain ; the fate of the Venetians and Portuguese, not to mention more ancient holders of monopoly, had overtaken still another aspirant for exclusive rights to trade. "In the case of the Spanish dependency, the bands binding it to the mother-country have been rigid and unelastic, so that they have

[1] The foregoing sketch of the Emancipation is condensed from Mitre, with some reference to Zimmermann, I, 444-475.

parted with the first considerable strain, and the colony has been irretrievably severed from its superior. The English dependencies, on the contrary, have found themselves at the end of an elastic tie. When they have tugged to be free, the cord has yielded, but has gradually drawn them backward when their discontent was past. . . . But Spain, or the Spanish king, insisted on an essential uniformity throughout the Spanish dominions; in other words, obedience to that policy which would contribute most to the selfish interests of the mother-country. The outcome of rigid adherence to Spanish policy has been the loss by Spain of her vast colonial possessions and abundant sources of wealth. . . . The traditions with which Spanish America began her career were the traditions of despotism, and any permanent advance towards liberty had to be made in opposition to these traditions." [1] And the separation was one which left ineffaceable scars behind it. Kindly feeling did not return, and commercial relations between Spain and her former colonies became practically nil; "to-day Spain takes less part in the commerce of Peru than does, for example, Sweden, not to mention Italy." In the shipping reports for 1876 Spain is found to be considerably behind Sweden and is included under "various," her shipping amounting in all to 8154 tons. The same is true in Chile and Argentina. "Thus the relations of Spain with her old colonies have nearly ceased; she furnishes still, however, immigrants in considerable number." [2]

SUMMARY OF SPANISH INFLUENCE

After what has been said, it is unnecessary to summarize at any length, in view of its results, the activity of the Spanish in America. It has been the order of the day to criticise them severely; recently, however, we have had a rehabilitation or an apologia representing the swing of judgment in the opposite direction. [3] Among patriotic Spanish writers, one of extraordinary ability and distinction has often been quoted — Colmeiro; and an ending may be made of specifically Spanish America by a quotation from him, representing probably the best he has to say. "We have dissimulated neither the faults nor the errors committed by the Spanish in America — from which the peoples who founded colonies in those days were

[1] Moses, pp. 305, 308–309.
[2] Leroy-Beaulieu, I, 38–40; Roscher, Sp. Col. Sys., p. 48.
[3] Bourne, Sp. in Amer.; cf. especially pp. 202–204, 242, 316–319.

not exempt, because they had their roots in the age and in the system. But those authors are writing with passion, and merit little credence, who paint us as ferocious wild beasts, or at least as barbarians thirsting for blood and gold, and forgetting good works. It was the Spaniards who introduced into the Indies the ox, the ass and the horse, pigs, sheep and goats, and a multitude of domesticated birds, for the comfort and pleasure of the inhabitants ; it was they who transplanted the vine, olive, pomegranate, orange, lemon, and almost all our fruit trees ; they introduced the sugar-cane and founded the first sugar-refineries ; they taught the art of raising silk, they sowed flax and hemp, and propagated various garden plants and vegetables ; they, in fine, purged the land of idolatry, eradicated the sacrifices of human blood, pursued the cannibals, and punished their cruelties and abominations." [1]

CUBA AND PUERTO RICO

Although Spanish America was lost in 1825, a Spanish colonial empire was destined yet to endure for over seventy years. Of the West Indies we have still to consider Cuba, which virtually was not reckoned as an important part of the empire until late in the eighteenth century ; and, of less importance, Puerto Rico. And there also remains the empire in the East, especially the Philippines, to which only casual attention has been accorded in the foregoing.

Cuba stands for the latest phases of the Spanish system and the latter-day resistance accorded to a prolongation of the anachronistic policy which led to the falling-away of the mainland colonies. Cuba actually suffered less beneath the old repressive system than did the other sections of Spanish America. She rebelled against the native laws as did the other tropical colonies, but, despite her almost unrivaled natural resources, she never attained a status of population [2] or of wealth, calculated to react with force against the enormity of the repression to which she was subjected, until the end of the eighteenth century. Cuba was revealed to the world only after Havana had been taken by the English in 1762 ; the possibilities of her commerce then became apparent. Although she had profited to some degree by the more enlightened policy of

[1] Colmeiro, II, 421–422.
[2] Cf. Humboldt, Isla de Cuba, chap. iii ; Saco, earlier chapters, *passim*.

the latter part of the eighteenth century, her economic awakening
was due largely to the impact of external forces. This is what
Leroy-Beaulieu means when he says that the history of Cuba
(and Puerto Rico) is of recent date : during the seventeenth and
eighteenth centuries Cuba was characterized by "a status of
mediocre and obscure prosperity, a rather general competency, a
mild civilization, good treatment of the slave population, slight
financial resources, and the need of aid and of subsidies from the
metropolis. A combination of exceptionally favorable circumstances," he adds, "brought about a radical change in the conditions of this colony and placed it in a few years above all the
Antilles." [1]

The English, during their ten months' tenure of Havana, had
opened the port to all English ships, and the immediate result was
that, during this period, instead of the usual five or six merchant
vessels, 727 entered the harbor. The same period saw as many
slaves (3000) imported as the preceding twenty years had afforded
under the privileged companies. "The enlightened Charles III of
Spain, profiting by this example, opened the trade of the islands
in 1765 and of Louisiana in 1768 to eight Spanish ports besides
Cadiz, and relaxed many of the regulations that had hampered
the merchants." [2] "The trade with Cuba, which in 1765 required
scarcely six ships, required over two hundred in 1778, after all
Spaniards had been allowed to share in it by paying a duty of six
per cent. From 1765 to 1770 the income from duties at Havana
trebled, while the exportation from the whole island increased
fivefold. Before 1765 this magnificent island, which was able to
provide all Europe with sugar, did not have even enough for the
consumption of the mother-country." [3] It can thus be seen that "the
prosperity of Cuba dates from the English capture of Havana"; [4]
that is to say, from the first direct subversion of stock Spanish
policy. Allusion need scarcely be made to the fact that such a
desirable end was regularly thus attained in Spanish America.

[1] Leroy-Beaulieu, I, 251, 252; cf. Humboldt, Isla de Cuba, p. 248. The latter
author considers in some detail the geographical and other natural advantages
possessed by the island, and especially by the port of Havana. See his chapters :
Consideraciones Generales, Extension, Clima, Comercio, *passim*. Merivale (quoted
by Leroy-Beaulieu, I, 253) notes that, by reason of its elongation, there is no productive part of Cuba which is over forty miles from the coast.

[2] Bourne, Sp. in Amer., pp. 296–297 ; Saco, p. 325; Zimmermann, I, 396.

[3] Roscher, Sp. Col. Sys., p. 36.   [4] Bourne, Sp. in Amer., p. 297.

But the great material advance of the island took place somewhat later and attained a sort of acme during the series of revolutions, first in Spain herself, and then in the colonies of the mainland. Cuba, therefore, seems in a way to have arisen from the collapse of the American empire, and its history to form a prolongation of Spanish American history after the great crisis. It is for this reason that the island has been singled out for separate treatment; a sketch of its nineteenth-century vicissitudes really exhibits the last phase, prolonged over seven decades, of Spanish American colonial policy and methods.

CUBA AFTER 1800

What differentiates Cuba after 1800 most sharply, for present purposes, from the rest of Spanish America, is the composition of its population. Indeed, the island long before that date formed a marked exception to the general rule in this respect. The fact that, besides lying farther to the north, it was an island, seems to have been determinative, in large degree, of its diverse destiny. With the rest of the Antilles it early lost its native population;[1] hence the rarity of the Spanish-American hybrid, the absence of race-conflicts and of the complex stratification into classes, the exclusion of the mission, and so on. Again, the more temperate climate, especially in the loftier interior, permitted and invited a larger settlement of Europeans. Despite the fact that Cuba was the Queen of the Antilles in the production of stock products of a warmer zone, she approached far closer to the type of the colony of settlement than did any other of the Spanish American colonies between the tropics. At the end of the year 1825 Cuba is thought by Humboldt to have had a population of 325,000 whites in a total of 715,000.[2] This was after a considerable importation of slaves, — the census of 1775 gives: whites, 95,419; mulattoes, 24,751; negroes, 50,200. In 1791, of 137,800 inhabitants of the jurisdiction of Havana, 73,000 were whites and 64,800 people of color. These figures may be compared with those already recorded[3] for different sections of Spanish America, and with those which Humboldt and others give for divers non-Spanish sections of

---

[1] On the disappearance of the Cuban natives see Humboldt, Isla de Cuba, pp. 126 ff.

[2] Rough estimates for 1850 are: 605,160 whites, 694,070 colored. In the latter part of the nineteenth century the whites constituted over half of the population. Leroy-Beaulieu, I, 254, 264.   [3] See pp. 215 ff., above.

the Antilles; for example, the proportion of colored population, negroes and mulattoes, amounted, it is said, for the whole of the Antilles, to 83 per cent of the total. And the suggestion of the colony of settlement becomes the more pronounced when it is realized, for example, that in 1775 there were 40,864 white women in Cuba to 54,555 white men.[1] Again, the percentage of Spaniards was raised by the flow of loyalists thither during the revolutionary period; Leroy-Beaulieu compares it to the movement of English loyalists to Canada during the American Revolution.[2]

Spain held in Cuba, therefore, after the falling-away of the mainland possessions, the nucleus of a real colony of Europeans, inspired, at least in good part, with loyalty to herself. Many of the blacks and mulattoes were free men,[3] and identified with the maintenance of Spanish rule. The island has been perhaps the most potentially productive section of any colonial empire. Here was yet another opportunity for Spain, recently chastened in a most suggestive and pointed manner, to develop a modern policy.

In addition to the benefits of the liberal policy of the early nineteenth century, Cuba fell upon still another piece of fortune, economically speaking, in the general abolition, in 1812 and following, of the slave-trade; upon her, "given the method of cultivation adopted in all the sugar colonies, it conferred, from the point of view of production, an incontestable advantage." For while the other islands lost their labor force, Cuba's was recruited; and the consequent decline of their production was pure profit for her. "She avoided that dismal transition which was to cost the English and French planters so dear. By a remarkable spirit of prudence and initiative, even while they were maintaining slavery, the planters of the Spanish islands introduced into their cultivation and their manufacture all the progress of which these were susceptible." Moreover, for the very reason that she was thus prosperous, Cuba drew to herself a large immigration of the European races. Again the passing of the "colonial pact" left Cuba undiscriminated against in France and England, and "the Cuban planters saw open before them two great markets in which the

---

[1] Humboldt, Isla de Cuba, pp. 97–109; cf. table, pp. 98–99; yet in the typical exploitation period in the middle of the nineteenth century Gallenga (p. 36) could call Havana a "city without women."

[2] Leroy-Beaulieu, I, 254.

[3] Humboldt, Isla de Cuba, pp. 100 ff.

natural and artificial conditions of their production assured them great advantages." [1]

It is plainly to be seen that the continued prosperity of the island, and so the progress of its cultivation, hinged upon the free utilization of the uniquely favorable economic advantages recounted. The fate of Cuba was bound up in that of her plantation production; but it was upon this that the attention of the metropolis was to be fixed. Hence the history of Cuba, for the present purpose, to the exclusion of most of such other topics as have engaged attention in the survey of other sections of Spanish America, narrows down to the attitude of the Spanish administration toward Cuban trade.

THE SUPPLY OF LABOR

For the moment, however, it will clarify counsel to devote a few words to the labor force over which the Cubans had control. That the whites themselves could labor to a certain degree with impunity seems undeniable; [2] there were, at any rate, too many of them for all to be owners or overseers. But the bulk of the heavy labor, in consonance with sub-tropical conditions, fell upon a more fully acclimatized race; and, the natives having disappeared, this was at first the African, imported in relatively small numbers under the familiar system of the asiento.[3] Cuba had in her early days very little use for slaves, inasmuch as the chief local occupation was cattle-raising. The Asiento of 1713 only slightly increased the importation; in 1763 there were but 32,000 slaves in the island; the whole number introduced between 1521 and 1763 is thought by Humboldt to have been no more than 60,000. But between 1763 and 1790 there were received at Havana 24,875, and elsewhere in the island some 6000. The prohibition of the slave-trade north of the equator (1817) and its entire abolition (1820) were preceded by the introduction of 225,574 slaves between 1790 and 1820, through the port of Havana alone. It is reckoned by Humboldt that the whole island received at least 320,000 negroes between 1791 and 1825, as against 93,500 in all the decades pre-

[1] Leroy-Beaulieu, I, 254–255. Even after the direct traffic was universally suppressed, Cuba still imported illicitly a considerable number of blacks.

[2] Cf. Leroy-Beaulieu, I, 264.

[3] P. 249, above; during the earlier centuries Cuba and Puerto Rico constantly demanded more slaves and at the same time feared slave-uprisings. Saco, earlier chapters, *passim*.

ceding. It is easily seen that the emergence of Cuba into a copiously productive status called for an immediate and large increase of the human labor force; and that the result was the creation of an important constituent of population with which reckoning had, in future, to be made. And it must be added that tolerance of race-mixture resulted in the formation of a considerable body of mulattoes; in 1775 there were some 24,750; in 1811, 70,000.[1] The conditions of the colored population were remarkably favorable: even Humboldt,[2] who hates the system of slavery so cordially, takes pains to demonstrate this. The possibility of attaining freedom is perhaps as good an evidence as any of the slave's status; and in Cuba, in 1825, one-third of the people of color were free. The free element, white and colored, reached in Cuba 64 per cent of the total population, as against scarcely 19 per cent in the English Antilles. These considerations will aid the American to a realization of the fact that Cuba in some respects more nearly resembled the southern states of his country than it did the rest of the Spanish colonies.[3]

Anticipating somewhat, it may be said that toward the middle of the nineteenth century[4] a strenuous effort was made to meet a growing need for a labor supply. Immigration of European families was encouraged, and Yucatecs, and especially Chinese, were introduced. Of the latter, 5560 were imported in 1859, and before 1860 some 17,000; of these, only seven were women. Further requisition upon the Chinese in 1860 resulted in the presence in Cuba, in 1862, of over 60,000; the regular cost of their introduction was $300 to $400 per head. In 1884 there were in Cuba

[1] Humboldt, Isla de Cuba, pp. 141–147, 109; between 1799 and 1803 there were imported into Havana 34,500 negroes, of whom seven per cent died per annum. Humboldt, Essai, I, 131. [2] Isla de Cuba, pp. 97–100.

[3] Leroy-Beaulieu (I, 256) states that the development of wealth and of the slave-trade changed the lot of the slaves. "The Spanish planter became more cruel and immoral than the other Europeans: the Cuban sugar-plantations are exploited, thanks to the slave-trade, at an enormous expense of human lives, losses which new recruits replace without cessation. The slave-trade being prohibited, commerce in slaves goes on as contraband, and their condition is rendered worse in default of the protection of the legal prescriptions which regulated the trade." He adds, upon the authority of Merivale: "The average life of a Cuban slave is only ten years; in Barbados, during the worst period of English slavery, it was seventeen years." On the later conditions of slave and free labor, emancipation, etc., consult Gallenga, pp. 75 ff., 91 ff., chap. vi. Cf. Bordier, Col., p. 78.

[4] For conditions of native population, sugar-production, etc., as they appeared at this time to a young Dane, see "Th.," Erindringer, etc., latter part, passim.

some 70,000 Chinese men; of women, only 1000. The usual abuses of the coolie system did not fail to appear, as well as the stock disadvantages to a colonial society of the presence of such aliens in its midst. Upon a revelation of the oppressiveness and rascality of the system there ensued uprisings in Canton against the coolie-agents and a formal protest to the European consuls from the governor of Shanghai.[1]

SPANISH POLICY IN CUBA

Having accentuated these main points of dissimilarity between Cuba and the rest of Spanish America, and refraining from the rehearsal of what they had in common, we now turn to the consideration of post-revolutionary Spanish policy in America, as applied typically to "The Pearl of the Antilles."

Early in the nineteenth century it seemed that Spain had learned her lesson, and that there lay before Cuba an unhampered development of great resources. Measures were taken in 1817 by Ferdinand VII which looked toward a continued moderation in the matter of government requisitions. But as time went on, the inveterate tendency toward exploitation and exclusion again manifested itself. Again Spain retrograded through failing to advance with the times. Tariffs which had been moderate ($7\frac{1}{2}$ to $33\frac{1}{2}$ per cent *ad valorem*) in 1809, became exorbitant when the other powers had deserted their former policy based upon the "colonial pact" and mercantilism; the planters found cause of complaint about their status when they came to compare it with that of the colonies of Jamaica, Martinique, and Barbados. One of their chief grievances lay in the unfavorable situation in which they were placed with their best customers, the people of the United States. For since the products of the northern republic, notably grains, were subject to differential duties upon entering Cuba, the obvious return-blow was the imposition of differentials upon Cuban sugar. But the United States formed the natural market for this sugar, taking 62 per cent of it; and England bought another 22 per cent as against 3 per cent taken by Spain. Yet upon the part which entered the United States the Cuban planters paid about two-thirds

---

[1] Leroy-Beaulieu, I, 255, 257–258; Gallenga, pp. 109, 127; for the place of the coolie system under the topic of tropical labor, cf. p. 11, above; Keller, Sociol. View, etc.

of the selling value. " Such were the deplorable results of a colonial régime which the metropolis, far from amending, rendered daily more rigorous : the planters had to pay very high for their flour, iron, fabrics, — for all those articles which were useful for existence and for manufacture, — and they found themselves in respect to sales in the great market of America under conditions far worse than those of their competitors from the neighboring islands. When the interests of colonists are thus manifestly injured, loyalism does not delay its departure." [1]

Naturally, as had been the case in the now revolted colonies, the creoles were allowed no share in their own government,[2] no chance to protest officially against treating Cuba like " a milch-cow which it [Spain] seemed to wish to exhaust." A complicated administrative mechanism whose various arms were sinecures with full lines of perquisites for Spaniards, and whose general character was corrupt to an exceptional degree, was saddled upon the Cuban producers. Captains-general made disgraceful fortunes ; high functionaries levied upon the people for their daughters' dowries and for their infants' baptismal finery. The budget augmented to the enormous figure of $30,000,000, covering expenses incurred by Spain in ways entirely disconnected with Cuba, and yielding a yearly profit of about $6,000,000 on her colonial budget. Cuban finance became disordered and the result was a forced circulation.[3]

INSURRECTION

Cuba's old proverbial loyalty was not proof against all this. The middle of the nineteenth century saw the inception of an insurrection, with independence as its aim, and numbering among its adherents not only the wealthy Cubans, planters, industrials, and merchants, but likewise the blacks. For the insurgents, taking advantage of the well-known willingness of the proprietors to emancipate their slaves, proclaimed, in February, 1869, the immediate and total abolition of slavery. Thus the negroes also came to espouse the cause of their liberators. The latent rebellion came to a head with the revolution of 1868 in Spain, which overthrew

[1] Leroy-Beaulieu, I, 255, 258–259; cf. Gallenga, pp. 42 ff.
[2] On class-animosity in Cuba, see Gallenga, pp. 39 ff., 62–66; cf. p. 360 and note 3, below.
[3] Leroy-Beaulieu, I, 260; Gallenga, pp. 13, 66 ff., etc. For the later vicissitudes of the depreciated currency, see Leroy-Beaulieu, I, 262, 266; Gallenga, pp. 44 ff.

the Spanish queen; of course this confusion provided only "the occasion, not the cause, for a conflagration which had been long smoldering in the colony." [1]

Spain's treatment of the insurgents was most ill-advised and tactless : all their claims were refused; no concessions to rebels were to be made by Castilian pride. "On March 21, 1869, 250 Cubans, selected from the élite of creole society, were torn from their firesides and deported to Fernando Po and Mahon. The indignation which seized the whole insular population at the spectacle of this unjustifiable barbarity, doubled the forces of the insurrection." The struggle was long and characterized by great atrocity; it was not until 1878 that the vigilant and apparently upright Campos managed to quell it, and then largely through buying off the insurgents. He is said to have paid, as a result of his agreement (*convenio*), as much as $8,500,000; he himself admitted such an expense of $850,000.[2] Reforms in general and in particular[3] were promised the Cubans, and overt hostilities were suspended.

The years of the insurrection had brought Cuban prosperity almost to ruin. For the island had had to suffer, not only the ravages of war, but also the insensate exactions of a suspicious and fearful government. Sugar-production was reduced by half; at the same time, however, the budget rose to $40,000,000, the equivalent of which for France, according to Leroy-Beaulieu, would be $1,000,000,000. Taxes of all kinds were capricious as well as heavy; simple merchants paid direct taxes of $2550; planters paid up to $60,000. Such taxes often surpassed income and infringed upon capital.[4] The only one of the promises wrung from Spain which had been fulfilled seventeen years later, was that which had to do with the slaves; they were definitively emancipated in 1880. The budget of 1884–1885 was certainly over

---

[1] Leroy-Beaulieu, I, 258. For a more detailed discussion of this insurrection, see Gallenga, pp. 14–22, chap. iii; on emancipation, see chap. vi. For the nineteenth-century history of Spain, see Hume, Modern Spain, or Clarke, Modern Spain, to which text-allusions, from this place on, refer. Upon topics connected with slavery Aimes is the latest authority.

[2] Leroy-Beaulieu, I, 261–262; see Gallenga on "Pacification," chap. vii.

[3] It seems unnecessary to rehearse the formal demands of the Cubans. Fellow-sufferers under the same rigid system wanted pretty much the same things. The reader is referred to the list of Filipino demands (p. 363, below), which included in general what they thought Cuba had gotten, or was about to get. Cf. also Zimmermann, I, 500.

[4] Leroy-Beaulieu, I, 262–263.

$32,000,000, a figure which would represent over $21 per capita;[1] it was divided as follows :

Interest and liquidation of debt	$10,000,000
War-expenses	9,000,000
Marine	2,204,000
Police { (*orden público*)	700,000
{ (*guardia civil*)	2,537,000
Various (*public works, public instruction, administration, etc.*)	5,000,000
Collection and financial organization	2,000,000

The meager provision under " Various " needs no comment.

" These charges were crushing. They came from a much too numerous military force, and from an administrative waste of which the figures of the budget scarcely give an idea." " If you treat the provinces of Cuba as enemies," said an orator in the Spanish senate in 1884, " 24,000 men are not sufficient to hold them under ; it would be necessary to send 100,000 men. If you treat them as friends, it is different." And this senator recalled the fact that England maintained only 6,000 troopers in the midst of 4,000,000 inhabitants of Canada. " Never has a colony been so pitilessly exploited by an avaricious and improvident mother country."[2]

It is plain that Spain had learned nothing from the separation of the colonies in 1825 nor from the hardly suppressed insurrection of the seventies. She blundered back into the old policy, and even accentuated it. It is a wonder that the final insurrection was so long delayed ; but it came at length in 1895 and found issue in the loss of what was left to Spain in America. Once again, however, Spain was destined to refer the collapse of her system and the loss of her colonies to the accursed foreigner. It seems unlikely that the insurgents could have realized their aims within any calculable period of time, had it not been for aid from without. In the earlier insurrection the " patriots " were as little able to take Havana as the royal forces were to pacify the island ; and the same situation recurred in the later revolution. An interminable vista of petty guerrilla strife afforded no prospect of future settlement and peace, while the economic interests, not only of Cuba,

[1] A Spanish senator, calling attention to the high per capita tax, gave the following comparative average rates : Canada, between $6.20 and $6.40 ; Martinique and Guadeloupe, $4 to $5 ; in the ensemble of the English colonies, $2.40 to $2.60. " No country in the world," he said, " attained to such a quota of taxation, not even France whose ordinary budget represents about 85 francs per French taxpayer." Leroy-Beaulieu, I, 265.

[2] Leroy-Beaulieu, I, 261–265, 266. For the earlier periods, see Humboldt, Isla de Cuba, pp. 250 ff., chapter entitled " Hácienda."

but of all the world that had to do with her commercially, suffered intolerably. And because the interests of the United States were so extensive, irritation in this country waxed ever greater, and gradually metamorphosed itself into the form of a crusade against misgovernment and oppression. Thus it was that, whereas the young Republic no more than held up the hands of England in helping on the emancipation of 1825, she became the protagonist in sweeping Spain finally from the New World.[1]

CUBA'S RELATIONS WITH THE UNITED STATES

That Cuba's destiny could not be disassociated from that of the country to the north appeared long ago to both practical men and to philosophic observers. The American colonists were deeply interested in the island, and there have been throughout later decades many occasions when half-stifled desire for its possession has flashed forth in plans of conquest. Geographical proximity and geological continuity have been the texts of those who professed a less material view-point. Of course the fundamental attraction was the complementary nature of the production of the two areas; as Leroy-Beaulieu asks, "Is not the American Union the natural market of Cuba?" Humboldt, long before, had answered this rhetorical query, for his statistics of Cuban commerce speak for the growing commercial affiliation of the two regions; as early as 1832 the flour of the United States, though severely taxed, could easily endure all competition.[2] The modern treatment of Leroy-Beaulieu[3] leaves no room for doubt as to the essentiality of the economic bond in question, and its potentiality in the creation of much closer relations. In his edition of 1891 the French economist, after noting the agitation, in 1884, for a commercial treaty between Cuba and the United States, adds[4]: "Let Spain make haste. If she does not profoundly reform the economic legislation

[1] Gallenga (pp. 117–118), writing in 1873, says that Cuba, by reason of its climate, would be "at all times an unprofitable possession" for the United States; that whites, "especially dram-drinking Yankees," would perish there like flies. Consequently the Cubans expect no overt act of hostility against Cuba. The policy of the United States, he says, "is simply, by worrying the Spanish Government — which, as she well knows, is here utterly powerless — so to aggravate the evils and hasten the disasters of the Island as to make her interference at some future period a matter of necessity for the Island itself, when she may be solicited to step in as a 'saviour of society.'" To what degree this passage is prophetic and to what degree cynical may be judged from the events of the succeeding decades.   [3] I, 259, 267–268.

[2] Humboldt, Isla de Cuba, pp. 221 ff., *passim* (231, 238, 241).   [4] I, 268.

and the administrative organization of Cuba, soon the Queen of the Antilles will be irrevocably lost to her."

The issue has justified the monition. For decades before the Spanish-American War the Cuban bond of economic and other sympathy with the United States had been viewed with hope and delight by the "patriots" and with suspicion and hatred by the Spanish. Americans lent furtive or even overt aid to the former, and in a few conspicuous instances [1] suffered the penalty. Whatever the exact truth of the matter may be, it is certain that the irritated feelings of the Americans awaited merely some such shock as they received in order to break forth into the fury of war. There could be but one result, for, while there had been an exaggerated notion of Spain's strength in earlier centuries, there was no possibility of a misconception respecting her subsequent decline and weakness. The unmatched struggle was carried out in reckless and holiday spirit by the Americans; target-practice upon the ill-kept and ill-manned fleet of Cervera was checked up with a view to the distribution of the meed of praise, as if the running fight of July 3, 1898, had been a mere tournament or diversion.

Puerto Rico

Spain lost, along with Cuba, not only the Philippines, of which more is to be said presently, but also the valuable dependency of Puerto Rico. The history of the latter island [2] offers several variants upon the course of Spanish colonial policy, together with an essential regularity. Up to the emancipation-period it was neglected or used as a place of exile for convicts; it profited during this period as an apt contraband station, and later its temperate climate and abundance of fertile soil attracted a considerable settlement of whites. Consequently the misfortune of absenteeism was, in Puerto Rico, reduced to a minimum. Merivale [3] says that the case of Puerto Rico is sufficient to disprove two universal and inveterate prejudices: that a European population cannot prosper and multiply freely in the West Indian climate, and that sugar and coffee cannot be produced by free labor and yet yield ample remuneration. Though a diversity of opinion is possible as to whether Merivale is

[1] For example, the *Virginius* case; cf. Halstead, chap. ii, etc., for the popular view of this episode and others; and Cabrera as an appeal to American sympathies.

[2] What is here said of Puerto Rico represents for the most part a summary of Leroy-Beaulieu, I, 269–271.

[3] Quoted in Leroy-Beaulieu, I, 270; cf. Humboldt, Isla de Cuba, pp. 26 ff., 64 ff.

not utilizing an exceptional case to disprove a matter of common observation,[1] yet the very exceptionality of the case would afford strong evidence as to the unusual conditions of Puerto Rican population.

Puerto Rico profited with Cuba from the reform in administration of the early years of the century; among other benefits conferred was the avoidance of great demesnes by the fostering of the system of small holdings. Taxes were lowered and the alcabala abandoned; and a period of prosperity like that of Cuba ensued. Toward 1835, however, these enviable conditions began to change for the worse: estates began to form; large subject populations, African and Asiatic, had to be dealt with. In the sixties Puerto Rico was going the way of Cuba and might have duplicated her history had she possessed the same attractiveness for the cupidity of the mother-country. However, she suffered but little from emancipation (1872) since it came about so easily. "As in Barbados, the smallness of the territory, the rarity of free and uncultivated lands,[2] and the relatively slight number of slaves occupied upon the plantations, facilitated the passage from slavery to freedom."

In the early nineties Puerto Rico was, for a Spanish colony, remarkably prosperous. It is noteworthy that her trade-relations were, like Cuba's, prevailingly with the United States, and secondarily with Great Britain; Spain, however, had a modest share. In 1891 Leroy-Beaulieu wrote: "It is probable that Puerto Rico may remain a dependence of Spain, if the metropolis is prudent and liberal; it will be perhaps the last remnant of the Spanish power in the New World." But the destiny of the island was absorbed in that of Cuba, in that it passed to the conqueror as spoil of war. And there seemed to be no serious protest anywhere against the final exclusion of Spain from the field of her secular blundering and humiliation.

THE PHILIPPINES

In an attempt to cover the important sections of the Spanish colonial empire, there yet remains to the recounter that group of trans-Pacific islands, discovered by Magellan in 1521, and later named *Filipinas*. It has been seen [3] that Columbus and the earlier explorers labored in the hope that they would presently discover

---

[1] Cf. p. 4 ff., above.

[2] The population of Puerto Rico was, in the nineties, six times that of Cuba (being 80 per square kilometer).   [3] Pp. 132, 177, 258, above.

some passage through America to the Orient, and that in this respect they encountered only disappointment. When, now, the actual experience of the Portuguese had demonstrated that the Spice Islands lay some fifty degrees east of Calicut, the old project of reaching them by sailing westward was revived. And it was shown that these islands must lie within the Spanish hemisphere as defined by an extension of the Demarcation meridian about the globe.[1] In pursuance of this object, and through the indomitable energy and resolution of " the first navigator of ancient or modern times,"[2] Spain actually reached, at last, the East, the final objective of her early efforts, the source of the coveted gain of Venice and of Portugal. Magellan and two-thirds of his companions perished, but " the cargo of spices brought by the little *Victoria*, consisting principally of twenty-six tons of cloves, exceeded in value the total net cost of the expedition."[3]

But the East that she found could scarcely stand to Spain in the hoped-for relation. Portugal was on the ground, and was determined ; she was able to concentrate resistance to encroachment upon her single and familiar, if widely extended, field better than Spain, already involved in America, could organize assaults upon a second and more than doubly-distant section of her half-world. Of a consequence, Spanish invasions of the Malay Archipelago were insignificant in result ; and even the Moluccas, the goal of desires, were speedily freed of their presence. When Charles V sold Spanish rights to the Moluccas and their trade, he also accepted a new north and south Demarcation Line seventeen degrees (297 leagues) on the equator east of the Moluccas. This renounced in reality all claim to the Philippines, but in practice it meant nothing of the sort. That actual conditions of possession and ability to defend formed the basis of the settlement respecting the Moluccas is rendered more probable by the fact that the Spaniards retained these northern islands almost unchallenged. " As they did not produce spices, the Portuguese had not occupied them, and they now made no effectual resistance to the Spanish

[1] Bourne, Hist. Introd., pp. 24–25; Sp. in Amer., pp. 41, 115, 118–119; on the Badajoz Junta, etc., see p 123, above.

[2] Bourne, Sp. in Amer., p. 128; for the voyage of Magellan, see id., pp. 119–130; Montero y Vidal, I, 9 ff. For the exhibition of " Spanish gratitude" in Magellan's case, see Foreman, p. 28.

[3] Bourne, Sp. in Amer., pp. 129–130. Cinnamon, sandalwood, etc., were also represented in the cargo. Foreman, p. 31.

conquest of the islands. The union of Portugal to the crown of Spain in 1580 subsequently removed every obstacle, and when the Portuguese crown resumed its independence in 1640, the Portuguese had been driven from the Spice Islands by the Dutch." [1]

The destiny of the Spanish in the East was metamorphosed when they were thus turned to the Philippines, as was that of the British when forced from Java to the mainland of India. Again, as in the case of America, they were to deal with uncivilized peoples,[2] again to miss, even in the Orient, the Oriental trade. Small wonder, then, to find their energy directed again into the primal activities of conquest and conversion. The results in the Philippines may therefore afford some idea of what might have occurred in America without the mines.

The conqueror of the Philippines was Miguel Lopez de Legazpi, one of the greatest of colonial pioneers. Starting in 1564 with four ships and 400 soldiers, and with a reënforcement of 200 in 1567 and of small contingents at irregular intervals, he effected results in the winning-over of the natives and in the repelling of the Portuguese which outdid in enduring quality those of any other Spanish conqueror except Cortés. In this he was much aided by the monks, but as representing a tactful, resourceful, and courageous directing spirit, he deserves the bulk of recognition.[3] The conquest was marked by none of the disastrous features of its American prototypes; Luzon was reduced (in 1579 and succeeding years by Salcedo) rather by persuasion and peaceable means than by force.[4] There was no pressing need of unwilling native labor as in the mines, and for a long time almost no plantation development took place; thus the relations with the natives were analogous to those which obtained in the early days of Buenos Ayres.[5]

[1] Bourne, Hist. Introd., p. 32; cf. pp. 24–25, 29–30; Sp. in Amer., pp. 131–132; Montero y Vidal, I, 6, 26 ff.

[2] For a brief ethnography of the Philippines, see Blumentritt, pp. 6 ff.; for the character of the Filipino, see also Scheidnagel, p. 59; Worcester, pp. 476–482; Foreman, chap. xi, *et passim*.

[3] Bourne, Hist. Introd., pp. 32–33. "It was owing to his heroism, his civic virtues, his superior genius, his grand patriotism and his noble disinterestedness that the Philippine Islands were incorporated quickly, pacifically and justly to Spain." Id., p. 43. Cf. Montero y Vidal, I, 35–43; Foreman pp. 33 ff.

[4] Montero y Vidal, I, 75–79; Bourne, Hist. Introd., pp. 38–40. Of course the Philippines were never thoroughly reduced, even excluding the Moro islands. Foreman, pp. 101 ff.

[5] P. 317, above.

The Moros

However, it must be noted that these early operations were directed mainly to the island of Luzon, and that the results signalized were attained among Malays whose natural development had been approximately uninfluenced from without. Farther south, on the contrary, the Spanish met a population already and definitely under the sway of the old arch-enemy Islam; for the Arabian influence had extended eastward through the preceding centuries and had just begun to make itself felt in the southern part of Luzon when the Spaniards arrived.[1] This state of affairs was recognized by the latter in the application to the Malays of the southern islands, particularly Mindanao and Joló (Sulu), of the generic term for Mohammedan, *Moro* or Moor. With these peoples the relations were those of persistent intermittent warfare. *Los piratas malayo-mahometanos*, as they were designated, descended periodically upon the coasts of Luzon, plundering the heretic in genuine Bedouin style; and Filipinos and Spaniards were always at one in their fear of these raids and in their determination to resist. For three centuries the chronicles are full of such piratic descents, and although Spanish expeditions took occasional nominal possession of Moro towns, destroyed the chiefs' sepulchers and the like, the succeeding repetition of attack and defense shows that such demonstrations were of small effect.[2] The Moros, with their

---

[1] Peschel, Races of Man, pp. 306–307; Blumentritt, pp. 18 ff. "The religion of the prophet had penetrated to Malacca in 1276, had reached the Moluccas in 1465, and thence was spreading steadily northward to Borneo and the Philippines. Joló (Sulu) and Mindanao succumbed in the sixteenth century, and when Legaspi began the conquest of Luzon in 1571, he found many Mohammedans whose settlement or conversion had grown out of the trade relations with Borneo. As the old Augustinian chronicler Grijalva remarks, . . . 'So well rooted was the cancer that had the arrival of the Spaniards been delayed, all the people would have become Moors, as are all the islanders who have not come under the government of the Philippines.'" Bourne, Hist. Introd., pp. 34–35. Montero y Vidal (e.g. I, 59–60) adverts to this view from time to time.

[2] Raids by malayo-mahometanos are chronicled by Montero y Vidal, I, 115, 117, 182, 201 ff., 242 ff., 273 ff., 434 ff., 482 ff., 540, 579; II, 344, 368 ff., 483, 500 ff., 559; III, 21, 87, 93 ff., 183 ff., 200 ff., 220 ff., 274 ff., 417 ff., 454.

"The year 1754 was fatal for the Philippine provinces by reason of the vandal attacks of the Moro Malays" (I, 515). There follows a list of damages for the year by months. "In 1789 the governor wrote to the king saying that the constant war with the malayo-mahometanos was an 'evil without remedy'" (II, 340). "According to official reports, the Moros captured per year over 500 persons, destining them to the most painful labor. The old, as of less value, were sold to the inhabitants of

lighter craft, regularly rowed into the eye of the wind, or took refuge in shallow waters, or, in the case of bombardment of their towns, simply evacuated them temporarily. It was not until the introduction of the steam-propelled gun-boats, about 1848, and the regular maintenance of a fleet of them in the eastern station (after 1861) that the seas were rid of the spoiler, and the course of commerce and travel became reasonably secure.[1] It is plain, therefore, that in the consideration of the Spanish system, one is justified in eliminating the Moros with slight notice as a people nominally subject but not actually so; indeed it may be said that the same condition of affairs has persisted to a considerable degree under the more masterful and vigilant system pursued by the United States.[2]

CONSTITUENTS OF POPULATION

With this brief notice the southern part of the archipelago may be dismissed from attention. Returning, now, to the actually subjected areas, it is proposed to give an account of the development of Spanish colonial policy in this new and, in some respects, very different field. In a general way, this policy was everywhere consistent with itself; many of the measures applied to the Philippines were the counterparts of those whose effects in Spanish America have just been reviewed. But, in part for reasons already suggested, there were variations in the East, which are instructive and significant to one who seeks the driving motives of the whole system.

In so far as emigration of Spaniards to the Philippines is concerned, it was almost negligible, being totally unsuited, in volume

Sandakan [in Borneo], who sacrificed them to the manes of their dead relatives or of important personages, preserving the skulls of the victims in proof of having fulfilled this barbarous custom " (II, 369). From 1778 to 1793, aside from incalculable losses in other ways, the expenses of pay for soldiers, for vessels, expeditions, etc., had amounted to 1,519,209 pesos fuertes (II, 369). The pirates were the "eternal question" as late as 1826 (II, 500); and even in case of victory the Spanish did not know how to handle them (III, 213 ff.). See also a special work by Montero y Vidal, Historia de la piratería malayo-mahometana en Mindanao, Joló y Borneo, Madrid, 1888.

[1] Montero y Vidal, III, 87, 135–136, 327 ff., 417 ff.; Foreman, p. 132. For the masterful administration of Arolas in Joló, see Worcester, pp. 168–188.

Joló was the most constant thorn in the flesh. "Precisamente es esa una isla que ha causado más males al comercio asiático que todas las demás Filipinas." Montero y Vidal, II, 559, note.

[2] On the Moros, see, besides Montero y Vidal, Foreman, chap. x; Blumentritt, 18 ff.

and quality, not only to constitute a new Spanish society, but even perceptibly to alter the ethnic type of the population. It was, from the first, composed almost exclusively of males, and these were practically all connected with military or religious establishments. For two centuries and a quarter the stock exclusion-policy of Spain forbade the establishment of any foreigner in the islands. About 1820 the ratio of whites to natives was about as one to 1600, and most of these whites lived in Manila. " As late as 1864 the total number of Spaniards amounted to but 4,050, of whom 3,280 were government officials, etc., 500 clergy, 200 landed proprietors, and 70 merchants." [1] During the last quarter of the nineteenth century the European Spaniards, apart from these functionaries, constituted scarcely a thousandth of the population; and the native Spaniards, or creoles, were about three in ten thousand (.03 per cent). Their influence upon the native strain was but slight; of Spanish mestizos (*mestizos privilegiados*) there were less than two per cent. Plainly the case is one quite divergent from that of America. If the Chinese be reckoned in at two and a half per cent,[2] and the Chinese mestizos (*mestizos de sangley*) at two per cent, the essential predominance of the native Malay stock is but accentuated;[3] the whites, at least, have been but transitory in the population. This is, of course, natural enough, when one reflects upon the essentially tropical type of environment represented by the Philippines;[4] there are no such corrections of latitude by altitude in the archipelago as rendered the sojourn of the Spaniards in Mexico and Peru more endurable.

[1] Bourne, Hist. Introd., pp. 59–60; cf. Foreman, pp. 4, 355. Filipino names are deceptive as a distinction of race. In 1849 a catalogue of Spanish names was sent out for distribution among the natives, a number of whom bore the same name, with the result of much confusion. Hence many Filipino families bear illustrious Spanish names. Montero y Vidal, III, 89.

[2] Foreman (p. 118) estimates the total number of Chinese in the islands just before the last insurrection against Spain (1896) as 100,000.

[3] Blumentritt, pp. 32, 35. Chinese and Spanish mestizos together constitute $3\frac{1}{2}$ per cent, but the former are more numerous.

[4] See pp. 7 ff., above. On the climate and diseases of the islands, see Worcester, pp. 64, 67–68, 313, 362–363, 434; Scheidnagel, 42 ff., 101 ff., 149–156. "It is unfortunately true," says Worcester (p. 67), "that the climate of the Philippines is especially severe in its effect on women and children. It is very doubtful, in my judgment, if many successive generations of European or American children could be reared there." Again (p. 478), " No one can work there as he would in a temperate climate and live."

Industrial Organization

Of industry there was but little in the islands and it was the result largely of the activity of the friars.[1] The chief products for export were those of the tropical plantation: sugar, Manila hemp, and tobacco; anything could be raised there, says Blumentritt,[2] which could be raised in the Dutch East Indies, but the trouble lay with the Spanish system. In any case, plantation-agriculture never attained any importance in Spanish hands; and the same may be said of mining and manufacture. Royal projects for the stimulation of industry and production were of no avail. The European Spaniards had no influence, wealth, or education; what local industry there was, was monopolized by the Chinese and the Chinese mestizos, who formed a noted contrast in vigor and enterprise with the Spaniards, creoles, and Spanish half-breeds. The Filipino (Malay) was an economic factor of small significance.[3]

The one economic activity of the Philippines, or, to be more exact, of Manila, was exchange — not of local products, but of those mainly of China; and it was naturally upon this trade that the hand of the regulator descended. From about 1576 the archipelago had profited by the visits of the mainland-dwellers; at the beginning of the Spanish domination, the Filipinos were trading with Japan, Cambodia, Siam, the Moluccas, and the Malay Archipelago. The Spaniards planned, in the absence of other means of accumulating wealth, to make of Manila the intermediary depot of trade between China and the Spanish world; and in this they seemed to be succeeding with some rapidity when the government, inspired by the Seville merchants, began to fear the competition of Chinese silks with those of Spain in the Lima market and a resultant movement of silver toward the East; and for this and other reasons began to introduce restrictions.[4] Whereas for thirty years there had been no limitations imposed, now came prohibitions of importation of Chinese fabrics from Mexico into Peru

[1] Montero y Vidal, I, 107; cf. p. 351, below.

[2] P. 6; cf. Worcester, pp. 73 ff., 503 ff. Foreman (pp. 269 ff.) discusses the commercial products in some detail.

[3] Montero y Vidal, II, 513–514; Blumentritt, pp. 32 ff.; Scheidnagel, pp. 70 ff.; Foreman, pp. 109 ff.; Worcester, pp. 516–517. Because of distance the home government was occasionally unable to check the enlightened policy of some active governor. One of these said of the government veto: " Afortunadamente había llegado tarde." Montero y Vidal, II, 288.

[4] Colmeiro, II, 405 ff.; Montero y Vidal, I, 456; Foreman, chaps. v, viii, pp. 247 ff.

(1587), of all direct trade between South America and the East (1591), limitations of shipments between Mexico and the Philippines (1593; rigorously enforced 1604), and restrictions to the Chinese of the trade between the islands and China. Because Chinese goods were smuggled into Lima, trade between New Spain and Peru was interdicted in 1636.[1] Finally, since the Philippines, as an appanage of New Spain, could trade with it only, Acapulco became a Seville for the Philippines; and the flotas were represented by one annual ship, — the *nao*.

For in actuality the commerce of the Philippines was crowded into one ship a year, and, thus confined, yielded the monopoly profits characteristic of the flotas. "In these great profits every Spaniard was entitled to share in proportion to his capital or standing in the community." The capacity of the nao was measured in bales of about seven cubic feet, and the right to ship numbers of such bales was represented by *boletas*, or tickets, the distribution of which was determined by a semi-political board. These boletas were worth in the later eighteenth century, in time of peace, from $80 to $100; and in war-time, about $300. Speculators bought up the tickets of poorer holders, borrowing money at 25 or 30 per cent from religious corporations, and hoping to clear 150 to 200 per cent. The voyage to Acapulco lasted in one instance 204 days; the ordinary time from Acapulco to Manila was 75 to 90 days.[2] The nao thus represented, on a small scale, the regular Spanish system as developed in the fleets and galleons, and with the same results. Large merchant-houses controlled the terminals, and the people at large profited little if at all — except that the command of the ship became a valuable piece of political patronage and that the pilots, mates, and even sailors made great gain in event of success. Individual enterprise was discouraged and the growth of population retarded; "the Acapulco ship has been the cause for the abandonment by the Spaniards of the natural and industrial resources of the Islands."[3]

There was no chance under such a system for the development or enrichment of a class of genuine merchants; corruption was invited. The old industries of the land declined; while the Dutch were enriching themselves in their eastern possessions, the Spanish

---

[1] Bourne, Sp. in Amer., pp. 289–290; Hist. Introd., pp. 61–63, 68, note.

[2] Bourne, Hist. Introd., pp. 63–65; Sp. in Amer., pp. 289–290; Roscher, Sp. Col. Sys., p. 35, note; Blumentritt, pp. 38 ff.; Montero y Vidal, I, 455 ff.; Foreman, pp. 243 ff.

[3] Bourne, Hist. Introd., p. 63, and notes.

and natives in the Philippines, even during the long peace succeeding 1648, grew poor in the most miserable fashion. Only Manila enjoyed spasmodic prosperity ; in fact, all the Spaniards but the monks and the province-governors removed thither to secure a share in the yearly lottery. The other settlements declined to mere villages.[1] And not only this : the nao, like the flotas, tempted the foreigner by its accumulation of valuables ; the booty taken from the Acapulco galleon in 1762, by the English admiral Anson, is said to have amounted to 3,000,000 piasters.[2] This system could not survive, of course, in the modern period ; the last nao sailed from Manila in 1811, making the final return-voyage in 1815. Trade then fell into private hands, and a port each in Mexico, Ecuador, and Peru was opened to it. Direct trade with Spain in a national vessel was allowed after 1766, the Cadiz ship continuing until 1783 ; but this system was replaced by a privileged company (*Real Compañía de Filipinas*) in 1785. The latter was embarrassed by the opposition of the Manila merchants, who resented the invasion of their monopoly of the export trade, and ceased to exist in 1830.[3]

It might also be mentioned, as paralleling the conditions in Spanish America, that the consistent policy was to keep the provinces apart ; even during the personal union with Portugal, the Portuguese might not trade from the Moluccas with the Philippines. Of the China trade it may be said that it was entirely in the hands of the Chinese and mestizos, and that if it prospered, together with trade with Japan, Borneo, Siam, and other eastern countries, it was due in no respect to assistance derived from the Spanish system.[4] In short, the regular policy of exclusion of foreigners obtained in full in the Philippines ; that it entailed, as in America, its inevitable results, will presently appear.

CLERICAL PREDOMINANCE

But the economic life of the archipelago was at most a secondary consideration : the islands were too far away, and promised too little of what the Spanish desired, as compared with America which lay

[1] Blumentritt, p. 38.

[2] Roscher, Sp. Col. Sys., p. 35, note ; Montero y Vidal, I, 456 ff. After the capture of the nao by Anson, the king ordered that, during war with England, no more ships should sail for Acapulco. Id., p. 481.

[3] Bourne, Hist. Introd., pp. 66–67 ; Montero y Vidal, II, 122, 297 ff., 446 ff., 481, 543 ; III, 539 ff. ; Zimmermann, I, 420–421 ; Foreman, chap. xv.

[4] Leroy-Beaulieu, I, 40 ; Bourne, Hist. Introd., p. 68, note.

between; the temptation to the merchant, especially under the restrictions recounted, was not large. But it was different for the votaries of the Church; and so the history of the Philippines came to be more purely mission history than was that of any other of the Spanish provinces except, perhaps, and in a different way, Paraguay. "From the beginning the Spanish establishments in the Philippines were a mission and not in the proper sense of the term a colony. They were founded and administered in the interests of religion rather than of commerce or industry." Spain knew that "a greater development of trade would only have hampered the progress of the missionaries and enfeebled the power of the convent." [1] In other words, the fathers had their way in the Philippines as they had not had it in Spanish or Portuguese America. There was no planter-class to oppose them. Consequently we miss in the Philippines, in any important form, all those topics of the encomienda-system, the decline of native population, the introduction of a substitute labor supply, and the like. Legazpi, it is true, followed the orthodox plan of apportioning encomiendas, but, in the absence of the exploiting class, these tended to become rather fields for the exercise of paternal and priestly influence than for the derivation of a labor force.[2] Laws favoring the natives were promulgated,[3] but there was no such occasion for reaffirmation, and no such disputes over enforcement, as in America. The representatives of the "practical," as against the "theoretical," were not in the field in the early times. Probably the treatment which the Filipino received would have appealed to Isabella as approaching the ideal; certainly the unrivaled feat represented by the wholesale conversion of the Malays [4] would, in retrospect, have filled her pious soul with joy. As a matter of fact, it was early discovered that the natives were eager to accept the new religion, at any rate in form, being impressed by its spectacular side. And so the friars, through their evangelistic enterprises, became active agents in the pacification of the country, religious advisers regularly accompanying the expeditions.[5] The extent and importance of their services cannot

[1] Bourne, Hist. Introd., pp. 48–49, 70–71; Leroy-Beaulieu, I, 40. For "forced cultures" in the Philippines, cf. Day, pp. 336–337.

[2] Cf. Montero y Vidal, I, 42, 87 ff., 380 ff.; Foreman, pp. 38, 212.

[3] Montero y Vidal, I, 380 ff.; II, 135 ff., 353 ff.

[4] Cf. Bourne, Hist. Introd., p. 37. On the "Domesticated Natives," see Foreman, chap. xi. Cf. also, on the treatment of the natives, Slosson, The Philippines Two Hundred Years Ago.   [5] Montero y Vidal, I, 17, 286; Foreman, p. 199.

be doubted, for during many decades the opinion prevailed that
"in each friar in the Philippines the king had a captain general
and a whole army." [1] Well on into the nineteenth century, in more
than half of the 1200 villages in the islands, "there was no other
Spaniard, no other national authority, nor any other force to maintain public order save only the friars"; this persuasion lasted as
a survival practically until the end of the Spanish domination.[2] It
was true enough that the monks knew far more of the nature of
the land and the people than almost any one else ; and their reputation along this line was the involuntary recognition on the part of
the home authorities, to whom, in the impotence of their real control, these matters were as a sealed book, of the value of acquaintance with a lower race's manners and customs.

The mission in the Philippines was on the plan of the reduction
in America. An efficient defense was organized against aggression,
in this case prevailingly that of the Moro pirates ; not a few of the
fathers had been seasoned soldiers, and rejoiced in the resumption
of military operations which bore the stamp of divine approval.[3]
They likewise supervised the tilling of the soil and laid the usual
stress upon the development of a higher industrial organization ;
beyond this they afforded the simple kind of education which they
judged suitable for the natives. Under their ministrations their
charges appear, as elsewhere in the absence of interference, to
have been comfortable and prosperous, and to have increased in
numbers.[4] The same attempt was made to exclude foreign influences ; trade with neighboring peoples, notably the Chinese, was
discouraged, and a European layman was a *persona non grata* in
the villages. The influence of the Church was so constant and
strong as to lead the more energetic governors to chafe beneath it.
Collisions between the secular and ecclesiastical authorities were
recurrent.[5]

[1] Bourne, Hist. Introd., p. 42 ; Blumentritt, p. 44.
[2] Bourne, Hist. Introd., p. 60 ; Blumentritt, pp. 44–45.
[3] Montero y Vidal, I, 242 *et passim* ; Blumentritt, p. 39.
[4] Bourne, Hist. Introd., pp. 32–34, 41–42, 57, 81–84, 85–86. Slavery was forbidden
by Philip II ; it lasted nearly up to the twentieth century, however. There are no
slaves now except among the Moros and wild tribes. Foreman, p. 191.
[5] Montero y Vidal, I, 380, 382, 384 ff. ; Bourne, Hist. Introd., pp. 49, 58 ; Blumentritt, p. 50 ; Foreman, pp. 51 ff., 209–210. The latter author asserts (p. 200) that up
to 1896 the monks were stronger than the law.

POWER OF THE CHURCH

Thus the power of the Church became established in the islands, and gained an inertia against which the political power, wherever it undertook to resume authority, beat in vain. Opposition to the monks might easily cost a man his whole career, if not his life. This immunity from control had, again, the usual effect of rendering the ecclesiastical authorities haughty and intractable, and finally ambitious and extortionate. Benefices were freely accepted, solicited, or demanded ; church-revenues were very large. Taken all in all, the friars have never possessed a more favorable large field for their activity than they had in the Philippines. Consequently, in view of their not having been seriously interfered with, it may be said that the present case demonstrates the outcome to be expected from such ecclesiastical control. Positively it may be asserted that the friars performed a great enterprise in converting *en masse* so large a body of heathen ; the magnitude of the exploit is unquestioned, however the term "conversion" be taken. But its real value and success must be otherwise measured, if at all. It is no particular service to a native people to supply them with a new set of fetiches, ceremonials, and so on; and wholesale baptisms can no longer be looked upon as guaranties of the general establishment of a new and improved frame of mind. The real effectiveness of the "conversion" lay in the fact that it brought the natives into permanent and friendly contact with the trained exponents of a new order of civilization. It is equally unscientific to hold the missions in contempt for the skin-deep Christianity which resulted from their ministrations, and to laud them for attaining at a blow, through modification of religious belief, what can be accomplished only through long and steady pressure brought to bear upon the ensemble of economic, social, and moral habitudes and customs.[1] The careful and minute discipline of the pious brothers undoubtedly started the natives in the direction of European civilization and its standards, but it never went very far ; it could train to a certain point only. "To prolong it beyond that stage would be to prolong carefully nurtured childhood to the grave, never allowing it to be displaced by self-reliant manhood. The legal status of the Indians [Filipinos] before the law was that of minors, and no provision was made for their arriving at their

[1] Cf. Bourne, Hist. Introd., pp. 36–40, 45–46.

majority. . . . The only thought was to make Christians and never citizens." [1] What the mission did was, here as in America, to ease the first relations of contact between a backward race and a modern world-economy; and it was the industrial and other by-products of their instruction that weighed infinitely over mere "conversion." The great speed with which the latter was carried out does not, therefore, form any measure of the real advance in civilization of the European type on the part of the Filipinos; it simply gave the friars a better chance.

They seem not to have improved the opportunity to promote civilization, partly because of the natural limitations set by their system of native education, and partly because they themselves diverged from the simple and unpretentious programme of their earlier years. As trade gradually opened up communication and diffused information, their pedagogic system was felt to be obsolete and a hindrance to advance; and to this was added active resentment of their encroachment upon the property-rights of individuals and of the community. In short, they became haughty and extortionate, and through means of various description they increased the holdings of the mortmain until, at the end of the Spanish domination, the friars held seven-eighths of the most valuable land in Luzon. [2] Their dispossession constituted one of the most serious problems of the American rule, and caused considerable embarrassment for the Holy See itself.

In the Philippines, as elsewhere, the case of the Jesuits was one, in many respects, apart from that of the other religious orders. As usual, they had been the most energetic and enlightened of the brotherhoods, but had exhibited here also the ambition and other qualities which rendered them universally obnoxious to the political powers. [3] They had accumulated properties to the amount of several million pesos and controlled a lucrative industry and commerce. In many ways they displayed their usual superiority over rival orders, for example, in education and culture. The natives

[1] Bourne, Hist. Introd., pp. 76–77; cf. pp. 73–74; Blumentritt (p. 28) says bluntly: "The national industry of the Filipinos at the time of the Spanish conquest stood upon a higher stage than it does now [1900]." On instruction in the Philippines, see Montero y Vidal, III, 536 ff.; Foreman, pp. 192 ff.

[2] Cf. Blumentritt, pp. 26, 53 ff.; Worcester, p. 315; Foreman, pp. 106–107; Bourne, Hist. Introd., pp. 73–74; The Nation, LXXII, No. 1857, pp. 82–83.

[3] Montero y Vidal, II, 141 ff., 180 ff.; Foreman, pp. 200 ff. In reading Foreman's account of the friars it should be borne in mind that his censure is not that of the Protestant.

were under their influence, and they displayed the regular contempt for royal control; after the English occupation they were accused of aiding the invasion. When their expulsion, for reasons already cited,[1] took place (1770), all their estates were confiscated and confided to the administration of a commission.[2]

The organization of the clergy was not so systematic as in America. Although the Archbishop of Manila was the head of the system, the orders, in their earlier numerical superiority, were unwilling to acknowledge subjection of any kind, and many sordid pages of the Philippine chronicles are taken up with accounts of refusals of visitation by the local head of the Church. During the last two centuries, however, the number of the secular clergy has increased. Another question in the archipelago was that of the native clergy, who were forbidden to enter the orders. It was asserted that they were not worthy of the high office of friar, lacking as they did both personal dignity and character, and being inclined to relapse, upon taking charge of a parish, into the indolent and barbarous habits of their previous years.[3] The seculars were also ill treated and repressed in all ways; they were given the inferior livings, and as soon as a parish became worth anything, it speedily fell into the hands of the clerical orders. This constituted a distinct political error, for the lower classes to whom the seculars ministered lost all sympathy with Spain. As will later be seen, the ill feeling thus engendered contributed not a little to the disintegration of the Spanish domination.

RESULTS OF CLERICAL RULE

On the whole, there seems to be little doubt that the experiment of control through the clergy worked out in a thoroughly disastrous way. The Inquisition (introduced in 1569) may never have gotten a strong hold upon the country; there were doubtless many of the clergy, the keepers of the Manila observatory, for example, who labored conscientiously and well, and even in an enlightened and scientific way; but the clerical régime by its intolerance and system of isolation certainly prevented the investment of foreign capital, and otherwise injured the economic and commercial

[1] Pp. 155 ff., above.

[2] Montero y Vidal, II, 36, 116, 141 ff., 180 ff. The re-suppression came in 1835. Id., p. 552, note. On the conditions of their return in 1859, see Foreman, p. 206.

[3] Bourne, Hist. Introd., p. 57; Montero y Vidal, II, 133–134, 318 ff., 362 ff., et passim; Blumentritt, pp. 46 ff.

prospects of the islands. And there is no doubt that there was, at least in more recent times, a liberal sprinkling of the low-natured, ignorant, and rapacious among the ranks of the clergy.[1]

One of the results of the dual activity of the commercial policy of jealousy and exclusion, and of religious prejudice, was the oppression of the Chinese. For them no need was felt, as for the negroes in America, as a substitute labor force; and they were cordially hated for the same reasons which have made them unpopular elsewhere : parsimony, business shrewdness, clannishness, religious differences, asserted immorality, and the rest. It is also noteworthy that the Filipinos and even the Chinese half-breeds (mestizos de sangley) exhibited this hatred in as bitter a form as did the Spanish themselves.[2] At the time of the discovery it was found that Chinese merchants visited the coasts of the islands ; and much damage was done in the early times by Chinese pirates. But the commercial relations were not cultivated, and the position of the Chinese who came to settle in the islands was rendered very dangerous by intermittent murderous outbreaks against them. In 1639 they were provoked to an uprising and 22,000 of them are said to have perished in five months of fighting. Despite preceding bad treatment, however, at the end of the sixteenth century about forty junks arrived at Manila for the month of March, in anticipation of the sailing of the nao in July.[3] But the Chinese were subject, not only to such irregular assaults, but also to the periodic attention of the government : the expulsion of the "infidel Chinese" was decreed for June 30, 1755, and it was again ordered in 1769 and in part was realized. They were allowed to return in 1778, and did so in large numbers. These periods of resentment of their presence, and of realization of its essential importance, alternated up to modern times ; but in the attempt to tax and otherwise discriminate against them, there was a steady consistency. Indeed, it was invited by the success with which they monopolized most branches of paying business ;[4] and the

---

[1] Cf. Bourne, Hist. Introd., p. 61 ; Foreman (pp. 202 ff.) devotes considerable space to their rascality. Cf. also Worcester, pp. 340 ff.; Scheidnagel, p. 62 ; Leroy, Phil. Life, chap. v.   [2] Blumentritt, pp. 33-35; cf. Scheidnagel, p. 199.

[3] Montero y Vidal, I, 24, 71-79, 144-147, 256-257, 461 ff. On early attempts at conquest by the Chinese, see Foreman, pp. 47 ff.

[4] Montero y Vidal, I, 532; II, 139, 289, 323 ff., 576 ff.; III, 150-152, 160, 171 ; Blumentritt, p. 33 ; Zimmermann, I, 416, 482, 485 ; Foreman, pp. 109 ff. The latter author notes the several massacres of the Chinese in his general chronological table, pp. 651 ff.

inveterate feeling of hostility to possible infringement which was involved in the monopoly and exclusion system lent energy to the movement.

ADMINISTRATION

But, before entering further upon the policy of exclusion, and the irruption of foreigners, it is in place to review the main lines of government policy in administration. In accordance with the Spanish theory whereby the king of Spain was also the sovereign of the external dominions, and was to rule them in consonance with the Peninsular system, the Philippine Islands became a kingdom under the charge of a governor and captain-general. They thus fell, for the most part, under the rule of military men, remaining, until 1819, a dependency of Mexico. As in America, the local executives were balanced and restrained by an audiencia and accountable through a residencia.[1] A local administration made connection with the subject races; the islands were divided into provinces under sub-governors (*alcaldes mayores*), the provinces into *pueblos* under an annually elected native or mestizo *gobernadorcillo*, and the pueblos into tributary groups (*barangay*) each under its head-man (*cabeza de barangay*).[2] Thus the type of administration was not in form essentially different from that of America; nor was the general attitude of suspicion, secrecy, and distrust any the less marked. The king suspected governors who showed initiative;[3] short-term functionaries rapidly succeeded each other. The same kind of spying upon the same kind of corruption took place; the same race-hatred separated classes;[4] the ignorance of the

[1] Bourne, Hist. Introd., pp. 49–50; Montero y Vidal, II, 323 ff.; Foreman, chap. xiii, 211 ff., pp. 306 ff., above. The salary of the governor-general was $8000 a year, with perquisites. Bourne, Hist. Introd., p. 50; cf. salary-lists in Foreman, pp. 214 ff.

[2] Bourne, Hist. Introd., pp. 53–56; Worcester, pp. 132 ff.; Scheidnagel, pp. 51–54; Foreman, chap. xiii.

[3] Foreman, p. 78. The following quotation (Foreman, p. 4) will recall conditions sufficiently treated under Spanish America, and will support the standpoint there occupied (e.g. p. 274, above) regarding the efficiency of benevolent legislation.

"The fundamental laws, considered as a whole, were the wisest desirable to suit the peculiar circumstances of the Colony; but whilst many of them were disregarded or treated as a dead letter, so many loop-holes were invented by the dispensers of those in operation as to render the whole system a wearisome, dilatory process. Up to the last, every possible impediment was placed in the way of trade expansion."

[4] Montero y Vidal (III, 566–567) says that the leaders in insurrections were mainly creoles; De Lanessan (p. 27) says the insurgents in both Cuba and the Philippines were mostly mestizos.

Spaniards regarding the islands was profound.[1] The main differences between Philippine and other colonial conditions were those of degree, such as became well-nigh inevitable in view of the greater remoteness of the islands from the center of rule, and the consequent augmented influence of the clerical orders. The isolation of the islands and the vexations of the residencia made it particularly difficult to get good officials; the friars were always ready to pursue a governor who crossed their desires, both during and after his term; and their opposition was a serious matter. Even after the regular residencia had become obsolescent, at the end of the eighteenth century, they still exercised a significant influence.[2]

In the Philippines the government had no such revenue-producing occupation to levy upon as it possessed in the mining-operations of America. It can scarcely be maintained that the government itself in earlier times oppressed the natives with taxes; if they were imposed upon, it was rather by the clergy. A certain revenue was raised by the taxation of the barangay through its head, who was held responsible; but the islands depended for the most part upon the regular subsidy from Mexico, which was, in a sense, the mother-country of the Philippines.[3] Up to 1884 all subdued tribes paid tribute, the sum varying; at the date mentioned the tax was $4.25 per year, $3 of which were remitted in return for 40 days' work rendered the government. There was also the system of the *cédula personal*, or personal certificate; every one over 18 years of age must possess one and pay for it from 50 cents to 25 dollars. Licenses of all kinds were purchasable at prices which were high in proportion to the wage, five to ten cents a day, received for labor. In later times, between the government and the priests, the natives were often involved in a life-long fruitless attempt to meet these obligations. And when it is realized that the government assured them of but few of the advantages for which taxes are paid — protection, education, harbor-works, roads and communications, sewers, etc. — the severity of the levies appears still

---

[1] Cf. Montero y Vidal, II, 305. Scheidnagel's book is largely a *vade mecum* for the newly appointed official. He prefaces his treatise with a disquisition upon prevalent Spanish ignorance of the islands (p. 204): "¡ Cuántas veces he oido decir á muchos de mis compañeros destinados á tal ó cual punto del Archipiélago, ¿ pero dónde está eso? ¿ por dónde he de ir? ¿ Cómo se hace el viaje? ¿ No habrá quien me dé noticias de aquello? etc. etc. !"

[2] Bourne, Hist. Introd., p. 52; Worcester, pp. 338, 340, 468, 471.

[3] Bourne, Hist. Introd., pp. 84–85; Sp. in Amer., p. 315; see note, p. 315, above.

greater.[1] Again the government held monopolies, particularly of tobacco, and regularly collected taxes whose operation was in restraint of trade.[2] Worcester[3] mentions a case in the island of Negros where it took a proprietor six years to get permission to build a tiny railroad and get his apparatus and materials through the custom-house. What little the rare efficient governor could do to assist industry and trade was before long upset by his successors.[4] As Scheidnagel[5] says, somewhat bitterly, a few Spaniards, in a vast territory, without prestige, protected even less by common law than the natives, often failing of aid from the local authorities, often subjected to the natives themselves, have been unable to execute any enterprises worth mentioning.

In short, for decades before the end of Spanish domination, the government was plainly and sordidly mercenary, corrupt,[6] and inefficient, and it takes an extremely benevolent observer to detect any more than ephemeral and accidental superiorities in its operations, from the period immediately succeeding the conquest up to 1898. It may have been relatively no worse at the outset than many of its contemporaries, but it showed no tendency to adapt itself to new conditions and thus incurred the reprehension and contempt of those nations which at least professed more modern ideals.

Foreign Aggression and Popular Discontent

Enough has perhaps been said to demonstrate the fact that the Spanish system in the Philippines was not essentially dissimilar, granted the changed conditions and their effects, to that applied in America. But the case of the Philippines, like that of Cuba,

---

[1] Montero y Vidal, I, 432–434; Foreman, chap. xiii; Worcester, pp. 93, 235–237; Scheidnagel, pp. 51–52, 195; Zimmermann, I, 478 ff., 486; Hilder, "The Present and Future of the Philippines"; cf. Bourne, Hist. Introd., pp. 42–43; Sp. in Amer., pp. 314–315. In regard to the roads, Scheidnagel (p. 55) passes severe judgment: "The system in vogue in the archipelago for so many years respecting this most important matter is undoubtedly the worst; for it depends purely upon the will, favorable or unfavorable, of the authorities and pueblos, without direct responsibility of any kind. The result is that commerce does not advance, wealth is not developed or augmented, and, as a last effect, civilization cannot be extended; innumerable and wide districts, as well as their inhabitants, remain in a completely wild state." On justice in the islands, see Scheidnagel, pp. 195–198; Foreman, pp. 239 ff.

[2] Cf. Montero y Vidal, II, 294–296, et passim; Zimmermann, I, 484; Foreman, pp. 293 ff.   [3] P. 259.

[4] Cf. the case of Basco y Vargas: Montero y Vidal, II, 286 ff., 315; III, 157; Worcester, pp. 168–188.   [5] P. 195.

[6] On Spanish Philippine finances, salary-lists, etc., see Foreman, chap. xiv, pp. 214 ff.

affords the student a view of the working-out of this system in the nineteenth century; for after 1825 Spain had more attention to give to her remaining colonies. One of the important consistencies in the history of all the main Spanish possessions lies in the fact that, while separation came as the direct result of foreign aggression, yet its essential and most significant antecedent was popular discontent in the colonies. Indeed, as respects the Philippines, it might be said that the aggression of the United States was almost fortuitous, being but part of a series of war-operations which had their storm-center in the Gulf of Mexico. Spanish control over the Philippines, as over Cuba, was almost illusory when the final shock with the foreigner precipitated the end.

The Portuguese caused Spain some uneasiness in regard to the archipelago in the early years of its domination; and the Dutch descended occasionally and at times in some force. Having seized Malacca in 1641, they moved on to the north the next year and took Formosa. But there existed a sentiment of loyalty to Spain which awoke to repel such invasion.[1] This was particularly evident during the English occupation, which began with Draper's sudden capture of utterly unwarned and unprepared Manila in 1762. The judge Anda y Salazar maintained a guerrilla warfare against which the English were unable to make headway, and they were glad to abandon the task after about sixteen months of precarious tenure of Manila and its immediate environs.[2] No other serious aggression is to be recorded until the arrival of the American squadron and the one-sided battle of May 1, 1898.

The real disaffection was internal, and was the direct outcome of the clerical encroachments and the governmental inefficiency and corruption of which an account has been given. And the positive and vital issue in the disaffection lay in the outcome of that monkish domination under which the islands fell, as has been seen, chiefly because of their geographical isolation. However, in the order of time, the first serious trouble arose in the Philippines as a sequel of the Napoleonic enterprises in Spain; the upheavals in the metropolis had their after-effects in the remotest of the colonies, in the form of uprisings. The natives thought the proclamation of the

[1] Montero y Vidal, I, 158 ff.; II, 261, 276 ff., 346 ff.; Foreman, chap. vi; Zimmermann, I, 411–412.

[2] Montero y Vidal, II, 13 ff., 382 ff.; cf. III, 347 ff.; Blumentritt, p. 41; Foreman, chap. vii.

political dogmas and constitution of 1812 meant exemption from tribute and public services, and were convinced that the measures of Ferdinand VII, after the restoration, emanated from oppressors in Manila.[1] The motives of unrest are implicit in the following proposals of the islanders, made at the time : they wished the suppression of the Acapulco nao ; the extension of the amounts of goods allowed to be exported ; the opening of Callao and Guayaquil to Philippine commerce ; concessions as to trade in national ships to the coasts of north-west California ; the amplification of permission regarding counter-cargoes ; and, finally, freedom from duties of all products of the Philippines carried in national ships, in all parts of the monarchy, for a period of ten years.[2] These proposals hinge chiefly, it will be observed, about the lightening of governmental interference with exchange. There was also, early in the nineteenth century, considerable trouble in the Philippine army, owing to the familiar Spanish policy of excluding the natives from positions of pride and influence ; almost all the officers were American Spanish. And there was exhibited a most bitter hatred between the Philippine Spaniards and the Peninsulars.[3]

Such conditions will be easily understood by one who has the driving principles of the Spanish system in mind. And when the sentiments were those of such discontent and bitterness, it is not surprising that every occasion of political overturning in Spain was seized upon to lend justification or to afford a chance for insurrection. Thus, in 1823, the announcement of the abolition of constitutional government was followed by strife ; and when, in 1868, Isabella II was dethroned, and the colonial personnel was thrown into confusion, we are already on the threshold of the insurrection of Cavité. The ensuing attempted introduction of "democracy," or what was vaguely but enthusiastically denominated such by La Torre, was a move which revealed a palpably mistaken idea of the

[1] Montero y Vidal, II, 421–426.

[2] Montero y Vidal, II, 429–430 ; the last proposal was virtually granted in 1820 ; id., p. 444.

[3] Montero y Vidal, II, 466 ff. ; III, 566 ff. The author referred to declares that from the very outset the Peninsulars regarded the Filipinos with great respect and that all the laws favored them. They could aspire to the highest places in the army, church, law, and civil administration. " Desde la llegada de los españoles, los filipinos han tenido el derecho de ocupar puestos en todos los órdenes administrativos, religiosos y militares, y los han ocupado, incluso la jefetura del Archipiélago, cosa que no sucede en ninguna otra colonia del mundo." III, 566, 601 (quotation). In any case, however, class hatred was present and wrought its inevitable results.

East and its prepossessions. In his rôle of plain democrat the governor, La Torre, was censured and ridiculed; to those who associated authority with magnificence and distance, the representative of Spain was a living confession of weakness.[1] And the uncertain and vacillating legislation based upon such inapt and veering idealism but strengthened the impression.[2]

ANTI-CLERICALISM : REVOLT

Returning now to the expressed opinion that it was ultimately the reaction against clerical invasions and aggressions which broke the bonds of the Filipinos with Spain, it is to be understood that this reaction began only in the nineteenth century.[3] As in America the upheavals in economic and political theories which marked the close of the eighteenth century, together with a greater dissemination of intelligence, led to a revolt mainly against commercial restriction, so in the relatively non-commercial Philippines they led, after 1812, to a restiveness beneath the local form of oppression — the sacerdotal. But, in one case as in the other, the direct counter-blow was launched against the political system which allowed the tyranny.[4]

The monks were always against reforms, for their monopoly and power were threatened by them, and speedily took up the trail of any publications which fostered agitation. Thus in 1871 they pursued and discovered a secret society of reformers, and were, by a piece of fortune, able to charge its members with overt acts of

[1] Montero y Vidal, II, 478 ff.; III, 487 ff., 557; Foreman, pp. 362 ff.

[2] Montero y Vidal, III, 530 ff. He quotes (p. 530) "El infierno está empedrado de buenas intenciones."

[3] Foreman remarks (p. 205), after describing the character and actions of the friars : "From the foregoing it may be readily understood how the conduct of the regular clergy was the primary cause of the Rebellion of 1896; it was not the monks' immorality which disturbed the mind of the native, but their Caesarism which raised his ire. The ground of discord was always infinitely more material than sentimental." But this author asserts elsewhere (p. 362) that there was really no friar question in the Philippines before 1812. Indeed, so far as his list of incipient insurrections goes (pp. 104–106), that of Cavité (1872) was the first serious anti-ecclesiastical demonstration.

[4] "Their [the Filipinos'] protest was not so much against the government of Spain as against the dominant influence of the obnoxious friars in the processes of that government. Even in their latest rebellion, that of 1896, the cry of the Filipino soldiery was, 'Viva España! Abajo los frailes!'" Robinson, pp. 19–20. This author's earlier chapters, containing the hastily assembled impressions of a clever staff correspondent on the spot, throw much light upon the last phases of Spanish rule.

sedition (Insurrection of Cavité).[1] They pursued their victims through the medium of the lay authorities, secured the execution of their leaders, and followed it up with other acts of vengeance upon the less deeply incriminated; many members of wealthy and influential families were thus banished to the Ladrone Islands. "There was, however, no open trial from which the public could form an opinion of the merits of the case, and the idea of subverting the Spanish government would appear to have been a fantastic concoction for the purposes stated. But from that date there never ceased to exist a secret revolutionary agitation which culminated in the events of 1898."[2] The reader is now in possession of sufficient preliminary and detail to pass on at once to the last revolt against the "official sacerdotal tyranny."[3] The friars, in a sort of confusion of bigotry and ignorance, had come to consider the native secret societies of reform or dissatisfaction as a local manifestation of "freemasonry."[4] They pursued them on this account the more systematically and relentlessly, and thus helped to secure the coherence, under pressure, of segregated societies into the so-called Katipunan ("League").[5] This society, driven beyond endurance, first prayed the Mikado of Japan to annex the archipelago; and then, upon the transmission by him of their petition, signed by 5000 disaffected persons, to the Spanish government, they planned for open rebellion. The latter project was prematurely discovered upon August 20, 1896, and military activities were at once initiated. Seizures of the richest and most prominent natives in Manila were not delayed.

The monks had learned nothing by the experience of preceding years; they held tenaciously to their old privileges and clamored against the humane and careful governor Blanco until they secured his recall in December, 1896. The few and not inexcusable executions sanctioned by him were now followed by acts of ferocity on the part of his monk-chosen successor Polavieja. During Polavieja's incumbency there occurred one of those acts of impolitic injustice which take hold upon the sentiment and imagination of an inflamed people : the execution of the brilliant surgeon, artist, poet, and novelist, José Rizal. Rizal was a man who had something of

[1] Cf. Montero y Vidal, III, 566 ff.

[2] Foreman, pp. 106–107, 108 (quoted), 363. The following sketch of the Tagálog Rebellion is mainly a condensation of Foreman, pp. 363 ff.   [3] Foreman, p. 364.

[4] The sympathy of republicans and freemasons in Spain really damaged the Philippine cause. Blumentritt, p. 52.   [5] Cf. Blumentritt, pp. 53 ff.

a European reputation, and who had conspicuously assailed the monks in two novels, published in Germany and Holland respectively, and widely read in the Philippines : *Noli Me Tangere*, and *El Filibusterismo*. The islanders were proud of Rizal, and his harrowing and romantic end stirred them to infuriation.[1] And in addition to their other motives for continued resistance they now began to realize the state of affairs in Cuba, and to profit by her example and by the necessary concentration in America of the Spanish forces.

In the spring of 1897 Polavieja was succeeded by Primo de Rivera, a former governor-general, who, it was hoped, would repair the damage done by his predecessor ; he issued a proclamation of amnesty which was, however, only partially effective. The insurgents in the field, here as in Cuba, were as safe from a definitive defeat as the Spanish were in the cities. Their demands, if one realizes that economic oppression in America had as its counterpart sacerdotal oppression in the East, read not unlike those of Spain's insurrectos of earlier years. The champions of reform, including the most notable men in the islands, called themselves *Asimilistas* or Assimilists, a name which is explained by the character of their demands ; they rebelled against unfavorable discrimination, especially as respects Cuba. First and foremost, the friars were to be expelled, their appropriations of land restored, and their incumbencies divided between the Peninsular and insular seculars. Parliamentary representation like Cuba's ; freedom of the press ; toleration of all religious sects; laws common with Cuba's, and administrative and economic autonomy ; equality in treatment and remuneration of Peninsular and insular civil servants ; abolition of governmental authority to banish citizens, as well as all other unjust measures against Filipinos ; legal equality of all persons, Peninsular or insular, under the civil as well as the penal code,

[1] Foreman (pp. 381 ff.) sketches the life of Rizal. Several detailed biographies are now in print; the latest and perhaps most authoritative is Retana's Vida y Escritos. Cf. Blumentritt, pp. 51, 57–58. In his first work, the one which really drew the venomous attention of the monks to him, Rizal attacks religion, showing the folly of the doctrine of Purgatory, charges the priests with atrocities, such as digging up the bodies of their enemies to insult them, and shows the fate of all who assault their power or even oppose them. He exhibits the *guardia civil* as their agent, and as a factor making for terrorism rather than order. But the tragedy of the book is really the hopelessness of a state of affairs where the persecuted, because of lifelong training and ancestral tradition, still stand up for their persecutors and assert that the presence of the monks is indispensable.

— these represent demands which the reader has met with before. But the background of all reform could be nothing less than the cessation of this "official sacerdotal tyranny," the root and stock of all Philippine woes.

In December, 1897, De Rivera negotiated the peace of Biac-na-bató, in connection with which he is said to have agreed to reforms and conditions "almost amounting to a total compliance with the demands of the rebels." An indemnity of 1,700,000 pesos was agreed upon, of which 800,000 were to be paid to Aguinaldo, the insurgent chief, under certain conditions.[1] But the reforms, together with a considerable portion of the indemnity, were not forthcoming, and the expatriated insurgent leaders, forming *La Junta Patriótica* at Hong-Kong, together with their friends in the islands, were filled with suspicion. Again hostilities began to break out; they were followed by savage reprisals on the part of the Spanish, and soon in the provinces north of Manila the rebellion was once more in full vigor. In April, 1898, De Rivera was recalled and Augustí succeeded him; but the reforms which he wished to introduce were too late. Petty warfare might have continued for an indefinite period, for the prospect of settlement, now that the reliance upon Spain's good faith was gone, was slighter than before. The outlook was not hopeful for foreign intervention, as in Cuba, and but little secret aid was afforded by coveters of the islands. However, as has been explained, the exigencies of a war begun halfway around the globe led to the seizure by the American fleet of the enemy's eastern stations, and in the succeeding treaty of peace they were not restored. The United States paid Spain some $20,000,000 for such claims to the islands as were not annulled by the counter-claim of conquest, and the Philippines became a dependency of the Republic.

It can scarcely be maintained that the islands ever constituted a Spanish colony; as Foreman says in the first sentence of his book: "During the three centuries and a quarter of more or less effective Spanish dominion, this Archipelago never ranked above the most primitive of colonial possessions." But its colonial history certainly furnishes the student of human society with a striking example of the phenomenon of the contact of races where such contact is controlled in its own way, with scarcely a trace of let or hindrance, by an organized priesthood.

[1] Cf. Blumentritt, pp. 59–60.

SPANISH AFRICA

A few words will suffice to indicate the present status of the once world-wide colonial empire of the Spanish. First of all, after the loss of the Philippines, Spain sold the part of the Micronesian archipelago which she still held (Caroline and Ladrone groups) to Germany (1899) and disposed of Guam and several other fragments to the United States, thus withdrawing finally from the Pacific.[1] The external possessions still remaining to her are several forts in Morocco, a section of desert sand upon the west coast of Africa (Rio de Oro and Adrar), and the islands (ceded by Portugal in 1778) Fernando Po and Annobom. They are practically value-less to Spain, and might well be disposed of. Spain has likewise, until recently, cherished a shadowy claim, in event of partition, to Morocco; but the Anglo-French agreement of 1904, and the ensuing negotiations of the Algeciras Conference of 1906, leave her with but slight hope of its realization.[2]

In short, Spain is, at the present day, practically bereft of colonies;[3] she has attained this position by four centuries of descent from the exalted station of a holder of half the world. And that her lesser and present condition is not fortuitous is indicated by the rather wide-spread persuasion that she is better off now than she was in 1898.

[1] Cf. Foreman, chap. iii.
[2] Keltie, Africa, pp. 247–248.
[3] The Canary Islands are, to all intents and purposes, part of Spain.

CHAPTER X

COLONIZATION OF THE NETHERLANDERS: BEGINNINGS, SETTING, THE ORGANIZATION OF THE COMPANIES

Having sketched the history of the Iberian colonial empires to their latter days or to their extinction, the narrative now returns to the story of their rivals of earlier times. Foremost of these, both in time and in importance, were the Netherlanders. It was in the order of events that they should next appear upon the field of commerce and colonization; the introduction of the northern European countries to the products of the warmer zones had taken place, in good part, via the Low Countries.[1] Even the Phœnicians penetrated the North Sea; and in much later times Flanders had been the objective of a regular Venetian fleet. When, now, the monopoly of Venice had passed westward to Portugal, and the routes of the Oriental trade had shifted to the Atlantic, the share of this exchange which fell ultimately to the region of the lower Rhine became proportionately greater. And the Netherlanders, being not unschooled in what had to do with the Orient, were enabled speedily to profit by all that changing conditions threw in their way. It may be noted, preliminarily, that the very policy of the Portuguese monopoly-holders operated as an active encouragement to the development of the Dutch into the position of rivals and, finally, of successors. It will be recalled [2] that the Portuguese, in the consciousness and pride of their monopoly, and in order to discourage the idea of direct approach to the East, practically renounced the European coastwise trade, preferring to gratify their sense of power and importance by forcing the ships of the northern

---

[1] The most useful survey of Dutch colonization is, in the present writer's opinion, that of Leroy-Beaulieu (I, book i, chap. iii; book ii, chap. iv). The topic, covering as it does mainly questions of commercial and financial organization, is singularly adapted to the genius of this noted economist. Few detailed references are given to Leroy-Beaulieu in the following chapters, but his general ideas will frequently receive expression in the text. The teacher will find his pages full of suggestions and of facts useful in the elaboration of what follows. Zimmermann (Vol. V) presents a useful but rather unsystematic and rambling account of Dutch colonization, full of facts, but lacking in perspective.   [2] Cf. p. 124, above.

countries, and, above all, of the Netherlands, to come to Lisbon
for the Eastern wares. The desire for these products of the tropic
lands was too strong to abide renunciation; and thus the Portuguese policy operated as a sort of process of pressure or forcing
which hastened the pace of the growth of Dutch shipping and
nautical knowledge, and overcame any reluctance which existed
toward the navigation of the ocean. Since, also, the navigation
of the Atlantic between the Low Countries and the Peninsula
demanded a more than ordinary courage and skill, at that stage
of the arts of seamanship, the momentum of advance to overcome
a sturdier resistance was necessarily increased. Thus it came
about that the conditions of the time provided a hard but effective school for the beginnings of the Dutch commercial power.

But, before entering into any further consideration of these
conditions, it is in place, in accordance with our method of treatment, to review the political, economic, and other conditions
amidst which the internal impulsion toward a colonial destiny
arose.

UNIFICATION

Politically, the Low Countries exhibit a gradually increasing degree of integration through the centuries succeeding the Crusades.
With the advance of civilization and the emergence from mediæval conditions, the formerly segregated communities began to settle
down under stronger local government and to learn something of
each other. The towns began to wax in importance and the gilds
and other forms of economic organization to make their influence
felt as against the military and atomistic forms of the Middle Ages;
"the future belonged to the burgher." Local merchant-leagues,
and finally the Hanse, stood as manifestations of the changes of
the center of gravity of society.[1] Thus the modifications of economic conditions impinged upon the political. But the actual
political bonds whose formation meant that there should at length
be a single state, where formerly there had existed isolated communities, were those created by the extension of the Burgundian
power. Starting from Flanders, the princes of this line gradually
added to their dominions the greater part of the Low Countries,
until, in the time of Charles V, when the house of Austria succeeded to them, "the unity of the Burgundian states seemed to

[1] Blok, I, 263 ff., 333 ff., 353; II, 29–30, 64 ff.; Pringsheim, p. 1.

be permanently established." [1] It does not conduce to our purposes to pursue the details of the Burgundian policy, or of its results; [2] it is enough to say that a certain degree of centralization was effected which had in it the possibilities of continuous and rapid growth. Local prejudices had not been aroused to an extent which precluded the sinking of local differences in a common cause; the several districts had been made to see the advantages of closer political union, and were well on the way toward state-formation. This is a condition which we have learned to know as an indispensable preliminary to any such exterior activity as colonization. Taking these general results of the Burgundian period as a basis, we are now briefly to follow the succeeding phases of the political drawing-together of the Netherlands.

It must not be understood that imposition of a common administration from without is enough to evoke a state from a number of scattered communities, with local ends and methods of attaining them. When, in 1515, Charles V took over the Netherlands, it rested largely with the character of his rule whether the promising movement toward union should continue. From what has already been said [3] of the emperor it is clear that he was entirely in sympathy with the Netherlanders; in fact, he was by birth and rearing, if not by ancestry, their fellow-countryman. He understood, and was understood by them; the very qualities which made him unpopular in Spain conspired to render him acceptable to the Netherlanders. Realizing the strength of local traditions and prejudices, he not only proceeded cautiously with his projects of centralization, but, to a certain degree, modified his own Catholic zeal in his treatment of the great religious problem of the day. The Low Countries formed, in his view, an integral part of his empire, and their interests were subordinate to those of the empire alone. He was cordially liked by the people, and his retirement took place amid scenes of profound feeling and regret. His reign tended, therefore, considerably to strengthen the bonds of growing nationality; in spite of subsequent happenings, the provinces were never again to manifest a distinct separatist tendency. [4]

Nevertheless, Charles did not feel secure as to the future of the provinces after his death. He had forebodings of disintegrating

[1] Blok, II, 114 ff.; cf. pp. 159, 204, 237, 292 ff., 316.
[2] Blok, II, 259 ff., 400 ff., 505 ff.   [3] P. 181 *et passim*.
[4] Blok, II, 305 ff., 317-319; Armstrong, Emperor Charles V, *passim*.

strifes of succession, and endeavored to anticipate such misfortunes by securing from the provinces a "pragmatic sanction," binding them to the Hapsburg succession. The readiness with which they accepted this arrangement shows their appreciation of the advantages of centralization and peace; it affords "strong evidence for the conviction that the feeling of mutual coherence, of common needs, was at length fixed in the inhabitants of these regions. . . . Above all, in the protracted war against France, people had learned to appreciate the advantage of the coherence of all the Netherlands."[1] And this conviction was not to be entirely lost, but rather strengthened by the events which were to follow. Philip was no such man as his father ; even during the short progress through the Netherlands which, as a young man, he undertook at the emperor's command, he made a distinctly bad impression upon the people. He was stiff and formal and could not assume such affection for the country as his father had cherished. He was a Spaniard of the Spaniards ; and in contradistinction to Charles, was unpopular in the Netherlands by reason of the very qualities which endeared him to Spain. As king, he ignored or crossed local privileges and traditions, and in no way masked his abhorrence of the form of religion which was now making its way in the provinces. Moreover, while to Charles the Netherlands had constituted an integral section of his empire, to Philip, who was simply king of Spain, they were no more than an appanage of that country, not to be considered where Spain's advantage forbade, and distinctly subsidiary in importance to Naples and other objective points in the south. "There was no independent Netherland state ; there was a congeries of Netherland states and statelets, dependent upon Spain." That this was Philip's view became increasingly evident after 1562, when his hopes of becoming emperor had collapsed.[2]

The possibility of further unification of the Netherlands under Bourbon or Hapsburg rule was thus eliminated ; it was to take place, as the fates decreed, not under, but in resistance to Charles's successor. This resistance was bred of anger which was roused against Philip mainly for two general reasons : because he hampered the economic development of the provinces ; and because he opposed in so inexorable, tactless, and ruthless a manner the spread of the Protestant movement. For one who is familiar with the economic policy of Philip in Spain a guess as to its aspect in the

[1] Blok, II, 316.   [2] Blok, II, 319 ff., 325.

despised Netherlands is attended with little hazard; and it is even easier to imagine what the gloomy, religious monomaniac would try to do to heretics for whom he had not even the sympathy of nationality. In either case Philip treated the Netherlanders as foreigners who sought to injure Spain. He rendered the sojourn of the Dutch merchants in Spain at least as unpleasant as that of other foreigners; and at home he subjected them to the heavy taxation and other discouragement of which, as applied in Spain, much has already been said. He created in the Netherlands a state of uncertainty, as well as an atmosphere of oppression, which struck at the heart of material development; and then, deaf to remonstrances, he visited manifestations of a rebellious spirit with arbitrary restrictions of customary privilege and with curtailment of political power.

The Struggle for Freedom of Faith

Of this attitude toward material development, and its results, more will presently appear. It was chiefly, however, Philip's policy of religious intolerance which ultimately brought about rebellion accompanied by a burning hatred which material oppression could hardly engender. And it was his savage repression of a growing religious persuasion, common especially to the northern provinces, which finally welded the latter together into a strong resisting confederation. In earlier times the Netherlands, with the rest of accessible Europe, had been inundated by the clergy. In Flanders, toward the end of the thirteenth century, there were forty-six cloisters, more than thirty associations of regular and lay prebendaries, and thirteen convents. The incomes of such religious establishments were very large. A growing indifference to the Church was manifested, however, as early as the twelfth century, and in succeeding time resentment against the clergy, on the part of princes and people, gained strength. Toward the end of the fifteenth century, Gansfoort and Erasmus won a number of adherents among the higher classes; but it was Luther who brought the unlettered into definite resistance against the Roman Church. The economic development of the provinces had tended to render the claims of the clergy anachronistic and exasperating, and the common people were angered at the gross abuses which they witnessed. A community with its face set toward economic progress and commercial development could not longer endure restriction which had been scarcely sensed in the mediæval period.[1]

Luther's ideas were introduced into the Low Countries about 1520; and Calvinism spread from Flanders and Henegouwen to Holland, Zeeland, and Utrecht shortly after the middle of the century. Lutheranism was met with determined opposition by Charles, for however much he loved the Netherlands and desired their prosperity, he could not, as a fervent Catholic, connive at the spread of heresy. The lay authorities succeeded to the religious orders, chiefly the Dominicans, as chastisers and inquisitors of the heretics; and after 1525 there was a systematic pursuit of the unfaithful, most of whose leaders were put to death, imprisoned, or banished, by 1530. Doubtless the number of executions has been grossly exaggerated; perhaps a thousand met death at the stake or otherwise. But many thousands were harassed and interfered with in the pursuit of their livelihoods. This persecution took place with especial thoroughness in the north, chiefly in Holland; and one of the results was a considerable emigration to hospitable England of valuable elements of the population. Thus, even in the time of Charles, discontent was strong enough to overcome the love of home and the inertia which opposes movement to alien lands.

But such persecution had but small effect in retarding a development called for by the spirit of the age and the people; it opposed, rather, a barrier which challenged and thus united the rising floods of opinion and resentment. This appeared almost immediately after the accession of Philip, being reënforced by the popular discontent which, as has been seen, his personality and economic policy called forth.[2] Philip was, of course, more severe than Charles, and speedily transformed the latent hostility of the Netherlanders into open resistance. Thus he united against himself, as king and as champion of the Church, a complex passion of hatred with a footing in both economic and religious discontent; and his subjects of the scattered provinces were forced to cohere as never before in common armed resistance to a common oppressor.[3] Or, envisaging the situation from the other side, we have now a series of formerly isolated communities, here forced into close coöperation in the mutual

---

[1] Blok, I, 277 ff.; II, 458 ff.   [2] Blok, II, 468–482.

[3] It was really under the stern hand of Alva that local differences between sections of the Netherlands were reconciled. He thus realized, in an unforeseen way, the policy of the Burgundians. Blok, II, 413.

defense of cherished habits and institutions. Material interest and religious sentiment were fused into a common group-feeling, for which patriotism is scarcely too strong a term; like the Spanish before them, the Dutch arrived at a certain sense of nationality in the process of defending themselves from alien aggressors on their own soil. And by reason of this strengthened habit of coöperation, they were the better prepared to develop into a state, and as such to form the center and directing power of an extended commercial and colonial empire.

Economic Strength

The other conditioning factor for such a destiny, for which we have come to look, is economic strength; for it is in proportion primarily to the degree of its political homogeneity and unity, and to the strength of its economic organization, that a state is likely to succeed or fail in the colonial field.[1] The Low Countries, with the rest of western Europe, were awakened by the Crusades to the extent of the outside world and to the variety and desirability of its products. They suffered with the rest the loss of population and destruction of labor forces consequent upon the enterprises in the Holy Land, but at the same time gained a conception of the value of trade, and a desire for gain and adventure.[2]

Agriculture in the Low Countries was favored by natural conditions, and early attained a respectable development. The local place-names of the Dutch indicate that they early concentrated attention upon the physical characteristics of the land; and it was, again, their natural environment which led to intensive methods of agriculture, forced the extended application of labor to land, and, among other things, made of the Netherlanders specialists in the treatment of marshy soils.[3] The proverbial industry and economy of the Dutch and Belgians testify to their earlier development along this line. When the towns began to form, the kernel of their population was composed of men trained in the school of careful and economical

[1] Blok (II, 482), while admitting and emphasizing the great political import to the Netherlands of unification under one ruler, thinks that their prominent rôle in the world-history of the fifteenth and sixteenth centuries fell to them rather more by reason of their development of industry and trade, that is, of economic strength.

[2] Blok, I, 183–184, 295.

[3] Many local names end in *loo, bosch, hout, woud, moer, poel.* Blok, I, 302, 305. Credit should be given to the monks for their early activities in diking, draining, etc.

intensive cultivation. This production of local food-supplies was a distinct element of national strength in the sixteenth century; and to such agricultural interests there was added a considerable development of sheep-raising, especially in Zeeland.

But agriculture could not keep pace, in such a country, with manufacture, especially after the development of a lively exchange. Towns formed early and became centers of gilds of artisans of all kinds. Especially in Flanders was there a strong development of manufactures, chiefly of fabrics; that province, alone of Europe, could vie with Spain during the period of prosperity of the Spanish textile industries; and it was the forced emigration of Flemish and other weavers that taught England much to her economic advantage. The forces of wind and water lent power to the manufacturers. As early as the fourteenth century, despite famines, wars, oscillations of prices, bad hygienic conditions, and the like, the position of the Flemish artisan was very strong; and the same thing may be asserted, in less degree, of artisans elsewhere in the Netherlands.[1] Even in the fourteenth century these industrial classes were prone to display their strength and independence in various uprisings and disorder which could not well be repressed. The type of the region was prevailingly industrial and commercial, and it became increasingly more marked, until, with the decadence of Venice and Spain, the Low Countries became industrially superior to all the rest of Europe. Thus at the outset of their colonial career the Netherlands added industrial solidity and force to their other elements of strength. Many of the details of their economic organization will appear in what follows.

GROWTH OF TRADE

Despite, however, the advancement of production and of industry, the Netherlands found their supreme advantage in commerce; and thus pursued exchange with a fervor, skill, and success unequaled before in the history of Europe. To "beat the Dutch" in trade became the high, but almost hopeless aim of their rivals of later centuries. The geographical and physiographical advantages of the Netherlands for the development of commerce have been touched upon before : they provided not only the point of outlet for central and northern Europe, but the convenient point of inlet

[1] Blok, I, 333 ff.; II, 3 ff., 64 ff., 483 ff., 495.

of sea-borne wares from the south. They were physically constituted to develop a people of middlemen. The Low Countries surrounded the mouths of the largest rivers of western Europe, the
Rhine, Maas, and Schelde, thus securing easy communication with
the inland. And on the sea they were only five or six days' sail
from Denmark and somewhat less from Norway; six to fifteen days
distant from the Spanish and Portuguese harbors; and only a few
hours from the French and English coasts.[1] Combined with this
advantage of position they possessed others of a more local nature
which conspired to train their population for its commercial destiny.
The flatness of the country; the navigability of the rivers; the ease
of canalization; the archipelago-like coast, especially in the north;
the location and good quality of the harbors; the prevailing winds;
the nearness, not to say imminence, of the sea — these are broad
environmental influences which nurture up sailors and fishermen
through the various stages of nautical skill and daring until they
venture upon the ocean. The Dutch early took to the sea and became daring skippers, so that other nations came to seek the services
of their ships and sailors; and this natural movement was fostered
under the Burgundians.[2] The immediate cause of the rapid development of trade lay, however, as has been intimated, in the fact that
the Netherlands formed the objective of the annual Venetian fleets,
and that the Dutch were thereby constituted a group of middlemen. As early as the thirteenth century these favorable conditions
were showing their effect in the concentration of population; and
the development of towns was reacting as a great stimulus upon
that of trade. Population increased rapidly, so that there were by
1500 a number of towns of 20,000 inhabitants, and many of half
that number. The total population of the Low Countries at this
time is estimated at 3,000,000; that of Holland (1514), at 400,000.
And together with this increase of numbers there went a development of municipal life and institutions, of schools and the like, and
a consequent evolution of a personal freedom which was to constitute the mainspring of reaction against an earlier and more cramping system. The Burgundian rule had proved a blessing for the
land; agriculture, cattle-raising, manufacture, and trade had been
encouraged and the Netherlands were rapidly coming to be the
" finest jewel " among Spain's possessions.[3]

[1] Blok, II, 483.   [2] Van Rees, II, 1 ff.; Blok, II, 417.
[3] Blok, II, pp. 505–522; cf. pp. 522 ff.; Pringsheim, p. 1.

Recurring specifically to trade, it is seen that local "hanses" began to take form in the thirteenth century, later to be absorbed into larger aggregations. Distributing activity began to extend from rivers to sea, and gradually strengthened until important commercial privileges were gained from neighboring states. The rulers of England, France, Sweden, Norway, Denmark, and Russia granted the Netherlanders exemptions from taxation, right of staple, use of their own laws and magistrates, and the like ; and to please them the strand-law was abolished in a number of regions.[1]

Commercial Predominance of the North

Thus far the Low Countries have been considered as a whole ; it is now in place to indicate the local shifting of the centers of trade which effected the dominance of the northern provinces, and which contributed in large part to assure to them alone the commercial and colonial career. In the twelfth, thirteenth, and fourteenth centuries Flanders and Brabant were far superior to their fellow-provinces. The Hanseatic League had a strong station at Brugge, which thus became the staple for all the river trade ; it was through Brugge that Lübeck and Hamburg made trade-connection with Italy ; through it passed the Oriental products from the south and east, French wines, grain from France and the Baltic region, Russian furs, Scandinavian woods, Spanish iron, and Italian silks. Naturally a considerable development of the machinery of exchange, of credit-instruments, etc., accompanied that of trade.[2] About 1400, however, the sanding-up of Brugge's sea-approach caused the diversion of the trade-routes, and they passed, from that period on, over Antwerp ; the latter had become, by 1550, the richest merchant city of Europe, with a steady population of 100,000 and a floating one of 50,000. Daily 500 ships entered and cleared from its harbor, and on occasions 2500 might be seen at one time on the Schelde ; 5000 merchants were day by day on 'change, and the European money market was centered here. The amount of Antwerp's trade is estimated as having been one and a half milliards (about \$600,000,000) annually.[3]

But Brabant as well as Flanders was falling upon evil days ; jealousies and factions, civil wars, the competition of the English,

---

[1] Blok, I, 350 ff.; II, 148–149.   [2] Blok, II, 483–485.
[3] Blok, II, 29–30, 486–487. For the development of the Dutch cities and trade, see also Wappäus, I, 328 ff.

and the difficulties in getting supplies of raw materials, caused chiefly by these same rivals, all conspired to check the development of the southern provinces. And a sturdier commercial power was rising in the north. Hollanders and Zeelanders were sea-faring as Flemish and Brabanters had never been; from 1400 on their herring-trade had been of great importance, constituting the chief means of livelihood of the coast districts. Of the 700 herring-craft in 1562, the Flemish owned 100, while Zeeland came in for 200 and Holland for 400, including the largest and best. The superior aggressiveness of the northerners in the sea-trade is indicated by the fact that while Brugge and Antwerp had been mere stations of the Hanseatics, the Hollanders and Zeelanders had been Hanseatics themselves. Thus they were not merely purveyors of their own products, or mere brokers; they were active transporters of merchandise from north to south. In the fifteenth century they had more trade in the Hanse towns than the Hanseatics in Brugge. By 1510 Holland and Zeeland were the great carriers between the Mediterranean and the Baltic; they sailed even to the polar seas; and in 1528 reached the Cape Verde Islands. From the middle of the fourteenth century they pressed Flanders and Brabant; and by 1560 Amsterdam had distanced the rest of the northern towns and was second only to Antwerp: in the sixteenth century it was the "Venice of the North." Holland particularly rejoiced in its fine situation, excellent and well-kept waterways and harbors, numerous and enterprising population, splendid cities, and rich lands. Combined with the poorer, ruder, but energetic sea-folk of Zeeland, the Hollanders were fitted to play a great rôle in the economic development of the world.[1] Money-conditions were coming to be better understood, and Charles V by his liberal policy contributed to this end; banking houses were established, and the mechanism of exchange became steadier and more secure; even life-insurance was developed. This was a situation which was forming during the time of Venetian trade-supremacy; and the extent and importance of Dutch commercial operations were only augmented after the discovery of the Cape route to the East, and of America. The Netherlands were much nearer now to the main ways of the Orient trade; and since the Venetians were still, and long remained, strong enough to block the free entrance of the Portuguese into the Mediterranean, the stream of tropical wares destined for central and

[1] Blok, II, 489–500.

western Europe, which naturally clung to the waterways, tended to flow almost undivided toward the north. Likewise the Hollanders gained control of practically the whole carrying-trade of Spain.[1] This meant that the Low Countries were to enjoy a still more extensive intermediary function, with its correspondingly increased profits. And when the policy of the Portuguese caused them, as has been seen, to renounce the coasting-trade, it further meant that the Dutch were to be obliged to develop a larger quantity and a better quality of merchant shipping, and to increase their nautical skill and confidence by regularly venturing across the stormy waters of the Bay of Biscay. They did this successfully, and their consequent wider activity in the field of commerce operated to accumulate opportunities for the exercise of a constantly increasing power to meet and utilize them. Development of trade toward the north was more difficult. The Hanse had to be met and overcome, and the taxes levied by the Danes paid or evaded. But by the end of the fourteenth century the Hanse was rapidly declining, and some alleviation from the Sound-tolls was secured. In any case there was peace in the north, for the most part, even if the heavy dues could not be evaded.[2] Relations with England, at first easy and free, became gradually more difficult and ominous. From 1430 on there arose contentions and competitions which could only issue in an ultimate struggle for trade-dominance ; but for many decades the Dutch retained an unquestioned supremacy. In short, by the end of the reign of Charles V the Dutch constituted potentially, if not yet actually, the strongest commercial power in the West ; the Netherlands had become "a member of great significance in the body of Europe." The population continued to increase rapidly and to display an energy and development superior to that of surrounding peoples ; and in Charles V the country was governed by a powerful prince in such a way as not to neglect the freedom-loving traditions of the subject nor yet to sacrifice the power of the central rule.[3]

RESISTANCE TO SPANISH POLICY

A people thus prosperous in material ways, and so independent of mind, had no grace to submit to the narrow and mediæval policy of Philip II. What the Prince of Orange and others, as

[1] Blok, II, 500.

[2] Blok, II, 491–494, 500–504 ; Pringsheim, pp. 20 ff.   [3] Blok, II, 436–437.

representatives especially of the malcontents of the northern provinces, complained of was the political and religious absolutism of that policy; in particular, they resented the injury to trade which Philip's attitude toward Denmark and England was sure to bring. "In short, they wanted a government in a Dutch, not in a Catholic or Spanish-Hapsburg sense; they did not want to see the Netherlands sacrificed to the king's religious and political purposes, which were not their own." [1] In other words, a progressive, enterprising people, alive to the conditions of national wealth, success, and growth, and not benumbed by a rigid subordination to an obsolete fetichism of King and Church, were ready to react violently against the same measures which Philip imposed upon the Peninsula to the ruin of all, and yet to the satisfaction also of all except a small and powerless minority. And as concurrence with Philip's mediæval policies led inevitably, as has been seen, to national degeneracy and final elimination from the concourse of the powers, so resistance thereto, representing as it did the awakening of the genius of a new age, elevated its exponents into a dominant position in the world. The Dutch exhibited the characteristics of an adaptable, and so viable, human society; they sensed the conditions of national existence and prosperity and attacked with resolution every artificial obstruction calculated to prevent or hinder speedy conformity with them.

What the provinces wanted was, above all, freedom from connection with that for which Philip so preëminently stood: regulation. And because the king was so much more obstinate and inexorable in the imposition of religious conformity than elsewhere, it was over this question that the storm-center so consistently hovered. At his accession the Protestants were not very numerous, especially in the south; but his measures against them were so severe that even the Catholics objected; and the reaction against his policy simply served to increase the rebellious element. The régime of Alva (1566–1573), including the execution of the popular counts Egmont and Hoorn, drove the country into the arms of the Prince of Orange and brought on open war. Hatred of the grasping and overbearing clergy increased; and all through the long ensuing conflict other issues were in the background as compared with that of religion. Occasional savage outbreaks such as the "Spanish Fury" (1576) left Catholic as well as Protestant

[1] Blok, III, 11.

in terror of indiscriminate slaughter and devastation. The insistence especially of the Hollanders and Zeelanders upon religious
freedom blocked many peace-negotiations, for Philip remained
bigoted and inexorable to the end ; but it was incorporated after
his death among the conditions of peace (1609).[1]

Thus it might be said that the struggle of the Netherlanders
was very largely for religious liberty, or, more exactly, for freedom
of thought. And it is unquestionably true that whatever aid was
lent in the war by other Protestant states, was to a varying degree motived by sympathy for the struggle of Protestant against
Catholic. Doubtless this consideration bulked largely in the minds
of the common people of England, and certainly among the Huguenot sympathizers. In a certain sense, Philip's Catholic bigotry, his
station as champion of the Faith, united against him all the most progressive elements of western Europe ; and they all later advanced
together by reason of the stimulus and inertia of their reaction
against his attacks. The other motives which impelled especially
England to lend aid to the struggling northern provinces will
presently become more clear ; recurring to these provinces themselves, it is evident that a war waged so largely for religious
liberty could not but effect a consolidation of interests calculated
to weld the participants into a more coherent national form.

MOVEMENTS TOWARD INDEPENDENCE

The resistance encountered by Philip was, however, based to
a large degree upon economic considerations. Nothing could blind
the Netherlanders to the chance of national gain or loss, and they
foresaw little but calamity from the application of Philip's system.
The correctness of this view was abundantly demonstrated to the
northern provinces through the fate of the southern ; for these fell
rapidly from their high estate with the strengthening of Spanish
control, and in consequence of the war which the attempted further
extension of that control brought on. The Dutch, for example,
resisted taxation for Spanish purposes : the attempt of Philip,
during the early days of Alva's rule (1569), to introduce the
alcabala as a regular tax encountered first active opposition, and
then, when this was quelled by stern means, a complex of evasion
and silent resistance. Yet the people had paid the " tenth penny "

[1] Blok, III, 15–23, 25–27, 37–48, 59–70, 89, 204–209, 258, 262, 313, 520 ff.

(*tiende penning*) on several separate occasions, where apparently its payment was without prejudice to their jealously cherished privileges. Again, in 1571, the attempt to impose this tax led to protests, — of which even Alva realized the justice, — that by this move the lower classes would suffer and trade be ruined; the opposition this time gave origin to an actual uprising and lent strength to the Prince of Orange. In all this period Holland had been particularly unmanageable; and that province remained under arms when the uprising had been elsewhere repressed.[1] Apart, also, from the direct injuries wrought by Spanish fiscal and other regulations, the provinces suffered greatly in the loss of valuable constituents of their population. Every striking exhibition of repressive action, especially in the line of religious intolerance, was followed by copious emigration of superior elements of the population, largely to England, or, during Spanish domination of the southern provinces, from that region to the resisting north. This movement meant likewise the emigration of considerable capital in the narrower sense.[2] And if war and its effects be reckoned in as sequels of Spanish policy, the economic consequences were of the most far-reaching upon the status and destiny of the provinces.

The aspect of this last assertion which bears most vitally upon our subject is the development of a separate destiny for the northern provinces as distinguished from those in the south which remained Spanish. It has been shown how Holland and Zeeland, as the most important of the northern provinces, had been gradually developing to succeed Flanders and Brabant as commercial centers; and it has been noted that, while not prevailingly Protestant, they were yet the strongholds of the reformed faith. Here it was that Spanish fiscal and religious oppression encountered the most determined resistance on the part of a population representing in exceptional degree the qualities and policies of a coming age; and it was hither that the resisting spirits of subdued regions fled, to further resist. The great contest lay between Spain and this kind of antagonism — that of a small but strong population, favored in its struggle by the lie of the land, led by an extraordinary captain, itself of stubborn character, insistent upon its rights, and, in this

---

[1] Blok, III, 83 ff., 101 ff.

[2] Blok, III, 59–60. He estimates the emigration from the Low Countries as 400,000 in 30 or 40 years. Cf. also III, 66, 89, 309, etc.

case, spurred to desperate endeavor by the savagery of repression. Of this people the determining factor was a minority ready to die for its beliefs and freedom, prepared to go into exile rather than submit to what it regarded as tyranny. Compared with such a nation, says Blok,[1] Spain was the earthen vessel contending with the iron, a colossus with feet of clay.

These northern districts increased in industrial and commercial importance with the decline of the south under Spanish rule, and especially under the blight of war waged largely within the same stricken region. After Alva's departure Antwerp was practically ruined, and the events culminating in the Spanish Fury of 1576 rendered prostration complete. At this time the southern provinces seemed about to throw in their lot with Orange and the northern districts; the Ghent *Pacificatie* of 1576 seemed to herald a complete union of all the Netherlands. But the opposition of the Catholic south to the increasingly Protestant north rendered the union of little permanent effect.[2] The north then united within itself in the *Unie* of Utrecht (1579), a defensive and offensive alliance;[3] and the two unions came to stand for diverse purposes: the Pacificatie for reconciliation with Philip, and the Unie for wholehearted support of the Prince of Orange and resistance to the end. Hence the south became virtually the supporter of Philip's great general Farnese (Duke of Parma) and the reaction in Holland and Zeeland took form in the practical abolition of Catholicism (1580). And so the final and, to a certain extent, unlooked for outcome was that it was the northern provinces alone, and chiefly Holland and Zeeland, which finally resisted Spain and thus came into the heritage of nationality and material prosperity which followed upon the successful defense of commonly cherished religious and economic ends. The conflict of thirty years, waged only in small part in the north, encompassed the complete ruin of the south, while Holland and the other northern provinces made such gain from it as scarcely to welcome for themselves conditions of peace.[4]

If this contrast has been drawn with sufficient clearness, it is now possible to eliminate the southern provinces from further

---

[1] III, 134–135; cf. p. 173.   [2] Blok, III, 127, 170–175, 196, 204–207.

[3] The uniting provinces, later the Dutch Republic, were Holland, Zeeland, Utrecht, Gelderland, Overijssel, Groningen, and Friesland.

[4] Blok, III, 228–234, 262, 297–305, 309, 400, 410, 448–449, 536–537.

consideration, and to concentrate attention upon Holland, Zeeland, and the other districts which coöperated in the formation of a commercial and colonial empire. Henceforth in this book the unmodified term "Netherlands" is taken to include them alone.

THE REVOLT

It seems unnecessary to follow in any detail the story of the war with Spain. The Spanish commanders were consistently handicapped by lack of funds, by the half-confidence, suspicion, and dilatoriness [1] of Philip, and by the rooted distrust of Spanish good faith.[2] The Dutch, on the other hand, persisted under all circumstances in the most stubborn manner, gradually developed a respect little short of worship for the great statesman who led them, supplied funds collected in copious streams [3] mainly from duties upon a constantly growing trade, received considerable countenance and but small actual aid from England and France,[4] and so labored on through reverses and successes, with steadfast purpose, inundating the country in the darkest hour, until their independence was finally wrung from Spain in 1609. After the defeat of the Invincible Armada in 1588, the hollowness of Spain's reputation became speedily apparent, and 1590 made a decided change in the character of the war; it ceased to be almost purely defensive, and the consummate soldier Maurits of Nassau began those offensive military operations whose extraordinary success soon filled his camp with young military men sent from many of the states of Europe to learn the art of war.[5] And, besides all their successes on land, the Dutch, in company with the English, began to harry the Peninsula with naval forays of greater or less vigor, thus terrorizing the coast towns, and not seldom garnering large booty; a little later they even overcame the garrison and seized the African island of Principé.[6]

[1] One high Spanish functionary in Italy is said to have remarked: "If death had to come from Spain, we should be certain of a long life." Blok, III, 160.

[2] Blok, III, 89, 135, 187, 282. The unpaid Spanish troops plundered right and left, exasperating the Netherlanders, and rendering the task of the Spanish governor doubly difficult (III, 209).

[3] Holland paid for some time 60 per cent of the war costs. These were very high, and were used to support 100 ships of war, 150 companies of infantry, and 58 troops of cavalry. Blok, III, 424–425.

[4] Blok, III, 79, 97–98, 105, 122, 249, 280, 324, 334 ff. (Leicester), 383, 386, 428.

[5] Blok, III, 258, 348, 401 ff. (Armada), 414–416, 420 ff., 466, 504–505.

[6] Blok, III, 437, 451, 457, 466–468, 504–505.

To the development of trade during the war time attention will presently be given. But one consideration, as bearing upon the development of national strength, yet awaits mention. Not only were the members of the resisting confederation bound by this protracted war into a more coherent whole, but there was likewise developed within the local and confederated governments a power of corporate action which made the Republic of the United Netherlands (recognized in 1648) something more than a name. During the early years of the war, in their more or less disunited condition, the provinces looked to the Prince of Orange as the father and savior of the country. Nevertheless the local parliaments maintained a locally uncontrolled function, and the States-General exercised considerable power despite a prevailing deference to the Prince. The result of this was that when the long-feared and finally encompassed assassination of the latter came, the States-General were able, after a new outburst of grief and rage against Spanish perfidy, to take the destiny of the United Netherlands into their own hands. Even during the life of Maurits, the bulk of real authority lay in the hands of Oldenbarnevelt, the State-Advocate of Holland, in his capacity as a leader of a parliamentary body.[1] So that we see here the partial explanation of the contrast soon to be drawn between Dutch colonial enterprise and that of the Portuguese and Spanish, namely, that the predominant factor in this movement is no longer royal initiative and support, but individual and above all corporate activity.

DEVELOPMENT OF TRADE: EARLIER VOYAGES

We recur now to the succession by the Netherlanders to the trade-monopoly of their Portuguese predecessors. It is natural that mere freight-carrying between the Peninsular ports and the north should not long have contented so energetic a sea-faring people; at first, however, attention turned to the north and east. The year 1577 marks a voyage to the White Sea, and 1584 the establishment of a factory at Archangel; after the defeat of the Armada, however, vessels began to penetrate to Venice (1590) and soon visited Alexandria and Constantinople. They also frequented from that period the Cape Verde Islands, at first for salt, and the coasts and rivers of Guinea. Moreover, in the earlier years Dutch sailors

[1] Blok, III, 264–265, 289–293, 321, 387–396, 475, 500 ff.

were employed by the southern nations; and Portugal and Spain even sent Dutch ships laden with northern merchandise on to Brazil and to other parts of America instead of unloading and reshipping their cargoes.[1] How dependent Spain speedily became upon the ships of foreign nations has already been pointed out.[2]

But for a considerable period the Dutch clung to their old routes and were seemingly unmoved by the report of Portuguese discovery and adventure. First of all there was no imperative need of change : wares could always be gotten on the Lisbon market, and thus the long, unknown voyage was obviated. The mistaken policy of the Portuguese in surrendering the European coastwise traffic was partially designed to preserve and confirm these conditions; when they forbade the exportation of India goods from Portugal in Portuguese ships it was largely with the idea of removing any stimulus toward undertaking the India voyage. And, for a time, the rest of Europe was quite willing to leave it to them. Moreover, the Netherlander received important commercial favors from Spain and Portugal in their rivalry for his trade. To encourage the visits and sojourn of the Dutch, Portugal conceded them, for example, security of person and goods, religious freedom, and judges of their own nationality, all on condition of agreement to trade with Portugal and not with Spain.[3] The value of this trade to both parties was such that even national hostilities could not quell it : Portuguese and even Spanish officials connived, and the Dutch held resolutely to it, in greater or less degree and against the representations of powerful allies, almost up to the peace of 1609. The grains of the north were so essential to the impoverished Peninsula that sudden stoppage meant little less than famine; while the Dutch practically paid their war-expenses out of their profits. Their claim to continuance during hostilities was that if they did not supply the grain, the Hanseatics and northerners would, and thus they could neither accumulate gain nor carry on war.[4] How much of speciousness this plea embodied let one familiar with commercial argumentation say.

Further hindrance to the attempt to reach India lay in the lack of proper ships, of capital, and of knowledge. European coasting vessels were thought unfit for such extended voyaging; and capital had not yet assembled into units large enough to finance heavy

---

[1] Blok, III, 452–453; Van Rees, II, 2 ff.
[2] Pp. 254 ff., above.
[3] Van der Chys, pp. 1–2.
[4] Blok, III, 305, 307–308, 440.

and protracted hazards. It was not until the fall of Antwerp in 1585 that large capitalists began to settle in the northern provinces. The ocean and its routes were little known before the publication, in 1595, of Linschoten's *Itinerarium ofte Schipvaert naer Oost ofte Portugaels Indien*, the first treatise on the subject in the Dutch language. Sporadic voyages to the East by Netherlanders had yielded as yet but little satisfaction; for it should be recalled that the Portuguese were strictly forbidden to give information which would tend to lift the veil of ominous secrecy with which they masked their operations in the East. It need hardly be said that they fashioned a series of "commercial myths," like the Phœnicians of old, which were calculated to play upon the superstitious ignorance of the age; these ranging from fairly accurate tales of strange winds and reefs, and of the deadly calms of the African coast, to the wildest flights which an unsophisticated credulity would tolerate. And even if information had been at hand, experience was lacking. Hence the "sure-going" Dutch were impelled by a complex of motives to cling to the humbler function of simple intermediaries. In addition to these natural hindrances two other inhibitions rested upon them : that of the Portuguese king, who threatened with death and confiscation of goods any one who should sail in Portuguese seas without royal permission; and that of the Pope, several times alluded to, which added religious sanction to the secular menaces of the lay authorities. It is understood that, prior to the accession of Philip to the Portuguese throne in 1580, Portugal was, nominally at least, a friendly power, in common cause with the enemies of Spain. Hence any attempt of the Dutch to evade the license-regulations would have been an unfriendly act toward a strong ally. But the Portuguese king in principle granted no licenses to foreigners; in short, it was made as hard to go beyond Lisbon as it was easy to come to that port. The same conditions long obtained in respect of voyages to America; these were undertaken but rarely by the Dutch before the last years of the sixteenth century.[1]

What finally enabled the Netherlanders to overcome all these obstacles was nothing less than the jeopardy of all their trade. In 1580 Philip II became king of Portugal, and at once manifested an intention of assailing the Dutch carrying-trade *in toto*. The

[1] Van der Chys, pp. 3–11; Blok, III, 453–454; Roscher, p. 258. On the earliest voyages to the East see art. "Tochten" in Encyl. Ned. Ind.

Dutch in Portuguese harbors now ran the risk of seizure and "examination" by the Inquisition, and although they did not give up their trade, but pursued it under a connivance which represented its real value to the Peninsulars, yet the state of insecurity engendered by the new conditions produced a restlessness and a close examination of all alternatives. Matters came violently to a head in 1595, when Philip seized such vessels of the Hollanders and Zeelanders as were then in Spanish and Portuguese harbors; these were 400 or 500 in number, manned by 5000 to 6000 sailors, and constituted about two-fifths of the whole merchant fleet of the northern Netherlands. Such a severe blow, threatening as it did the solvency of their large merchant houses, awoke the Dutch to the perils of the situation and the futility of their dreams of its betterment.[1]

One other alternative to the Cape voyage, it should be noted, had been attempted with ill success — that of the north-east passage. As early as 1580 adventurers had requested aid of the state in an attempt to discover this route to the Indies. It was reckoned that it would be shorter by 2000 miles, would avoid the loss of life attendant upon tropical voyages, and would be pursued without molestation of any kind. But it was not until 1594 that a beginning was made; in that year one Moucheron discovered what he supposed was a passage, and a second expedition was at once prepared and fitted out for the China trade; it is noteworthy that the policy of exclusion of other nations from this commercial bonanza was at once adopted. But the expedition of 1595 ended in no more than a small and but slightly edifying extension of geographical knowledge concerning the region of Spitzbergen and Nova Zembla. Hopes were not given up, however, until 1601, by which date Houtman's voyage by way of the Cape had been made, and interest diverted permanently toward the southern route.[2]

THE VOYAGE TO INDIA

By 1585 improvement had been made in ships and methods of navigation, and a flow of capital had set in toward Amsterdam. Linschoten returned in 1592; and as far back as 1579 and 1587 Drake and Cavendish had reached respectively the Moluccas and Java, thus providing examples of contempt for the Portuguese,

[1] Van der Chys, pp. 13–14; Van Rees, II, 4; Blok, III, 436, 458; De Reus, p. xi.
[2] Van der Chys, pp. 16–51; Blok, III, 454–455.

Spanish, and the Pope.[1] The reformed religion, together with opposition to Catholicism as almost personified in its royal champion, had freed the Dutch from any strong religious scruple in
the matter of infringement of the Church-sanctioned monopoly
now held by Philip; and it was at this favorable juncture that the
inevitable individual who was destined to precipitate the situation
came into prominence. This was Cornelis Houtman, a man who
seems to have had long experience in Portugal and Spain, and
whose consequent influence was considerable. A company of nine
merchants was organized and there were laid the keels of four
ships to be built on the English plan, small but manageable; they
carried over 100 cannon and 248 men, their entire cost reaching
290,000 florins.[2] The undertaking was of something more than a
private character; the cannon were borrowed from the government,
under security for their return, this being in the nature of a subsidy which should not weigh upon the general population; there
were likewise furnished from the government stores powder, guns,
spears, etc. Further, exemption was extended from licenses and
taxes, it being understood that no goods were to be taken in
or unloaded west of the Cape. The commander carried letters of
introduction from Prince Maurits and from him received injunctions
not to attack any one, but to defend only at need; to accomplish
his ends through friendly means, realizing that his mission was
mercantile, not military; to strike his flags when suspected ships
approached; to make a treaty of peace at Bantam; and so on.
All these considerations lend to the operations of the nine mer-
chant-adventurers a certain political status; in these negotiations
little mention is made, however, of the States-General. At the
advice of Linschoten, Java was selected as the objective, much to
the future advantage of the Dutch in the extension of their power
over the Archipelago.[3]

Houtman sailed April 2, 1595, arriving in Bantam June 22, 1596,
and returning home in July, 1597. He brought back with him
three of the four ships, but only a third of his men, and a very
small cargo; lack of knowledge and divisions of opinion had lengthened the voyage and perturbed its course, while a parsimonious
trade-policy had lent confirmation to the representations of the

---

[1] Van der Chys, p. 15.
[2] Van der Chys (p. 31) reckons this sum as equivalent to 362,000 florins of
modern money.　　　[3] Van der Chys, pp. 28–37; Van Rees, II, 6–7.

Portuguese and enabled them to convince the Javanese that the Dutch were simply pirates, with no real desire to trade. Nevertheless a conception had been gained of the lucrativeness of the direct trade; another company was at once founded in Amsterdam, and two in Zeeland, and in 1598 twenty-two vessels sailed for the East Indies. By July, 1599, of nine ships in one of these fleets four had returned richly laden, the voyage having covered the incredibly short time of fifteen months.[1] By the end of 1601 fifteen fleets, comprising sixty-five ships, had sailed, some by way of the Cape and a few through the Straits of Magellan, and had returned with cargoes of great value. In some cases they not only made treaties with native princes but expelled the Portuguese and built Dutch strongholds. A passion for the India trade, long regarded as a hopeless dream, piled capital on capital for its prosecution; and to these new enterprises the government was persuaded, chiefly by Oldenbarnevelt, to lend some such assistance as it had granted the first. Before the end of the century the loss of the trade with Spain and Portugal was no longer regretted; direct connection with the East was far more profitable, and the old routes to the Peninsula were deserted. Great misery ensued for Portugal and Spain, thus robbed of an almost indispensable supply of food-products; it began to be seen even more clearly that the new venture was a deadly blow at an old enemy, and the government granted aid the more gladly to an enterprise of national importance. Sailors were put under oath of service and the force of law was lent to punishments of their misdeeds. The state did not yet grant commissions as against Spain, but great changes had nevertheless occurred since the time of Houtman's instructions.[2] It is certain that neither government nor people intended to yield the great prospects opening up in the direct eastern trade; they were inured to war, which had become an almost normal condition, especially for Holland and Zeeland, the leaders of the Unie. Hence they resolutely refused any peace which did not leave them free to trade

---

[1] It was joyfully exclaimed that never had such richly laden ships returned since Holland had been Holland. Bells were rung and great excitement prevailed. The Portuguese in Amsterdam said that the fleet could not have visited India in so short a space of time, and must have looted the cargoes at some intermediate station. These cargoes included, as most important constituents, 600,000 pounds of pepper, 250,000 of cloves, 20,000 of nutmegs, 200 of mace, and 100 of long peppers. "The merchants admitted to have made easily two penninck on one." Van der Chys, p. 74; cf. Roscher, p. 262 and note.   [2] Van der Chys, pp. 64–69; Blok, III, 457–458.

in the East, and they won their point in the negotiations preceding the cessation of war in 1609; negotiations which led to a settlement modeled all along the line upon the principle of *uti posside-tis*,[1] a practical acceptation of the actual status in the last years of the war.

We may pause here to indicate the effects of this long-delayed peace upon the fortunes of the northern Netherlands. Danger of sudden attack disappeared; the perennial strain upon finance ceased; the number of troops might be diminished; extraordinary protection was no longer needed by merchant vessels; internal disorder could be sternly suppressed; credit could be restored; the public debt, reaching 12,000,000 guilders, and which carried up to 10 and 14 per cent interest, could be diminished; arrangements might now be made with England and France regarding advances which amounted to 14,000,000 or 15,000,000 in the case of the latter, and over 8,000,000 for the former; the peace was sure to redound to the ultimate advantage of industry and trade.[2] Such considerations more than outweighed the gains incident to a state of war, especially since the peace-settlement upon the principle of holding what was held in 1609 assured the Netherlanders of practically all the advantage which the successful last years of the war had gained for them. They were now recognized participants in the trade with the Orient and the directors of their own fortunes in both economic and religious lines, which were the main points of issue all through the conflict. And this conflict had consolidated them in such fashion that, despite sectional bickerings, the United Provinces now constituted a new state and nation.[3]

FOUNDATION OF THE EAST INDIA COMPANY

As early as 1598 it was seen that for the prosecution of the East India enterprises a coalition of all participators was necessary; and the rapid formation of local companies[4] ensuing upon the return of Houtman rendered coöperation the issue of the day. There were at the end of the century four companies in Amsterdam

---

[1] Blok, III, 520–525, 534–536; cf. p. 436 (return of the seized ships).

[2] Blok, III, 536.

[3] The provinces which formed the *Vereenigde Nederlanden* are named in note 3, p. 381, above.

[4] The companies grew, says De Reus (p. xii), "wie die Pilze aus der Erde"; they "sailed the money out of each other's purses and the shoes off each other's feet."

alone, two in Rotterdam, one in Delft, one in Hoorn and Enkhuizen. In a short time the mischief of competition, which had
been dimly foreseen, began to work concrete effects; despite the
warnings of the States-General the companies, having only gain as
their object, commenced to work against each other both at home
and abroad. In the East Indies the ships were loaded as quickly
as possible at the cost of a general elevation, under competition
of buyers, of the local prices; and so the Dutch merchants came to
be at the mercy of the greed of native chiefs. And in Holland the
competition of sellers caused a great decline of prices. Thus the
diversity of the conjuncture, so profitable in the frontier-trade, was
being reduced at both ends toward a mediocrity of profit. The
companies went so far as even to seek a monopoly of the best captains, each striving to pledge them to itself. On March 20, 1602,
a resolution was passed in the legislative assembly of Holland
denouncing the contemporary conditions of the East Indian trade
as a harm and a shame to the United Provinces.[1]

The difficulty experienced, in such a condition of affairs, and the
valuable time wasted in efforts to effect a union of the several companies, is evidence for the persistence, even after years of coerced
common defense, of local interests and narrow selfishness. Despite
the pressure of the powerful Oldenbarnevelt it was not until September, 1600, that an actual movement toward union was set on
foot. Nothing but failure and a redoubled bitterness of competition resulted. In December, 1601, the representatives of the several companies were finally assembled and induced to submit in
writing proposals for the establishment of union; but Holland opposed the union as under the protection of the States-General, and
Zeeland and other districts feared the richer and more powerful
Holland. No terms could be agreed upon. Finally, in the last
days of 1601, the delegates were again summoned by the States-
General, and listened to a crafty exhortation from Oldenbarnevelt
wherein the weight of argument for union was shifted to the political field. The king of Spain was hoping, it was stated, for just such
quarrels and disagreements in the Netherlands; he was always
eager to see his purposes furthered by disintegration of the provincial Union. Combination must be made against the ancient
enemy, and would issue in an aggravation of his already deep humiliation. By union and agreement the maritime interests of the

[1] Van der Chys, pp. 70–71, 75, 130–131; Van Rees, II, 9–11; Blok, III, 488–489.

Netherlands would be strongly furthered and damage consistently done to Spain without cost to the country. Resistance was weakened by this appeal, but the towns still stood to their rights, clamoring against the proportion of their proposed representation on the board of directors. As a last resort the authority of Prince Maurits, the Stadhouder, was called in; pressure was brought to bear upon the most stubborn, and at length, on March 29, 1602, the union was pushed through and the companies coalesced into one grand organization, chartered for twenty-one years, the East India Company.[1] For many decades the history of the commerce and colonization of the Dutch is the history of this chartered corporation and of its offshoot, the West India Company.

The Charter

This being the case, when once the driving motives of their activity are known, the results attained appear, in many ways, singularly consistent and inevitable. The character and policy of the East India Company, of which the West India was but an aftertype, come out clearly in the provisions of its charter. This instrument is both historically significant and remarkable of its kind; it constituted one of the first weighty experiments in the definition of the powers and obligations of a large corporate body. It is the more important, likewise, to attend to the provisions of this charter inasmuch as they continued for nearly two centuries to form the recognized expression of a set of principles upon which the Company's policy was consistently based. These gradually took on the force of a stereotyped commercial creed, resisting modification and steadily thwarting projects of adaptation to altering conditions.[2]

It is not probable that the charter borrowed anything from that of the English East India Company, formulated two years before. Movements in England toward establishing a company may have exercised some general influence in the Netherlands;[3] but any alignment of the two organizations has the value of a comparative study of the simultaneous reactions of two similarly minded peoples

[1] Van der Chys, pp. 76–97; Van Rees, II, 12; Blok, III, 488–490; Day, pp. 40 ff.; cf. Colmeiro, II, 453.

[2] Cf. De Reus, p. 1; this author says (p. vii) that the Company had no history, no development in organization or policy. Changes occurred in the extent of its operations, its financial status, etc., but its principles remained the same. Cf. Day, p. 39.

[3] Van Rees, II, 19; Van der Chys, p. 129.

upon similar conditions, rather than that of an exercise in the detection of mutual borrowings.

The charter, excluding the preamble which recites the reasons for the Company's formation, and the last article (46), which commands all good subjects, under pain of severe punishment, to respect the charter-provisions, and enjoins upon all officials to let the Directors benefit without molestation from the fruits of their activities, falls roughly under seven main heads or topics : the organization of the Company (§§ 1–6); participation (§§ 7–11); interrelation of the Chambers (§§ 12–14); relations with shareholders (§§ 14–17); the Directors (§§ 18–33); grants of monopoly (§§ 34–35); relation to the state (§§ 36–45).[1] The history of the Company, as it functioned in the metropolis, may well be assembled about the explanation and further development of these topics, taken in such order as to insure clearness and sequence of narrative.

THE MONOPOLY

First, then, as to the crucial feature of the charter, the granting of a monopoly. Why were exclusive rights of any kind conferred, and why did the state create within its own body an *imperium in imperio* which was able, within a comparatively few years, to bid it defiance ? That this was done is the more remarkable as the Dutch harbored a positive distaste for monopolies, and ran all to individualistic enterprise.[2] It has been shown in what precedes that the formation of a company was not easy ; that it required, indeed, strenuous governmental pressure to bring the several jealous companies into union, and this too, although they all realized that they were dragging each other down to ruin. Left to themselves it is difficult to see how unification could have come about within any definable period; it was, indeed, the very hopelessness of the situation that overcame prejudices against the erection of a monopoly as the least of several alternative evils. In view of the total disorder in East Indian affairs it was at first proposed that the state should send a fleet to occupy certain stations, afford protection, and keep order; but, involved as it was in a desperate

---

[1] The charter is reproduced by Van der Chys (pp. 98–115), and translated, largely literally, into German, by De Reus (pp. 5–12). Van Rees (II, 23 ff.) and Van der Chys (pp. 116 ff.), as well as De Reus, give an extended discussion of the organization. Cf. Day, pp. 82 ff.   [2] Van Rees, II, 13–15 ; Van der Chys, p. 117.

struggle for independence, it could not spare the necessary forces. Again the possibility was considered of establishing something on the order of the Portuguese Casa da India, which should regulate colonial affairs from home ; but this meant that the government was to function as did the Portuguese king, owning all the ships and working through its own agents ; and, in addition to the fact of the government's preoccupation with Spain, the Dutch were unwilling to concede it such power. The government distrusted itself; it was only newly and provisionally a centralized one, and it felt its own ignorance and incompetence to manage the affairs of the East Indies, at that time so strange and distant. The only other practicable alternative was to leave the enterprise in the hands which had shown so much zeal in opening up the East and had secured such important national advantages through their activities. The Netherlander salved his prejudice against monopolies with the reflection that the States-General could keep an eye upon the running of this one, which would, moreover, proceed to discomfit Spain without it costing the state anything.[1] The public felt the safer inasmuch as the charter was to run only twenty-one years,—a provision designed to render the Company powerless at the end of that period, — and so acquiesced with small objection in the monopoly. Thus it was enacted that for twenty-one years no Dutch competitor was to sail east of the Cape of Good Hope or through the Straits of Magellan, under the penalty of confiscation of ship and cargo, the clause as to the Straits-voyage becoming null if the Company did not utilize its privileges in that section inside of four years (§ 34). Within the area of its monopoly, moreover, the Company was granted practical sovereignty : power to make treaties with native rulers in the name of the States-General, to build strongholds, appoint governors and military and judicial functionaries ; in short, to take all measures called for in the interest of trade, and looking to the maintenance of order, government, and justice.[2] That the States-General strove to retain a voice in the destiny of the functionaries, who were required, moreover, to swear their oaths of allegiance before the States-General previous to doing the same before the Company (§ 35), is, as will be seen, interesting as theory rather than as practice. As to India, the Directors could really do anything they

[1] Van Rees, II, 17–22 ; Van der Chys, pp. 118–119 ; De Reus, pp. 2–5 ; Roscher, pp. 257–258.

[2] Cf. Van der Chys, p. 110 ; De Reus, p. 10 ; Colmeiro, II, 453–454.

chose except establish a government wholly apart from that of the Netherlands ; their oath of allegiance prevented this.[1]

But around the scheme of the monopoly here granted there arise certain other considerations of especial interest from the comparative view-point. Unlike the monopolies that went before, that of the Dutch was to be enforced regarding only a portion of the seas ; and not against the world, nor against the adherents of another religion, nor even against any special foreign nation, but against fellow-countrymen as potential competitors. This consideration, sometimes taken[2] to show the changed attitude of the Dutch with respect to the "free sea," witnesses rather to the essentially local character of the charter as a document calculated to obviate only intra-national competition. Spanish and Portuguese alike were enemies, and the plain intention, however much disowned in earlier times of weakness and when the Dutch were novices, was to smite them anywhere and everywhere, including of course the eastern seas ; and the subsequent temper of the Dutch toward English, and other interlopers,[3] leaves no doubt as to their working theories. Since, however, the Dutch were too sensible to go on record with any such impossible project as general exclusion, they have had far less word-swallowing to do than had their immediate predecessors in the field. The idea of a generally exclusive monopoly was just as attractive as it had been to the Venetians, but the Dutch had emerged far enough from mediæval ignorance and provinciality to perceive its impracticability in the world as it was coming to be. Their efforts to realize as much of monopoly as possible will appear through subsequent pages.

RELATIONS OF COMPANY AND STATE

Much in the foregoing has already suggested the close relationship of the Company with the state ; formed under political pressure, it acted as a substitute for the direct extension of the state's control, and stood forth to fight its battles for it. It is doubtful if unification of the companies could so soon have been brought about if the argument for a company as an arm of war had not proved so compelling ; again, as has been noted, the state was expected, by constant control of the Company, to guard against the foreseen evils of a monopoly. Aside from the national and inevitable predominance

[1] Van der Chys, p. 126.   [2] Id., p. 121.   [3] Pp. 418 ff., 492 ff., below.

of the creator over its creature, the States-General are represented once and again in the charter as the arbiter of the Company: for example, if the Directors fail of agreement, the States-General will decide (§ 6); if the Company incurs losses, it can appeal to the States-General (§ 36). Other articles define more exhaustively the Company's relation to the government; the state is to receive twenty per cent of the gain from seizure of Spanish and Portuguese ships (§ 37); likewise it holds receivable from the Company 25,000 guilders with which it is credited on the Company's books, in order to share gains with the rest (§ 44); it levies export and import duties on existing lines upon the Company's goods, and it will allow certain irregularities (§§ 38, 41);[1] it will not take away the Company's artillery, ammunition, etc., without its consent (§ 39); it enforces a common system of weights and measures (§ 40); it will not allow the seizure of the person or goods of a Director, but will assure him a hearing before a regular judge (§ 42); it delegates the Company a certain police power in apprehending its sailors in Dutch ports, but with proper deference to local officers (§ 43); it requires of commanders of fleets or ships a full report of the conditions in India, and of the voyage, before the States-General (§ 45). Several of these provisions are scarcely more than the assertion of the ordinary rights of a government; others convey favors or exemptions; but a warning that control is to be exercised inheres throughout.

This topic of state-control may here be pursued into its subsequent and virtually typical and final stage. The founders meant well, but they could not reckon with the forces of avarice and corruption which were prompted by the prospect of enormous gain. Instead of the government controlling the Company from without, in the interests of the shareholders, governmental officials came to control it from within for the benefit of their own class, the political and commercial aristocracy. The directors of the state and of the Company became almost identical in personnel, and nearly all of the popular attempts to control the latter were foiled by the States-General. All objections were evaded by adducing reasons of state: the Company constituted the safety of the nation against Spanish aggression, and must not be subject to let or hindrance. Such willful abdication or abuse of the controlling function on the

---

[1] Freedom from taxes, licenses, etc., had likewise been granted to the earlier separate companies. Cf. Van Rees, II, 15–16.

part of the state left the Company all but independent; in fact the Directors, upon the occasion of their opposition to the founding of the West India Company, stated bluntly that the Company's East India possessions were theirs and could be sold to the king of Spain if they so desired. It took the state two centuries, and endless effort and trouble, to lay hands upon the directive power.[1]

INTERRELATION OF THE CHAMBERS

Another significant aspect of the situation out of which the unification of the companies grew, is to be found in the provisions dealing with the interrelations of the Chambers, that is, the local bodies representative of the formerly independent trading centers. These retained such independence that they could at any time have gone on by themselves as separate organizations had The Seventeen, the visible bond of their union, been done away with;[2] hence they were not willing to merge their identity in the union, and their jealousies and strivings with each other, which meant generally the opposition of province to province, betray the newness and instability of the " United Netherlands " This separatist tendency comes out plainly in the charter, which both recognizes it and seeks to minimize its effect. The general board of Directors ("The Seventeen") was granted the widest of powers and affiliated with the States-General;[3] the Chambers were to keep each other fully informed as to business done and projected (§ 14), and those whose ventures came out well were even to provide their unlucky fellows with spices and other eastern wares in event of uneven fortune attending their respective enterprises (§ 13). Such provisions were designed to increase solidarity; nevertheless the separate Chambers practically controlled themselves. A ship was to return to its port of departure if possible; and if it was obliged to enter another Dutch harbor, the Chamber which fitted it out was to send Directors to attend to all the details of its homecoming, unless it seemed advisable to delegate this business to the local Chamber (§ 12). Again, if a Director became bankrupt, his own Chamber had to shoulder the losses incident, not the general treasury (§ 32); and

[1] Van der Chys, pp. 116, 119, note; Day, pp. 86–88.

[2] Van der Chys, p. 128. " So war auch die Comp. nichts anderes als eine künstliche Vereinigung von verschiedenen Handelsgesellschaften welche unter den Namen 'Kammern' selbstständig bestehen blieben." De Reus, p. 19; cf. pp. 20–22.

[3] Cf. p. 398, below.

such employees as bookkeepers were to be paid by the Directors of the several Chambers, their maintenance not coming from the body of shareholders (§ 31). All such provisions clearly indicate the rudimentary nature of the union and a reluctance to accept the full consequences of centralization; and this not only in the case of the companies but also of the provinces which they represented. Such a condition of affairs is perfectly normal, as is shown for example by the history of the confederation of the American colonies; that the initial advances toward nationality are imperfect and slowly traversed does not impair the general consequences of such development.

The Chamber of Chambers was constituted by The Seventeen, a body which united the constituent companies as the States-General united the Provinces,[1] and whose constitution and function will presently be explained.

INTERNAL ORGANIZATION

Having cleared away the more general aspects of the charter, we now turn to the actual organization of the Company and to its relations with the public who took up its shares. The basis of organization was, of course, the constituent companies, operating in the several chief cities of the Republic. These were grouped according to location and came under the administration of local directors whose appointment was assigned to the "States" or parliaments of the several provinces. The body of local directors thus constituted was called a Chamber, and represented the interests of what had been the companies of its district. Naturally, then, the size of the local Chamber was proportional to the commercial strength of its district, as represented by the antecedent formation of companies: Amsterdam had 23 Directors, Zeeland 14, Delft 12, Rotterdam 9, Hoorn 4, and Enkhuizen 11 (§§ 18–23). This made a total of 73, which was later to be reduced to 60, of which Amsterdam was to have 20, Zeeland 12, and the rest 7 apiece. When it came to equipping fleets, etc., a similar proportion of contribution was fixed, namely: Amsterdam one-half, Zeeland

---

[1] "Ebenso wie in dem Niederländischen Staate die sieben fast unabhängigen Provinzen in der Versammlung der Generalstaaten zu *einer* Republik verbunden wurden, ebenso wurden auch die sechs selbstständigen Kammern durch die Versammlung der Siebzehner zu *einer* Compagnie vereinigt." De Reus, p. 39.

one-quarter, and the rest one-sixteenth each (§ 1).[1] Thus else-where the proportion is maintained (cf. § 29). The extent of the powers of these local Chambers and their relation to each other have been already indicated.

When the companies merged, a general directorate was created which was called The Seventeen, or, for brevity's sake, The XVII; of these the Chamber of Amsterdam appointed 8, that of Zee-land 4, those of the rest one each, while the seventeenth was to be elected from the Chambers of Zeeland, of the Maas region (Rotterdam and Delft), and of the "North-Quarter" (Hoorn and Enkhuizen) in turn.[2] To The Seventeen was comprehensively dele-gated the management "of all affairs touching these united com-panies" (§ 2). It decided the times and destinations of voyages, the number of ships to be sent, and, in general, was sovereign of the East Indian trade (§ 3). Its sessions were regularly fixed in Amsterdam for a term of six years, then in Zeeland for two, and so on in alternation (§ 4); but irregularities occurred, especially when it was deemed needful to engage in political activities at the capital. The several functions of The Seventeen will appear throughout the ensuing narrative; in general, this body supervised the trade as a whole, the carrying-out of its policy being left to the local Chambers; it was administrative in its activity, not judicial.[3]

It is unnecessary here to pursue the organization of the Com-pany into its finer ramifications.[4] But a word may be given to the chief director by way of further clarification of the relation of the Company to the state. The Stadhouder Maurits van Nassau had, as has been seen, considerable influence in effecting the coalition of the companies, and both he and his successors exerted a certain important influence, as in some sort heads of the government, upon the Company as a state-organ; but it was not until 1674 that the Princes came into permanent office in the Company, drawing divi-dends from it. Willem III was at that time formally constituted Chief Director and was to receive one-thirty-third of the total divi-dends declared. This move, however, though it indicates the grow-ing political trend of the Company, had no essential significance, says De Reus,[5] for its internal prosperity or external reputation;

---

[1] De Reus, pp. 8, 5.   [2] Cf. De Reus, pp. 5–6.   [3] De Reus, pp. 19, 44.
[4] De Reus (pp. 51 ff.) treats of the Bookkeeper and other more special functionaries.
[5] P. 69; cf. pp. 59–67.

the Prince was simply the nominal head of the Directorate, but
without special powers.

In fact, there were no essential changes in the Company's home
organization until the years of its downfall, toward the end of the
eighteenth century.[1]

Before coming to the conditions covering general participation
in the Company, it remains to summarize the provisions of the
charter which were designed to control the local Directors, the
active agents in carrying on the actual operation of trade. These
were, of course, the managers of the constituent companies. The
names of the 73 are given (§§ 18–23) and are immediately followed
by the provision that vacancies are not to be filled (§ 24) until
the total number is brought down to 60, apportioned as explained
above (§ 25); after that time vacancies are to be supplied through
selection by the local legislatures of one name out of three presented by the Company (§ 26). It may here be remarked that with
the growth of political influence this selection passed into the
hands of the burgomasters, who were supposed to possess a more
intimate knowledge of the candidates and their qualifications; they
did possess such knowledge, at least so far as they and their political friends were concerned, and so the local Directors, and consequently The Seventeen, came presently to be the political leaders
of the cities and state, and were able as officers to guard themselves as Directors from many unpleasant consequences.[2] Nevertheless it was intended to control the Directors and so avoid the bad
effects of monopoly; they had to take a solemn and pious oath to
act honorably, render honest accounts, and not to prefer one shareholder over another (§ 27). They must be interested in the enterprises which they managed, to a certain amount varying with the
importance of the trade of their local Chambers (§ 29). They could
not make free with the Company's money in any way (§ 30) nor
shift expenses upon the shareholders (§ 31); they were responsible
for the administration of their several treasuries (§ 33). How effective these safeguards were to be will shortly appear. They were
paid on the basis of one per cent on the outfit of the fleets and on
the return-cargoes, apportionment of such profits to be on the lines
already cited: the Amsterdam Chamber receiving one-half, that of
Zeeland one-quarter, and the rest one-sixteenth each (§ 29). Thus
a careful attempt was made to guard against the weakness of human

---

[1] Alterations are discussed by De Reus, pp. 12 ff.   [2] De Reus, pp. 26–30, 37.

nature and to obviate what the slang of the present age terms "graft"; even private correspondence was forbidden, in later times, between a Director and any one in India.[1] If the Directors had lived up to the spirit of the charter provisions, no such tale would follow as that which is to tell; but they were practically irresponsible and their actions do not belie the fact.

Rights of Shareholders

The definition of shareholders' rights as against the Directors' really amounts to further restrictions and control over the latter. It was provided that at the end of ten years a general public accounting should be held in the presence of the shareholders (§ 14); and, further, that local provinces or cities interested to the extent of 50,000 florins could demand an accounting, even of incoming cargoes (§ 15), and that several provinces together could appoint an agent who should have the right of thorough examination (§ 16). It was also provided that dividends should not be held back; they should be declared when five per cent profit lay in the treasury (§ 17). These provisions of restraint fall in with the ones just considered, and their evasion or nullification forms part of the same mournful and sordid tale. It is to be noted that there was no way provided for deposing a Director.[2]

Participation

The provisions respecting participation in the Company remain; and the most general of these was that any citizens of the United Netherlands could invest in shares, with sums small or great. Smaller investments were encouraged; for it was provided that if the shares were over-subscribed, the larger investors should yield to the smaller (§ 10). Certain generous and fair-appearing articles were added, allowing any shareholder to withdraw his money at the end of the first decade when the first general accounting was to take place (§ 7); similarly any one dissatisfied with the early ventures was to be permitted to withdraw, receiving back his investment with seven and one-half per cent (or more) interest for

---

[1] De Reus, p. 24. The Chambers were not to receive presents (p. 24); cf. Day, pp. 84–86, 88–91.

[2] Van der Chys, p. 125. This author thinks (p. 128) that the defective provisions respecting the shareholders resulted from there being no shareholders at the time of the foundation to develop this side of the charter.

the period of investment (§ 9). Provision was made in apparently perfect fairness for the subsequent entrance of new participants (§ 11); and there seemed to be foresight and conservatism in the arrangement whereby the naturally larger outlays of the first decade were to go over, to the extent of "half or less," upon the participants of the second ten-year period (§ 8). It is noteworthy here, as bearing upon the attitude of the Dutch toward a national monopoly, that only Netherlanders might hold shares; in fact it was likewise enacted that prospective Directors should declare under oath their entire disassociation with any competing foreign company.[1]

Conflicts between Directors and Shareholders

Of the topics based upon charter-provisions and now before us, the one about which most of the history of the Company, at the European end, was made, was that of the relations between Directors and shareholders; and it is to the phases of this relationship that return will constantly be made.

The reputation of the Company was so high that shortly after subscription to its shares was opened, 6,450,000 florins had been brought together, Amsterdam alone furnishing something over half of this sum. A few days after the Company's establishment seventeen vessels sailed for the East, the last of them returning richly laden in 1607. The new organization seemed to justify all the high expectations of the country: in 1605 it returned dividends of fifteen per cent, in 1606 seventy-five per cent, and in the following four years forty, twenty, twenty-five, and fifty per cent respectively — a total of two hundred and twenty-five per cent in eight years. But this tremendous showing was evidently deceptive, for the shares, having risen to 140 in 1605, fell to 80 in 1607.[2] And it was not long before voices of protest against the Directors were heard. The latter had already found that their task was not entirely simple. In the effort to keep up the Company's early reputation they had been lavish in dividends; they were

---

[1] De Reus, p. 34.

[2] Van Rees, II, 22–23, 27; De Reus, pp. 175–179; Blok, III, 492, 495–496, 498; Roscher, p. 277, note 4. De Reus (p. 178) shows that the older writers were incorrect in believing that these dividends came out of the Company's earnings subsequent to its formation. The accounts of The Seventeen give 1609 as the date of the first real Company payments. But whatever the source of the dividends, the Company could scarcely fail to get the credit for them, especially among the uninstructed. For the reputation of the Company, see Colmeiro, II, 453–454.

moved by considerations of immediate gain, and paid little attention to the preservation of their capital and to the meeting of their debts. They became unscrupulous as to the source of the dividends, and began to borrow money at high rates of interest in order to be able to declare them. The expenses of the Company as a militant organization encroached deeply upon their funds and left them ill prepared to take advantage of commercial opportunity; for example, the dispatch of two large war-vessels to conquer the Moluccas cost them 150,000 guilders. They commenced to fear competition, and, asserting that the government did not afford them security in this respect, they began impudently to refuse payment of money which, according to the grant, they owed to the state.[1] The sort of procedure of which these are specimens could not have failed to arouse suspicion and distrust in a people who had embarked on the way of monopoly with misgivings.

HOSTILITY TO THE COMPANY

The critical attitude toward the Company was exemplified in Le Maire. Le Maire had been elected a Director, but had quarreled with his colleagues and resigned, a move which frightened them more than it should have done had their operations been irreproachable. They feared that he would use his inside information to aid others, or against the Company, and they placed him under a penalty if he should so do. It can be seen that Le Maire was an excellent authority upon any point of the Company's policy about which he cared to speak. But he was far more than a scandal-monger; he was an independent-spirited man and a farsighted merchant. He complained of the narrowness of the Company's policy, directed as it was toward the exploitation of the proximate source of gain, the spice-trade, alone; it was interested, he said, only in Bantam and the Moluccas; the east coast of Africa had not been approached, and the Japanese trade was left to the Portuguese. The Company, moreover, was not truly loyal; warfare was with it merely a means to get gain; it did nothing from love of the fatherland; it managed its great monopoly without conscience, appealing to its charter to exclude all better-minded people. From having been one of its Directors, Le Maire emerged as a determined enemy of its monopoly. He was even in communication

[1] Van Rees, II, 28, 31.

with Henry IV of France in regard to a French company when the latter suddenly died, in May, 1610, and the plans broke up.[1]

The Company being in such bad repute, there were not a few who, though they saw in the prospective peace with Spain the probable dissolution of the Company, were yet quite ready to consent to its sacrifice. But the government, now largely involved in the organization, — for, as has been seen, the political oligarchy had gradually filled the Directorate, or translated the Directors into its own ranks, — had no such purpose ; and the Company was well assured of this fact. But there was no certainty that the latter could keep up in any case : if there should be peace with the grant of access to the East, other European nations would press in whose competition was already a menace ; and if war continued, its expenses would only increase. In any event, now that France and England had made peace with her, Spain was free to cause the more trouble and cost. Again, were the state obliged to send warships and defend the Indies, it would attain a power of supervision not to the liking of the Directors; if the people as tax-payers had to carry on the operations in the East, there would be an accounting despite all political quietism. Hence the Directors felt that to keep the monopoly they must themselves hold to the East Indies, pay high dividends, and pose the Company as an institution too valuable to sacrifice.[2]

But peace was made in 1609 and the Company did not cease to be. However, it was in wretched shape and was, moreover, face to face with the approaching decennial report and accounting due in 1612. Conscious of its desperate condition, and fearing withdrawal of capital if anything approaching the truth should get out, it employed the subterfuge of asking for an extension of time, so that it might make its reckoning of 1612 along with that of the second decade, in 1622. This request was clothed with a show of reasonableness and with an appeal to loyalty by the explanation that the expenses of the first decade had naturally been heavier, and the gains less, than were to be expected from the second ; and by the warning that unless all the capital could be held together, successful opposition to Spain in the East Indies would be impossible. This request provoked a storm of hostility : Le Maire, for example, declared it to be "out and out absurd and impertinent." As

[1] Van Rees, II, 33–37, 45 ff. ; De Reus, pp. 67 ff. ; Blok, III, 496–497.
[2] Van Rees, II, 38–40.

spokesman of many others, he denounced retention of shareholders' capital, under such pretexts, as tyranny; and when the Directors suggested that shares were marketable for any who did not wish to retain them,[1] he retorted that the right to sell them was valueless, as they would at once fall if the Company attained its demands. Despite all opposition, however, the States-General indorsed the proposition of the Directors; they were not yet able to send a fleet to the Indies, and judged the aid of the Company to be indispensable in harming the Spaniards and preserving trade for the Republic. An assault upon the Company was construed to be an attack on the state. Also, as must constantly be borne in mind, the legislators were themselves largely interested in the destiny of the Company.[2]

This proceeding was not calculated to allay the suspicions and discontent of the shareholders, now virtually constrained to remain in a questionable venture. The revelations of the fearless governor-general of the Indies, Coen,[3] but confirmed their fears, as did the eccentric succession of dividends. These were, in 1611, 50; in 1612, 25; in 1613, 12; and in 1614, 3 per cent. Then up to 1619 no more were paid, though several high percentages were declared and interest upon them promised. Thus it appears "that the wrong principle of declaring dividends, even if there were no profit, is almost as old as the Company itself." The dividend for 1620 was $37\frac{1}{2}$ per cent. The charter had required a declaration of dividends whenever there should be five per cent profit in the treasury, though it had unfortunately neglected to determine the maximum percentage to be paid.[4] This fluctuation of returns reacted upon the value of the shares, causing great instability, a condition aggravated by the actions of Le Maire and others, who in disgust and anger threw their shares on the market, causing great decline in quotations. The Directors asked the help of the government to stop this panic and the latter responded by forbidding the sales of futures in shares and by other measures, and thus further aroused the ire of those who asserted that freedom in buying and selling was the great privilege of the country. Le Maire was so

[1] Cf. also De Reus, p. 72. The Company's policy was to make the transference of shares difficult. Id., p. 176.

[2] Van Rees, II, 47–48. Holland especially supported the Company. De Reus, pp. 69, 74.   [3] Cf. p. 423, below.

[4] Van der Chys, p. 127; De Reus, pp. 178–179. For an excellent brief sketch of the Company's finances, see Day, pp. 70 ff.

hounded by legal persecution that he had to leave Amsterdam. But instability of the shares continued; the renewal of dividend-payment in 1620, together with the influence of an agreement with the English,[1] brought quotations from 166 to 250, but for the next two years, under non-payment of dividends, they fell to 165. The conviction gained strength that the Directors were utilizing their inside information regarding the issue of dividends in shameless speculation; that they were acting "neither trustworthily nor prudently." During the second decade also the Company had been led to invest a million toward the proposed West India Company, and this without reference to the shareholders at all; it was correctly objected that the charter contemplated no such use of funds.[2]

Hence all the malcontents and any neutrals among the shareholders were very anxious to see the double decennial report of 1622. But there was no intention of making any such accounting. The Directors had by this time attained a position of equanimity respecting state supervision which measured their real identity with the government; and when the participants went to them to get information, they were snubbed right royally as "shameless men who wanted to mix in everything and were presumptuous enough to call to account their own lords and masters." They were informed that if they did not compose themselves they would get no dividends for seven years. Memorials to the Directors and representations to the States-General were of no avail; the petitioners were denounced as Flemings and Brabanters, ungrateful for the hospitality they enjoyed, or even as friends of Spain who were trying to destroy the agency that did Spain so much damage. Hope was held out, however, that after the extension of the charter, from 1623, attention would be given to grievances of the shareholders. This was small satisfaction, especially when it leaked out that the Directors wanted the charter extended for fifty years, and that they all should retain their offices. An appeal was made, in the fashion of the time, to public opinion; pamphlets were printed and circulated broadcast, showing how the Directors had taken advantage of their position. Vacancies had not been filled, in order that the survivors might divide the Directors' percentage among fewer claimants; this percentage had been raised through extravagant outlays and purchases; more Eastern wares also had been bought

---

[1] Cf. p. 419, below.   [2] Van Rees, II, 65–67, 145–147 ; De Reus, p. 177.

than could be sold with advantage in Europe. The Company was known to be in considerable debt, and the million advanced to the West India Company was supposed to be merely a way of securing to the Directors a good share of the latter's profits. In any case, many of the Directors became suddenly and inexplicably rich, some were known to have done private business in the Company's ships, and others to have been "shamelessly solicited with gifts and presents." They had failed to observe the articles of the charter dealing with accounting, declaration of dividends, etc.; and they had proved untrue to their oath of office. They were plainly escaping more and more from the choice and oversight of the shareholders.[1]

The answers of the Directors to all this were specious : they harped on the fact that the Company's records were "material of state "; that the heavy expenses had been incurred in waging the country's wars, latterly against the English ; that their borrowings really advantaged the country, affording as they did such excellent investments ; that the decline of the shares was really due to speculation, crushed in 1610 by the state, but rife again in 1621. They also resorted to bluster, branding some of the strongest pamphlets as seditious and disorderly libels, and offering rewards for the discovery of author or printer. The state seconded these measures ; in Holland the courts were even forbidden to take cognizance of complaints regarding the extension of the charter and allied subjects. These gag-measures, however, did not frighten the people, who were coming to perceive the true inconsistency of the Company's existence ; they did not demand its dissolution, but the separation of politics and trade ; they were willing to leave their money in the Company, but they wanted the Directors to be responsible. Let the state do the war-making, if need be (ran the plea), for it could do that better than the merchants ; and let the latter run the business, which they could do much better than the state.[2]

It is not to be denied that the Company was in good part a victim to experimentation in a new field of economic organization, or, perhaps more exactly, to experimentation upon a much larger scale

---

[1] Van Rees, II, 147 151 ; De Reus, pp. 70 ff.

[2] Van Rees, II, 157–161. This seems to have been prophetic. " The fiscal history of the Company can be roughly summarized by saying that in its early period, when it was more trader than ruler, it made money on the whole ; that in its later period, when it was more ruler than trader, it lost." Day, p. 73 ; cf. Roscher, p. 286 ; p. 560, below.

in an old field. The Company was always serving two masters : the shareholders and the state. The returning fleets had been obliged by the charter to report to the States-General, and gradually the Directors fell into the discussion of war-policy with the authorities. Thus the Company's archives came really to be state-documents ; and its credit and strength were synonymous with those of the United Provinces. And with the increasing degree of identity between the controllers of the state and of the Company, already noted, this inherent condition became the more pronounced.[1]

RENEWALS OF THE CHARTER ; DECLINE

But the state was not willing to resolve this union of inconsistent functions by itself taking up the war-making in the East ; there was no doubt that the charter would be renewed and the Directors continued. But when, in December, 1622, the renewal for twenty years was made, public opinion was recognized in the attachment of certain conditions having to do with the relation of the Company to its participants. The Directors were to present to certain chief shareholders, within six months, a general reckoning " according to the style and fitting form, as it is wont to be done among merchants "; this was to be public, and was to be repeated every ten years. Again, the Directors were to retire according to schedule, becoming eligible again after three years, and their selection was to fall slightly more into the shareholders' hands. They should not be preferred purchasers from the Company. Also the chief shareholders should choose nine out of their number to supervise the annual accounts of their Chamber, while The Seventeen should ask their advice concerning sales and other important matters.[2]

The shareholders had to acquiesce in the charter-extension, and made the best of the new conditions, electing the inspectors of accounts and sending them to Amsterdam in 1623. But the Directors would give them only the most general of the records, refusing the detailed India accounts, letters, etc. An appeal to the States-General brought a command to turn the latter over (April, 1624) ; but on the return to Amsterdam all these documents were gone and effort to find them was vain. The searchers were informed

---

[1] Van Rees, II, 155-156. The state assisted the Company in diplomatic ways also ; and when it was feared that sailors would go into foreign service, it forbade experienced mariners to take service in other lands. Yet the policy of the Company really drove talent out of its service. Id., pp. 28-32, 37.   [2] Van Rees, II, 161-164.

that they would not be able to satisfy their curiosity that time, nor earn big vacation pay ; the accounting did not take place. A similar fate awaited the nine auditors of annual accounts. The Directors tried to use undue influence in their choice and insisted that they should have at least a thousand Flemish pounds[1] invested in the Company ; they received in their resistance and obstruction such political support, especially from Holland, that the participants had finally to give it up. Thus the struggle for the renewal of the charter left the Company still more free from the duty of responsibility to shareholders, and the Directors practically permanent and unimpeachable.[2]

Each succeeding extension of charter found the Directors ever farther advanced upon the way they had taken, and the resistance encountered by them ever more languid. The Company itself got into worse straits financially, declaring dividends in the latter part of the century in question when there was nothing to declare them with except a debt; they gave the shareholders, to quiet them, interest-bearing obligations on the Company (at four per cent) in 1679, 1680, 1681, 1682, 1697, 1698. The speculation in shares, which began early in the history of the Company and was graphically described as a " Windhandel," went on through all the later periods. Quotations were up to 400 in the middle of the seventeenth century, and rose at times, after a succession of dividends, to 1080 and even 1720. Again, after bad news from the East, they fell to 60 and 48 ; 1730 was a " dark time " for the Company. But as late as 1720 shares reached 1260, and in such unfortunate years as 1672 and 1781 they were quoted at 250 and 215 respectively. During the latter half of the eighteenth century they rose as high as 750. It is clear that these were thoroughly fictitious values.

The last dividend was paid in 1782. During the 198 years of the Company's existence the sum total paid to shareholders is figured at $3600\frac{1}{3}$ per cent, or an average of 18 per cent a year. This seems very high ; but it must be realized that the Company constantly operated with a capital in excess of the par value of its shares, and that the state of mind of the shareholders was one of constant insecurity. No one knew where the dividends came from and they lent no solid value to the shares.[3] In its latter years, the

[1] About $2400 ; cf. De Reus, p. 20, note 2.   [2] Van Rees, II, 165–169.
[3] De Reus, pp. xxxii-xxxiii, 175–180; Van Rees, II, 294 ; Blok, III, 495–499.

only ones beside the Directors who seem to have drawn steady profit from the Company were the members of a commission of the States-General, who received generous gifts of money, spices, and the like, for an indulgent examination and certification of shaky accounts. The charter was extended from period to period without any strife, on condition at times of a goodly contribution to the state or an addition to the fleet. From 1782 to 1794 the debts increased nearly 8,000,000 florins, amounting to a grand total of 74,000,000 in 1789, and the aid of the government was asked, in humility, over and over. But the Directors would not renounce their petty perquisites,[1] caring little really for the Company; after 1790 the latter was entirely dependent on the state. Thus it continued to lead a dishonorable and sordid existence, growing steadily weaker until the war with England in 1781 revealed its true condition, and the events culminating in the fall of the state before the French power, in 1795, swept it away.[2]

FOUNDATION OF THE WEST INDIA COMPANY

We have thus far observed the Company's operations and policy in Europe, and have yet to exhibit its other and even more characteristic aspects, or phases of the same aspect, in its Eastern dominion. But, by way of throwing similar topics into proximity, it seems advisable first to consider the formation and, in many respects, parallel organization and career in Europe of the West India Company.

Although the older Company had made little or no use of its monopoly of the Magellan Straits passage, it had consistently resisted all efforts to utilize this route of approach to the East. The most serious of such attempts had been made by the archenemy, Le Maire, who, smarting under his persecutions, conceived the idea of hunting for a passage to the Pacific farther to the south. He attained from the state assurances of rights in any passage he might open up, and an expedition was fitted out which discovered the Straits of Le Maire (January 24, 1616) and later the passage around the Cape. A ship was now dispatched to the Moluccas by the new route, but upon arrival its papers were seized by the Dutch governor-general and the crew shipped home. A

---

[1] Their "Zuckerbrot," as De Reus (p. 31) calls it.

[2] Van Rees, II, 171–172, 210, 217; De Reus, pp. xlvi, 27–33; Fortanier, pp. 39 ff.; Day, pp. 73 ff.

protest from Le Maire before the States-General secured restitution and damages; but the whole incident made it clear that the Company would brook no competition, that it was ready to do the same thing over again. About a century later a second attempt with a similar history took place, after which there was no further competition on the part of Dutchmen while the Company lasted.[1] With regard to America itself, however, in so far as enterprises thither directed did not threaten the East, the Company was far more indifferent. This appeared in its half-contemptuous attitude toward the agitation preceding the West India Company's formation.

WILLEM USSELINCX

The man above all others who kept the project of an American company before the Dutch public was Willem Usselincx,[2] an enthusiast, in many respects far in advance of his age, and who pursued a plan of his youth varying only in its details, through a long life. "This plan was in the main very simple, and consisted in the founding of settlements without slaves in America, not in order to seek gold and silver there, but to establish a profitable reciprocal exchange of manufactures for raw goods between mother-country and colony." He likewise hoped thus to transfer the field of strife between the Netherlands and Spain to a distance, and to undermine the power of the enemy by cutting off the sources of his strength. Thus he thought to benefit the Netherlands in a positive way, and also to honor God by spreading the holy evangel; and since segregated traders could do little, he proposed a great West India Company. These ideas were presented to the public as early as 1591, and in 1600 there seemed to be some likelihood of their realization, though the tendency was always toward organization on the lines of the East India Company, a fact which gave Usselincx great anxiety. For this man was in several respects like Le Maire, and was dominated by a similar hatred of the older organization. However, the question of war or peace with Spain was to the fore in the first decade of the seventeenth century, and the foundation of a new Company was made to await its issue. The war-party, realizing that such a move would destroy all hope of peace, favored the project, but the peace-party, headed by Oldenbarnevelt, was unwilling to organize such an expensive war-machine,

[1] Van Rees, II, 67–72.   [2] On the life of Usselincx, see Jameson.

which, besides, offered no prospect of gain. The temper of the
country decided for peace and it was concluded in 1609 with
little attention to Usselincx or his partisans.[1]

However, what with the growth of confidence as against Spain
and the widening conception of commercial possibility, the idea of
the Company was not allowed to drop. The state toyed with the
project, and asked a good deal of advice from Usselincx, who seems
to have possessed a wide practical knowledge of the Indies, both
East and West. Thus matters developed until 1621, when the
Company was actually founded. Its charter, following closely that
of the East India Company, realized the worst apprehensions of
Usselincx, who had been a severe critic of the older Company and
who believed that "merchants have gain for a pole-star and greed
for a compass, and are unfit to rule." It is of little utility to
follow his criticisms of the charter, for they were of no avail; it
may simply be said that his views were of a distinctly modern
type, and so, to his own age, visionary and in many respects really
impracticable. To get booty, to found strongholds, and to conquer,
were the colonial goals set before the peoples of that age; the
slow, costly, and laborious foundings of true settlement colonies
presented no attraction at all. Again, when the power of Holland
among the Provinces is realized, and it is borne in mind that the
most influential Hollanders were also Directors of the East India
Company, it is little wonder that such innovations in policy were
promptly rejected. Thus Usselincx's advice and warnings went
for naught; they even called him a friend of Spain, which hurt
him more than all else. He suffered the fate of a man who is in
advance of his time; he became bitter in his disappointment, fell
into debt, drifted into the service of Gustavus Adolphus of Sweden,
and assisted him in his schemes for a South Sea Company until
the death of the monarch put an end to this also. He came to
regard himself as a martyr, speaking continually of his unpaid
services, but gradually dropped out of sight, and died, probably in
1647, at the age of eighty.[2]

[1] Van Rees, II, 72–96.

[2] Van Rees, II, 98–103, 112–122, 129–132, 134–142. Jameson's monograph on
Usselincx covers many details of the founding of the West India Company, as well
as of that of the Swedish company. Into the story of the latter, because it possesses
curious interest rather than importance to the general student of colonization, it has
seemed unnecessary to go. In all essentials Jameson supports Van Rees.

Organization of the West India Company

The monopoly granted to the West India Company in 1621 was for twenty-four years; it covered most of the west coast of Africa, all of the east coast of America from Newfoundland to Cape Horn, and a large part of the west coast of South America, as well as all Atlantic islands included within these boundaries and all " southern lands" from the Cape of Good Hope westward to New Guinea. There were constituted five Chambers which met at Amsterdam and Middleburg (Zeeland), and a directorial college, "The Nineteen." Reports were due every six years. The state by virtue of subsidies given was to have a large share in the gain to be gotten, and was to insure the safety of the Company with sixteen large and four small war-vessels. The Company was essentially a fighting organization, with sinister designs upon Spanish and Portuguese America.[1] In view of the prospective expense of this military function, and because there was no immediate promise of gain, as in the spice-trade, the subscriptions for shares came in very slowly; people had taken warning from the East India Company and feared to invest. But the government granted the new Company the monopoly of West India salt (1622); state-officials subscribed and urged the richest citizens to do so. The East India Company was forced to put a million into its younger contemporary, and subscriptions were solicited in foreign countries. Despite all this pressure, however, the subscription-list stayed open until September, 1623; finally there were gotten together 7,108,106 florins, of which half came from Amsterdam, and in November the new Company had fifteen ships at sea.[2]

The history of the West India Company is in one distinctive respect different from that of its East India contemporary: of the two inconsistent functions of trade and war, it accentuated the latter, while the East India Company, despite all its talk of patriotism, was above all a trade-organization. Hence the West India Company assisted the state against Spain to a greater extent, and more as a matter of avowed policy, and thus debated its operations with the government and was supported by national ships-of-war and troops. It was thus far less independent than the East India Company, which, after the early strifes over the charter,

---

[1] Van Rees, II, 110–112, 121; Roscher, pp. 270 ff.
[2] Van Rees, II, 125–128, 133–134.

had practically gone its own way. Nor was the monopoly of the western Company so complete; there was from the outset a great deal of illicit trade in America which the extent of coast-line and the absence of any natural point of supervision made it impossible to prevent. As early as 1631 certain rights of voyage were allowed to private persons under provision that they should use only well-armed ships and should pay a recognition of 20 per cent to the Company; and in 1634 the whole of Brazil, with a few reservations, was opened under like conditions. The gain to these private traders was so great that by 1636 The Nineteen considered limitation of freedom, but the Amsterdam Directors opposed this, and won their point; in 1638 the Directors, in conjunction with the States-General, left commerce free to the Dutch and the inhabitants of Brazil under payment of 10 per cent for European and 30 per cent for American wares. But one trip a year was allowed to each vessel; and the Company reserved for itself the trade in slaves, Brazil-wood, and necessities of war.[1]

MALADMINISTRATION AND DECLINE

The Company had attained a strong footing in Brazil during the early years of its existence, but was unable, largely for lack of funds, to hold it.[2] Reckoning on state-subsidies it had expended nearly all it possessed in dividends, and so ran out of money·just at a time when new enterprises and war demanded large outlays. In 1629, after the capture of the Spanish silver fleet, dividends had reached 50 and 25 per cent; but already in 1631 aid was of necessity sought from the state. It was given in the form of a loan of 700,000 guilders and later repeated. But after a time the subsidies began to fail and to be replaced by bad debts. In 1629 the Company had stood by the state, furnishing ships and men, and contributing, besides other aid, 600,000 guilders; in 1631 the States-General were in debt to the Company 1,250,000 guilders for money advanced. Holland alone had been prompt in payments, but, when the rest had fallen behind, refused to pay till they did; in 1638 Holland alone owed over a million. By 1636 the Company, having been forced to borrow, was in debt 18,000,000 guilders, and by 1640 the case was hopeless. There was too little unity of purpose in the States-General; the several Provinces were always

---

[1] Van Rees, II, 179–180, 183–188.   [2] Cf. pp. 146 ff., above, and 453 ff., below.

pursuing their selfish interests, and set them aside only in times of the utmost need. As long as the war with Spain was located within its district the Company was favored; now hostilities were on the southern boundaries of the Republic and its services were no longer needed.[1] In 1644 the charters of both companies came to an end, and a union was proposed. Strong objection immediately developed on the part of the East India Company, which declared that it could not go in for the war-projects of its fellow, and asserted its absolute rights in the East Indies. The West India Company recalled other combinations, among them that by which the East India organization had itself been formed; and it called to mind its own services. From 1623 to 1636 it had fitted out over 800 ships, with 67,000 men, and had maintained 24,000 men in service at a cost of 45,000,000 guilders. It had captured or destroyed over 600 Spanish ships, 98 of which were "famous galleons," and had brought the king of Spain 75,000,000 guilders' worth of trouble. The winnings of the Company from ships captured and from booty had been about 37,000,000 guilders from 1623 to 1636. These operations had aided the East India Company, also, by diverting Spain's attention from the East; and now that the king of Spain had heard of the proposed union of the two companies he was the more eager for peace. The conqueror of Brazil, Count Nassau, was convinced that Spain could not stand against the two in union, but would lose all she had in the New World. The pamphlets of the time appear to have favored the West India Company,[2] and men like Usselincx opposed the union on the ground that thereby *all* the trade would fall into dishonest and disreputable hands. The older Company had involved the country with the English and was out of favor; it was even seen that the West India Company's trade in raw goods and manufactures was more solid and valuable than that in the spices of the East.[3]

During this discussion the charters were periodically renewed for brief terms, until finally decision was made against union (March, 1647). The charter of the East India Company was then extended for twenty-five years, but it was to pay a million and a half guilders to the West India Company. In July the

[1] Van Rees, II, 180 ff., 190–193; Roscher, p. 272.

[2] The king of Spain regarded the West India realm as his "true spouse," while that of the East Indies was only his "mistress." Hence the greater damage wrought against him by the West India Company. Van Rees, II, 202.

[3] Van Rees, II, 193–205; Watson, II, 21.

latter's charter was extended, also for twenty-five years, although its shares were down to 30 and the state of affairs in Brazil was lamentable, the families of the Dutch functionaries actually suffering from hunger. This situation was charged up to extravagance and questionable practices adopted after the example of the East India Company ; but it was against the constitution of the Republic and the spirit of the time for the state to take over colonies, however wretched, so it merely propped up the old organization. Creditors began to make trouble in 1655, and in 1667 sale of the charter to the highest bidder was considered ; in 1674 the state of the Company was so bad that it was decided to give it up. A new one was then erected, with certain provisions regarding triennial accounting and the separation of war and trade ; commerce was to be open to all on condition of a recognition to the Company, thus become a mere incubus upon private trade. In 1730 further limitation of the monopoly took place. Shares had sunk from 92 in 1723 to 35, and the dividends between 1730 and 1780 averaged about one and one-half per cent ; the Company was living upon the dues paid by private traders, and the opinion was growing that it was useless. In 1791, when the question of charter-renewal came up, it was disbanded ; the council of the Company was succeeded by a Council of the Colonies, and the shares at 30 were converted into three-per-cent obligations of the state.[1]

The story of these companies seems a sorry enough affair ; yet the Dutch rather unanimously regarded them as " the two pillars upon which the status of these lands rests." They appeared to constitute a necessary part of a government unable to attend to distant possessions and interests. " During the second half of the seventeenth and almost the whole of the eighteenth century no one doubted that the possession of the East India trade was dependent upon the existence of the great Company." [2] But before attempting any more general estimate of these chartered monopolies, or trying to arrive at a conception of their influence upon the life of the metropolis, it still remains to treat of their activity within the regions assigned to their control.

[1] Van Rees, II, 209–211, 213, 218–223.
[2] Van Rees, II, 213, 216 ; cf. Colmeiro, II, 453–454.

CHAPTER XI

THE COMPANIES IN THEIR FIELDS

Immediately after the formation of the East India Company, as has been seen, a fleet of seventeen vessels sailed for the East; these were followed in 1603 by one of thirteen, well-armed; and in 1606 by a third. The first established a factory at Bantam, where a head-merchant and sub-officials were left. Thence ships plied in all directions, to Banda, Atjeh, Borneo, Siam, and China. The second visited Goa and Calicut, concluding a treaty with the Zamorin of the latter district; went to the Moluccas, where conquests were made and a governor left; founded a factory at Banda and penetrated as far as New Guinea. The third, under Matelief, defeated the Portuguese near Malacca but could not take the place, and thence pushed on as far as Tidore, Ternate, and even Macao. In 1607 a stronger fleet, under an admiral, departed to fight the Portuguese in Malacca and the Moluccas; it visited and made treaties in Mozambique and Farther India, seized many Portuguese ships, and was just ready to assault Malacca when the peace of 1609 was announced.[1] Matelief's idea in attacking Malacca had been to close the Straits of Singapore to rivals, Portuguese above all; but he intended to shut out both Arabs and Chinese as well, and then to drive the Spanish from the Philippines. Coen elaborated the same idea in his plan of forcing the Chinese to allow free trade along their coast and to keep out of the archipelago except in so far as they came to Batavia to trade with the Dutch. This project, it may be added, was partially realized; in 1624 the Dutch occupied Formosa and a lively trade with the Chinese ensued; but the arrogance and greed of the Dutch disgusted the Orientals, and after 1661, when the Chinese private Coxinga seized Formosa, the Chinese trade was confined to the taking of tea to Batavia. However, there was no more serious competition from east and south Asia and, after the conquest of Malacca (1641), the straits remained closed.

[1] Blok, III, 493-495; Van Rees, II, 226-228.

CENTRALIZATION OF ADMINISTRATION

All through this early period the Company proceeded upon the regular mercantile programme of making treaties and founding factories on an extensive scale. Gradually, however, these establishments began to display a lack of unity of purpose, heads of factories acting independently of each other as far as their instructions permitted. Local management was proved a failure and the need of centralization shown; it was likewise desirable to present a strong front to the Spanish and Portuguese, and, as the latter had done, to impress the natives by a magnificent court. Thus, in 1609, a governor-general, Pieter Both, was appointed, who arrived in Bantam and began actual Dutch rule in the Indies on December 19, 1610. From this time on, the office thus created was almost that of a monarch. The governor was expected to follow the orders of The Seventeen, and there was attached to him, as a sort of check, a council (*Raad van Indië*) of five men, later (1617) increased to nine.[1] In general, however, The Seventeen were too far away, especially since the imperfection of means of communication as compared with those of to-day multiplied distances as now reckoned, to dictate more than general policies. In the seventeenth century it was ordinarily more than a year before a governor could get an answer from home, and even as late as 1769 a prize of 1200 guilders was offered by The Seventeen for the skipper who should reach Batavia within six months; as for the Raad, only five members were stationed at Batavia, the other four being governors of districts outside of Java, and so too far away to do much. And the governor had his own ways of evading their control. At first he was to confer with the Raad when there was no special instruction from The Seventeen; later he was merely its president, with casting vote. But as head of fleet and army he far outdid his advisers in importance; and he could easily get the upper hand by reference to secret advices of The Seventeen, or on the pretext of awaiting instructions. The Seventeen were willing to grant large powers, thinking that thus only could unity be secured; and realizing their own ignorance of local Indian affairs, they were glad to

---

[1] This was called: " Het Collegie van regeering over alle actiën en zaken van gansch Indië, de Nederlandsche Compagnie betreffende." De Reus, p. 83; cf. Day, pp. 42–43, 91–94. Encycl. Ned. Ind., arts. " Gouverneur-generaal," " Raad van Nederlandsch-Indië."

depend upon the man on the spot.[1] Thus the history of administration in the East is largely a record of the governors-general.

THE CRUSHING OF COMPETITION

One of the first duties that fell to the governors was the crushing of all competition within the areas of spice-production. The
States-General held strongly to the idea that the Company was the
proper organ with which to keep up trouble with Spain, and so gave
it large power against the enemy; a discretion which it used so
energetically as to foil all hostile projects and to establish itself
strongly in factories and forts. The status of the Portuguese
power in the latter half of the sixteenth century was, as has been
shown,[2] deplorable; in particular the natives, in their hatred of
their oppressors, were all ready to go over to the Dutch or any one
else hostile to the Portuguese. The whole structure of the empire
was ready to collapse at a slight shock; and the Portuguese themselves were the more apathetic inasmuch as the Indies now belonged
to Philip II as king of Portugal. The Dutch captured Malacca in
1641, and were thereafter masters of the archipelago, possessing
its keys in the straits of Malacca and Sunda; the Portuguese continued to hold Timor only, and the Spanish soon (1663) turned
their faces east from the Philippines to Mexico, both alike fearing
and avoiding the Dutch. But the latter were not content with anything short of a closed monopoly, and determined to expel friendly
nations also. The French possessed small capacity and little capital, and their East India Company, founded in 1604, rapidly declined. The Company did not balk at the use of force, although it
was willing to pay damages after the object had been gained. After
1682 the French kept out of the archipelago, and the Danes confined themselves to the mainland.[3] With the English the struggle
was sharper, not only because they were stronger, but because
England had been and was the traditional friend of the Netherlands.
But this consideration was not allowed to weigh overmuch; and
in any case strife between their "colonies" was not proof of the

---

[1] Van Rees, II, 48–50; De Reus, pp. xiii–xiv, 80–85; Day, pp. 88–91.

[2] Pp. 115 ff., above.

[3] Van Rees, II, 51–52, 63; cf. Danvers, II, 105 ff. For more detailed accounts of
these various nations in the East, see Encycl. Ned. Ind., arts. "De Denen," "De
Engelschen," "De Franschen," "De Portugeezen," "De Spanjaarden in den Maleischen Archipel."

enmity of two nations; the English did not hesitate to provoke or even aid the natives of the Moluccas against the Dutch. They hesitated to consider combination with the latter, fearing that the Netherlanders' superior energy and capacity would come more and more to limit the number of English participants. But some such pooling of interests was being brought to definite form in 1619, and was favored by the Dutch Company in the hope of thus securing extra insurance against mishaps due in a few years, when war broke out in the East Indies. The Dutch then determined upon the expulsion at all hazards of their rivals from the Moluccas; and in 1619 the governor-general, Coen, was instructed to attack them at all points. He treated the English as a sort of subject nation; and early in 1623, on the occasion of a conspiracy of English agents in Amboina, he openly broke with them. The conspirators were executed ("Amboina Massacre") and the English forced to leave the Moluccas, and also, in 1624, Batavia. From this time on the policy was one of absolute exclusion; the Dutch, despite all efforts of their enemies, remained in full possession, and in 1667 (Peace of Breda) the English gave up their last hold in the Moluccas and upon the spice-trade; in 1683 they surrendered Bantam and their exclusion from the East Indies was complete. There were no other foreign rivals.

The Dutch had started out, as novices, with Hugo de Groot's theory of freedom of the sea, which conveniently demonstrated their own right to approach and trade in the Indies. But the situation appeared so altered when viewed from the inside that they ended by giving the world an exemplar of the old exclusion policy carried out in truly orthodox form. Having come to occupy the situation and to be appealed to by the conditions of the Spanish and Portuguese, they speedily reacted in a fashion identical with theirs, but with an energy and thoroughness that realized what had been the dreams rather than the hopes of the Iberians. And this was after all but the local application of the principle of exclusion universally applied by the Dutch; in the trade-history of the seventeenth and eighteenth century "the fundamental starting-point for our merchants is simply this: for us the greatest possible freedom, for our competitors the greatest possible obstruction, here and elsewhere. To this end our trade-legislation and trade-policy were directed." [1]

[1] Van Rees, II, 53–63; Blok, II, 504 (quoted); cf. 346–349, 502–504; Day, pp. 51–55.

MONOPOLY POLICY; OPPRESSION OF THE NATIVES

In their increasing freedom from interference on the part of the outside world, The Seventeen and their governors-general were enabled to turn more attention to the objects, or rather the object, for which they labored. This was commercial gain, conceived to be derivable first and foremost, and to the exclusion of all else, from the spice-trade. Like the Portuguese the Dutch were determined to get the spices at a low price, and thus their policy was to cajole or coerce the natives, through treaties or by war, to sell their products to them at a fixed price and to have no trade-relations with other nations. With Ternate, one of the few centers of clove-production, a treaty was made to the effect that the cost of expelling the Spaniards was to be borne by the natives and that they were then to sell to the Company at prices arranged between the States-General and the local king. Strongholds were to be erected to keep the natives in order and to repel the foreigner. This arrangement was on the whole a peaceable one, but usually violence was not long restrained. The Bandanese, who displayed a greater sense of freedom and more energy than is usual with Easterners, and had even developed to the extent of holding folk-assemblies to consider policy, had agreed in 1602 to sell all nutmegs and mace to the Dutch, but with no special condition as to price. They had likewise stipulated for the right of trade in their junks wherever they wished. But they speedily discovered that the Company could force them to take low prices by refusing to buy at higher figures; and they came to make more and more use of their stipulation, trading with the English and Portuguese, and even receiving aid from the former against the Dutch assertion of monopoly. The governor-general, Coen, put an end to all this insubordination; in 1621 he assembled a large force and made himself master of the Banda Islands, and then proceeded to depopulate them with relentless cruelty. Those of the Bandanese who remained in the islands were obliged to live on the coast, where it was impossible to keep up their agriculture; others were removed to Java and located near Batavia, to cultivate rice. Some escaped to other islands and stirred up hatred against the Dutch, and some fled to the bush in their own islands and died of hunger. The Directors approved entirely of these measures. The sequel of the tale likewise throws its light upon Dutch trade and native policy. Coen tried to populate the islands again, and sent there four hundred men and women, mostly whites, a number which increased in ten years to one thousand. The Company was to furnish them slaves to till the soil and sell them rice and cloth at cost price; they, for their part, were to sell nutmegs and mace for a fixed price to the Company. But the latter could not see enough in the rice-trade to continue it, and so decided, in the latter part of the seventeenth century, that the slaves would have to live on sago and fish, which the islanders could procure for themselves from the Moluccas. This food was insufficient, the slaves died in great numbers, and the consequent rise of their price gave impetus to the slave-trade. Meanwhile the sago and fish gatherers had utilized their opportunities to engage in illicit traffic and were getting rich. This trade was discovered in the early years of the eighteenth century and crushed by force.[1]

In some such way the whole archipelago was rendered subservient[2] to the paramount consideration, and, at least at first, the gains were very large. The Dutch bought nutmegs at a stiver and a half and less per pound in the Indies, and sold them in Holland and Zeeland for three guilders and a quarter, making in some cases up to five thousand per cent. The cloves also of Amboina and Ternate yielded heavy profit; a half million pounds, purchased at four stivers, sold at four guilders, and even in the early part of the eighteenth century the Company still got the cloves for six stivers a pound and sold them for almost four guilders. But in the case of the cloves also the contraband traffic naturally arose, for the clove was a favorite spice in the East itself; and since smuggling was carried on by native skippers in their elusive small-craft, it was difficult to check by ordinary means. Hence arose the Company policy of uprooting the trees wherever its mastery was not complete, on the pretext that the natives had not kept to their agreements with the Dutch. A sort of annual voyage of as many as sixty-four vessels was organized and natives were taken along to

---

[1] Van Rees, II, 229–232.

[2] The ease with which the Dutch appear to have extended their power recalls the experience of the Portuguese, detailed above (pp. 107 ff.). According to Day (p. 10), who makes a survey of the native organization a prime factor in his argument, the native institutions in Java were "not fresh and in a course of vigorous development, but old and worn, going through their cycles of change only to return to the starting-point. Nothing else would explain the ease with which the Dutch conquered and ruled the island."

destroy trees; if these were found where they were unauthorized, the adjacent towns were burned. When, for a certain year, the Company had need of more cloves, there was either no round made or a short one; if the spice was in plenty, a long one. The Amboinese natives on occasion of the long voyage were unable to return in time to sell their own spice and so suffered want. This extirpation was in general the destruction of livelihood itself, for the trees had need of years of careful tending before they bore.[1] The bitterness that such inhuman greed had caused aided the illicit traffic, a result which the Company met with new severity; the seventeenth-century history of the Indies is that of brave but hopeless defense of liberty on the part of the Malays against the cupidity of the Dutch. The latter did not stop with severity but employed deceit and treachery to effect their ends. Coen brought fulfillment of the monopoly policy; nutmegs were thereafter raised on the Banda Islands alone and cloves in Amboina. In Ternate the extirpation found less resistance because of the local interest in tobacco, but in 1680 the people, discouraged by the collapse of their trade, took up arms. After they had been quelled in blood, prosperity never returned to the island; it remained a costly Company post, maintained for reasons of monopoly and war. In Amboina, after some strife, the Company had its way, uprooted such trees as it chose, and forced the inhabitants to live under the guns of the forts; from being a fairly civilized, energetic, brave people, they were reduced to a poverty-stricken group of slaves. By these varied means the production of cloves was reduced to one-fourth of what it had been. Then ensued a direful policy of vacillation: first the Dutch had misgivings as to there being enough trees, and encouraged the natives of Amboina to plant more, and then the fear of low prices caused them to force submission to the destruction of the young trees; and "so it went on through the whole of the eighteenth century."[2]

Policy toward Private Trade

But it was not enough to destroy the trees — the native merchant shipping must also be annihilated, if the *raison d'être* of the Company was to be vindicated. At the period of the arrival of the

[1] Van Rees, II, 232–234, 238–239. For details of the spice-trade see Encycl. Ned. Ind., arts. "Amboina," "Notenmuskaat," "Peper," "Kaneel," "Nagelen (Kruid-)," "Ternate," etc. [2] Van Rees, II, 234–235.

Dutch in the East they had found a prosperous merchant shipping in the hands chiefly of Javanese and Macassars. This had not been disturbed by the Portuguese because of their dependence upon it for the assembling of their cargoes; but the Dutch felt no such need. The Javanese were rather easily disposed of; in 1646 a treaty with the sultan of Mataram forbade his subjects from going to the Moluccas. Passes from Batavia were demanded as a condition of passing Malacca; and it was finally ordered that the Javanese should follow the coasting-trade only, their ships and cargoes to be confiscated if they were found more than five miles from the shore. The Macassars of southern Celebes were more stubborn; their *praus* visited the whole archipelago, and in vain did the governor, De Vlaming, threaten intercourse with the Moluccas with hard labor for life. But by 1667, through sowing disaffection, the Company reduced the strong Macassar state, and thereafter, since all trade had to be done under a pass, the Moluccas were secure.[1]

This determined policy toward foreigners and natives assumed a form scarcely less truculent and inexorable as against the private trade of the Netherlanders in the archipelago. The trade-areas of the East were roughly divided into two classes : the region actually held by or treaty-bound to the Company, and the outlying districts. For the first class, Company functionaries could be used, but for the second they were less valuable since they lacked the spirit of individual enterprise. Hence there was in the latter case something less of opposition to private traders; Coen, in 1623, attempted to demonstrate to The Seventeen that such exchange was better intrusted to individual enterprise under a recognition-fee to the Company. India must maintain and feed itself, his argument runs, and so men, ships, and capital must be attracted to India and put in a position to help themselves and the Company through free trade. Coen partially won over The Seventeen and the Chambers, but illness delayed him from setting his own hand to the work, and the complaisant attitude of the Directors suffered speedy alteration. The reaction in 1631 was signalized by a determined assault on freedom of trade, and another period of generosity in 1662 was again followed by a tightening of restriction. The Company gradually strengthened prohibitive ordinances until the years 1771 to 1774, when a good deal of relaxation took place; but it was then too late. The Directors seemed to miss the significance of the

1 Van Rees, II, 236–238.

fact that even a delegate from their own body, when sent to the
Indies as governor to effect measures of restriction, was shortly
made over, once in touch with local conditions, into an advocate
of freedom.[1] The results of their consistent narrow-mindedness
will appear the more clearly when actual attempts at colonization
under the Company are considered.[2]

LIMITATION OF PRODUCTION

Thus far the activity of the Company in doing away with rivals
of all kinds has received the bulk of attention, although incidentally some idea has been given of the processes by which the natives
were reduced and of the profits subsequently secured. We now
turn to the business policy of the Company in the regions which
it had cleared of all resistance. The keynote of this policy, struck
almost at the beginning, was the counterpart of that which dominated at the European end; and its underlying motive was the
preservation of diversity of conjunctures. The supply of spices
was kept down on the European market in order to realize high
returns, this procedure extending to the actual destruction of crops
and even to the burying and burning of large quantities of spice;[3]
and in the East the theory always prevailed of purchase at the
lowest prices and sale of the Company's goods to the natives or
resident Dutch at the highest. The old ideal of large percentages
of gain on a small movement of trade still persisted, and had been
strengthened by the happenings of the first few years when, in
consequence of the competitive activity of the disunited companies,
the price of pepper had been brought low in Europe.[4]

What has been said as to the clove-production and its limitation applies in general to all the products in which the Company
conceived it worth while to trade. The raising of pepper was
forbidden elsewhere than under Company control; and since the

---

[1] Van Rees, II, 246–247; De Reus, pp. 246–249, 259–261.   [2] P. 433, below.

[3] "Some years . . . many hundred pounds of cloves are openly buried, and in part,
also, burned." Valentijn (IV, 251) in Van Rees, II, 285; cf. Roscher, pp. 280–281.
Leroy-Beaulieu exhibits the folly of staking everything on the spice-trade; its great
profits were illusory. In 1840, he says (I, 275), the spice-trade was insignificant. The use
of substitutes for the monopolized articles cut deeply into profits. Van Rees, II, 286.

[4] Van Rees, II, 283 ff.; De Reus, p. xxi; Blok, III, 496; Day, p. 62. In 1623 the
shareholders complained that the Directors asked such high prices that much of their
goods remained in the warehouses, the capital invested lying idle in the meantime.
But price-regulation was a cardinal tenet, and elevation of prices was a popular expedient for covering losses. Van Rees, II, 285–286.

plants grew slowly and could not quickly respond to the mood of the Directors, determined as this was by the momentary ups and downs of European demand, the culture was gradually given up and after the dissolution of the Company practically ceased. Coffee was earlier procured in Mocha, but when the price rose and the Arab government made some trouble, it was introduced (about 1700) into Java. To incite its culture the Company paid at first ten stivers a pound; but it speedily got down to six, and then set out to eliminate individuals from the production. Thus arose the regular monopoly; but, since coffee could be bought cheaper in Ceylon, it was necessary now to reduce the purchase price to two stivers. Further, in order to prevent the inevitable resistance here encountered, the Directors proceeded now to limit production to the region of Batavia, where control was easy; elsewhere the plants were to be uprooted. Thus through meddling and oscillation of policy the industry was destroyed in Javanese districts. Indigo, again, had been a successful product of the Javanese before the Dutch arrived, and trade in it quickly arose; but the prices the Dutch were willing to pay were too low and the forcing system came again into operation. Sugar-production suffered in the same manner. The Company held also the monopoly of the opium and salt industries, which were let out at handsome sums to the Chinese.[1] Plainly there was little economic chance for the natives under such a system.

What prices the Company paid in the East were largely in money. This was theoretically unfortunate; the Dutch thought to make double gain if they could barter linen and other textiles and manufactures for the spices. But the Easterners had little need of food; and their clothing was made so well and cheaply at home as to render European competition, in these centuries that preceded the use of steam-driven machinery, impossible. Nor must it ever be lost sight of that, especially in its later period, a very large proportion of the Company's wares "came to it in a political rather than an economic way, as tribute and not by exchange."[2] Thus the exports of the Company to the Indies were mainly the necessities of life for the Europeans, a few cloths, and some gold and

---

[1] Van Rees, II, 279–282; Day, pp. 65–70. See Encyl. Ned. Ind., arts. "Indigo," "Koffie," "Tabak," "Rijst," "Suiker," "Opium," "Zout."

[2] Day, p. 63. The "contingents" and "forced deliveries" are regarded by this author (pp. 63–64) as essentially the same.

silver articles that pleased the natives ; upon these goods the Company forced the payment of high prices, not only from the natives, but also, where it could, from the Europeans. These imports to the colonies were not of very great volume, never exceeding, apparently , a value of 3,000,000 guilders a year. Payment for the spices was largely in gold and silver ; in the latter half of the eighteenth century a value of 4,000,000 to 6,000,000 guilders was sent yearly to the East, and as high as 450,000 at a voyage. In accordance with the prevailing mercantilism of the day, this export of metal from the Netherlands was looked upon with a misgiving, which but reënforced the tendency to make a little of it go a great way. Later it seemed the part of policy to pay in copper duits, which were worth in the East twice as much as in Europe ; between 1771 and 1780 over 100,000,000 of these were sent to the Indies.[1]

CORRUPTION OF THE SERVICE

Such a penurious, catch-penny policy could not but have its effects upon the morale of the Company service.[2] The functionaries were, first of all, very poorly paid ; the principle here was to exact the maximum of service for the minimum of actual outlay. The local agents lived not infrequently in a condition of real misery ; and gradually their quality deteriorated, not only because good men would not come but because they did not remain honest when they did come. There was a provision that no one could enter the Indian service who had failed or committed crime at home, or who had once been sent back from the Indies ; but such criteria were not maintained. Officers cashiered for incompetence were given refuge in the Indies, and no evidence was demanded as to the quality of the immigrant or sojourner except that he must not be French, Scotch, or English. Here the policy of the Dutch must be compared, to its plain disadvantage, with that of the Spanish. Wonderment is with reason expressed that so much as the Dutch did could have been accomplished with the human agencies they employed. But whatever the quality of the functionary, he was practically forced, in order to exist, to prove false

---

[1] Van Rees, II, 245, 283–285; Van der Chys, p. 79 and note; Encycl. Ned. Ind., art. " Scheepvaart en Handel."

[2] For a list of the Company officials in India, see De Reus, pp. 97 ff.

to his bounden duty; and this was to some degree recognized by his employers. The functionaries took to dishonest methods, especially to illicit trade; and they had no scruples as time went on about oppressing the natives. Officers both high and low engaged in contraband traffic even in the ships of the Company; clergymen were often deeply involved, and both they and their wives could give instruction in method to expert merchants. The Company's agents were too few and were too widely separated to be under much control, and the evil became so all-pervasive that it was practically impossible to identify and punish the guilty; as the years · went on the honest man became more rare. All this was seen to harm the Company, but the latter reasoned that the evil would be the worse if the waters were opened for freedom of trade.[1] Thus the policy deliberately adopted was one calculated thoroughly to demoralize the local agents.

The damage thus done extended to the personnel of the army and the merchant marine. The military force, which was under the civil power, was kept small through the parsimony of the Company; the whole army was not over 10,000, and of these but few were Europeans. Its quality was lower still, for the idea seems to have been to get certain numbers of men into uniform, with no respect to their race or character; the European contingent was composed largely of those who for various reasons found life in Europe impossible. Wages were extremely low and prices of supplies purchasable by the soldiers high; clothing cost enough to allow the Company alone to make upon it seventy-five per cent gain. The men were systematically cheated. The navy was much better in all ways, for a good marine, here as at home, was a strict necessity; yet conservatism entered to undermine its effectiveness. For one thing, the routes of the ships were strictly prescribed, and, despite all protests, they were obliged by the Directors to sail around Scotland on their home voyages. The ships were too large and unwieldy, though too few in number. The quality of the captains speedily declined and numerous complaints were raised against them on the score of their ignorance, uselessness, and infidelity to · trust. The increase of illicit traffic testifies to the justice of the latter charge; but rascals consistently got off with impunity. The sailors were in a condition similar to that of the soldiers; their

<hr />

[1] Van Rees, II, 248–249 and note, 293; De Reus, pp. 24–25, 94–95; Day, pp. 89–91, 93–106; Encycl. Ned. Ind., art. "Opleiding van Indische Ambtenaaren."

numbers were larger, running up to 4000 sailing to the East yearly, but their position was wretched, whether they voyaged between East and West, or remained in the Indies.[1]

Hence the natural tendency of the European sojourner in tropical countries — to accumulate with speed and ruthlessness, in order presently to return home[2] — was strongly accentuated by the characteristic policy of the Company, itself animated by like desires.

NATIVE POLICY

To one who has gotten before his mind a clear conception of the aims of the East India Company, the inevitable destiny of the native can scarcely come as a surprise. Indeed it has already been seen how native life was subjected to all sorts of economic shock ; how native industry was cynically cramped or crushed in order to assure the profit of a closed monopoly. The Dutch came, without question, to regard the native as simply one of the factors entering into the making of money, a factor to be treated in the same objective way as water, soil, or any other non-sentient or inanimate element. To find the Company harboring any idea of benefiting the native peoples is to surprise it acting out of character ; and yet some such benevolent intent existed, at least in theory, at the outset of its career. There was no lack of instructions from home to treat the natives well and kindly, these being dictated by political as well as humanitarian considerations. In respect of religion in particular it was desirable " to enlighten the poor, blind heathen, eager to learn, through the grace of God, and to bring them out of blind darkness into the knowledge of the holy evangel." The Dutch had scarcely finished a struggle in which religious ardor was a driving factor ; and national honor, if no more, demanded that they do no less than the Spanish and Portuguese. The Seventeen accordingly began to bestir themselves that the natives might, through spread of the Holy Scripture, be defended against the superstitions of Moors, atheists, and their kind.

[1] De Reus, pp. 108–117, 120–124 ; Day, pp. 107–108 ; Roscher, p. 286. For the carrying-trade of the Company, see Day, pp. 61 ff. For the early instructions to sailors, and the rules governing life on ship-board, see Van der Chys, Bijlagen, I, II, and III. Cf. Encycl. Ned. Ind., arts. " Kaarte," " Leger," " Scheepvaart en Handel," " Triangulatie," " Verdediging," " Zeekarten," " Zeemacht." The mortality in the crowded ships was very high. Roscher, p. 275.

[2] See p. 11, above.

There had been an eye to business in all this. The Company thought to bind the natives to itself through a common religion and thus enforce in them the moral obligation to fulfill contracts. It was found, however, that, after the pious exploits of the Portuguese, religious instruction was regarded with hostility and fear; that the surest way toward confidence and good will was to interfere as little as possible with religion or government, and to confine efforts purely to trade. This was a comfortable conclusion, and instructions came to convey the praiseworthy maxim of non-interference. When, now, the question arose as to whether the church or the Company should take the superintendence of religious instruction, the latter felt that one might go further in religious fervor than the aims of trade would justify; where the people were absolutely subject little harm could be done, but elsewhere Mohammedans and others might become distrustful. Nothing could be lost by intrusting such matters to the discreet and practical. Finally the Company had its way; general instructions to the functionaries provided that they should see that the Christian religion was spread abroad, good schools founded, and so on. The results were slight, for, except in Ceylon, the Moluccas, and Formosa, where there were preachers, the natives were left pretty much to themselves. Discontent arose among the pious at home, and in 1645 it was proposed not to renew the Company's charter until it had had the Bible translated into the native languages. But the government refused to bind the Company. Thus all preachers and schoolmasters came to be Company dependents, and were even thus few in number, owing to the indisposition of the Directors to assume the cost and trouble incident to energetic missionary endeavor.[1] What the Company did for religion and education in the East was therefore practically nothing. All such activities were calculated to detract from the commercial well-being of the organization. If they had hoped by religious means to influence the natives to keep their low-priced contracts, the Dutch were in this disappointed; it was found that complete conquest alone could make the natives fulfill their obligations as interpreted by the Dutch. This had not been the attitude at the outset; there was then no desire to get ground except for factories, for it was proposed to proceed through treaties and contracts. But the Orientals, perceiving the over-reaching

---

[1] Van Rees, II, 239–244; Van der Chys, p. 62; Encycl. Ned. Ind., arts. "Christenen," "Eeredienst," "Evangelisatie," "Zending."

which lay in the essence of these agreements, were brought to a deceit and enmity that could be quelled through conquest alone.[1] Constant reference of all projects back to the dominant trade idea thus choked the development of generous impulses and high motives, and reduced the relation with subject peoples to one of sordid exploitation, pure and simple.

CONQUESTS; NATIVE SERVICES

Through the seventeenth century the Dutch became ever clearer upon the subject of acquiring territory. They found the factory insecure without a fort, the fort imperiled without mastery of the surrounding district. Native princes paid the costs of war on the Company by the cession of domain, or of income of the same; petty tribal wars where the foreigner was haled in as an ally yielded a like return. Thus in 1677 the Company forced entry into Mataram through special privileges accorded, becoming the only seller of opium, sugar, and linen in that region. Later (1743) the Dutch gained such control that the native officials swore allegiance to them rather than to their own rulers; the people were to cultivate what the Company wished, and sell or give their products to it. A succeeding uprising played further into Dutch hands. Similarly in Bantam and Cheribon: a foothold was gained in the former, securing trade advantages; and this was later followed by conquest. The sultan then received back his lands in fief, under the promise to sell to the Company at low prices all the pepper that should be raised. Thus the Company came to impinge upon the masses of the Javanese natives through their princes, who were to have rice, and, above all, coffee, pepper, indigo, sugar, turmeric, etc., raised and sold to the Dutch at a figure yielding the latter a large profit.[2]

The native princes turned out to be lax in their duties, knavish and oppressive to the people; hence the Company came to prefer land sales to more responsible parties; and, together with the soil, the natives were passed over to private supervision. But they were not thereby released from service to the Company; all the natives in the region of Batavia were obliged to perform certain tasks on its account, such as attending to roads and bridges and transporting persons and goods. Beyond this they had to give a part, usually a tenth, of their products to their landlords, and work one day

[1] Van Rees, II, 240, 271.
[2] Van Rees, II, 271–276; Day, pp. 43–50; cf. p. 43, note 3.

in the week for them; otherwise they labored for wages, with the Chinese and slaves. They were not bound to the soil but could go and settle where they would. The status thus defined does not look so bad on the face of it; but it was hard to keep track of the landlords and much oppression occurred. More service and higher contributions were exacted than was lawful, this being done through native chiefs who received a commission on the business; and army service was often required. Thus the natives labored under a three-fold yoke, and the authorities were always averse to supporting them against their landlords.[1]

In the actual domain of the Company the Javanese were left under their own chiefs, as that plan was found to be cheaper; and certain conditions as to the sale to the Company of specified products at low prices were imposed. The chiefs were bound to call the people to war when the Company wished it. These local rulers were not paid by the Dutch; indeed they had to bid for the tenure of their position through gifts to the governors. Son usually succeeded father, but the succession might be perverted if another party offered more. Naturally all the expenses of the chiefs, legitimate and illegitimate, had to come out of the people, through ways direct or devious. Here the latter had really two masters to serve. They got little or nothing for their goods or services from the Company; where by exception a decent price was paid, it emerged from the hands of the functionaries reduced beyond recognition. The Company paid little attention to the needs of the natives, interfering only in cases of crying injustice on the part of the chiefs, or, more commonly, when the contingents failed or when scarcity and dearness of products indicated some perversity to be corrected. As for the dishonest functionaries, it was more profitable to connive at their rascality — such as demanding more of the people than the Company itself, and appropriating the differences — and then tax them for it.[2]

Although the average status of the natives appears to have been that of an abject servitude, nothing has hitherto been considered which bears the actual designation of slavery. But there were, in the Indies, up to January 1, 1860, what were called house-slaves

---

[1] Van Rees, II, 277-278. For a closer examination of the Company's administration, see Day, pp. 108-121; this author regards the activities of the Dutch as on the whole beneficial to the natives. Cf. pp. 36-37, 121 ff.

[2] Van Rees, II, 278-279; Day, pp. 108-121.

and Company-slaves. They were held at first in default of other means of securing service, and were reckoned in with the " dead effects," such as gold and silver, food, ammunition, houses, furniture, etc. In September, 1694, the Company had 1273 slaves, men, women, and children, and certain private persons possessed a great many. Strange to say, as regards these slaves, the Company seems to have suppressed its characteristic greed ; they were treated on the whole very humanely, were paid for service, and allowed to accumulate funds to buy their freedom. They were really better off than free people under their regents. Slaves who turned Christian must be sold to Christians, and a freed man could even demand aid of his old master ; slaves, however, could not make wills, and, among other minor disabilities, might not wear a hat unless they could speak Dutch. They did the rougher work, especially of agriculture ; it was largely the cost of providing them for the prospective colonists, who had been proved incapable of performing such heavy tasks in the hot regions, that made the parsimonious Seventeen oppose colonization as a policy. There was no feeling whatsoever against the institution ; use of slaves was allowed in the Old Testament and was not forbidden in the New ; and the imperial Roman law recognized it. Moreover the slaves could, here as in America, be converted and no longer remain " slaves of the devil." The system was indorsed by such jurists as De Groot. And, above all, it was demanded by economic necessity, however this might be veiled, just as it had been in the case of the Portuguese and Spanish. Nevertheless, owing chiefly to the slight development of plantation agriculture and industry under the direction of actual Dutch settlers, the extent of what went by the acknowledged name of slavery was never great in the Indies.[1]

Enough has been said to demonstrate the deplorable situation of the native peoples ; it could not have been otherwise under the control of a corporation governed by motives both sordid and selfish. The account of the further fortunes of the natives under the later " culture system "[2] will serve to reflect additional light upon their previous status as here indicated in its general outlines.

[1] De Reus, pp. 127–131, 289; Van Rees, II, 321–322; cf. pp. 258 ff., above.
[2] Pp. 473 ff., below.

POLICY TOWARD COLONIZATION

A single phase of the Company's activity in the East remains to be noticed : its relation toward actual settlement and colonization in the stricter sense.[1] In the charter there was no idea whatsoever of settlement; naturally, however, the ordinary factories demanded for their support a certain number of Dutch residents ; and the larger the factory became the greater was the number of Europeans who were required in order to provide stores and lading for outgoing vessels and to receive those that arrived. Thus a certain amount of population, however shifting as respects its units, was rendered inevitable. Some one of these factories was bound to gain an ascendency over the rest, and this mainly because of its favorable location. The Dutch with unerring skill picked the straits as the dominant situations and at first cast their eyes on Malacca, which had been under the Portuguese the chief entrepôt of the East. There were at first and for some decades great difficulties in seizing Malacca, and attention turned toward the Sunda straits, where it was hoped to build a fort " serving as a rendezvous of the whole Indies navigation." In 1619 Coen conquered the whole province of Jacatra and the local fort took the name of Batavia, becoming the great deposit-station for all Company funds and goods, and the residence of the governor-general. At first its site lay in a waste, for all the natives had been swept away, and the Dutch were confronted with the need of population. This they recruited largely from the Chinese by securing them preferential rights, and gradually, as the factory-interests grew, both other Orientals and Dutch functionaries became relatively numerous. To attract the Dutch, private trade was allowed by Coen even to the west of the Straits of Malacca ; and the Netherlanders thus and otherwise attracted were the first free citizens of Batavia.[2]

The projects of Coen[3] deserve to be dwelt upon with brevity, even though they came to little more than naught, for this governor-general, standing at the parting of the ways, cruel and ruthless though he was, was a man of great keenness, and probably

[1] Cf. Encycl. Ned. Ind., art. " Kolonisatie."

[2] Van Rees, II, 252–255, 304 ; De Reus, pp. 276–277 ; Day, pp. 56–61. In 1632 Batavia had 8058 inhabitants, including the garrison, etc. ; of these the number of Dutch in the service of the Company, with wives and children, was 1912 ; the number of burghers, with wives, children, and slaves, 1372. De Reus, p. 251, note.

[3] For the life of Coen, see Encycl. Ned. Ind., art. " Coen."

the best informed of his generation. He is found to have been the
advocate of settlement, and, by way of promoting and supporting
the latter, of freedom of trade. The Directors had sent only men,
and of these but a few; and both the men and women whom they
finally forwarded at his solicitation were, in Coen's judgment, the
"scum of all nations." They were too lazy, he protested, to put
food in their mouths, or even, when it was once there, to chew it.
He wanted several hundred boys and girls from charity-houses
who should grow up to regard Java as their fatherland; he rebelled
against the sole dominant idea, to return home with full pockets.
Believing that labor could do little without capital, and that consequently the entrepreneur was a necessity to economic development, Coen urged also that peoples of the leisure classes should
be induced to go to the Indies. In other words, he seems at first
sight to have risen in opposition against some of the normal characteristics of the tropical colony.[1] In so far as he desired to see a
transplantation of the European race it is probable that his views,
despite the favorable island-position of Java, were visionary. Probably the Directors had some reason in their refusal to send European women "from whom no permanent and healthy offspring
arise in India." It was not denied, in somewhat later time, that
"hitherto Dutch children born in India, especially the half-breeds,
have been accustomed to lead a somewhat dissolute and disorderly
existence"; and very likely the Company may be excused for not
standing the cost of the great number of slaves needful for plantation agriculture and cattle-raising. But Coen did not base his whole
argument, nor any essential part of it, upon premises thus easily
and rationally swept aside. He understood that the immediate
source of livelihood for Dutch settlers must lie in exchange, and
it was a freedom of trade adequate to meet these needs for which
he contended. He wished trade to be free to his settlers even from
the Cape of Good Hope to Japan.[2]

But such a suggestion could meet with no lasting accord on the
part of the Directors; nor were the costs of real colonization such
as they could contemplate without aversion. Hence, as has been
seen, the policy of trade-restriction speedily came to its own, to be
modified only at rare intervals and for brief periods.[3] It is during

[1] Cf. pp. 4 ff., above.
[2] Van Rees, II, 255–256 and notes, 258–260 and notes, 307; De Reus, pp. 277–278.
[3] Van Rees, II, 306–315; cf. p. 423, above.

these sporadic periods only that any movements of settlement took place. Dutch colonization under the Company may then be divided roughly into three periods : that of 1618–1630, including Coen's activities ; that of 1662–1700 ; and that of 1742–1752, covering mainly the term of Van Imhoff. When the settlers of the first period had come to realize that they could not cultivate without capital, nor compete in the industries with the Chinese, and were not to be allowed to trade, they migrated back to the Netherlands ; colonial enterprises remained in abeyance for a generation or more, and then were resurrected to a hopeful though short-lived popularity. In 1662 the Chamber of Amsterdam offered free transport to prospective settlers in the Indies, and assured them, under certain conditions, of freedom of trade ; in 1669 action still more favorable was taken respecting settlement in Ceylon, Mauritius, at the Cape, and elsewhere. The effects of this policy at the Cape are yet to be recounted ; but in the tropics success could not be attained. The Dutch suspected any favors ; if any one sought fortune in the Indies it was as a Company agent, not as a freeholder subject to the caprices of officials. By 1684 Ceylon presented the regulation picture of misery ; the Company would not transport the locally grown tobacco for fear of encouraging contraband traffic, and would not allow the producers to seek their own markets. Even where trade was ostensibly free, passes were refused, or granted only in cases where the profit could not be large. Trade was left free in those articles only which the Company could not hope to monopolize ; and if an article not proscribed, like sugar, became important, the Company had a way of interfering and destroying all opportunities. Insecurity thus engendered paralyzed the little enterprise that remained ; toward the end of the seventeenth century all effort of the Company directed toward colonization had been proved an entire and dismal failure. During the general misrule of the first half of the eighteenth century no further action was taken. Then under Van Imhoff transportation and some actual aid in securing a start were offered, which were the basis of later settlement in Java ; but after the death of the governor, in 1750, there was no great advance. Robber-raids from Bantam, motived by local dissatisfaction under Company rule, destroyed what little had been done and the government abandoned the colonies.[1] In 1778 Batavia had a population of 110,816, but of these

[1] Van Rees, II, 261–264 ; De Reus, pp. 282–285.

only 468 were free citizens; 33,408 were Javanese, and of the remaining 76,940, all Orientals, 20,072 were slaves and 23,309 Chinese. Outside of Batavia there was, of course, an overwhelming preponderance of the native element.[1]

It is unnecessary to pursue such melancholy attempts into their details, for these amount, as has been seen from examples given, to little more than a catalogue of instances of ineptitude, selfishness, and greed on the part of the Company. There was bound to be no society of a pure European type in the Indies, for, besides the very grave menace of the physical environment,[2] the Company constantly threw obstacles in the way of the emigration of women from the Netherlands. This being the case, the only alternative, if the agent or settler were to have a home, was to marry a native woman; but to this procedure also discouragement was opposed, for the native wife could not go back to Holland with her husband. In the case of the higher functionaries, moreover, those who contracted marriage had to bind themselves to twice the regular length of service.[3] It is, therefore, not at all strange that inter-race marriages did not take place with any frequency. Miscegenation on a large scale was nowhere present, and half-breeds born of unions legitimate or otherwise played no such prominent part in the destiny of the Dutch Indies as in that, for example, of Spanish America.

From what has been said of the destiny of private trade and of settlement, it is clear that the only real administration in the Indies was the imposition of the Company's will. The burghers, such as they were, had no share worth mentioning in the government, which was, in last analysis, the governor-general alone. In general the colonization was not a state enterprise at all. Pamphlets speak of necessities for emigration rooting in over-population and poverty at home, and they discuss the various problems connected with state-favored colonization; but the state turned over

[1] Van Rees, II, 264–265, 268–270; De Reus, pp. 285–289. Even in 1892 the Europeans were a vanishing quantity outside of the main centers. In Atjeh, for example, there were in that year 252 Europeans as against 525,579 natives and 3159 Chinese. Encycl. Ned. Ind., art. "Atjeh."

[2] De Reus, who was perhaps anxious to write what the German colonial societies would like to hear (cf. his introduction), states (p. 290) that the experience of the Dutch proves nothing as to the possibility of European colonization of the tropical highlands. Cf. Van Rees, II, 258, note 4; De Lanessan, p. 34; Bordier, Col., p. 47; Engler, p. 154, note; Van der Aa, De Gids, 1860, I, 837.

[3] Van Rees, II, 265.

the direction of the movement in all its details to the Company, with results recounted, as to their main lines, in what precedes.[1]

THE CHINESE

But if the colonization of Europeans was almost steadily discouraged, the same cannot be said of settlement by the Chinese, at least in the earlier periods. By 1617 instructions to the governor not only permitted their presence in the Moluccas, but urged that they should be attracted, as being industrious and peaceable; in 1632 it was the policy to draw their trade, so far as possible, to Batavia. Coen said, " There is no people in the world that serve us better than the Chinese "; and asserted that too many could not be attracted to Batavia. They were of benefit to agriculture and the mechanic arts, and could be ruled the more easily as they would not appeal to their own country. The Chinese came then to function as the local transporters and middlemen of the Dutch possessions, and in time became owners of large sugar-plantations and refineries, etc., chiefly in the region of Batavia. But the Company could not renounce the opportunity of preying upon them, and they were taxed if poor, and ruthlessly blackmailed if wealthy; then came the Company's agents, each with itching palm. The success of the Chinese was their undoing; embittered, they finally rebelled (1740) against this oppression, and united many Javanese to their cause. The governor, Valckenier, broke their resistance, and for two days Batavia was a scene of blood and death; even the prisoners and those sick in the hospitals were put to death. The Chinese quarter was plundered and burned; 600 dwellings were destroyed and 10,000 defenseless Chinese were killed. Similar exhibitions of inhuman ferocity elsewhere in Java have left a lasting disgrace upon the name of Valckenier.[2] By 1743, however, the Chinese and their allies were reduced to subjection; the former returned to Batavia, for they could not be spared, and later spread over all Java. They lent money to the improvident natives and gained great profit; they lived under their own rules and customs, in separate quarters, and almost the whole of the interior and coast trade drifted into their hands. Indeed, in both earlier and later times, the commercial privileges accorded them by the Company, which represented its estimate of

---

[1] Van Rees, II, 305, 308.   [2] Cf. Encycl. Ned. Ind., art. " Valckenier."

their indispensability, are contrasted with the much slighter favors extended to individual Dutch traders. Of the later fortunes of the Chinese the main outlines will appear in subsequent pages.[1]

Foreign Aggressions

Certainly the Company had had its way; it had been allowed to develop a great predatory activity, varied by but few impulses of a more generous nature, within the range of its monopoly. Government by a body of merchants had been permitted to proceed in its extremest form. Something of its influence upon the destiny of the human life beneath its control may have appeared in the foregoing; it seems to have desired to subserve no interests save its own. The question as to whether it realized its own aims, however the latter may present themselves to later ages as respects worthiness or unworthiness, may now engage attention. These aims may be summed up conveniently under two heads: maintenance of monopoly, and so realization of profits; and — for it must not be lost to view that the Company was in one of its most significant aspects a political agency — support of the state.

After the expulsion of the English from Batavia, in 1624, the Company was not seriously annoyed by foreign competition for a century and a quarter, and after the Peace of Breda (1667) the Netherlanders were practically alone in the Indies for well-nigh a hundred years. The time of Van Diemen (1636–1645) represents the first period of expansion and the disclosure of new sources of profit. The rest of the century saw the extension of the Company's power from Ceylon to New Guinea, and of its influence and trade from Persia to Japan. But the eighteenth century brought a reversal of destiny, for reasons presently to appear, although the vertex of the prosperity-curve was not sharp. The French, English, and Danes began to pluck up courage again and to invade the Dutch seas. In consideration of international rights and courtesy, their vessels could not be refused the privilege of making repairs and laying in provisions in Dutch harbors, and thus, under revelation of the richness of the Company's monopoly, was offered the temptation to illicit trade. The real impotence of the Company was likewise discovered, and its existence was not long allowed to remain as a merely curious or astounding academic consideration;

[1] Van Rees, II, 265–267; De Reus, pp. xxxiv–xxxvi, 250–251, 281–282; Encycl. Ned. Ind., art. "Chineezen"; cf. p. 488 ff., below.

from 1750 on the Company was forced to meet an aggression to which it could offer no adequate resistance. The war between the Netherlands and England in 1781 was the beginning of the end; Dutch stations fell without a blow, and the English came to control the Coromandel coast and Ceylon. The events that followed the French Revolution, whereby the Netherlands were made over into the Batavian Republic (1795), completed the dissolution. The Stadhouder Willem V, exiled to England, urged that the colonies be placed under the protection of that country; and this was a signal for a weak yielding of most of the Indies. In 1795 Malacca and other posts in Farther India were lost; in 1796 Ceylon, Amboina, Banda, and other stations. Ternate and Timor alone of the islands were defended, and Van Overstraten struggled on in Java; but the monopoly was gone and the course of the Company's history as a controller of vast territories was run.[1]

BANKRUPTCY AND RUIN

Such an exhibition of weakness argues internal deterioration and a prostration of finances. Enough has been heard of the "hook-handed" functionaries of the Company and of its generally costly, ineffectual, and disreputable internal organization and personnel; so that a realization of these elements of weakness may be assumed. Aside from the incessant drain of peculation and embezzlement of funds, however, the Company had found that the very attainment and preservation of monopoly constantly defeated its end; before they knew it the Directors were led into a costly conquest-policy that ate up profits with awe-inspiring celerity. Wars in Europe likewise obliged the Company to come to the state's aid. With the later growth of competition, prices in Europe were brought down, and in the East even the Arabs and Chinese dared again to take advantage of the Company. By 1676 there existed a large unfavorable balance in Batavia, yet the Directors learned nothing and proceeded with even increased severity against the private trade of the Dutch settlers, imposing penalties in the way of heavy fines, public whipping, exile, and even death, to stop it. At the end of the seventeenth century the Directors were pursuing the "ostrich-policy" of suppressing unfavorable reports, and

[1] Van Rees, II, 288–291 ; De Reus, pp. xvi–xxviii, xxxix–xlvi; Encycl. Ned. Ind., arts. " Verdediging," " Verovering van Java door de Engelschen in 1811." ·

the early part of the eighteenth saw the golden age of illicit traffic.[1] When the competition of other nations had at length become confident and strong, the expenses of maintaining the monopoly became naturally heavier; according to Van Imhoff they rose from 680,-000 guilders in 1715 to 990,000 in 1739, and yet prices were constantly sinking in Europe. The French and English left the local trade of the East free under a recognition-duty, and the Dutch could not combat this kind of competition, backed by the zeal, daring, and knowledge of the private adventurer; for because such trade had no rules of prescribed action it could adapt itself to new or altering circumstances as the Company could never do. The Dutch even emulated the Portuguese in forming (of Batavia) a staple where all returning ships must report; thus their cargoes suffered from deterioration, their tea, for instance, coming upon the European markets several years later than that brought direct from China by the Danes.[2] Deficits accumulated: the credit balance of 40,000,000 of 1693 was all gone by 1724, after which time the course was steadily toward bankruptcy. From 1750 to 1760 the income gotten from the Indies was 750,000 guilders; from 1760 to 1770, 680,000; and although it was 500,000 for the next five-year period, debts were always mounting, for the Directors kept paying out dividends of $12\frac{1}{2}$ to 20 per cent through the whole second half of the century. By 1779 the Company owed 85,000,000, and the war with England brought it in 1782 to ask aid of the state. It received loans from this source, for its reputation was still great as the essential factor in preserving the East Indian trade. After 1790 it was entirely dependent upon the government; in 1795 its debt was 112,000,000 guilders. War had cut communications with Holland and all profits disappeared; even interest on debt could not be paid. The Company ships became antiquated and were sold; at the end of the century scarcely any of them were usable, and Dutch ships and products ceased to arrive from the East. The last sale of East Indian wares took place in 1797. There was even talk of reforming the Company, semi-defunct as it was; but, as has been seen, its end was nigh, for the conviction was becoming confirmed that war and trade were inconsistent functions.[3]

[1] De Reus, pp. 253–257; Day, pp. 73 ff.   [2] Van Reès, II, 288–289.
[3] Van Rees, II, 294–297; De Reus, p. xlvi. On the income of the Company in India, see De Reus, pp. 202–232.

One of the reasons why the essential weakness of the Company was not earlier discovered at home lay in its system of secrecy, especially in regard to its finances. We have already viewed the twistings and turnings of the Directors and how they were able bluntly to defy public scrutiny. The utmost secrecy was maintained regarding especially the income and outgo in the Indies; the very accounts of the Company were merely unrelated expenses, orders, etc., and such announcements as were made were issued with a purpose. The functionaries were forbidden to keep with them maps, journals, and the like; all such documents were to be deposited where the governors-general or the Chambers could guard them well. It was the middle of the eighteenth century before regular news was sent from the East, and the medium, a newspaper, was suppressed in 1746 after running a year. The people at home had their curiosity satisfied, if at all, with respect only to the flora, fauna, and inhabitants of the East; this diverted them from more intimate topics. Thus almost to the end the financial situation remained unknown to the body of the Dutch people, and the Directors had free hand in their sinuous operations.[1]

The profits went largely to individuals, who, in their dual capacity of controllers and controlled, saw to it that investigation remained irrelevant and innocuous. Yet even they could not have so often adduced reasons of state to prevent examinations, if there had been no political services of the Company with which to weight the argument; there seems to be no doubt that the Company did confer tangible and concrete benefits upon the fatherland. The Netherlands were made the staple of the Indies trade, with all that implied of economic importance and opportunities for the increase of public wealth. In the first half of the eighteenth century the servants of the Company brought into the country each year 2,500,000 guilders in addition to the dividends of 1,300,000 guilders dispensed annually. That the spending of such sums or their investment in Holland conferred an economic benefit upon the nation at large seems never to have been seriously doubted;[2] all such services of the Company were highly rated. But there were relations between it and the state of a still more intimate character, for, during the seventeenth century, the latter was often directly assisted in its straits by the former. It was said that the state,

[1] Van Rees, II, 297–300.
[2] But cf. p. 460, below.

by way of revenue, received three times the gain from the Company that the participants had derived. The whole matter of the Company's finances is a troubled question, but if these general statements are accepted, it becomes clearer why the government was willing to extend for period upon period the monopolistic corporation whose collapse, with all it revealed, became then a disgrace even to the state itself.[1]

But before attempting any further summary of the Company's characteristics, and of its reflex influence upon the life of the metropolis, two topics should engage attention : first, that of the settlement at the Cape of Good Hope ; and, second, the history of the West India Company within its monopoly-area. The alignment of the West India Company beside the elder organization is of especial importance, for not only do the two show a strong similarity in essential points, but they also exhibit a significant diversity resulting from their disparate conditions. From a composite set of impressions taking in both organizations, a clearer idea can be formed of the politico-commercial corporation of the centuries under review.

THE CAPE SETTLEMENTS

In any topical treatment of the activities of the East India Company, what it did at the Cape would fall under its function as a colonizing agency. For there were in the Cape region none of those products from which it thought to derive large profit. In fact, for the dominant commercial purpose the Cape was worth nothing except as a way-station upon the predestined route of trade ; and the same may be said of Mauritius and other points in the Indian Ocean. For this purpose the Dutch appropriated the Cape region from the enfeebled Portuguese in 1652.[2] At first there was no intention of founding a settlement or colony ; it was simply a secure port of call that the needs of trade seemed to demand. But quarrels with the Hottentots, followed by a war (1659), left the Dutch the possessors of territory which they must needs defend against both natives and Europeans. In the early years of possession an attempt to raise grain and vines met with

---

[1] Van Rees, II, 286–287 ; De Reus, pp. 275–276.

[2] The Portuguese in reality never made any use of Table Bay; South Africa offered them no inducements. But after 1616 the Dutch put in at the Cape nearly every season. Theal, I, 13, 30, 40.

little success, for the labor supply was unsatisfactory and the Company's policy toward colonization was discouraging; later negro slaves were introduced in considerable numbers, and, as in the East, humanely treated. After thirty years the colony showed a total of 663 Dutch settlers; and the fact that of these 162 were children witnesses for climatic and other environmental conditions far more favorable than those of the Indies. Relatively little, however, in the way of settlement was projected or encouraged until the " second period " of attention to colonization. Then the opportunities offered to prospective settlers [1] chanced to coincide with the sudden increase of human material in Europe. After the Revocation of the Edict of Nantes in 1685, numerous Huguenots had fled to the Netherlands, and these, with certain Piedmontese peasants and vine-growers, seized the favorable chance to begin life over again; by 1689 nearly 200 French émigrants had settled at the Cape. In 1687, likewise, in response to an appeal to the Directors, many of the free burghers had been furnished with wives; and they and their families numbered nearly 600, in addition to 439 other Europeans, mainly Company employees. The success of the new cultivators was marked; by 1690 they could ship wine to the Netherlands. " If the Company had gone on in the same way the Cape would undoubtedly have become one of the most beautiful and rich of the Dutch possessions." [2]

But as soon as the Company had secured a good harborage for its ships, it ceased to have any interest in colonization, and speedily slipped back into the typical attitude of exploitation. Land was assigned more sparingly and the grants were to be separated from one another by a clear space of three miles. Then the Company began to enforce its rights as the only trading agency; the settlers were obliged not only to sell it their products at a low price, but to buy from it at rising prices. Since it was found profitable to barter with the natives toys and trinkets for cattle, the colonists were prohibited from this source of gain under pain of whipping and branding. Freedom from taxes, assured at first, gave way to high taxation; all goods had to be painfully transported to Cape Town to sell, hand over to the Company, or pay taxes upon. And

[1] P. 435, above.
[2] Van Rees, II, 261–262, 375–376 ; De Reus, pp. 282–283 ; Johnston, pp. 67–72 ; Theal, I, 82, 88 ff., 337 ff., 358 ff. For the population in 1672, 1691, etc., see Theal, I, 221, 335, 370, etc.

since this provision applied chiefly to grain, agriculture was confined within the narrow limits defined by the crudeness and slowness of means of communication.[1] Naturally the temptation to evade such restrictions soon led to a development of illicit traffic. That the people should have any share in the government lay in the plan of the Company as little here as elsewhere; gradually almost all the conditions necessary to the prosperity of a colony, even where these had once existed, were withdrawn, and the Cape ceased to attract any movement of colonization. Yet the Company, despite all its restrictive and oppressive measures, could not bring the local revenue to balance expenditure.[2]

The settlers already established in South Africa, who, with the absorption of the Huguenot strain, were prevailingly Dutch, could not endure the exactions of the Company and gradually "trekked" away from the coast. For a certain distance the officials followed and sought to prey upon them, but they gradually escaped surveillance of any kind. In 1788 the boundary of the colony was extended to the Great Fish River. It was during this movement toward the interior that the settlers came first into direct contact with the Bantus who were migrating from the north-east, and who from that time on have formed an important factor in the history of South Africa. The Company, naturally enough, provided no protection for the farmer-settlers (Boers); and owing to the relatively small numbers of the latter, in comparison with the Kaffir invaders, the native situation was a constant peril. The Dutch appear to have practiced miscegenation with little or no repugnance, both with the Hottentots of the Cape and the Bantus; the result being in the first case the so-called Bastaards, of whom there are at present some tens of thousands.[3] But the bulk of this race-mixture, which befits the tropical rather than the temperate colony, is probably assignable to the absence of European women; for the latter were not likely to come of their own accord to so uncertain and hazardous a frontier,

---

[1] Communication by sea was also very slow; up to 1750 a voyage from the Netherlands to South Africa which consumed less than 120 days was regarded as a fortunate one. Theal, I, 40.

[2] Van Rees, II, 375–378; Johnston, pp. 73, 75; Theal, I, 188, 276 ff., 322 ff.; II, 1 ff., 41–43, 71 ff., 121, 155, 231 ff., 284 ff., 299 ff., 332 ff.

[3] Keane (Africa, II, 187) reports 1000 Bastaards for German Southwest Africa, and says (II, 238) respecting the Cape Colony region that it contains not greatly over 180,000 Hottentots pure and mixed, but that of these the mongrels and half-castes form the immense majority. Cf. Schmidt, II, 233–234; Letourneau, Guerre, p. 59; Ratzel, Hist. of Mankind, II, 295.

and the Company was not willing, and, later, was unable to undertake the cost of their transportation. In actual results the Company had little to show when, in 1790, it became practically a financial ruin. There was at that time a population of 14,600 Europeans owning 17,000 slaves, but it was not ready to support its rulers. Indeed the Boers of the interior expelled their magistrates and proceeded to govern themselves in a rude fashion; and the people of the Cape, while they joined with the Company agents in an attempt to beat off the covetous British, were really half-hearted and quickly yielded. For in 1795, as a sequel of European upturnings and political readjustments, the Netherlands had come to be the enemy of England, and the latter had at once set out to seize the Cape. The West African stations were passed over as being relatively worthless since the abolition of the slave-trade. The Cape was taken with little effort, and, except for three years (1803–1806), when it was, by a short-lived agreement, restored to Holland, it has remained British ever since.[1]

THE BOERS AS A PRODUCT OF COMPANY RULE

The history of the burghers who had isolated themselves in the interior in consequence of Company oppression presents a sociological phenomenon in many respects unique. Here is a case, namely, of a strong European stock suffering degeneracy in a temperate colony. It may seem fanciful to refer phenomena so far subsequent in time to the policy of the long-extinct Company; but it is none the less true that the Boers of 1900 presented in no visionary sense the logical and finished product of the system imposed so strictly by the Company. They were the products of the isolation and attendant influences forced upon their ancestors as recalcitrants against the policy of greed and exploitation. For these progenitors had been led to plunge "ever more deeply into a rude and harsh natural environment, wherein they came into contact with a grade of civilization, or non-civilization, much cruder and coarser than their own. Like all frontier societies placed in similar conditions and almost wholly segregated from the outside world, they sunk in large degree to the level of their surroundings." And they did not then progress. "In 1880 the bulk

[1] Fortanier, pp. 69–70; Johnston, pp. 72, 74–80 ; Keltie, p. 79; Theal, II, 359; III, 1 ff., 96–97.

of the Boers of the Republics were, to most intents and purposes, of a pronounced seventeenth-century type of civilization; indeed, in many cases they were inferior in education, general culture, etc., to the Hollanders, and especially to the Huguenots, from whom they derived their descent." Thus they were primitive in their industrial organization, in their manners and customs, religion and morals, law and government.[1] Whatever the merits of the recent struggle between these backward peoples and England, it cannot but be admitted that they stood for the narrowness and ignorance of the past, even though their antagonist seemed often to be championing the ruthless aggressions of modern capitalism rather than the greater blessings of a later and higher stage of human culture. In any case the trend of the age is sure to sweep away what the Boer stood for, and the Boer himself, if he proves unadaptable. The conflict was one of civilizations, not races, except as they represented different ideals of civilization. Had the Cape been colonized upon liberal lines of policy, with a slowly advancing frontier closely connected with and so supported by a freely increasing settled population, there could have been no such isolation, with its attendant results of ignorance, bigotry, and general maladaptation to the altering conditions of life. In South Africa the Company had a chance to work out its colonial policy for over a century almost undisturbed; and it has left to the student of societies its human "results" sealed in an isolation virtually unpenetrated until the discovery of gold in the Transvaal toward the end of the nineteenth century.

It is no wonder, therefore, that under Dutch rule South Africa gave little promise of what it was to be. The old type of policy, continued through the eighteenth century, with brief respites that served only to increase uncertainty, allowed of no natural development. Details are scarcely necessary, after what has been said of colonization in Java and elsewhere, and in view of what is to come respecting the West India Company's policy in the New

---

[1] Keltie, Africa (chapter by the editor, on "Africa since 1895"), pp. 275–276. " Der Boer ist ein Stock-holländer, der um zwei Jahrhunderte hinter der Cultur zurückgeblieben ist, und einen Beigeschmack von Katterthum angenommen hat. . . . Herr von Weber rühmt ihm zwar nach, dass er die Bibel stets auf dem runden Tische liegen hat und sein Tagewerk mit einer Hymne beginnt, aber neben seiner Frömmigkeit trachtet er danach die Schwarzen mit Scorpionen zu züchtigen, und seine Bibelfestigkeit äussert sich meist in alt-testamentarischen Citaten über die Vertilgung der Heiden, d. h. der Kaffern." Philippson, p. 35.

World. One important consideration must, however, be noted, namely, that inasmuch as South Africa has later been proved colonizable, it is not possible to minimize the Company's responsibility in any degree, as was done in the case of Java, by reference to unfavorable natural conditions. Rather does the case of South Africa demonstrate the truth of what De Reus has been quoted as asserting,[1] that the experience of the Dutch proves nothing as to the possibility of colonization of such regions as Java. The Company's policy was a sufficient cause for ill-success in the Indies, as it was the sole cause for the same at the Cape.

The narrative turns now to the operations of the West India Company within the field of its monopoly, and may be the more condensed in that points of general similarity between the policies and enterprises of the two companies need little more than a recording allusion.

POLICY OF THE WEST INDIA COMPANY IN NEW NETHERLANDS

The younger Company, having been organized in the manner described,[2] began to survey its field in order to locate promising sources of gain and possible points of attack upon the arch-enemy whom it was designed to discomfit; it turned its attention first of all to the northern continent. The East India Company, with the purpose of rendering its monopoly perfectly secure, had sent out Hendrik Hudson (1607) to discover a north-west passage to the Orient; and this unfortunate explorer had opened up the waters that bear his name. Then, in 1614, the district of the New Netherlands, between the fortieth and fiftieth parallels of north latitude, had been granted to certain shipowners of Amsterdam and Hoorn for purposes of discovery and trade. In 1621 the newly formed West India Company took over the station that had been located upon Manhattan Island, as well as certain smaller ones farther up the Hudson River. The Director Minnewit purchased the island from the natives and founded New Amsterdam (1626).[3]

But the new Company, like that of the East Indies, was entirely given over to commerce, and proposed to make of the fur-trade an analogue to the spice-trade of the East. The early years were promising: in 1624 there were exported 27,000 guilders' worth of

---

[1] P. 436, note 2, above.　　[2] Pp. 412 ff., above.　　[3] Van Rees, II, 42-43, 332.

beaver-skins, and in 1627 twice that value. This, however, did not pay the costs of the settlement, and the Company began to seek some way to avoid such burden without losing hold of the fur-trade. It seemed clear that the colonists must be put in the way of self-support through agriculture, and the Company aimed to encompass this end while leaving the costs of colonization to individuals. In 1629 it was enacted that any shareholder who, within four years after announcing his purpose, should found a colony of fifty persons over fifteen years of age, bound to temporary service, should receive the title of *patroon* over the land thus settled. Such an estate might front for four miles on the coast, or two miles on a navigable river, with no limits set toward the interior; the land must be purchased from the natives, and was then to be governed by the patroon under the Company. Free colonists who were able to come to America could have all the land they could cultivate, and were to be immune from taxation for ten years.[1] These terms appear very favorable for colonization; but the trade policy and monopoly were yet to be attended to. Both the colonist and the patroon were forbidden to engage in the fur-trade, except where the Company had no station; and even in the latter case all pelts had to be brought to Fort Amsterdam and taxed a guilder apiece before they could be taken to the metropolis. All exported wares, likewise, had to be taken to the same point of departure and loaded upon Company ships. The patroons might trade along the coast from Florida to Newfoundland, but must at every turn put in at Fort Amsterdam and pay a duty of five per cent. As for the import trade, the Company reserved that for itself; it engaged to bring necessities from home at a reasonable price, and any patroons who wished to do this were obliged to pay large recognition-dues. The colonists must not trade in this way at all; nor could they weave or otherwise compete with home-production, on pain of penalties that went as far as banishment. In the colonists' trade with the natives and in the disposal of their own products they were consistently obstructed. It is plain that the Company was out for gain, and cared for colonization only as it was conceived to conduce to that end.[2]

[1] Van Rees, II, 332–333.

[2] Van Rees, II, 333–334. It is noteworthy that the West India Company, owing to the length and accessibility of the American coast-line, always suffered more from the competition of illicit traders than did the East India Company. Van Rees, II, 128; Roscher, pp. 273, note 3, 274.

Administration: the Patroons

The government of the new stations was a purely Company affair; there was no thought of civil freedom. A council, or Raad, composed of the director-general and five members chosen by him from the most important Company agents, wielded all power, legislative, executive, or judicial; the lives, property, honor, and freedom of the colonists were surrendered unconditionally into such partisan hands. The director-general, or governor, was really all-powerful, for the men he selected could not oppose his will. Despite this centralization of power, however, and the fact that the patroons were simply vassals, the latter had sufficient opportunity, in so unsettled a country, to dupe the Company and escape its oversight; for they had no schemes of colonization at heart, but intended merely to barter with the natives under the loop-hole conditions of the decree. Some even of the Directors of the Company had bought through agents the best places along the Delaware and Hudson rivers, an underhand policy which deterred better men from settlement or investment. The patroons got presently a great deal of the native trade and simply refused to fulfill the conditions attendant. But the Company resisted such an invasion of its monopoly and took measures, under the administration of the weak Van Twiller (1633–1637), which so incensed the patroons that they came to resist even the conditions with which they had formerly complied. Both parties appealed to the States-General.[1]

The actions of the patroons and the Company seem to have convinced the colonists that there was something in the fur-trade for them too; thus agriculture was deserted in favor of barter with the Indians. Colonization was neglected, even the patroons, in disgust, selling their rights back to the Company. Restrictions of industry and trade, and interference with the colonist's choice of a means of livelihood and with his power of disposal of the products of his own toil, led to general discouragement and impatience. In 1638, after fifteen years of Company rule, the New Netherlands showed few traces of cultivation. And what incensed the settlers the more was that, while the Company, intent on gain alone, could do nothing for agriculture in its own colony, it was importing oxen, horses, and sheep into the near-by settlements of the English. But about all that could be at once accomplished

[1] Van Rees, II, 335–337.

was the recall of Van Twiller;[1] any alteration of policy took more time, and it was not until 1640 that substantial changes were effected. Then the coast trade was made free from Newfoundland to Florida and the fur-monopoly was given up, the Company retaining as in 1629 the practical control of exchange with the mother-country. The States-General insisted also that the patroons should not be exclusively shareholders in the Company, but that any citizen of the land could make use of the same privileges under similar conditions. The rights of individuals to pass in their own ships between metropolis and colony were widened, and to any one who should take over five persons besides himself there were assured not only 200 acres of land, but even the right to hunt and fish. The prohibition upon the manufacture of fabrics and other articles was removed. It looked as if the Company had at last become a sponsor of colonization; it even agreed to provide free passage, tools, cattle, and the like, for a yearly payment of 100 guilders and 80 pounds of butter, the Company to take back the number of cattle given after six years; it even suggested advances to the settlers of money and necessities on credit. Results began at once to appear: first of all the Company agents, who had regularly gone home at the end of their service, took advantage of the new liberality and set about raising corn and tobacco, or building ships to trade with New England and Virginia; population likewise increased through immigration from New England caused by religious intolerance in Massachusetts. Everywhere land was cleared and farming begun.[2] But the Company had yielded only to need and the demands of the States-General, and as soon as the attention of the authorities was relaxed it returned stealthily to its old policy; it saw in every settler a competitor and proceeded against him as of old. The documents conferring rights to land were given under conditions of submission to exactions and dues; they were recalled under pretense of errors in form, and when returned were altered to suit the Company. Churches, schools, and courts of justice that had been promised were withheld; and a general colonization was effectually opposed, for none would venture to settle under such a system. Then the Company set to work to regain the export trade: the 1640 duties of ten per cent on pelts and five per cent on other wares were gradually

---

[1] Van Rees, II, 337–338.
[2] Van Rees, II, 339–341.

raised, the latter to sixteen per cent; and the regulations were strongly enforced under penalty of confiscation of ship and cargo.[1]

The cruelty and injustice to the Indians of Kieft, a bankrupt and evil man who succeeded Van Twiller, brought on a destructive war from 1641 to 1645, wherein the farmers' establishments were ruined and the population reduced from 3000 to 1000. There resulted a bitter strife between the governor and his council, upon whom he had to depend for aid, but whom he treacherously dismissed when trouble seemed to be over. English soldiers were hired to defend the colonists and were to be paid by Kieft through the imposition of a tax on beer. In 1645 the government called the Company to account and found its condition miserable; for, despite its oppressive policy, it had suffered heavy losses. The debit-balance of the period 1626 to 1645 was 500,000 guilders. It was a question whether the New Netherlands should not be given up; but a further effort was decided upon. Trade was opened generally to private persons, and colonization was to be encouraged; Stuyvesant, a more intelligent and energetic man, was sent out as director-general. But the latter, being of extreme obstinacy, and opposed to civil freedom in principle, began by simply repeating in slightly different form the oppressive measures of his predecessors. Representations to the States-General again secured (1652) better conditions for the colony, and, as usual, the removal of pressure was followed by a relatively large natural inflow of population. Manufactories started up; in 1659 trade with France, Spain, Italy, and the Caribbean islands was made free, though, as a survival of the old monopoly policy, beaver-skins had to be taken direct to Amsterdam.[2]

BELATED REFORM

Prosperity redoubled the desire of the colonists for autonomy; they wished, as the price of their endurance in creating a colony from which the metropolis derived great benefit, to possess the same rights as their fellows who stayed at home. Seizing an occasion when Stuyvesant needed support in war, they presented a memorandum of demands and comments which shows the whole story of their grievances. They asserted that it was not right that the people's lives, property, and all the rest should be in the power

[1] Van Rees, II, 341–343.   [2] Van Rees, II, 344–353.

of one man or several who would act with caprice or with little understanding; they complained that the Company left them without protection from their enemies; they demanded that each locality should have its own local government; they asserted that, since obsolete laws and enactments were not expunged, they knew neither their own rights nor duties; and they charged the colonial government with caprice and favoritism in its land grants. Despite the ire of Stuyvesant, who declared these representations to be seditious, there resulted some betterment from their publication.[1]

But that which infused a belated haste into reforms was the imminence of the English, who had moved down the Connecticut River, driving the Dutch outposts before them, and were already strong on Long Island. When it dawned at last upon the Dutch government that the English colonists were eager to seize Dutch territory, and that the British government was a party to their endeavors, nothing was omitted which might incite the settlement of defenders. The Directors saw that a mistake had been made, and that their possessions with few inhabitants lay open to encroachment. Huguenots, Waldenses, and Germans, who were present at this time in great numbers in Holland, were shipped over by hundreds; religious freedom became the policy. The population of the New Amsterdam region increased under Stuyvesant (1647–1664) from 2000 to 10,000.

But a change of heart at the eleventh hour, after fifty years of selfish neglect, was in this case unavailing. The Connecticut colony was laying a strong hold upon Long Island when, in 1664, the English king, Charles II, gave the whole of the New Netherlands to his brother, the Duke of York. Stuyvesant was unable to protect Long Island even against the Connecticut colony, and when the duke had sent without delay four ships-of-war to assume possession of New Amsterdam, there was no defense; it was given over under a treaty.[2]

Such, in brief, are the salient features of the Company colonization in the New Netherlands. Analogies with the colonization of Java and South Africa under the East India Company crop out at every turn; they display the same policy based upon the same

---

[1] Van Rees, II, 354–355. It was during the administration of Stuyvesant (1655) that the Dutch took possession of the colony of New Sweden. For an account of this colony, see Acrelius and Campanius.

[2] Van Rees, II, 355–357.

motives, in a slightly different setting. The present case demonstrates, says Van Rees,[1] that the Dutch lacked neither the will nor the skill to found colonies. Religious or political persecution was not necessary to drive them to it; as soon as it was known that labor and capital might make great gain across the ocean, many were ready to go. The less rich were content to settle if they received free passage and reasonable assistance in overcoming the early obstacles; the wealthy were ready to invest if they were assured the rights they had at home. But the Company was not in a state of mind to grant either of these essentials. Whether this argumentation absolves the Dutch from the charge of being unable to colonize successfully, may be susceptible of doubt; certainly the rank and file were bent on "great gain" as the most successful colonizing peoples have not been. It is doubtful if they could ever have withstood the racial elements that surrounded them and have founded a new Dutch nation. But it is at least true that, both here and in Africa and in Brazil, the Dutch labored under an incubus, in the shape of the two India Companies, with which few other colonizing peoples have had to contend.

The Company in Brazil and Surinam

The case of the Dutch in Brazil provides almost a surfeit of demonstration along this line. Since, also, the story of their attempted settlement in that country has been told already, from the standpoint of the Portuguese defenders,[2] it may be dismissed in a few words, the only attempt being to fit this exhibition of Company policy in with the rest of its class.

One of the strong motives, if not the strongest, in the founding of the West India Company had been to do damage to the king of Spain; and since he was, from 1580 to 1640, king also of Portugal, the Portuguese colonies were as desirable points of attack as any others. During the first years of its existence the Company had made an attempt to get footing upon the coast of Brazil; and its activities were encouraged in 1629 by the capture of the Spanish silver fleet. In 1636 the determination to conquer Brazil was so strong that the Count of Nassau-Siegen, Joan Maurits, was sent for its prosecution. His successes have been elsewhere noted; by 1640 the West India Company held the best six provinces of Brazil,

---

[1] II, 357–358.   [2] Pp. 146 ff., above.

extending from Sergipe in the south to Ceará in the north, Recife (Pernambuco) being the seat of its government and commerce.[1] The need of colonists at once appeared, and the usual policy of opening up trade under dues to the Company, and under reservation of certain profitable articles, was evolved. As noted above, Dutch and Brazilians could make one voyage per year, paying ten per cent on European and thirty per cent on American wares, but were to let the trade in slaves, Brazil-wood, and war articles severely alone. The Count of Nassau established order and discipline and attended to school-facilities and the like. Brazil began to be prosperous; the revenues, chiefly from a thirty per cent tax on the product of the sugar-mills, paid nearly all the expenses of the war.

But this could not long satisfy the Company. Nassau's religious tolerance, in consequence of which numerous Jews had flocked to Brazil, was not to the taste of the Directors, and they began to throw obstacles before him. The prices of the necessities of life were kept high; the military force of about 6000, employed mainly in garrison-duty, was reduced, and the pay and even the food-supplies for the army were held back. In a country whose cultivators had been largely driven away and which was dependent upon supplies from Europe, the results of this exhibition of cramping avarice were fatal. Nassau returned discouraged to the Netherlands in 1644; then the troops, no longer restrained by his presence, fell to plundering and abusing the Portuguese, who had come to regard Nassau as their protector, with the result of a revolution and the loss of the colony, as detailed in a former chapter.[2]

In the same year that the Dutch lost the New Netherlands, they lost also Cayenne to the French, after holding it since 1656; but in 1667 this was made up for by the Zeelanders' conquest of the English province of Surinam. In the administration of this new possession the Dutch seem to have tried to keep in mind the lessons they had just been obliged to learn. But naturally conditions were far less favorable here than in Java or the New Netherlands, and reversions to the old policy were sure to occur.

In 1682 the West India Company took over Surinam from Zeeland, paying for its rights the sum of 260,000 guilders. To attract

[1] Van Rees, II, 180–182; Watson, II, 1–2, 21, 28–29.
[2] Van Rees, II, 182, 186–190; Watson, II, 28–35, 43, 46–48, 74–75, 118; Zimmermann, pp. 142–152.

colonists the Company granted generous terms on the analogy of those temporarily and successfully employed elsewhere; taxes and dues were to be kept down in the early years, free trade encouraged, and rights similar to those enjoyed under the English were decreed. But the Company recoiled before the costs attendant upon this system, and had, by 1683, sold two-thirds of its rights to the city of Amsterdam and one Cornelis van Aerssen. The new controlling body was called the Chartered Society of Surinam, and Van Aerssen became governor. He was an able, energetic, and good man, and his policy of stimulating emigration was effective in promoting the settlement especially of foreigners temporarily located as religious refugees in the Netherlands. Plantations speedily increased in number from 50 to 200. The special skill of the Dutch in dealing with wet and swampy regions stood them in satisfactory stead, and the sugar-plantations and mills began to put out a good product.[1] But the new Society, whatever its intentions, soon fell heir to the reputation of Dutch colonial governments, and was believed to be working for the maximum income. The citizens thought they had too little share in governing themselves, and they knew they were insufficiently protected. In 1712, when the French undertook to reduce Surinam, the burghers were obliged to buy them off at a cost of 700,000 guilders, which the Society refused to refund. It also afforded little protection against escaped slaves, the so-called bush-negroes, who fell upon their old masters at every opportunity; and the peace concluded with these outlaws in 1761–1762 was regarded as ineffective, besides being dishonorable.

All this might have been endured if the conditions of production had remained favorable. In the tropical region, here as elsewhere, the indispensable factor in production was the acclimatized laborer, the negro. There was no opposition to slavery as a system; in fact the complaint was that there were not enough slaves.[2] The West India Company had reserved the slave-trade for itself, agreeing to supply enough negroes — at least 2500 yearly. But the Company could not renounce the old policy of raising prices by limiting the supply, and in some of the years imported no slaves at all; and when, later, the captured African posts had been

---

[1] Van Rees, II, 361–367; Fermin, I, 3 ff. For a brief treatment of the Dutch in Guiana, see Leroy-Beaulieu, I, 299–302.

[2] Van Rees, II, 319–324. "On the whole, colonization is not possible in Surinam with Europeans alone, in the absence of an intermediate negro population." Hostmann, I, 257.

lost,[1] it was unable to keep its word if it had so willed. Thus the only labor force was lacking, although the prevalence of slavery injured the position of the free laborer. In addition to this trouble with labor, the absenteeism of proprietors, in the latter half of the eighteenth century, began to produce its regular effects. Bad local management then induced the owners to sell; debts increased, and misery resulted in the colony.[2] While Surinam was at times rated as superior to the East Indies, it steadily declined under the stock policy of shortsighted greed and exploitation so characteristic of tropical establishments. Its history came to afford only another variation upon the stock destiny of the Dutch colony.[3]

ASPECTS OF THE CHARTERED COMPANY

The general aspects of the chartered company, as they appeared in the Netherlands and in the over-sea possessions, tempt one to digression from the main subject of colonization. Considered, however, as expedients for the furthering of colonial enterprise, the story of the companies affords reason for several broad observations upon a phase of colonial endeavor.

In a country whose people were averse in principle to monopoly, there arose in these companies one of the most striking cases of monopoly in history. And this development was, so far as can be seen, inevitable in the conditions of the age. For, first, there appeared in the decades succeeding the Discoveries a need of accumulation and concentration of capital such as had never before been experienced. This necessity led, in the case of Spain and Portugal, to a monopoly lodged in the hands of the only master of

---

[1] Cf. p. 127, above: 15,000 slaves brought an annual profit to the Company of 2,000,-000 guilders; in the latter half of the eighteenth century the yearly demand called for about 8000 slaves. Van Rees, II, 325. Fermin (pp. 120 ff.) says that in 1762 there were 425 plantations in all in Surinam, and that each of these contained at least 180 slaves. The whole number of blacks, including escaped slaves (*marrons*), was about 109,500. Cf. chaps. xi ff. Hostmann discusses the question of emancipation in a rather impassioned manner. He treats of the details of the ordering of the slave's existence (I, 212 ff.), of the missions (I, 197 ff.); discusses the bush-negroes quite at length (I, 240 ff.); and gives a list of the chief negro stocks imported into Surinam (II, 247 ff.).

[2] On climatic and vital (and moral) conditions, see Fermin, chap. iii, and especially Hostmann, II, 228, and chap. xii. Both Fermin and Hostmann were physicians. On the government, see Fermin, pp. 30 ff.; Hostmann, II, 433. Of the policy of confining production to one staple crop (sugar) Hostmann has many bitter criticisms (II, 255; chap. xiii). For a general treatment, see Zimmermann, V, 148–168, 267–286.

[3] Van Rees, II, 368–375; cf. pp. 314–324.

sufficient capital, the king. But in the Netherlands there was none such. Hence the function of financing the new and hazardous ventures descended upon individual initiative, and could be discharged only through some form, at first local, of incorporation of capital. But the competition of these local capitals which speedily ensued, enforced a larger consolidation, and finally, as a means of protection to those who were discharging what was conceived to be a weighty public and patriotic function, a grant of absolute monopoly. There was no other expedient at hand, and theories and prejudices bent before inexorable concrete fact. That such monopoly was now used in a way ill-befitting, lay also in the conditions of the time, as well as in human nature. For by the very constitution of the companies there could be but one object before them, and that was present gain; and because of the height of popular expectation, the need of self-justification in a new and suspected enterprise required that profits must be large. All the urge and stress of the situation tended in this direction; returns must be immediate and high, and so policies in any case quick-acting, if the investing participants were to be satisfied. The latter were in the organization, not for theoretical or humanitarian aims, not for the benefit of posterity or the heathen, but for material return. Even the patriotic desire to injure Spain was not without its background of visions of treasure-ships and of seas free to trade. Naturally the situation was too much for the as yet unformulated ethics of corporate management, and there ensued the often crude and sometimes singularly modern spectacle of wholesale rascality and general corruption.

If such a system existed in the metropolis, nothing more enlightened could be expected in the distant possessions. The companies could not pursue farsighted policies, as a state of modern times is thought to do, awaiting slowly-maturing results, or even renouncing actual returns in the pursuit of cosmopolitan, not to say cosmic, ends. And so the companies' history shows little attempt to better the natives, to colonize in the stricter sense — in a word, to lay strong foundations for future political, social, or even commercial structures. They not only neglected such matters, but, under the increasing stress of yielding constant and high dividends while confronting and somehow solving problems in transportation, administration, race-contact, and the like, but newly presented to man (and many of them still unresolved), they fell back upon expedients hurtful to the ruled as well as destructive of the permanency of empire. Thus it came about that they challenged the well-known comment of Adam Smith, that " of all the expedients that can well be contrived to stunt the natural growth of a new colony, that of an exclusive company, is undoubtedly the most effectual." [1] This author, writing at a time slightly preceding the total collapse of the East India Company, clearly perceives the inconsistency of its double rôle of ruler and merchant. " It is in the interest of the East India Company, considered as sovereigns, that the European goods which are carried to the Indian dominions, should be sold there as cheap as possible ; and that the Indian goods which are brought from thence, should bring there as good a price, or should be sold there as dear as possible. But the reverse of this is their interest as merchants. As sovereigns, their interest is exactly the same with that of the country which they govern. As merchants, their interest is directly opposite to that interest." He then goes on to show how the administration in India must pursue the same ends as the direction in Europe, and how it is vain to prohibit the functionaries from trading on their own account. " The regulations . . . which have been sent out from Europe, though they have been frequently weak, have upon most occasions been well-meaning. More intelligence, and perhaps less good meaning, has sometimes appeared . . [in] those established by the servants in India. It is a very singular government in which every member of the administration wishes to get out of the country, and consequently to have done with the government as soon as he can, and to whose interest, the day after he has left it and carried his whole fortune with him, it is perfectly indifferent though the whole country was swallowed up by an earthquake." [2]

INFLUENCE OF DUTCH COLONIZATION

These reflections may reveal the character of the companies in its broader and most general lines. It is clear that the trade-motive was the dominant and almost the sole consideration, the function of government being exercised as an " appendix " [3] to the prime activity of commercial enterprise. Here again, then, is found the

[1] Book IV, chap. vii, part ii (II, 77 of Cannan's ed.) ; cf. De Reus, pp. 292–310.

[2] Book IV, chap. vii, part iii (II, 137, 139–140, of Cannan's ed.).

[3] Smith, Book IV, chap. vii, part iii (II, 136 of Cannan's ed.). " Als souverein, niet als koopman, is de Compagnie te kort gekomen." R. Fruin, " Nederlands Rechten en Verplichtingen ten opzichte van Indie." De Gids, 1865, II, 45.

isolation of the motive of material self-interest, as in the case of the Phœnicians of old. But the effects are certainly not to be compared with those wrought by the ancients. There are several changed factors in the situation which preclude the attainment of like results. It will be recalled[1] that the chief point of difference between the colonial enterprises preceding the Discoveries period and those subsequent to it, was that the former were not called upon to meet any of the conditions of tropical colonization, while the latter encountered new and strange environmental exigencies at every turn. There appeared not alone the need of acclimatization, and its attendant evils, but also the baffling question of relationship with strange, uncongenial, and largely Mohammedan native races. The equation was set in odd and difficult terms and with a number of unknown quantities; it was no longer one Mediterranean people dealing with another. The possibilities of such a situation in engendering mutual misunderstanding, contempt, and hostility, and so in undermining that attitude of tolerance which conduces to the growth of trade-relations, need no development in this place. Yet, even so, it is probable that, if the Dutch had confined themselves to exchange and had exhibited a tithe of the adaptability of the Phœnicians and their successors, they might have left some such record of culture-dissemination as that of the Mediterranean merchants and colonists. Where they were unable to conquer, they applied their undoubted business sagacity with results more favorable to the spread of civilization than in their immediate domain. That the people of the East were, after all, receptive of the germs of a higher culture as implanted in their economic life is proved by the widespread peaceful influence of the Chinese, the "Phœnicians of the East," throughout what became Netherlands-India. But, although the idea of the Dutch was gain pure and simple, as has been seen, the methods which they employed were those of force; in this respect they followed the Portuguese, whose notorious ill-success where conquest and conversion were added to the motive of trade-exploitation has furnished the subject of previous pages. And when the consideration is included that the Malays were a tropical people, with all that that means of divergence from the European races upon which the ancients exerted influence, the comparative inefficiency of the trade-motive as a civilizing factor in the East becomes immediately explicable.

[1] Cf. pp. 74 ff., above.

Influence of the Companies upon the Metropolis

One further consideration respecting the companies remains: their reflex influence upon the life of the metropolis; and the first and main reflection to be made is an obvious one. By the introduction into the life of the nation of a large element of uncertainty and hazard, their tendency was to divert the economic habitudes of the country into forms less solid and sure. The speculation to which they gave an unheard-of impetus, and the corruption into which Directors and government fell, could not but react unfavorably upon industry of all kinds, and make for inefficiency where preceding conditions had called for courage, initiative, skill, and strength. Even maritime enterprise was on the wane; it was too far to the Indies and the voyage demanded too much capital for the individual to undertake it. Freight-carrying along the coast of Europe gave quicker returns and appeared more profitable; this was the reaction after the fevered excitement of earlier years. The case is, *mutatis mutandis*, that of the Portuguese and Spaniards over again, except that it is the more clearly marked because the Dutch were so far superior to their predecessors in industry and trade, and in the qualities that lay behind them. Wealth became unequally divided; and where there had been practically no dependent class there was nurtured up a horde of hangers-on of the wealthy. Every one who had power used it ruthlessly, and internal dissension, political and industrial, was already common after 1650. In other words, there ensued upon the activity of the companies a significant change for the worse in the economic and moral character of the nation.[1]

How far the persistence of the companies was effective in retarding consolidation of the provinces and government it may be hard to say, but it certainly contributed to foster local attachments which were detrimental to national development. One writer asserts that "before 1795 the Netherlander knew no father-land, but merely a father-city."[2] If this is the case, and if it took the French Revolution to make over the Netherlands from a city-economy into a modern state, certainly the companies can be said to

---

[1] Cf. Pringsheim, pp. 59–70; Van Rees, II, 213–214.

[2] Blok, Eene hollandsche stad in de middeleeuwen, 1883; quoted in Pringsheim, p. 2, note 5.

have failed after what looked like a splendid start toward promoting national unification.[1]

But the final ills that reduced the Netherlands from a position of preëminence were directly connected with the attempts of the companies, especially that of the East Indies, to maintain their exclusive monopolies. The great period of Dutch commercial power came early in the seventeenth century; then began the attacks of rivals, especially England, whose Navigation Acts, combined with the operations of Colbert (1664 and 1667), struck a blow from which, under the conditions indicated, there was only partial and intermittent recovery. For the old monopoly ideas were not abandoned in the face of competition, and so the process of sinking into the commercial background went on apace. Had the colonial raw products entered the Netherlands in any sufficiency, the Dutch industries could have better weathered the rising competition; but as it was, the height of prices and of taxes made it impossible for them to keep their place in the world. The India trade was really of inferior importance, never being over 11,000,000 guilders' worth of importation per year; and the total export of Holland to the West Indies for the period 1623 to 1636 was worth somewhat less than 7,000,000 guilders. But the trade of the Indies was a sort of fetich and the monopoly principle a dogma; and so the Dutch went on in the now traditional system until war with England in 1780 completed their humiliation, and rendered the company-system moribund.[2]

COLLAPSE OF THE MONOPOLY

Thus is added yet another case to those which demonstrate the inevitable outcome of the monopoly system. The closer the monopoly, and the more successful it is in securing the elevation of prices for which it aims, the greater is the temptation to its infringement; but because of the waste and costliness of the system, such infringement means ruin. Thus, toward the end of the

[1] Cf. Pringsheim, pp. 2–9; De Reus, p. 292. "The condition of this Company in India was the thermometer of the political life of the Netherlands, exactly as this political life can be regarded as the cause of the conditions of the Company with which it kept pace." De Reus, p. 310. Leroy-Beaulieu (I, 79) remarks: "Ce n'est jamais impunément qu'un peuple commet des fautes nombreuses et persistantes dans une des branches principales de son activité: toute la vie économique et politique d'une nation s'en ressent à la longue."

[2] Pringsheim, pp. 11–15, 36–39; De Reus, pp. 290–293.

eighteenth century, the course of the Dutch as a colonial power seems to have been run. That they did not lose all their external possessions shortly thereafter, and relapse into the status of Portugal and Spain after their monopolies were broken, was due in part to the real superiority of their economic and social organization over that of the Peninsular countries, and also to the newer and larger outlook upon the relations of nations which was gradually replacing the narrow purview of earlier centuries. The world was opening up under the influence of developed means of communication, and other broadening factors; and the old fetich of monopoly was being shattered thereby, and through the growing prevalence of ideals reflecting the changed material conditions.

But the commercial and maritime preëminence of the Dutch was as irrevocably gone as was that of their predecessors. It remained for them to try in what was left of their colonial empire to work out some system that should be in closer harmony with the spirit of modern times. Such a system became then as inevitable in its time as the monopoly régime had been in its own day and generation, although the new long retained traces of derivative relationship with the old.

CHAPTER XII

DUTCH COLONIZATION IN THE NINETEENTH CENTURY

The attempts of commissions to probe into the abuses of the East India Company during the last years of its existence met such opposition as totally to defeat their purpose. The charter's last extension came to an end on December 31, 1798; and in the following year there was formed a Council of the Asiatic Possessions, responsible to the government of the now Batavian Republic. But upon the accession of the Napoleonic dynasty (1806) what was left of the Eastern possessions was practically turned over to a local autocrat in the person of Governor-General Daendels. During the period of French predominance, as has been seen, certain parts only of the Dutch possessions resisted the encroaching English, and presently Java alone remained.[1] It is chiefly with this island that the colonial activity of the Dutch in the last century was concerned.

REORGANIZATION : DAENDELS

The period from 1807 to 1830 engages attention chiefly as one of reaction away from the company-system, followed by a gradual resumption, in changed form, of what was essentially the old exploitation based upon the dominant consideration of commercial gain. This troubled period would be of less importance to the subject were it not that subsequent counter-movements tended to return in some degree to the theories and methods essayed at this time. But it is necessary to realize, first of all, that in a vexed and hurried period of reorganization attention must still be pre-occupied with the same subjects which engaged the Company to the exclusion of all others, namely, commerce and administration. The spirit of the reaction against Company-policy lies in the fact that emphasis was shifted from one of these purposes to the other, so that whereas a company of individuals had been pursuing gain and keeping up a semblance of government, a state, partly under

[1] P. 439, above; cf. Fortanier, pp. 40–46, 65–70.

the stress of need of defense, now set about the reorganization of government while striving still to gather revenue to support its own existence and to favor the life of trade. At first the Dutch state was substituted for the Company, then for five years (1811–1816) the island was ruled as a dependency of British India, and finally (1816–1830), "during the first period of the Dutch restoration, Java was managed on a mixed system in which the traditional methods of the East India Company were employed to exploit it for the benefit of the crown.[1] This explains why the narrative of Dutch colonial policy during the period preceding 1830 is so largely one of administrative changes and development, however much these were based upon commercial and fiscal considerations. Other aims than these were excluded, not only because necessity demanded concentration upon immediately vital issues, but also because the frame of mind of the Dutch still for decades led them to hold that "colonies exist for the mother-country, and not the mother-country for the colonies."[2]

The first move toward administrative betterment was the dispatch of Daendels by King Louis, who had dissolved the Council of the Asiatic Possessions, substituting a minister of his own, and thus centralizing the whole matter of colonial administration. Daendels was no colonial expert, but a man of energy and independence of mind, who had seen military and political service under the French in the Netherlands; he was bound by no traditions, and, because of the belated and defective character of his instructions, was practically uncontrolled. His methods were direct and were designed for the securing of immediate results; he "saw many things going wrong, and set about in a rough-and-ready fashion to right them."[3]

The first and most evident evil was the inefficiency and corruption of the colonial service. Both men and methods were of poor quality; there was no intelligent division of function, nor was there coöperation between officers and departments. Into this

[1] Day, p. 128.

[2] From a State Commission's report of 1803, quoted in Pierson, p. 8. Day (pp. 129–146) gives a number of carefully written pages to the analysis of the opinions of the period respecting reform and the lines upon which it should be pursued. He summarizes the charter of 1803, and assigns it great weight in the history of Java in that "it outlines with substantial correctness the Dutch policy and the ideals of the Dutch government in the following period, while its accompanying report gives an insight into the reasons that determined the decisions" (p. 146).

[3] Day, pp. 148–149.

chaos Daendels introduced system and centralization, considerably extending the power of the governor-general through his prefects. Payments and promotions were so altered as to make the colonial career a field for an honest man; and the corrupt were resolutely pursued. Daendels had no fleet, and his army was treacherous; but although he could do little to better the former, he whipped the latter into a passable shape. He also made of Batavia a relatively wholesome place for Europeans, and developed, too often regardless of the means employed, facilities for internal communication.[1] The courts and justice were placed upon a trustworthy footing for the first time. Upon the native organization likewise the influence of Daendels was strongly exerted, though with less beneficent result. "Regents were henceforth to hold the position, not of protected rulers, but of government officials, bearing the honorable title of 'the king's servants'; they were to stand no longer in the relations of contract with the government but subject to it." The will was present to curb their oppression of the people, but seems not to have been realized. As for the fiscal system, it went back to the traditional expedient of contingents, for Daendels saw no practicability in a system of taxation; he was advanced in many of his measures, but in the most vital ones touching production, he could do little better than persist in the controlling and forcing system. Again, though he protected the natives against the Dutch, he laid upon the regents many heavy burdens which were then shifted over upon the people he tried to aid; the latter were overwhelmed with forced services and were miserable. Daendels gained the name of "the tyrant of the East"; his system was described as "the most vigorous attempt ever made, at least in Dutch India, to get from a people by force and by forced labor all that can be demanded not alone for commerce but for public works, for a strong defense, for ample payment of officials, and for the unhampered establishment of all departments and branches of administration."[2] Nevertheless, in view of the unsettled times and the absence of, as well as the danger to carriers of the revenue-bringing products, Daendels was always in straits financially, while facing the menace of a British attack which he saw to be inevitable. Thus he resorted to loans and confiscations, depreciation of the currency, sale of government rights in land, and the like, and was

[1] Encycl. Ned. Ind., arts. "Daendels," "Wegen."
[2] Muntinghe, in Day, p. 160.

naturally none too tender toward the natives when it came to raising revenue.

"He shows throughout the brief period of his rule the methods of a politician rather than of a statesman, making his decisions suit the needs of the moment with little regard for the future." Thus, though he really reorganized the administration, was conscious of abuses and inclined to work for their rectification where heavy necessity did not oblige him to renounce wise and farsighted plans, yet he reverted in many cases toward the old exploitation policy of the Company, in some cases even exaggerating it, and finally left the island, so far as economic and social status go, pretty much as he found it.[1] His administration possesses for our subject, then, the importance of an unsuccessful attempt to break with the past; and the details of these years that might be given are of less significance inasmuch as they do not contribute in any constructive way to the evolution of later stages of colonial theory and policy.

BRITISH DOMINANCE: RAFFLES

The first sharp break with the past was made under British dominance through the undaunted energy and persistence of Stamford Raffles.[2] Daendels had been the object of much complaint to Napoleon and had asked for and finally obtained honorable release from his post in 1811. Later in the same year the British conquest of the island took place with ridiculous ease,[3] and Raffles became lieutenant-governor; this position conferred virtually absolute power, for although he was nominally subordinate to the governor-general in Calcutta, in practice he was a local autocrat. He himself was the government, and his period of rule was marked by varied expressions of his personality. This was in general an intelligent and forceful one, and his personal qualities were supported by an extended experience and by scientific and linguistic attainments of a high order. What makes him of such marked significance as a factor in the destiny of Java was rather the projection of this personality than the definite results

[1] For the administration of Daendels, see Day, pp. 148–163; cf. Fortanier, pp. 71–76.

[2] On Raffles's administration, see Pierson, chap. i; Day, chap. v; cf. Fortanier, pp. 77–88; Leroy-Beaulieu, I, 277–278.

[3] Cf. Encycl. Ned. Ind., arts. "Verdediging," "Verovering van Java door de Engelschen."

for which he was responsible. " His efforts should be judged . . . by direction as well as distance. Raffles was great, not in the results which he achieved, but in the ideals that he established, which have been a power in all later reforms. He tried to do alone, in a few years, and with the uncertainty of his position constantly before him, what generations of later workers have accomplished." It was doubtless his eagerness to see these reforms through before the restoration of the island to the Dutch, that led him into a course somewhat headlong, with results sometimes bearing the marks of his want of time for mature deliberation. " Viewed in the light of the difficulties under which he worked, the faults of Raffles's career as Lieutenant-Governor grow smaller, and his failure appears only as a deferred success." [1]

RAFFLES'S REVENUE SYSTEM

The most significant change upon which Raffles was bent was an alteration of the government's fiscal policy toward the natives. He felt that there must be public loss through the delivery of produce, for it entailed unavoidable waste and expense, and yet there was no certainty of sale ; he saw that the revenue must suffer during its passage through a number of intermediate hands, just because it was likely to produce the further evil of irregularity and corruption ; and he was concerned not only that there was no security for the people against the oppression of the regents, but that incitement to industry must be absent. Hence he planned the establishment of perfect freedom in cultivation and trade, — this to entail the abolition of forced deliveries at inadequate rates, and of feudal services ; the assumption by the government of the superintendence of lands together with their revenues and rents, — this to do away with the intervention of the regents who should be restricted to public duties ; and the renting out of such lands in large or small parcels on moderate-term leases. The many chances for petty oppression which occurred along the tortuous ways of native procedure in these matters were to disappear under the European system of dues proportioned to the rental value of the lands. Moreover, indirect taxation was to be reformed in the interest of free industry and trade ; internal tolls were to be abolished, customs duties regulated by the government, and the salt tax no longer farmed out. The " whole process of assessment and collection was

[1] Day, pp. 169, 170.

to be brought under the control of European ideas of honesty, economy, and justice,"[1] this being effected by direct contact of the government, to the exclusion of more or less independent native officials, with the people.

" The central part of Raffles's system was the land-tax, which was to absorb all the multiform dues and services paid by the people under native rule, and was to be, as it has been in British India, the mainstay of the government treasury."[2] Into the details of the collection of this tax it is not necessary to go. Its application was a failure, not only because it had certain faults that only experience could mend, but because of Raffles's own limitations in the matter of time and resources. Geographical and ethnological conditions were insufficiently known, and any logical application of the system was locally thwarted by the emergence of numberless obstacles, small though some of them may seem to have been. The tax-collectors, confused before the difficulties of the new system, fell back upon the principle that it is better to get, in any case, and presently the inequities of the old régime were again in almost full swing. And the whole situation was perturbed inasmuch as Raffles could not cut loose absolutely from the old practices, such as the contingents, until the tax had begun to yield. This did not take place in any degree sufficient to cover expenditures. Hence with all his good intent Raffles really contributed to make " the reversion to the Company's policy much more easy and natural in the time of the culture system by preserving the most important cultures to that time."[3]

Here is where the British governor was forced, in a sense, to a better appreciation of the Company's situation, although the conditions he faced were largely created by the misbehavior of the Company in its straits. Raffles had no clamoring shareholders to satisfy, and yet, if the natives were to be treated rightly, he could not balance his budget. How the Javanese must have been exploited before and after his time may be left to the imagination.

Raffles's Administrative System

The fiscal phase of Raffles's activity may be taken to correspond to the commercial preoccupations of the Company; but the Englishman also governed, as the Company did not, and mainly in

---

[1] Day, p. 181. [2] Id., p. 174. [3] Id., p. 190.

an enlightened and beneficent manner. He proceeded directly to the strengthening of the position of European officials, who were, of course, largely Netherlanders ; he nearly doubled the number of residents, and informed them so well as to their powers and duties that his instructions were retained entire after the Dutch restoration. Among the first of the prescribed duties was the making of periodic journeys and reports ; at last the residents were to know their districts. Again, Raffles greatly bettered the administration of justice, establishing " the principles upon which the judicial relations of the natives were afterward developed." [1] With his attempted reorganization of the native government Raffles was decades in advance of his time, and succeeded only in leaving a series of vigorous and pregnant suggestions for later reflection and action. Briefly speaking, he meant to relieve the regents [2] of functions and privileges which had been oppressively employed, making them government officials with carefully defined powers and duties. They were to profit in a material way by reason of such renunciation, but through a definite grant or salary ; they were no longer to help themselves from the property of the people. But here again resources to carry the new system failed ; native officials soon renewed their relations with the cultivators, and the old exactions continued as before. Thus it was likewise in the less sweeping aspects of Raffles's reorganization.

If the English governor had had the maximum of extraneous aids in his work, and could have possessed a secure tenure of several times five years, it is yet entirely unlikely that posterity would have been robbed of the privilege of finally realizing some of his advanced ideas. Under such favoring circumstances he might, indeed, have made some impression upon the Company system, with but two centuries of time and a correspondingly and relatively slight inertia behind it ; but the attempt vitally to alter the native organization, especially in the matter of its traditional habitudes, its *mores*, given both time and other resources, rests yet upon a forlorn hope. It is sanguine to expect to modify the industrial organization except over a long period; and to look for anything of the kind in the secondary social forms within a brief five years is rather ridiculous than visionary. If Raffles knew as much of the East as he is given

---

[1] Day, p. 195; Encycl. Ned. Ind., art. " Rechtswezen."

[2] The regents were the old native authorities. The need of curbing such superseded chiefs was felt also by the Spanish in America. Cf. p. 283, above.

credit for, he could not have been much depressed by what looks in cold type like failure almost all along the line. What he did was to discharge the function of the strong, clear-seeing, independent man : he caused the customary discomfort and upheaval produced by the application of candid rationality to that which is growing obsolete and anachronistic. That the movement was one of the man and not of the time, place, and people, is shown by the speedy settling-down of the situation into old lines as soon as this perturbing personality was removed.

The Commission of 1816

In 1815, according to antecedent agreement, the Dutch East Indies, and, chief among them, Java, were restored to their former owners ; [1] and in 1816 officials were sent out to resume possession. These men had behind them a colonial constitution which was to serve them as a guide in the reëstablishment of Dutch rule, a document which went back to the more liberal principles that succeeded, in the early years of the century, those of the Company ; it allowed free cultivation except of spices and opium, reserving the question of the forced deliveries as maintained under Raffles for future attention. The implication was that the landtax was to cover most of the fiscal relations with the natives. Now these Commissioners fell upon an evil situation, succeeding as they did to the half-completed and confused application of the English reformer's work, and unable as they were to retain his English agents. The treasury was empty and the deficit constant.

The first question which arose was whether labor should be compulsory or free ; that is, whether the land-tax principle should be rejected or retained ; the Commissioners decided for its retention, though planning improvement of its administration. The laws of 1818 and 1819, which were based upon the Commission's reports, continued to regulate the land-tax until 1872 and after. The chief alterations made in Raffles's plan were : the imposition of the tax upon village-groups rather than upon individuals ; assessment not upon a fixed principle, but in accordance with local conditions ; and the allowance of payment in money or in kind. These relaxations from a rigid system naturally eased the conditions of

[1] For the period of the Dutch restoration the present treatment follows Day, chap. vi, and Pierson, chaps. ii and iii. Cf. Fortanier, pp. 90 ff.

the natives who were in a position to suffer from any rigorous application of pure theory. At the same time the Commissioners "stood squarely on the ground that the home country had full right to all returns that could be got from the natives without infringing their claims to liberty and protection." [1] And, like Raffles, they were obliged to retain the system of forced service in a number of cases until the land-tax should have demonstrated its fiscal utility. In the matter of administration the system and ideas of Raffles were pretty generally followed; in particular the Commission insisted upon better quality and training in the colonial service. The attitude of the government toward native officials was developed into more definite form, and in 1820 found expression in the following paragraph, conceived in part, as will be seen, in apt native terminology : " In matters concerning the government of the natives the regents are the confidential advisers of the resident, and he shall treat them as his younger brothers." [2] How far this attitude allowed the regents power and the abuse of it will appear when the culture system is considered. Certainly the attempt was made to introduce the salary régime so far as practicable; payments through grants of land were abolished in 1819, and the regents were forbidden to engage in trade or otherwise to use their positions to get irregular gain from the people.

REVERSION TO COMPANY POLICY

The Commissioners held office for three years (until 1819), and naturally saw during their term but few positive results, in vindication or otherwise, of their policy. The yield of the land-tax increased from 3,259,933 guilders in 1818 to 3,876,221 in 1819, and then rather steadily to almost 6,000,000 in 1829; but any general justification of measures was long delayed, not only through the natural inertia of things, but because the years 1820 to 1830 saw what might be taken as a slowing-up, if not a partial reversal, of the process of development of the preceding decade. "In the period after the departure of the Commissioners in 1819 there is observable a tendency in India to gravitate back to the Company's policy, though it was never strong enough to lead to the open sacrifice of the tax system to that policy, and would not have led to the culture system except for the influence of the home government." [3]

[1] Day, p. 213.　　　[2] Quoted in Day, p. 219.　　　[3] Day, p. 226.

The tendency to reversion lay not only in the withdrawal of the influence of the English, but in the fact that the Dutch officials had somewhat resented their inmixture in affairs and felt it more patriotic, especially when they found it easier and more profitable, to return to the system under which they had been trained.

This spirit seems to have been embodied in Van der Capellen, the governor-general who succeeded the Commission, who "in the seven years of his rule entirely ignored the principles that had been established for his guidance and reverted step by step to the old system."[1] Among other things he did not favor the tendency toward the settlement of Europeans, and the promising beginnings of organized industry and private trade. "The government had returned to the jealous attitude of the East India Company, and could tolerate no industry, however much it might conduce to the welfare of the people, so long as it seemed likely to affect the immediate interests of the treasury."[2] And as for foreigners, the imposition of relatively heavy differential duties, although they did not restore to the Dutch any great share in the trade of the island, yet betrayed the survival of the old exclusion policy, and deprived the colony of the higher degree of material prosperity to which it seemed ready and able to attain.

In fact a return to the company system took place, not only in essence but likewise in name. Although trade after 1816 was for a time left in private hands, the old conviction of the superiority of the corporation remained and regained strength; thus in 1824 the Dutch Trading Company (*Nederlandsche Handelsmaatschappij*) was founded to further "the national trade, navigation, ship-building, fisheries, agriculture, manufactures and business."[3] The king took one-third of the stock originally designed to be issued and guaranteed the other stockholders a return of four and one-half per cent; and such was the popularity of the Company that "the public over-subscribed to the remainder of the stock nearly nine-fold on the first day that it was offered to them, and the capital was greatly increased to meet their demand." It is to be noted, however, that the Company was to be denied full monopoly and was to possess no sovereign power such as the East India Company had held. It could not impose forced cultures nor own its own vessels; the latter must be chartered and its profits were to be those gained as an ordinary trader. "The main advantage that

[1] Day, p. 233.   [2] Id., p. 236.   [3] Quoted in Day, p. 241.

the articles of agreement promised it was the chance to contract for government business, and until the culture system built up this business the Company's books showed an unprofitable balance." [1]

The Culture System

Attention now turns to this new method, or rather modification of an old method of securing to the mother-country a favorable balance from its colony; for the Dutch continued to regard Java and the rest of their East Indies from the standpoint of what is in essence almost unmixed national egoism. Hence it is that the narrative of Dutch colonization seems so barren and sordid, so unrelieved by the dramatic or romantic, almost empty of the play of passion, of personal highmindedness and renunciation in the pursuit of perhaps unwise ideals; for it is almost exclusively a record of accountings and cheatings, a tale of consistent exploitation. Thus the topics to be considered as period follows period are variations upon the same monotonous theme: commercial policy. Even where the subject of administration enters it is generally an account of the maintenance or alteration of conditions as they directly or indirectly affect the *batig slot,* the favorable balance, the desirable plus quantity in the national ledger.

Such another expedient was the *cultuur stelsel,* or culture system, once from insufficient and unreliable evidence adjudged the philosopher's stone of colonial policy, not only because it yielded material gold, but because it was likewise thought to embody all other desiderata in a colonial policy such as, in particular, the assurance of native welfare and happiness and the spread of civilization. Because, however, of the recent publication in English [2] of the truth in regard to this system, together with an abundance of convincing detail, it is possible for the present treatment to confine itself largely to generalities now demonstrated. The attempt will be made to throw the salient features of the system into line with the general aspects of colonization as heretofore developed.

---

[1] Id., pp. 241–242; Encycl. Ned. Ind., art. " Handelsmaatschappij, De Nederlandsche."

[2] Day, The Dutch in Java, 1904, especially chaps. vii-xii. This is evidently a very careful and able treatise; in addition it possesses the special confidence of the present writer because of his personal knowledge of the author and of his scholarly temperament and methods and sound judgment. Pierson, Koloniale Politiek, chaps. iv-x, covers the same period, for a reader of Dutch, in a most enlightening manner.

The reasons which lay at the bottom of the reaction toward
Company policy represented by the culture system were of a predominantly fiscal nature. The land-tax had nearly doubled its return in the period 1818 to 1829, it is true; but its satisfactory
condition was not duplicated elsewhere on the credit side of the
budget. And the expenses of an imprudent administration and, in
particular, the cost of the native war in central Java which broke
out in 1825, overbalanced any increase of income to such an extent
that by 1830 the Indian government was over 30,000,000 guilders
in debt. But the sentiment in the Netherlands was for immediate
and constant gain, not loss ; and impatience with the situation and
fear of having a weak dependency saddled upon the country led
to a policy of decisive interference on the part of the metropolis.
Thus it happened that General Van den Bosch, an official who
recognized the exigencies of the situation and was prepared to
meet them in what looked like, and proved to be from the fiscal
standpoint, an effective way, was left in virtually undisturbed control of the East from 1830 to 1839 ; and was then succeeded by a
man of like mind, Baud, who maintained the system of Van den
Bosch until 1848.

Plan of the Culture System

" The plan of the culture system, as proposed by Van den Bosch
in 1829, was in brief as follows : Instead of paying to the government a certain proportion of their crops, the natives were to put
at its disposal a certain proportion of their land and labor-time.
The revenue would then consist not in rice, which was almost universally cultivated and which was of comparatively little value to
the government, but in export products grown under the direction
of government contractors on the land set free by the remission
of the former tax. According to the estimate, the natives would
give up only one-fifth of their time in place of two-fifths of their
main crop. The government proposed to bear the loss from failure
of crops if this was not directly due to the fault of the cultivators,
and moreover promised to pay the natives a certain small price for
such amounts as they furnished. The government proposed in this
way to secure products suited for export to the European market,
on which it expected to realize profits largely in excess of the prices
paid to natives and contractors, and of the costs of administration.

To the natives it promised increased prosperity and a lighter burden of taxation, as a result of the fuller utilization of their chances under the far-sighted management of Europeans. The labor that before through carelessness and ignorance would have been wasted in idleness or in the cultivation of some cheap and superfluous crop was to supply a product of great value in the world market, and the natives were to share in the resulting profits. Van den Bosch justified his proposal not only by the benefits it would heap upon all parties, but by reference to previous history and the character of native institutions which made it seem not only impolitic but unjust to cling longer to the land-tax as the basis of government revenue." [1]

REAL CHARACTER OF THE SYSTEM

Because of the great renown of the culture system [2] as a sort of miracle in colonial history this summary of its character as proposed is set before the reader. Not that any such programme may be taken as a basis for the attempt to figure the plan in action; it merely throws light upon the motives of the system's adoption or of the support accorded it by people who knew it only from its prospectus. It looks philanthropic, but was in reality mercenary; in its application all the features that interfered with revenue speedily dropped away. For example, the fifth of the people's working-time which was put under requisition lengthened out indefinitely, and they often bore the land-tax besides, from which the system was supposed to free them. Moreover the government evaded shouldering the losses both by a specious use of the proviso attached and otherwise; and paid the natives, if at all, in the scantiest and stingiest manner. The system was unworkable in any way profitable to all parties because of general ignorance of conditions, poor organization of labor, injudicious selection of locations, and lack of roads and vehicles sufficient in quantity and adequate in quality to meet the needs of transportation. [3]

It is not to be understood that the system was universal in its application either to products or in places. After experimentation and exclusion of the least profitable cultures the government settled down mainly to coffee, sugar, and indigo. The system was applied

---

[1] Day, pp. 249–250.

[2] Cf. Brunialti, pp. 161–162; and Keltie, p. 452, as examples of the prevalent view.

[3] Cf. Encycl. Ned. Ind., arts. "Nijverheid," "Wegen," etc.

chiefly in Java, but even here only partially; and it never affected all the population where it was introduced. "In 1845 the cultures occupied about 5.5% of the total cleared land . . . , in 1854–57 about 3.2% of the total agricultural land of the native population." [1] Something more than one-half of the population in the districts of its introduction came beneath the system. Elsewhere some close approximation to the centuries-old arrangements persisted.

Even the selected products failed to pay except as the system was turned into one of virtual enslavement of the natives; to yield profit the products had to be gotten for nothing or next to it. It was really worse than this, for the actual damage done the natives converted the fictitious or meager payment into a minus quantity, and one of certainly great magnitude even though, like all such social loss, it could not be measured in money. For the native habits of steadiness and industry, such as they were, were demoralized by insecurity and always imminent interference; and the very life of the people was imperiled by the failure of such crops as sugar and indigo which had been made to replace native food-products.[2] Moreover, the system worked out into an inequality of burdens, despite the ostensible fairness of its principles; some cultures were more onerous than others and the same culture would vary in its weight on the native with the type of the official who imposed it. Again the native was required to apply labor or to deliver products in places appointed by the government, a demand which could not but impose great hardship. The result of all this was that the native in his unenviable position lost all stimulus to industry; he gave his labor grudgingly and made no attempt to acquire skill or check waste. These are characteristics of slave-labor; the returns of the government cultures were notably less than those of free industry. Products also suffered deterioration in the factories, for under governmental monopoly there was no competition and the output was of inferior quality.

All this is the old policy of exploitation under a new form. A further ear-mark of the old system is to be found in the treatment accorded to private trade and production, which resembles that beneath which they languished under the Company. Natives were discouraged from the production of articles that might compete with the government monopoly, and were hampered in the disposal

---

[1] Day, p. 259, note 1.
[2] Cf. Encycl. Ned. Ind., arts. "Nijverheid," "Koffie," "Indigo," "Suiker," etc.

of what did not thus compete. The same kind of obstruction was offered to the European planter, with the result that the Dutch who supported themselves in entire independence of the government were very few in number; in 1856 in all Java and Madura these numbered only 608 out of a total Dutch population, exclusive of soldiers, of about 20,000; foreign Europeans engaged in gainful occupations numbered in the same year less than a hundred. Without entering further into detail it may be said that the incentive to the development of individual enterprise and of actual settlement in the colony was about as small under the government as it had been under the Company.

A further evidence of the similarity of old and new systems was the ease with which the Dutch Trading Company slipped into the position of the old Company when once the culture system was well started. Before that time it had languished; now it became the sole agent of the monopoly-holding government, transporting its products to the Netherlands and selling them there on the account of its principal. Great gains were thus made, as in former days, at the expense of private enterprise and public interest.

Oppression and Corruption

It is plain from the above that the Dutch were still endeavoring to reconcile the two historically inconsistent functions of trade and government. In its original programme the culture system bore the aspect of a benevolent attempt to secure a good return to the government through assuring the natives a life of opportunity and advance. It was the very betterment of the natives which was to place their relation with their rulers upon such a plane as to render the new system profitable to the latter. The whole scheme was a " prosperity-policy " which, with the minimum of pain, was to secure general satisfaction for all parties. But the nature of human life is such that losses and gains are balanced, and that the strong inevitably utilize their power to seize the latter and shift off the former, even though this may mean, in the end, losses for both sides. And since the advantages which the Dutch were contemplating in their relations with the Javanese were still pecuniary, and not composed to any extent of pleasurable sensations to be experienced in the discharge of a civilizing and humanitarian function, their governing activity was regularly subordinated to the commercial. Hence the relative unimportance of Dutch "colonial administration" during the period under survey.

The land-tax was continued as a source of revenue, and was imposed not only upon the districts where the culture system had been introduced, but also upon the natives who, by coming under the system, had in form released themselves from the land-tax. "It is certain that many, probably most, of the natives bore the double burden of culture services and taxes too." [1] Outside the region of the cultures the land-tax continued in the old way, meeting the passive resistance of the natives and growing in its yield at about the same rate as formerly. Its collection was mostly in the hands of natives, for the government's attention was for the time concentrated upon the system newly introduced, and was haphazard and irregular. The most important change for the natives not under the culture system was the increased demand for labor services which they had to meet. The government spent ready money with chagrin and found it much cheaper to pay nominal wages for required native labor; and officials wasted a great amount of such labor in the effort to exhibit zeal before their superiors. One estimate reckons the time of the natives which was taken up in services as at least a quarter of their working hours. And the waste was the greater for utter lack of organization, and for general capriciousness, inefficiency, and lack of good will on the part of the directors of labor.

The system of administration was thoroughly bad, as it had been before; greed and parsimony vied with inefficiency and infidelity to trust. The welfare of the natives, so speciously proclaimed as the real object of the culture system and so thoroughly advertised, especially among foreigners, as being a result of it, formed no part of the working programme of the system. Practically nothing was done for the natives. In general the whole preoccupation of the government was commercial, not administrative; it was willing to multiply functionaries in the revenue service, but would make no extension of the purely governmental departments. "Officials soon learned that their careers depended on the fiscal showing their districts could make; they attended to the business of raising revenue, and did not worry the government overmuch with accounts of the sacrifices of the natives." [2] The fact that a percentage upon the product of a district was divided among the directing officials,

---

[1] Day, p. 281.   [2] Id., p. 293.

tended to focus the attention of all upon the yield of the government cultures; purely administrative duties became flat and irksome, and the function of government constantly dwindled as its parallel and inconsistent function of trade increased. "Neither in the training of officials nor in the regulation of their careers by promotion did the government take any measures sufficient to counteract the bad influence of its fiscal policy upon them. In character and abilities they were below standard."[1] Favoritism played a great rôle in their selection and location; they were demoralized by the presence of many sources of illicit gain, as well as by the culture-percentages. All this could not have failed to exercise a malign influence upon the native officials, who, in general, were apter to acquire the vices than the virtues of their European superiors. To these regents, besides, the system of Van den Bosch had restored a considerable portion of the power which Raffles and his immediate successors had desired to take from them; they gradually acquired land-grants in return for services to a government always reluctant to pay in cash, and, since the grants carried rights of taxation over the natives that lived upon them, the people were thus turned over again to the mercies of their own chiefs under the old native customs. The main difference between the conditions of this restoration as compared with the old aboriginal status was that the chiefs had taken during their period of eclipse a course in luxury, greed, and dishonesty on the European model. And the subordinate native officials, who had always been poorly paid, were not behind in practicing on the petty scale what their superiors did on the large. Every demand of the European government increased as it passed through native hands. "They multiplied tenfold and more the demands which the government in theory allowed them to make on the labor services of the population;"[2] and the Dutch officials, though on oath to protect the natives against their chiefs, could do little, even when they willed, in the face of governmental greed and apathy.[3] All this demoralization had its effect upon the village government and thus penetrated still more intimately into native life. Up to 1840 the

---

[1] Day, p. 294; Encycl. Ned. Ind., art. "Opleiding van Indische Ambtenaaren."

[2] Day, p. 300.

[3] Cf. the career of Max Havelaar in the story of that title, by Edouard Douwes Dekker. For a picture of the dissoluteness of the Dutch and native officials, and the suffering of Europeans as well as of the Javanese in consequence of it, see Van Wijk's story, De Goeie Jo.

villages had chosen their own head-men, but after that time deposition was utilized as a punishment for non-extortion of what the government wished, and election became a mere form. Tools of the Dutch were instated as village-chiefs, and were protected in all sorts of wrong-doing, or at most subjected to slight or formal punishments for superlative rascality.

CONDITION OF THE NATIVES

The situation of the Javanese native under all this oppression was pathetic, but after a realization of the uselessness of complaint or resistance, he settled down to a fatalistic endurance of his lot. The Dutch, wanting money, transmitted pressure through their officials, and it finally impinged, far down in the lower strata of the social structure, upon the unknown and for the most part unseen wretch whose life on earth was thereby rendered the more onerous and unhuman. " It is probable, from what is known of the nature of village governments, that the cases of injustice and oppression in the workings of the culture system that were brought to the notice of the Dutch and put on record were as nothing compared with tyrannies and extortions by petty officials, by the comparatively well-to-do, by village cliques, wrought inside the villages and never known to the outside world. ' The little man never makes open complaint,' said a native witness at an investigation in 1850, when asked why the gross abuses discovered had not sooner been brought to the attention of the government." The native bore his sufferings in silence, and it was mainly through unconscious manifestations of his distress, such as appeared in famine and pestilence and in his flight from the land, that the government came in time to realize the faults of the system. [1]

In other words, the pressure of the struggle for existence had to be deduced for the native as it is deduced for the dumb animal or plant, from the observed consequences of his presence in an unendurable environment. That the native had been treated for the most part with the same detached egoism with which man approaches the lower organisms has been sufficiently demonstrated. This is the keynote of the Dutch system, taken as a whole, in its relation with the natives : they were exploited like the coffee-trees

---

[1] Day, p. 307.

or the carabaos, as soulless organisms designed to minister to the well-being of a dominant species. There were absent, for the most part, in their treatment, those elements of sympathy and humanity by which the struggle for existence between men has come through ages to some amelioration. The Spanish and Portuguese may have proceeded in many cases with a more conscious ruthlessness, but no one can deny the essential highmindedness and self-sacrifice for immaterial ends exhibited by certain of their men and measures. The Dutch, on the contrary, uninspired by any ideal considerations, in the prevailing materialism of their aims substituted for positive action of any kind an immense indifference and detachment as regards the fate of their native subjects. There is perhaps in theory some room for argument as to which course is ultimately best for humanity : to allow full swing to the natural conflict of races, or to alter and mollify the struggle to the advantage of the weaker race, this meaning naturally the material disadvantage of the stronger. But, taking a narrower purview and confining ourselves to the four centuries since the first meeting on the large scale of races of different grades of civilization, the Dutch appear to have carried out in the East, under the Company and the culture system, a distinctly low and unprogressive development of native policy. Out of a promising native population they had made nothing except sordid profit. The fact that their system was not worthy of a modern age, that it did not suit the *mores* of a later day, was recognized by the Dutch themselves in their efforts to reform the culture system, which began about the middle of the nineteenth century.

Reputation of the Culture System

One of the reasons why the Dutch were so long regarded as masters in colonial practice was because they proved an exception to that regular rule that, in modern days, states suffer fiscal loss from their colonies. Other governments were always balancing colonial budgets through substantial subventions ; but here were the Dutch, under, apparently, a thoroughly modern system, receiving a yearly dividend from their colony. No wonder the culture system received reverential handling from Germans and English. The system did return, in fact, a regular net profit (*batig slot*) of 22,333,003 guilders a year from 1840 to 1874, or, all together,

781,000,000 guilders for the period.[1] Of this amount 639,000,000 came from coffee, and 115,000,000 from sugar. Other cultures brought loss or slight gain ; and it is shown by Day that the profit on coffee was due largely to price-conditions in Europe upon which the culture system could have had no influence. Nevertheless the regular annual profit was not the object of analysis either by the Dutch or their admiring competitors ; it stood for success, and for the success of a modern and enlightened policy. How far from the truth this last conviction was, has been sufficiently explained.

Nor was it the foreigners alone who were in the dark as to the real results of the culture system. The Dutch knew practically nothing of conditions in Java, for the policy of secrecy of the Company had been succeeded by a similar governmental reticence. The Dutch may have known the favorable-appearing fact that population was increasing in Java at about the regular old rate, but they did not know of the flight of population from the culture-districts, nor of the recurring and severe famines and pestilences due to a diminished food-supply. For the natives could get neither time nor land for raising food, nor were they given wages to buy it. The very absence of armed revolts might have been construed as an evidence of prosperity and contentment, whereas it was due to habits of obedience and subjection, and, perhaps, to weakness as well. That revolts occurred elsewhere with regularity[2] was plausible proof of the excellence of the system in Java. The fact of it was that the people of the Netherlands were not supposed to know anything about the colonies ; they were under the sole control of the king. Even the government was but slightly informed, for " practically no one outside the colonial office had any knowledge or interest concerning colonial affairs." Europeans who did not hold office were not welcomed in Java, and the news from the East was carefully touched up before being published. The press was not allowed to agitate questions that might embarrass the government ; in fact the censor was so active in the East that the newspapers could get no facts had they desired to agitate. One writer exclaims that " the Dutch, unlike the English, had neither

---

[1] According to an estimate of Pierson, p. 148. This is quoted, with additional matter, in Day, pp. 309–310. Leroy-Beaulieu (I, 292) remarks : " Jusqu' à des temps assez proches de nous, Java avait été pour la mère patrie une vache à lait dont le gouvernement hollandais pressait soigneusement les mamelles. C'était, avec Cuba, la seule colonie qui fût productrice d'un gros revenu pour la métropole."

[2] See pp. 493 ff., below.

the desire to make known the facts about their Eastern possessions, nor even the desire to know themselves." Thus it came about, says Day, that "no government industry was ever so free from the supervision of the general public, or so unchecked by the public criticism that keeps governments in the right track, as was the culture system." [1] If some exception be taken to the comprehensiveness of this assertion, with the cases of the earlier colonizing powers in mind, it must yet be admitted that, in the nineteenth century at least, any such system of secrecy, supported by any such incurious disposition on the part of the public, is unique.

REFORM: METHODS OF INDIRECTION

The way in which the colonial skeleton was extracted from its closet was an involved one, and started with an upheaval in home politics by which the States-General attained to a more important function than it had held; it laid hand at last upon the colonial budget. But even then there was no direct penetration beyond the fact of the *batig slot*; "it was generally assumed that the increased revenues from the East were due to the prosperity of the natives, and that the culture system was conferring on them all the benefits that its founder had promised." [2] What the liberal party was contending against was not the colonial policy but the lodgment of all governmental functions in the king. By 1848 the point was being carried against the king; but even after constitutional changes had occurred there was really no colonial policy. Ignorance of conditions still ruled; what had been done had been the preparation of the legislative body, through the introduction of modern men into its halls, to cope with modern questions, and, among them, with colonial problems. Then followed (1854) the relaxation of press-regulations, the abolition of slavery, projects of native education and of regulation of services and land-tax. The legislators struggled between the desire for the net yearly profit on the one hand, and, on the other, the wish to extend opportunities to European planters, and to protect the natives from an oppression they were gradually coming to realize.

A paragraph was introduced into the colonial constitution of 1854 which provided (1) that the cultures should not interfere with

---

[1] The preceding quotations are from Day, pp. 319, 318, and 316 respectively.
[2] Day, p. 322.

the production of sufficient means of subsistence; (2) that lands cleared by natives for their use and then occupied by cultures should be disposed of with justice and with respect for existing rights and customs; (3) that in the assignment of labor the same rules should hold; (4) that in general the pay of the natives should be such that the government cultures should return them with the same labor at least the same advantages as free cultivation; (5) that oppressions of the cultures discovered by a careful investigation, be, so far as practicable, remedied; (6) that a regulation be then prepared, based on voluntary agreements with the communities and individuals concerned, as a transition to a condition where government intervention may be dispensed with.[1] The carrying out of such ideas meant the realization of Van den Bosch's promises; but it likewise meant the abolition of the system. For, as has been seen, the system had nothing to give apart from the exploitation of the natives; it could not assure them fair play and still live. "The Dutch must choose between making money by the sacrifice of the natives and protecting natives at the sacrifice of fiscal interests. . . . Little by little Dutch legislators perceived this, and began to range themselves in parties sharply defined on the question of the maintenance or abolition of the culture system."[2]

"MAX HAVELAAR": DECLINE OF THE SYSTEM

Some of the more flagrant abuses had been corrected between 1845 and 1851; and this 1854 constitution set a new and higher standard for continued reform. But, as is so often the case, an appeal to popular emotion was necessary in order to accelerate the more deliberate development of rational conviction and to cut the entanglement produced by a conflict of interests and opinions, candid or otherwise. This appeal came in 1860 with the publication of "Max Havelaar, or The Coffee Auctions of the Dutch Trading Company," by Edouard Douwes Dekker, writing under the significant pseudonym of "Multatuli.[3]" It is the story of a young Dutch colonial official to whom the abuses of the culture system became intolerable, and who then, owing to the impolitic

[1] Translation in Day, p. 328.
[2] Day, p. 329.
[3] Translation by Nahuijs (Edinburgh, 1868); selections in Warner's Library, VIII, 4513–4520.

expression of his views, fell out with the colonial administration and suffered in consequence all the persecution, petty and other, that falls to the share of the isolated and indiscreet reformer. As a piece of literature it is of little value, being repetitious, fantastic, and surcharged with the weakly emotional; but in these respects it is not unlike the performances of many enthusiasts whose influence upon their time lies in the fact that they have made exaggerated appeals to men's feelings, consciously or unconsciously acting upon the principle that in these rather than in the intellect are to be found the springs of human action. Dekker is in this respect classifiable with the authoress of "Uncle Tom's Cabin," and other such purveyors of real kernels of wheat in bushels of chaff, rather than with the more rational protestants against local or general conditions. "Dekker took sides neither with the conservatives for forced labor, nor with the liberals for free labor; he had but one refrain — the Javanese is given over to the oppression of his chiefs and they abuse him in the name of the King."[1] The very earnestness of the author, coupled with the evident fact that he spoke from bitter personal experience, lent force to his appeal, for, as has been seen, the time was ripe for the rejection of the existing system.[2]

The colonial question remained well to the fore during the decade 1860 to 1870, and at its end the liberals had carried the day and the culture system was formally superseded by that of "free labor." In 1818 the slave-trade had been forbidden; slavery was abolished, with reimbursement of loss to applying owners, in 1860, after which time it existed, except in disguised form, only in New Guinea.[3] Between 1860 and 1865 the less important government cultures (tea, tobacco, indigo, pepper, cinnamon) were given up; the sugar-culture alone remained to occupy arable land of the natives, for coffee was grown on the waste areas. Natives were freed from the passport-system which impeded easy movement of labor, and

[1] Day, p. 333.

[2] For a contemporary estimate of Max Havelaar by a thoroughly competent authority see P. J. Veth, "Multatuli vs. Droogstoppel," etc., De Gids, 1860, II, 65 ff., 233 ff. Veth says the eccentricity of the work is against it among cool, calm Hollanders; that it is a little wild; that the story "wat verdichtsel is in het bijzonder, waarheid is in het algemeen." Other utterances regarding the culture system, by this excellent authority, are to be found under the review-heading: "Nieuwste Literatuur over Nederlandsch-Indië," in De Gids, 1862, II, 841; 1863, I, 19; 1864, III, 150; 1865, IV, 385, et al. Cf. R. Fruin, "Nederlands Rechten en Verplichtingen ten opzichte van Indië," De Gids, 1865, II, 28.

[3] Encycl. Ned. Ind., arts. "Slavernij," "Ternate," "Nieuw-Guinea."

were protected against excessive demands for their services; the culture-percentages were abolished, the payment of native officials in land restricted, and the village heads restored to their old position.[1] And it was of still greater importance that the system of official secrecy weakened as there was less need for concealment. Naturally enough parts and survivals of the culture system have lasted on in dwindling or altered form to the present day.

With the decline of the culture system yet another, and this time much-heralded, expedient for the development of the tropics is proved, at least under modern theories of justice and ethics, inadequate. All such expedients that have any chance at all represent compulsion in some form; but compulsion is, for reasons of humanity, morality, and the like, disallowed. Hence as system after system passes, return is made to the original dilemma, and a new way must be evolved of securing a tropical labor force otherwise than through unsensed economic stimulation or forbidden physical coercion.[2]

"Free Labor"

It is perhaps as well to continue this topic up to recent years[3] before attempting to go back and gather up for brief mention certain other lines of Dutch colonial development hitherto thrust one side by reason of preoccupation with relatively far more important issues in Java. The "free labor" system which succeeded the culture system has not escaped the inevitable tendency to revert to a mitigated form of compulsion; it is really credit-bondage, voluntarily or unwittingly entered by the natives, and is not at that very successful. For the Dutch had not trained the native to labor for the purpose of getting something he wanted, but rather did he toil to avoid that which he did not want, namely, punishment or other discomfort. It was found to be a long swing of the pendulum from this extreme of the negative through the traditional position of rest across to the positive. The most that could be done

[1] Cf. Encycl. Ned. Ind., arts. "Amboina," "Nijverheid," "Heerendiensten," "Indigo," "Koffie," "Rijst," "Suiker," etc. In an utterance in the States-General during this period two principles were set down as "the two corner-stones of the colonial structure — respect for the institutions and customs of the people under our rule, and the maintenance of the prestige (*aanzien*) of their princes and chiefs." Van der Aa, "Koloniale Politiek," *De Gids*, 1860, I, 461. [2] Cf. Keller, Sociol. View, etc.

[3] For the recent system of the Dutch in Java, Day (chaps. x-xii) remains the chief authority; cf. also Id., pp. 1–4.

was to set over against the vaguely perceived discomforts of future labor the present lure of immediate material benefits, and when the bait had been unintelligently but voluntarily taken, to insist upon the fulfillment of the contract; as high as three years' wages were thus advanced against future services, which then became compulsory. In form, of course, this is merely a subterfuge; and doubtless it often proved so to be in reality, despite the provisions as to limitation and recording of contracts and the like. Such provisions were in force in the coolie-system,[1] but they did not prevent abuses sufficient to cause the Chinese and British authorities, and those of the Dutch themselves to repudiate it, at least so far as allowing their subjects to serve in colonies of foreign powers was concerned. The system was in reality one of debt-slavery, and as such was perfectly comprehensible to the native, who had known it under what the Dutch called *pandelingschap*[2] for many preceding periods of his history. Debt-slavery to one's chiefs is common enough among uncivilized peoples, but is generally mitigated by the irregularity or mildness of the service imposed; Europeans, with a different and more energetic temperament, and intent on speedy gain, are likely to insist upon a strenuosity and accountability which effect a total metamorphosis of the institution. But reiterated complaints as to the capricious breaking of contracts by natives leave us to understand that in Java the compulsion was not rigorous enough for the system still to deserve the name of slavery; indeed the very lamentations that denote the absence of coercion indicate a return to the original dilemma of tropical production. The problem of tropical labor seems still to be set for the Dutch in its original terms — terms which are, indeed, more unfavorable if anything than at first, because of the results of several centuries of crude and inapt manipulation.

Yet, despite all theory, in practice a good deal of compulsion along old lines is exercised over the natives to bring them as producers under the modern economic system. For though the government allows to the landed proprietor no such powers utilizable for oppression as he formerly possessed, yet he still holds "a semipublic position; he exacts dues in labor and in kind from the natives, and, subject to the approval of the State, he appoints and pays the head-men who exercise the most important function of

[1] Cf. Encycl. Ned. Ind., art. "Koelie."
[2] Cf. Encycl. Ned. Ind., art. "Pandelingschap."

communal government." [1] Abuses must arise under these conditions; the government plainly recognizes their existence, though it has as yet devised no means for their eradication.

THE CHINESE

The most effective and natural agency for the economic education of the natives, in Java and elsewhere, is formed by the Chinese. It has been shown [2] that Coen and others early recognized their importance and favored their immigration; and then how they became hated and were subjected to persecution. Their peculiar value as educators of less-developed races lies in the fact that they are culturally near enough to them to understand that in their lives which is a closed book to the European. They are natural mediators between two diverse types of civilization.[3] A Javanese could hope and desire to attain to what of superiority the Chinese has, while he could not even regard as desirable or superior much of that for which the European strives. Moreover, the Chinese were long experienced over all the East before the European arrived. Their intelligence, industry, and reliability led to the delegation to them of functions like that of the tax farmer, where they were oppressive indeed, under a conniving government, but effective for its purposes. "Even in the eighteenth century they were recognized as indispensable in their capacity of manufacturers, traders, and money-lenders; they alone showed the ability to stimulate production, not by political pressure, but by economic means such as characterize the modern system of labor.

"In modern times the Chinese have lost much of their importance as tax farmers, but their place in the commercial organization is secure." [4] Thus they continue to come into constant and close contact with the natives; they are the peddlers, the small-scale suppliers who depend for their existence upon the stimulation of those petty demands which precede others and larger. Their work is in many striking respects a counterpart of that of the Phœnicians or the mediæval Jews; they are similarly hated, bearing as they do a like reputation. But these "Phœnicians of the East" are exerting an analogous influence because their point of attack is, like that of their prototypes, the only logical one; it is

---

[1] Day, p. 368.   [2] Pp. 437 ff., above.
[3] Cf. Keller, Sociol. View, etc.; Encycl. Ned. Ind., art. "Chineezen."
[4] Day, p. 362.

the industrial organization alone that they influence, and that in simple, understandable ways, and holding out benefits which, though dearly purchased, seem worth the price.   The Chinese really extract products from the natives ; " the petty trader should have the credit for the total amount produced for export by the industrial natives, and for a large proportion of that which is produced by natives under European direction." [1] Thus are the natives being gradually drawn into the outskirts of the world-market and afforded some hope of such adaptation to modern conditions as will allow them a modest share in its system and perhaps ultimately save them from the extinction that follows failure to conform.

In this process the Dutch have had little share ; nevertheless their recent efforts to improve the native's position, whatever the results, must not be overlooked.   The general easing-up on services, and other measures dating from about the middle of the nineteenth century, were followed by attempts to better the education not only of the colonial service but of the natives as well.   Likewise an increased attention was given to religious matters, although " among the Javanese the opinion is dominant that the government does not wish a chief (*hoofd*) to become a Christian."   In 1770 there were 500,000 native Christians in the domain of the Company, and at its fall 70,000 within the area of the present Netherlands-India.   In 1903 there were 445,950 native Christians in the same region, of whom 28,368 were Catholic.   Naturally the Dutch have steadily opposed the extension of the Roman faith from the time they succeeded to the Portuguese and Spanish.[2]

RECENT FISCAL AND OTHER CONDITIONS

If the government intended to see the natives rightly treated according to modern criteria, it could not hope for the old fiscal returns.   But it was unwilling, naturally enough, to surrender these ; after 1864 the home government fixed the Indian budget, and for some years the contributions ranged between 10,000,000 and 40,000,000 guilders a year.   But, in consequence of the Atjeh

---

[1] Day, p. 365.   The total number of Chinese in Netherlands-India is given (for 1893) as 443,945, of whom 290,449 are males.   Encycl. Ned. Ind., art. " Chineezen."

[2] Encycl. Ned. Ind., art. " Christenen "; cf. arts. " Onderwijs," " Opleiding van Indische Ambtenaaren," " Heerendiensten," " Eeredienst," " Evangelisatie," " Zending."   For the character of training for the colonial service, see Lowell, chap. ii, 113 ff., and Bourne, Col. Civ. Serv.

War which broke out in 1873, this Indian surplus declined and, in 1878, had disappeared. Later schemes regarding the budget " have had in common the idea that the Indies should be held to contribute each year a fixed sum which should recompense the home government for its expenditures on colonial account, while any surplus above that should be appropriated by the States General to objects of direct interest to the people in the East." [1] Recent budgets seem to indicate a considerably increased attention to the formerly neglected public works, local administration, native welfare, and the like.

In considering the source of the government revenues, return is made from another standpoint to the modification of the culture system. After the less important cultures were abolished those of sugar and coffee alone remained. In the case of the former a gradual transition from forced- to wage-labor was begun in 1870, and by 1890 the transition was fully effected. The taxes levied from the planters were sufficient for some years to cause the government but slight loss ; but misfortunes, entirely apart from the change of system, which overtook the industry toward the end of the century brought heavy loss to the planters and led to the abolition of the sugar-tax, after some years of suspension, in 1898. The coffee-culture is still continued ; to it the government held because of its productiveness, striving to remedy abuses and increase efficiency by changes of detail. It was seen that, since the industry was, unlike that of sugar, almost entirely in native hands, there would be little production for export under a free system ; the European entrepreneur was lacking and so could not be made responsible or taxed. Culture-percentages for European officials were abolished, however, in 1865, although those for native supervisors were continued. But the industry is rather feebly carried on ; fall of coffee-prices leaves the culture less desirable and destined to pass away. The coffee-culture, like all the rest, could have been abolished any time the government chose to forego the revenue derived from it.

Thus far little has been said of mining ; but although it formed no very considerable part of the interests of the Dutch up to 1867, and contributed therefore but slightly to the labor question, it deserves some reference in view of present-day conditions. In early times Java had the reputation of a " gold and silver island," and

[1] Day, p. 384.

the precious metals were a sort of vague secondary lure to the European discoverers; but the Portuguese and Spanish found little to attract them, and the East India Company, after some experimentation, allowed such enterprise to drop. In the course of time, however, the extension of information about the Dutch possessions recalled attention to their metal wealth; for, in accord with more modern ideas, it was now possible to conceive of such resources as consisting of something besides gold and silver. There is gold in Netherlands-India, but the metallic attraction has come to be the more useful ores, and, above all, tin; to have tin mines in their colonies is for the Dutch a rather unique distinction, and a profitable one. This ore occurs chiefly in the islands of Banka and Billiton, and is mined through the agency, under the resident of Banka, of Chinese resident communities (*kong-si*).[1] Concessions for mining have been granted in considerable numbers since 1873, but only to Netherlanders or subject natives or to companies formed in the Netherlands or in the Dutch islands. The exigencies of steam-navigation have lent importance to the mining of coal; and iron and petroleum seem to promise well. Thus in the field of the extractive industries, as of the productive, the center of gravity is moving away from the costly and luxurious toward the cheap and practical.[2]   In any case mining in Netherlands-India has never cost the native, in loss of vitality and in misery, what it wrung from the Indians in America.

With the decline of forced services[3] of all kinds the Dutch have come to look to taxes on the European model as sources of revenue. The land-tax was the chief of these, and it has remained in approximately its old form, although growth of population and strengthening of the administration have contributed to make it more endurable. The Dutch are now engaged upon an investigation of the whole tax system, which will probably end by sweeping away the greater part of the survivals of antique and poorly

---

[1] Cf. p. 25, above.

[2] Cf. Encycl. Ned. Ind., arts. "Mijnbouw," "Billiton-maatschappij," "Petroleum," "Steenkolen," "Tin," "Ijzer," etc.

[3] Another species of service demanded by the government as a sort of commuted tax was that which included labor on public works, maintenance of order, labor for the personal enterprises of native government (*pantjen* services) and village officials. These services were wasteful and ineffective, as they were given grudgingly and directed inefficiently. From 1864 to 1890 they were progressively restricted; then it was realized that general regulation was ineffective, and since 1890 forced services have been prescribed according to the local conditions of the various residencies.

adapted measures. It would appear from all this that they have finally decided for the formerly neglected alternative in the dual policy of trade and government; they have certainly moved in that direction since the days of the Company. Yet there are those who assert that the Dutch policy is still that of greed and gain. It is stated, for example, with a good deal of evidence, that the government is actively fostering the greatest curse of the East, the opium-traffic, and that, though the form of the drug's disposal has been changed from time to time, it is being offered to, or rather forced upon, an increasing number of East Indian districts.[1] It would be strange indeed if some such ugly aftermath of the old mercenary policy did not persist. No one believes all the protestations of parliamentary speeches, least of all those of defenders of their own policy. But for the present it is safe to say that in recent years the colonial policy in Java has certainly more closely approached the modern type, where measures are, openly at least, based less upon considerations of gain.

In pursuance of the early policy of exploitation one of the strongest persuasions of the Dutch was that foreigners should be rigidly excluded from the entire archipelago; and it has been seen how they forced an entry and finally for a time held almost the whole of the Dutch possessions. Of course the modern ideas, based upon the working of a modern system with its developed communication and transportation, no longer allow of a closed monopoly or an attempt at one. Nevertheless the Dutch are yet strict in such measures as are calculated to discourage foreign enterprise in their own territories, or, what is much the same thing, to restrict the relations between foreigners, European and Oriental, and their native subjects. "According to a formula which has been framed to describe the policy of the Dutch, the native is major in his relations to the other natives; he is a minor in his relations to the rest of the world." [2] For example, there can be no valid sale of land-rights from a native to a foreign Oriental or European; the most the alien can hope to get, on land cultivated by natives, is a short-term lease, and this is hedged about with varied restrictions. The theory of the relations of natives to foreigners is that the former are not yet able to hold their own in bargaining with Chinese or Europeans; hence government activity

[1] J. F. Scheltema, in *Amer. Jr. of Sociology;* cf. Encycl. Ned. Ind., art. "Opium."
[2] Day, pp. 372-373.

in keeping the foreigner at his distance is viewed as an expression of benevolent paternalism.

As regards their Malay possessions, and chiefly Java, the Dutch have in later years developed a far more intelligent and modern view-point in respect to the improvement of means of defense, communication, and the like. One of the great evils which they had to combat was the prevalent piracy of the Malays; in fact they were obliged, like the Spanish, to increase their local navy, and, in particular, to introduce steam-boats (1835), in order to put an end to this menace of trade. The Spanish efforts against Joló (Sulu) had by 1876 afforded considerable relief to the Dutch, and since 1888 the pirates have been practically suppressed. Moreover, to aid navigation the Dutch have directed attention to the charting of sea-ways and the erection of lighthouses; and by the lowering of duties and the establishment of free harbors they have done commerce a service scarcely inferior. Posts and telegraphs have been multiplied. The organization of scientific expeditions and the establishment of many journals and newspapers dealing with Netherlands-India have all contributed to a better knowledge of the country and to the extension of scientific information along various lines.[1]

The East Indies other than Java; the Atjeh War

Apart from Java, which, as the center of activity and interest, has claimed so large a share of the foregoing, the history of the Dutch possessions in the nineteenth century is relatively unimportant. But the narrative returns to them briefly in order to gather up a few of the aspects of Dutch colonization as exhibited outside of Java. After the Napoleonic wars practically all the Dutch East Indies were restored; but in the exhaustion of the Netherlands little effort could be expended where it did not return or promise the maximum of result. Elsewhere than in the region of application of the culture system an ineffective extension of trade and administration after the eighteenth-century model persisted. In the perpetuation of the trade-motive there had been but little interest taken in those regions whose productions did not figure

[1] Cf. Encycl. Ned. Ind., arts. "Kaarte," "Kaartebeschriving," "Stoomvaart," "Scheepvaart en Handel," "Post en Telegraafdienst," "Rechten (In-, uit- en doorvoer-)," "Sumatra-Expeditie," "Triangulatie," "Tijdschriften," "Vrijhavens," "Wegen," "Zeekarten," "Zeemacht," "Zeeroof."

profitably in the world-market. Thus a good deal of attention had been accorded the Spice Islands, much to their detriment. The Dutch never penetrated very deeply into Borneo, Celebes, and the islands to the eastward, but exercised over their local chiefs a species of protectorate, exacting a certain tribute in the form chiefly of contributions in products. Treaties were made from time to time and formed the basis of a loose relationship between Dutch and natives. Naturally uprisings were frequent and, though often brief of duration, cut deeply into the income of the government. The most disastrous of these was the war with Atjeh, which began in 1873 and whose history is a type on a larger scale of many of the conflicts that took place in the "Outer Possessions."[1] At all times the Dutch, and the Portuguese before them, had suffered at the hands of this relatively strong native state. They had proceeded on the plan of treaties and agreements which the native princes promptly broke when it seemed to their advantage; Dutch relations with Atjeh were in many respects, and for similar reasons, like those of the Spanish with the Moros.[2] Under the Company, Sumatra was but little regarded, and it was not until 1824 that Van den Bosch developed the idea of reducing the whole island. This project was realized in but slight degree, but the faltering efforts put forth did not add to the good feeling of the natives. When now, with the development of trade, the piratic propensities of the people of Atjeh had come to be a distinct menace to all nations alike, it became necessary for the Dutch to put an end to their depredations unless they wished some other powers, by doing so, to gain claims to indemnity and so to territory. It was plain that the sultan, even if he so desired, was unable to check his subjects in their deeds of violence; despite the treaty of 1857 covering these matters, they continued to prey upon peaceful traders and to keep up a constant turmoil among the native adjacent states. It was also clear that there was double-dealing on the part of the native government; in 1868, for example, it tried to yield its allegiance to the sultan of Turkey, and later, while negotiating with the resident of Riouw over a new treaty, it was secretly dealing with the agents of foreign powers at Singapore. In consequence of these and other reasons war broke out with the sultan in 1873; and the Dutch, who had miscalculated the strength

---

[1] Cf. Veth, Atchin; in particular the chapter on the causes of the war (pp. 104 ff.); Encycl. Ned. Ind., arts. "Atjeh," "Sumatra."　　　[2] Cf. pp. 344-345, above.

of the natives, suffered immediate and costly reverses, which have
been repeated at intervals up to the present day. The effect of
all this upon the Netherlands-India budget has been alluded to ;
war expenditures, chiefly with Atjeh, have been the significant
item for many years. But the Dutch, like so many other colonial
powers, have comforted themselves with the reflection that they
are fighting the battles of civilization and humanity against barbarism and savagery, and continue to spend money and lives with but
slight prospect of securing a decisive and enduring result.

With this sort of thing the student of modern colonization is
sufficiently familiar. The Dutch present other instances on a
smaller scale.[1] In general the history of the Dutch in their " Outer
Possessions " is fragmentary and unessential. It cannot be summed
up except in the statement that it has varied with different localities ; a description even of administration and regulation must go
into endless detail if it is not to misrepresent.[2]

In short, the Dutch tropical lands are, like those of other nations,
practically undeveloped ; and that by reason at bottom of the same
deterring element — climate — which has prevented other nations
from such consummation. For, as has been shown,[3] the climatic
conditions draw others in their train which effectually, as yet, check
the activity of the dominant races from attaining in the tropics
anything comparable to its results in the cooler zones. Doubtless
the shortsightedness and selfish preoccupations of the Netherlanders have cost them much. But even these were natural in their
time ; and the more enlightened policies of other nations have not
brought them appreciably nearer the common goal, namely, the
inclusion of the tropics within the world-market.

[1] See Knoop, W. J., " Bijdrage tot de Kennis der Indische Krijgszaken,"*De Gids*,
1849, II, 245 ff.; "Indische Krijgsgeschiedenis," Id., 1860, II, 189 ff.; arts. " Bali,"
" Borneo," " Nieuw-Guinea," etc., in Encycl. Ned. Ind. New Guinea is now divided
between Dutch, Germans, and British, in the percentages 48.6, 28.3, and 23.1
respectively.

[2] De Louter, pp. 355–366; cf. pp. 220, 433, 477, etc.

[3] Cf. pp. 4 ff., above.

CHAPTER XIII

THE COLONIES OF THE SCANDINAVIANS

The colonial history of the Norwegians and Danes, unimportant though it is from most standpoints, yet possesses a peculiar interest to one who would understand colonization as the process of founding new human societies. For here again he has an experiment performed for him, — the old problem set in different terms. Hitherto the colonizing peoples have been prevailingly southern Europeans, and their colonizing enterprises have been directed mainly along their own lines of latitude or toward the south. In the case of the Scandinavians, however, we have, first, attempts at tropical colonization on the part of northern Europeans; and then the striking case of colonization in polar regions. Therefore, although historical data be meager and somewhat vague, it is with a peculiar interest that one turns to the Danish West Indies and to Danish Iceland and Greenland.

The Danish East India Company

The Danes early entered the competition for the trade of the East, and a word upon their East India Company may serve to align their enterprises with those of the peoples whose colonial history has been sketched. This organization (*Dansk-Ostindiske Compagni*) was chartered in 1616, and in 1618 the India voyage was attempted on its account. Seafaring folk that they were, the Danes were not without some experience even in the remote East; but as for the Company, many of its functionaries and servants were Dutch. In 1620 the fort of Dansborg was founded on the Coromandel coast; in 1625 a rather important station was established in Macassar; in 1633 a factory in Atjeh. Other stations were located here and there in the archipelago. The Danish programme was trade pure and simple; it included no political aims of any kind. A certain amount of gain was made, much of it in smuggling and in other ways detestable to the Dutch East India Company. And since the Danish Company received at most lukewarm support from home, it was entirely unable to withstand the pressure of the Dutch. Thus the Danes were gradually crowded out and by 1682 were virtually excluded from the archipelago and the East.[1] The last Danish possessions in the East were transferred in 1845 to the English East India Company. At its dissolution in 1634 the first Danish Company was just able to pay its debts; but a second was organized at once, a third in 1686, and a fourth, with extraordinary privileges, in 1732. In general, the Danes prospered when stronger rivals were at war; thus Company shares issued at 500 rose in 1782 to 1800 and 1900, to descend, by 1790, to 420. Both Danes and Swedes held certain isolated way-stations on the west coast of Africa, as their predecessors and models had done; the Danish forts in this region were sold to England in 1850 for $50,000.[2]

THE DANISH WEST INDIES

The operations of the Danes in the eastern tropics were thus incidental and short-lived, never advancing far toward the deserving of the name colonization. In the West Indies, however, they did create a miniature "empire," which they hold at the present time. And because of the fact that, though it is a miniature empire, it yet reflects in perhaps the more striking simplicity some of the fundamental phases of tropical colonization, and because, likewise, its history is especially difficult of access, the present treatment enters into somewhat more of detail than is usual, and allots a disproportionate amount of space to a relatively insignificant subject.[3]

There was no pressing reason for Denmark's colonial activity in the seventeenth century. No overplus of population or capital demanded new fields into which to expand; no religious or political strifes existed in the home-land, to create a body of exiles to foreign parts. Commerce was not such as to require new regions of supply

[1] Øverland, IV, 786 ff., 800 ff.; also *sub* " Ostindien" in indexes; art. " De Denen in den Maleischen Archipel," in Encycl. Ned. Ind.; p. 418, above.

[2] Keltie, pp. 68, 77; cf. also Lindsay, I, 345–347, on the shipping of the Danes. A Swedish company formed in this period (cf. p. 411, above) was dissolved in 1671 with a considerable deficit. Roscher, p. 278; Leroy-Beaulieu, I, 182–184.

The most recent book upon the Danes in the East — inaccessible to the author at the time of writing — is that of Larsen.

[3] The following matter on the Danish West Indies is from an article by the author, entitled "Notes on the Danish West Indies." This study has been checked and supplemented by an examination of an unpublished (Yale) thesis of Dr. H. J. Thorstenberg, and of the treatise of Knox. The bibliography of the original article, with some additions, will be found in the general bibliography. Cf. Leroy-Beaulieu, I, 182–185.

and demand. The acquisition of the islands St. Thomas and St. John, and later, St. Croix, was due very largely to a desire to imitate the activities of Holland and England, and to reap, if possible, the direct and indirect results of such a policy. The movement is an artificial one, therefore, at the very outset; as far as Danish trade with the tropics was concerned, it could hope for little advance of profit under the new conditions.

St. Croix, the largest of the islands, was occupied by the Danes in 1733; already it had been successively in Dutch, English, Spanish, and French hands. Under Colbert a company, invested with the usual trade-monopoly, was formed, which, however, had been compelled to turn to the king for aid; and the island had been deserted (1695) by the 147 whites and 623 slaves who had inhabited it. For thirty-eight years it had been neglected and masterless. St. Thomas, the second in size of the Danish islands, was seized in 1667 by the English, and its few Dutch colonists were forced to depart; except for the visits of pirates, the island was then deserted until 1671. In that year there was formed the *Dansk Guineisk-Vestindiske Compagni*, under whose auspices St. Thomas was at once occupied by the Danes, in spite of England's protest. This Danish Company was managed by six directors, who were required to invest two thousand rigsdaler [1] in the enterprise; shares were sold at one hundred rigsdaler. The first governor, Iversen, reached the island in 1672. His earliest proclamation dealt, in its first articles, with religious matters: fines were fixed for nonattendance at divine service, for Sunday labor, and the like. There follow strict prescriptions as to drill and use of arms in defense. All persons were forbidden to leave the island, or take anything away from the island without the governor's permission. Heavy fines [2] were to be exacted for attempts to entice away another's indentured servants, i.e. whites who had sold their liberty for passage. Negroes were not allowed to leave a plantation after dark; if a strange negro was found on a plantation at night, he was to be arrested, taken to the fort, and punished. Other injunctions calculated to insure internal cohesion and order, and an efficient defense, were published. The necessity of such defense was made apparent by the robberies of the Spanish from Puerto Rico, and by the presence of French and English buccaneers on the island of Tortuga.

[1] The specie rigsdaler was worth, at the end of the seventeenth century, about $1.02. It rose a few cents in value during the ensuing period and was worth, in 1844, $1.11. [2] All fines were payable in tobacco, the natural currency of the colony.

EARLY CONDITIONS: THE WEST INDIA COMPANY

To the Danes, now in possession of their tropical islands, the familiar difficulty of tropical colonization — lack of an adequate labor supply — began to make itself felt as early as 1679. Complaint was made to King Christian V, who promptly established slave-stations on the Gold Coast, and under pressure increased the number of shareholders of the Company in Copenhagen; a tax was levied on coaches, for example, when the owners could not show certificates of participation to a certain figure in the Company. Naturally enough, the importation of slaves into the islands increased perceptibly and with it the prosperity of the plantations. The slaves came, however, of restless and unruly stocks, and in an exceptionally short time the Danish islanders are found to be in terror of revolts and deeds of violence; laws were enacted which could not have been enforced, else all the slaves would have perished by the halter. The evil, because of the essential weakness of the Danish Company, was not at this time of such proportions as it later displayed. Possessing meager capital, the Company could send but one ship a year to the African coast; this vessel transported slaves to St. Thomas and then loaded with colonial wares for Denmark. For the purpose of increasing trade and also to encourage the settlement of the colony, a thirty-year treaty was concluded with the duchy of Brandenburg, in accordance with which a trading-company of Germans, most of whose shares, however, were in Dutch hands, was to undertake settlement. The immediate result of this movement was the appearance of fifty workmen in the islands and of five ships, sailing on the Company's account. This company suffered much from French pirates shortly after its erection, but made such large gains as to excite the envy of the Danes, to whom small consideration was shown. Its privilege ran out in 1715 and was not renewed; members of the Company who desired to stay were required to take the oath of allegiance.

After the revocation of the Edict of Nantes (1685) the islands were fortunate enough to receive as settlers a number of Huguenot fugitives from St. Christopher; these were noted, as usual, for frugality, industry, and fear of God. In general during all this period efforts were being made to attract a larger immigration; at one time young unmarried women were forbidden to leave the colony without special permission. A number of privileges were guaranteed to settlers, including religious tolerance, freedom from taxes for eight years, grants of as much land as could be put under cultivation, needed aid in agriculture, etc. Imported and exported products were to be free of customs for eight years. The policy was liberal and the results were good; in 1688 St. Thomas numbered ninety plantations, with 317 whites and 422 slaves. To show the ethnic mixture in the population, it may be mentioned that of the white families, nineteen were Danish, sixty-three Dutch, thirty English, seventeen French, three Swedish, two German, and one Portuguese; this diversification was maintained into the nineteenth century, and was plainly evident to an observer in the forties.[1] Many local names on the island recall to mind the varied nationality of its early settlers.

The monopolistic trading Company, as time went on, did not fail to prove its kinship with its prototypes; it ran the usual course of inglorious inefficiency. In 1692, as a relief measure, the island of St. Thomas was leased to a merchant, Thormohlen by name, for ten years; the lessee was to maintain a garrison and was to have full control of all the island's affairs and income. The characteristic independence of the colonial society was here witnessed, for the colonists resolutely refused to pay taxes to Thormohlen, whose activity was not prolonged beyond the original period of lease. After the disappearance of this adventurer, the Company led a humdrum existence for some years. In 1736 it was found that, to keep itself above water, it had in the matter of trade consistently favored the Dutch and excluded its own countrymen; eight Dutch ships were engaged in the trade to one Danish. A countermovement of merchants in Copenhagen succeeded in forcing an entrance into the West India Company and the Dutch were in turn excluded. But the Company was nearing its end. The burdens which its manipulations had laid upon the colonists were intolerable, and frequent complaints were lodged with the king. The Company had secured a thorough-going monopoly of raw sugar in Denmark and, by opening a refinery there, virtually commanded the market; prices were driven very high and sugar became a luxury no longer in common use. The shortsightedness and greed of this policy impressed themselves upon the government and in 1755 King Frederik V bought out the Company's entire plant, including the islands, the equipment, and the Copenhagen refinery.

[1] Erindringer, etc., p. 150.

The price paid (1,418,000 rigsdaler) was entirely incommensurate with the good effects that appeared at once, and with the general gratitude of the oppressed colonists.

PURCHASE BY THE KING

One of the chief causes of rejoicing to the planters was the removal of the restrictions laid by the Company on the importation of slaves. Slaves were a necessary evil, and one with which the colonists played as with fire. Early in the eighteenth century and before, precautions had regularly to be taken regarding runaways and fear of uprisings was constantly displayed. All the boats, for instance, were drawn up at night under the guns of the fort. The Spanish of Puerto Rico enticed the runaways and hypocritically explained, in answer to complaint, that the slaves had come "to be baptized." The fear of the blacks had grown until the colonists had become panicky, and consequently needlessly cruel and arbitrary. In 1733 an edict appeared which betrayed this terror; such punishments as branding, loss of limbs, hanging, and breaking on the wheel were threatened for what appear to us to be comparatively trivial offenses. By this cruelty an uprising was brought about late in 1733 on the island of St. John, for the suppression of which it was found necessary to call in the French from Martinique. The desperation of the negroes is shown by the fact that they preferred death to capture; a body of three hundred, finally shut in and sure to be taken, deliberately shot each other, so that the victors found their dead bodies lying in a circle about their last camp. The suppression of this revolution cost 7900 rigsdaler, besides costly gifts to the French officers. But the St. John planters refused to bear a share in the expense, asserting, among other things, that the fort was poorly prepared for resistance.

When the king had taken over the powers of the Company and slaves began to come in with greater rapidity, the native question became still more threatening. Partially in consequence of this the slave-trade was declared illegal (1792). Thus the Danes became the forerunners of the great philanthropic movement of the early nineteenth century; the slave-trade went on, none the less, with the connivance of the authorities, for half a century.[1] Finally, on

[1] After 1792 slaves were continually imported, and premiums were paid for strong and healthy ones. Burt, En Stemme, etc.

the queen's birthday, June 28, 1847, all children born of slaves were declared to be free; the whole slave system was to be abolished in twelve years. But this move failed to win the confidence of the slaves, who were suspicious of the twelve-year term. Indications of a conspiracy appeared in 1848 and an incipient and dangerous revolt in St. Croix, in July of that year, encouraged by English sailors, forced an immediate emancipation; 1892 whites were opposed to 22,000 negroes in desperate mood, who carried the English flag as a symbol of freedom.

Administration; Social Conditions

We have here, then, with unimportant variations, the stock history of tropical labor up to emancipation; the measures that followed were likewise of a familiar general type. Contracts for paid labor were to date from October 1 of each year, and would be renewed only at that time; notice of such intention was to be given in August. No discharge was to be without ground, and no strikes were to be allowed; work was to last from sunrise till sunset, as a rule, and for only five days in the week, liberal allowance of time for meals (three hours) being granted. The laborer was given a small plot of ground and was to be paid per day fifteen, ten, or five cents according as he belonged to the first, second, or third grade of workmen. Extra labor during harvest was to be compensated, and no one was to be forced to work on Saturday; a maximum wage of twenty, thirteen, or seven cents was to be paid for voluntary Saturday labor. Fines, levied in labor, for absence and tardiness, were designed to oppose the tendency to vagabondage. Women were to be excused from work for seven weeks after confinement. Other provisions dealt with the treatment of the sick and weak, and with the punishment of those who incited a stoppage of labor. Certainly these St. Croix provisions were mild ones as they appear on the statute books. It is likely that they represent the actual treatment of the freedmen with approximate correctness. The conditions of forced labor of all kinds have been regularly harder on islands than upon the mainland where escape was easier; but, inasmuch as the position of the Danish islands favored evasion, it is likely that the planters, prizing their comparatively few laborers higher, took pains to retain them. The absence of the coolie system is scarcely remarkable, when one realizes the poverty of Denmark and the generally discouraging attitude of the British, Dutch, and Chinese governments toward this form of semi-slavery.

In spite of the laws, vagabondage, and with it crime, increased notably, especially in the towns of St. Thomas. In the country, master and former slave often worked side by side, winning a precarious existence under a somewhat disjointed system. For a long time no indemnity to former slave-owners was granted, owing to embarrassments of the home-country during the Slesvig-Holstein war.[1] In 1855 the working classes of St. Thomas were earning from five to twenty dollars per month. Many of them were great bunglers; few felt much obligation or displayed much fidelity to their masters. The regular effects of emancipation upon the character of the negro did not fail to appear; work was felt to be lowering; the negroes held the conviction that to be a "gentleman" one must command others and exact obedience. Domestic tyranny and cruelty resulted when this wish could not be gratified otherwise. Shameless begging was preferred to labor, and no attempt was made to provide for old age; alms of less than a dollar were regarded as petty, and the donor was despised. Aid was asked by able-bodied men as a matter of course. Vanity was a characteristic all too common; servants would not appear on errands until time had been taken to append to the person all the finery the individual in question possessed. Marriage was most lax, among the higher as well as the lower classes, and three-quarters of the children born on the island were illegitimate. The sentiment

[1] Under date of August 24, 1852, we have a letter of considerable interest, written by a St. Croix planter to the Danish Parliament (J. H. Burt, Jr., En Stemme, etc.). The author, after recalling the prosperity of the islands during the European wars, states that they are now struggling for existence: labor is insecure, insufficient, and costly; production is declining, and prices are low. He regards the labor regulations mentioned above as wise and beneficial, but explains that the planters could not have carried out the provisions demanded of them unless the labor supply had been made steady and secure. The main contention of the letter is that the Danish government should not so far prove false to its honor as to refuse indemnification to slave-owners after emancipation. The planters had been to considerable expense in the erection of schools, etc., for the betterment of the negroes, and yet it was proposed by some that they should in addition bear the entire amount of the loss incident to the freeing of the slaves. Any distinction between Danish and foreign planters in the matter of indemnification, such as seems to have been proposed, was doubly dishonorable. Other grievances of the colonies are touched upon, the letter concluding with the following paragraph: "A just indemnification, a sufficient immigration of free labor, an influential Colonialraad, and a strong government are the fundamental points upon which the future well-being of the colonists rests."

of the Danes seems to have been decidedly against formal marriages with blacks or mulattoes.[1]

The government of the islands after the fall of the Company appears to have been of a careful and reasonable type. Desire for an expansion of territorial possessions and a wish to aid the Company had led Christian VI to purchase St. Croix (1733) from the French. The price paid was 750,000 livres.[2] The miserable administration of the Company on this island conspired with the rest to bring about the purchase of its rights by Frederik V. In the negro troubles that followed, the government seems to have displayed clemency and thereby to have saved itself much expense and its island-citizens much loss of life and property. Complaints were not lacking, however, and the government became passive, rather than active, in later times. No successful effort was made to further education in the colonies, nor to establish adequate sea-connections. The school-fund was used up in St. Croix, and Sunday schools, maintained by private persons, formed almost the sole educational agency in the other two islands. Postal arrangements were particularly inadequate; letters were left at the nearest store and often lay there for long periods, until the recipient happened to be apprised of their presence. Many were lost; how letters from North America, coming always via Havana, managed to reach their destination has remained something of a mystery to the islanders themselves. Other details of administration were better managed. Tolls, harbor dues, etc., seem rarely to have been excessive under the royal government. The first *Colonialraad* was formed in 1852, under the governor as presiding officer. Its members were twenty in number, four from the king's selection and sixteen elective in the islands. Municipal affairs were in the hands of a council of five citizens, who received no remuneration save honor, and were not responsible to any one; they were regularly selected from the best men of the islands and seem to have served with fidelity and economy, although they held no open session, but simply submitted an annual report. The governor received under the Company a very small salary, but his position carried with it, of course, a number of fees and perquisites. In spite of economy, however, the royal budget of the islands shows for 1850–1851 a deficit of $48,662.[3]

---

[1] Erindringer, etc., pp. 114 ff.   [2] The livre of the period was worth about 19½ cents.
[3] For modern administrative and fiscal conditions, see Tooke.

The climate of these islands is well known. Its baleful effect upon the morals, and so the health, of the Danish colonists, was pronounced. Intemperance of all kinds was prevalent, and gambling for high stakes aided in the general demoralization. Of the diseases noted by the Danes, malaria, yellow-fever, influenza, and small-pox were the most serious, fatalities occurring chiefly among the lower classes of the population. Tables of mortality for the years 1835–1850 inclusive show an average yearly death-rate of about 38 per thousand, or 416 in an average population of 11,000. Earthquakes are frequent, though hitherto harmless; but hurricanes are prevalent (127 in the 352 years from 1494 to 1846), and very destructive; the islands are in the direct track of these storms.

TRADE-CONDITIONS

The trade-history of St. Thomas, which stands as a fair type for the other colonies, exhibits certain characteristics incident to its geographical location and political history. It is to be noted, first of all, that the harbor of St. Thomas formed an admirable haven, entirely adapted to the safe concealment that was so often a desideratum in the days of privateering and contraband traffic. This harbor was situated at the cross-ways of the trade-routes of that day. To these natural advantages were added others of a political nature: an almost constant neutrality and a free-haven status. The abbé Labat, writing in 1701, notices these favorable conditions, and states that the Danes derived great profits from the constant European wars, as prizes of both sides, and of freebooters, were brought in to be sold; the island also enjoyed benefits from the silver-trade with South America. St. Thomas was, in a word, a West Indian market-place of the first rank. The production of the island, with its light soil, was small, and prices were regularly high; but on the other hand, acquisition of wealth was easy and many resident foreigners had already grown rich. Though St. Thomas's harbor was declared a free haven for the first time in 1724, it had been so in reality for years.

The Company's influence upon the island's prosperity has been noted; an indirect evil result was seen, when, at the demise of this organization, Danish merchants were for some years too timid to seize upon the palpable advantages of the trade; during 1756 not one Danish ship entered the harbor. In fact, a number of merchants left the island, and circulating currency became so scarce as to lead to an issue of paper money for which the authorities were responsible. Depopulation was so much feared that a law was published according to which any one who left the island must surrender to the government 2½ per cent of his income and real property. In 1773 St. Thomas had 39 sugar and 43 cotton plantations, and 4233 inhabitants; of these 265 whites, 336 colored, and 1067 slaves lived in the town. St. John boasted 104 whites and 2330 slaves. Expenses slightly exceeded income; from 1755 to 1792 trade amounted to little. In 1792, however, a great change occurred, coincidently with European wars; trade rose to unhoped-for heights, and between 1792 and 1801, 1569 foreigners were naturalized in the island. A number of fugitives likewise came from San Domingo, and at the end of the century the population numbered about 7000. But between 1801 and 1815 the advantageous neutrality of the Danes was broken by forces which they could not control; from April, 1801, to February, 1802, St. Thomas was in British hands, and though trade revived again promptly after the restitution, a second violent break came in 1807. The Danes having refused England's proffered defensive alliance, the islands were seized and held until 1815. That some, at least, of the Danes valued their possessions highly in 1801 is shown by contemporary authority; [1] the feeling against England was exceedingly bitter. During the English occupation, English merchantmen alone were to be seen in the harbor and trade was very small. American products were diverted and passed over St. Bartholomew, [2] which at this time enjoyed an ephemeral importance; St. Thomas retained the direct trade of British North America alone.

DECLINE OF THE ISLANDS

After 1815 events again conspired to render St. Thomas prosperous. During the wars of emancipation of the Spanish continental

[1] Werfel, for example. Oxholm gives considerable detail as to the condition of the islands at the end of the eighteenth century. His book is an answer to certain "Breve fra St. Croix" containing articles upon the management of the islands.

[2] This diminutive island was the one venture of Sweden in tropical colonization. Cf. Euphrasen and Dahlman for some details of its conditions and history. The latter author is hopeful that the Swedish island may yet emulate the at his time enviable position of St. Thomas. For "The Swedish Legend in Guiana," see Edmundson under that title. There were some Swedish stations on the west coast of Africa, and several Swedish settlements in Delaware and New Jersey. The latter were taken by the Dutch in 1655, the African stations declined, and St. Bartholomew was ceded back to France in 1878. See Leroy-Beaulieu, I, 182–185.

colonies, many native Spaniards emigrated to the island, and the harbor was a resort of freebooters flying the flags of Buenos Ayres and Colombia; the year 1824 has been regarded by some as the culminating point of St. Thomas's prosperity. But the conditions which created this status were short-lived. The evil day was delayed for some years by the opportunities afforded for trade with the neighboring Puerto Rico and for the financing of its early development; many sugar-raisers in Puerto Rico could not have begun or prosecuted their industry without the credit afforded from St. Thomas. But as soon as this aid was no longer indispensable it was rudely put aside by the levying of heavy import-dues against the Danish island, and otherwise. In 1855 imports to St. Thomas (half from Europe and half from America) were valued at $5,000,000; St. Thomas merchants still continued to finance Puerto Rico to some extent, but the Danish island was evidently and surely on the decline. Denmark has been willing to part with her colonial possessions for a sufficient consideration several times since the middle of the nineteenth century; later years have witnessed no revival of trade. And this appears only natural when one reflects on the conditions which lent the former prosperity. The rise of modern transportation facilities, and the substantial peace of the world, implying as they do the passing of the narrower system of the former centuries, render a free, neutral harbor, and even a harbor of such central position as that of St. Thomas, of comparatively less importance. Way-stations and hiding-places are less in demand. Even the piercing of a waterway between the continents does not promise much for the future of these islands. As the city of small harbors has given way to the port like New York, which possesses, virtually, no harbor in the old sense of the term, so the small and local way-station has fallen away in a commerce on a grand scale in world-wide markets. True colonization in the West Indies was clearly beyond the strength of Denmark, as it was beyond the strength of the Portuguese in India. The mother-country was too remote and too small, the competition of greater peoples was too strong. A decision to part with the islands would seem to be the conclusion of wisdom, and considerations of national pride alone can oppose it.

This exceptional experiment in tropical colonization by a Scandinavian people runs, therefore, through most of the characteristic phases to which the student of colonies is used. In so far, it goes to show that the general course of events has followed the order of a natural and inevitable evolution. No particular virtue in avoiding stock errors, nor vice in committing peculiar and unusual mistakes is to be found in the Danes above other nations; economic evolution runs its course for them all alike, and they submit, each in his own way, to inevitable conditions and movements. In isolated cases, such as that of the Danes, though the local setting of the experiment is of curious rather than of vital interest, essential economic and political truths are not unlikely to emerge with especial simplicity and definiteness.

POLAR COLONIES OF THE SCANDINAVIANS

The history of the Danish colonies of Iceland and Greenland affords what is in some respects a distinct anomaly in colonization; and so, though of little practical importance, these dependencies may deserve some notice. Colonization toward the far north is an unprecedented enterprise and its annals cast a certain side-light upon the general process of the movement and re-formation of human societies.

POPULATION AND LIFE-CONDITIONS OF ICELAND

Strictly speaking, the first settlement of Iceland [1] was the result of emigration rather than of colonization. Discovered toward the end of the eighth century, about seventy years passed before it began to receive attention on the part of the Norse (860–870 A.D.); but within the subsequent sixty years, in consequence of a mass-emigration of political malcontents, the island had its full quota of population, that is, all that it could support upon that stage of the arts of life. This settlement was due largely to the movement toward state-integration in Norway by which losing factions were forced into exile; the settlers were prevailingly Norwegians. But owing to the very exigencies of the situation the emigrants recognized no bond of dependency, and, because of the natural isolation of Iceland, imposition of rule was all but impossible. Hence a rude and hardy race, schooled to courage and independence by the severity of the struggle for existence, at home as well as in the new land, took its fate into its own hands and formed a republic which

[1] On ancient Iceland the authorities here used are Maurer and Sars; for more modern conditions they are Otté and Øverland (passages referred to under "Island" in the indexes).

remained independent up to the year 1262. During the early part of this period the Norwegian kings had made several ineffectual attempts to persuade the Icelanders to acknowledge their sway; their purpose was resisted, but, by setting leader against leader, and through the partisanship of the clergy, they had gradually gained an ever greater influence. The internal government of the island was by the end of the thirteenth century in a state of demoralization, and the various districts yielded one by one until, between 1262 and 1264, a general fealty was sworn to the Norwegian King Haakon.[1]

It does not fall within the scope of the present book to describe the organization of the republic which the Icelanders created out of the confusion of their beginnings;[2] it is enough to say that the type of the society was Norse and that political coalescence with the land of origin was in the order of events. " Such a conformity cannot have been a chance one; it goes to show that the two societies, of which the one proceeded out of the other, . . . continued to belong together; that their public life was nurtured from the same source, and rested essentially upon the same foundation; that antitheses between republican Iceland and monarchical Norway were more seeming than real; and that the aristocracy of birth . . . continued to be, in later times as well as in earlier, in Norway as in Iceland, the actual support of the life of the state and society."[3] Here then we have in Norway a metropolis which has attained the political integration and the influence necessary to take to itself independent settlements of its own emigrants. Iceland was now a true Norwegian colony, and it so remained until 1380; thereafter it became a Danish possession and was destined so to remain when Norway had become united with Sweden and finally had attained independence.[4]

The interest of the student of colonization leads him to consider first of all the life-conditions of such a colony and to seek the

<hr/>

[1] Cf Øverland, III, 421 ff.

[2] Details of the organization of the republic and its decline are to be found in Maurer and in Sars, I, chap. vii.

[3] Sars, I, 196. " The colonial character of the Icelandic society — the whole unbroken spiritual cohesion in which it remained with the rest of the Norwegians — appears most clearly in the way in which Icelanders write Norway's history. For it is seen that they never regard her history otherwise than as their own, that they have conceived the whole in the same manner as do all other Norwegians, and have fully shared the sentiments and opinions that prevail in Norway." Sars, II, 325.

[4] Sars, II, chap. vi. Danish rule was rather easily established. Øverland, IV, 440.

motives which lay behind the policy of the mother-country toward it. The population of Iceland was small in earlier times and has so remained; as late as 1870 its 40,000 square miles supported not quite 70,000 souls; and in 1890 there were but a thousand more. The island is one-quarter desert and only a third of it can support sheep even in the summer; two-fifths are of better quality, but the cultivation of even the hardiest grains is precarious; all bread-stuffs are still imported.[1] In 1853, a year nearly normal, there were in Iceland 23,663 horned cattle, 40,485 horses, and 516,853 sheep. Fishing is one of the most profitable occupations; in 1853 the islanders owned 3506 boats. Other food-supply than flesh and fish is of a primitive character; the eggs of sea-birds may be mentioned.[2] The isolation of the country militates against trade: communication has been of so faulty a character that the shortest and cheapest route between certain parts of the island has been via Copenhagen; in the favorable season sailing-vessels take six to eight weeks to reach Iceland, and in winter it is practically cut off from the world.[3]

Evidently the Norwegian colonists were an industrious people, and chiefly sheep-raisers, desiring above all, from the government to which they had sworn allegiance, conditions of peace and order. In type the settlements represented the "farm colony";[4] there were no precious metals, no native-question, no large staple products; the emigrants were of both sexes and in general had come to found homes; in the absence of natives the society fostered no half-breed stock. Naturally, however, environing conditions precluded any development of numbers; hardships had their inevitable effect in keeping down the standard of living; and other local factors conspired to render the society but a feeble representative of the flourishing farm colony. Indeed, the absence of agriculture itself makes the term "farm colony," except as it connotes a type of social organization, a misnomer. There has been a possibility of but little favorable change in the economic life of Iceland up to the

---

[1] Otté (p. 203) says nine-tenths of Iceland are unfit for human habitation.

[2] Maurer, pp. 1-11, 16-19; Otté, pp. 203 ff. The Statesman's Year-Book (for 1906; sub "Denmark") gives the proportion of the population in 1850 which was dependent upon cattle-raising and fishing as 82 per cent and 17 per cent respectively; in 1890 these had changed to 64 per cent and 18 per cent.

[3] The death of Frederik VII (November 15, 1863) was reported in Iceland upon April 4, 1864; meanwhile the late king's island-subjects had been praying all winter in orthodox fashion for his health. Maurer, p. 33.

[4] Cf. pp. 4 ff., above; Øverland, III, 504.

present time; indeed, there has been in several periods a distinct retrogression. Iceland has been frequently visited by famines and pestilences, those scourges of a population pressing overhard upon land; and volcanic outbursts followed by copious lava-flows have destroyed large sections of habitable country. In 1786 the desertion of the island was seriously considered.[1] Few resources have been added to elevate the standard of living. The salting of meat and of salmon has provided some extra employment and gain, and certain sulphur-deposits have been worked. The latter, however, were leased to an English company in 1872 for fifty years. Since the early seventies there has been a relatively large emigration from Iceland to Canada, especially to the province of Manitoba; meanwhile the population (1901) had increased to nearly 78,500, a conjunction of facts calculated to show the society able to more than reproduce itself.

GOVERNMENT

When Iceland came under Norwegian rule there was made a proviso — whose terms bespeak the severity of life-conditions — that the new king should send at least six ships every year with meal and like necessities. It was partly by reason of this condition that the later Norwegian rulers, and, after the personal union with Denmark (Kalmar-union,[2] 1397), the Danish sovereigns, came to regard the trade with Iceland as their own prerogative and sold or leased it at will. Until the fourteenth century the trade of the island had been in the hands of the Icelanders and Norse; during the fifteenth the English and during the sixteenth the Hanseatics had secured a large proportion of it. But it had been subject to little restriction, and the royal monopoly came gradually to press hard upon the struggling islanders.

To follow the history of Iceland during the centuries of its subjection to Norway and Denmark is a rather profitless task. Norwegian rule seems to have brought a period of decline which is not all referable to plagues and other such calamities.[3] The impression gained from reading scattered notices of Iceland in

---

[1] In 1783 occurred an eruption of the Skaptar Jökull, which overwhelmed plains and inhabited villages and caused the death of 9500 out of 50,000 inhabitants. Barney, p. 38, note. The second eruption of the same volcano, in 1873, was one of the principal causes for the ensuing emigration. [2] Sars, III, chap. ii.

[3] Øverland, III, 716 ff. For a list of plagues, volcanic eruptions, etc., between 1284 and 1390, see id., p. 507.

histories of Norway is that the island was treated with indifference except in so far as it might provide a small increment to the royal revenues. Later times have seen the development of a more liberal policy ; in 1854 the trade-monopoly was renounced and commerce was made free. In 1874 Iceland was restored to virtual independence and remains locally republican in its government, though nominally ruled by the king in conjunction with a legislative assembly. It is designated as an inalienable part of the Danish monarchy and its legal system is mainly Danish. The Icelanders have endured much from their rulers in the past, but have insisted upon their rights with the characteristic steadiness and firmness, yet with the same remarkable self-restraint exhibited by the Scandinavian peoples on the occasion of the recent separation of Norway and Sweden. Iceland is civilly and nationally independent in all but form, and constitutes a strong if small society, singularly free from crime and intensely attached to its inhospitable island-home. The religion has been of the reformed type since the early part of the sixteenth century.[1] Denmark gets no gain from her Norwegian-founded colony : the average annual revenue is 200,000 kroner and the expenditure 188,000 ; in the former item was reckoned for many years a Danish subsidy of 60,000 kroner. Imports for 1904 were valued at 2,466,000 kroner and exports at 3,417,000.

It would be an evidence of narrow interest on the part of any narrator of Icelandic affairs to neglect to mention the astonishing intellectual and especially literary productiveness of these northern islanders. An antique tongue has been safeguarded by them and they have originated or preserved ancient sagas that are a heritage of the race. They are more Norse than the Norse. In modern times they have furnished their full share of men superior in learning and otherwise. Taking into consideration the drawbacks of environment and the necessary depression of the standard of living, Iceland's contribution to the world ranks with the most notable.

Colonization and Life-Conditions of Greenland

Greenland[2] presents another instance of polar colonization by the Norwegians whose fruits, such as they are, have fallen to the Danes.

---

[1] For the Reformation in Iceland, cf. Øverland, IV, 422 ff.

[2] The chief authority for the history of Greenland is Rink. Some use has been made of Crantz, Gravier, Peyrère, Wilhelmi, Otté, and Øverland (references *sub* "Grønland" in indexes). For more modern conditions Nansen has been followed.

The only striking point of difference between the case of Greenland and that of Iceland is that in the former colony there have existed conditions of race-contact and mixture. The discovery of Greenland goes back probably into the eighth century, and was made from Iceland, according to old chronicles, by Eric the Red ; it then served as an intermediary station for the attainment of America. Christianity was introduced about the year 1000 and in 1023 the country was tributary to Norway ; an attempt at revolt (1256) led to its full subjection with the aid of the Danish king, in 1261. After this time but little attention seems to have been accorded to Greenland, and concern in Europe over the ravages of the Black Death (1347–1351) reduced that little to nothing ; decades of virtual oblivion followed. It was only with the discoveries of Columbus that interest was reawakened in possible lands or passages toward the west. Succeeding Frobisher (1578) and Davis (1585), the Danes — for Norway was now under Danish rule — made some ineffectual attempts to reach the old settlements ; a Greenland Company was formed in 1636 and dispatched vessels. But what little hold the Norwegians had possessed was now lost : the Eskimo, and even Atlantic pirates, had done their share to effect general ruin.[1] And it appears that during the long period of neglect the royal power, jealous of even its well-nigh valueless monopoly of the Greenland trade in oil, ivory, and furs, had prohibited the approach of private adventurers to the region.[2]

The re-colonization of Greenland took place largely as a result of the activities of a clergyman, Egede, who had been for years agitated over the fate of the Norwegians and their descendants left in the old settlements. In 1721 Frederik IV was led to found Godthaab (Good Hope) and Egede began his religious labors in Greenland. Since that time the natives have had Christianity preached to them, often not wisely but too well ; in 1733 the Moravian Brothers took up Egede's work.[3]

[1] Nansen (pp. 11–12) does not believe that the Eskimo waged a war of annihilation against the early settlers.

[2] " All these details are confused and contradictory. But there emerges, nevertheless, one fact : the pirates made common cause with the cold, the Eskimo, the pest, and the lawyers of Margaret [of Denmark] in ruining the colonies founded by the Scandinavians on the coasts of America and of Greenland." Gravier, p. 223. Cf. Rink, pp. 20 ff., 29 ff.

[3] Crantz's book is mainly a chronicle of the Moravians' religious work. From the time he reaches this topic (I, 315) his book loses all interest for the scientist or historian. The missionaries spent a deal of misdirected zeal in " correcting " native

The life-conditions in Greenland are an extreme variation upon the Icelandic type; even the hardy vegetables fail to thrive, and the dog is the only domestic animal of any value.[1] Europeans are interested only in trade or in the mission; the former yields a "trifling but sure profit." Under the royal monopoly, dating from 1774, prices have been fixed, the Danes paying to the Greenlanders about 22 per cent of the value of their products (train-oil, whale-bone, pelts, etc.) in the European market; it is said that the gain on goods sold to the Eskimo is not exorbitant, reaching only 20 per cent as a maximum. From 1870 to 1874 the mean annual value of products received from Greenland was about $228,000; that of cargoes destined for Greenland, about $120,000. The representatives of Denmark are mainly factors whose duty lies in the drumming-up of trade; there were in 1877 eleven agents and eighteen clerks. The net revenue of the Greenland trade for the period 1853–1874 was about $705,000, the cryolite tax for the same years amounting to $295,000. "The whole amount of net revenues from the present Trade during the period from 1790 to 1875, the interest of the capital as well as the income from the cryolite being subtracted, has been estimated at about 160,000 l."[2]

RACE-CONTACT

There have never been many Scandinavians in Greenland. In early times some criminals were deported there, and later orphan boys were sent out to become teachers or to recruit the inferior clergy. But as late as 1881 there were only 200 Danes among a native population of some 10,000; in 1870 there were 237 Europeans, of whom 95 were traders, 19 missionaries, and 38 employed in the cryolite mines. Until the time of the missions there were practically no white women in Greenland, and there have been very few since; thus Greenland has never become a settlement-colony like Iceland. In fact, the population-conditions more closely

habits which really represented a natural adaptation to the local environment; they tried, for instance, to render the Eskimo sedentary and to force them to wear clothing in their *igloos* or huts. They ruthlessly annihilated the often harmless or even beneficent influence and the respectability of the *angakoks* or medicine-men. Cf. Rink and Nansen, *passim*, and Rink, p. 143.

[1] There were in Greenland, in 1855, 30 to 40 horned cattle, 100 goats, and 20 sheep. Rink, p. 97.

[2] Rink, pp. 138, 280–282, 312, 313 (quoted).

resemble those of the tropical colony: the natives are indispensable to the whites and if they died out, Greenland would become uninhabited. Here likewise is found a wholesale miscegenation; it is difficult to find a pure-blooded Eskimo on the west coast. Half-breeds were reckoned as constituting 14 per cent of the population in 1820, and 30 per cent in 1855; the blending has now become imperceptible. The native women prefer the worse Dane to the best Greenlander and the half-breeds are the more eligible for their strain of white blood; illicit relations with white men are rather a glory than a disgrace.[1] The Danish government favors the race-mixture; even at the present time officials are not discouraged from marrying Eskimo women, although upon return to Denmark under pension they must leave wife and children behind. The mongrels resulting from these mixed unions appear to form no very great improvement upon the native stock.

Relations between the two races, aside from intermarriage, began with the absurd and often cruel interference of the missionaries; but they have been on the whole so friendly as to be almost unique. Doubtless this was due in part to the kindly temperament of the natives, and also to a realization often brought home to the Europeans, of their dependence upon a clever and generous people. Nevertheless, despite such friendliness, the Eskimo have declined in number and degenerated in their habits of life. Egede reckoned 30,000 as the number of natives; allowing a large discount for ecclesiastical mendacity, the decline is evident and rapid. Both Rink and Nansen advert repeatedly to the feeling of superiority of the European toward the native as in some sense a key to the situation, and both refer to the missions in slighting terms. It is shown, especially by Nansen, how the very gifts of the white men have occasioned a decline in native prowess, inventiveness, and the like; the rifle, for example, is a curse in that it renders possible a reckless slaughter of wild animals for purposes of momentary gain. Also, although the Danish government prohibits the sale of brandy to the natives, other European products, notably coffee, have produced ill effects. The increase of native population in late years is said to be illusory, and the Greenland Eskimo appear to be on the highroad to extinction, at least as a pure race.[2]

[1] Rink, pp. 166, 169, 175, 162, 296 ff., 163, 151; Nansen, pp. 12, 20, 165.
[2] Rink, pp. 145 ff., 158 ff., 168, 227-228, 283, 286; Nansen, pp. 88, 97, 105 ff., 166, 307-308; chap. xv; pp. 313, 328 ff., 342 ff.

The natives are all nominally Christians; they are by nature happy and contented, peaceable and harmless, and thus tractable in an extraordinary degree. Owing to the efforts of Rink they have some voice through their local councils in the administration of their villages.[1] Admirably adapted as they have become, through centuries of vicissitudes, to a difficult environment, their continuance, or at least the retarding of their disappearance, seems to hang upon their power to exist and propagate where the dominant race cannot. The purity of their blood may be threatened or sacrificed, but for the present their manner of life and other tribal characteristics seem likely to persist for an indefinite period to come.

[1] Nansen, pp. 321–322.

CHAPTER XIV

MODERN ITALIAN AND GERMAN COLONIZATION

ITALIAN COLONIZATION

The history of the colonial ventures of modern Italy is brief and inglorious ; at the present time, after much bloodshed and expense, it can hardly be said that Italy possesses any real colonies from whose administration and development an economic or political lesson or warning can be gained. And yet the struggles of Italy, during the latter part of the nineteenth century, to found a colonial empire after the manner of other European states possess a peculiar interest for the student of colonization ; for she seems to have approached the self-appointed task in a novel, and, as the result proved, a disastrous way. Italy is a nation which hoped, by taking thought, to add unto her stature. Granted that England's greatness is emphasized and augmented by her colonial possessions, it is at best a logical *non sequitur* to conclude that Italy, by acquiring colonies and possessions, will thereby take her place among the Powers. And yet the Italians seem to have believed it possible to substitute for the long and toilsome road from cause to effect a convenient short-cut from effect to cause. Colonies were not only to increase Italy's political importance ; they were also to build up her trade, develop her merchant marine, and make her rich. Thus the normal order of evolution was reversed in this suddenly evoked colonial policy, and the consequences, in this case little ameliorated by circumstances, ran out into the usual misery of confusion and humiliation.

DISQUALIFICATIONS OF ITALY

This is the fundamental judgment to be passed upon the Italian so-called colonization. Italy was not prepared to take her place among colonizing states ; she lacked the internal cohesion and organization necessary to the political unit that turns its arms against the outside world. On the eve of her colonial efforts the

517

nation was united in no such way as were England, France, the Netherlands, Spain, and Portugal, just before their colonial expansion. Italy lacked capital and, in a certain sense, superfluous population for external colonization; what forces she had could better have been used for internal development, which, in turn, would have aided national organization and prosperity. She lacked the objective knowledge of lands, peoples, and processes which most of the great colonizing nations had attained from the actual experience of their traders and navigators before their colonial empires were even begun. She was unfit for colonization because she was without those things which she hoped the possession of colonies would bring her.

One more disqualification must be noticed in order to get a perspective of the short and disastrous history of Italian expansion: the Italians, together with the other Latin nations, suffer from a race-temperament unfortunate in colonizers. They are generally dominated too much by feeling and too little by judgment; they are attracted too much by abstract theory, military glory, and all that which caters to national vanity; they cannot accept defeat with dignity, renounce a high-sounding ideal, and bide their time in patience. They have shown themselves incapable of such steadiness and foresight as, for instance, was exhibited in the withdrawal, quiet preparation, and final overwhelming return of England in the Egyptian Sudan.[1] Italy's colonial development, however, retarded by so many wars, has not as yet reached that stage of civil administration where the characteristic defects of Latin policy are wont to appear; judging from the organization of the Red Sea possessions during a short period of peace and security, the Italians might have been expected to adopt a somewhat better adapted policy than did Spain, Portugal, or France.

MOTIVES OF EXPANSION

It is significant that poverty, rather than overflowing wealth, first caused United Italy to desire a colony. The individual emigrated because of poverty and misery; the state sought a penal colony because of poverty and social disorder. On March 13, 1865, the Chamber of Deputies abolished the capital penalty, and a substitute was at once considered. The example of England was cited

---

[1] Cf. De Saussure, chap. xi, p. 208, etc.

in support of adopting deportation, and the position of those who favored this substitute was strengthened by the grave condition of public security in the sixties and seventies. Prison population grew by more than 1500 annually, and increased from 52,000 in 1862 to 67,000 in 1870, averaging 104 per 100,000 population. Prisons were insufficient in number and all in wretched state; it was estimated that 100,000,000 lire and twenty years' time would be necessary to construct new edifices. Deportation seemed an anchor of safety. A hot controversy was waged over the employment of this penalty, and for a long time desire for such a place of exile formed the chief motive for acquisition of external possessions. A government agent tried to get possession of locations in the Far East suitable for penal establishments, and other private or semi-official travelers reported on the same project. But in 1874 the enemies of deportation had increased in number, and conditions in Italy were ameliorated; discussion lasted on till 1888, when it was dropped.[1] The question of deportation was therefore a temporary one, not connected with later developments, except as it directed the attention of the Italians to conditions without; deportation was never popular. Prospecting for a commercial or naval station, which to a certain extent accompanied the search for a penal colony, was even more feeble, vague, and unproductive. Up to 1880 expansionists talked to the empty air. Even the opening of the Suez Canal (November, 1869) effected little, though through the urgency of a small party, who insisted upon the necessity of a station on the new Indies route, the government half-heartedly acquiesced in the purchase of Assab, a sterile tract on the Red Sea coast.[2]

"The search for colonies, therefore," Brunialti says, "had conducted to no serious conclusion"; further efforts were made to arouse interest, but "we sang to the deaf." After 1873 there was no more talk of colonies and even Assab fell into oblivion; in 1882

[1] Brunialti, pp. 271 ff., 527 ff. Brunialti's book affords, besides a sketch, chiefly historical and political, of the colonies of modern Italy, also a history of the mediæval Venetian and Genoese trading-colonies and an account of the great Italian navigators of the period of Discoveries. The author treats the modern possessions from an authoritative position, inasmuch as he was personally involved in the discussions and projects which preceded and accompanied the late colonial policy.

[2] Through the agency of the Rubattino Steamship Company for 15,000 Maria-Theresa dollars (about $16,000), with some extra fees and payments to recalcitrant sheiks. Brunialti, pp. 324, 532.

Italy refused an advantageous opportunity to coöperate with England in reducing Egypt, explained her action to Europe with virtuous self-complacency, and wished to have nothing to do with Africa.[1]

Suddenly, in February, 1885, in consequence of the massacre of the Italian scientific party of Bianchi, the government at Rome roused itself and occupied the port of Massowah. The effect upon the national mind was unexpected and astonishing, affording a marked illustration of the changefulness of public opinion. Before the occupation, "the less enthusiastic were precisely those who had a more exact idea of colonial policy and its exigencies, who feared that public opinion would cast itself upon this acquisition, increase its importance, and make an unique objective of what ought to be a small episode and nothing else." This fear was realized, for the country faced about from indifference to military ambition, parliamentary calculation, and political delirium; there resulted "a whole artificial elaboration of public opinion, such as would scarcely be believed possible in a free and civilized modern state."[2] These are the symptoms of "colonial fever," which was not slow to discover itself in pronounced form; nor was the country, smitten with the passion for expansion, tardy in presenting reasons to justify the satisfaction of that passion. Were not the Romans the first of colonizers? Could the Italians acknowledge themselves degenerate sons of those hardy Venetians, Genoese, and Pisans who were the mediæval lords of trade and of commercial factories? This pride of ancestry was united with what Laveleye and others call "megalomania," as the main motive forces in a disastrous expansion.[3] With the eye ever upon England and the Netherlands, the endeavor was made to construct a Greater Italy. To these high ambitions, however, were joined the most absurd fears, an unsettled policy, and general weakness and indecision — qualities seldom exhibited in any degree by a people ripe for colonization.[4]

Attention, it has been said, turned to emigration, the merchant marine, and national production. As for the first of these, a brief study of Italian emigration suffices to show it an unstable foundation upon which to build a colonial edifice. During the early days of the colonial agitation, the Italian consul at Nice, one of those

[1] Brunialti, pp. 323–326, 422 ff.   [2] Id., pp. 15 ff., 433.
[3] Cf. the articles of Laveleye, Nash, Mezzacapo, and Pittaluga.
[4] Brunialti, pp. 228 ff., 261–297.

whose opinion concerning the new policy was officially asked, opposed such a movement, saying that for colonization, capital, heads,
and hands were needful, but that Italy possessed only the last
of these requirements.[1] This concisely expresses the character of
Italian emigration ; only the poverty-stricken and the ignorant emigrated, and their exodus was a species of flight. It may be true
that unprincipled agents worked upon the credulity of the over-
taxed and underpaid *contadini* and often allured them to a fate even
more wretched than that of remaining in Italy ; but it is significant that whole villages were ready to emigrate, with their parish
priests at the head, while acres of productive ground were falling
into waste in the home-land. This emigration of Italian labor cannot be regarded as a natural and inevitable flow, due to purely
natural conditions of population and land ; private initiative counted
for little ; the emigrant would in most cases have stayed at home
if, after paying his heavy dues, he had had enough to eat.[2]

Not until 1884 was the Italian marine able to provide proper
postal facilities for the settlements along the Red Sea ; its condition, then, can be imagined, during those years when the government was vaguely seeking, even from Denmark in Greenland, and
from Russia in Behring Straits, those colonies which should by
some magic set commerce upon its feet. The Italians awakened
to find their wooden sailing-ships contending in a losing competition with modern vessels of iron, propelled by steam. Italy had
at her disposal neither coal nor iron, neither mechanics nor engi-
neers. To wait for trade to develop its carriers was too slow a
process ; the marine called for colonies, which would then call for
a marine ; and the government began to spend large sums in subventions and other aid.[3]

The remaining reason for Italian expansion was economic ; the
growth of protection in Europe and America seriously threatened
Italy's trade, and colonies were sought as outlets and markets.
The government was also in the search for stations in the Far
East in order to profit by treaties concluded in the sixties with
China, Japan, and Siam.[4] This was, perhaps, the most rational of
the reasons assigned for the development of the colonial policy.

---

[1] Brunialti, pp. 231, note, 289.   [2] Id., pp. 261 ff. ; Laveleye.
[3] Brunialti, pp. 283 ff. ; " The Merchant Marine of Italy," *The Nation*, August 31,
1882, XXXV, 171.
[4] Brunialti, p. 524.

At all events, Italy became aware in 1885 of the fact that she had lost Tunis to the French, after most favorable beginnings, had childishly refused England's offer, fraught with possibility, of a dual campaign in Egypt, and had sacrificed numerous possible possessions in the Far East. She fixed her eyes on Tripoli and gave more attention to the flourishing natural colonies in the Plata region of South America; though, sad to say, she allowed these districts to take an entirely secondary place in relation to the new acquisitions in eastern Africa.[1]

THE AFRICAN ACQUISITIONS

Real expansion, then, began with the occupation of Massowah. Assab had cost in all about two-thirds of a million lire, the territory extending thirty-six miles along the coast and having an area of about two hundred and forty square miles. But after Massowah had been occupied by force, the method of purchase lost all popularity; the way of conquest was more "essential to our position as a Great Power"—it was more theatrical.[2] Little attention was paid to the safeguarding of an indispensable friendship with the Negus, or King of Kings, of Abyssinia. There followed in rapid succession the occupation by force of Habab and Beni-Amer (1887), Cheren and Asmara (1889), Cassala, Coatit, and Senafé (1894), and Tigré (1895), until the Italian possessions comprised about 96,000 square miles, with 200,000 native and 3500 European inhabitants.[3] In 1889 a protectorate was assumed over the sultans of Obbia and Migertini; and by the treaty of Ucciali (May 2, 1889) the whole kingdom of Abyssinia came under Italian influence. A protectorate was officially recognized in Europe, and, to a certain extent, by the Negus;[4] later, however, the latter repudiated the article of the treaty upon which Italy based her claim to a protectorate, alleging misrepresentation and fraud. Under such strains, and because the Abyssinians were incensed at the occupation of their ancient capital, Adowa, in the holy country of Tigré, war speedily broke out; and on March 1, 1896, Italian expansion was brought to a sudden close in the battle of Abba Garima, where

---

[1] Brunialti, chap. xi; pp. 298 ff., 422.　　　　[2] Id., pp. 16, 409, 430.

[3] Id., p. 466; Appleton's Ann. Cyc., 1895, *sub* "Abyssinia."

[4] This made the total area under Italian influence about 550,000 square miles, with more than 6,000,000 inhabitants. Cf. Statesman's Year-Book, 1891; Appleton's Ann. Cyc., as above.

12,000 Italians rashly attacked the Abyssinian army of 80,000 and were almost annihilated.[1] In the treaty that followed, the protectorate over Abyssinia was given up, Cassala was ceded to Egypt, the Abyssinian territory which had been occupied was evacuated, and Italy paid a heavy indemnity for the maintenance and return of prisoners. This decisive check may be considered as bringing the ten years' period of Italian expansion to a close, for since 1896 no further move toward aggrandizement in Africa has been attempted. Indeed, it is said that the tenure of Italian Somaliland, in view of the attitude of Menelek, is precarious.

From the military and political standpoints, therefore, Italian expansion was a failure. Results also failed to meet the expectations of those who were looking for a more profitable regulation of emigration, a development of commerce and of the marine, and a notable spread of civilization. Here one must do justice to the small minority of clear-headed statesmen who constantly opposed the current of popular folly, or with it were unwillingly and resistingly borne along. It was in vain that they reiterated objections against the popular projects — objections since proved only too valid. In fact, as was at the time pointed out, only those parts of Africa were allotted to Italy which fall to the weak late-comer; while England, the generous giver, drew considerable advantages from occupation by a friendly nation. These possessions, which from Crispi received the pompous collective name of Eritrea, were entirely unsuitable for agricultural or plantation colonies. The soil is, in general, arid, sandy, and unproductive; rain is infrequent; even drinking-water is extremely scarce and brackish. The climate, especially near the coast, is almost insupportable for Europeans; the Italian army was forced by the heat to take refuge upon the interior plateaus. The sharp contrast of temperature between night

---

[1] This battle and other reverses were due largely to the ambition of the Crispi and preceding ministries, which needed victories to hold their place; it was also due to gross geographical and ethnographical ignorance and insufficient preparation. Brunialti says the Italian statesmen had "a sacred horror of geography," and that one of the most responsible could not "read a geographical chart in the proper manner." Upon Crispi, however, falls the heaviest weight of indignation and contempt: he called the war "my war," and, according to Brunialti, his chief reason for desiring it was that his "personal necessities . . . impelled him to hide too many things, and himself as well, behind a series of victories." The war was very unpopular in its later stages; protests came in from the women of Pavia and other cities; troops were transported in secret, "in the dead of night, through a window or down an exterior stair," and "despatched hurriedly by goods-trains to Naples for embarcation." Brunialti, pp. 435, 497, 506 ff.; art. by "Ouida."

and day affects cattle disastrously. The flora is meager, consisting mostly of acacias and the like, and the better parts of the country are infested by destructive and dangerous wild beasts.[1] Yet even these unalluring prospects were less discouraging than the ethnic environment. The Italians found themselves face to face with the only strong and organized African state — a state whose warlike population prided itself upon its independence and its successes against invaders; the Italians, however, looked upon the Abyssinian army as a "horde," an easy prey for five hundred Italians with a little artillery. They found it armed with rapid-fire guns and drilled by French tacticians.[2]

POLICY AND ADMINISTRATION

In such a state of affairs the security necessary for the development of permanent agricultural settlements was never attained. All experiments resulted in dismal failure; emigration could not be attracted from America. Under the best conditions of peace, with gratuitous concessions of land, subsidies in money, intelligent direction and disinterested counsels from men who knew the Italian peasants well, all attempts to settle them in Eritrea came to naught. Harvests failed to meet expectations and life in Africa could develop no alluring features; the *contadini* could exist there, as in Italy, and no better. There was no prospect of making one's fortune, that chance which prompts one to choose a dangerous possibility in place of a tame certainty, and which has regularly led Italians to brave the unknown in America. "Therefore the colonization of Eritrea was ever an official project, a work of beneficence, and as such could yield no serious and important result, even though the fortune of arms had been quite different." The case was worse than a negative one; destitute emigrants were sent out, on the verge of the great disasters, to "do homage to the ideas of the government regarding the future of the Eritrean colony, to make believe that Africa, through so many years ignored and feared, had become all at once the land of Bengodi."[3]

But if a producing colony, receptive of a large and successful emigration, was impossible, there still remained the alternative of developing a trading-settlement. Even if this aided emigration

---

[1] Arts. by Rossi, Edwards, and Capucci.   [2] Brunialti, p. 449; Frassati.
[3] Brunialti, p. 472; Rossi.

little, it would yet assist the home-country's commerce and marine. It was claimed by the sponsors of Eritrean expansion that Assab, and to a greater extent Massowah and Cassala, were the keys to the trade of the eastern Sudan, Abyssinia, and central Africa; it was expected that caravans would make an easier passage to these stations than to others, and it was proposed to afford facilities in the shape of roads, magazines, etc., and to remove hindering trade-restrictions.[1] To a certain degree this more modest purpose succeeded, though, of course, trade never attained the proportions expected. Assab and Massowah are good harbors, protected from the prevailing monsoons; the commerce of Assab rose from nil in 1880 to some 525 each of arrivals and clearances in 1883; as for Massowah, the value of its imports fell from 1887 to 1893, then to rise with some rapidity. The figure for 1896 is the largest, showing an increase of more than 100 per cent over 1895.[2] Some valuable roads were opened, and a salt industry, founded at Assab, was very important as looking toward trade with the interior. Had peace prevailed and security been permanently maintained, it seems likely that Italy would have gotten a modest share in the interior trade. But capital refused to emigrate; in 1887 Massowah had not a single merchant house. Many were afraid of finding in Masso-wah a "new Tonkin"; it had "all the disadvantages and none of the advantages of a territorial colony." [3] It is evident that Italians at the present time cherish no enthusiasm for the Eritrean trade, and that the powerful neighbors of Eritrea fear and envy its commerce but little. The development of the marine and of home production would seem not to have been greatly stimulated as a result of the African colonial career.[4]

The brighter pages of the history of Eritrea are those which deal with the organization and incipient administration of the colony, especially under General Baratieri. The Italians were a bit theoretical withal, but set out to avoid "Spanish formalism, Dutch egoism, French concentration, and the too diverse conditions

---

[1] Brunialti, pp. 409 ff., 416, 430 ff.

[2] Brunialti, pp. 414 ff.; Statesman's Year-Book, 1890 and following years; Almanach de Gotha, 1889 and following.   [3] Brunialti, pp. 446–448; Rossi.

[4] From 1884 to 1896 the total tonnage of Italian seagoing vessels slowly declined; but during the same period the tonnage of Italian steamships rose from 107,542 to 220,508. Something over one-half of the vessels entering and clearing from Massowah were under the Italian flag. Entries to Italian ports increased slowly during the period. Statesman's Year-Book, 1885–1896; Almanach de Gotha, same years.

of English colonization." They regarded the first need of a country barely out of savagery as that of a simple justice, with rapid and economic procedure, without distinction of legal qualification and backed up by a prompt and vigorous execution. They intended to respect religion, family relations, etc., where not irreconcilable with *morale universale*, and to maintain a full and severe custody of public order; they hoped to become *non dominatori, non tutori, non innovatori, ma amici ed aiutatori,* guiding new fellow-citizens toward a betterment that was comprehended and desired. Certain high-sounding phrases about making the Italian name a synonym for honesty and loyalty, concerning Italian sympathy with others' patriotism, and so on, were declaimed; but they were mere words, most clearly set at naught in the dealings with the Negus. For "the Italian government always proceeded towards Abyssinia as toward a people ignorant and barbarous, whom they thought it not only allowable, but easy to deceive." [1]

Before 1892 the colonial government was rather chaotic; a municipal and military tax imposed in 1888 by the military governor was stoutly resisted. The military was replaced by a civil government in 1890, troops were withdrawn, and an attempt was made to organize commerce and profitable cultivation; the condition of the colony was far from satisfactory, however, and in 1891 the minister, Di Rudini, initiated the non-extension policy and sent a commission to examine matters in Eritrea. On February 8, 1892, General Baratieri was appointed civil governor of the province. The condition of the colony changed at once for the better. Baratieri was well fitted for the office conferred upon him, being familiar with the region and well versed in the duties required. He appointed picked men as the leaders of native troops, established friendly relations with the Negus Menelek and all the chiefs who proffered friendship, and he incited Italian residents to a sharp watch over all "protected" territories. He established within a short time stations of *carabinieri* with natives under them, dispelled all fear of raids, set about making roads, and, the opportunity presenting itself, dealt the slave-trade a crushing blow. "The colony was divided into the district of Massowah, where the administration, judicial, social, and political, is carried on as in Italy, and into dependent territories, where the native laws and usages are respected and applied as far as possible; tribunals of

[1] Brunialti, pp. 409–412, 448.

arbitration were set up at Cheren and Asmara, judges of the peace
in the villages, and everywhere residential officials bound to keep
the governor 'up to date' on all military and local matters." The
roads were made chiefly by native labor, and artesian wells were
driven and lighthouses erected by the same means. Hygiene was
attended to; water was analyzed and food inspected. Cisterns
were built to preserve the scanty rains and in house-building stone
succeeded straw. Schools were established for girls and boys,
teaching Italian, Arabic, arithmetic, hygiene, and gymnastics. The
division of lands was commenced, defining tribal and ecclesiastical
property, and marking out such parts as the state could take possession of and distribute to the natives and to Italian emigrants.
The entire military department was reorganized; Baratieri insisted
that if Italy were to succeed in Africa, it must be with native troops
under Italian officers. The governor did not stay in Massowah; he
lived with his soldiers; he had a strong influence over the natives,
and suffered no defections of the indigenous forces in battle.[1]

Creditable Success

The right man in the right place, evidently; in November, 1892,
the crown expressed itself as well pleased that the colony had
been entirely pacified and was ceasing to be a drain on the finances
of the mother-country. Baratieri had aided agriculture and commerce and systematized the public service; it was hoped that
the time was not far off when the costs of civil management in the
colony would be paid with the colony's own products. The influence
of the Italians was extending peacefully, and the neighboring tribes
were attracted to them by gifts, by the surety of order and peace
and of impartial and prompt justice. Brunialti[2] calls this a modest
but true success, without exaggeration, uncertainty, or weakness.
A special budget was instituted for the colony and attached to
that of Foreign Affairs. On December 8, 1892, the powers exercised by the minister of the marine over civil services in Eritrea
were withdrawn and the corresponding funds inscribed in the
colonial budget. Gradually there were added to this budget other
expenses formerly charged under the heads of finance, treasury,
posts and telegraph, public works, etc. In consequence, an expenditure of 8,000,000 lire was recognized as necessary for all the

[1] Brunialti, pp. 464 ff., 473 ff.; "Italy in Africa," *The Nation*, March 7, 1895, LX, 179.
[2] Pp. 474, 480.

services for which provision had at first been made fragmentarily, and which finally were to come under the oversight and responsibility of the governor. A distinction was made between civil and military expenses, by which ministerial control and responsibility to parliament were made less difficult. Attention was directed to tax and customs reforms, security and justice were more firmly established, and public instruction made an advance, to the advantage of both Italians and natives. The Massowah Chamber of Commerce heartily coöperated, suggesting plans for the development of local trade and industry for the benefit of Italy. More roads, commercial as well as strategic, were laid out; a bank of credit was founded at Massowah; construction of markets, magazines, and better facilities for ships were regarded as paramount objects. The abolition of customs dues; more frequent postal and caravan communication between Italy and Massowah, Massowah and the principal centers of Abyssinia; the protection of interests, which was always efficacious — all these advantages worked toward civilization and success. The population seemed to have perfect faith in the government and a beginning of agriculture was made, even among the native nomads. The suggestions of the governor to the ministry show a clear comprehension of the situation and its needs. Among other desiderata he wished the lands to be studied so that the most successful methods of working them might be developed; he also insisted that holdings, assigned by choice or lot to Italians, individual or in common, should be guaranteed against the evils of speculation. Anticipations of money without interest, a regulated water supply, paternal care of Italian settlers, including religious and medical attention — these were among the suggestions of the governor, and many of them were promptly adopted. By 1894 the Eritrean administration was autonomous and the management of its finances independent. The imperial government was represented only by the civil governor and three counselors, all royally appointed. Military and naval commanders were, of course, under direction from the Italian ministry.[1]

Considering the ground she had to work on, Italy had certainly made a creditable showing. But it must not be imagined that this liberal administration cost nothing; deficits appeared annually in the colonial budget and the lower ones of prosperous years were inadequate to keep down a very high average when the whole period

[1] Brunialti, pp. 472 ff., 480–484; Statesman's Year-Book, 1894, etc.

of colonial possession is considered.   There have been repeated struggles to reduce the yearly expenses of the colony to 9,000,000 or 8,000,000 lire ; no such scheme seems to have succeeded.   The deficit has averaged considerably more than this figure ; during the whole period of colonial expansion up to 1896, losses are esti- mated by Brunialti[1] as 10,000 men and 500,000,000 lire.   For a country whose debt was in the thousand millions, which, out of every hundred lire expended, paid thirty-three lire interest on debt and thirty-three lire for the maintenance of army and navy, this colonial policy was certainly what one of its opponents called it, *une poli- tique de luxe.*[2]   For a rich nation to expend great sums in the work of civilization or extermination may be wastefulness ; for a poverty- stricken, debt-burdened nation, full of internal strife and uproar, it is almost suicide.   If the disaster inflicted by Menelek has taught this lesson, perhaps the experience was not too dearly bought.

" Megalomania," however, was not yet cured ; the incident of San Mun Bay, where Italy thought of taking another useless burden upon her shoulders, in order to prove herself a Power, is a happen- ing of the more recent past.[3]   In this case, however, right counsels prevailed, and perhaps the fever has abated.   As for Eritrea, little enthusiasm is expressed regarding it ; since the shock of 1896 the colony has come under discussion from time to time, and if it is not restricted to narrower boundaries or quite abandoned, it is largely because of national pride.   In 1897 an attempt was made to take up again the organization of the district and the stimulation of industry, but the colony has never fully recovered ; it is accepted as an inevitable burden which some would gladly exchange for a share in the nearer and more congenial Tripoli.[4]   Whether Eritrea

[1] P. 519; it is elsewhere stated that about 125,000,000 lire were spent in the mili- tary operations of 1895–1896.   The budget for 1895–1896 is given as follows (in lire):

Receipts: from colonies, 1,700,000; from state, 10,000,000.
Expenses: colonial troops, 9,351,000; other expenses, 2,349,000.

It is difficult to get exact information on these particulars, but the above figures show general conditions. Even with elimination of the heavy military expense, the colony is far from paying its own way. See Statesman's Year-Book and Almanach de Gotha, 1897, etc.; Appleton's Ann. Cyc., 1898.

[2] " The Financial Condition of Italy," *The Nation*, October 1, 1891, LIII, 255; arts. by "An Observer," "Ouida," Geffcken, and Rossi.

[3] See Lombroso, art. in the *Nuova Antologia*, as well as various other articles and editorial comment in the earlier issues of this publication for 1899.

[4] " Rassegna Politica," in *Nuova Antologia* during 1897 ; little interest in Eritrea has been exhibited since that year; Brunialti, pp. 516 ff.; Traversi, Primerano, Rossi, and Capucci.

is in the future even to pay for itself, remains to be seen; it is
hoped rather than expected.

ITALY'S "NATURAL" COLONIES

If Italy were intent upon the essence of colonization rather than
the name, her field of action would not be far to seek; she has a
series of natural colonies in America, surrounding the lower course
of the Plata River, which evince a vigor of growth and a prosperity
that ought to have been the pride of the mother-country while she
was squandering resources on the sand-dunes of the Red Sea coast.
The essence of the mutual sympathy of two countries lies, not in
political union, but in those racial affiliations of blood, language,
religion, customs, and manners, the mutual possession of which
renders intercourse between groups of men easy and enjoyable.
After the Revolution the American republic turned, not to
France, but to England with her favors of trade and intercourse.
So the Plata settlements, with no serious encouragement, and with
memories not the most pleasant of the native land and its extortions, have nevertheless benefited Italy commercially to an infinitely
higher degree than did Eritrea at its best. As an illustration of
the normal growth of national offspring, the development of these
perhaps happily neglected settlements deserves a paragraph of comparison with the above-described "colony for a purpose." First
and most important, the Italians have succeeded there, and that
without aid, as nowhere else in the world. They were the first to
own inns, cafés, boats, etc., and have kept industrially in advance
of a people inferior to themselves in culture. Italians have founded
and operated banks, and in Buenos Ayres they owned in the nineties
62 per cent of the businesses. The Italian language is spreading,
and Spanish is supreme only in public administration; probably one-
fourth (4,000,000) of the population of Argentina have Italian blood
in their veins. The current of emigration to these regions is growing ever stronger, and in its wake are following advantages to Italian trade and industry; in 1889 the importation from Italy to the
Argentine Republic represented 5 per cent of the total; in 1894,
9 per cent. In later years of crisis (1889–1894) Italian trade suffered less than that of any other nation. And it is seen that the
Italian emigrants, who are largely from the north of Italy, do not
lose their native good qualities in the new country, but transmit

them, along with Italian ideas and tastes, to a people who need them and are able and often willing to profit by them.[1]

It is toward this Plata region that some of Italy's more responsible advisers have long been attempting to direct her attention, not with a view to the extension of imperial power — for sufficient barriers exist, fortunately for the colonies, to restrain any such interference — but in the hope of developing, without expense or bloodshed, close commercial and industrial relations and a national sympathy which may some day assist in assuring existence to that which is Italian. The Italians, like other Latin peoples, feel a sense of weakness before the tremendous energy and the power of expansion and of assimilation displayed by the Anglo-Saxon race. To the end of establishing these desired relations, a more strict supervision of emigration and a more developed consular service are advocated; the ideal is that the South American colonies shall stand to Italy as the United States to England. At present, and neglecting the crying necessity for the internal reorganization of Italy, this idea seems by far the most practical and realizable of Italian colonial projects.

GERMAN COLONIZATION

Among German writers on colonization there has existed a consensus of opinion as to the tardiness of Germany's entrance upon the colonial field. The common cry of " Too late ! " has been voiced in all accents, from those of the reproachful complainer to those of the belligerent partisan and agitator. Among certain of these parties there has been manifested a disposition to hold some person or policy responsible for such national backwardness; others have disdained to assail the past, have accepted the situation as inevitable, and have directed their thoughts and efforts toward the future. Upon reflection it is seen that Germany's past indifference toward organized expansion and colonization has been perfectly natural, and could hardly have been otherwise. During the last few centuries and up to the borders of our own generation Germany has been in no position to devote attention and effort to matters of this

---

[1] Brunialti, chap. x. The official figures of the commissioners of immigration for 1857–1889 give for the number of Italian immigrants 646,086 as against 144,654 for the Spanish and 91,719 for the French. The Italians have regularly maintained the lead in numbers, and have figured for 70 per cent of the total. Daireaux, I, 45–46; II, chaps. i and ii; especially p. 11.

kind; internal conditions and external relations have alike impeded
the development of colonial activity in distant lands. Periodically
through the earlier centuries and during part of the nineteenth, frequent, long-continued, and devastating wars reduced the population
and destroyed accumulated wealth; industrial development was indefinitely postponed; political centralization and national unity were
rendered impossible in a continuous strife of petty local interests.
External relations were such as to discourage and cripple the trade
of a country whose geographical position was and is most unfavorable
to the development of shipping and trans-oceanic commerce. Everything was narrow, local, and self-centered; horizons were limited,
and ignorance of the external world was dense. Whatever may
have been the intellectual life of the higher classes as exemplified
in Humboldt, Goethe, and others, the masses of the people had
acquired no such cosmopolitan freedom of outlook, nor such enterprise and experience of the outside world as distinguished the industrial and commercial population of England and Holland during
the same periods.[1] Germany was looked down upon by many of
her own greatest men as irretrievably provincial and uncultured.

Earlier Colonial Projects

The impracticability, in the earlier periods, of German colonial
ventures across the seas is shown by the history of an actual attempt at colonization dating from the end of the seventeenth century.[2] Frederick William, the Elector of Brandenburg, a man of
theories, who had picked up many foreign ideas during a period of
study in Holland, conceived the scheme of making Prussia prosperous by creating colonies after the manner of the Dutch. He
maintained a fleet under the command of a Dutch pirate, Raule,
in order to secure his prospective commerce from the depredations and tyranny of the Swedes and Danes. After the peace of
St. Germain (1679), finding his hands free from war, he turned his
whole attention to colonization; the Guinea coast of Africa was

---

[1] This condition lasted far down into the nineteenth century. See Wohltmann in
the *Indische Gids*, 1897, II, 1387.

[2] Germans like to recall also the memory of how the famous Augsburg Welser
undertook to develop and colonize Venezuela. This was a sort of miniature *conquista*
after the Spanish model, depending upon warlike methods "without any serious prospects of commercial advantage." It took place about the middle of the sixteenth
century, and suffered continually from the enmity of the Spaniards. Ehrenberg,
I, 200; cf. pp. 242 ff., above.

his immediate objective, and there he hoisted his flag in 1683. An African Company with a trade-monopoly had been founded in 1682, which for a time made considerable profit by a vigorous participation in the slave-trade. Negotiations were made with the Danes for the establishment of a slave-station or mart on the island of St. Thomas in the West Indies, and a small island between St. Thomas and Puerto Rico was actually seized. For the direction and prosecution of his project Frederick was obliged to have recourse to foreign agents. This was disastrous, for the numerous Dutchmen in his service seem to have jeopardized his undertaking about as much as their professedly hostile countrymen did. The local African management was incompetent and dishonest, and the settlement became a refuge for smugglers, broken men, and outlaws. The Company was always hovering on the verge of bankruptcy, and the Elector confessed that every new ducat of Guinea gold cost him double its value. In the midst of complications with Holland the prince died; his successor had little sympathy with colonial projects, and after some half-hearted attempts to revive the Africa Company, the heavily involved colony was sold to the Dutch West India Company in 1720. The West India settlements were abandoned.

This ill-starred exploit was a private project, attracting at its best but few supporters; its collapse "was the failure of a strong personal initiative to overcome the tastes and prejudices of a whole people." [1] It is in no way to be reckoned as a display of collective activity, but demonstrates rather the utter hopelessness of trying to force a people out of its natural course of development. The German people, as a whole, were under the domination of social forces which were acting along lines of least resistance, and were impelling them, as it were instinctively, in the earlier period toward the east, and from the time of Louis XIV toward America. Historically the eastern movement goes back to the exploits of the Teutonic Knights (thirteenth century), and needs little mention here except as it throws light upon the sometimes questioned capacities of the German people in the field of colonial expansion. It was steady and strong, causing the Slav much apprehension; Russian and Polish novelists have shown how formidable it appeared to their countrymen, even in recent decades. It would have been strange, then as

[1] Meinecke, pp. 1–3; Perry, "Traditions," etc.; Keltie, pp. 68–69. Details in Schmidt, I, x–xxi. The first experience of the Germans with African fever was most disastrous.

now, if this people had neglected what was at its very doors in order to acquire unknown possessions beyond the seas. In the nature of the case it little mattered to the average German that fellow-countrymen on the opposite side of the globe were compelled to seek protection beneath the British flag, because the fatherland possessed neither colonies, consuls, nor navy; the fact that counted was that gradual expansion into Poland and Lithuania demanded little outfit, mental or material, and little adaptation of any kind.

As for America, emigration was less easy : conditions were less familiar, some capital was almost indispensable, and a greater effort and decision were demanded. But positive benefits were such as to attract a people noted for its expansive force and not unready to quit its native soil in order to better its conditions of life. In America, especially in the English colonies, later the United States, one could live in a congenial climate, acquire land in certain tenure, and pursue his labors with the assurance of a livelihood and more. The vexatious and oppressive European system, with its crystallized distinctions and exactions, could not exist where land was plenty, conditions primitive, and cultivators few. In the new states that were rising, an individual might cut loose from his past history and start anew under conditions of virtual equality of opportunity ; he might hope to realize, at least for the generations to come, advantages of wealth and position which it had been impossible for preceding generations to secure for him in Europe. This was felt, at first more or less vaguely ; evidence was soon accumulated from instances of the phenomenal successes of the first bolder adventurers. However much conditions have changed in America, this primal impulse toward self-betterment is as ever a most powerful element and has regularly neutralized efforts to divert the stream of German emigration. The immense importance to both Americas of this desirable inflow is well known.

UNIFICATION OF GERMANY

No other enterprises like Frederick's occurred to interrupt the normal course of events. Prussia remained innocent of any serious maritime or colonial policy from the time of the Brandenburg episode till the middle of the nineteenth century.[1] The factors which make for industrial development continued to be but feebly

[1] Perry, "Traditions," etc.

represented; wars of all kinds and finally the crushing blows of Napoleon I kept the Continent in a state of insecurity, ferment, and demoralization, and allowed England and America to monopolize commercial and industrial progress. Germany suffered with the rest under the blight of war, but when at last the upheavals were over, it was seen that a powerful country and people were emerging; the narrowness of the past was disappearing, and, under the régime of peace, population, capital, and industrial and commercial activity were advancing at an accelerated speed. With the expansion of national interests came a widening of popular horizons, and Germany of the sixties displayed almost all the characteristics usually associated with a " colonizing nation." A series of judiciously managed wars under the guidance of a great statesman created the indispensable element of national unity, and the state, coherent within, was ready to try its arms in more distant fields and to enter upon a world-activity which should in time include the extension of control over distant territory.[1] During the period preceding the culmination of Bismarck's policy of unification, noteworthy omens for the future began to appear in the form of unofficial foreign undertakings in the commercial, missionary, and scientific fields. The German trader and missionary became ubiquitous, and the Hamburg and Bremen merchant-houses extended their activity to South America, Africa, and Australasia. Emigration of men and capital went along with the growth of a merchant marine and the formation of wide interests in foreign parts. Treaties were made with eastern nations. German explorers and scientific travelers commenced to publish results of investigations pursued with a method and thoroughness to which the world was not used. Prussian men-of-war began to multiply and to appear on cruises of discovery and survey.[2]

Agitation for Colonies

After the war with France had welded the German nation into a still more coherent whole and had inspired it with the elation of victory and the sense of important individuality, voices began to be

[1] Leroy-Beaulieu, I, 307.

[2] Der Deutsche Export, pp. 1 ff.; Meinecke, pp. 4–5; Blum, pp. 8 ff.; Pfeil, Studien, pp. 10 ff.; Johnston, pp. 206 ff.; Keltie, pp. 167 ff.; Philippson, pp. 61 ff. "Colonies are in our present development a natural and inevitable consequence of a vigorous trade across the seas." T. Fabri, p. 10.

heard which demanded the official extension of German control over external territory. These views were opposed from many prudent sources, and a controversy arose, where, as usual, enthusiasm scored heavily against foresight — if one is to judge by the sequence of events. A couple of pamphlets, published late in the seventies,[1] initiated the awakening of popular enthusiasm. The arguments of the colonial agitators centered about the questions of emigration, extension of markets, protection of trade-interests, development and use of a marine, and establishment of penal colonies.[2] These were varied by the *argumentum ad hominem* and the heated appeal to patriotism and popular passions. Too often efforts were made to enlist the emotions rather than the intellect; the spirit of '71 ran riot, and much was heard of *"das kanonenfeste Deutschland,"* of Germany's *"Weltberuf,"* and so on. The political symbol or catchword was ardently reiterated, and other concomitants of political hysteria were in evidence.[3]

Of arguments that pretended to a rational basis, that which had to do with over-population and emigration was most often heard. The stock form of statement was to the effect that Germany lost every year the equivalent of a large army, fully equipped, inasmuch as those young, able-bodied emigrants who regularly quitted the fatherland, each with his $100 or so, ceased forever to be Germans, and devoted their strength and capital to the augmentation of a ruinous competition with their former fellow-countrymen.[4] The net loss in labor power and capital was variously footed up, but always reached a very high figure.[5] Fabri and Weber raised a great

[1] F. Fabri, Bedarf Deutschland der Colonien? Eine politisch-ökonomische Betrachtung, Gotha, 1879; E. von Weber, Die Erweiterung des deutschen Wirtschaftsgebietes und die Grundlegung zu überseeischen deutschen Staaten, Leipzig, 1879. Philippson (pp. 6 ff.) states the arguments of these writers and answers them.

[2] Wohltmann, *Indische Gids,* 1897, II, 1387; Philippson, pp. 7 ff.

[3] Engler, pp. 77, 133; T. Fabri, pp. 8, 12, etc.; Oberländer, pp. 167 ff.; cf. Philippson, p. 83.

[4] Considerable complaint is made of the speedy amalgamation of German emigrants with their new fellow-countrymen. Engler, p. 114, note; Philippson, p. 6. Bismarck himself frequently expressed his contempt for Germans who could shake the dust of the fatherland thus indifferently from their feet. Cf. Poschinger, p. 237. Emigration to the all-assimilating United States has naturally been the most dispiriting feature of the question. Between 1870 and 1890 the emigration to the United States was never under 90 per cent of the total. Geffcken, in *The Forum,* XIII, 200; cf. Der Deutsche Export, etc., p. 2.

[5] T. Fabri, p. 22; Philippson, p. 25. Geffcken (in *The Forum*) estimates the total emigration from 1820 to 1888 as 6,000,000; if each emigrant carried off an average of $100, the loss of actual money was very great, not to mention that incurred in the education of the departing citizens, and otherwise.

outcry over this and predicted rise in prices, decline in wages, over-importation, and aggravation of pauperism, social need, and socialism. They thought to cure all this evil by directing German emigration to German colonies. Here it was proposed to create a field for the youthful professional men, technicians, and others, who found their chances narrowed in the overstocked market of the home-land. These colonies need not be joined politically with the metropolis, but should constitute essentially German communities, preserving the national language and traits in foreign lands.[1]

Other arguments were brought forward on the ground of trade-interests. It is noteworthy that the Germans, as a rule, put forth such pleas on their own merits; there was little attempt to cloak them in the hypocritical garb of humanitarianism and disinterested-ness. The penetration of foreign, especially tropical, products into Germany turned the attention of certain classes to the need of a direct relation of the empire with its supply region; at the same time the rapid development of home industries and shipping seemed to demand the widening of existing markets. It was felt that Germans must try to insure themselves against the hostility of tariffs and other trade-regulations by creating colonies which should act as a unit with the mother-country, supplying her with raw materials and increasing the demand for her manufactured products. It was also asserted that German trade-interests in dis-tant lands needed the protection and standing which it was thought a possessor of colonies was peculiarly fitted to give.[2] This, of course, easily passed over into jingoism and megalomania; "the victors of Königgrätz and Sedan" could not disavow their manifest destiny. Agitators spent much of their time railing against the provincial small-mindedness of a people which, even in the midst of victories, could not perceive its "mission."[3]

The navy was anxious, of course, for the addition to its growing importance which the supervision of trading-posts and colonies would afford; numerous shipping interests hungered for subsidies and other favors; there were those who complained that the navy had not enough to do, though objections to the increase of naval expenditures were stifled. But, in general, there was no inverse

---

[1] Oberländer, p. 170; Philippson, pp. 13 ff.; T. Fabri, pp. 20 ff.

[2] Jannasch, pp. 423 ff.; Oberländer, p. 168; Philippson, pp. 7 ff., 61 ff.

[3] "In der That, wer in aller Welt soll es denn wagen, ohne Scheu vor fremdem Neid Thaten zu thun, wenn nicht der Sieger von Königgrätz und Sedan?" T. Fabri, p. 17.

process contemplated; colonies were not expected to create trade and a merchant marine, but were rather to represent the flower and culmination of the growth of foreign trade and other interests. This attitude may have been due to the strong common sense of Bismarck, which so often held in check the extravagances of the multitude; at any rate, it was impressed upon the state policy. Arguments in favor of penal colonies, based upon exaggerated estimates of criminality and the dangers of socialism, were also to be heard in pre-expansion days.[1]

It is to be noted, however, that many and worthy names were to be found in the anti-expansionist ranks. In the period of popular agitation there were those who withstood the current, pleaded for deliberation, and brought counter-arguments to meet the assertions of the dominant faction. It was shown that Germany was far from over-populated; that emigration took place from the comparatively under-populated rural districts; that the trend of prices, taking a reasonably extended period, was downward, while that of wages was upward; that rise of the standard of living and growth of new needs explained much of the increasing importation; that the departure of the farmers was due chiefly to an oppressive military service and difficulties in acquiring holdings of land; that painful reminiscences were at the bottom of the Germans' speedy forgetfulness of the fatherland under the more enlightened system of other nations, and especially of the United States. The self-contradiction of those who decried emigration and yet complained of over-population was exposed. The folly of schemes looking to the regulation of the German population resident under a foreign flag was held up to ridicule, and the flimsiness of a mere political tie was shown from the experience of England, the very country whose example had been most frequently invoked by the colonial agitators. The weakness of Germany's geographical position, the dangers of European complications, the inexperience of the Germans in governing external territory, the expense of such government with no experienced colonial soldiers and functionaries to back it, its trials and disillusionments, were not hidden from the eyes of the historian and social philosopher. Such critics urged the necessity of reform at home and of development of those arts of life which make possible the maintenance of a larger population on the same soil. This would effectually dispose of the emigration

[1] Philippson, pp. 50 ff.

and penal colony arguments.[1] They urged the nation not to accept the propositions of hot-brained young enthusiasts whose ardor scorned to discriminate between the possible and the utterly illusory.[2] If argument or biting satire had counted for anything, the Germans would have been deterred from their precipitate rush into the colonial field.[3]

POLICY OF BISMARCK

They had little or no effect; apparently Germany had become already a "colonizing nation." There was no thought of pause or deliberation in the ranks of the *Kolonialmenschen*; they organized themselves into colonial societies (1882–1884), and began to besiege the government with demands for action.[4] That attention was called more sharply to the regulation of emigration and the development of the consular service, was apparently a real benefit to the country.[5] In despair of acquiring unoccupied lands fit for colonies of settlement, the furtherers of the colonial movement directed attention to Brazil, Argentina, Paraguay, and other parts of South America, already more or less under German influence; they were willing to fight the United States, if necessary, over the Monroe Doctrine, or to insist upon England's allowing an essentially German settlement in Australia. Some bluster was heard regarding the seizure of French colonies, particularly Pondichéry, together with twenty ironclads, as indemnity of the Franco-Prussian war; this project shipwrecked against the imperturbable opposition

[1] " Jeder Schritt, den wir zur Aufklärung des Volkes, zum Ausbau der Freiheit und zur Versöhnung der socialen Gegensätze thun, wird unsern Staat und unsere Gesellschaft mehr kräftigen, als das Schreckmittel der Strafcolonien." Philippson, p. 60.

[2] Weber even suggested artificial restriction of the growth of cities. Philippson, p. 29.

[3] Jannasch, pp. 378–399, 403 (Roscher on German emigration, same volume, 327 ff.); Philippson, pp. 7 ff., 25 ff., 38 ff., 61 ff.

[4] Schmidt, Deutschlands Kolonien, I, 1–2. This work is the most comprehensive of those cited in the present chapter. It is written by a soldier and exhibits the virtues and defects incident to its authorship. The first volume is on East Africa, where the author's own experience enables him to go into considerable detail; the second is a compilation from reliable and important original sources. The work impresses the reader as a trustworthy and honest production.

[5] Jannasch (pp. 452 ff.) asserts the ineffectiveness of the consular service; he says the selection of the consuls was most vicious — if a man had squandered one estate, he was fit to be consul; if three, to be consul-general. Merit received little reward beyond cheap medals and the like, and the best men kept out of the service.

of Bismarck. The colonial societies were very much in earnest and were even willing to put their hands into their pockets, if necessary; their influence was powerful and became an important factor in the development of the imperial foreign and colonial policy.[1] The government, however, was too deliberate to meet their wishes; statesmanship and its requirements did not enter into their stock of ideas. The government was, of course, Bismarck, and the Chancellor's tardiness came in for many recriminations and caused much disillusionment; criticism of the government took on a personal tinge. Whatever may have been his later views, for years Bismarck certainly presented the figure of a reluctant, hardly persuaded adherent of a colonization policy. That his finger was ever on the pulse of Germany goes without saying, and it is certain that he saw fit to yield, willingly or regretfully at the outset, to the swelling sentiment of the empire. But however much his original attitude may have changed, there is little cause to wonder that the brakes were put on with a firm hand and kept on until the farsighted statesman could more confidently reckon with the national future. A young nation, scarcely yet united, was eager to enter a field where shocks and strains were in the order of events, and where inexperience was likely to feel their force with peculiar intensity. Collision with nations whose friendship was all but indispensable was more than a possibility. It is scarcely surprising if the prudence of age hesitated to expose an unseasoned people to all these chances and trials. And the conservatism of the Chancellor was radicalism from the standpoint of the Reichstag. This body consistently opposed all colonial schemes and naturally became a mark for incessant abuse and complaints of narrow-mindedness. Even after Bismarck began to advocate the acquisition of colonies, the Reichstag was not won over, but continued to offer hateful obstruction to the wide-reaching plans of the expansionists. There was besides a large indifferent element among the people to provoke these "patriots"; the peasant stolidly emigrated as before, and the general populace needed many a warm and specious appeal before it swung into line with the agitators and the interested merchant circles. It was danger to the interests of the latter class which most directly stimulated governmental activity.

[1] Lowe, II, 203; Philippson, pp. 38 ff.; Jannasch, pp. 399 ff.; F. Fabri, Fünf Jahre, etc., p. 135.

Bismarck seems to have foreseen the ultimate colonial destiny of his country, but to have regarded the first projects as ill-timed. To the earliest approaches of colonial partisans he gave no satisfaction.[1] In his opinion the merchant should precede the official, whose entrance upon the function of administering young societies should take place relatively late. Colonies without a fleet he regarded as so many vulnerable and undefended points.[2] But he was always open to all suggestions looking to the development of trade. Trade was an immediate advantage; whether it would lead in time to the official occupation of colonies was a question for the future to decide. Bismarck sounded the public mind in regard to trade with considerable regularity. In 1883 he put forth a request to merchant societies for reports and recommendations on the attitude to be taken by the government toward German commercial interests in foreign parts; some of the reports submitted urged vigorous action, but no action resulted. In 1880, with the failure of the old Godeffroy house, the time seemed ripe for more positive measures; the extinction of German trade in Polynesia, where it was predominant, was threatened, unless a substitute for this well-known house could be maintained. Bismarck accordingly asked the Reichstag to guarantee the dividends of a new South Sea Company by a maximum annual grant of 300,000 marks, for twenty years. The demand was refused by a small majority. Evidently the time was not yet; but Bismarck's change of attitude was attested by his bitter complaints of this lack of support "even in the beginnings of colonization"; he felt that the time for action had almost come. The next move was the proposal of a mail-steamer subsidy bill; this was rejected by the Reichstag, but warmly applauded by the country at large.[3] At this juncture, feeling sure of popular support, but desiring to stimulate it to the pitch of blind partisanship, and thus once for all decide the issue, Bismarck deftly smote that one of the

[1] To those who wished to relieve France of colonies and battleships, he said : "I want no colonies. They are good for nothing but supply-stations. For us in Germany, this colonial business would be just like the silken sables in the noble families of Poland, who have no shirts to their backs." Lowe, II, 203. In the Reichstag (January 22, 1889) he announced, "Ich war von Haus aus kein Kolonialmensch." Andler, p. 270; F. Fabri, Fünf Jahre, etc., Vorwort. He was studying the subject of colonization, however, as early as 1876. Lowe, II, 210.

[2] The phenomenal growth of the German navy (1871–1885) seems to have done away in part with this objection. Lowe, II, 203.

[3] It was passed in the next (1884–1885) session.

national heart-strings which vibrates to national vanity. He departed from his avowed custom and published a White Book (1884) detailing with gross one-sidedness his grievances and maltreatment at the hands of the English diplomatic office, in connection with questions of trade-interests and protection in Southwest Africa. These virtuous plaints gained him the sympathy not only of his own countrymen, but that of English circles as well. In Germany the opponents of colonial expansion were no longer heeded; a force stronger than reason had been invoked and the path was cleared for the realization of what had become one of Bismarck's chief aims.[1]

This Southwest Africa incident was the crisis in Germany's development of a colonial policy. It was not approached by the government precipitately; numerous petitions of missionaries and traders in those parts for protection had been pigeon-holed before the pressing appeals in the early eighties. These and the uncertain position of Lüderitz[2] virtually forced representations to be made to England. Her shuffling and evasive answers and her dilatory conduct in response to straightforward inquiries concerning English intentions in the country about Angra Pequena seem finally to have exhausted Bismarck's patience. He had spent fruitless months in polite negotiations whose net result was practically nil, and though evidently appreciating to the full the value of England's friendship, he at last suddenly and peremptorily declared a protectorate over the Lüderitz possessions of Southwest Africa.[3] All intentions of conquest were disclaimed. After this step it seems that the Rubicon had been crossed. England protested, but finally acquiesced as gracefully as possible under awkward circumstances,

[1] Lowe, II, 211 ff.; Meinecke, p. 17; Philippson, pp. 66 ff.; F. Fabri, pp. 15–16; Keltie, chap. xii; Andler, p. 272; Geffcken, in *The Forum*, XIII, 200.

[2] Lüderitz was a Bremen merchant who acquired in 1883 by purchase from native chiefs about 215 square miles of land on the bay of Angra Pequena, with all rights of supremacy. His ostensible purpose was to found a trading-station, but there is little question that he was inspired by the inner circles of the colonial societies. He was soon beyond his depth in this undertaking—this necessitating the formation of a company for Southwest Africa. The extreme caution and the noncommittal character of the government's attitude toward Lüderitz are especially to be noted. Schmidt, II, 257 ff.; Keltie, chap. xii, 178 ff.; Oberländer, pp. 148 ff.; Büttner, pp. 115–116; F. Fabri, Fünf Jahre, etc., pp. 3 ff.

[3] He instructed the German consul at Cape Town (April 24, 1884) to declare officially that Lüderitz and his settlements were under the protection of the German Empire. A naval officer hoisted the imperial flag over Angra Pequena August 7, 1884. Schmidt, II, 261; Keltie, chap. xii; Johnston, pp. 249 ff.

and the colonial party at home in Germany forgot its grievances and demonstrated vigorously.

But Bismarck still clung to his enunciated policy; he announced that Germany was not going colony-hunting: " German colonies would, like the English, have to trust to individual effort and natural growth, not, like the French, to artificial forcing and state patronage." [1] This common-sense doctrine was characteristic of Bismarck's whole colonial activity; he departed from it only under the strongest pressure. When he is found favoring projects of expansion, one may be sure there is some preëxisting commercial interest to be safeguarded; he never believed in colonies for the sake of colonies. Throughout his period of power he seems consistently to have kept the history of England and her example before his eye. Though a man of quick decision and daring action, self-confident as few statesmen have the right to be, he prepared for entrance upon the untried colonial field modestly and as a student.[2] To him statesmanship meant wise direction of popular impulse; he risked and lost much popularity because he kept his head cool and his hand firm, and insisted upon postponing colonization until the time was ripe.

Colonial Acquisitions

When, in 1884, the reins were slackened and the colonial movement had been concentrated and directed toward an immediate success through the enlistment of popular prejudice and self-esteem, further developments were not slow to manifest themselves. The latent and gathering forces of the preceding period were transformed into actual energy and momentum, and within four months of the establishment of a protectorate over Southwest Africa the clamor of trade-interests in West Africa had brought about the official occupation of Togo (July 5, 1884) and Kamerun (July 14, 1884), and the representations of South Sea merchants [3] had led

[1] Perry, "Traditions," etc.; F. Fabri, p. 100; Leroy-Beaulieu, I, 307; Lowe, II, 213.
[2] Lowe, II, 210.
[3] Complaints were made of an imminent English and Australian expansion over German trade-districts. Bismarck, at the same time, had become distrustful of the sincerity and value of British protection of German interests and felt that the situation called for speedy action in the establishment of a German foothold in the threatened region. The South Sea projects were furthered through the influence of Hansemann and other important financiers. Lowe, II, 231; F. Fabri, Fünf Jahre, etc., p. 9; Andler, p. 273; Schmidt, II, 292 ff.

to the virtual seizure of Kaiser Wilhelmsland and the Bismarck Archipelago (August 20, 1884). Here, as in Southwest Africa, the missionaries had played their part.[1] In these cases it may be said that the Chancellor's policy of trader first, government afterward, was carried out; but a wide deviation from this system was yet to come. On October 1, 1884, three young adventurers, under assumed names and disguised as laborers, undertook for the *Gesell-schaft für deutsche Kolonisation* the seizure of what is now German East Africa. No German interests worth mentioning existed in this part of the earth. The objects of this expedition were attained with extraordinary celerity; so-called treaties were made with a number of native princes, who were cajoled into agreements which they understood very imperfectly, if at all, and concessions of land and administrative privileges were obtained to which imperial protection was extended through charter, February 27, 1885.[2]

In the middle of 1884 Germany had had no possessions beyond the seas; early in 1885 she found herself a great colonial power, possessing an external empire of over 1,000,000 square miles and exercising dominion over more than 10,000,000 subjects, mostly of lower races.[3] The tide had been taken at its full, and the nation had been guided through a dangerous passage without war and without loss of prestige or dignity. The issue once joined, Bismarck's policy had been of a daring and decisive nature; he had handled the English with scant respect, in marked contrast with his former courtesy and patience, and had resorted to stratagems, ambiguities, and evasions which had been completely successful in throwing the unsuspecting and self-satisfied British government off the track until it was too late. The German commissioner, Nachtigal, had snatched Togo and Kamerun from under the very nose of the English commissioner, and no apologies were made for the seizure of East African districts which Great Britain had long regarded as prospectively her own. It is noteworthy that the

---

[1] Schmidt, II, 51 ff., 173 ff., 292 ff.; Von Stengel, pp. 10 ff.; Keltie, chap. xiii; F. Fabri, Fünf Jahre, etc., pp. 9 ff.; Johnston, pp. 249 ff.; Oberländer, p. 156; Müller, pp. 2 ff. Büttner (p. 68) says the missionaries had commenced their activity in Southwest Africa as early as 1864.

[2] Schmidt, I, 1–18, 28–29, 43; Keltie, chap. xv; F. Fabri, Fünf Jahre, etc., pp. 7 ff. Two of the young men in question were Karl Peters and Graf Pfeil.

[3] Statesman's Year-Book, 1897 (estimates of 1896); these figures are, of course, only approximate. Estimates for 1899, subtracting areas and population acquired since 1886, give the total area of possessions as 1,025,110 square miles; the total population as 14,556,000. Statesman's Year-Book, 1900.

attitude maintained toward France and French colonial suscepti-
bilities during this period was markedly conciliatory and courteous.[1]

The Chartered Companies

Such progress in expansion as has been described ought, one
would think, to have satisfied colonial partisans and given them
faith in the government as represented by Bismarck. Perhaps
their appetites had been whetted too long ; at any rate they grum-
bled still. The Chancellor was too conservative for them ; they
chafed under his guidance and were unable to forgive him his lack
of warmth and energy. They hailed his retirement with undisguised joy and welcomed the advent of the young emperor into
sole power with high hopes. They greeted the perpetrators of unspeakable horrors in the new possessions as heroes, and knew no
measure in their loves and hatreds.[2] Nevertheless, the Reichstag
refused to be fired by their excitement ; the proposals of Prince
Bismarck looking to the direct management of the protectorates
by the imperial government were rejected. The public purse was
not to be opened, and of necessity recourse was had to the old
expedient of monopolistic companies of trade and exploitation.
These companies undertook severally the management of East and
Southwest Africa, the New Guinea region (including Bismarck
Archipelago and the Solomon Islands), and the Marshall Islands,
under the protection of and under responsibility to the German
Chancellor.[3]

These sudden and successful moves of Germany initiated a wild
scramble for what was left of Africa, and, indeed, of the world at
large — a contest ended for Africa with the Berlin Conference of
1884, in which the respective spheres of influence of the nations

[1] Bismarck seems to have become so impatient with England as to have contemplated a *rapprochement* with France. He could not afford to antagonize both at once.
Lowe, II, 169, 244; Keltie, pp. 202, 206. Keltie (pp. 191–192) says, " The contemptuous
dog-in-the-manger policy of the Cape authorities did much to arouse the wrath of
Prince Bismarck and the German people and to strengthen the resolve of the former
to throw himself heart and soul into the Colonial movement." Bismarck thought
that if the dog would n't get out of the manger, he must be pelted out. Lowe, II, 219.

[2] Wilhelm II in his youth is said to have been fired with zeal for colonial expansion by the example of his distant predecessor, the Elector of Brandenburg.
Cf. *Spectator*, LXXXI, 481; Perry, "Traditions," etc.

[3] Togo and Kamerun were taken directly under imperial rule. On the companies,
see pp. 555 ff., below. The Marshall Islands were occupied in 1886. Von Stengel,
p. 17.

were delimited and the opportunity for further exploits and adventures in land-grabbing reduced practically to nil.[1] With the seizure of New Guinea and adjacent islands, the occupation of "unoccupied " lands has virtually come to an end on earth. Germany, after centuries of indifference, has completed the race among the very first ; in extent her colonial empire is inferior only to those of England and France ; but its quality is that which usually marks the portion of the late-comer.

CHARACTER OF THE COLONIES

Preceding their official occupation, all of these colonies [2] except East Africa had been more or less familiar to the German missionary and trader. Substantial commercial interests existed in Kamerun and Togo ; the missionaries of Southwest Africa were predominantly Germans ; and beginnings of both trade and missions had been made in the South Sea possessions. Upon the continent of Africa, Germans had been famous for many years as explorers and pioneers, while German missionaries had dared and suffered in the very centers of savagery. The extension of protection to German interests was real in West Africa and plausible in Southwest Africa and New Guinea ; asserted in regard to East Africa, it was a mere pretense. The major possessions of the German Empire may be roughly divided according to latitude into two classes, the tropical and the sub-tropical ; all belong to the first class except Southwest Africa. Of the conditions of these colonies dependent on latitude, climate [3] is the most decisive and the most unfortunate ; the climate of all the colonies in low latitudes is typically tropical, with the exception of alleged sanatoria in the mountains of Kamerun and New Guinea, and of the Kilima Njaro slope in East Africa, where altitude corrects latitude to some extent.[4] All these tropical colonies are abodes of fever and malaria ; Kamerun and Togo have an especially evil reputation for the worst

[1] Von Stengel, pp. 10 ff.; Keltie, chap. xiv.

[2] Strictly speaking, the German possessions are neither colonies nor protectorates. They have as yet too few settlers to deserve the name of colonies; and, in reality, there were no reasonably stable native governments to protect. Von Stengel, pp. 3, 20.

[3] For climatic conditions, flora and fauna of the German colonies, see Schmidt, *passim*; Meinecke, *passim*; Keane, Africa, II, *passim*; Keltie, chaps. xii, xiii, xv, xvii, xxii. The following treat separate colonies more in detail: Blum, pp. 84 ff., 104; Boshart, pp. 161 ff., 225 ff.; Büttner, pp. 10 ff.; Hagen, pp. 13 ff.; Hermann, pp. 66, 94; *Globus*, LXXIX, 3 (January 17, 1901).

[4] Schmidt (I, 148) says that heights of 1000 meters protect in no way.

forms of African fever. Dysentery abounds throughout the tropical possessions. Acclimatization is an illusion — all suffer from the tropical diseases, even natives and animals.[1] Aside from the fever, the moist heat, the inevitable hardships and coarse food, not to mention loneliness and homesickness, induce nervous disorders, melancholia, and insanity. In short, the regular characteristics and influences of the genuine tropical climate are everywhere in evidence, and we shall see that the Germans have been as little able as any other people to treat their physical environment with indifference. The soil of the tropical possessions, excepting East Africa, likewise presents slight variation from the type. Rainfall is heavy and vegetation luxuriant, especially in Togo and Kamerun. Valuable woods are common. Palms, rubber trees, bananas, yams, taro, etc., are everywhere at hand, and coffee, tea, tobacco, and cotton will, as a rule, flourish and yield abundantly.[2] East Africa is much less favored in the matter of soil and rainfall. Wissmann said that four-fifths of the country was barren waste, and of the remaining fifth not all was available for plantations. Dry seasons occur and are severe. The savanna is characteristic. In the German tropical colonies, as in all others, genuine agriculture after the fashion of the temperate zone is impossible, but the plantation system is said to promise much with good management and persistence.

The climate of the sub-tropical colony, Southwest Africa, is reported to be very wholesome and invigorating, especially in the southern part. In spite of the extreme dryness, however, it is acknowledged that fever in a milder form is very common.[3] To neutralize this relative advantage of climate, there is an almost entire absence of rainfall, especially near the coast, and the soil is of such porous quality as rapidly to absorb the water from occasional cloudbursts and showers. Of a consequence, the country is largely desert, in many places more arid and desolate than the Sahara, and for miles inland no water or vegetation of any kind appears.[4] At best

[1] Boshart, pp. 229 ff. This author is convinced by long experience that animals' deaths are more often caused by malaria than by the dreaded *tsetse* fly. His treatment of tropical diseases and hygiene is quite full and satisfactory. It should be supplemented with the very valuable treatise of Hagen, an experienced physician of the tropics.

[2] Schmidt (II, 328) and Blum (p. 93) think that northern New Guinea bids fair to rival Java in the raising of tropical products.

[3] In the recent military operations in Southwest Africa, the mortality due to fever is reported to have been high.

[4] Büttner (pp. 12 ff.), a veteran missionary, describes the southern part of the coast of Southwest Africa as practically bereft of rain. At a distance of 50 km. from the

the flora is limited to sparse grass-tufts and dwarfed trees except in a few more favored localities. Anything approaching a systematic development of agriculture would demand stupendous expense and labor in irrigation and otherwise. Cattle-raising, however, is said to flourish in the inner districts; it is necessarily of a nomadic order. Unfortunately pulmonary disease is rife, and as yet unyielding to treatment or inoculation with germ-cultures.[1]

In the matter of fauna, the African possessions may be considered together. The most important beast, the elephant, is being rapidly exterminated wherever it is found; the ostrich, too, has been ruthlessly hunted down in Southwest Africa, so that it has withdrawn to relatively inaccessible retreats and even there often refuses to brood. Dangerous and predatory animals are being rapidly done away with; other species whose influence on man's life is of any significance are common enough, though on the decline before civilization. New Guinea shares the commercially unimportant fauna of its part of the world. Fish are plentiful off the coasts of Kamerun, Southwest Africa, and New Guinea.[2]

From the standpoint of commercial geography, the line of distinction is between African possessions and others. The African continent, with its unindented coast-line and table-land formation, offers few harbors and still fewer rivers with uninterrupted course. Other factors enter to make the case still more unfortunate. In Kamerun large estuaries offer harborage, but the surf runs so high along the whole of the gulf coast that ships are exposed to great danger in landing. Off Togo they are frequently forced to anchor in open sea and depend on native skill to land the cargoes piecemeal. Southwest Africa has one good harbor, Walfisch Bay, but it is in British hands; Swakopmund is said, however, to offer good prospects with skillful engineering.[3] East African harbors are not suitable for large commerce; Dar-es-Salaam, for instance, though

coast it may rain once a year; at 100 km. twice or three times; at 200 km. seven or eight times. He says the eastern slope of the country sheds rain like a tile roof. He knows of no water supply at Walfisch Bay nor within a considerable distance of it. According to Schmidt (II, 213), the first grass for cattle appears 50 km. from the coast in Damaraland. In view of such conditions, difficulties in the way of opening up the country are self-evident.

[1] Hermann, pp. 25 ff.; Büttner, p. 45. Parts of East and Southwest Africa also come within the habitat of the *tsetse* fly. Oberländer, p. 155; Pfeil, Vorschläge, p. 15.

[2] Reichenow, p. 6; Büttner, p. 10; Schmidt, II, 332; Boshart, p. 176.

[3] Schmidt (II, 201) says that Swakopmund will succeed Walfisch Bay as the chief harbor of the district, as the latter is filling rapidly with sand.

it possesses a deep basin, is reached only through a narrow, tortuous channel. Other " harbors " are largely beaching-places for Arab *dhows*.[1] The rivers of the African protectorates are almost all broken by falls not far from their mouths. In Togo the best river-courses are under French or British supervision; in Southwest Africa there are no rivers : the courses of occasional torrents, coming after rain in the back-country, are marked by dry beds of sand. The rivers of East Africa and Kamerun are comparatively insignificant. In Africa there are no natural communications with the interior, no arteries of trade; the native caravan roads are mere paths a few feet wide.

In the South Sea region, chances for trade-development are a little better; good harbors are to be found, and one or two large streams are navigable far into the interior.[2] Penetration by land is unfortunately most difficult throughout New Guinea and the other larger islands; the mountain ranges are much broken, and deep chasms impede advance. Reefs and soundings along the coast have been insufficiently marked as yet; when reliable charts have been made, New Guinea will hold a respectable chance in the trade of its region; but extreme remoteness from Europe and from established Oriental trade-routes will interfere seriously with its commercial development for years and decades to come.[3]

From time to time reports of the discovery of gold in this or that colony are noised abroad; a little has been found here and there, but as yet the longed-for stimulus of the yellow metal fails the German possessions. Copper has been mined in some quantities in Southwest Africa and iron ore of a high quality is not uncommon, but the nature of the country prevents much progress. Ambitious attempts in the mining of copper have failed signally, and systematic development of the mines will become possible only when better means of transportation shall have been introduced.[4]

The native population of the German possessions, taken as a whole, is sparse and of a distinctly inferior stamp. Hottentots and

[1] On Dar-es-Salaam, see Davis, in *Scribner's*; Pfeil, Vorschläge, p. 50.

[2] The Kaiserin Augusta River, in New Guinea, is navigable to a point distant about 180 miles (as the bird flies) from the coast. Schmidt, II, 316.

[3] On the commercial geography of the German colonies, see Schmidt, I, 134 ff.; II, 2 ff., 156 ff., 198 ff., 302 ff.; Keltie, chap. xxii; Keane, Africa, II, 3 ff., 189 ff., 522; Blum, pp. 102, 186 ff.; Pfeil, Studien, pp. 3 ff.; Vorschläge, pp. 6–7; Finsch, Samoa-fahrten, p. 132.

[4] Keane, Africa, II, 175; Büttner, pp. 43 ff.

Bushmen in Southwest Africa, and Papuans in New Guinea represent some of the least developed races on the globe. The Bantu peoples of East and Southwest Africa and Kamerun are of a higher order, as are the natives of Togo and the Sudanese of Kamerun; the Bismarck and Solomon Islanders are peoples upon whom some hopes are based. Where the tribes are not unspeakably stupid and lazy, they are generally warlike and far from docile : the Somali and Galla, who border East Africa, are in constant feud and render the northern districts of this protectorate extremely dangerous to life and property; in New Guinea there is constant fighting between the coast population and the mountaineers ; likewise in Southwest Africa the Herero and Hottentots have struggled for generations, pausing now and then, but only long enough to get breath and recruit strength. The Solomon Islanders are extremely hostile to all Europeans ; their archipelago has regularly been the scene of savage outbreaks and massacres. In native Africa there is little settled rule ; in Togo and Kamerun alone is there to be found anything approaching a native government, and even this is of no advantage to the Germans, as both rulers and ruled are devout Mohammedans, with all that implies of hostility to European culture. The further difficulties of the native question will appear in later pages, but enough has been said to characterize the native situation as most unfortunate.[1]

Summary of the Beginnings

Taking a general view, then, of the Germans and their colonies, we find a people as fully equipped as any other in the matter of national character, numbers, and culture, and superior to all but the most advanced in commercial and industrial enterprise and in accumulated wealth. National unity is recent but strong, and national discipline is without its European equal. For colonial undertakings the Germans seem to lack only experience with its accumulated precepts of practical wisdom.[2] The strength of Germany

---

[1] For the natives of the various colonies, see Ratzel, Hist. of Mankind, chiefly I and II, *passim*; Schmidt, I, 160 ff., II, 13 ff., 162 ff., 221 ff., 334 ff. ; Keane, Africa, II, *passim*; Meinecke, *passim*; Reichenow, pp. 25 ff.; F. Fabri, Fünf Jahre, etc., pp. 33 ff.; Engler, p. 135; Finsch, Eth. Erfahrungen, *passim*; cf. pp. 573 ff., below.

[2] " The German settler has all the qualities which distinguish the Englishman with somewhat less initiative, whilst he is less inclined to adventures. He is calm, sober, economical, striving less to become quickly rich, and better educated. After all, the

as a young colonial power can best be seen by a comparison with the weakness of Italy, whose modern colonial activity began but slightly before that of the more northern people, and whose tentatives and early colonial development remind one in many ways of the German beginnings sketched above. Often such comparison is suggested by the almost absolute contrasts involved. Other interesting resemblances and differences might be discovered if one were to compare German colonization with the recent artificial expansion of the United States. As for the colonies themselves, which this new nation was to try to develop and make profitable, they were among the most difficult to deal with in the whole world. Nowhere was there a refuge for pilgrims from the fatherland; the questions of over-population and emigration had been settled in no respect. The current of emigration did not swerve from its old course. Natural difficulties stood in the way of hoped-for trade advantages and there was practically no native population to depend upon for coöperation in economic development. To be sure, the "patriotic" and "liberal" spirit had been somewhat appeased — a great demonstration had been made and England had been over-reached and snubbed into the bargain. This was undoubtedly something; it was as balm to the souls of certain of the colonial following. But the more rational could not but see that their efforts had brought them little nearer than before to the substantial results for which they had hoped; among such men there were grave misgivings as to the outcome. Whatever else may be said, Germany's colonial future was exceedingly problematic in 1885, when the last great possessions had been appropriated. It devolved upon the nation to demonstrate its capacities in the new and strange field.

General Character of the Colonial Policy

The responsible directors of Germany's early colonial policy labored under no illusion regarding the grave difficulties of the task set before them. Their view of the colonies was anything

German and the Anglo-Saxon emigrants are of the same value. All unbiassed observers pronounce them to be *pares inter nationes*. This is particularly the case in the most important branch, agriculture — the German and the Scotch are considered the best farmers." Geffcken, in *The Forum*, XIII, p. 204, note; Philippson, p. 5; Der Deutsche Export, p. 8. Cf. also F. Fabri, Fünf Jahre, etc., p 13; Jannasch, p. 368; [Bastian], Einiges, etc., p. 59.

but sanguine; they were oppressed, rather, by a sense of responsibility for the outcome of an extremely hazardous series of undertakings, initiated under unfavorable conditions in an unknown field. When the wave of national excitement had subsided, counsels of caution were heard, even from the mouths of erstwhile agitators.[1] Problems that went unheeded in the ardor of conquest now reappeared and demanded a practical solution, in cold blood; it was only the least rational of the *Kolonialmenschen* who refused to profit by the study of other nations' experiences, and who clamored for the development of a distinctly "German policy."[2] It is not always easy to specify exactly what a party means when it calls for a genuinely "national" policy. There is an element of symbolism about the term which baffles definition. In the present case — one not without its parallels — a national policy was invoked as a convenient short-cut to avoid all the uninteresting and unpleasant exigencies which had marked the history of other peoples' colonial undertakings. The fundamental assumption of those who clamor for a national policy is that the experience of the past counts for little or nothing; national vanity and unreflecting patriotism foster the belief that a royal road lies open to the genius of the particular people in question. The irrationality involved in such a view, is, of course, a necessary attendant upon popular sentiment unbridled by intelligence or judgment.

As a matter of fact the policy really developed was, in several important respects, a genuinely German one. Who but the Germans, for example, have approached the colonial question from the "learned" standpoint, discarding with decision, on the one hand, the empirical, and on the other the "metaphysical" methods of their seniors in the art? This learned attitude may seem amusing — it has furnished much material for the facetious, even in Germany, and, at first sight, it does provoke a smile to find the *Dr. phil.* and the *Dr. juris* so generously represented in the humbler categories of the colonial service; but it is none the less an attitude marked by individuality and without its parallel in the history of incipient colonial activity. Perhaps with the Germans such an

---

[1] F. Fabri, Fünf Jahre, etc., pp. 13, 28, 144. Some of the larger Hamburg and Bremen firms looked on colonization with coolness or distrust. Id., p. 18.

[2] An official organ of the colonial party declared that "Germany had nothing to learn from England or any other colonizing nation, having a method of handling social problems peculiar to the German spirit." Perry, "Traditions," etc. But cf. F. Fabri, Fünf Jahre, etc., p. 28.

attitude was logically to be expected, though the historian could doubtless cite many striking instances of a people scorning its national traditions and superior advantages, and electing rather to revive obsolete and exploded fallacies and flounder about in the vaguest indecision. To assert that the Germans have tried at the outset to profit by the study of the records of the past, and by the enlistment of the services of the best contemporary science, is not to extend them unqualified approval; but because they have attempted, with a fair degree of consistency, to use against their new environment the knowledge and experience accumulated by man's centuries of struggle with adverse nature, the history of their colonial activity possesses a certain added interest. The student of the social sciences feels this interest, perhaps, with especial force; he is always looking for a social experiment from which the tiresome and reiterated errors of the past shall have been eliminated, and where the distrusted conclusions of political and economic science can be fairly confronted with hard fact. In any case, whatever else may be said of the Germans, they cannot be accused of holding their own inexperience as a matter of slight moment, to be put aside with a wave of the hand.[1] There seems to have been considerable candid self-searching at the bottom; then an honest effort to offset serious disadvantages of many kinds by calling into requisition the most modern and approved of methods and expedients. One cannot fail to detect the hand of Bismarck in the development of this rational and practical side of the early colonial policy.

Germany was, of course, surpassingly fitted for scientific colonization — absolutely and relatively better equipped than any other country has been. The reputation of her historians, explorers, and professional men of science, who have accumulated knowledge and imparted it *ex cathedra*, needs no remark; more significant still as witness to the nation's intellectual life and vigor are the treatises of her army officers, missionaries, and colonial administrators, written under the stress of strenuous lives of action, and yet ranking among the very best contributions to science, in their keenness of observation and soundness of conclusion.[2] Such studies in

---

[1] Meinecke, p. 104; cf. [Bastian], Einiges, etc., pp. 59 ff.

[2] E.g. those of Pfeil, Boshart, Wissmann, Krieger, Hagen, Schmidt, Klose, Von François, Büttner, and many others mentioned in Giesebrecht's compilation. The high scientific value of officers' reports is well recognized (Schmidt, I, 282). On Germany's readiness to adopt modern scientific methods see also *The Athenæum*, No. 3812 (November 17, 1900).

commercial geography, physiography, geology, meteorology, tropical hygiene, and ethnography have added much to the sum of human knowledge, and cannot but contribute to the future efficiency of German colonial methods. Unfortunately, experiments in the field of the social sciences cannot proceed by isolation of factors. Demonstration of cause and effect in a complicated social problem is all but impossible, and the captious logician can always come forward with his "multiplicity of causes" or his "inconsistency of effects." Thus might it be in the case in hand : one might be censured for exaggeration of the intellectual element in German colonial policy, in view of the present-day, often unedifying picture of the German colonies. It is none the less true that Germany has stood for scientific method in colonization, and it is only a pity that she has stood, at the same time, for other things which have tended to neutralize and obscure her successes and to cast ridicule upon the social sciences and their conclusions.

The most unfortunate factor in the German attitude toward the colonial question has been as characteristic as the most enlightened element : if the Germans are great scientists, they are likewise confirmed militarists and bureaucrats. Owing their national existence to rigid discipline and vigorous use of the " mailed fist," they are disposed to believe in the universal effectiveness of inflexible system and peremptory action. Education, military and other, strengthens this conviction. But, though not without their place in the management of dependencies, inflexibility and governmental rigor are about as ill adapted to young and chaotic societies as the frontier-system would be to the Prussian state. The vital error in the German policy has been the attempt to carry over to .the colonies the complex military and administrative system of the home-land. Here it was that the rational régime broke down; such a proceeding was unscientific to the last degree, and its vicious effects have cast copious discredit upon the solid worth of other parts of the German system.[1]

[1] Jannasch (pp. 368 ff.) comments at length on the Germans' lack of education for colonization, and especially attacks the system of government through the agency of jurists and other specialists of narrow horizons. It is interesting to note the change of attitude toward imperialism and bureauracy of the " business-minister," Dernburg, since his accession to power.

The Modern Chartered Company

When the colonies had been officially annexed to the empire, Bismarck, always a close student of effective methods, desired to give them an organization modeled on that of the British crown colony, directly responsible to the Chancellor; this seemed to him the most thoroughly tested and successful system when one had to deal with colonies such as those of the Germans. It was evident, however, that such a system must entail upon the imperial government a responsibility for the colonies that it could not well disavow, and under which there might well arise calls for armed interference and financial support, together with other costly and unpleasant contingencies. These considerations alienated the support of the still half-hostile Reichstag, and, except for Togo and Kamerun, where German interests were more substantial and promising, such a form of organization was decisively rejected. This amounted to a refusal of the representative branch of government to ratify actions to which the executive branch was committed. The position was awkward, but it was promptly relieved by the support of the colonial societies. The expedient of the monopolistic trading company[1] was invoked from a dishonorable oblivion, and again set upon a characteristic career of incompetence and final dissolution. Companies undertook the management of all the possessions except Togo and Kamerun, under charters which granted them, in general, exclusive rights of rule under the general supervision of the empire, exclusive rights of trade, of the occupation and development of new land, and so on. Thus the German state was initially saved the expense of administration and the colonies were still held virtually beneath the German flag.

Before entering upon the history of the German companies, it should be stated that these chartered monopolies of the nineteenth century, though strikingly similar to those of the seventeenth, were destined to subserve purposes considerably different. The same political and economic causes which created the companies of the earlier century have been effective in their recent development: the modern companies have been confined regularly to countries of a rudimentary development, inhabited by peoples of

[1] Blum, p. 41; F. Fabri, Fünf Jahre, etc., pp. 7, 119; Hermann, p. 31; Meinecke, pp. 5–8; cf. Van Dene in *Indische Gids*, 1888, I, 134–142.

a low economic and political organization. The privileges granted under modern charters have been, in many particulars, strikingly similar to those vouchsafed by the older documents.[1] In the course of time, however, general economic and political conditions have been so modified as to sap the independence of such an organization, with the result that the modern monopolistic society is but a shadow of its former self. Belonging in its prime to an age of small, segregated, and relatively feeble political unities, it is quite out of its element amidst present-day movements toward commercial and political world-dominion. Its independent political functions have been lopped away and its commercial powers are not adequate to the tasks and stress of contemporary life. Its monopoly, that is, its reputed source of gain and power, is no longer possible.[2] As has been seen, the East India Company of the Dutch (and the same may be said of that of the English) was founded for the purpose of securing mutual protection of ships and cargoes and to prevent ruinous competition between buyers in the Indies. The companies were, to a great extent, militant bodies, providing for themselves by force of arms, in distant seas, a security of trade which their countries of origin could not afford They soon came to exercise the tyranny of independent political powers, and could not well be brought to account, not only because of their actual strength, but also because of the crudeness of contemporary means of communication. Their object was actual, mercantile gain, for which end no means were too violent or underhanded. The case of the trading-companies of our own day, well represented by the German examples, is somewhat different; they are subordinate organizations for a conscious political purpose rather than essentially independent organizations for purely commercial ends. The actual powers which they are able to wield are not sufficient to afford them more than a relatively ephemeral independence. Extension of the market and its protection, the development of commercial usages and norms, the suppression of war, the "reach" of communication with its attendant diffusion of information, an extended power of home-control, rendered the more redoubtable by the development of swift national navies ready to enforce with speed the provisions of a government which is, as it were, on the spot — all these factors conspire to render a company little more than the servitor of the political power of the metropolis. As a

[1] Leroy-Beaulieu, II, book ii, chap. v.　　　　[2] Geffcken, in *The Forum.*

servitor, however, its functions are most significant, in these days; as Leroy-Beaulieu says,[1] the modern companies should not be judged merely from the standpoint of commerce and finance. They offer unrivaled opportunities as a means of entrance and occupation of new lands; they afford an agency which is simple and elastic, which does much with little, and which works in silence without having its doings undesirably advertised in parliamentary discussion. Not only that; the company forms a screen behind which the government can pursue its purposes of annexation until it sees fit to assume in actuality the power which it has merely delegated until the time is ripe. In the development of a new country such an expedient is most salutary for the preservation of the world's peace. Disavowals in consequence of rash or over-zealous action are thereby rendered plausible; the company is the pioneer and represents the not unfortunate scapegoat of international differences, whose existence is but for a time and whose wounds are easily healed, however loudly and bitterly it sees fit to bleat over its lot before the world.

The German Companies: Function and Administration

The German companies perfectly exemplify this general type — although their existence has been arrested considerably short of the average term of twenty-five to fifty years allotted by the French economist. All but one of the German companies, and that a comparatively insignificant one, have surrendered their political functions into the imperial hands and remain in a more or less private capacity in their respective regions.[2] This history of the various companies in their dual capacity shows some variation of detail, but presents, on the whole, a consistent picture of incompetence and failure. They were constructed after British and Dutch models, without, however, adequate account having been taken of the different environment in which it was their lot to be cast. Where they would accept them, the companies were granted the essential rights, and allowed to exercise the typical functions, of a state, under a slight imperial supervision. These included the levying of taxes and tolls, the coining of money, the erection of banks of issue, the maintenance of a police force, the administration of justice, exclusive rights in the occupation of unoccupied

[1] II, 662–663.   [2] Von Stengel, pp. 41–42.

land and in the closing of treaties and agreements with natives, certain mining rights, railroad concessions, and so on.[1] In short, the rights assured to the companies answered to the necessity to which they owed their existence — they obtained all the privileges necessary to private societies whose main *raison d'être* was to relieve the home-government from expense on account of the protectorates until such time as necessity or reconsideration should bring the people as represented by the Reichstag to a more tractable frame of mind.

The administration of the colonies under the companies was vested nominally in a *Landeshauptmann*, who was assisted by the supervisors of the various districts into which the protectorates were divided.[2] In reality, however, this functionary had very little freedom of action. He was both too near to and too distant from the "green baize": too near because his measures were ever subject to revocation by cable, too distant in that detailed orders from Berlin were, for the most part, antedated ere their arrival. The directors at home were ever ready to take a hand in the settlement of local colonial questions, and too often their interference and recommendation took the shape of poorly informed but confident meddling, productive of endless confusion and contradiction; this was flagrantly the case in New Guinea, the most distant and least known of the protectorates. Blum[3] says that not one of the directors or council of the New Guinea Company ever saw the island; that Hansemann, the chief director, was a type of the modern moneyed aristocrat, who resented advice from any one; that to his self-sufficiency the fiasco in New Guinea is chiefly to be charged. One administrator succeeded another in rapid succession, each new arrival being of a different calling and having different interests; and alteration of system went with change of personnel.[4] No sound

[1] Von Stengel, p. 42; Schmidt, I, 16; II, 300–301; Hermann, pp. 33–51; Meinecke, p. 8. The legal status of the companies is concisely treated by Von Stengel; see also Der Deutsche Export, pp. 50–51.

[2] Von Stengel, p. 68; Schmidt, II, 394 ff.; Fitzner, Kolonial-Handbuch, I, 265, etc. This manual gives full and minute details of the colonies and their stations (including telegraph lines, railroads, postal facilities, etc.); it also includes a catalogue of the personnel of the service

[3] Pp. 41 ff., 60.

[4] Blum, p. 43. Here is given a catalogue of changes in personnel and system. A quotation from Schmiele on this subject is particularly noteworthy. Several stories illustrating the pitiful weakness of the judiciary follow. For further details of the Company's management, see Krieger, pp. 231 ff.; Schmidt, II, 399.

governmental system of any kind was introduced, no agreements
were made with the natives, no dignity was lent to the administration of justice. Occasionally an administrator of rare personal
force managed to triumph in part over his difficulties, but this was
the exception.[1] Boshart[2] tells a like story of the Company for
Southwest Africa. He says that the colonial societies, though
they number among their members some of the greatest capitalists of the empire, get scarcely enough funds together to maintain a dozen poorly paid and, for the most part, useless officials.
The funds go for the local "plant" in Berlin, for clerk-hire, and
for occasional festivities; no money is applied to actual colonial
purposes.

In any land the evils of such a system of government are
apparent on its face; they are the more disastrous in a young
and undeveloped colony. In a new country there constantly arise
administrative contingencies which cannot be foreseen, risks which
cannot be systematized or distributed; conditions demand fertility
of resource and promptness of action, and success has often been
proved to vary with the strength of these qualities. The experience of all successful colonizers seems to point to the system of
local direction and responsibility as the most practicable in a field
where, in any case, action must be largely empiric. If, for its
welfare, adult trade demands security and a maintenance of the
status quo, and suffers severely from the entrance of caprice and
irregularity, certainly the beginnings of commerce ought to be
assured against such disturbing factors. In still another way did

[1] Blum, (pp. 121 ff.) describes the truly heroic attempts of Von Hagen to accomplish anything under this system. He says there was a tendency to refer all, even the
smallest questions, to Berlin. The system of accounting was most lax, and constant
conflicts arose from the commercial and political powers being lodged in one hand;
when the function of governing had been given up by the Company, a wholesome
trade set in. Blum calls the activity of the New Guinea Company, "Tappen und
Tasten ohne Sinn und deshalb ohne Gewinn" (p. 146). F. Fabri (Fünf Jahre, etc.,
p. 24) says the policy has been "von Fall zu Fall"—a system well enough in European diplomatic entanglements, but utterly out of place in a new country where the
"Fälle" are different in kind and should not be allowed to exist. Dr. Hahl, in the
Bismarck Archipelago, managed to initiate a better system. The German administration in these parts had a living reproof ever before it in the admirable system of
Sir W. MacGregor, in British New Guinea (Blum, p. 54).

[2] Pp. 159, 177. Boshart was an officer sent by the Company in 1887 to investigate
the political and commercial possibilities of Southwest Africa and vicinity. It is to be
noted that the Southwest Africa Company refused the *Hoheitsrechte*. Complaints of
parsimony are made by Engler also (p. 112).

the insecurity and instability of company administration make themselves felt in the German colonies : they complicated the native situation. To this question further attention will be subsequently given ; it is one of the most vital issues, if not the most important and menacing, in the history of the German colonies.

It would appear, then, in the matter of government, that the companies furnished a system scarcely worthy of the name. They benefited commerce to a very slight degree only, and devoted themselves chiefly to the occupation, such as it was, and ruthless exploitation, of the lands and their native products. Starting out with great plans and well-equipped scientific staffs,[1] they later found themselves embarrassed for funds and forced to reduce their scale of operations. Never having really grappled with the essential issues in the development of trade with the tropics, the financial strain grew upon them along with the political, until it was greater than they could bear. Then they were severally forced to request the imperial government to take over the administrative function — earlier, perhaps, than had originally been contemplated or desired. Inefficiency of administration, therefore, and of commercial methods and measures, acted and reacted upon one another, creating a vicious and disastrous round, and almost precluding the possibility of advance. The fact was demonstrated anew that there exists an essential contradiction and incompatibility between the governing and the trading functions, whether or not these are united in the same individual or society.[2] In trading one reckons for the proximate gain, for advantage realizable certainly within the life-time of the operator ; the function of governing, on the contrary, is the more perfect and dignified, according as it discounts present conditions and labors for that distant future good which, through disinterested statesmanship, it foresees. A state may endure immediate losses and sacrifices — it can do that because of its longevity and extended credit — but the individual or company can follow only afar off and to the extent of its narrower means and limited credit. This contradiction was perhaps less perceptible in the seventeenth-century prototypes of the nineteenth-century chartered companies, because, properly speaking, administration in the colonies was in their time a mere adjunct to trade-exploitation. The later developing ideas of colonial government

[1] Keltie, pp. 252, 319, etc.; Schmidt, I, 135 ff.; II, 322.
[2] Cf. F. Fabri, Fünf Jahre, etc., pp. 7, 18 ff., 120; pp. 456 ff., above.

which clothe it with responsibility for peace, humanity, and civilization, and make it thereby the regulator of trade, were yet to come. In the German colonies there was no longer any opportunity to occupy rich land, dig treasure, or maintain a spice monopoly; in a difficult country, under adverse conditions, the initial labors preparatory to occupancy must have, in a large measure, preceded the advance of trade. The companies could not open up the land for themselves, and establish security, order, and law. Again it was demonstrated that a colonial policy could not be built on trade-relations, nor a stable government on mercantile principles.

It has already been noted that the colonies of Togo and Kamerun passed directly under the imperial power, and were organized after the general type of the British crown colony.[1] The actually existing German interests in these colonies were substantial enough to effect this result; indeed, the well-known "Kamerun" was popularly all but synonymous with "colony" in early German colonial times.[2] The entrance of the imperial power into Southwest Africa was an unwilling one; although originally a company had been formed to carry forward the projects of Lüderitz, it promptly declared itself unwilling to assume the *Hoheitsrechte*, forcing, by such action, an occupation at imperial expense, at least in part, and under imperial officials.[3] East Africa next passed under the imperial power (1891); an insurrection which broke out in 1888 had proved too much for the East Africa Company's resources, and, indeed, kept an able imperial commissioner's hands full for several years.[4] New Guinea presents a more checkered history. Owing to financial embarrassment, the Company, in 1889, asked the Chancellor to take over the government. This was done; but by 1892 it was found that double expense for officials was being incurred under the existing system, and the imperial government withdrew. In 1899, however, the Company was again in a most wretched state of financial embarrassment and economic collapse, and the imperial rule was again requested

---

[1] F. Fabri, Fünf Jahre, etc., pp. 7, 23 ff.; Keltie, pp. 326, 330; Geffcken, in *The Forum*.

[2] "Der Volksmund kennt vor allem nur Kamerun, der gewissermassen alle unsere Schutzgebiete repräsentiert." Engler, p. 157.

[3] F. Fabri, Fünf Jahre, etc., p. 23. Hamburg and Bremen firms were not at all sanguine as to the chartered company scheme. Schmidt, II, 265; Geffcken, in *The Forum*.

[4] F. Fabri, Fünf Jahre, etc., pp. 23, 36 ff.; Schmidt, I, 1 ff.; Andler, p. 273.

and established.[1] The remaining society, the small Jaluit Company of the Marshall Islands, has naturally better fulfilled its mission than any of the others, if retention and control of its territory be considered its mission; it has paid all regular expenses of government and has enjoyed a fair measure of reputation and prosperity.[2] It may be said, then, of the German companies, that they were really makeshifts pending the readiness of the government to take control; their origin in the colonial societies should of itself indicate this. As makeshifts they have no doubt discharged important political functions and done their share towards neutralizing the dangerous friction caused by direct contact of sovereign states on exterior territory.

Imperial Administration

When the imperial government succeeded to the possessions of the various companies, colonial policy began to take on the definite outlines which it had already displayed in Togo and Kamerun. The new government found itself on its own ground where there was fighting to be done; the insurrection in East Africa, which had cost the local company its political existence, was reduced by a vigorous and relentless swinging of the sword. The martial spirit of discipline soon seized upon and pervaded the administrative system; where the Spaniards had worshiped the dogma of religion and the French had set up the ideal of "assimilation," the Germans invoked the panacea of strict order and inflexible discipline. It was natural and almost inevitable that this should be so, but one sighs to think that this social experiment of a gifted people should have been crossed by another of those inexorable dogmas which time and again in history have neutralized and set at naught interesting social movements — processes which were seemingly sure to prove or refute through striking instances the practical value of science and rational method. Over-government through a system of bureaucracy was about as bad for the colonies as the interference of the home societies had been, during the period of the chartered companies. If there is anything that is proved

---

[1] Müller, pp. 38 ff.; Blum, p. v; Schmidt, II, 40 ff., 394. Of course the companies received some compensation for their surrender of rights, in this case four million marks and some share in deciding upon measures of rule under the empire. Krieger, pp. 231 ff.

[2] Von Stengel, p. 200; Meinecke, p. 8; Loeb, p. 61.

by the history of colonies, it is that they cannot flourish under an inelastic and stereotyped system. In the colonies the individual and the society stand once more in closer and more vital relation with their physical environment ; a return to a less evolved system of government is found necessary, and the application of minute regulation is felt to be a detriment and an anachronism. The rough-and-ready methods of frontier government and justice have their place in the development of a new country, and if external power is able permanently to impose a much more highly refined system, it is the misfortune of the colony involved.[1] German writers are almost unanimous in condemning this bureaucracy, and their re-monstrances have borne some fruit. They have rebelled against the military caste-system, the imposition of petty regulations and fines, the direction of affairs from Berlin, the inexperience and self-confidence of the colonial functionaries, and in general against the arbitrary conduct of a governing organization which did not know its ground.[2]

As usual, however, good is mixed with evil ; the services of the imperial domination must not be overlooked. Under the strong arm, peace and security have been established, and the slave-trade has been largely suppressed in its ancient strongholds by the power which holds the coasts. Expense in lives and in money has not been spared in the exploration of the *Hinterland* and in pushing forward the permanent outposts of civilization. Scientific investi-gation of the most valuable kind has been made coincidently with the advance of expeditions and of administrative stations.[3] The same conscientious and painstaking effort has been universally put forth. When the errors incident to inexperience shall have been recognized and eliminated — and the Germans, hampered by no false pride, seem to be adept at this process — it will be hard to find a people better equipped for the management of dependencies.[4]

[1] Bismarck's views on the value of the bureaucratic system in the colonies were pronounced ; he said in 1876 that no success was to be attained by transplanting the Prussian government assessors and bureaucratic system to Africa ; that work at the green table was the last thing suitable to that sphere. Poschinger, p. 242 ; cf. F. Fabri, Fünf Jahre, etc., pp. 27, 100.

[2] For some details of German officialism and its workings, see Blum, pp. 140 ff. ; Witt, in *Blackwood's*, CLXIII, 788 ; *Globus*, LXXVII, 229 ; Pfeil, Vorschläge, pp. 39 ff. ; Keltie, p. 258, etc.

[3] This was particularly true of Kamerun, where the unexplored region of Africa is nearest the coast. Engler, p. 89 ; cf. Keltie, pp. 260 ff.

[4] See Brunialti, pp. 171 ff. ; F. Fabri, Fünf Jahre, etc., p. 29.

Under the imperial rule, the *Schutzgebiete* "are substantially colonies in the same sense as the British crown colonies, forming an integral part of the empire as regards other states, although of course German laws are not applicable to them except by express enactment, and their natives are not German citizens." [1] The actual power of administration is vested in a governor (or commissioner) who is responsible primarily to the German Chancellor. Unfortunately he was at first responsible to other officials as well, inasmuch as a colonial office had not yet been differentiated.[2] This led to conflicts, and finally to a serious over-burdening of the Foreign Office with colonial business. The Colonial Department of the Foreign Office was established April 1, 1890, and finally, in very recent times, a Colonial Minister has been appointed; the governor is responsible through this officer and the Chancellor, to the emperor, in whom is vested the general function of rule in the colonies. The imperial Chancellor is empowered to summon a colonial council, consisting of experts in all departments of knowledge bearing on colonies, to advise with him in such questions as he desires. This council passes on the draft budget.[3] In the colony the governor is assisted by subordinates in the different provinces or districts, is head of the military power, of the judiciary, etc. High centralization, therefore, prevails. The administration of justice follows one general plan in the protectorates: minor disputes of natives are left, as far as possible, to the native chiefs as arbiters; secondary courts try the remaining minor cases; and death sentences and appeals are the province of the governor, with or without council, as chief judge.[4]

The commercial position [5] of the colony with reference to the German government is that of most favored country. The colonies rank as *Zollausland*, and their exports are subject to the imposition of duties, both at the German ports and at the boundaries of the other colonies; export duties also are collected, except in

---

[1] Geffcken, in *The Forum*.

[2] Schmidt, I, 276 ff.; F. Fabri, Fünf Jahre, etc., p. 123.

[3] Von Stengel, p. 66; Loeb, p. 49.

[4] Details are given in Von Stengel's work; it is a standard treatise on legal relations in the colonies. See also, for less detailed treatment, Fitzner, *passim*; Loeb, pp. 45 ff.; Schmidt, II, 194; Meinecke, p. 14. Of late there has been a movement looking to the adoption of English and French systems of colonial government; the establishment of the local council and the independent colonial budget have been much discussed. *Annals Amer. Acad. Pol. and Soc. Sci.*, XIX, No. 1 (January, 1902), p. 162.   [5] Von Stengel, pp. 97 ff.

Togo and Kamerun. The tariff on imports is levied on a revenue basis, and seldom exceeds a low percentage ($1\frac{1}{2}$–20 per cent); many and important articles are placed on the free list at both ends.[1] Prohibitions affect only arms and ammunition, and spirituous liquors. It will be noted also that some of the German territory comes under the rulings of the Berlin conference,[2] by which the conventional basins of the Congo and Niger were opened to free navigation by the ships of all nations. Freedom of trade was established and only such duties were to be levied as would pay expenses incurred in the interests of trade, no differentials being allowed. These provisions are, of course, active to a limited degree only in the German possessions.

POPULATION

The settlement of the new colonies has not proceeded apace. It is generally recognized that, with the exception of Southwest Africa, they are unfitted to receive any permanent European settlement; their lot is that of the trading or plantation colony, supporting a shifting population of European traders and planters, whose interest in the country can never be that of a people for its home. Southwest Africa, as far as climate is concerned, might allow of European settlement; but, as has been seen, the region is anything but inviting to the settler; and in addition to this, the action of the Company for Southwest Africa has interposed artificial obstacles of the most serious kind. Where it has not itself pursued the selfish policy of appropriation of the best lands, it has allowed speculators to gain possession; the price of land [3]

---

[1] Details in Fitzner, *passim*; Der Deutsche Export, pp. 34 ff., 41 ff.; Loeb, pp. 59 ff. The customs-dues of Togo were admittedly modeled upon those of the English Gold Coast colony. Klose, p. 547. Scientific apparatus, the property of the missions, etc., were regularly free.

[2] Keltie, chap. xiv.

[3] The government price is 1 M. per ha. for the lands it has retained. The Southwest Africa Company charges about the same. Other companies ask a prohibitive price, as they are waiting for a rise. Prices are reckoned in lump-sums with no regard to the quality of the land, of which, indeed, the companies are oftentimes as ignorant as the settlers. The conditions of payment are very hard (10 per cent down, two years free, then 10 per cent a year). Hermann, who gives this information from personal experience, says that, considering the defective protection of the government, the arid quality of the land, etc., the price should be put down to 50 pf. (10 cents) per ha., to be paid up in fifty years. There are only two settlers near Windhoek who deserve the name, and, though economical and industrious, they find it hard or impossible to pay. Hermann, pp. 5–11.

is, in view of existing conditions, exceedingly high, and the pur-
chaser can never be sure that his title is secure and that the land
he has bought is not an arid sandhill. Worst of all, the delays and
expense incident to settlement are so great that immigration of the
German peasant is out of the question. The expenses due to delays
alone (in journeying by ox-wagon to Windhoek and there waiting
on the convenience of the far from strenuous Company official) is
estimated by a competent critic at $100; the same writer asserts
that a capital of over $2300 is indispensable, and that, even with
this, and neglecting the never remote possibility of drought, "rinder-
pest," and bad years, the settler would still be in debt $800 in the
fifth year of his cattle-raising activity.[1] Agriculture on any respectable scale is debarred by physical conditions; in the neighborhood
of Windhoek, where prices are extremely high, it is only with great
painstaking that horticulture on the small scale can be made to pay.
The fact of the matter is that the German emigrant avoids the German possessions because of the virtual extension thither of the
national "system." Often this system is exactly the incubus which
he is trying to throw off; why should he subject himself anew to
military conscription and petty regulation when so many of his fellow-countrymen are leading free and prosperous lives across the
Atlantic? It is no doubt true that labor is deterred from entering
Southwest Africa, the only German colony possible of settlement,
because it is well known that the competing native of that colony
will work (after a fashion) for merely food and drink — or the latter
alone; but at bottom, the attempted artificial direction of German
emigration is ineffective against the innate desire of man to be his
own master.[2]

According to late official statistics, the total white population of
the German dependencies is not above 7000; of these the greater

[1] Hermann, pp. 2 ff., 13 ff. This author, himself a settler in Southwest Africa, has
several times come into collision with the Company and its powerful manipulators in
Berlin (see Giesebrecht, p. 121). He writes a very interesting and detailed account
of the productive possibilities of Southwest Africa. Novelties proposed and partially
adopted are ostrich-raising and the culture of the silkworm (Hermann, pp. 63–64).

[2] Hermann, pp. 1–2; cf. *The Nation*, LXV, 471. Engler (pp. 98–99) distinguishes
six classes of emigrants to the colonies: (1) merchants in the colonies and their supporters at home; (2) enterprising youths, tired of home, and on their travels; (3) former
soldiers, who are weary of garrison life and impatient of slow promotion, and who
want to fight; (4) young men through school, who covet rank and honors unattainable
at home; (5) older men who want to be something at home and cannot — who wish
to speak or write; (6) merchants who want to get into political life.

part are officers, officials, and traders. In Southwest Africa, the *Kolonial-Handbuch* claimed before the recent uprising of the natives 3388 German and foreign settlers.[1] It should here be mentioned that the Germans have anticipated for some years, and with a mixture of feelings, the influx of a large Boer population into the Southwest African colony. The Boers are hardy enough, and rich enough in cattle, to become a permanent and increasing element of the population; but the Germans dislike their character and have regularly repelled advances looking to the establishment of a German protectorate over certain regions farther to the south.[2]

Colonial Trade

In the development of the colonial trade,[3] Germany has succeeded little better than in the attempt to direct emigration. The companies did practically nothing toward opening up their respective regions by means of road-making, clearing of river-courses, and the like. They did not attempt to minimize the risks of commerce by the erection of lighthouses, the making of charts, and the dredging of harbors. Communication with the outside world, especially for New Guinea, was fitful, being rendered possible, for the most part, by Dutch and English vessels. Only as the imperial government came forward with subsidized lines, was regular communication with Europe established. All these works were beyond the strength of the companies, and, it may be said, considering their actual political nature and purpose, beyond their province; they were to hold the colonies and try to pay expenses some way till the government could relieve them. There was really no incentive for the investment of capital in Southwest Africa and New Guinea, for they provided neither supply stations nor markets;[4] a scanty and inelastic export of hides and ivory from Southwest Africa, and of copra from New Guinea, was all that could be reckoned on. The crudeness of the means of communication in these two possessions

---

[1] Fitzner, p. 141. These estimates agree, except in the case of Southwest Africa, with those of the Statesman's Year-Book (1901). The latter gives the number of Europeans in Southwest Africa as 1840 (1557 Germans), which seems a more reasonable estimate than that of the (perhaps inspired) Kolonial-Handbuch. Hauser says (p. 114) that there are not over 3400 Germans, functionaries and all, in the *Schutzgebiete*.

[2] Büttner, p. 105; Engler, p. 112; Hermann, p. 12; *Globus*, LXXIX, 3 (January, 17, 1901).   [3] See Fitzner, *passim*, for details; also Der Deutsche Export.

[4] The Germans call Southwest Africa their "Schmerzenkind." Hauser, p. 41; Leroy-Beaulieu, I, 324.

and the distance of the latter colony were fatal obstacles to the development of trade. Valuable woods in New Guinea could not be transported to the coast and still yield a profit, and the cotton of the island, though of splendid quality and long staple, could not realize a price on European markets which would cover the cost of production and freight charges,[1] and still leave a reasonable margin of profit. In Togo[2] and Kamerun trade-interests had long existed, and from East Africa also many valuable products could be drawn; choice woods, palm-oil and kernels, tropical fruits, copra, sugar, ivory, and caoutchouc were among them, although the last two articles named were becoming more and more scarce under a system of ruthless exploitation. Cacao, coffee, tea, and a promising quality of tobacco (from New Guinea) were raised in the several tropical colonies, and seemed to point to future gains as recompense for present toil and sacrifice. As a supply region, then, the colonies were eminently unsatisfactory; nor did they afford a profitable market for German wares. The native peoples either had little to give in exchange for German goods, or their needs were so few and their improvidence so great that they did not care to take advantage of resources which they possessed. This was the case particularly in Southwest Africa and New Guinea. The Herero of the former country clung to their one form of wealth, cattle, with religious fervor, and would sell only those beasts that were old, sick, or bewitched;[3] the Papuans of New Guinea were quite satisfied with their lot, and desirous only of such minor articles as iron hatchets and knives.[4] Most of the native peoples under the German flag confined their demand to powder and guns, and to alcoholic spirits, goods which the government was unwilling to supply.

[1] Blum (p. 103) says the *plus* in the transport costs must be made up for by a *minus* in the cost of production or a *melius* in quality of product — for all of which practice and experience are needed. The wide fluctuations of the European markets are exceedingly harmful to the development of cotton-raising (p. 171). Cf. Schmidt, II, 409.

[2] An exceptionally full treatment of the economic possibilities of Togo is given by Klose, pp. 547 ff.   [3] Büttner, pp. 25 ff., 86.

[4] For ages Papuans have traded only when absolute need has frightened them out of their laziness. This trade was carried on by means of periodical, rotating markets and festivals. As usual, the folk of the smaller islands have become the industrial specialists and traders. Papuan manufactured articles of export are largely "objects of ethnological interest." Hagen, pp. 214 ff.

One of the irritating features of the native trade is the amount of dickering necessary. Long discussions are to the native a favorite diversion; he insists upon bartering each article separately and prolongs his enjoyment to the despair of the unhappy German. Schmidt, I, 187.

East Africa and Kamerun present certain additional trading conditions which entitle them to separate mention. In Kamerun the Germans were long irritated by the Dualla tribe, a people of middlemen, who insisted upon retaining for themselves the privilege of trading between widely diverse conjunctures — the essential advantage of the frontier-trade. During the earlier years of occupation, they offered much open and covert opposition to the expansion of German trade with the interior; of late, however, their power has been weakened by the extension inland of the imperial arms. In East Africa trade has remained for centuries in the hands of Arabs and natives of India, and attempts of the East Africa Company to lay hands upon the commercial routes and caravans for purposes of trade and taxation have been, for the most part, futile.[1] The tremendous inertia of custom and the redoubtable power of Islam, vested in the sultan of Zanzibar, have been encountered, in active or passive resistance, at every turn; the East Africa Company never got much beyond the invasion stage.[2]

On the whole, then, the trade of these new possessions has not justified the eager expectations, nor satisfied the longings, of the acquisition-period. The possession of "colonies" seems to have been as unsatisfactory in the solution of commercial problems as of those of emigration. Nor has the development of commerce with the colonies been such as to afford any convincing instances to those who asserted that trade would follow the flag. If truth be told, the tendency of trade seems to have been to follow the British, and for obvious reasons. It was only by the use of English trade-marks, for example, that the Germans managed to get any hold at all in Southwest Africa; their goods were regarded as "German trash,"[3] and the demand for them under their own mark and form was very small. Here again the Germans brought up against the barrier of century-old and time-hallowed custom, as well as against the superior elasticity and development of the British commercial system. The tariff regulations mentioned above, however moderate, could not but have had their effect upon an incipient trade which called for the utmost freedom of

---

[1] The Indians (especially the Banians) are sly and bad, but indispensable to the Germans for the present. Schmidt, I, 181.

[2] Cf. Leroy-Beaulieu, I, 327.

[3] This was about 1840, when Germans first appeared as merchants in Southwest Africa. Keltie, p. 171.

development.[1] Statistics of Germany's trade with her colonies exhibit, on the whole, an uninteresting dead-level. It is found that while exports have remained practically stationary, imports, especially of manufactured wares, have increased somewhat in volume. The decline of caoutchouc and ivory under a system of ruthless destruction has already been alluded to. In general, Germany's share in the exports and imports of the *Schutzgebiete* is insignificant; it appears, however, to be on the increase.[2] But, though the development of the German colonial trade has not been such as to satisfy the inflated hopes of the colonial party, the recital of its story need cause no shame to the Germans. They were working against overwhelming odds. The companies, however culpable, cannot with justice be held to full account for all the mismanagement and mistakes incident to their performance of temporary and inconsistent functions; even if the directors were seriously at fault, the evil occasioned was rather local than general in its incidence. There was a singular moderation and care displayed by the government in the whole matter; this, again, in all probability, must be referred to the influence of Bismarck; fortunately for the Germans, the governor of the mechanism seems to have discharged its function with rare precision.

Internal Improvements; Budget

After the government had gathered the reins of power into its own hands, commercial matters were set at once upon a better footing. The companies themselves, especially that of East Africa,[3] began to feel themselves more nearly equal to the discharge of their business functions now that the incubus of administration had been removed. The imperial government operated, if not with skilled hand, certainly with farsighted purpose. Scientific expeditions were systematically organized and experiment stations were

[1] The manufactured articles imported into East Africa are mostly from England, America, Switzerland, and India. Arms and (inferior) powder are about the only articles demanded of the Germans. Schmidt, I, 179 ff. Philippson (pp. 32, 44) had predicted (1880) that colonies could not be permanently retained by a country of such unfortunate geographical position as Germany; he prophesied that they would fall into England's market.

[2] The import trade of Germany with West Africa attained its high-water mark in 1891 (M. 5,600,000). Since 1896 its rise has been due to imperial subventions, especially for Southwest Africa. The statistics here involved are admittedly poor and corrupt. Only general tendencies can be shown. For details, see Der Deutsche Export, pp. 56 ff.; Fitzner; Statesman's Year-Book, etc.   [3] Schmidt, I, 122 ff.

founded for the investigation of conditions of soil, climate, etc.; the acclimatization of various grains, vegetables, and fruits became a subject for study and experiment. The *Hinterland* of West and Southwest Africa had been vigorously opened up in the early years of the imperial government; East Africa, and later New Guinea, now offered a fresh field for exploits and advance. Military and commercial roads were built and carefully patrolled.[1] In general, however, trade from the interior still passes over the narrow native "paths," as it has done from time immemorial;[2] the solution of the question of communication still looms up as a *sine qua non* of effective occupation and development. The imperial coin has been made legal tender in most of the colonies. In Southwest Africa, it is said, the once prevalent British coin is becoming more scarce; but in Togo, where trade-interests have been better developed, British currency is much preferred.[3]

In the matter of transmarine communication, the government's hand has been active from the first. Liberal subventions[4] were granted to African lines, and by the early nineties fair communications had been established. New Guinea and the Bismarck Archipelago were dependent solely upon Dutch and English lines until recently; the New Guinea Company did nothing to facilitate local or European connections and the government could, at that time, accomplish little. At present the German colonies do not suffer to any great extent from absence of external communication.[5] Railroads in the colonies are a more crying need, and are no more than in their beginnings. Railroad development can do much for Southwest Africa, where the chief obstacles to the opening-up of the interior lie in the time, danger, and cost of transport across the sandy desert that borders the coast. Cable connection is now made with all the African protectorates and

---

[1] They have generally been of an unnecessary width and quality, inasmuch as length and penetration have been sacrificed. Natives of Togo cannot see the use of a road several meters in width; they solemnly march in " goose-order " along the edges, in the good old ancestral way. Meinecke, p. 16.

[2] Cf. Hauser, p. 13. Where there are no native paths (e.g. in parts of New Guinea) a passage has to be hacked out, step by step, through the dense jungle. Krieger, p. 243.

[3] Loeb, p. 53; Meinecke, p. 43; Klose, p. 127.

[4] The first subvention was legalized April 6, 1885; after this time subventions became more and more common. Der Deutsche Export, pp. 47–48.

[5] Fitzner, I and II, *passim*. An account of then existing connections is to be found in *Globus*, LXXIX, No. 9 (March 7, 1901), p. 146.

limited telegraph and telephone lines (largely military) are found in all the colonies.[1]

On the whole, considering the obstacles which the Germans have had to meet, and their inexperience in governing dependencies, it must be admitted that they have coped manfully with an extremely troublesome situation, sparing neither money, effort, nor lives in the solution of commercial and other problems, presented in their most forbidding forms. Throughout, the attitude of the colonizing power has been that of modesty and of dogged persé-verance, of willingness to learn and to correct errors. There has been no extravagance countenanced, and yet the expense has been grievously heavy. Many brave lives have been lost in battle, and many more sacrificed to the deadly climate, with its fatal fevers and dysentery.[2] In comparison with such irreparable losses, expenses of administration may seem slight; but, as has been seen, they were such as to discourage the enthusiastic and reasonably strong colonial companies. From the time of their annexation until the late nineties, Togo and Kamerun managed to pay their own way; since that time, however, they have been the recipients of rapidly increasing imperial subventions. The small Jaluit Company is the only one which has regularly balanced its budget without state aid. The expense incurred by the empire in the entire or partial administration of East and Southwest Africa and New Guinea has been heavy from the first, and manifests a tendency to increase steadily.[3] The heavy debt item of the budget is, of course, the expense of military occupation. The credit items consist of the subventions, and of various taxes, — e.g. on natives, on business firms, etc., — customs dues, income from railroads, and other minor income. The receipts from the customs form by far the largest of these items, excepting always the subventions.

[1] Fitzner, I and II, *passim.* All the *Schutzgebiete* are in the *Weltpostverein.*

[2] The story goes that there were always two governors en route between the English West African possessions and the home-land; one, in his coffin, being carried home for burial, and the other hastening to take his vacant place.

[3] According to Loeb (p. 61), expenses in behalf of the colonies rose from M. 9,497,000 in 1896–1897 to 25,200,000 in 1899. The full estimates, he says (p. 63), were never allowed by the imperial legislature. He notes (p. 70) the interesting fact that Kamerun alone has been required to repay subventions, on a basis of annual installments, to the imperial treasury. The budget and debt-contracting powers have been in the hands of the imperial legislature since 1892, although here the emperor's hand is still very powerful (p. 48 ff.). For details, see Fitzner, I and II, *passim,* and Loeb, pp. 56 ff. In the former are to be found details of taxation, tax-collection, expenses of various kinds, and the like.

To the Germans, then, as well as to other peoples, world-dominion has proved itself to be an expensive luxury. They seem to regard it as worth the cost; indeed, it has been charged by certain recalcitrants[1] that the popular mind is unsettled in the matter of the colonies to the verge of megalomania. The criticism is made that improvements of unquestioned value at home are delayed by reason of excessive and imprudent grants for questionable enterprises in the colonies. But by this lavishness the Germans thought to raise the importance of the empire in the eyes of the world.

THE "NATIVE-QUESTION"

The native-question in any colony is one which, for the attainment of any adequate results, must be attacked at the same time from the general and from the specific points of view. Its satisfactory solution, if such solution is ever possible, must call into requisition the results of the most advanced thought in the fields of ethnology and the science of society. In this place, however, a specific study, with but casual reference to general principles, is less out of place, because of the homogeneous character of the natives of the German colonies; the typical virtues and defects of the German system stand out, therefore, more consistently, and lend themselves to a briefer and less involved treatment.

As in other issues of colonial policy, so here, the successes and failures of the Germans are intimately bound up with the national character and disposition. Theoretically, German administrators should have known a great deal about native peoples and their life; if they remained ignorant in any cases, it was certainly not for lack of portly volumes on these subjects, constructed with the usual laborious *Gründlichkeit*. An acquaintance with such sources, on the part of colonial administrators, is far from exceptional; but the most important contribution of scientific training to the handling of the native-question, as presented to the Germans, appears in the distinctly sane view which the administrators as a class are enabled to take before this troubled issue. Most of them have realized that the German possessions, in common with all other tropical countries, find in the presence of native races an essential, even though variable, and often merely potential, factor in public wealth. Years have served to strengthen the conviction that the

[1] Speech of Herr Richter in the Reichstag (New York *Times*, January 10, 1902).

Germans are thrown back upon the native peoples for what assistance they are to get, even though that be slight, in the development
of colonial resources.[1] Little false sentiment is to be found and
few grandiloquent expressions of purely humanitarian aims. The
problem is approached with ˙cool head and with a method that is
scientific, even though over-academic in its first expressions.

This promising attitude was compromised first by the eminently
temporizing policy of the chartered companies, and, later, by bureaucratic narrow-mindedness and military rigor. The administration of the companies, with its shifty and uncertain policy, was about
the worst system to which the fate of the native could have been
intrusted. They exercised both too much and too little power;
they imposed upon and irritated the native, without being able to
enforce wholesome discipline, or, indeed, caring to do so. They
were in the field for very tangible and immediate ends, and had
no inclination or ambition to foresee the future and prepare for it.
No predetermined and settled policy existed under their régime;
they took little or no account of the character and customs of the
native peoples of their districts. In New Guinea and the Pacific
islands the results of their inefficiency were, of course, less notice-
able, amounting only to the death of a number of brave men; but
in Southwest and East Africa the outcome has been more momentous. The losses occasioned by the hostility of Witbooi and of
Maharero may not have been directly chargeable to the arrogance
and stupidity of Company officials;[2] the uprising in East Africa,
however, which finally cost the local Company its political existence,
had its immediate cause in tactless and oppressive measures, motived by a curious combination of greed, timidity, and parsimony.
No attention was paid to the warnings of British officers who knew
well the dangerous mood of the Arabs and Swahili; these resentful

---

[1] The value of the native peoples is recognized by almost all the authorities; the
case is stated most strongly by Blum, pp. 47, 102, 162; Pfeil, Vorschläge, 60 ff.; Hermann, p. 82.

[2] The earlier uprisings have been, of course, relatively overshadowed by the troubles
in Southwest Africa which have been going on now for some years and at a grave
cost of resources and lives. Military operations against the Herero and their allies
have been most difficult owing to the physical character of the colony; and despite
the adoption of the arduous "hunting-out" style of campaign, the end is not nearly
in sight. The voting of extra credits for Southwest Africa has cost the Kaiser and
his ministers much trouble from the opposition. The modest progress that the colony
showed is now set back for an indefinite period to come, and the whole colonial programme has been rendered distasteful to a large number of Germans.

peoples were handled with entire lack of caution and of fair consideration, and were not long in discovering and profiting by the
essential weakness of their oppressors.[1]

SEVERITY AND CRUELTY : MALADAPTABILITY

The companies had no native policy, therefore ; but with the
entrance of the imperial rule there appeared, full-fledged, a most
simple and definite system. The invincible Prussian army would
put these reckless and insubordinate savages down, once and for
all. This was, again, the military spirit fostered by German life
and training ; and it was not without its salutary effect in the case
in hand. Much objection may be had to the bureaucrat, with his
petty powers and small tyranny, who followed along with the imperial rule, but little can be urged against the German doctrine of
force. The native understands force ; it is about the only thing
that is permanently and wholesomely imposing to him ; and any
colonizing people does well to flash the blade from out the scab-
bard now and then. The effect can generally be produced without
striking often and cruelly ; in the case of the Germans, however,
it appears that resort to actual bloodshed has shown itself to be
necessary again and again. Dismissal of incompetent and insolent
company officials and of *"schneidige Lieutenants"* would, doubtless, have been in the nature of the ounce of prevention, but, under
the circumstances, these were an inevitable incubus of the system.
Much must be set down to the account of inexperience of contact
with native races, and consequent ignorance of and contempt for
their customs and prejudices, on the part of the average colonial
functionary ; taken all in all, however, this severity was far better
than a wavering policy and indecision.[2]

Too often, however, condonable military strictness has been
called upon to account for conspicuous examples of individual

[1] F. Fabri, Fünf Jahre, etc., pp. 65 ff., 85 ff. ; Keltie, pp. 254 ff. ; Johnston, p. 256;
Keane, Africa, II, 180; Dove, pp. 160 ff., 178; *Globus*, LXXIX, No. 9, p. 134. The
native princes felt that they had been hoaxed by Peters and others in the matter of
the " treaties " in which they had signed away land and power. They had never understood the import of these documents, which were, indeed, of the most flimsy sort.
Schmidt (I, 12–13) gives a typical example of Peters's treaties.

[2] F. Fabri, Fünf Jahre, etc., p. 111 ; Pfeil, Vorschläge, pp. 65 ff. ; Studien, etc.,
p. 256; Boshart, p. 184. Keltie (pp. 259–262) compares German activity in East Africa
with the efforts of the British in the same region, to the great disadvantage of the
latter.

cruelty. From time to time tales of indescribable tortures inflicted upon natives in the Kamerun region have shocked the civilized world. Insignificant faults have been punished with wanton and senseless cruelty. Flagrant cases of the eighties seem to have found their aftertypes at the beginning of a new century.[1] The Germans seem to feel that there is something abnormal about these bursts of murderous rage. They are not countenanced,[2] and the feeling of the responsible administrators and colonists about them is one of anger and shame. They are regarded by some as evidence of a distemper for which the significant term *Tropenkoller* has been coined.[3] There really appears to be something pathological about these cases. No doubt the German subordinate officer is inclined to be tyrannical in the exercise of petty power, — the German system is hardly calculated to instill ideals of self-restraint in the treatment of inferiors, — but it is hard to believe that any man in his right mind could enjoy poking a ramrod down a defenseless negro's windpipe, or that he would feel it necessary, for the sake of discipline, to whip numbers of women publicly and brutally, before the eyes of their men. This is not the wild burst of sudden anger; it is barbarous and insane torture. These examples are not the worst. And a reasonable physical cause for it all is really not far to seek : the Germans are naturally maladaptable to an unfamiliar physical environment, and, as a rule, take no pains to neutralize this weakness by artificial adaptation. All experience of the white race with equatorial Africa goes to show that it is about as unlikely a region in which to keep health and sanity as any on the globe ; the Belgian Congo State, as well as the German protectorates, has its tale of shame to tell. Here is a region, then, where special care in matters of tropical hygiene and dietary are demanded of a European population, even though it come from the

[1] New York *Times*, December 22, 1901. The earlier cases were those of Leist, Wehlan, and Peters ; in Giesebrecht's collection are found letters from a number of scientists and administrators, condemning the above native-torturers, together with a communication from Peters, in which he seeks to defend his course. The case of Peters has received special attention because of his prominence in German colonial history. See also Schmidt, II, 96 ff. ; Johnston, p. 258 ; Hermann, p. 84 ; New York *Times*, April 15, 1894. Giesebrecht (p. 23) mentions a study of his own on " Kolonialgreuel," in *Neue Deutsche Rundschau*, 1895, Heft ii.

[2] The three culprits mentioned above were cashiered. The New York *Times* (December 15, 1901) reports light punishments, but according to Sir H. H. Johnston, · (p. 258), publicity was given to these cases, prosecution was vigorous, and the punishments proportional to the offenses. Later years exhibit the same policy.

[3] Der Deutsche Export, p. 91 ; Schmidt, II, 74–76 ; Pfeil, Studien, etc., p. 252.

Mediterranean states. With the Germans, much more of caution is necessary, for they are a people that has always acclimatized poorly in low latitudes, as statistics, even of Algeria, will show.[1]

However, either from ignorance or from willfulness, the Germans are found to have neglected certain prime essentials of tropical hygiene. The more self-evident rules, regarding clothing, marching in crowded ranks, and the like, were perforce observed, but, as the reports of importations into the German colonies and the tales of eye-witnesses unite to show, the German absolutely refused to renounce in tropical colonies the heavy alcoholic drinks of the fatherland. No people can endure the continued use of these liquors under the equator; the Spanish and Portuguese had to learn to be sparing in the use of even the light wines to which they had been accustomed. Doubtless heat, hardship, and coarse food do their share in wrecking the digestive and nervous systems, but intemperance in the tropics — and this may well be temperance at home — must certainly be taken into grave account. It should be reckoned in with the climatic agents which induce such frequent melancholia and consequent insanity or suicide in the equatorial districts of Africa.[2] Another unfortunate factor is present in the iron inflexibility of the social system in the colonies. Distinctions of rank, social position, and the like are rigorously maintained; nothing short of imminent annihilation seems likely to modify the strictness of etiquette and caste. There are no "clubs" in the German colonies; each military circle of a few members herds by itself and gulps down its steins of Bavarian beer in lonely and dignified seclusion. Homesickness plays its familiar rôle in inducing gloom and despair, and consequent deterioration of resistive power. It is generally admitted that a cheerful disposition and good-fellowship do much to ward off maladies in any part of the earth, and especially in the tropics, where home influences and the society of women and of friends are but rarely to be enjoyed.[3]

These are some of the factors that render the German less master of himself in the colonies than he is at home, and predispose him to gusts of passion on slight occasion. They also accentuate the irritable and petty tendencies of a shortsighted bureaucracy, and are, to a great extent, responsible for an ill grace of manner which is sure to awaken resentment in a native population, particularly

[1] Bordier, Col., pp. 55, 91, 155–157, 184–187; Leroy-Beaulieu, I, 383.
[2] Boshart, pp. 225 ff. [3] Bigelow, in *Harper's*, C, 577–590.

if the latter is already restive under a brand-new harness of ill-fitting, cramping, and generally trivial restrictions. The contact of such a bureaucracy with a savage or semi-civilized population can easily be figured in imagination; police regulations calculated for Berlin, bundles of acts whose transgression is a matter of daily occurrence among the unwary sojourners in German towns — all these formed a system whose application to the Sudanese and Bantus was incongruous even to the local official.[1] Reiterated appeals on the part of opponents of this system, so ill-suited to its environment, have not failed entirely of effect.

STRENGE MIT GERECHTIGKEIT

A change which created, as it were, a new ideal of the treatment of the natives came with the downfall of the companies and the consequent presence in the colonies of well-chosen imperial commissioners and commanders. The typical case is that of Wissmann, in East Africa, where the expiring Company had, by its oppression and its indiscreet attitude toward native and Arab prejudices, roused a rebellion with which it was utterly unable to cope. To this scene of disorder and uproar Bismarck sent the scientist and explorer, Dr. von Wissmann, a man chosen rather for his knowledge and personality than for any distinctive military achievements. He quelled the insurrection in a masterly manner, promptly executing the leader. Not only that; he gained the confidence of the natives, together with their wholesome respect, so that his succeeding administration of the colony in peace only added to his reputation as an "*Afrikakenner*." [2] His successes led to imitation of his methods on the part of his subordinates and brother-administrators; there was established a new fashion, as it were, in colonial management. The formula of this system was simplicity itself: "sternness with justice." In dealing with the rebels in East Africa, Wissmann's first object was to teach a "*gründliche Lehre*," to make an imposing display of European superiority and power. The effect upon the native population was instantaneous.[3] This

---

[1] Boshart, pp. 182–183, 186; *Globus*, LXXIX, No. 9, p. 134.

[2] Bismarck referred to Wissmann as "the man who knew how to deal with natives." Poschinger, p. 244.

[3] The natives said of his rule: "Bisher war bei euch Deutschen alles Spielerei, jetzt sieht man doch, dass euer Sultan ernst macht und da wird es euch gelingen, wirklich die Herren des Landes zu werden." Schmidt, I, 64; cf. Geffcken, in *The Forum*.

administrator knew also how to temper severity with mercy and to use his prestige to secure in time of peace what he had gained in war. The " Wissmann system " has been complained of by those whose humanitarian feelings are wounded by violence of any kind in dealings with the noble savage; but it is not without its sound elements of common sense and science. Where practices abhorrent to the civilized world were found to exist, they were resolutely eradicated; Wissmann dealt blows to the slave-trade of East Africa from which it will scarcely recover.[1] In less essential matters, however, a wise moderation was displayed; the bureaucratic system was discouraged and no attempt was made to interfere with cherished institutions and customs of the indigenous tribes. The Arab *wali* and *kadi* were retained; and, while German discipline was enforced, it was rather along general lines than in matters of detail.[2] The system rested upon a correct recognition of conditions, intelligent judgment, and respect for the natives' rights and for their chiefs' authority. The gifts and geniality of Wissmann himself played a great part in his successes; he possessed the qualities both of leader and organizer. He had the reputation of selecting realizable aims, and always realizing them, and his prestige was marred by no fiasco of any moment; his subordinates were held strictly to duty and were at the same time assured of power to fulfill the task assigned. Their loyalty to this leader is something exceptional, taking into account the extreme hardships of the service in the East African country. It speaks well for the Wissmann system that it has made out of this difficult district a relatively peaceful colony; later difficulties in the attempted application of civil rule in East Africa led to the re-adoption and consequent vindication of this system. At the accession of Hohenlohe, Wissmann, who had been recalled by Caprivi, was returned as governor-general of the protectorate.[3]

[1] Giesebrecht, p. 22; Schmidt, I, 188 ff., 224 ff. An interesting passage in F. Fabri (Fünf Jahre, etc., p. 55) shows how a development of methods of transportation in East Africa will necessarily bring about the complete downfall of the slave-trade.

[2] Bitter complaint is made that the German functionaries take no pains to learn the native languages, not even spending the time on shipboard on the long journey to New Guinea in study. The Germans revolt at the "pidgin English" that forms the only universally understood language of New Guinea and environs. They combat it also in Africa. Blum, pp. 165–166; Engler, p. 114; Keane, Africa, II, 19; Pfeil, Studien, etc., pp. 128–130; R. L. Stevenson, In the South Seas, chap. ii.

[3] Schmidt, I, 232 ff., 243–244; Giesebrecht, pp. 19 ff. More tact has been displayed of late by the German officers. Johnston, pp. 257–258. It appears that the climate

A number of writers who have criticised the administration of the German colonies have complained of an insufficient display of military and naval power on the part of the home-government. They have also asserted that the opening up of the *Hinterland* has followed no settled plan and has worked from no stable and selected base of operations.[1] The number of imperial troops has indeed been small; but since the time of Wissmann, and especially in East Africa, it has been the policy of the government to utilize native auxiliaries about a relatively insignificant nucleus of regulars. The warlike tribes who would, in any case, lend themselves unwillingly to the régime of industry, are glad to be mustered in and to fight under European officers. The Sudanese have been particularly useful in this line, completely outclassing the Bantus; and the Solomon Islanders are also regarded as suitable material for the same ends.[2] The idea is that the warlike tribes shall hold the more docile natives to work, thereby effecting a division of labor of which all shall reap the good results.[3]

THE TROPICAL LABOR ISSUE

Here we touch upon the question of labor in tropical colonies; it is rightly recognized as the vital issue, and strenuous, if unsuccessful, efforts have been put forth in attempts at its solution. It is a modern riddle of the Sphinx at which the various nations have guessed, each in its characteristic way. The conclusions of the Germans, as a well-informed people, new to the subject, singularly free from bias and open to new truth, possess an especial and peculiar interest to the student of this vexed problem. It seems, in the

and hardships finally told upon Wissmann so as to impair health and temper, and to a certain extent, former reputation.

[1] See Schmidt, I, 94; Boshart, p. 183; Pfeil, Vorschläge, p. 43; F. Fabri, Fünf Jahre, etc., pp. 71 ff.; Sievers, Afrika, p. 405. Complaint is also made of governmental parsimony, which F. Fabri (p. 89) declares to be false economy; " es geht in solchen Dingen häufig wie beim Ankauf der sibyllinischen Bücher."

[2] Unfortunately the Sudanese insist upon the presence of their families on any extended expeditions. While the women are useful in some ways, they form an undesirable camp-following. It is noted that the negro soldiers, although they were soon able to manipulate the mechanism of the breech-loading rifles, are likely to shoot high and erratically in action. Apparently they have not as yet full confidence in the new weapon. See Schmidt, II, 374, 385; Pfeil, Vorschläge, pp. 66 ff.

[3] Pfeil, Vorschläge, pp. 60, 67; cf. Studien, etc., p. 239. No satisfactory system of taxing the natives has been devised. The Germans have decided, however, in favor of a hut-tax versus a poll-tax; the hut, they say, is something that cannot evade taxes by a timely disappearance. A small portion only of the colonial income is derived from this source.

first place, that the Germans have been regularly unsuccessful in creating a supply of free labor by the stimulation of wants; the ground upon which they work is unpropitious, and no support for their economists' theories, in the shape of actual results, is yet forthcoming. The natives are almost all tropical peoples, whose needs are few and will continue so to be, except in the matter of intoxicants and implements of war which the sentiment of the civilized world refuses to supply.[1] The native, as a factor in economic supply and demand, is, as has been seen, a virtual nonentity. There is need of ages of slow development, or of some effectual forcing process, before the Papuan and his ilk begin to respond to stimuli which are calculated to appeal to anything higher than momentary desire or caprice. But the tropics, *ex hypothesi*, must be developed, and Europeans are, of themselves, unable to effect such development; if this be granted, nothing remains as alternative except the adoption of some form of compulsory labor imposed upon the tropical peoples. Avowed slavery is, of course, inhibited by forces too strong to be opposed. Substitution of more advanced races is costly and has been rendered well-nigh impracticable by the attitude of the governments which sway the fates of the peoples available for coolie service. The system of compulsory labor under contract remains; a system which, like coolie labor, is a partial return, in the form of semi-slavery, to the rough-and-ready methods of the ancient world.

The Germans did not reach this alternative, which seems to so many of their competent writers a last and inevitable resort, without exploring all the *culs-de-sac* along in the way, in the hope of discovering some other solution less repugnant to themselves and others. The attempt to introduce a wage system was early shown to be futile; what little labor was thus secured was both low in efficiency and extremely irregular. Even the Krumen who were available along the Togo and Kamerun seaboard refused to enter upon contracts of over one year's duration; at its expiration they insisted upon returning to their own tribes with what they had earned, and it was only in consequence of the reckless expenditure which ensued that a labor force could again be recruited from this source.[2] The labor supply was similarly intermittent in the rest of the African colonies, while in New Guinea it was

[1] Cf. Finsch, Samoafahrten, pp. 26, 62.

[2] The labor of the Krus was relatively expensive, and its cost was enhanced by the periodic need of double transportation. See Keane, Man, etc., pp. 53–54;

practically impossible to enlist any workers whatsoever under a voluntary system.[1]

After this disillusionment, recourse was had, especially in East Africa and New Guinea, to imported labor of various types. In the latter protectorate the system was really one of slave-transfer, whereby the ruling chief of a limited area, or the old men of a village, sold the vital forces of captives or subjects (debtors, oftentimes) for a consideration; that some form of compulsion on the part of the Melanesian native authorities was usually present, even though it was not actually demonstrable, is commonly conceded by the German writers themselves. This system of slavery for a term, which carried with it the so-called " Labor Trade," had been shamefully abused by the Queenslanders, and was already under universal condemnation; the missionaries in the South Sea were bitterly opposed to it. The Germans honestly attempted, therefore, to carry out regulations which would give the appearance, at least, of fairness and humanity.[2] They intended also to keep clear of the many possible misunderstandings with the native peoples, and thus avoid the inevitable vendetta with its consequent unpopular punitive expeditions, and other evil and dangerous consequences.[3] An attempt was made to give Kaiser Wilhelmsland a better reputation among those islanders whose services could be secured.[4] But results were not commensurate with the effort put forth; the death-rate of the laborers, though lowered, was still believed to be high, and the " trade " in natives still continued to be carried on in unseaworthy ships. Inadequacy of transport facilities often left

Reichenow, p. 44. Hermann (p. 86) says that native labor has been relatively overpaid in Southwest Africa.

[1] The best reports of native labor come from Togo and Kamerun, but even here it is found that the natives regularly choose such minor occupations as demand little physical effort. The Dualla were always energetic traders, and continue to be so, but there is a conspicuous absence of smiths, wheelwrights, etc. See Pfeil, Vorschläge, pp. 54 ff.; Schmidt, II, 89–90, 168 ff.

[2] Pfeil, Studien, etc., pp. 241 ff.; Finsch, Samoafahrten, p. 26; Egerton, p. 396; Blum, pp. 47, 78; Schmidt, II, 410–412. Krieger enters somewhat upon the details of the labor trade (pp. 244 ff.). The native never believed in the Anwerbemodus. Blum, p. 162.

[3] If a native died during his term, the vendetta came at once into play, and the next Europeans to meet the relatives of the deceased were exposed to unexpected attack and murder. Money-commutation for such a death, together with accrued wages, were, as a rule, promptly forwarded to the relatives or village-authorities of the dead man. Krieger, pp. 244–245.

[4] The native laborers said of Kaiser Wilhelmsland: " No kaikai [food], no sunday, plenty fight, plenty die." Blum, p. 135.

the government burdened with an unruly crowd of recruits : those who had arrived previously and whose wages must be paid from the time of arrival, and those whose terms were served out and who were eager to leave the neighborhood of the whites forever. Few cases of renewed contracts are to be found.[1] And when all these difficulties had been somehow met or evaded, the character of the labor supply was, after all, completely inadequate. The natives could be forced to an occasional activity in fetching and carrying, and could be induced to dig the earth in a more or less desultory fashion, but for the finer kinds of labor, in the raising of coffee and cacao, it was necessary from the first to employ the higher-class labor of the Javanese and Chinese.[2]

Moreover, the problem of holding the native to labor, when his presence had been secured, was not yet solved.[3] The Melanesian could not be effectively controlled by a system of fines ; he had no idea of the value of money, and whether he received a little more or a little less was a matter of complete indifference to him. In any case his earnings went to the authorities of his native village. And it was found that penalties in the form of extra hours taxed the European overseer far more than they did the nonchalant native ; the unsophisticated functionaries were likewise astonished to find that the orthodox German system of imprisonment was absolutely ineffective. "To lie eight days long upon his back, to receive his meals regularly, and every other day to take a walk, is, for the Kanaka, a life of good cheer ; and one can easily conceive the wrath of the settlers when protracted and costly legal proceedings found their conclusion in such a

[1] The natives reckoned their terms by "fellow-moons," of which they counted ten to the year ; this difference of standard led to frequent misunderstandings. Blum, p. 135. Too much seems to have been made of a few cases of renewed contracts.

[2] Blum, p. 166. The government was also obliged to furnish a particular kind of food to the Melanesian coolies: yams and taro. Pfeil, Studien, etc., pp. 238, 242. Blum (p. 136) thinks the natives may be educated through the agency of Chinese and Malay overseers and middlemen. Not long ago it was announced (New York Times, March 30, 1902) that the Tuskegee Institute had been called upon by the German Colonial Economic Society to send five graduates to Togo ; these young negroes were to assist three predecessors, sent eighteen months before, in teaching the natives the arts of agriculture.

[3] Some German writers have accused the authorities of spending their time in deciding how to hold the native to labor, when the vital question was how to secure the native at all. The Germans seem to have had a way of settling a problem before they were perfectly sure of the actual terms in which it was to be presented. Pfeil, Vorschläge, p. 60 ; F. Fabri, Fünf Jahre, etc., p. 79.

chastisement." [1] The planters, naturally enough, insisted upon the right of private corporal correction. The courts were distant and uncertain, and the struggle for commercial existence near and sure. Beating exactly met the natives' ideas of punishment, and, as a rule, no grudges were cherished if the causes for such correction had been set forth with requisite clearness and emphasis. But the grant of such privilege would amount to the legalization of one of the most characteristic and most odious marks of slavery. Humanitarian sentiment would be wounded in distant Europe; and thus what the actors on the spot, with few exceptions, regarded as necessary, could not but be permanently disallowed. Infringements of this prohibition have doubtless occurred, but they have been relatively few; the missionaries are alert to denounce any possible faults of the system. It is no wonder that the situation has remained unaltered for some years back.[2] In this embarrassing and hopeless situation, the government turned to the time-honored coolie system. Javanese and Chinese were enlisted in Batavia and Singapore; and, though the costs, including, of course, double transportation, were excessive, the new arrivals seemed to promise much for the future of the colony. Political complications and national jealousies, however, have closed the several sources of supply. In the early nineties, alleging the unhealthfulness of the New Guinea settlements, both Holland and England forbade the further export of coolies from their colonies, after having rendered that export as costly and as inconvenient as possible.[3] The Germans later cherished some hopes of deriving a supply of labor directly from China; but the well-known hostility of the Chinese authorities to the coolie system soon put an end to this expectation.[4]

[1] Pfeil, Studien, etc., p. 254; for the other aspects of the question of punishment, see pp. 252–256, *passim*.

[2] According to Pfeil, an officer of long experience (see Giesebrecht, p. 130), in view of the failure of coolie importation, the defective system just described must be maintained, with all its difficulties, for some time to come. Studien, etc., p. 244.

[3] The resentment of the Germans attaches with especial bitterness to the British; tales are not lacking which, if true, establish serious charges of the breaking of neutrality, of the stirring up of native passions, etc. British missionaries come in for a good share of this accusation. As for the coolie question, it is asserted that the British were especially proficient in the selection of crippled and diseased natives, whose subsequent deaths or ailments were then charged to the deadly climate of New Guinea. Blum, pp. 118, 168; Schmidt, II, 66 ff.; Pfeil, Studien, etc., p. 240; Egerton, pp. 400–402; Krieger, p. 250.

[4] Blum, p. 166. Krieger (pp. 236 ff.) gives facts concerning the enlistment of Javanese and Chinese coolies and their life in the colonies.

Compulsory Labor

Nothing remained, then, if the colonies were to be developed — and Germany would scarcely renounce this object so close to her heart without a struggle — but to organize some system of forced labor, and render it as palatable as possible to European tastes.[1] Many of the best administrators and writers on colonial questions openly support this system and justify their views by fairly consistent lines of argument. The orthodox position, viz., to renounce all force, is represented chiefly in the writings and utterances of the older scientists and missionaries,[2] though several of the latter have come out strongly for the enforcement of regular labor as, in any case, indispensable for the natives' advancement in civilization.[3] The model before the eyes of the advocates of forced labor was the overrated culture system of the Dutch, as developed chiefly on the island of Java.[4] They wish, in effect, to enforce native labor through the agency of already constituted native authorities, whether those authorities are chiefs or village elders.[5] But

[1] A brief account of attempts to do away with the virtual slavery existing in East Africa, by allowing the purchase of "*Freibriefe*," is given in *Annals Amer. Acad. of Pol. and Soc. Science*, XIX, No. 2, p. 164.

[2] A collection of opinions on the native question has been made by Giesebrecht; this work has been done very completely, and appended biographical sketches of the various contributors enable the reader to make correction for the personal factor with some ease. Expressions were elicited from prominent scientists, colonial officials, and missionaries; the whole collection is extremely valuable and readable. According to the author, the question is still *sub judice*; he believes that the more favorable views of the older scientists are due to the fact of their having met the native before he had been irritated and rendered hostile by contact with Europeans. The more modern officers, administrators, and travelers are unanimous in advocating strictness and sternness, though they all insist upon pairing these with justice; *Strenge mit Gerechtigkeit* is the typical formula. It is curious how the opinions differ according as the writer is a military man, a missionary, or a planter. Some of the judgments rendered are exceedingly strong pieces of work, notably those of Pfeil, Denhardt, Holub, Peters, and Hübbeschleiden. Though the author professes to have reached no definite conclusions, it seems to the present writer that the impressions left by the work, though perhaps a little indistinct because of minor differences and contradictions, are of undeniable value to the colonial administrator and the student. Cf. Müller, p. 32. Finsch (Samoafahrten, pp. 64 ff.) says he had little difficulty with the New Guinea natives, for he followed in the steps of the "moon-man," the Russian scientist, Miklukho-Maclay, who always got along well with native peoples.

[3] Besides the opinions in Giesebrecht's collection, see especially Pfeil, Vorschläge, p. 64.

[4] Cf. pp. 473 ff., above. Pfeil (Studien, etc., pp. 248 ff.) is an advocate of this system.

[5] The idea of holding the more tractable tribes to work under compulsion exercised by more warlike natives, officered by Germans, is likewise a part of the

conditions in the German protectorates differ so widely from those in Java that the outcome of such a system must remain an enigma until it is tried ; the Bantus and Papuans have, as a rule, no chiefs of an extended and despotic power,[1] and it is extremely doubtful if any of the native peoples subject to Germany could be managed under the Dutch system. The islander of the Dutch possessions is a great advance in character and civilization over anything the German colonies can produce. The blacks of the latter districts do not understand what is demanded of them ; they are incorrigibly improvident. The prevailing conviction among the natives of New Guinea was that the foreigners would soon depart, — indeed, a preliminary division had already been made of the habitations and the personal effects likely to be left behind. The negro believes that the white man will soon grow weary of all this useless activity and let things return to their former and natural course.[2]

No system of forced labor has yet been organized ; such a move would undoubtedly encounter bitter opposition among philanthropists at home and abroad. But the reasons for their faith have been set forth so clearly and convincingly by some of the most capable administrators, that they cannot fail to find converts to their views as time goes on and conditions grow more intolerable. Given the need, real or imaginary, of developing tropical colonies under German rule, and, in consequence of considerations already stated, the inevitable outcome is compulsory labor. A compulsory labor system, though abhorred as an infringement of the " rights of man," is, it is claimed, from the standpoint of society's life and weal, perfectly justifiable. No more is required of the savage than

proposed system. Pfeil is a special advocate of a rotating labor supply, whereby certain sections of a village population are drawn upon in successive periods. Much difficulty has been experienced in " localizing" the labor supply, and this had led to a curious proposition involving the resurrection, in certain respects, of the characteristic provisions of the Spanish encomienda system, as developed in America. The experience of the Germans goes to show that colonizing powers are rarely able to invent anything new and revolutionary in the treatment of century-old problems, even when the sum of modern science and historical research can be drawn upon. Pfeil, Vorschläge, pp. 57, 69 ff. ; Hermann, p. 88.

[1] If there is no chief to exercise compulsion, force of some other nature must be called into requisition. Pfeil, Vorschläge, p. 72. It is occasionally stated that this or that people possesses a tribal organization which is comparable to that of the Javanese, but, inasmuch as nothing has been made out of these tribes, it is probable that the eagerness of hope has led to exaggeration. See Blum, p. 21 ; Pfeil, Vorschläge, p. 60 ; Globus, LXXIX, No. 9, p. 134 ; Schmidt, I, 160 ff. ; Sievers, p. 409.

[2] Pfeil, Studien, etc., pp. 238 ff. ; Blum (p. 102) says that the labor force of New Guinea must come from elsewhere.

has been and is demanded of his civilized superior; there is no more reason why black drones should be tolerated in the hive than white drones; vagabondage is, in any case, a disease in the body of society. European philanthropists have no compunctions about enforcing industry at home and coercing each member of society to render his share of service to the public; but as soon as a hand is outstretched to impel the distant, and therefore somewhat idealized, savage to vary his life of tranquillity, the cry of "Taboo!" is heard at once. But labor, say these writers, is the basis of all advance in civilization; the experience of years has persuaded all rational missionaries of this.[1] Only by *forcing* in the thin edge of the wedge can you open up the possibilities of a higher civilization. Moreover, along with this alternative of advance, the native stands unwittingly before another and more serious one, not less to be dreaded by his friends : that of more or less speedy degradation and retrogression, if not extinction. It is useless to rail at the presence of a new human environment which means for the native the necessity of unwonted activity and the pain of change; it is present in response to the action of nature-forces, and the consequences are inevitable. The most valuable service is rendered to the native by him who will force him, as a child is forced, to live up to the requirements of the next stage of growth. This is the gist of the arguments of the advocates of forced labor;[2] in theory, at least, they do not lack a certain convincing force, and

[1] Especial attention has been directed to the activity of the veteran Hahn in Southwest Africa. After some years of disappointing experience, he frankly gave up the attempt to influence the natives through purely religious means. He felt and acknowledged that an impulse must first be given to the economic life of the native people, and so devoted his efforts almost exclusively to the teaching of trades and the improvement of material conditions. Schmidt, II, 280 ff.; Büttner, pp. 51 ff.

[2] The arguments of Pfeil carry the most weight, not only because of his high reputation as an administrator, but because of the clarity and vigor of his statement and the exceptionally pleasing quality of his style. He was one of Peters's coadjutors in the seizure of East Africa, and has been active in the colonial service ever since. His arguments are to be found in Vorschläge, pp. 60 ff.; Studien, etc., pp. 238 ff.; and in his letter in Giesebrecht's collection (p. 130). Cf. Dove, pp. 239 ff. Pfeil says of his own successes: " Dies erkläre ich mir nur daraus, weil ich im Principe streng, im Einzelnen stets mild war und allezeit mich bemüht habe, gerecht zu sein. . . . Aber ich habe den Muth als Princip Ernst und Strenge aufzustellen : ὁ μὴ δαρεὶς ἄνθρωπος οὐ παιδεύεται." Vorschläge, p. 74. This view is expressed more sternly elsewhere : " Wir verlangen eine Gegengabe (i.e. service) für unseren Verzicht auf das Recht des Stärkeren im Kampfe ums Dasein." Studien, etc., p. 246. Boshart is, as usual, radical to the extreme, and sees nothing before the native population except annihilation, which he is not adverse to furthering (pp. 181 ff.). See also Geffcken, in *The Forum* ; Finsch, Samoafahrten, pp. 170-172; Dove, pp. 44-45.

in practice, as far as the German has exercised a master's power, he seems, with comparatively few exceptions, to have wielded it well. The present labor conditions are thoroughly unsatisfactory; whether a better system can be devised and carried out, is for the future to show. The Germans are well fitted in many ways to deal with this most difficult and probably insoluble question.

MISSIONS AND EDUCATION

It must not be thought that the natives have met only officers and soldiers in the colonies; they have been longer acquainted with the bearers of the staff and scrip than with the wearers of the sword. German missionaries early extended their activity to those parts of Africa which later became German colonies. Their "converts" have been few,[1] but their efforts looking to the advance of material civilization have been far from fruitless. With the exception of certain visionaries, whose folly and ridiculous results are recorded,[2] they have taken an exceptionally sensible view of their own activity and its prospects, and are almost universally commended by the colonial administrators.[3] They have also, though in far less degree than the British missionaries, labored for the political predominance of the fatherland. Some friction with the government has been caused by their sectarian squabbles in the South Sea possessions, and also by their abuse of privileges, and exemption from customs dues, a grant which they utilized in a way calculated to retard the advance of trade.[4] On the whole, however, they seem to share in a remarkable degree the freedom from ultra-conservatism and dogma which characterizes the general attitude of the Germans toward the native tribes.

[1] Finsch (Samoafahrten, p. 171) says that in seven years 215 natives of Kaiser Wilhelmsland had been "converted," at an expenditure of 350,000 marks. From 1842 to 1861 not one Herero, in Southwest Africa, was baptized, for here ability to read and write formed a condition of baptism. This wise and exceptional condition seems characteristic of German missionaries; in their freedom from the worship of *numbers* of baptisms, confirmations, etc., they form an edifying contrast to their Anglo-Saxon brethren. See Meinecke, p. 37; Boshart, p. 173; Krieger, p. 248; Schmidt, II, 289; Blum, pp. 63 ff.   [2] Pfeil, Studien, etc., pp. 247, 262 ff.

[3] Pfeil, Studien, etc., pp. 246 ff.; Finsch, Samoafahrten, p. 170; Krieger, pp. 247 ff.; F. Fabri, Fünf Jahre, etc., p. 82; Schmidt, I, 237-241; II, 288-289, cf. Büttner, p. 120. They enjoy an especially high reputation with both Germans and natives in Southwest Africa; they can carry on a peaceful commerce with both sides, at all times. Büttner, p. 118.

[4] Schmidt, II, 403; Müller, pp. 33-35; Pfeil, Studien, etc., pp. 11-12; Blum, pp. 63 ff., 76-83; Dove, p. 26.

The education of the native has not proceeded apace. Schools in the colonies are of two types, governmental and missionary. The latter were, of course, of earlier establishment. In the governmental schools in East Africa attendance has been made compulsory between the ages of six and fifteen; two hours per day for about ten months in the year. The Mohammedans of East Africa at first opposed the requirements of school-attendance, fearing that their children would be instructed in Christian doctrines; the governmental schools are, however, non-sectarian, and of late attendance has increased. The "curricula" are generally rational ones; the rudiments — reading, writing,[1] etc. — are taught, and supplementary education is generally along the line of trades. Negroes who can play the piano and converse on such esoteric subjects as the Shakespeare-Bacon controversy are at a discount with the Germans; they think they are considerably ahead of the British here, and boast that in teaching they do not insist upon German political history, the dates of the Crusades, and the like. Their experience is that a highly educated negro is a rascal and absolutely useless for all practical purposes, and they do not mean to turn out such products.[2] The Germans, in their first contact with African peoples, made some embarrassing and regretted errors in their fulsome treatment of native " kings' " sons,[3] but these mistakes have been speedily recognized, and they seem to be settling down into an earnest and intelligent attitude toward the grave complexity of difficulties inherent in the contact of widely separated stages of culture.[4]

[1] German is the language of instruction in one school only (Victoria, Kamerun); elsewhere it is merely a branch of instruction. *Globus*, LXXIX, No. 9, pp. 140–141; Engler, p. 114.

[2] The other colonizing nations accuse the Germans of insincerity in the alcohol-prohibitions; they say that the colonies are inundated with *Schnaps*. This view is resented by the Germans, who assert that the increasing import of alcoholic drinks is for German consumption, however much they deprecate that; they say that, at any rate, conditions are no worse than in the colonies of other nations. Der Deutsche Export, pp. 67 ff.; Schmidt, II, 291–292. In the German colonies it is often hard to refuse the natives whisky and tobacco when these are the only rewards for which they will put forth real effort in labor. Schmidt, II, 228.

[3] Schmidt, II, 90–92; Meinecke, p. 25.

[4] For these questions of native education and kindred topics, see Meinecke, p. 37; Schmidt, II, 91–92. The government schools are designed in part to fit natives for the discharge of minor duties in the colonial service. *Globus*, LXXIX, No. 9, pp. 140–141.

THE COLONIAL SERVICE

The general character of the colonial service has already been indicated; it was found to possess both the virtues and the defects of a rigid disciplinary system. Relatively little favoritism appears in the selection of either the superior or the subordinate imperial officials. At first there were, of course, no facilities for securing a special education for the prospective colonial servant; the earlier officials of the government had been, as a rule, subjected to a rather strict and technical military training, but it is hard to say whether this was an advantage or a disadvantage in the colonies. If the service was performed in a spirit more cosmopolitan and enlightened than such training would lead one to expect, it was doubtless due to the incidental and unprofessional education which all Germans received. As time went on, the universities attempted to meet a newly felt need by improvising courses of instruction bearing on the colonial career. The Oriental Seminar in Berlin undertook training in languages; scientific investigation was directed and regulated, and lectures were arranged on tropical hygiene and kindred subjects. This training was likely to be over-academic in character; practical ends were subordinated to the establishment of "principles," and to elaborate schematization. In the formation of the colonial personnel too much importance was at first attached to superficial "experts"; too little weight was given to personal qualities indispensable in administrators. The essential qualifications of youth and health were too often overlooked. In the course of time, however, these errors were detected and rectified; they were the results, for the most part, of misconceptions inseparable from incipient activity in an entirely new and strange field.[1]

It was not until the year 1899 that a special colonial school was called into existence. It was founded at Witzenhausen, near Göttingen, by a corporation with limited liability, under the protection of the Prince zu Wied. The semi-private nature of the enterprise, it was hoped, would make for such unrestricted opportunity and unhampered development as would be impossible under a rigorous

[1] Schmidt, I, 278 ff.; II, 74 ff.; Andler, pp. 281–282; Pfeil, Vorschläge, pp. 32 ff.; *The Nation*, LXXII, No. 1860, p. 158; *U. S. Con. Reports*, No. 1285 (March 10, 1902), p. 2. F. Fabri (Fünf Jahre, etc.), writing in 1889, says that up to that time officers had been selected at random; there was no thought of special training. Dove (p. 174) says conditions of rank and title have too often outweighed those of personal qualification.

governmental direction. This hope has been, at least partially, realized in the brief period of the institution's existence. The school was modeled after what was considered the best and wisest in the English, Dutch, and French types; and its avowed object is to train up experts in plantation-agriculture, commerce, mining, etc. The institution is open, however, to evangelical missionaries and to government officials who wish to qualify in a more special manner for the colonial service. It has been found that the demand for experts, such as the school proposes to turn out in years to come, has been far in excess of the supply. Requests for trained overseers and managers have poured in, not alone from the German protectorates but from Brazil and Central America, where, as is well known, considerable settlements of Germans are to be found. Up to October, 1900, a year and a half after the founding of the school, of sixty-four young men who had matriculated, sixteen were already active in foreign parts. The greatest importance is attached to the *character* of the finished product, and several dismissals of unsatisfactory novices are already recorded, for the institution, to judge by its motto, professes to work

> Mit Gott für Deutschlands Ehr'
> Daheim und überm Meer!

It forms, therefore, one more of those expedients which are calculated to keep alive a sense of German nationality and love of the fatherland, among emigrants in foreign parts.[1]

Other Colonial Possessions

To complete the picture of German colonization, it remains to speak of the smaller possessions of the East. Among these, Samoa alone approaches the type of settlement-colony; Germans have long had substantial interests in these islands and have contributed largely to their European population. Great complaint has been made in Germany because the archipelago was not annexed in 1877; instead of that, a tripartite agreement, insuring neutrality of the islands, was concluded with Great Britain and the United States (1889), succeeding the several treaties of friendship and trade of the late seventies. It is well known how the strifes of rival kings all but drew these interested parties into hostilities,

---

[1] For a somewhat detailed description of the school, see *Globus*, LXXIX, No. 9, pp. 144–146.

and how the archipelago was finally peaceably divided.[1] The possessions of Germany in the South Sea were augmented in 1899 by the purchase from Spain of the Caroline, Palao (Pelew), and Ladrone (Marianne) islands, for which 16,750,000 marks were paid.[2] None of these islands promise much for the future as colonies or markets; their value lies in their position.[3] They are coral formations with a small population and few valuable products. Their lot and purpose fall in with those of Kiautschou. This port, "leased" in 1898 for ninety-nine years, was seized (1897) to meet the need of a foothold in China after the Chinese-Japanese war; the murder of two German missionaries formed the pretext for seizure.[4] Here, again, we have a possession which can scarcely become a colony in the strict sense of the word. The district of Shantung is one of the most populous of the Chinese provinces, but no success in the settlement, even of merchants, has been attained. For very slight material prospects an enormous price has been paid.[5]

These late acquisitions have been held for too short a period for any sweeping approval or condemnation to be passed. In the islands conditions are not materially altered since the German occupation; in Kiautschou, however, considerable activity has been displayed. The testimony as to results is conflicting; it seems, however, that the military system has been introduced in all its strictness, and that the "red devils" are already cordially hated by the natives. Among the Germans themselves there is considerable diversity of opinion about Kiautschou; this disagreement is due, it appears, to the different points of view, economic and political, occupied by those passing judgment. As sources of direct commercial gain, and as localities for settlement, it is evident that the late acquisitions are a failure. There may be some development of the coalfields back of Kiautschou, which may thus form an admirable naval

[1] F. Fabri, Fünf Jahre, etc., pp. 146 ff.; Schmidt, II, 413 ff.; *Illustrierte Zeitfragen: Samoa*, Leipzig, 1900; Statesman's Year-Book, 1901; Hauser, pp. 87 ff.; Philippson, pp. 61 ff.

[2] Germany and Spain disputed the possession of the Carolines in 1885, but the Pope, selected as arbiter, decided for Spain. Blum, p. 88.   [3] Engler, p. 163.

[4] "The event gives rise to the soliloquy attributed by a comic paper to the German Emperor, 'If my missionaries only hold out, I shall soon own the earth.'" Bigelow, *Harper's*, C, 577–590.

[5] The subventions have been regularly very large. Trade is mostly in cheap Japanese wares, imported by Chinese middlemen. Local companies are always in need of government aid; to a bankrupt electric company, for example, there was recently proposed a government credit of 350,000 marks. New York *Times*, January 10 and 29, 1902; Hauser, pp. 102 ff.

station; and it is possible that some minor outlet may be formed for Chinese foreign trade. But Hong-Kong and Shanghai will continue, for very conclusive reasons of all-around superiority, to provide the main channels for the movement of products.[1] There is another, however, and more grandiose way of looking at these matters, and for those who possess this second-sight, the outlook is nothing if not brilliant and promising. For the fatherland now possesses a "naturally rounded-out area in the Pacific" — a series of bases of operations on the long sea-way. Having the way-stations, it will be less difficult, it is thought, to secure the terminals.[2] Such political advantages, together with the opportunity of infusing the genuine *"deutsche Sitte"* into uncontaminated aboriginal minds,[3] far outweigh the unproductiveness and costliness of the new possessions, as of the old.

COLONIAL PROSPECTS

But what are to be the termini, the *ultima ratio* of all this sacrifice and endeavor? The occupation of Kiautschou is significant of German ideas in this direction. Germans have seen clearly enough how national juvenility deprived them of a full share in the earth-division of the eighties; they are tired of tropical "leavings" and desire to feed upon the real loaf. They have realized that no further division of unoccupied land is possible; but they have seen the probability of a new kind of division in the Far East. China is a country of endurable climate and might afford opportunity for

[1] Native proprietors were displaced under the payment of valuations fixed by the German authorities (Bigelow). Kiautschou is a "free port" and is governed under the Department of the Marine. Meinecke, pp. 96 ff.; *Globus*, LXXIX, No. 9, pp. 141–143. Richthofen (Shantung, etc.) gives much detail concerning the province; his view seems to be more sanguine than that of Hesse-Wartegg (Shantung, etc.). The latter (p. 29) says, "Ich habe nunmehr Deutsch-China in fast allen seinen Teilen durchzogen und weiss aus eigener Anschauung, dass dort nichts für Europa zu holen ist." Richthofen (id., p. 242) regards Kiautschou as a valuable port of entrance into northern China.

[2] Blum (p. 62) congratulates his countrymen that New Guinea is on the road from Australia through the Pacific to Asia, and adds, "möchte die Zukunft diese neue Strasse des Weltverkehrs weiter ausbauen, und über die nunmehr deutschen Karolinen gen Japan, über Samoa nach dem deutschen Südamerika führen — aber unter deutscher Flagge!" Hesse-Wartegg (Samoa, etc.) makes a great effort to arouse enthusiasm over the Pacific colonies. His position is bitterly hostile to Great Britain. Cf. Hauser, pp. 69 ff.

[3] The "culture mission" of the Germans is, of course, one of the most portentous watchwords of the colonial party; the floutings and the damaging facts of the opposition diminish its effectiveness but slightly. Cf. T. Fabri, p. 12.

trade, if not for settlement.   The bitterness of national loss by emigration to the Americas is in nowise ameliorated of late, and, in view of a possible share in land where Germans *could* go and settle, it has seemed best to secure a "front seat" in Kiautschou. It is hoped that future gains will compensate for the costly holding of this point of vantage.[1] Germany is weary of the tropical colony ; golden dreams of new spice monopolies and metal treasures have been rudely broken. The signs of the times are anxiously scanned for indications of weakness in the tenure of present holders of temperate lands : if the bonds of the British Empire should loosen, Germany would expect to emerge from the ensuing scramble far from portionless ; the status of Brazil and other South American countries, with a large and unassimilated German population,[2] are narrowly watched ; the Monroe Doctrine is only as strong as the power that stands its sponsor. A peculiar interest attaches to German undertakings and hopes in the old culture-land of Mesopotamia ; there may be undefined designs on Transylvania and Turkey, but something has already been done in the Euphrates valley. Certain railroad concessions are in German hands and trade-interests are carefully fostered ; there are not lacking those who insinuate that the Kaiser's pilgrimage to Palestine several years ago had other than religious and artistic motives. Here, certainly, is a wholesome climate, and a soil which should respond to modern methods, taking into account its former exceeding fertility under crude and shortsighted management.[3]

The time is full of possibilities, and the German people are endowed with steadfastness and tireless energy. Who can say what the future will bring forth ? The Germans have a high reputation as settlers, and, in the opinion of most rivals, need only the chance, to become great colonizers. To the weaker nations they stand as a sort of international safeguard against the predominance of Great

---

[1] *The Nation*, LXXI, 46; New York *Times*, March 16, 1902.

[2] It is observed, however, that the German population of Brazil looks with little favor on these projects; they do not wish to "replace themselves under the sway of the police and drillmasters of Prussia." *Spectator*, LXXXI, 481, October 8, 1898.

[3] *Spectator*, LXXXI, 481, October 8, 1898; Geffcken, *The Forum*, XIII, 200; F. Fabri, Fünf Jahre, etc., pp. 135–139; *Advanced Sheets, U. S. Con. Reports*, Nos. 1273 and 1315 (1902); New York *Times*, March 16, 1902; Hauser, pp. 115 ff., 127 ff.; Leroy-Beaulieu, I, 332. Engler (p. 164) exhorts his fellow-countrymen (in 1889) : ". . . schauen wir uns jetzt schon recht sorgsam nach den Kolonien allen um und widmen wir ihnen ein besonderes Studium, damit wir bei Gelegenheit auch wissen, wo zuzugreifen ist und wir nicht vorher noch lange tasten und sondiren müssen."

Britain. The Dutch desire their presence in the East, the Italians cling to alliance with them and believe in their future, and even the French view their activity with complacency and a certain scientific approval.[1] Russia must perforce bear witness to the effectiveness of their presence as settlers;[2] a high respect for the German components of their population is freely acknowledged by the several important states of the New World. Even the British, forgetting the grievances of the eighties, say flattering things of them.[3] Whatever may be the fate of their colonies,[4] the Germans are destined to accomplish their full share in the settlement of new countries and in the formation of the effective races of the future.

[1] "Duitschland als Kolonisierende en Koloniale Mogendheid," in *Tijdschrift voor Nederlandsch-Indië*, No. 13, 2, pp. 218–220; Brunialti, p. 168 ff.; Leroy-Beaulieu, I, 333. Some French writers congratulate themselves on the increasing attention given by the Germans to a study of French colonial methods and policy. Hauser, p. viii. It is a striking commentary on this view when a prominent and popular German writer on colonies is found urging his fellow-countrymen to renounce the British model and imitate the French. He says that neither the French nor the Germans have succeeded in their efforts to adapt British methods. " Die britischen Einrichtungen haben bei der Verpflanzung stets eine vollständige, oft ihr innerstes Wesen zerstörende Umwandlung erfahren." This is the case above all with the British system of self-government in the colonies. Zimmermann, IV, Vorwort.

[2] See the novels of Russian writers, especially of Tolstoi and Turgenev; Tikhomirov, I, 85 ff.

[3] Keltie (p. 333) says that Germany has scarcely gotten beyond her *Sturm und Drang* period in colonization; that there is no reason for discouragement. Johnston (p. 258) looks upon the unmixed Teutons as good colonizers; the German in particular " is on first contact with subject races apt to be harsh and even brutal, but . . . he is no fool and wins the respect of the negro or Asiatic, who admire brute force, while his own good nature in time induces a softening of manners when the native has ceased to rebel and begun to cringe. There is this that is hopeful and wholesome about the Germans. They are quick to realize their own defects and equally quick to amend them. As in commerce, so in government, they observe, learn, and master the best principles. The politician would be very shortsighted who underrated the greatness of the German character, or reckoned on the evanescence of German dominion in strange lands." It is a little hard to subscribe to all of this. A curious mood of self-depreciation in comparison with other nations seems of late to have taken possession of many British writers and travelers. But it is undeniable that, with all their faults and lack of experience, the Germans can well stand comparison with all colonizing peoples except the very most successful.

[4] A strong and bitter opposition to colonial expansion has regularly been encountered in the Reichstag, — especially from the Socialists. Bebel and Richter have said many damaging things about the colonies, and the recent disclosure of corruption in the Colonial Office, taken together with the disasters in Southwest Africa, has added strength to the opposition. This does not, however, seem to prevent the realization of the imperial programme in most of its details. The Kaiser is determined and resourceful, qualities never more clearly shown than by his recent elevation of a business man, reputed to be a Hebrew, Director of the Colonial office, and later Secretary of State for the Colonies.

APPENDIX

MONEY–EQUIVALENTS

The difficulty of fixing upon coin- and price-equivalents is alluded to in note 1, p. 94. The following valuations are taken mainly from Dye's Coin Encyclopædia,[1] and agree fairly well with the isolated equivalents given here and there by the regular authorities quoted. No attempt has been made to attain corrections for contemporary purchasing-power or the like, as most of the sums quoted are estimates in modern money. Cf. Note at end of Chapter IV. Where dollars are quoted in the text, the estimate is generally that of the authority used. The more unusual valuations have been noticed in the footnotes. Figures are, of course, only roughly approximate.

Conto (of reis)	= $1000.00	Lira	= $0.20
Cruzado	= 0.40	Maravedí	= 0.0025
Ducat	= 2.25	Mark (M.)	= 0.25
Duit	= 0.0025	Milreis	= 1.00
Duro (see Peso)		Peseta	= 0.20
Florin (see Guilder)		Peso	= 1.00
Guilder	= 0.40	Piaster (see Peso)	
Gulden (see Guilder)		Real	= 0.05
Krone	= 0.27	Stiver	= 0.02

[1] Dye, J. S., Coin Encyclopædia, Philadelphia, 1883; Cf. F. W. Clarke, Weights, Measures, and Money of All Nations, New York, 1875. Lea (Inquis., I, 560–566) gives a detailed account of Spanish coinage.

BIBLIOGRAPHY

NOTE. In this book, based upon such lines [1] and covering a field so wide, it has not been thought necessary in general, nor indeed has it been possible, to go behind a fairly limited number of secondary authorities, when these had once been selected with an eye to their essential correctness; in fact, the book is based almost entirely upon treatises rather than sources. The aspects of colonial history essential for the present purpose have been developed satisfactorily by writers (Colmeiro, for example) whose lesser statements may have been shown to be inaccurate by later and technically better equipped scholars. There has been, then, no attempt made to cover a comprehensive bibliography; the great aim was to get at what was wanted as speedily and economically as possible. Hence the number of titles of works consulted bears in general an inverse relation to the accessibility of information; and so the bibliography of the several sections will be seen to be uneven as respects quantity. For example, it was found necessary to read almost everything that one could lay hand to in writing of the Portuguese and Danish colonies; while, on the other hand, although the Hooykaas-Hartmann *Repertorium* was at hand, and although the Dutch publishing houses put forth thick volumes merely of titles of works on the Dutch colonies, it was thought sufficient to rely upon Blok, De Reus, Van Rees, Day, Pierson, and a few others for the essentials of the subject.

Certain books are referred to over several sections of the text, but these have been set down under that section of the bibliography to which they seem chiefly to belong. The titles of the authorities most frequently used by the present writer are preceded by an asterisk. Abbreviations of titles used in the text are self-explanatory, except in a few cases to be indicated in the following bibliography.

GENERAL WORKS

American Economic Association. Essays in Colonial Finance. Third Series, I, 3. August, 1900.

D'Avenel, G. Histoire économique de la Propriété, des Salaires, des Denrées et de tous les Prix en général depuis l'an 1200 jusqu'en l'an 1800. 4 vols. Paris, 1894, 1894, 1898, 1898.

Bordier, A. Géographie Médicale. Paris, 1884.

—— La Colonisation Scientifique et les Colonies Françaises. Paris, 1884.

Bourne, E. G. A Trained Colonial Civil Service. *North American Review* (1899), CLXIX, 528.

Cheyney, E. P. European Background of American History, 1300–1600. New York, 1904.

Clarke, F. W. Weights, Measures, and Money of All Nations. New York, 1875.

[1] See the Introduction.

Darwin, C. The Descent of Man and Selection in Relation to Sex. 2d edition. New York, 1898.

—— The Origin of Species by Means of Natural Selection or the Preservation of Favored Races in the Struggle for Life. From sixth and last English edition. 2 vols. New York, 1898.

—— The Variation of Animals and Plants under Domestication. 2 vols. New York, 1899.

Day, C. A History of Commerce. New York and London, 1907.

Dye, J. S. Coin Encyclopædia. Philadelphia, 1883.

Egerton, H. E. A Short History of British Colonial Policy. London, 1897.

Essays in Colonial Finance. By Members of the American Economic Association. New York, August, 1900.

Galton, F. Hereditary Genius: An Inquiry into its Laws and Consequences. New York, 1870.

Griffin, A. P. C. List of Books (with references to periodicals) relating to the Theory of Colonization, etc. 2d edition. Washington (Library of Congress), 1900.

Gumplowicz, L. Der Rassenkampf. Innsbruck, 1883.

Ireland, A. Tropical Colonization. New York and London, 1899.

Johnston, H. H. A History of the Colonization of Africa by Alien Races. Cambridge, 1899.

Keane, A. H. Africa. In Stanford's Compendium of Geography and Travel. 2 vols. London, 1895.

—— Man Past and Present. Cambridge, 1900.

Keller, A. G. A Sociological View of the " Native Question." *Yale Review* (November, 1903), XII, 3.

Keltie, J. S. Africa. The History of Nations, Vol. XIX. Edited by A. G. Keller. Philadelphia, 1907.

—— The Partition of Africa. 2d edition. London, 1895.

(References to Keltie are to the second of the above, excepting when the present author refers to his supplementary chapter in the first.)

Lanessan, J. M. A. de. Principes de Colonisation. Paris, 1897.

Lavisse et Rambaud. Histoire Générale du Quatrième Siècle à Nos Jours. 12 vols. Paris, 1893–1900.

Le Bon, G. Lois Psychologiques de l'Évolution des Peuples. Paris, 1894.

*Leroy-Beaulieu, P. De la Colonisation chez les Peuples Modernes. 5th edition. 2 vols. Paris, 1902.

Letourneau, Ch. L'Évolution du Commerce dans les diverses Races Humaines. Paris, 1897.

Lewis, G. C. An Essay on the Government of Dependencies. London, 1891.

Lindsay, W. S. History of Merchant Shipping and Ancient Commerce. 4 vols. London, 1874–1876.

Lippert, J. Kulturgeschichte. 2 vols. Stuttgart, 1886.

Lowell, A. L. Colonial Civil Service. The Selection and Training of Colonial Officials in England, Holland, and France. New York and London, 1900.

Payne, E. J. Age of Discovery. In Cambridge Modern History, I, Chap. I. Cambridge, 1902.

Peschel, O. The Races of Man and their Geographical Distribution. New York, 1896.

Ratzel, F. History of Mankind. 3 vols. New York, 1896–1898.

—— Politische Geographie. München und Leipzig, 1897.

Reinsch, P. S. Colonial Government. An Introduction to the Study of Colonial Institutions. New York and London, 1902.

*Roscher, W., und Jannasch, R. Kolonien, Kolonialpolitik und Auswanderung. 3d edition. (Third part by Jannasch.) Leipzig, 1885.

*Ruge, S. Geschichte des Zeitalters der Entdeckungen. Berlin, 1881.

Saco, J. A. de. Historia de la Esclavitud de la Raza Africana en el Nuevo Mundo, etc. Barcelona, 1879.

Schäffle, A. Deutsche Kern- und Zeitfragen (pp. 168 ff.). Berlin, 1894. (Reference and summary of his classification of colonies in Reinsch, pp. 19–20.)

Schallmayer, W. Vererbung und Auslese im Lebenslauf der Völker. Jena, 1903.

Smith, A. An Inquiry into the Nature and Causes of the Wealth of Nations. Cannan's edition. 2 vols. London, 1904.

Statesman's Year-Book.

Sumner, W. G. Folkways. A Study of the Sociological Importance of Usages, Manners, Customs, Mores, and Morals. Boston, 1907.

—— Unpublished Lectures on the Industrial Revolution of the Renaissance Period.

Tylor, E. B. Anthropology: an Introduction to the Study of Man and Civilization. New York, 1903.

United States Daily Consular Reports.

THE ORIENTALS, ANCIENTS, AND MEDIÆVAL ITALIANS

Arnold, W. T. The Roman System of Provincial Administration to the Accession of Constantine the Great. London, 1879.

*Beloch, J. Griechische Geschichte. 3 vols. Strassburg, 1893–1904.

Boulger, D. C. History of China. 3 vols. London, 1881–1884.

Brandt, M. von. China. Vol. II of Helmolt's History of the World. 8 vols. New York, 1902–1904.

Brodrick, G. C. Political Studies (Roman colonies). London, 1879.

Brown, H. F. Venice (1100–1484). In Cambridge Modern History, I, Chap. VIII. Cambridge, 1902.

Busolt, G. Griechische Geschichte bis zur Schlacht bei Chaironeia. 2 vols. Gotha, 1885–1888.

Caillemer, E. In Daremberg et Saglio's Dictionnaire des Antiquités Grecques et Romaines. Sub "Colonie." Paris, 1887.

Canestrini, G. Il Mar Nero e le Colonie degli Italiani nel Medio Evo. Archiv. Stor. Ital., Nuova Serie, Tomo Quarto, Parte Iª. Firenze, 1857.

Cibrario, G. A. L. Della Economia Politica del Medio Evo. 2d edition. 3 vols. Torino, 1842.

Cicero, M. T. De Lege Agraria (Contra Rullum).

Cicero, M. T. De Re Publica.

*Coulanges, F. de. Histoire des Institutions Politiques de l'Ancienne France: la Gaule Romaine. Paris, 1891.

Daremberg et Saglio. Dictionnaire des Antiquités Grecques et Romaines. Paris, 1887.

Duncker, M. History of Antiquity. 4 vols. Berlin, 1855–1857 and Leipzig, 1874–1886.

Encyclopædia Biblica. T. K. Cheyne and J. S. Black, editors. New York and London, 1899–1903.

Ersch, J. S., und Gruber, J. G. Allgemeine Encyclopädie der Wissenschaften und Künste. [Hopf, Carl, sub "Giustiniani" (Familie aus Genua).] Leipzig, 1818–.

Freeman, E. Greater Greece and Greater Britain. London, 1886.

Groot, J. J. M. de. Het Kongsiwezen van Borneo. 's Gravenhage, 1885.

Herodotus. Ἱστορίαι.

Hertzberg, G. F. Kurze Geschichte der altgriechischen Kolonisation. Gütersloh, 1892.

*Heyd, W. Geschichte des Levantehandels im Mittelalter. 2 vols. Stuttgart, 1879.

Hopf, C. Sub "Giustiniani" (Familie aus Genua) in Ersch und Gruber's Encyclopädie.

Humbert, G. In Daremberg et Saglio's Dictionnaire des Antiquités Grecques et Romaines. Paris, 1887.

Ihne, W. Roman History. 5 vols. London, 1871–1882.

Keller, A. G. Homeric Society. New York and London, 1902, 1906.

Kugler, B. Geschichte der Kreuzzüge (Oncken). Berlin, 1880.

Letourneau, Ch. La Guerre dans les diverses Races Humaines. Paris, 1895.

Liddell and Scott. Greek Lexicon. 6th edition. New York, 1869.

Livius, T. Rerum Romanorum ab Urbe Condita Historia.

McCurdy, J. F. History, Prophecy and the Monuments. New York and London, 1894–1901.

Maspero, G. Histoire Ancienne des Peuples de l'Orient. 2d edition. Paris, 1876.

*Meltzer, O. Geschichte der Karthager. 2 vols. Berlin, 1879 and 1896.

Meyer, E. Article " Phoenicia " in the Encyclopædia Biblica.

—— *Geschichte des Altertums. 5 vols. Stuttgart, 1884–1902.

Movers, F. C. Die Phönizier. I (Bonn, 1841); II, Pts. I–III (Berlin, 1849, 1850, 1856).

Munro, D. C. Christian and Infidel in the Holy Land. International Monthly, IV, Nos. 5 and 6 (November and December, 1901).

Pauly-Wissowa (Pauly, A. F. von; and Wissowa, G., editor). Real-encyclopädie der classischen Altertumswissenschaft. Sub "Colonatus" and " Coloniae." 6 vols. Stuttgart, 1901–1903.

Pietschmann, R. Geschichte der Phönizier (Oncken). Berlin, 1889.

Pigeonneau, H. Histoire de la Commerce de la France. 2 vols. Paris, 1887.

Plato. Νόμοι.

Plinius, C. Secundus. Naturalis Historia.

*Prutz, H. Kulturgeschichte der Kreuzzüge. Berlin, 1883.

Raoul-Rochette, D. Histoire Critique de l'Establissement des Colonies Grecques. 4 vols. Paris, 1815.

*Ratzel, F. Die Chinesische Auswanderung. Ein Beitrag zur Cultur- und Handelsgeographie. Breslau, 1876.

Rawlinson, G. History of Phœnicia. London, 1889.

Richter, W. Handel und Verkehr der wichtigsten Völker des Mittelmeeres im Altertume. Leipzig, 1886.

Richthofen, F. von. China. Ergebnisse eigener Reisen und darauf gegründeter Studien. 4 vols. Berlin, 1877–1882.

Saussure, L. de. Psychologie de la Colonisation Française dans ses Rapports avec les Sociétés Indigènes. Paris, 1899.

Seymour, T. D. Life in the Homeric Age. New York and London, 1907.

Simonsfeld, H. Der Fondaco dei Tedeschi in Venedig und die deutschvenetianischen Handelsbeziehungen. 2 vols. Stuttgart, 1887.

Smith, R. B. Carthage and the Carthaginians. London, 1878.

Speck, E. Handelsgeschichte des Altertums. 3 vols. Leipzig, 1900–1906.

Thucydides. Ξυγγραφή.

Van der Aa, R. Koloniale Politiek. De Gids, 1860.

Wappäus, J. E. Untersuchungen über die geographischen Entdeckungen der Portugiesen unter Heinrich dem Seefahrer. Göttingen, 1842.

Winckler, H. Die Bedeutung der Phönizier für die Kulturen des Mittelmeeres. Zeitschrift für Socialwissenschaft, VI, 337, 434 (1903).

THE PORTUGUESE

Adams, G. B. Civilization during the Middle Ages. New York, 1894.

Azurara, G. E. de. The Chronicle of the Discovery and Conquest of Guinea. Edited by C. R. Beazley and E. Prestage. 2 vols. (Introduction by Beazley in Vol. II.) London (Hakluyt Society), 1896 and 1899. (References are mainly to Beazley's Introduction.)

*Bourne, E. G. Essays in Historical Criticism. New York and London, 1901.

Branco, M. B. Portugal na Epocha de D. João V. 2d edition. Lisboa, 1886.

Corvo, J. de A. Estudos sobre as Provincias Ultramarinas. 4 vols. Lisboa, 1883, 1884, 1885, 1887.

Danvers, F. C. The Portuguese in India. Being a History of the Rise and Decline of their Eastern Empire. 2 vols. London, 1894.

*Hunter, W. W. A History of British India. 2 vols. London, New York, and Bombay, 1899, 1900.

Major, R. H. The Life of Prince Henry of Portugal the Navigator — and its Results. London and Berlin, 1868.

*Martins, J. P. O. Historia da Civilisação Iberica. 3d edition. Lisboa, 1885.

—— *Historia de Portugal. 6th edition. 2 vols. Lisboa, 1901.

—— *O Brazil e as Colonias Portuguezas. 6th edition. Lisboa, 1888.

—— Os Filhos de D. João I. Lisboa, 1891.

Meneses, D. de. Don Duart de Meneses the Vice-roy, his tractate of the Portugall Indies, containing the Lawes, Customes, Revenues, Expenses, and other matters remarkable therein: here abbreviated. Purchas His Pilgrimes, IX, ch. X. Glasgow, 1905.

Nevinson, H. W.   A Modern Slavery.   New York and London, 1906.

Parkman, F.   Pioneers of France in the New World.   16th edition.   Part I of France and England in North America.   Boston, 1879.

Rio-Branco, Baron de.   Esquisse de l'Histoire du Brésil.   Chap. V of Le Brésil en 1889 (Paris Exposition publication).   F.-J. de Santa-Anna Nery, editor. Paris, 1889.

Rogers, J. E. T.   A History of Agriculture and Prices in England.   8 vols. Oxford, 1866–1902.

Schäfer, H.   Geschichte von Portugal.   5 vols.   Hamburg, 1836–1854.

Southey, R.   History of Brazil.   3 vols.   London, 1822.

Stephens, H. M.   The Story of Portugal.   New York, 1891.

*Varnhagen, F. A. de.   Historia Geral do Brazil.   2 vols.   Rio de Janeiro, 1854 and 1857.

Vasconcellos, E. J. de C. e.   As Colonias Portuguezas.   Lisboa, 1897.

*Watson, R. G.   Spanish and Portuguese South America during the Colonial Period.   2 vols.   London, 1884.

*Whiteway, R. S.   The Rise of Portuguese Power in India, 1497–1550.   Westminster, 1899.

Zimmermann, A.   Die Kolonialpolitik Portugals und Spaniens.   Vol. I of Die Europäischen Kolonien.   Berlin, 1896.

THE SPANISH

Aimes, H. H. S.   A History of Slavery in Cuba.   1511 to 1868.   New York and London, 1907.

Arce, G. N. de.   El Haz de Leña.   Schevill's edition.   Boston, 1903.

Argensola, B. L. de.   Conquista de las Islas Malucas al Rey Filipe Tercero Nuestro Señor.   Zaragoza, 1891.

Armstrong, E.   The Emperor Charles V.   2 vols.   London and New York, 1902.

D'Avila, G. G.   Teatro de las Grandezas de la Villa de Madrid, etc.   Madrid, 1623.

Blumentritt, F.   Die Philippinen.   In *Sammlung gemeinverständlicher wissenschaftlicher Vorträge*, herausgegeben von R. Virchow.   Neue Folge, fünfzehnte Serie, Heft 337/338.   Hamburg, 1900.

*Bourne, E. G.   Historical Introduction to Blair and Robertson's The Philippine Islands: 1493–1803.   Cleveland, 1903.

—— *Spain in America, 1450–1580.   New York and London, 1904.   (This volume contains a noteworthy critical bibliography.)

Cabrera, R.   Cuba and the Cubans.   Translated from Cuba y sus Jueces.   Philadelphia, 1896.

Clarke, H. B.   Modern Spain, 1815–1898.   Cambridge, 1906.

—— The Catholic Kings.   In Cambridge Modern History, I, Chap. XI.   Cambridge, 1902.

(References to the author's name alone are to the latter.)

*Colmeiro, M.   Historia de la Economia Política en España.   2 vols.   Madrid, 1863.

Cunningham, W.   Economic Change.   In Cambridge Modern History, I, Chap. XV.   Cambridge, 1902.

Daireaux, E. La Vie et les Mœurs à La Plata. 2d edition. 2 vols. Paris, 1889.

Fabié, A. Ensayo Histórico de la Legislacion Española en sus Estados de Ultramar. Madrid, 1896.

*Foreman, J. The Philippine Islands. A Political, Geographical, Ethnographical, Social, and Commercial History of the Philippine Archipelago. 3d edition. New York, 1906.

Gallenga, A. The Pearl of the Antilles. London, 1873.

*Haebler, K. Amerika. In Helmolt's Weltgeschichte, Vol. I. Leipzig und Wien, 1899.

—— *Die wirtschaftliche Blüte Spaniens im 16. Jahrhundert und ihr Verfall. Berlin, 1888.

Halstead, M. The Story of Cuba. Chicago, 1896.

Hilder, F. F. The Present and Future of the Philippines. *The Forum*, XXIX, No. 6 (August, 1900).

*Humboldt, A. von. Essai Politique sur le Royaume de Nouvelle Espagne. 3 vols. Paris, 1811.

—— *Ensayo Político sobre la Isla de Cuba. Paris, 1827.

Hume, M. A. S. Modern Spain, 1788–1898. New York and London, 1900.

—— *Spain. Its Greatness and Decay, 1479–1788. Cambridge, 1898.

(References to Hume, *Spain*, are to the former.)

Lea, H. C. A History of the Inquisition of Spain. 4 vols. New York and London, 1906–1908.

—— An Historical Sketch of Sacerdotal Celibacy in the Christian Church. Philadelphia, 1867.

—— The Indian Policy of Spain. *Yale Review*, VIII, No. 2 (August, 1899).

—— The Moriscos of Spain. Their Conversion and Expulsion. Philadelphia, 1901.

Leroy, J. A. Philippine Life in Town and Country. New York, 1905.

Lowery, W. The Spanish Settlements within the Present Limits of the United States, 1513–1561. New York and London, 1901.

Memorias de los Vireyes que han gobernado el Perú durante el tiempo del Coloniaje Español. 6 vols. Lima, 1859.

Mitre, B. Historia de San Martín y de la Emancipación Sud-Americana. Segunda edición. 4 vols. Buenos-Aires, 1890.

—— The Emancipation of South America. Being a condensed Translation by William Pilling of The History of San Martin, by Gen. Don Bartolomé Mitre, first Constitutional President of the Argentine Republic. London, 1893.

*Montero y Vidal, J. Historia de la Piratería Malayo-Mahometana en Mindanao, Joló y Borneo. Madrid, 1888.

—— Historia General de Filipinas, desde el descubrimiento de dichas Islas hasta nuestras dias. 3 vols. Madrid, 1887, 1894, 1895.

Moses, B. The Establishment of Spanish Rule in America. An Introduction to the History and Politics of Spanish America. New York and London, 1898.

Nation, The (New York). On Property of Religious Orders in the Philippines. Vol. LXXII, No. 1857 (January 31, 1901), pp. 82–83.

Recopilacion de Leyes de los Reinos de las Indias. Madrid, 1841.

Relaciónes de los Vireyes y Audiencias que han gobernado el Perú. 3 vols. Lima, 1867; and Madrid, 1871 and 1872.

Retana, W. E. Vida y Escritos del Dr. José Rizal. Madrid, 1907.

Rizal, J. Noli me Tangere (Novela Tagala). Berlin, 1886.

Robinson, A. G. The Philippines : the War and the People. New York, 1901.

Roscher, W. The Spanish Colonial System. Edited by E. G. Bourne. New York, 1904.

(This translation is regularly used in the text excepting where the author desired to revise the rendering into English. In such cases the note, referring to the German edition, gives simply the author's name.)

Scheidnagel, M. Las Colonias Españolas de Asia — Islas Filipinas. Madrid, 1880.

Slosson, E. E. The Philippines Two Hundred Years Ago. *Popular Science Monthly*, LVIII, No. 4 (February, 1901).

Velasco, J. L. de. Geografía y Descripción Universal de las Indias (desde el año de 1571 al de 1574). Zaragoza's edition. Madrid, 1894.

Woodward, W. H. A Short History of the Expansion of the British Empire (1500–1902). 2d edition. Cambridge, 1902.

Worcester, D. C. The Philippine Islands. New York and London, 1899.

THE DUTCH

Blok, P. J. Eene hollandsche Stad onder de Bourgondisch-Oostenrijksche Heerschappij. 's Gravenhage, 1884.

—— *Geschiedenis van het Nederlandsche Volk. 7 Dl. Groningen, 1892–1907. (References to the author's name alone are to the latter.)

*Day, C. The Policy and Administration of the Dutch in Java. New York and London, 1904.

[Dekker, E. D.] (Multatuli). Max Havelaar, of de Koffiveilingen der Nederlandsche Handelsmaatschappy. 9. Druk. Amsterdam, 1900.

De Opiumpolitiek der Regeering en de Vrijheid der Drukpers in Nederlandsch-Indië. Verfolging en Veroordeling van den gewezen Hoofdredacteur van het Bataviaasch-Nieuwsblad, J. F. Scheltema. 's Gravenhage, 1903.

*De Reus, G. C. K. de. Geschichtliche Ueberblick der administrativen, recht-lichen und finanziellen Entwicklung der Niederländisch-Ostindischen Compagnie. Batavia, 1894.

Edmundson, G. The Dutch in Western Guiana. *Engl. Hist. Rev.*, XVI, 640 (1901).

—— The Dutch Power in Brazil. *Eng. Hist. Rev.*, XI, 231 ff. (1896); XIV, 676 ff. (1899); XV, 38 ff. (1900).

*Encyclopædie van Nederlandsch-Indië. Met Medewerking van verschillende Ambtenaaren, Geleerden en Officieren samengesteld door P. A. van der Lith (and others). 's Gravenhage and Leiden, 1905.

Fermin, P. Description générale, historique, géographique et physique de la Colonie de Surinam. 2 vols. Aamsterdam, 1769.

Fortanier, A. Geschiedenis van het Ontstaan en de Ontwikkeling der Neder-landsche Kolonien. Amsterdam, 1869.

Fruin, R. Nederlands Rechten en Verplichtingen ten Opzichte van Indië. *De Gids*, 1865.

Hostmann, F. W. Over de Beschaving van Negers in America door Kolonisatie met Europeanen. Amsterdam, 1850.

Jameson, J. F. William Usselinx. Am. Hist. Association, II, 3. New York and London, 1887.

Knoop, W. J. Bijdrage tot de Kennis der Indische Krijgszaken. *De Gids*, 1849.

—— Indische Krijgsgeschiedenis. *De Gids*, 1860.

Louter, J. de. Handleiding tot de Kennis van het Staats- en Administratief Recht van Nederlandsch-Indië. 4th edition. 's Gravenhage, 1895.

Multatuli. See Dekker.

*Pierson, N. G. Koloniale Politiek. Amsterdam, 1877.

Pringsheim, O. Beiträge zur wirtschaftlichen Entwickelungsgeschichte der Vereinigten Niederlande im 17. und 18. Jahrhundert. *Schmoller's Forschungen*, X, 3. Leipzig, 1890.

Scheltema, J. F. The Opium Trade in the Dutch East Indies. *American Journal of Sociology*, XIII, Nos. 1 and 2 (July and September, 1907).

Stuers, H. J. J. L. Ridder de. De Vestiging en Uitbreiding der Nederlanders ter Westkust van Sumatra. Edited by P. J. Veth. 2 vols. Amsterdam, 1849, 1850.

Theal, G. McC. History of South Africa. 5 vols. London, 1888–1893.

*Van der Chys, J. A. Geschiedenis der Stichting van de Oost-Indische Compagnie. 2e Druk. Leyden, 1857.

*Van Rees, O. Staathuishoudkunde. Vol. II: Geschiedenis der Koloniale Politiek van de Republiek der Vereenigde Nederlanden. Utrecht, 1868.

Van Wijk, G. O. De Goeie Jo; Roman uit het Indische Leven. Amsterdam, 1893.

Veth, P. J. Atchin en zijne Betrekkingen tot Nederland. Topographisch-Historische Beschrijving. Leiden, 1873.

—— Multatuli vs. Droogstoppel. *De Gids*, 1860.

—— Nieuwste Literatuur over Nederlandsch-Indië. *De Gids*, 1862, 1863, 1864, 1865.

Wallace, A. R. The Malay Archipelago. London, 1872.

Warner, C. D. (editor). Library of the World's Best Literature. 30 vols. New York, 1896–1898.

Wilken, G. A. Vergelijkende Volkenkunde van Nederlandsch-Indië. Leiden, 1893.

Zimmermann, A. Die Kolonialpolitik der Niederländer: Vol. V of Die Europäischen Kolonien. Berlin, 1903.

THE SCANDINAVIANS

Acrelius, I. Histori af Nya Swerige. English Translation in Memoirs of the Historical Society of Pennsylvania, XI.

Austin, O. P. The Danish West Indies, 1621–1901. Commerce, Production, Population, Area, etc. (Summary of Commerce and Finance.) Washington, 1902.

Bonney, T. G. Volcanoes, their Structure and Significance. New York and London, 1899.

Burt, J. H., Jr. En Stemme fra St. Croix. Breve til den danske Rigsdag. Kjøbenhavn, 1852.

Campanius, T. Nya Swerige. English Translation in Memoirs of the Historical Society of Pennsylvania, III.

Crantz, D. The History of Greenland. 2 vols. London, 1767.

Dahlman, S. Beskrifning om S. Barthelemy Swensk Ö uti Westindien. Stockholm, 1786. (Bound with Euphrasén.)

Edmundson, G. The Swedish Legend in Guiana. *Eng. Hist. Rev.*, XIV, 71 (1899).

Euphrasén, B. A. Beskrifning öfver svenska vestindiska ön St. Barthelemi, samt öarne St. Eustache och St. Christopher. Stockholm, 1795.

Gravier, G. Découverte de l'Amérique par les Normands au Xe Siècle. Paris, 1874.

Høst, G. Efterretninger om Øen Sanct-Thomas og dens Gouverneurer, optegnede der paa Landet fra 1769 indtil 1776. Kjøbenhavn, 1791.

Keller, A. G. Notes on the Danish West Indies (incorporated in the present volume). *Annals of the American Academy of Political and Social Science*, XXII, 99 (July, 1903).

Knox, J. P. A Historical Account of St. Thomas, W. I., and Incidental Notices of St. Croix and St. Johns. New York, 1852.

Larsen, K. De dansk-ostindiske Koloniers Historie. Kjøbenhavn, 1907.

Leo, H. Einiges ueber das Leben und die Lebensbedingungen in Island in der Zeit des Heidenthumes. Historisches Taschenbuch, sechster Jahrgang. Leipzig, 1835.

*Maurer, K. Island von seiner ersten Entdeckung bis zum Untergange des Freistaats. München, 1874.

Nansen, F. Eskimo Life. Translated by William Archer. London, 1893.

Otté, E. C. Denmark and Iceland. London, 1881.

Øverland, O. A. Illustreret Norges Historie. 5 vols. Kristiania, 1885–1895.

Oxholm, P. L. De Danske Vestindiske Øers Tilstand i Henseende til Population, Cultur og Finance-Forfatning. Kjøbenhavn, 1797.

*Petersen, B. von. En historisk Beretning om de dansk-Vestindiske Øer St. Croix, St. Thomas og St. Jan. Kjøbenhavn, 1855.

Peyrère, I. de la. Translation from Histoire du Groenland (Paris, 1663), in Hakluyt Society Publications. "A Collection of Documents on Spitzbergen and Greenland." London, 1855.

*Rink, H. Danish Greenland : its People and its Products. Edited by Robert Brown. London, 1877.

Sars, J. E. Udsigt over den Norske Historie. 4 parts in 3 bound vols. Christiania, 1873, 1877, 1887, 1891.

*Th,—(full name withheld). Erindringer fra et sexaarigt Ophold paa St. Croix og Cuba. Kjøbenhavn, 1866.

Tooke, C. W. The Danish Colonial Fiscal System in the West Indies. In Essays in Colonial Finance, q. v.

Werfel, J. Efterretning on de danske-Vestindiske Øers St. Croix's, St. Thomas's og St. Jan's. Kjøbenhavn, 1801.

West, H. Bidrag til Beskrivelse over Ste. Croix med en kort Udsigt over St. Thomas, St. Jean, Tortola, Spanishtown og Crabeiland. Kjøbenhavn, 1793.

Wilhelmi, K. Island, Hvitramannaland, Grönland und Vinland. Heidelberg, 1842.

THE MODERN ITALIANS

Almanach de Gotha. 1889 *et seq.*

"An Observer." Italy of To-day. *Fortnightly Review*, LXI, 225 (1894).

Appleton's Annual Cyclopædia. Article "Abyssinia." 1895.

*Brunialti, A. Le Colonie degli Italiani. Torino, 1897.

Capucci, L. La Politica Africana in Africa. *Nuova Antologia*, August 1, 1897.

Edwards, F. E. The Italians in Africa. *Westminster Review*, CXLVIII, 477 (1897).

*Frassati, A. Il Pericolo Abissino e Inghilterra, Francia ed Italia. *Nuova Antologia*, April 1, 1899.

Geffcken, F. H. The Economic Condition of Italy. *Contemporary Review*, LVIII, 609 (1890).

Laveleye, E. The Foreign Policy of Italy. *Contemporary Review*, LXI, 153 (1892).

Lombroso, C. L'Italia in China. Il pericolo giallo. *Nuova Antologia*, March 16, 1899.

Mezzacapo, C. L' Eritrea e i suoi Confini. *Nuova Antologia*, December 1, 1897.

Nash, F. P. Italy as a "Great Power." *The Nation* (New York), LXV, 146 (August 19, 1897).

Nation, The (New York). Italy in Africa. LX, 179.

—— The Financial Condition of Italy, LIII, 255.

—— The Merchant Marine of Italy, XXXV, 171.

Nuova Antologia. Rassegna Politica. 1897 *et seq.*

"Ouida." The Italian Awakening. *Fortnightly Review*, LXV, 541 (1896).

Pittaluga, G. L' Eritrea Giudicata in Francia. *Nuova Antologia*, July 16, 1897.

Primerano, D. Che cosa fare dell' Eritrea? *Nuova Antologia*, October 16, 1897.

*Rossi, A. La Incerta Politica Africana. *Nuova Antologia*, November 16, 1897.

Traversi, Dottor. L' Etiopia d'oggi e l' Eritrea. *Nuova Antologia*, May 16, 1897.

THE GERMANS

Andler, C. Le Prince de Bismarck. Paris, 1899.

Annals of the American Academy of Political and Social Science, XIX, Nos. 1 and 2.

[Bastian, A.] Einiges aus Samoa und anderen Inseln der Südsee. Mit ethnographischen Anmerkungen zur Colonialgeschichte. Berlin, 1889.

Bigelow, P. Germany's First Colony in China. *Harper's Magazine*, C, 577.

*Blum, H. Neu-Guinea und der Bismarck-Archipel. Berlin, 1900.

Boshart, A. Zehn Jahre afrikanischen Lebens. Leipzig, 1898.

Büttner, C. G. Das Hinterland von Walfischbai und Angra Pequena. Heidelberg, 1884.

Davis, R. H. Along the East Coast of Africa. *Scribner's Magazine*, XXIX, 3, 259 (March, 1901).

Dove, K. Südwest-Afrika. Berlin, 1896.

Ehrenberg, R. Das Zeitalter der Fugger. 2 vols. Jena, 1896.

Engler, G. Koloniales. Eine umfassende Darstellung der Colonialverhältnisse des Deutschen Reiches und der übrigen europäischen Staaten. Hamburg, 1889.

Export (Der deutsche) nach den Tropen und die Ausrüstung für die Kolonien. G. Meinecke, editor. Berlin, 1900.

Fabri, F. Bedarf Deutschland der Colonien? Eine politisch-ökonomische Betrachtung. Gotha, 1879.

—— Fünf Jahre deutscher Kolonialpolitik. Gotha, 1889.

Fabri, T. Kolonien als Bedürfnis unserer nationalen Entwickelung. Heidelberg, 1884.

Finsch, O. Ethnologische Erfahrungen und Belegstücke aus der Südsee. Wien, 1893.

—— Samoafahrten; Reisen in Kaiser-Wilhelmsland und Englisch Neu-Guinea in den Jahren 1884 und 1885. Leipzig, 1888.

(Any references to the author's name alone are to the latter.)

Fitzner, R. Deutsches Kolonial-Handbuch. 2d edition. 2 vols. Berlin, 1901.

Geffcken, F. H. The Germans as Emigrants and Colonists. *The Forum*, XIII, 200 (1892).

Giesebrecht, F. Die Behandlung der Eingeborenen in den deutschen Kolonieen. Berlin, 1897.

Globus. LXXVII, 229 (1900); LXXIX, 3 (1901); LXXIX, 9 (1901).

*Hagen, B. Unter den Papuas. Wiesbaden, 1899.

Hauser, H. Colonies Allemandes Impériales et Spontanées. Paris, 1900.

Hermann, E. Viehzucht und Bodenkultur in Südwestafrika. Berlin, 1900.

Hesse-Wartegg, E. von. Samoa, Bismarck-Archipel und Neu-Guinea, 1902.

—— Shantung und Deutsch-China im Jahre 1898. Leipzig, 1898.

Illustrierte Zeitfragen: Samoa. Leipzig, 1900.

Jannasch, R. See Roscher, W.

Keller, A. G. Essays in Colonization (incorporated in the present volume). New Haven, 1902.

Klose, H. Togo unter deutscher Flagge. Reisebilder und Betrachtungen. Berlin, 1899.

Krieger, M. Neu-Guinea. Berlin, 1899.

Loeb, I. The German Colonial Fiscal System. In Essays in Colonial Finance, q. v.

Lowe, C. Prince Bismarck. 2 vols. New York, 1886.

Meinecke, G. Die deutschen Kolonien in Wort und Bild. Leipzig, 1900. See also " Export."

Müller, G. Land und Leute in Bismarck-Archipel. Leipzig, *circa* 1893.

Nation, The (New York). LXV, 471 ; LXXII, 1860.

Oberländer, R. Deutsch-Afrika. Leipzig und Berlin, 1885.

Perry, H. A. The Traditions of German Colonization. *Macmillan's Magazine*, LXII, 113 (1890).

*Pfeil, J., Graf. Studien und Beobachtungen aus der Südsee. Braunschweig, 1899.

—— *Vorschläge zur praktischen Kolonisation in Ost-Afrika. Berlin, 1888.

*Philippson, F. C. Ueber Colonisation. Volkswirtschaftliche Zeitfragen, Jahrgang 2, Hefte 4 und 5. Berlin. 1880.

Poschinger, H. von. Conversations of Prince Bismarck. Edited by Sidney Whitman. New York, 1900.

Reichenow, A. Die deutsche Kolonie Kamerun. Berlin, 1884.

Richthofen, F. Schantung und seine Eingangspforte Kiautschou. Berlin, 1898.

*Schmidt, R. Deutschlands Kolonien. 2 vols. Berlin, 1895–1896.

Sievers, W. Afrika. Leipzig und Wien, 1891.

Spectator, The. LXXXI, 481 (October 8, 1898).

*Stengel, K., Freiherr von. Die Rechtsverhältnisse der deutschen Schutzgebiete. Tübingen und Leipzig, 1901.

Stevenson, R. L. In the South Seas. New York, 1901.

Tijdschrift voor Nederlandsch-Indië. Duitschland als Kolonisierende en Koloniale Mogendheid. No. 13, 2.

Tikhomirov, L. Russia Political and Social. 2 vols. London, 1888.

Times, The (New York). Speech of Herr Richter. January 10, 1902.

—— On Kiautschou. January 10 and 29, and March 16, 1902.

—— Tuskegee Graduates called to Togo. March 30, 1902.

Vane Dene, S. Duitschlands Kolonien. *Indische Gids*, 1888, i, 134.

Weber, E. von. Die Erweiterung des deutschen Wirtschaftsgebietes und die Grundlegung zu überseeischen deutschen Staaten. Leipzig, 1879.

Witt, R. C. An Experiment in Colonization. *Blackwood's*, CLXIII, 788.

Wohltmann, Dr. Over de Duitsche Koloniale Politiek. *Indische Gids*, 1897, ii, 1387.

Zimmermann, A. Die Kolonialpolitik Frankreichs. Vol. IV of Die Europäischen Kolonien. Berlin, 1900.

INDEX

MAPS.

NOTE. The following set of specially prepared maps is designed to cover all portions of the text. No references to the maps occur in the footnotes, but it is supposed that the teacher, upon whom the vital importance of the constant use of charts must have been impressed by experience, will desire to make consistent use of these aids to study. The arrangement of the maps follows roughly the main divisions of the text; however, to secure compactness, the conditions of different historical epochs are sometimes indicated upon the same sheet.

LIST OF MAPS

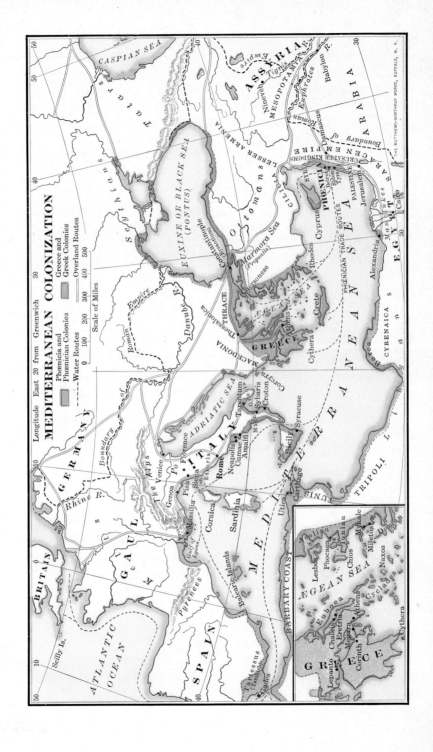

MEDITERRANEAN COLONIZATION

Longitude East 20 from Greenwich

Phoenicia and Phoenician Colonies

Greece and Greek Colonies

Water Routes

Overland Routes

Scale of Miles

0 100 200 300 400 500

THE MATTHEWS-NORTHRUP WORKS, BUFFALO, N. Y.

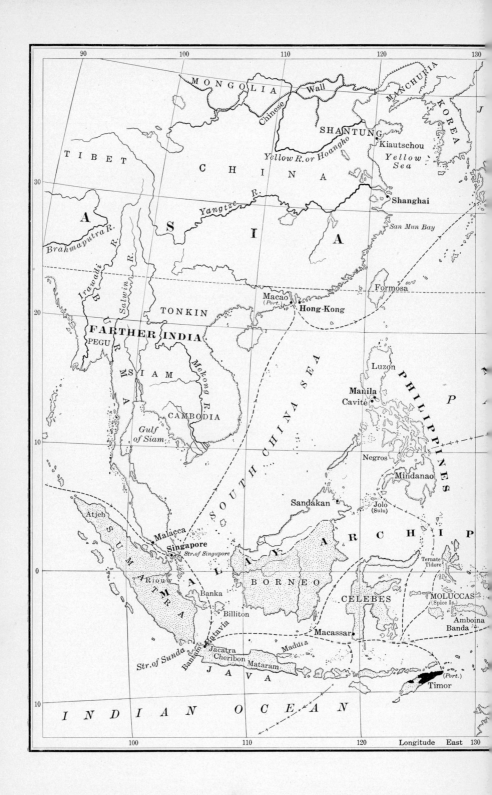

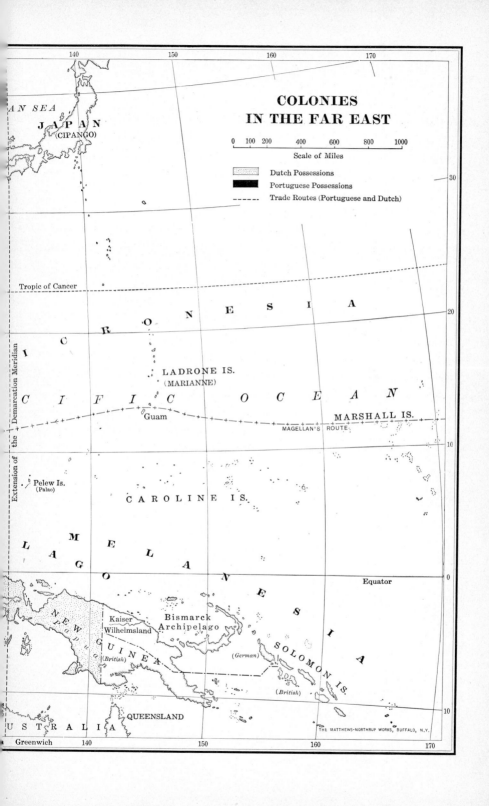

COLONIES
IN THE FAR EAST

0   100 200   400   600   800   1000
Scale of Miles

Dutch Possessions
Portuguese Possessions
- - - - Trade Routes (Portuguese and Dutch)

AN SEA

JAPAN
(CIPANGO)

Tropic of Cancer

M I C R O N E S I A

LADRONE IS.
(MARIANNE)

P A C I F I C   O C E A N

Guam
MAGELLAN'S ROUTE

MARSHALL IS.

Pelew Is.
(Palao)

CAROLINE IS.

M E L A N E S I A

Extension of the Demarcation Meridian

Equator

NEW GUINEA

Kaiser
Wilhelmsland

Bismarck
Archipelago

(British)   (German)

SOLOMON IS.

(British)

QUEENSLAND

AUSTRALIA

Greenwich   140   150   160   170

THE MATTHEWS-NORTHRUP WORKS, BUFFALO, N.Y.

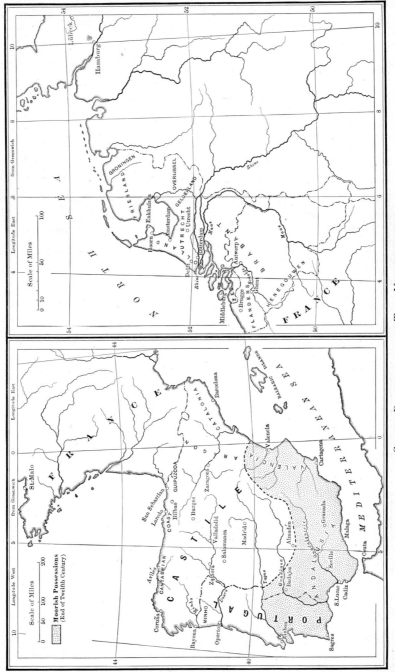

SPAIN, PORTUGAL, AND THE NETHERLANDS

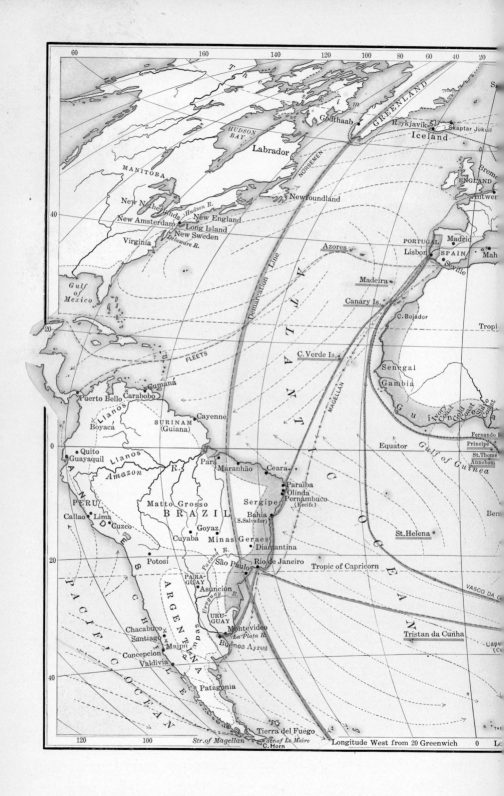

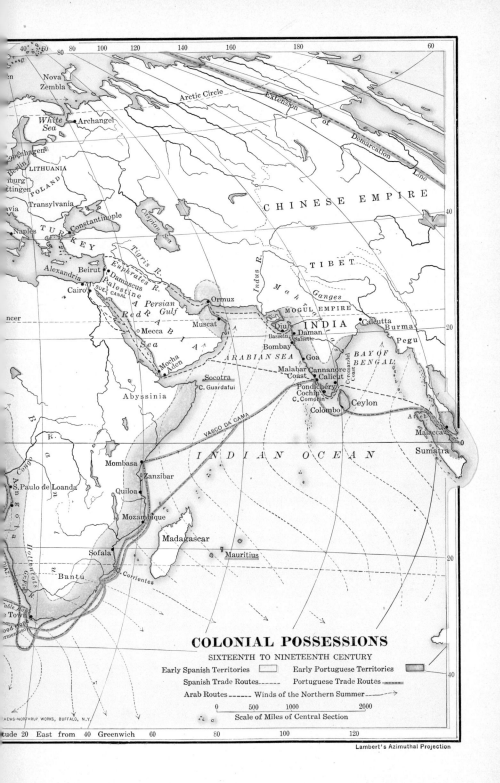

COLONIAL POSSESSIONS

SIXTEENTH TO NINETEENTH CENTURY

Early Spanish Territories ☐ Early Portuguese Territories ▨

Spanish Trade Routes ------ Portuguese Trade Routes -·-·-

Arab Routes -·-·- Winds of the Northern Summer -------→

0   500   1000   2000

Scale of Miles of Central Section

Lambert's Azimuthal Projection

THEWS-NORTHRUP WORKS, BUFFALO, N.Y.

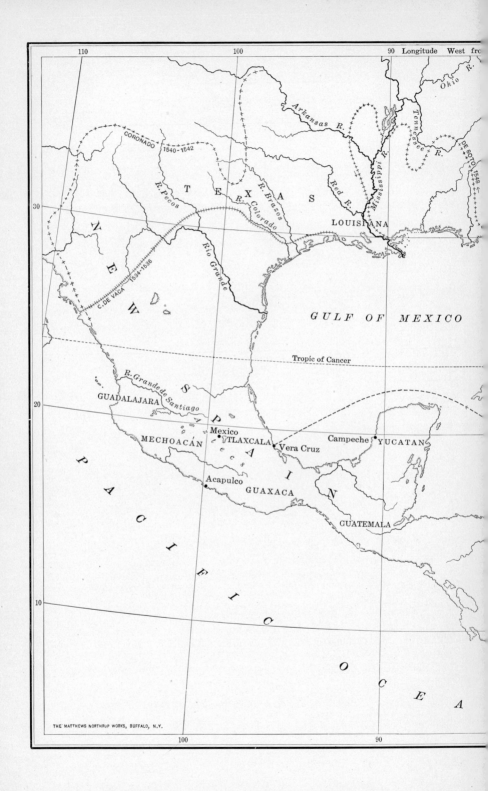

MEXICO
AND
THE ANTILLES

0   50   100   200   300   400   500

Scale of Miles

30

A T L A N T I C

FRENCH SETTLEMENTS
1564
St.Augustine

F L O R I D A

P. DE LEON

O C E A N

C

B A H A M A S

Havana

C U B A

20

A N T

Santiago

Tortuga

JAMAICA

ESPAÑOLA

HAITI

S.DOMINGO

PUERTO RICO

St.Thomas

St.John

St.Bartholomew

St.Croix

St.Christopher
(St.Kitts)

FLEETS --- AND --- GALLEONS

Dominica

I L L E S

Martinique

St.Lucia

St.Vincent

Barbados

C A R I B B E A N   S E A

Curaçao

Grenada

Tobago

Trinidad

10

Nombre de Dios

Cartagena

Maracaibo

Caracas

Cumana

Puerto Bello

Panama

R. Magdalena

R. Cauca

T I E R R A   F I R M E

Orinoco R.

V E N E Z U E L A

GUIANA

N E W   G R A N A D A

(COLOMBIA)

R. Meta

Bogotá

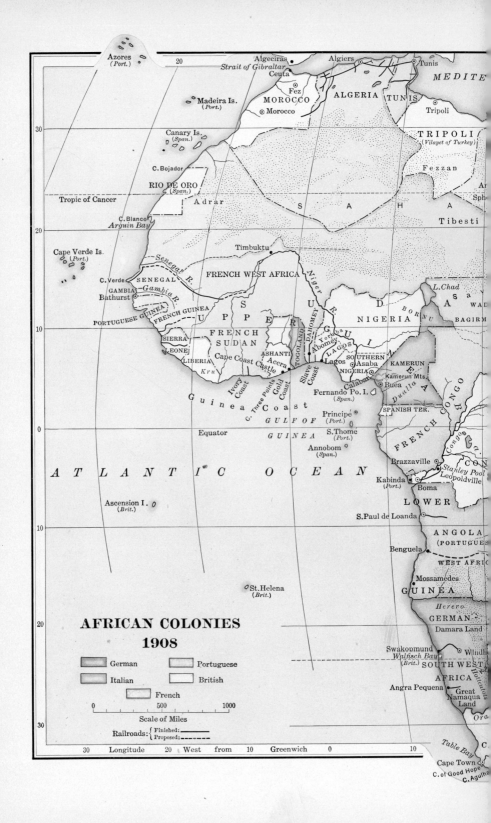

Azores
(Port.)

Strait of Gibraltar
Algeciras
Ceuta
Algiers
Tunis
MEDITE

20

Madeira Is.
(Port.)

Fez
MOROCCO
Morocco

ALGERIA

TUN IS.

Tripoli

TRIPOLI
(Vilayet of Turkey)

30

Canary Is.
(Span.)

Fezzan

C. Bojador

RIO DE ORO
(Span.)

Adrar

S A H A

A

Tropic of Cancer

Tibesti

Sph

C. Blanco
Arguin Bay

20

A

Cape Verde Is.
(Port.)

Senegal R.

Timbuktu

Niger

FRENCH WEST AFRICA

D

L. Chad

A S A

C. Verde
SENEGAL
GAMBIA
Bathurst
Gambia R.

U

P

P

E

R

NIGERIA

BOR

WAD

BAGIRM

PORTUGUESE GUINEA
FRENCH GUINEA

10

G

U

I

SIERRA
LEONE
LIBERIA

FRENCH
SUDAN

Kru

Cape Coast Castle

ASHANTI
Accra

Gold
Coast

TOGOLAND

DAHOMEY
Abomey
Yoruba

Lagos

SOUTHERN
NIGERIA
Asaba

LAGOS

Calabar

KAMERUN
Buea

Kamerun Mts.

E

A

Dualla

CONGO

Ivory
Coast

C. Three Points

Slave
Coast

Fernando Po. I.
(Span.)

SPANISH TER.

FRENCH

Guinea
Coast

GULF OF

Principé
(Port.)

Congo
Ga

Equator

GUINEA

S. Thome
(Port.)

0

Annobom
(Span.)

Brazzaville

CON

Stanley Pool
Leopoldville

A T L A N T I C

O C E A N

Kabinda
(Port.)

Boma

Ascension I.
(Brit.)

LOWER

S. Paul de Loanda

10

ANGOLA
(PORTUGUES

Benguela

WEST AFRIC

St.Helena
(Brit.)

Mossamedes

GUINEA

Herero

GERMAN

Damara Land

20

AFRICAN COLONIES
1908

Swakopmund
Walfisch Bay
(Brit.)

Windh

SOUTH WEST

	German		Portuguese
	Italian		British
		French	

AFRICA

Angra Pequena

Great
Namaqua
Land

Hottento

0   500   1000

Scale of Miles

Railroads: { Finished: ———
{ Proposed: ---------

30

Ora

Table Bay

30   Longitude   20   West   from   10   Greenwich   0   10

Cape Town
C. of Good Hope
C. Aguthe

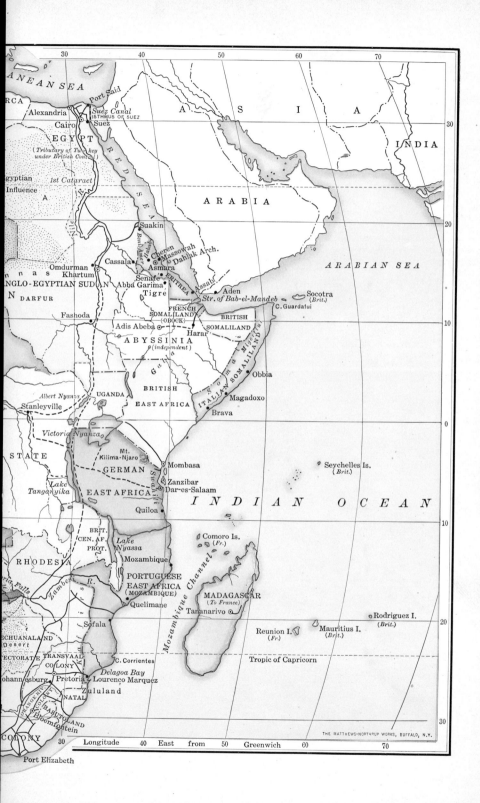

MEDITERRANEAN SEA

Alexandria
Port Said
Suez Canal
ISTHMUS OF SUEZ
Cairo
Suez

EGYPT
(Tributary of Turkey
under British Control)

Egyptian
Influence

1st Cataract

A S I A

ARABIA

INDIA

RED SEA

Suakin

Cassala
Cheren
Massowah
Dahlak Arch.
Asmara
ERITREA
Omdurman
Khartum
Senafe
ANGLO-EGYPTIAN SUDAN
Abba Garima
Tigre

DARFUR

ARABIAN SEA

Fashoda

Aden
Str. of Bab-el-Mandeb
Socotra
(Brit.)
C. Guardafui

FRENCH
SOMALILAND
(OBOCK)
BRITISH
SOMALILAND
Adis Abeba
Harar

ABYSSINIA
(independent)

Gallas

SOMALILAND in a Midjurtin
ITALIAN SOMALILAND
Obbia

BRITISH
EAST AFRICA
Magadoxo
Brava

Albert Nyanza
UGANDA
Stanleyville

Victoria Nyanza

Seychelles Is.
(Brit.)

Mt.
Kilima-Njaro
GERMAN
Mombasa
STATE
EAST AFRICA
Zanzibar
Dar-es-Salaam
Lake
Tanganyika

I N D I A N   O C E A N

Quiloa

BRIT.
CEN. AF.
PROT.
Lake
Nyassa
Comoro Is.
(Fr.)

RHODESIA
Mozambique

Victoria Falls
Zambesi R.
PORTUGUESE
EAST AFRICA
(MOZAMBIQUE)
Quelimane

Mozambique Channel

MADAGASCAR
(To France)
Tananarivo
Rodriguez I.
(Brit.)

Sofala
Reunion I.
(Fr.)
Mauritius I.
(Brit.)

BECHUANALAND
Desert
PROTECTORATE
TRANSVAAL
COLONY
C. Corrientes
Tropic of Capricorn

Johannesburg
Pretoria
Delagoa Bay
Lourenço Marquez
Zululand
ORANGE RIVER COLONY
NATAL
BASUTOLAND
Bloemfontein
COLONY
Port Elizabeth

THE MATTHEWS-NORTHRUP WORKS, BUFFALO, N.Y.

Longitude   40   East   from   50   Greenwich   60   70